Maine

AN EXPLORER'S GUIDE

Maine

AN EXPLORER'S GUIDE

CHRISTINA TREE & ELIZABETH ROUNDY

Eighth Edition

The Countryman Press
Woodstock, Vermont

Dedications

To Timothy Alfred Davis
—C.T.

To the memory of Nancy Gilles
—E.R.

Library of Congress Cataloging-in-Publication Data
Tree, Christina.
Maine : an explorer's guide / Christina Tree & Elizabeth Roundy. — 8th ed.
p.   cm.
Includes index.
ISBN 0-88150-387-8 (alk. paper)
1. Maine—Guidebooks.   I. Roundy, Elizabeth.   II. Title.
F17.3.T73 1997
917.404'43—dc21
96-48306
CIP

Maps by Alex Wallach, © 1997 The Country-
man Press
Book design by Glenn Suokko
Cover painting by Jill Anise Hoy
Author photo on back cover by Gordon Pine
Published by The Countryman Press
PO Box 748, Woodstock, Vermont 05091
Distributed by W.W. Norton & Company, Inc.,
500 Fifth Avenue, New York, New York
10110
Printed in the United States of America
10 9 8 7 6 5 4 3 2 1

Explore With Us!

We have been fine-tuning *Maine: An Explorer's Guide* for the past 15 years, a period in which lodging, dining, and shopping opportunities have more than quadrupled in the state. As we have expanded our guide, we have also been increasingly selective, making recommendations based on years of conscientious research and personal experience. What makes us unique is that we describe the state by locally defined regions, giving you Maine's communities, not simply her most popular destinations. With this guide you'll feel confident to venture beyond the tourist towns, along roads less traveled, to places of special hospitality and charm.

WHAT'S WHERE

In the beginning of the book you'll find an alphabetical listing of special highlights and important information that you may want to reference quickly. You'll find advice on everything from where to buy the best local lobster to where to write or call for camping reservations and park information.

LODGING

We've selected lodging places for mention in this book based on their merit alone; **we do not charge innkeepers for inclusion.** We're the only travel guide that tries personally to check every bed & breakfast, farm, sporting lodge, and inn in Maine, and one of the few that do not charge for inclusion.

Prices: Please don't hold us or the respective innkeepers responsible for the rates listed as of press time in 1997. Some changes are inevitable. The 7 percent state rooms and meals tax should be added to all prices unless we specifically state that it's included in a price. We've tried to note when a gratuity is added but it's always wise to check before booking.

Smoking: Many B&Bs are now smoke-free and many inns and restaurants feature smoke-free rooms. If this is important to you, be sure to ask when making reservations.

RESTAURANTS

In most sections, please note a distinction between *Dining Out* and *Eating Out*. By their nature, restaurants included in the *Eating Out* group are generally inexpensive.

KEY TO SYMBOLS

☞ The special-value symbol appears next to selected lodging and restaurants that combine quality and moderate prices.

✐ The kids-alert symbol appears next to lodging, restaurants, activities, and shops of special interest or appeal to youngsters.

We would appreciate any comments or corrections. Please address your correspondence to Explorer's Guide Editor, The Countryman Press, PO Box 748, Woodstock, Vermont 05091.

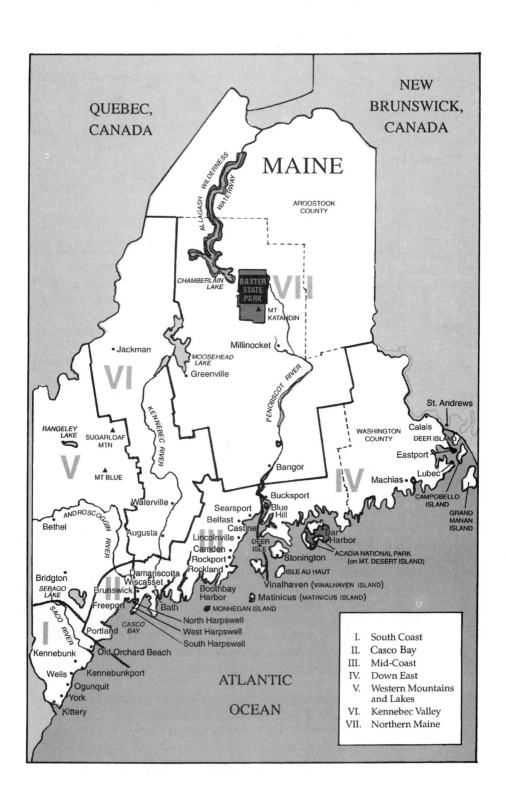

Contents

Introduction

He who rides and keeps the beaten track studies the fences chiefly.
—*Henry David Thoreau*, The Maine Woods, 1853

Back in the 1920s, "motor touring" was hailed as a big improvement over train and steamer travel because it meant you no longer had to go where everyone else did—over routes prescribed by railroad tracks and steamboat schedules.

Ironically, though, in Maine cars have had precisely the opposite effect. Now 90 percent of the state's visitors follow the coastal tourist route as faithfully as though their wheels were grooved to Route 1.

Worse still, it's as though many tourists are on a train making only express stops—at rush hour. At least half of those who follow Route 1 stop, stay, and eat in all the same places (such as Kennebunkport, Boothbay or Camden, and Bar Harbor)—in August. Although this book should help visitors and Maine residents alike enjoy the state's resort towns, it is particularly useful for those who explore less frequented places.

When *Maine: An Explorer's Guide* first appeared in 1982, it was the first 20th-century guidebook to describe New England's largest state region by region rather than by tourist towns listed alphabetically. From the start it critiqued places to stay and to eat as well as everything to see and to do—based on merit rather than money (we don't charge anyone to be included).

In the beginning it didn't seem like a tall order; but over the years—which coincided with a proliferation of inns, B&Bs, and other lodging options—we've been including more and more of Maine from Matinicus to Madawaska and from the White Mountains to Campobello, not to mention all of Route 1 from Kittery to Fort Kent.

In all, we now describe more than 500 places to stay, ranging from campgrounds to grand old resorts and including farms as well as B&Bs and inns—in all corners of the state and in all price ranges. We have also checked out many hundreds of places to dine and to eat (we make a distinction between dining and eating); and, since shopping is an important part of everyone's travels, we include exceptional stores we've discovered while browsing along the coast and inland. We have opin-

9

MAINE OFFICE OF TOURISM

Sailboats in Bar Harbor

ions about everything we've found, and we don't hesitate to share them. In every category, we record exactly what we see, again because we charge no business to be included in the book.

Guidebooks either atrophy and die after an edition or two, or they take on a life of their own. We are relieved to report that by now *Maine: An Explorer's Guide* has introduced so many people to so many parts of Maine that it has become a phenomenon in its own right.

Chris is a Bay Stater addicted to many Maines. As a toddler she learned to swim in the Ogunquit River and later watched her three sons do the same in Monhegan's icy waters—and then learn to sail at summer camp in Raymond and paddle canoes on the Saco River and down the St. John. Before beginning this book, she thought she "knew" Maine, having already spent a dozen years exploring it for the *Boston Globe*, describing the charm of coastal villages and the quiet of inland mountains and lakes. For the *Globe*, she continues to write about a variety of things to do, from skiing at Sugarloaf and Sunday River and llama trekking in Bethel to sea kayaking off Portland and windjamming on Penobscot Bay. But after 16 years, some 80,000 miles, and eight editions of the book, Chris no longer claims to "know" Maine. What she does know are the state's lodging places (she also coauthors *Best Places to Stay in New England*), restaurants, and shops, from Kittery to Calais and from Matinicus to Kokadjo and Grand Lake Stream.

Elizabeth was born and raised in the Bangor area, and she took Maine for granted, never appreciating its beauty and uniqueness until she returned after moving out of state for a few years. She has lived in the Bangor area, Augusta, Bar Harbor, and the Portland area and has spent time in "camps" on lakes with her family as a child; one of her favorite spots remains a large lodge overlooking the ocean on Sandy Point, where she spent many special summers. She, too, thought she knew Maine, but in the course of this research realized that she was wrong, that there are many less traveled areas that even a native can overlook, places she had avoided with misconceived notions of how they would be, only to be pleasantly surprised. She also discovered some amazing history she had been missing but won't soon forget.

Maine's history continues to fascinate both of us. We are intrigued by the traces of ancient Native American habitations and pre-Pilgrim settlements, by colorful tales of 17th-century heroes like Baron de St. Castin (scion of a noble French family who married a Penobscot Indian princess), and by the state's legendary seafaring history, well told in the Maine Maritime Museum in Bath (where a total of 5000 vessels have been launched over the years) and at the Penobscot Marine Museum (in Searsport, a small village that once boasted of being home to a full 10 percent of all American sea captains). And, of course, there is the heady saga of the lumbering era (dramatized in the Lumberman's Museum in Patten), which finally ensured Maine's admission to the Union in 1820, but not until Massachusetts had sold off all unsettled land, the privately owned "unorganized townships" that add up to nearly half of inland Maine.

We are also fascinated by the ways in which 150 years of tourism, as much as any industry, have helped shape Maine's current landscape: by the fact, for instance, that long-vanished trains and steamboats still determine where you stay in Maine. With the exception of Sugarloaf/USA (one of New England's largest ski resorts), all resort villages date from the time when visitors from Boston, New York, and Philadelphia were ferried directly to the tips of peninsulas and coastal islands or deposited at inland train depots, frequently to board boats bound for lakeside hotels.

Cars have altered this picture only to a degree, narrowing the number of towns geared to accommodating any volume of visitors. Nineteenth-century resorts like Stonington, Castine, Pemaquid Point, and Christmas Cove, all of them too far off Route 1 to attract much traffic today, contentedly cater to yachtsmen and inn lovers. And of all the inland villages that once welcomed summer "rusticators," only Bridgton, Bethel, Rangeley, and the Moosehead area still serve non-cottage owners in any number.

This book's introductory section, "What's Where in Maine," is a quick reference directory to a vast variety of activities available within the state. The remainder of the book describes Maine region by region. The basic criterion for including an area is the availability of lodging.

Note that "off-season" prices are often substantially less than those in July and August. September is dependably sparkling and frequently warm. Early October in Maine is just as spectacular as it is in New Hampshire and Vermont, with magnificent mountains rising from inland lakes as well as the golds and reds set against coastal blue. It's also well worth noting that the inland resorts of Bethel and the Sugarloaf area are "off-season" all summer as well as fall.

Maine is almost as big as the other five New England states combined, but her residents add up to fewer than half the population of Greater Boston. That means there is plenty of room for all who look to her for renewal—both residents and out-of-staters.

We would like to thank Laura Jorstad and Helen Whybrow of The Countryman Press for shepherding our manuscript through the many stages to publication of this, the eighth edition. Chris owes thanks to Virginia Fieldman of Jonesport, Joanne Williams of Machias, Linda Pagels of Milbridge, Marion Stocking of Marlboro, Peter Ebeling of South Brooksville, Mark Hodesh of Castine, Alan and Jean Davis of Newcastle, Bud Warren of Phippsburg, Rick Griffin and Karen Arel of Kennebunkport, Diana Schmidt of Ogunquit, David Lusty and Sue Antal of York, Jane Staret of Bridgton, Wende Gray of Bethel, Marti Strunk of Weld, Bud Dick of Kingfield, Melinda Molin of Portland, and her ever-helpful husband, William Davis. Elizabeth thanks her family for their tremendous support. She also owes thanks to John Johnson and Marjory Wright at the Maine Office of Tourism, Peter Thompson of Augusta, Austin Griffin of Old Orchard Beach, Cathy Latham of Camden, and Toni Blake of Greenville.

We would also like to thank all the people who have taken the time to write about their experiences in Maine. We can't tell you how much your input—or simply your reactions to how we have described things—means to us. We welcome your comments and appreciate all your thoughtful suggestions for the next edition of *Maine: An Explorer's Guide.* Note the postage-paid insert in the book for that purpose. You can also contact us directly by e-mail: ctree@worldnet.att.net.

What's Where in Maine

AGRICULTURAL FAIRS

The season opens with the small, family-geared **Pittston Fair** in late June (pig scrambles, antique tractor show) and culminates with the big, colorful **Fryeburg Fair** during the first week of October. Among the best traditional fairs are the **Union Fair** (late August) and the **Blue Hill Fair** (Labor Day weekend). The **Common Ground Country Fair** (late September at the fairgrounds in Windsor) draws Maine's back-to-the-earth and organic gardeners from all corners of the state, and the **Full Circle Summer Fair** at the Union Fairgrounds (mid-July) is a smaller, even less "commercial" gathering. Request a pamphlet listing all the fairs from the Maine Department of Agriculture (287-3221), State House Station 28, Augusta 04333.

AIRPORTS AND AIRLINES

Portland, with connections to most American and Canadian cities, is an increasingly important gateway to northern New England. Bangor International is also served by major carriers. Bar Harbor/Hancock County Regional, Rockland/Knox County Regional, and Northern Maine Regional (Presque Isle) are served by smaller planes from Portland, Augusta, and Boston.

AIR SERVICES

Also called flying services, these are useful links with wilderness camps and coastal islands. Greenville, prime jump-off point for the North Woods, claims to be New England's largest seaplane base. In this book, flying services are also listed in the Rangeley, Moosehead, and Katahdin chapters. From Rockland, air taxis also serve some islands.

AMUSEMENT PARKS

Funtown/Splashtown USA in Saco is Maine's biggest, with rides, water slides, and pools, and **Aquaboggan** (pools and slides) is also on Route 1 in Saco. **Palace Playland** in Old Orchard Beach is a classic with a 1906 carousel, a Ferris wheel, rides, and a 60-foot water slide. **York's Wild Kingdom** at York Beach and **Funland** in Caribou are small areas offering kiddie rides and arcades.

ANTIQUARIAN BOOKS

Maine is well known among book buffs as a browsing mecca. Within this book we have noted antiquarian bookstores where they cluster along Route 1 in Wells and in Portland. More than 75 are described in a directory available from all the antiquarian dealers mentioned in this guide.

ANTIQUES

A member directory listing more than 100 dealers is produced by the Maine Antiques Dealers' Association, Inc., and available from the Maine Publicity Bureau (MPB) (623-

GORDON C. PINE

0363). Another useful resource is the monthly *Maine Antiques Digest*, available in many bookstores.

APPLES

Fall brings plenty of pick-your-own opportunities across the state, and many orchards also sell apples and cider. For a list of orchards, contact the Department of Agriculture (287-3491) for their brochure "Maine Apples."

AQUARIUMS

The **Maine Aquarium** in Saco is open daily year-round, exhibiting seals, penguins, sharks, and tide-pool animals. There is also a small branch of the aquarium at the end of the Old Orchard Pier. The **Mount Desert Oceanarium** has three locations: Southwest Harbor has 20 tanks exhibiting sea life; Bar Harbor features everything you ever wanted to know about lobsters; and the working lobster hatchery in downtown Bar Harbor is where thousands of lobsters are raised for later release. **Marine Resources**

Aquarium in Southport is also an excellent small facility.

AREA CODE
The area code for Maine is **207.**

ART GALLERIES
Commercial galleries selling work by local artists have proliferated so in recent years that the Maine Publicity Bureau (623-0363) has compiled a partial list of more than 75. Within this book, look for detailed listings in "Ogunquit," "Portland," "Brunswick," "Wiscasset," "Rockland," "Rockport," "Blue Hill," "Eastport," and "Bar Harbor and Acadia."

ART MUSEUMS
Portland Museum of Art (775-6148), 111 High Street, Portland, has an outstanding collection of American paintings. The **Farnsworth Museum** in Rockland represents the prime collection of specifically Maine art and is drawing art lovers from throughout the country. The **Ogunquit Museum,** the **Bowdoin College Museum of Art** in Brunswick, and the **Colby College Museum of Art** in Waterville are also well worth checking out. For descriptions of outstanding museums see "Portland," "Monhegan," "Deer Isle," "Bar Harbor and Acadia," and "Bangor."

BALLOONING
Hot-air rides are available across the state from **Balloons Over New England** (499-7575; 1-800-788-5562) in Kennebunk; **Hot Fun** (799-0193) in South Portland; **Balloon Rides** (761-8373) in Portland; **Freeport Balloon Company** (865-1712) in Pownal; and **Sails Aloft** (623-1136) in Augusta.

BEACHES
Just 2 percent of the Maine coast is public, and not all of that is beach. Given the sum-

NANCY G. HORTON

mer temperature of the water (from 59 degrees in Ogunquit to 54 degrees at Bar Harbor), swimming isn't the primary reason you come to Maine. But Maine beaches can be splendid walking, sunning, and kite-flying places (see York, Wells, the Kennebunks, Portland, Popham, and Pemaquid). At **Ogunquit** and in **Reid State Park,** there are also warmer backwater areas in which small children can paddle. Families tend to take advantage of the reasonably priced cottages available on lakes, many of them just a few miles from the seashore (see *Lakes*). Other outstanding beaches include 7-mile-long **Old Orchard** and, nearby, state-maintained **Crescent Beach** on Cape Elizabeth; **Scarborough Beach** in Scarborough; and **Ferry Beach** in Saco. The big, state-maintained freshwater beaches are on **Lakes Damariscotta, St. George, Sebec, Rangeley, Sebago,** and **Moosehead;** also on **Pleasant Pond** in Richmond. All state beach facilities include changing facilities, rest rooms, and showers; many have snack bars. The town of Bridgton has several fine little lakeside beaches. In 1996, state beaches charged $2 per person entrance; $2.50 at Crescent Beach, Montpelier and Range Ponds, and Sebago Lake.

BED & BREAKFASTS

We visited hundreds of B&Bs and were impressed by what we saw. They range from elegant town houses and country mansions to farms and a fisherman's home. Prices vary from $30 to $450 (on the coast in August)

for a double and average $85 in high season on the coast. With few exceptions, they offer a friendly entrée to their communities. Hosts are usually delighted to advise guests on places to explore, dine, and shop. The *Maine Guide to Inns and Bed & Breakfasts,* available from the Maine Publicity Bureau (623-0363), includes close to 300 descriptive listings for 1996.

BICYCLING

Mountain biking has become a widely popular sport and is often the best way to explore islands, trails, and country roads. The carriage roads in **Acadia National Park** are particularly well suited for mountain biking. Routes are outlined in local handouts, and rentals are available. **Sunday River's Mountain Bike Park** offers high-altitude trails and a bike school (see "Bethel"); **Sugarloaf/USA** also rents bikes and suggests trails. A few Maine islands are best toured by bike; see Casco Bay islands and Islesboro. Bicycle rentals are also available in Bar Harbor, Kennebunkport, and Ogunquit. **American Youth Hostels** maintains nominally priced, bicyclist-geared hostels in Portland, Carmel, and Bar Harbor; contact AYH, Greater Boston Council, 1020 Commonwealth Avenue, Boston, MA 02215 (617-731-5430). Another good resource for bikers is *25 Bicycle Tours in Maine* by Howard Stone (Backcountry Publications).

BIRDING

The **Maine Audubon Society** (781-2330), based at Gilsland Farm in Falmouth, maintains a number of birding sites and sponsors nature programs and field trips, which include cruises to Matinicus Rock and to Eagle Island. (For details about the **National Audubon Ecology Camp** on Hog Island, see "Damariscotta.") The most popular coastal birding spots are the **national wildlife sanctuaries** between Kittery and Cape Elizabeth, especially the area now preserved as **Laudholm Farm** in Wells. **Biddeford Pool, Scarborough Marsh, Merrymeeting Bay,** and **Mount Desert** are the other top birding sites. **Monhegan** is the island to visit. The **Moosehorn National Wildlife Refuge** (454-3521) in Washington County represents the northeastern terminus of the East Coast chain of wildlife refuges and is particularly rich in bird life. We recommend *A Birder's Guide to the Coast of Maine* by Elizabeth Cary Pierson and Jan Erik Pierson (Down East Books). (Also see *Puffin-Watching* and *Nature Preserves*.)

BLUEBERRYING

Maine grows 98 percent of America's lowbush blueberries. More than 40 million pounds are harvested annually from an estimated 25,000 acres. Because of pruning practices, only half the acreage produces berries in a given year, and there are absolutely no human-planted wild blueberry fields. Lowbush blueberry plants spread naturally in the present commercial fields after the forests are cleared or by natural establishment in abandoned pastures. Unfortunately, very few berries are sold fresh (most are quick-frozen), and few growers allow U-pick, at least not until the commercial harvest is over. Then the public is invited to go "stumping" for leftovers. On the other hand, berrying along roads and hiking paths, under power lines, and on hilltops is a rite of summer for all who happen to be in southern Maine in late July or farther Down East in early August. For a look at the **blueberry barrens**—thousands of blueberry-covered acres—you must drive up to Cherryfield, Columbia, and Machias (site of the state's most colorful blueberry festival in August) in Washington County. For more about Maine's most famous fruit, write: Wild Blueberry Association of North America, 142 Kelley Road, Orono 04473.

BOATBUILDING

Wooden Boat School (359-4651) in Brooklin (see "Blue Hill") offers more than 75 warm-weather courses, including more than 24 on various aspects of boatbuilding. The **Maine Maritime Museum** in Bath offers an apprenticeship program; the **Landing School of Boatbuilding & Design** in Kennebunk offers summer courses in building sailboats; and the **Washington County Vocational-Tech Inst. Marine Trades Center** at Deep Cove attracts many out-of-staters.

BOAT EXCURSIONS

You don't need to own your own yacht to enjoy the salt spray and views, and you really won't know what Maine is about until you stand off at sea to appreciate the beauty of the cliffs and island-dotted bays. For the greatest concentrations of boat excursions, see "Boothbay Harbor," "Rockland," and "Bar Harbor and Acadia"; there are also excursions from Ogunquit, Kennebunkport, Portland, Belfast, Camden, Castine, and Stonington. (Also see *Coastal Cruises, Ferries, Sailing*, and *Windjammers*. See "Sebago and Long Lakes," "Rangeley," and "Augusta and Mid Maine" for lake excursions.) A partial list of more than 100 cruises, ferries, and deep-sea fishing options is published in Maine Publicity Bureau's annual free magazine, *Maine Invites You* (see *Information*).

BOAT RENTALS

Readily available in the Belgrade Lakes, the Sebago Lake area, in Rangeley, Jackman, Rockwood, and all other inland lake areas. (Also see *Canoe Rentals* and *Sailing.*)

BOOKS

Anyone who seriously sets out to explore Maine should read the following mix of Maine classics and guidebooks: *The Maine Woods* by Henry David Thoreau, first published posthumously in 1864, remains very readable and gives an excellent description of Maine's mountains (we recommend the Penguin edition). Our favorite relatively recent Maine author is Ruth Moore, who writes about Maine islands in *The Weir, Spoon Handle,* and *Speak to the Wind* (originally published in the 1940s, reissued by Blackberry Books, Nobleboro); happily the '40s books by Louise Dickinson Rich, among which our favorites are *The Coast of Maine: An Informal History* and *We Took to the Woods,* are now published by Down East Books in Camden, along with Henry Beston's '40s classic *Northern Farm: A Chronicle of Maine.* Sarah Orne Jewett's classic, *The Country of the Pointed Firs and Other Stories,* first published in 1896, is still an excellent read, set on the coast around Tenants Harbor (W.W. Norton, New York). The children's classics by Robert McCloskey, *Blueberries for Sal* (Viking Children's Books, 1948), *Time of Wonder* (1957), and *One Morning in Maine* (1952), are as fresh as the day they were written. John Gould, an essayist who wrote a regular column for the *Christian Science Monitor* for more than 50 years, has published several books, including *Dispatches from Maine,* a collection of those columns, and *Maine Lingo* (with Lillian Ross), a humorous look at Maine phrases and expressions. E.B. White has some wonderful essay collections as well, along with his ever-popular children's novels, *Charlotte's Web* and *Stuart Little.*

Recent classics set in Maine include Carolyn Chute's *The Beans of Egypt, Maine* (1985), *Letourneau's Used Auto Parts* (1988), and *Merry Men* (1994), and Cathie Pelletier's *The Funeral Makers* (1987) and *The Weight of Winter* (1991). *Maine Speaks,* an anthology of Maine literature published by the Maine Writers and Publishers Alliance (see "Brunswick") contains all the obvious poems and essays and many pleasant surprises; *The Maine Reader,* edited by Charles and Samuella Shain, is an anthology of writing from the 1600s to the present.

Guides to exploring Maine include the indispensable *Maine Atlas and Gazetteer* (DeLorme Publishing Company) and, from Down East Books, *A Birder's Guide to the Coast of Maine* by Elizabeth Cary Pierson and Jan Erik Pierson, *Walking the Maine Coast* by John Gibson, and *Islands in Time: A Natural and Human History of the Islands of Maine* by Philip W. Conkling. Serious hikers should secure the *AMC Maine Mountain Guide* (AMC Books, Boston); also *50 Hikes in the Maine Mountains* by Cloe Chunn and *50 Hikes in Southern and Coastal Maine* by John Gibson (Backcountry Publications). Also worth noting: *The Wildest Country: A Guide to Thoreau's Maine* by J. Parker Huber (AMC Books). *Maine,* by Charles C. Calhoun (Compass American Guides), complements this guide with its superb illustrations and well-written background text.

CAMPING

Almost half of Maine lies within "unorganized townships": wooded, privately owned lands, most of which are open to the public on the condition that basic rules be observed. These rules vary with the owners. See the "Northern Maine" chapters for details about camping within these vast fiefdoms, also for camping in **Baxter State Park** and in the **Allagash Wilderness.** For camping within **Acadia National Park,** see "Bar Harbor and Acadia." For the same within the **White Mountain National Forest,** see "Bethel." For private campgrounds, the booklet "Maine Camping Guide," published by the Maine Campground Owners Association (782-5874), lists most privately operated camping and tenting areas in the state and is available from the Maine Publicity Bureau (623-0363). Reservations are advised for the state's 13 parks that offer camping; phone 287-3821. We have attempted to describe the state parks in detail wherever they appear in this book (see Damariscotta, Camden, Cobscook Bay, Sebago, Rangeley, and Greenville). Note that though campsites can accommodate average-sized campers and trailers, there are no trailer hook-ups. Warren Island (just off Isleboro) and Swan Island (just off Richmond) offer organized camping, and primitive camping is permitted on a number of islands through the Island Institute (see *Islands*). (Also see *Parks, State.*)

CAMPS, FOR ADULTS

The **Appalachian Mountain Club** maintains a number of summer lodges and campsites for adults and families seeking a hiking and/or canoeing vacation. Intended primarily for members, they are technically open to all who reserve space, available only after April 1. The full-service camps in Maine (offering three daily meals, organized hikes, evening programs) are at **Echo Lake** and **Cold River Camp** in Evans Notch (near the New Hampshire border within the White Mountain National Forest). For details about all facilities and membership, contact the AMC (617-523-0636). **Outward Bound** (594-5548) in Rockland and Bethel offers a variety of adult-geared outdoors adventures. **Audubon Ecology Camp** on

Hog Island off Bremen offers a series of weeklong courses; contact the registrar (203-869-2017). The **University of Maine at Machias** (255-3313) is a summer center for ornithology workshops. **Maine Folk Dance Camp** (647-3424) in Bridgton has been a center for international dance and customs since 1950. Nine weekly sessions start the last week in June; before then phone 516-661-3866. Photographers should check out the **Maine Photographic Workshop** in Camden; also check boatbuilding schools (**Wooden Boat** offers much more than boatbuilding); **Elderhostel** (617-426-7788), which offers a variety of programs throughout Maine for everyone over age 60; and **Merle Donovan's Maine Coast Workshops** (372-8200), Port Clyde.

CAMPS, FOR CHILDREN

More than 200 summer camps are listed in the exceptional booklet published annually by the Maine Youth Camping Association, PO Box 455, Orono 04473 (581-1350); also available from the Maine Publicity Bureau (623-0363).

CAMPS, RENTAL

In Maine, "camp" is the word for a second home or cottage. See *Cottage Rentals* for inexpensive vacation rentals.

CANOEING, GUIDED TRIPS

Saco Bound, just over the New Hampshire line (Box 1, Conway, NH 03813; 603-447-2177), offers guided tours on the calm (great for beginners) Saco River, as well as white-water canoeing and rafting. A number of "outfitters" specializing in Allagash Waterway and other wilderness trips are listed in the *Outdoor Guide to Maine,* published by the Maine Professional Guides Association and available from the Maine Publicity Bureau (623-0363), which also publishes a list of canoe and kayaking outfitters in *Maine Invites You.*

CANOEING THE ALLAGASH

The ultimate canoe trip in Maine (and on the entire East Coast, for that matter) is the 7- to 10-day expedition up the Allagash Wilderness Waterway, a 92-mile ribbon of lakes, ponds, rivers, and streams through the heart of northern Maine's vast commercial forests. Since 1966 the land flanking the waterway has been owned (500 feet back on either side of the waterway) by the state of Maine. A map pinpointing the 65 authorized campsites within the zone (and supplying other crucial information) is available free from the Bureau of Parks and Lands (287-4984), State House Station 22, Augusta 04333. A more detailed map, backed with historical and a variety of other handy information, is DeLorme's "Map and Guide to the Allagash and St. John." Anybody contemplating the trip should be aware of blackflies in June and the "no-seeums" when warm weather finally comes. For further information, check *Camping* and *Guide Services*.

CANOE RENTALS

Rentals are under *To Do* within each chapter.

CHILDREN, ESPECIALLY FOR

The Maine Publicity Bureau booklet "Fun for the Whole Family" lists over 90 activities that are good to do with children. Within this book, note that we have marked a number of sites and activities that have special child appeal with a "✐."

CLAMMING

Maine state law permits the harvesting of shellfish for personal use only, unless you have a commercial license. Individuals can take up to ½ bushel of shellfish or 3 bushels of hen or surf clams (the big ones out in the flats) in 1 day, unless municipal ordinances further limit "the taking of shellfish." Be sure to check locally at the town clerk's office (source of licenses) before you dig, and make sure there's no red tide. Some towns do prohibit clamming, and in certain places there is a temporary stay on harvesting while the beds are being seeded. In a few places clamming has been banned because of pollution.

COASTAL CRUISES

"Cruise" is a much used (and abused) term along the Maine coast, used chiefly to mean a boat ride. *Maine Invites You* has a list of over 100 cruises, ferries, and deep-sea fishing choices, most of them described in the appropriate chapters of this book. We have also tried to list the charter sailing yachts that will take passengers on multiday cruises and have described each of the windjammers that sail for 3 and 6 days at a time (see *Windjammers*).

COTTAGE RENTALS

Cottage rentals are the only reasonably priced way to go for families who wish to stay in one Maine spot for more than a week (unless you go for camping). Request the booklet "Maine Guide to Camp & Cottage Rentals" from the Maine Publicity Bureau (623-0363). The 1996 booklet's weekly rates for coastal cottages in July and August begin at $350. If you have your heart set on one particular area and cannot get satisfaction through the booklet, we recommend obtaining a printout of real estate agencies just for that county, then sending notes off to agents in the precise area in which you are interested. The printouts are available for a small fee by writing to the Maine Department of Business Regulation, Central Licensing Division, State House Station 35, Augusta 04333 (287-2217).

COVERED BRIDGES

Of the 120 covered bridges that once spanned Maine rivers, just 9 survive. A leaflet guide is available from the Maine Publicity Bureau (623-0363). The most famous, and certainly as picturesque as a covered bridge can be, is the **Artist's Covered Bridge** (1872) over the Sunday River in Newry, northwest of Bethel. The others are: **Porter Bridge** (1876), over the Ossipee River, 0.5 mile south of Porter; **Babb's Bridge,** recently rebuilt, over the Presumpscot River between Gorham and Windham; **Hemlock Bridge** (1857), 3 miles northwest of East Fryeburg; **Lovejoy Bridge** (1883), in South Andover; **Bennett Bridge** (1901), over the Magalloway River, 1.5 miles south of the Wilson's Mills Post Office; **Robyville Bridge** (1876), Maine's only completely shingled covered bridge, in the town of Corinth; and the **Watson Settlement Bridge** (1911), between Woodstock and Littleton. Carefully reconstructed **Low's Bridge** (1857), across the Piscataquis River between Guilford and Sangerville was added in 1990.

CRAFTS

"Maine Cultural Guide," published by the Maine Crafts Association, is available by writing to Box 288, Deer Isle 04627, or phoning 348-9943. The free, 80-page booklet describes hundreds of studios, galleries, and museums in Maine. For a shorter listing of craftspeople and juried crafts shows, write to Directions, PO Box 10832, Portland 04104. United Maine Craftsmen Inc. (621-2818) also sponsors several large shows each year.

CRAFTS CENTERS

Haystack Mountain School of Crafts (see "Deer Isle") is a summer school nationally respected in a variety of crafts, offering 3-week courses beginning mid-June and continuing through mid-September. Applicants must be more than 18 years old; enrollment is limited to 65. Work by students is displayed in the visitors center, which also serves as a forum for frequent evening presentations. The surrounding area (Blue Hill to Stonington) contains the largest concentration of Maine craftspeople, many of whom invite visitors to their studios.

DEEP-SEA FISHING

Cruises, Ferries, and Deep-Sea Fishing, available from the Maine Publicity Bureau (623-0363), describes many boats throughout the state. We have described specific boats within appropriate chapters.

DIVE SHOPS

The Maine Publicity Bureau keeps a statewide list (see *Information*).

DOGSLEDDING

Although racing is a long-established winter spectator sport, the chance actually to ride on a dogsled is relatively recent and growing in popularity. Tim Diehl at **Sugarloaf/USA** offers half-hour rides throughout the day during ski season (you ride behind a team of friendly, frisky Samoyeds), **Bethel Outdoor Adventures** (1-800-533-3607) offers dogsled workshops and tours, and in Newry, Polly Mahoney and Kevin Slater **(Mahoosuc Mountain Adventures)** offer multiday treks with their huskies. Diehl also offers summer rides. See the "Sugarloaf" and "Bethel" chapters for details.

EVENTS
We have listed outstanding annual events within each chapter of this book, and leaflet guides to events are published by the state four times a year. Check with the Maine Publicity Bureau (623-0363).

FACTORY OUTLETS
See the "Kittery" and "Freeport" chapters.

FACTORY TOURS
Tours range from Tom's of Maine in Kennebunk (toothpaste) to Rackliffe and Rowantrees Pottery-makers (Blue Hill), and include Blueberry Processors & Growers (Cherryfield) and Maine Wild Blueberry Company (Machias).

FALL FOLIAGE
Autumn is extremely pleasant along the coast; days tend to be clear, and the changing leaves against the blue sea can be spectacular. Many inns remain open through foliage season, and the resort towns of Ogunquit, Kennebunkport, Boothbay Harbor, Bar Harbor, and Camden all offer excellent dining, shopping, and lodging through Columbus Day weekend. Off-season prices prevail, in contrast with the rest of New England, at this time of year. *Maine Invites You* outlines some particularly beautiful tours, as does *Maine Fall Foliage Tours*, published by Down East Enterprise, Inc., and available at Maine Publicity Bureau information centers.

FARM B&BS
In 1996, 19 farms are described in a brochure available from the Maine Farm Vacation B&B Association, RR 3, 377 Gray Road, Route 26, West Falmouth 04105 (797-5540). Note that this is a promotional association, not an officially approved and inspected group. Properties vary widely. Some are just what you might expect: plenty of space, animals, big breakfasts, friendly, informal atmosphere, and reasonable prices. Others are more formal. Some are not farms. The properties are scattered across Maine. Though we haven't made it to all of those listed yet, the ones we have seen are recommended in their regions. We wish there were some in Aroostook County.

FARMER'S MARKETS
The Maine Federation of Farmer's Markets, RFD 1, Box 234 Hebron 04238, publishes a pamphlet listing over 25 farmer's markets statewide.

FERRIES, TO CANADA
Portland to Yarmouth, Nova Scotia: **Prince of Fundy Cruises** offers nightly sailings (departing 9:30 PM) late April through the Columbus Day weekend. The ferry itself is a car-carrying cruise ship with gambling, restaurants, and cabins aboard (1-800-482-0955 in Maine; 1-800-341-7540 in the United States). The ***Bluenose*** (1-800-341-7981) runs between Bar Harbor and Yarmouth, Nova Scotia, nightly year-round. Note that it's very possible to use these ferries as part of a loop: going on one and returning on the other. Mid-June to mid-September **East Coast Ferries Ltd.** (506-747-2159), a small car ferry based on Deer Island, serves Eastport (30 minutes) and Campobello (45 minutes), and the small provincial (free) **Deer Island–L'Etete Ferry** (506-453-2600) also connects the island with the New Brunswick mainland. The 65-car **Coastal Transport Ltd. Ferry** (506-662-3724) runs year-round from Black Harbour, not far east of L'Etete, to the island of Grand Manan.

FERRIES, IN MAINE

Maine State Ferry Service (1-800-521-3939 in-state; 207-596-2202 outside of Maine), Rockland 04841, operates year-round service from Rockland to Vinalhaven and North Haven, from Lincolnville to Islesboro, and from Bass Harbor to Swan's Island and Frenchboro. For private ferry services to Monhegan, see "Boothbay Harbor" and "The Islands"; for the Casco Bay islands, see "Portland"; for Matinicus, see "The Islands"; and for Isle au Haut, see "East Penobscot Bay Region."

FIRE PERMITS

Maine law dictates that no person shall kindle or use outdoor fires without a permit, except at authorized campsites or picnic grounds. Fire permits in the organized towns are obtained from the local town warden; in the unorganized towns, from the nearest forest ranger. Portable stoves fueled by propane gas, gasoline, or sterno are exempt from the rule.

FISHING

"The Maine Guide to Hunting and Fishing," published by the Maine Publicity Bureau (623-0363), is a handy overview of rules, license fees, and other matters of interest to fishermen. (Also see *Deep-Sea Fishing*.) Detailed descriptions of camps and rustic resorts catering to fishermen can be found in chapters under "Western Lakes," "The Kennebec Valley" and "Northern Maine." A 1-day fishing license cost nonresidents $9 in 1996; 3-, 7-, and 15-day licenses are also available at most general stores and sporting-goods outlets or by writing to the Maine Department of Inland Fisheries and Wildlife, 284 State Street, Augusta 04333 (287-3371).

FLYING SCHOOLS

The Maine Publicity Bureau keeps a list (see *Information*).

NEAL PARENT

FORTS

To be married to a fort freak is to realize that there are people in this world who will detour 50 miles to see an 18th-century earthworks. Maine's forts are actually a fascinating lot, monuments to the state's unique and largely forgotten history. Examples: **Fort William Henry** at Pemaquid, **Fort Edgecomb** in Edgecomb, **Fort George** in Castine, **Fort Kent** and **Fort Knox** near Bucksport, **Fort McClary** in Kittery, **Fort O'Brien** near Machias, **Fort Popham** near Bath, and **Fort Pownall** at Stockton Springs.

GOLF

The Maine Publicity Bureau publishes a statewide list of golf courses in *Maine Invites You* (the list is also available as a separate brochure). Within this book, we list golf courses for each area. The major resorts catering to golfers are the **Samoset** in Rockport, the **Bethel Inn** in Bethel, **Sebasco Estates** near Bath, the **Country Club Inn** in Rangeley, and **Sugarloaf/USA** in the Carrabassett Valley.

GORGES

Maine has the lion's share of the Northeast's gorges. There are four biggies. The widest is the **Upper Sebois River Gorge** north of Patten, and the most dramatic, "Maine's Miniature Grand Canyon," is **Gulf Hagas** near the Katahdin Iron Works (see Katahdin Region). Both **Kennebec Gorge** and **Ripogenus Gorge** are now popular whitewater-rafting routes.

GUIDE SERVICES

There are more than 1000 registered Maine guides—men and women who have passed a qualifying test. Finding the guide to suit your needs, be it fishing, hunting, or canoeing the Allagash Waterway, can be a confusing business. A list of guides is available from the Maine Professional Guides Association (785-2061), 18 White Street, Topsham 04086.

HIKING

For organized trips, contact the Appalachian Mountain Club's Boston office (617-523-0636). In addition to the *AMC Maine Mountain Guide* (available from AMC Books Division, Dept. B, 5 Joy Street, Boston, MA 02108) and the AMC map guide to trails on Mount Desert, we recommend investing in *50 Hikes in Southern and Coastal Maine* by John Gibson and *50 Hikes in the Maine Mountains* by Cloe Chunn (both from Backcountry Publications), which offer clear, inviting treks up hills of every size throughout the state. The *Maine Atlas and Gazetteer* (DeLorme Publishing Company) also outlines a number of rewarding hikes.

HISTORIC HOUSES

The Maine Publicity Bureau's outstanding booklet "Museums and Historic Homes" is worth requesting (623-0363). Within this book, dozens of historic houses open to the public are listed by town.

HORSE RACING

Harness racing can be found at **Scarborough Downs** (883-4331), US 1, or exit 6 off the Maine Turnpike, April through November. The **Bangor Raceway** is open late May through late July. **County Raceways** has several scheduled dates in June, July, and August. The leaflet guide "Maine Agricultural Fairs" also lists harness racing dates for the current season. Contact the Maine Harness Racing Commission (287-3221) for more information.

HORSEBACK RIDING

Northern Maine Adventures (see "Moosehead Lake") offers entire days and overnights as well as shorter stints in the saddle. For trail riding, check "Old Orchard Beach," "Boothbay Harbor," "Sebago and Long Lakes," and "Moosehead Lake." *Maine Invites You* publishes a list of stables.

HUNTING

Hunters should obtain a summary of Maine hunting and trapping laws from the Maine Department of Inland Fisheries and Wildlife, 284 State Street, Augusta 04333 (287-3371). For leads on registered Maine guides who specialize in organized expeditions (complete with meals and lodging), contact the sources we list under *Fishing, Guide Services, Canoeing,* and *Camping.* You might also try the Moosehead Region Chamber of Commerce (695-2702). A handy "Maine Guide to Hunting and Fishing" booklet, published annually by the Maine Publicity Bureau (623-0363), is filled with information and ads for hunting lodges, guides, and the like.

INFORMATION

The Maine Publicity Bureau (623-0363; 1-800-533-9595 outside of Maine), PO Box 2300, Hallowell 04347, publishes *Maine*

Invites You, as well as "Exploring Maine," "Maine Guide to Hunting and Fishing," *Maine Guide to Winter,* and a variety of other guides noted here under specific headings. Write or call the bureau's office if you have a special query, or stop by one of the MPB year-round information centers: on I-95 in Kittery (439-1319); just off coastal Route 1 and I-95 in Yarmouth (846-0833); both northbound and southbound on I-95 in Hampden near Bangor (862-6628/6638); in Calais (454-2211); and in Houlton (532-6346). There is also a seasonal information center on the New Hampshire line on Route 302 in Fryeburg (935-3639).

INNS

In this book, we have been more selective than in earlier editions because there are simply so many more new places to stay out there. While researching this book, we personally inspected more than 400 inns and B&Bs. Realizing that "inn books" tend to focus on the higher end of the price spectrum, we have tried to include more reasonably priced, equally appealing options in the same area. The booklet "Maine Guide to Inns and Bed & Breakfasts" is useful, free from the Maine Publicity Bureau (623-0363). *Best Places to Stay in New England* by Christina Tree and Kimberly Grant (Houghton Mifflin) also includes a wide range of places to stay in Maine.

ISLANDS

In all there are said to be over 3000 islands, most uninhabited, ranging from oversized rocks to several thousand acres. The state owns some 1500 of these islands, totaling 800 acres (the average size is a half acre), and 45 are open to the public; so are 15 privately owned islands. Access is through the **Maine Island Trail Association** (596-6456). For a $40 membership fee you receive a map guide to the 74 islands scattered

NEAL PARENT

over 325 miles from Casco Bay to Machias Bay. For details about camping on state-owned islands, contact the **Bureau of Parks and Lands** (287-3821) and request the brochure "Your Islands on the Coast." The islands that offer overnight accommodations are Chebeague and Peaks in Casco Bay (see "Portland"), Monhegan, Vinalhaven, North Haven, Matinicus (see "The Islands"), Isle au Haut, Islesford and Islesboro.

LAKES

Maine boasts some 6000 lakes and ponds, and every natural body of water over 10 acres—which accounts for most of them—is, theoretically at least, available to the public for "fishing and fowling." Access is, of course, limited by the property owners around the lakes. Because so much acreage in Maine is owned by paper companies and other land-management concerns that permit public use provided the public obey their rules (see *Camping*), there is ample opportunity to canoe or fish in solitary waters. Powerboat owners should note that most states have reciprocal license privileges with Maine; the big exception is New Hampshire. For more about the most popular resort lakes in the state, see Bridgton, Rangeley, Greenville, and the Belgrade Lakes. The state parks on lakes are **Aroostook** (camping, fishing, swimming; Route 1 south of Presque Isle), **Damariscotta Lake State Park** (Route 32 in Jefferson), **Lake St. George State Park** (swimming, picnicking, fishing; Route 3 in Liberty), **Lily Bay State Park** (8 miles north of Greenville), **Peacock Beach State Park** (swimming, picnicking; Richmond), **Peaks-Kenny State Park** (Sebec Lake in Dover-Foxcroft), **Rangeley Lake State Park** (swimming, camping; Rangeley), **Range Ponds State Park** (Poland), **Sebago Lake State Park** (swimming, picnicking, camping; near Bridgton), **Mount Blue Lake State Park** (Weld), and **Swan Lake State Park** (Swanville). Families with small children should be aware of the many coastal lakes surrounded by reasonably priced cottages (see *Cottages, Rental*).

LIGHTHOUSES

Maine takes pride in its 63 lighthouses. The most popular to visit are **Portland Head Light** (completed in 1790, automated in 1990, now a delightful museum featuring the history of lighthouses) on Cape Elizabeth; **Cape Neddick Light** in York; **Marshall Point Light** at Port Clyde; **Fort Point Light** at Stockton Springs; **Pemaquid Point** (the lighthouse keeper's house is now a museum, there's an art gallery, and the rocks below are peerless for scrambling); **Owl's Head** near Rockland (built 1826); **Bass Harbor Head Light** at Bass Harbor; and Lubec's **West Quoddy Head,** the start of a beautiful shore path. On **Monhegan,** the lighthouse keeper's house is a seasonal museum, and at **Grindle Point** on Islesboro there is also an adjacent seasonal museum. True lighthouse buffs also make the pilgrimage to **Matinicus Rock,** the setting for children's books. Lighthouse aficionados tell us that **East Quoddy Head Lighthouse** on the island of Campobello, accessible at low tide, is the ultimate adventure to get to; it is also a prime whale-watching post. Captain Barna Norton (497-5933) runs charters from Jonesport to lighthouses on Libby Island, Moose Peak, Nash Island, and Petit Manan, as well as to Machias Seal (see *Puffin-Watching*).

LITTER

Littering in Maine is punishable by a $100 fine; this applies to dumping from boats as well as other vehicles. Most cans and bottles are redeemable.

LLAMA TREKKING

The principle is appealingly simple: The llama carries your gear; you lead the llama. From the **Telemark Inn** (836-2703), surrounded by semi-wilderness west of Bethel, Steve Crone offers day and multiday treks. At **Pleasant Bay Bed & Breakfast** (483-4490) in Addison, guests can walk the property's waterside trails with the llamas, and at **Maine-lly Llamas Farm** (929-3057) in Hollis, guests can also take a nature trek with llamas.

LOBSTER POUNDS

A lobster pound is usually a no-frills seaside restaurant that specializes in serving lobsters and clams steamed in seawater. The most basic and reasonably priced pounds are frequently fishermen's co-ops. The Pemaquid Peninsula (see "Damariscotta") is especially blessed: Check out both the **New Harbor Co-op** and neighboring **Shaw's,** the **Pemaquid Fisherman's Co-op,** and, in nearby Round Pond, both **Muscongus Bay Lobster** and **Round Pond Lobster. Cod End** in Tenants Harbor, **Miller's Lobster Company** on Spruce Head, and **Waterman's Beach Lobsters** in South Thomaston are also the real thing. Expect good value but no china plates and salads at **Chauncey Creek** in Kittery, **Harraseeket Lunch & Lobster Company** in South Freeport, and the **Fisherman's Landing** in Bar Harbor; other lobster-eating landmarks include **Nunan's Lobster Hut** in Cape Porpoise, **Eaton's** on Deer Isle, **Robinson's Wharf** at Townsend Gut near Boothbay, the **Lobster Shack** on Cape Elizabeth, the **Lobster Pound** in Lincolnville Beach, the **Lobster Shack** in Searsport, **Trenton Bridge** on Route 3 at the entrance to Mount Desert, and on the island: **Oak Point** and **Thurston's.** The **Ogunquit Lobster Pound** in Ogunquit and **Beal's** in Southwest Harbor tend to be the state's priciest pounds.

LOBSTERS TO GO

The Maine Publicity Bureau (see *Information*) keeps a list of firms that will ship lobsters anywhere in the world.

THE MAINE FESTIVAL

Maine's biggest, splashiest cultural happening of the year, the festival is held for 4 days around the second weekend in August at Thomas Point Beach in Brunswick. Performing artists are from everywhere, but the Maine folk artists are definitely local, as are the craftspeople; children's entertainment, a food garden, and plenty of outdoor sculpture are also part of the scene. Sponsored by Maine Arts: 772-9012; 1-800-639-4212.

MAINE TURNPIKE

For travel conditions, phone 1-800-675-PIKE.

MAPLE SUGARING

Maine produces roughly 8000 gallons of syrup a year, and the Maine Department of Agriculture publishes a list of producers who welcome visitors on **Maine Maple Sunday** (also known as Sap Sunday) in late March.

MOOSE-WATCHING

Moose have made a comeback from their near-extinct status in the 1930s and now number more than 20,000. Your chances of spotting one are best in early morning or at dusk on a wooded pond or lake or along logging roads. If you are driving through moose country at night, go slowly because moose typically freeze rather than retreat from oncoming headlights. For details about commercial moose-watching expeditions, check the "Rangeley" and "Moosehead Lake" chapters. The Moosehead Lake Region Chamber of Commerce sponsors **"Moosemainea"** mid-May through mid-June, with special events and a huge moose locator map. Suspicious that this promotion coincided with Moosehead's low tourist season,

BILL SILLIKER JR.

we queried the state's moose expert, who assures us that moose are indeed most visible in late spring. Last season 5200 moose were spotted.

MUSEUM VILLAGES

What variety! Open seasonally as a commercial attraction, **Willowbrook** at Newfield is a 19th-century village center consisting of 31 buildings that have been restored by one man. Other attractions include the old village center of **Searsport,** restored as a fine maritime museum; **Sabbathday Lake Shaker Museum,** still a functioning religious community; **York Village,** with its Old Gaol, school, tavern, church, and scattering of historic houses open to the public, all adding up to a picture of late-18th-century life in coastal Maine; **Norlands,** a former estate with a neo-Gothic library, school, and farm buildings, as well as a mansion that invites you to come and live for a weekend as if you were in this particular place (Livermore) in the 1870s.

MUSEUMS

Also see *Art Museums*. Easily the most undervisited in the state, the **Maine State Museum** in Augusta has outstanding displays on the varied Maine landscape and historical exhibits ranging from traces of the area's earliest people to rifles used by State of Mainers in Korea; you can also see exhibits on fishing, agriculture, lumbering, quarrying, and shipbuilding. Our own favorites also include the **Peary-MacMillan Arctic Museum** at Bowdoin College in Brunswick, the **Seashore Trolley Museum** in Kennebunkport, the **Owl's Head Transportation Museum** near Rockland, the **Robert Abbe Museum** in Acadia National Park (outstanding for its regional Native American artifacts), the **Wilson Museum** in Castine, the **Patten Lumberman's Museum** in Patten (which surprises you with the extent and quality of

its exhibits), and the **Colonial Pemaquid Restoration** in Pemaquid (which presents fascinating archaeological finds from the adjacent, early-17th-century settlement). The **Maine Maritime Museum** in Bath stands in a class by itself and should not be missed.

MUSIC CONCERT SERIES

Among the most famous summer concert series are the **Bar Harbor Festival** (288-5744) and the **Mount Desert Festival of Chamber Music** (276-5039); the **Sebago/Long Lakes Region Chamber Music Festival** in North Bridgton (627-4939); the **Bay Chamber Concerts,** presented in the Rockport Opera House (236-2823); the **Round Top Center for the Arts** (563-1507) in Damariscotta, a series of outdoor picnic concerts; **Kneisel Hall** chamber concerts in Blue Hill; **Bowdoin College Summer Concerts** in Brunswick (725-8731, ext. 321); and **Machias Bay Chamber Concerts** in Machias (255-8685). There is, of course, the **Portland Symphony Orchestra** (773-8191), which also has a summertime pops series, and the **Bangor Symphony Orchestra** (945-6408). Music lovers should also take note of the **Annual Rockport Folk Festival** in mid-July, the **Downeast Jazz Festival in Rockland** every August, the **Lincoln Arts Festival** of classical and choral music held throughout the Boothbay Harbor Region in summer months, and the **Bluegrass Festival** at Thomas Point Beach in September.

MUSIC SCHOOLS

Notable are **Bowdoin College Summer School** (see *Music Concert Series*), **Kneisel Hall** in Blue Hill (call 725-8731 only after June 24; prior inquiries should be addressed to Kneisel Hall, Blue Hill 04614); the **Pierre Monteux Memorial Domaine School** in Hancock (442-6251); **Salzedo Summer Harp Colony** in Camden (236-2289); **New**

England Music Camp in Oakland (465-3025); **Maine Summer Youth Music** at the University of Maine, Orono (581-1960); and **Maine Music Camp** at the University of Maine, Farmington (778-3501).

NATURE PRESERVES, COASTAL

The **Rachel Carson National Wildlife Refuge** is a total of nine separate preserves salted between Kittery and Cape Elizabeth along the Atlantic Flyway. Request a leaflet guide from the Parker River National Wildlife Refuge, Newbury, MA 01950. The Maine Audubon Society headquarters at **Gilsland Farm** in Falmouth (open year-round) has 70 acres with nature trails through woodlands, meadows, and marshes. The **Maine Audubon Society** maintains a nature center at **Scarborough Marsh** and offers canoe tours, bird walks, and a variety of other summer programs (883-5100). The society also maintains self-guiding nature trails (cross-country-ski trails in winter) and facilities for picnicking and tenting at the 150-acre **Mast Landing Sanctuary** in Freeport. **Birdsacre,** a 40-acre preserve in Ellsworth, harbors 109 species of birds in and around a network of nature trails and maintains a museum that honors pioneer ornithologist Cordelia Stanwood, open June 15 through October 15 and other times by appointment (667-8683). **Acadia National Park,** with its miles of hiking trails and extensive naturalist-led programs, is the state's busiest preserve (see "Bar Harbor and Acadia"). Some 30 miles east of Ellsworth, in Steuben, is **Petit Manan National Wildlife Refuge** (1999 acres), a peninsula offering two hiking trails. At the extreme eastern end of Maine, the **Moosehorn National Wildlife Refuge** in Calais (454-3521) consists of two units, roughly 20 miles apart. The bigger (16,065 acres) is partially bounded by the St. Croix River, and the 6600-acre Edmunds Unit overlooks Cobscook Bay; a visitors center is open May through September, and there are hiking trails. The largest private landowner of preservation land in Maine is **The Nature Conservancy** (729-5181), protecting 82 preserves adding up to more than 22,000 acres throughout the state. For details, request "Maine Forever: A Guide to Nature Conservancy Preserves in Maine," available through the Maine chapter of The Nature Conservancy, 14 Maine Street, Suite 401, Brunswick 04011. (Also see *Islands* and *Birding*.) Recently acquired preserves are summarized in "Land for Maine's Future," a brochure worth requesting from the Maine State Planning Office (287-3261; ask for "LMFB"). **The Maine Coast Heritage Trust** (729-7366) also protects some 66,000 acres, including 173 islands and 250 miles of shore, through conservation easements.

NATURE PRESERVES, INLAND

Steve Powell Wildlife Management Area, described in a booklet available from the Maine Department of Inland Fisheries and Wildlife, 284 State Street, Augusta 04333 (289-3651), consists of two islands and several hundred acres of intervening tidal flats at the head of Merrymeeting Bay. Southeast of Fryeburg, the **Brownfield Bog Wildlife Management Areas** (5454 acres) are a mix of marshland, floodplain, and upland that invites exploration by canoe; a campsite at Walker's Falls is maintained by the Appalachian Mountain Club (see *Hiking*). In the Bridgton area there is the **Hiram Nature Study Area** maintained by the Central Maine Power Company (647-3391), some 60 acres of woodland in Baldwin with a trail along the Saco River and picnic facilities. **Vaughan Woods,** a 250-acre state preserve, offers a few fine miles of wooded hiking trails along the Salmon Falls River, good for cross-country skiing and birding as well as hiking and picnicking (see "Kittery"). The greatest inland preserve is **Baxter State Park** in Maine's North Woods (see "Katahdin"). (Also see *Camping, Fishing, Hiking,* and *Hunting,* and The Nature Conservancy and "Land for Maine's Future" under *Nature Preserves, Coastal.*)

PARKS AND FORESTS, NATIONAL

Acadia National Park (288-3338), which occupies roughly half of Mount Desert, plus scattered areas on Isle au Haut, Little Cranberry Island, Baker Island, Little Moose Island, and Schoodic Point, adds up to a 44,000-acre preserve offering hiking, touring, swimming, horseback riding, canoeing, and a variety of guided nature tours and programs as well as a scenic 56-mile driving tour. Note that an entry fee is now charged to drive the Loop Road on Mount Desert and that camping is by reservation only. See "Bar Harbor and Acadia" for details. The **White Mountain National Forest** encompasses 41,943 acres in Maine, including five campgrounds under the jurisdiction of the Evans Notch Ranger District, Bridge Street, Bethel 04217 (824-2134). For details see "Bethel Area."

PARKS, STATE

The Bureau of Parks and Lands (287-3821), Station 22, Augusta 04333, can send a packet of information describing each of the parks and camping facilities. In the text, we have described parks as they appear geographically. In 1997 day-use fees are between $1 and $2.50 per adult, children 5–11 $.50, free for children under 5 and for seniors over 65; camping fee is $8–12 for residents, $10–16 for nonresidents. There is also a $2-per-night reservation fee for camping. Call (Monday through Friday) at least 7 days in advance to make a campground reservation. (Also see *Lakes.*)

POPULATION

Approximately 1.2 million.

PUFFIN-WATCHING

Atlantic puffins are smaller than you might expect. They lay just one egg a year and were heading for extinction around the turn of the century, when the only surviving birds nested either on Matinicus Rock or Machias Seal Island. Since 1973 the Audubon Society has had nesting areas on Eastern Egg Rock in Muscongus Bay, 6 miles off Pemaquid Point. Since 1984, there has been a similar puffin-restoration project on Seal Island in outer Penobscot Bay, 6 miles from Matinicus Rock. The best months for viewing puffins are June and July or the first few days of August. The only place from which you are allowed to view the birds on land is at Machias Seal Island, where visitors are permitted in limited numbers. Contact **Barna Norton** in Jonesport and **Bold Coast Charter** in Cutler. With the help of binoculars (a must), you can also view the birds from the water via tours offered by **Lively Lady Enterprises** based on Vinalhaven, **Offshore Passenger & Freight** in Rockland, **Cap'n Fish Boat Trips** in Boothbay Harbor, **Sea Bird Watcher** in Bar Harbor, the ***Hardy III* Tours** out of New Harbor, and the **Maine Audubon Society**.

RAILROAD RIDES & MUSEUMS

Boothbay Railway Village delights small children and offers railroad exhibits in its depot. For rail fans there are other sites to see: the **Sandy River Railroad** in Phillips, the **Belfast & Moosehead Lake Railroad Company** in Belfast, the **Maine Coast Railroad** in Wiscasset, and the **Maine Narrow Gauge Railroad Company & Museum**, Portland.

RATES

Please regard any prices listed for *Lodging, Dining Out,* and *Eating Out,* as well as for museums and attractions, as benchmarks in the rising tide of inflation. Call ahead to confirm them. MAP stands for Modified American Plan: breakfast and dinner included in rate. AP stands for American Plan: three meals included in rate. EP stands for European Plan: breakfast included in rate. B&B stands for bed and breakfast: continental breakfast included in rate.

ROCKHOUNDING

Perham's Maine Mineral Store at Trap Corner in West Paris, which claims to attract an annual 90,000 visitors, displays Maine minerals and offers access to its four quarries. The store also offers information about other quarries and sells its own guidebooks to gem hunting in Oxford County and throughout the state. Open year-round 9–5 daily except Thanksgiving and Christmas. For other rockhounding meccas, check the

NINA KENNEDY

"Bethel" chapter. Thanks to the high price of gold, prospectors are back-panning Maine streambeds; a list of likely spots is available from the Maine Geological Survey, Department of Conservation, State House Station 22, Augusta 04333 (289-2801). A helpful pamphlet, "Maine Mineral Collecting," lists annual gem shows and gem shops as well as quarries and is available from the Maine Publicity Bureau (623-0363).

SAILING

Windjammers and yacht charter brokers aside, there are a limited number of places that will rent small sailing craft, fewer that will offer lessons to adults and children alike. **Blue Seas Adventure Co.** in Camden rents sailboats by the day or longer, as does **Mansell Boat Company,** Southwest Harbor. Learn-to-sail programs are offered by **Wooden Boat School** in Brooklin and in Camden by both the **Camden Yacht Club** and **Bay Island Sailing School.** Sailboat rentals and day sails are listed throughout the book. (Also see *Windjammers.*)

SEA KAYAKING

Sea kayaking is the fastest growing sport along the coast of Maine, and outfitters are responding to the demand, offering guided half-day and full-day trips, also overnight and multiday expeditions with camping on Maine islands. Paddling a kayak is a comfortable way to sit—not crouching, as in a canoe, or arched over, as in a rowboat. You're also low, so low that you can stare down a duck or a cormorant, or study the surface of the water and its kaleidoscopic patterns. Maneuverable in as little as 6 inches of water, kayaks are ideal craft for "gunkholing" (poking in and out of coves) around the rocky edges of Maine islands. The leading outfitters are **Maine Island Kayak Company** (766-2373), on Peaks Island off Portland, and **Maine Sport Outfitters** (236-8797) in Rockport, both of

TAMSIN VENN

which specialize in multiday camping trips and offer introductory lessons. Others include **Kayak Adventures** (967-5243) in Kennebunkport, **H2Outfitters** (833-5357) on Orrs Island near Brunswick, **Tidal Transit** (633-7140) in Boothbay Harbor, **Indian Island Kayak Co.** (236-4088) in Camden, **Outward Bound School** (1-800-341-1744), **The Phoenix Center** (374-2113) in Blue Hill Falls, **Coastal Kayaking Tours** (288-9605) in Bar Harbor, **Schoodic Kayak Tours** (963-7958) in Corea, and **Norumbega Outfitters** (773-0910) in Portland. **L.L. Bean Sea Kayak Symposium,** held in early July at the Maine Maritime Academy in Castine (by reservation only), is New England's oldest and still its biggest annual kayaking event: a 2-day program geared to neophytes and all levels of ability, with lessons and equipment demonstrations. **L.L. Bean's Coastal Kayaking Workshop,** held the beginning of August at the University of New England, Biddeford, is a smaller, more skills-oriented event. For details and reservations call 1-800-341-4341, ext. 2509. *Sea Kayaking Along the New England Coast* by Tamsin Venn (Appalachian Mountain Club, 1991) includes detailed guidance to kayaking routes from Portland to Cobscook Bay; it also offers tips on local lodging and dining as well as an overall introduction to the sport. *Atlantic Coastal Kayaker* (508-774-0906), a monthly magazine ($2) based in Wenham, Massachusetts, is a source of outfitting information and equipment buys.

SKIING, CROSS-COUNTRY
Carrabassett Valley Touring Center at Sugarloaf is the largest commercial Nordic network in the state. Bethel, with four trail networks (**Sunday River Inn, the Bethel Inn, Carter's X-C Ski Center,** and **Telemark Inn & Llama Treks**), offers varied terrain. The trails at **Saddleback Mountain** in Rangeley are the highest in Maine and may, in fact, be snow-covered when no place else is. The most adventurous touring is found in the Katahdin/Moosehead area in Maine's North Woods. **The Birches** in Rockwood and **Little Lyford Camps** near Brownville Junction offer guided wilderness tours. **Mahoosuc Mountain Adventures** in the Bethel area also offers guided trips with dogsleds toting gear for overnight camping. The *Maine Guide to Winter*, published by the Maine Publicity Bureau (see *Information*), lists most Nordic areas, and the Maine Nordic Ski Council (PO Box 645, Bethel 04217) publishes its own guide and maintains a snow phone: 1-800-754-9263.

SKIING, DOWNHILL
Sugarloaf/USA in the Carrabassett Valley and **Sunday River** in the Bethel area, both owned by the Bethel-based American Skiing Company, vie for the title of Maine's number one ski resort. The two are very different and actually complement each other well. Sugarloaf is a high, relatively remote mountain with New England's only lift-serviced snowfields on its summit and a classy, self-contained condo-village at its base. Sunday River, just 1 hour north of Portland, consists of eight adjoining (relatively low altitude) mountains; snowmaking is a big point of pride, and facilities include a variety of slope-side condo lodging. **Saddleback Mountain** (in the Rangeley area) is a big, relatively undeveloped mountain with a small, enthusiastic following. **Mount Abram** (also in the Bethel area) is a true family area with a strong

MAINE OFFICE OF TOURISM

ski school and some fine runs. **Shawnee Peak** in Bridgton is a medium-sized, family-geared area that offers night as well as day skiing. **Squaw Mountain** in Greenville and the **Camden Snow Bowl** in Camden are also medium-sized but satisfying. Locally geared ski hills include **Lost Valley** in Auburn, **Mt. Jefferson** in Lee, **Titcomb Mountain** in Farmington, and **Eaton Mountain** in Skowhegan. At this writing, Maine offers toll-free ski reports: out-of-state callers dial 1-800-533-9595; in-state, 773-SNOW. The annual magazine *Maine Guide to Winter*, profiling all ski areas, is available from the Maine Publicity Bureau (see *Information*).

SNOWMOBILING

Maine has reciprocal agreements with nearly all states and provinces; for licensing and rules, contact the Fish and Game Department. The **Maine Snowmobile Association** (MSA) represents 270 clubs and maintains some 10,500 miles of an ever-expanding, cross-state trail network. Aroostook County, given its reliable snow conditions, is a particularly popular desti-

nation, geared to handling visitors. In the Upper Kennebec Valley, Jackman is a snowmobiling mecca; for details contact the MSA (622-6983), Box 77, Augusta 04332. For maps and further information, write to the Snowmobile Program, Bureau of Parks and Recreation, State House Station 22, Augusta 04333; MSA maintains a trail condition hotline: 1-800-880-SNOW.

SPA

Northern Pines in Raymond is the only fully developed spa program of which we are aware in Maine.

SPORTING CAMPS

The Maine sporting camp is a distinctly Maine phenomenon that began appearing in the 1860s—a gathering of log cabins around a log lodge by a lake, frequently many miles from the nearest road. In the 19th century, access was usually via Rangeley or Greenville, where "sports" (urbanites who wanted to hunt wild game) would be met by a guide and paddled up lakes and rivers to a camp. With the advent of floatplanes, many of these camps became more accessible (see *Air Services*), and the proliferation of private logging roads has put most within reach of sturdy vehicles. True sporting camps still cater primarily to fishermen in spring and hunters in fall, but since August is neither hunting nor a prime fishing season, they are increasingly hosting families who just want to be in the woods by a lake in summer. True sporting camps (as opposed to "rental camps") include a central lodge in which guests are served all three meals; boats and guide service are available. The Maine Sporting Camp Association (PO Box 89, Jay 04239) publishes a truly fabulous map/guide to its more than 50 members.

THEATER, SUMMER

The **Ogunquit Playhouse** (646-5511) is among the oldest and most prestigious summer theaters in the country. The **Hackmatack Playhouse** in Berwick (698-1807) and **Biddeford City Theater** (282-0849) are other South Coast options. In Portland note the **Portland Stage Company** (774-0465); and in Brunswick the **Maine State Music Theater** and **Children's Theatre Program** on the Bowdoin campus (725-8769), and the **Theater Project** (729-8584). Farther along the coast, look for the **Camden Civic Theatre** based in the newly refurbished Opera House in Camden (236-4866), **The Belfast Maskers** in Belfast (338-4427), **Cold Comfort Summer Theatre** (326-8830) in Castine, the **Surry Opera Company** in Surry (667-2629), the **Acadia Repertory Theatre** (244-7260) in Somesville, **Down River Theater Company** (255-4997) in Machias, and the Eastport Arts Center (853-4133) in Eastport. Inland look for the **Theater at Monmouth** (933-2952). **Lakewood Theater** (474-7176) is in Madison, **Deertrees Theater** (583-6747) is in Harrison, and **Celebration Barn Theater** (743-8452) is in South Paris.

THEATER, YEAR-ROUND

Acadia Repertory Theater in winter performs in Bangor (942-3333). Other companies are the **Performing Arts Center** in Bath (442-8455), the **Camden Civic Theatre** in Camden (236-4885), and the **Kennebec Performing Arts Center** in Gardiner (582-1325). **Portland Performing Arts Center** is at 25A Forest Avenue, Portland 04112 (774-0465). Also, the **Portland Players** (799-7337) present a winter season of productions, as does the **Maine Acting Company** (784-1616) in Lewiston.

WATERFALLS

The following are all easily accessible to families with small children: **Snow Falls Gorge** off Route 26 in West Paris offers a beautiful cascade (ask for directions at Perham's Gem Store); **Smalls Falls** on the Sandy River, off Route 4 between Rangeley and Phillips, has a picnic spot with a trail beside the falls; **Step Falls** is on Wight Brook in Newry off Route 26; and just a ways farther up the road in Grafton Notch State Park is **Screw Auger Falls,** with its natural gorge. Another Screw Auger Falls is in Gulf Hagas (see *Gorges*), off the Appalachian Trail near the Katahdin Iron Works Road north of Brownville Junction. **Kezar Falls,** on the Kezar River, is best reached via Lovell Road from Route 35 at North Waterford. An extensive list of "scenic waterfalls" is detailed in *The Maine Atlas and Gazetteer* (DeLorme Publishing Company). Check out 90-foot **Moxie Falls** at The Forks.

WHALE-WATCHING

Each spring humpback, finback, and minke whales migrate to New England waters, where they remain until fall, cavorting, it sometimes seems, for the pleasure of excursion boats. One prime gathering spot is **Jeffrey's Ledge,** about 20 miles off Kennebunkport, and another is the **Bay of Fundy.** For listings of whale-watch cruises, see "The Kennebunks," "Portland," "Bar Harbor," and "Washington County." The East Quoddy (Campobello) and West Quoddy (Lubec) lighthouses are also prime viewing spots.

WHITE-WATER RAFTING

White-water rafting is such a spring-through-fall phenomenon in Maine today that it's difficult to believe it only began in 1976, coincidentally the year of the last log drive on the Kennebec River. Logs were actually still hurtling through Kennebec Gorge on that day in the spring of 1976 when fishing guide Wayne Hockmeyer (and eight bear hunters from New Jersey he had talked into coming along) plunged through it in a rubber raft. At the time, Hockmeyer's rafting know-how stemmed solely from having seen *River of No Return,* in which Robert Mitchum steered Marilyn Monroe down the Salmon River. Needless to say, Hockmeyer's **Northern Outdoors** and the more than a dozen other major outfitters now positioned around the tiny village of The Forks, near the confluence of the Kennebec and Dead Rivers, are all well skilled in negotiating the rapids through nearby 12-mile-long Kennebec Gorge. Numbers on the river are now strictly limited, and rafts line up to take their turns riding the releases—which gush up to 8000 cubic feet of water per second—from the Harris Hydroelectric Station above the gorge. Several rafting companies—notably **Northern Outdoors, New England Whitewater Center, Crab Apple White Water,** and **Unicorn Rafting Expeditions**—have fairly elaborate base facilities in and around The Forks, while **Wilderness Expeditions** offers facilities both here and at The Birches, a family-geared resort on nearby Moosehead Lake. Several outfitters—including **Northern Outdoors, Wilderness Expeditions,** and **Unicorn**—have established food and lodging facilities for patrons who want to raft the Penobscot near Baxter State Park. **Downeast Whitewater,** based on the Maine/New Hampshire border, rafts five different rivers. **Windfall Outdoor Center** is based at the luxurious Sky Lodge in Jackman. **Moxie Outdoor Adventures** is located at one of Maine's oldest sporting camps on pristine Lake Moxie. Some 80,000 rafters a year—including thousands of women, children, and grandparents—now raft in Maine each year. For information about most outfitters, call RAFT MAINE: 1-800-723-8633.

WINDJAMMERS

In 1935 a young artist named Frank Swift fitted a few former fishing and cargo schooners to carry passengers around the islands of Penobscot Bay. At the time, there were plenty of these old vessels moored in every harbor and cove, casualties of progress. Swift called his business **Maine Windjammer Cruises,** and during the next two decades it grew to include more than a dozen vessels. Competitors also prospered through the '50s, but the entire windjammer fleet almost faded away with the advent of rigorous Coast Guard licensing requirements in the '60s and the increased cost of building and rebuilding schooners. The '70s and '80s have, however, seen the rise of a new breed of windjammer captain. Almost every one of those now sailing has built or restored the vessel he or she commands. Members of the current Maine windjammer fleet range from the *Stephen Taber* and the *Lewis French,* both originally launched in 1871, to the *Heritage,* launched in 1983, to the *Kathryn B* (a luxury version of the others), launched in 1996.

Taber co-captain Ellen Barnes recalls her own joy upon first discovering the windjammers as a passenger: "No museums had gobbled up these vessels; no cities had purchased them to sit at piers as public-relations gimmicks. These vessels were the real thing, plying their trade as they had in the past with one exception: The present-day cargo was people instead of pulpwood, bricks, coal, limestone, and granite."

Windjammers offer a sense of what the Maine coast and islands are all about. Most sail with the tide on Monday mornings with no set itinerary; where they go depends on the wind and the tide. Clad in old jeans and sneakers, passengers help haul a line and then lounge around the decks, gradually succumbing to the luxury of steeping in life on the face of Penobscot Bay. As the wind and sun drop, the schooner eases into a harbor. Supper is hearty Yankee fare, maybe fish chowder and beef stew with plenty of fresh corn bread. Before or after supper, passengers can board the vessel's yawl for a foray into the nearest village or onto the nearest road (most landlubbers feel the need to walk a bit each day). By Wednesday, the days begin to blur. Cradled in a favorite corner of the deck, you sun and find yourself seeing more: flocks of cormorants and an occasional seal or minke whale, eagles circling over island nests. The sky itself seems closer, and you are mesmerized by the ever-changing surface of the sea.

Choosing which vessel to sail on, in retrospect, turns out to be the most difficult part of a windjammer vacation. All have ship-to-shore radios and sophisticated radar, and some offer more in the way of creature comforts; some are known for their food or a captain with great jokes or songs. Within the "Rockport, Camden, and Lincolnville" chapter, we have described each vessel in the kind of detail we devote to individual inns. Windjammers accommodate between 12 and 44 passengers, and the cost of 3- to 6-day cruises ranges $300–700 (the *Kathryn B* charges $496–1295). Excessive drinking is discouraged on all the vessels, and guests are invited to bring their musical instruments. Children under 14 are permitted only on some vessels. See the "Rockland" and "Rockport" chapters for details and toll-free numbers for the various vessels. Questions you might like to ask in making your reservation include the following: (1) What's the bunk arrangement? Double bunks and cabins for a family or group do exist. (2) What's the cabin ventilation? Some vessels offer cabins with portholes or windows that open. (3) What's the rule about children? On some vessels passengers must be at least 16, on others 10, but several schooners schedule special family cruises with activities geared to kids. (4) What's the extent of weatherproof common space? It varies widely. 5) Is smoking allowed? (6) Is there evening entertainment of any kind?

WORKSHOPS
See *Camps, For Adults*.

I. SOUTH COAST

The beach at Ogunquit

TOM JONES

South Coast

The smell of pine needles and salt air, the taste of lobster and saltwater taffy, the shock of cold green waves, and, most of all, the promise of endless beach—this is the Maine that draws upward of half the state's visitors, those who never get beyond its South Coast. The southern Maine coast comprises just 35 miles of the state's 35,000 coastal miles but contains 90 percent of its sand.

Beyond their sand these resort towns—and the villages within them—differ deeply. York Village and Kittery are recognized as the oldest communities in Maine, Wells dates from the 1640s, and Kennebunkport was a shipbuilding center by the 1790s. All were transformed in the second half of the 19th century, an era when most Americans—not just the rich—began to take summer vacations, each in his or her own way.

Maine's South Coast was one of the country's first beach resort areas, and it catered—as it does today—to the full spectrum of vacationers, from blue-collar workers to millionaires. Before the Civil War, Old Orchard Beach rivaled Newport, Rhode Island, as the place to be seen; when the Grand Trunk Railroad to Montreal opened in 1854, it became the first American resort to attract a sizable number of Canadians.

While ocean tides are most extreme way Down East, the ebb and flow of tourist tides wash most dramatically over this stretch of Maine. Nowhere are the '30s motor courts thicker along Route 1, now sandwiched between elaborate '90s condo complexes with indoor pools and elevators. Most of the big old summer hotels vanished by the '50s, the era of the motor inns that now occupy their sites. But in the past few decades hundreds of former sea captains' homes and summer mansions have been transformed into small inns and bed & breakfasts, rounding out the lodging options. Luckily, the lay of the land—salt marsh, estuarine reserves, and other wetlands—largely limits commercial clutter.

GUIDANCE

The **Coalition of Southern Maine Chambers of Commerce** maintains a toll-free number that connects with each of the six chambers: 1-800-639-2442.

Kittery and the Yorks

The moment you cross the Piscataqua River you know you are in Maine. You have to go a long way Down East to find any deeper coves, finer lobster pounds, rockier ocean paths, or sandier beaches than those in Kittery and York.

Both towns claim to be Maine's oldest community. Technically Kittery wins, but York looks older . . . depending, of course, on which Kittery and which York you are talking about.

Kittery Point, an 18th-century settlement overlooking Portsmouth Harbor, boasts Maine's oldest church and some of the state's finest mansions. The village of Kittery itself, however, has been shattered by so many bridges and rotaries that it seems to exist only as a gateway, on one hand for workers at the Portsmouth Naval Shipyard and on the other for patrons of the outlet malls on Route 1. The Kittery Historical and Naval Museum is worth searching out, as are the dining, strolling, and swimming spots along coastal Route 103.

In the late 19th century, artists and literati gathered at Kittery Point. Novelist William Dean Howells, who summered here, became keenly interested in preserving the area's colonial-era buildings. He, his friend Sam Clemens (otherwise known as Mark Twain), and wealthy summer people began buying up the splendid old buildings in York, where the school, church, burial ground, and abundance of 1740s homes comprised Maine's oldest surviving community.

In 1900 Howells suggested turning the "old gaol" in York Village into a museum. At the time, you could count the country's historic house museums on your fingers. In the Old Gaol of today, you learn about the village's bizarre history, including its origins as a Native American settlement called Agamenticus, one of many settlements wiped out by a plague in 1616. In 1630 it was settled by English colonists, and in 1642 it became Gorgeana, America's first chartered city. It was then demoted to the town of York, part of Massachusetts, in 1670. Fierce Native American raids followed, but by the middle of the 18th century the present colonial village was established, a crucial way station between Portsmouth and points east.

York is divided into so many distinct villages that Clemens once observed, "It is difficult to throw a brick . . . in any one direction without

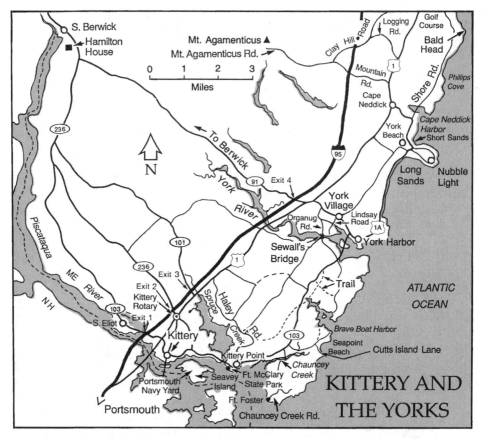

danger of disabling a postmaster." Not counting Scotland and York Corners, York includes York Village, York Harbor, York Beach, and Cape Neddick—such varied communities that locals can't bring themselves to speak of them as one town; they refer instead to "the Yorks."

The rocky shore beyond York Village was Lower Town until the Marshall House was opened near the small, gray sand beach in 1871 and its address was changed to York Harbor. Soon the hotel had 300 rooms, and other mammoth frame hotels appeared at intervals along the shore. All the old hotels are gone. All, that is, except the 162-room Cliff House, which, although physically in York, has long since changed its address and phone to Ogunquit, better known now as a resort town.

Still, York Harbor remains a delightful, low-key retreat. The Marshall House has been replaced by the modern Stage Neck Inn, and several dignified old summer "cottages" are now inns and B&Bs. A narrow, mile-or-so path along the shore was first traced by fishermen and later smoothed and graced with small touches such as the Wiggly Bridge, a graceful little suspension bridge across the river and through Steedman Woods.

Landscaping and public spaces were among the consuming interests of the 19th-century summer residents, who around the turn of the century also became interested in zoning. In *Trending into Maine* (1935), Kenneth Roberts noted York Harbor's "determination to be free of billboards, tourist camps, dance halls and other cheapening manifestations of the herd instinct and Vacationland civilization."

A York Harbor corporation was formed to impose its own taxes and keep out unwanted development. The corporation's biggest fight, wrote Roberts, was against the Libby Camps, a tent-and-trailer campground on the eastern edge of York Harbor that "had spread with such fungus-like rapidity that York Harbor was in danger of being almost completely swamped by young ladies in shorts, young men in soiled undershirts, and fat ladies in knickerbockers."

Libby's Oceanside Camp still sits on Roaring Rock Point, its trailers neatly angled along the shore. Across from it is matching Camp Eaton, established in 1923. No other village boundary within a New England town remains more clearly defined than this one between York Harbor and York Beach.

Beyond the campgrounds stretches 2-mile Long Sands Beach, lined with a simpler breed of summer cottage than anything in York Village or York Harbor. There is a real charm to the strip and to the village of York Beach, with its Victorian-style shops, boardwalk amusements, and The Goldenrod—known for its taffy "Goldenrod kisses." This restaurant is still owned by the same family that opened it in 1896, about the time the electric streetcar put York Beach within reach of "the working class."

During this "Trolley Era," a half-dozen big hotels accommodated 3000 summer visitors, and 2000 more patronized boardinghouses in York Beach. Today's lodgings are a mix of motels, cottages, and B&Bs. There are beaches (with free or metered parking), Fun-O-Rama games and bowling, and York's Wild Kingdom, with exotic animals and carnival rides. York Beach, too, has now gained "historic" status, and the Old York Historical Society, keeper of the half-dozen colonial-era buildings open to the public in York Village, now sponsors York Beach walking tours.

GUIDANCE

The **Kittery Information Center** (439-1319), Maine's gatehouse in a real sense, is on I-95 northbound in Kittery, a source of advice on local as well as statewide lodging, dining, and attractions. It's open daily except Christmas and Thanksgiving, 8 AM–9 PM in summer months, otherwise 9–5 (bathrooms open 24 hours daily). We usually stop by the center for information and a weather update (press a button outside the men's room to get a full report).

The **Kittery-Eliot Chamber of Commerce** (439-7545; 1-800-639-9645), just north of the Route 1 rotary (across from the Kittery Historical and Naval Museum), publishes a guide to lodging, dining, and sights.

York Chamber of Commerce (363-4422; via the Southern Maine link: 1-800-639-2442), PO Box 417, York 03909. On Route 1 just off exit 4 (York), a handsome information center modeled on a Victorian summer "cottage" is open year-round 9–5 (later on Friday and Saturday) in summer; shorter hours off-season.

GETTING THERE

Trailways serves Portsmouth, New Hampshire, some 12 miles south. **Little Brook Airport** in Eliot serves private and charter planes.

GETTING AROUND

From late June through Labor Day, 10 AM–8 PM, an **open-sided trolley** links York Village, Harbor, and Beach with Cape Neddick and Route 1. Narrated tours are offered every hour. For details, check with the chambers of commerce (see *Guidance*).

MEDICAL EMERGENCY

York Hospital 24-Hour Emergency Services (363-4321), Lindsay Road, York Village.

TO SEE

In Kittery

Kittery Historical and Naval Museum (439-3080), Route 1, just north of the Route 236 rotary. Open May through October, daily except Sunday 10–4. $3 adults, $1.50 ages 7–15; senior, family, and group rates. A fine little museum filled with ship models, naval relics from the Portsmouth Naval Shipyard, and exhibits about the early history of this stretch of the South Coast. Displays include archaeological finds, ship models, early shipbuilding tools, navigational instruments, trade documents, and mariner's folk art, including samples of work by Kittery master ship's carver John Haley Bellamy (1836–1914).

Portsmouth Naval Shipyard (open 1 day a week and by appointment: 438-3550), sited on Seavey Island at the mouth of the Piscataqua River. Also known as the Kittery Navy Yard, it is very visible from downtown Kittery. Established in 1806, it was the site of the treaty ending the Russo-Japanese War in 1905 and was responsible for building half of all American submarines during World War II. Today the navy yard remains an important submarine maintenance point. The PNS Command Museum has exhibits from the yard's past.

Fort McClary, Route 103. A state park open seasonally (grounds accessible year-round). A hexagonal, 1846 blockhouse on a granite base, it was the site of fortifications in 1715, 1776, and 1808. The site was first fortified in the early 18th century to protect Massachusetts's vessels from being taxed by the New Hampshire colony. This is a good place to picnic, overlooking Portsmouth Harbor, but the formal picnicking area is across the road.

Also see *Scenic Drives*.

In York

Old York (363-4974), Box 312, York 03909. This nonprofit society maintains seven historic buildings, open to the public from mid-June
through September, Tuesday through Saturday 10–5, Sunday 1–5;
$6 adults, $2.50 children includes admission to all buildings; free
Wednesday in July and August. The society also sponsors walking
tours and special events and offers a local historical research library
and archives in its headquarters, a former bank building at 207 York
Street in the middle of York Village. **Jefferds Tavern Visitors Center,** Route 1A. Begin your tour here: a 1759 building moved from
Wells in 1939. Watch the orientation video for Old York and purchase
tickets to other museum buildings and tours. Exhibits change, and
food is frequently cooking on the hearth at the tavern kitchen. The
Old School House next door, an original, mid-18th-century York
school, contains an exhibit on education of the period. **Old Gaol,** York
Village center. Dating from 1719 and billed as the oldest remaining
public building of the English colonies, it once served the whole prov-
ince of Maine and continued to house York County prisoners until
1860. You can inspect the cells and jailer's quarters and learn about
York's early miscreants. **Emerson-Wilcox House,** Route 1A. Dating
in part from 1742 and expanded over the years, period rooms and
gallery space trace the development of domestic interiors and decorative arts in York from the Revolutionary period to the 1930s. Exhibits
include furniture, ceramics, glass, and a complete set of bed hangings
embroidered by Mary Bulman in 1745. **Elizabeth Perkins House,**
Lindsay Road (at Sewall Bridge—a replica of the first pile bridge in
America, built on this spot in 1761). Our favorite building, this 1730
farmhouse is down by the York River. It is still filled with colonial-era
antiques and the spirit of the real powerhouse behind York's original
Historic Landmarks Society. It was Miss Perkins who saved the
Jefferds Tavern. She's buried under the simple plaque that's in a boul-
der at the edge of the lawn overlooking the river. **John Hancock
Warehouse and Wharf,** Lindsay Road. An 18th-century warehouse
with exhibits of 18th-century life and industry on and around the York
River. **George Marshall Store** (a former chandlery at which large
schooners once docked), 140 Lindsay Road, houses exhibits relating
to the maritime history of the region. **First Parish Church,** York
Village. An outstanding, mid-18th-century meetinghouse with a fine
old cemetery full of old stones with death's heads and Old English
spelling. **Civil War Monument,** York Village. Look closely at the
monument in the middle of the village—the soldier is wearing a rebel
uniform. The statue commissioned for York stands in a South Carolina
town because the sculptor made a mistake. At the time, both towns
agreed that freight rates were too high to make the switch, a consensus
that continues to prevail every time a swap is seriously considered.

In York Harbor and York Beach

Sayward-Wheeler House (603-436-3205), 79 Barrell Lane, York Harbor. Open June through October 15, Wednesday through Sunday 12–5; $4 adults, $3.50 seniors, $2.50 children 12 and under; maintained by the Society for the Preservation of New England Antiquities (SPNEA). A fine, early-18th-century house built by Jonathan Sayward—merchant, ship owner, judge, and representative to the Massachusetts General Court—who retained the respect of the community despite his Tory leanings. It remained in the same family for 200 years and retains its Queen Anne and Chippendale furnishings, family portraits, and china brought back as booty from the expedition against the French at Louisburg in 1745. It overlooks the river and is accessible from York's Shore Path, near the Wiggly Bridge (see *Walks*).

☞ **Nubble Light,** York Beach. From Shore Road, take Nubble Road out through the Nubble (a cottage-covered peninsula) to Sohier Park at the tip of the peninsula. It includes a parking area, rest rooms, and a seasonal information center and overlooks an 1879 lighthouse perched on a small island of its own.

✎ **York's Wild Kingdom** (363-4911; 1-800-456-4911), York Beach. Rides open daily at noon, late June through Labor Day weekend (weekends only in June and September); zoo is open 10–5 May through Labor Day. This is a combination amusement area and zoo with paddleboats, midway rides, and over 200 animals including some real exotica. There are also miniature golf and both pony and elephant rides. It's expensive: $12.50 per adult, $9.50 per child 4–10, and $3.50 for 3 and under for zoo/ride admission (in 1996).

SCENIC DRIVES

Kittery Point, Pepperrell Cove, and Gerrish Island. From Route 1, find your way to Route 103 (see map) and follow its twists and turns along the harbor until you come to the white First Congregational Church and a small green across from a striking, privately owned Georgian-style house. An old graveyard overlooking the harbor completes the scene. Park at the church (built in 1730, Maine's oldest), notice the parsonage (1729), and walk across to the old graveyard. The magnificent house was built in 1760 for the widow of Sir William Pepperrell, the French and Indian War hero who captured the fortress at Louisburg from the French. Knighted for his feat, Pepperrell went on to become the richest man in New England. For a splendid view of the harbor, continue along Route 103 to Fort McClary, and for the same view combined with good food, stop up the road at Cap'n Simeon's Galley (see *Dining Out*) in Pepperrell Cove, where everyone seems to be named Frisbee. It's hidden behind **Frisbees Market,** which claims to be America's oldest family-run grocery store. Four large hotels once clustered in this corner of Kittery, but today it's one of the quietest along the South Coast. Beyond Pepperrell Cove, note the turnoff for Gerrish

Island (see Fort Foster Park under *Parks,* Chauncey Creek Lobster Pound under *Lobster,* Seapoint Beach under *Green Space*). Route 103 winds on by the mouth of the York River and into York Harbor.

South Berwick. A short ride north of the Route 1 outlets and clutter transports you to a bend in the Salmon Falls River that is capped by a splendid, 1780s Georgian mansion, restored through the efforts of local author Sarah Orne Jewett; a formal garden and riverside trails through the woods add to the unusual appeal of this place. From Kittery, take either Route 236 north from the I-95 Eliot exit or Route 101 north from Route 1 (through high farmland to join Route 236). From York, take Route 91 north. Hamilton House and **Vaughan Woods** are the first left after the junction of Routes 236 and 91 (Brattle Street); follow signs. **Hamilton House** (384-5269) is open June through October 15, Tuesday, Thursday, Saturday, and Sunday 12–4, with tours on the hour ($4); grounds open every day dawn to dusk, Sunday-afternoon garden concerts in-season. The foursquare Georgian mansion built in 1785 on a promontory above the river had fallen into disrepair by the time Sarah Orne Jewett was growing up in nearby South Berwick; she used it as the setting for her novel *The Tory Lover,* and persuaded wealthy friends to restore it in 1898 (the same period that William Dean Howells was involved in restoring nearby York Village). The SPNEA also maintains the **Sarah Orne Jewett Birthplace** (384-5269) farther up Route 236, smack in the middle of the village of South Berwick. This is another fine 1774 Georgian house that has been preserved to look much as the author knew it. She actually grew up in the house next door, now the town library.

TO DO

BOAT EXCURSIONS

Lobstering Trips (call between 5 and 6 PM: 363-3234), Town Dock #2, York Harbor. When he's not teaching science at the local school, Tom Farnum offers 1-hour lobstering trips around York Harbor in his 22-foot, wooden lobster skiff. **Isles of Shoals Steamship Co.** (603-431-5000) in Portsmouth offers daily cruises in-season to the Isles of Shoals. (Also see "Ogunquit and Wells" for excursions from Perkins Cove.)

FISHING

Check with the York Chamber of Commerce (see *Guidance*) about the half-dozen deep-sea-fishing boats operating from York Harbor. Surf casting is also popular along Long Sands and Short Sands in York Beach.

GOLF

York Corner Golf (363-5439), Route 1, York. Nine holes, par 3.

Highland Farm Golf Club (351-2727), Route 91. Driving range, putting green, nine-hole course.

HORSEBACK RIDING

Mount Agamenticus Riding Stables (361-2840), summit of Mount

Agamenticus (turn off Route 1 at Flo's Hot Dogs). Open daily late June through October, 8–8: 1-hour trail rides, extended rides, corral rides, private lessons.

MOUNTAIN BIKING

The **Mount Agamenticus base lodge** is a source of rental bikes to use on the mountain's trails. For details, call 363-1040.

SCUBA DIVING

York Beach Scuba (363-3330), Railroad Avenue, York Beach. Guided dives around Nubble Light, boat dives, rental equipment, and instruction are all offered.

GREEN SPACE

BEACHES

Long Sands is a 2-mile expanse of coarse, gray sand stretching from York Harbor to the Nubble, backed by Route 1A and summer cottages. **Short Sands** is a shorter stretch of coarse, gray sand with a parking lot (meters), toilets, and the Victorian-era village of York Beach just behind it. **York Harbor Beach** is small and pebbly, but pleasant. Limited parking. This is the western terminus of the Cliff Walk. **Cape Neddick Beach,** Shore Road just east of Route 1A, is smallest of all, at the river's mouth, sheltered, and a good choice for children. **Seapoint Beach,** Kittery, is long with silky soft sand. Parking only for residents right at the sand, but limited public parking 0.5 mile back.

PARKS

Fort Foster Park. Beyond Pepperrell Cove, look for Gerrish Island Lane and turn right at the T on Pocahontas Road, which leads, eventually, to this 92-acre town park. The World War I fortifications are ugly, but there is a choice of small beaches with different exposures, one very popular with windsurfers. There are extensive walking trails and picnic facilities. Entrance fee.

Mount Agamenticus (363-1040), open weekdays 8:30–4:30. Just 580 feet high but billed as the highest hill on the Atlantic seaboard between York and Florida. A defunct ski area now owned by the town of York, it can be reached by an access road from Mountain Road off Route 1 (turn at Flo's Hot Dogs; see *Eating Out*). The summit is cluttered by radio and TV towers, but the view is sweeping. Rocks mark the grave of St. Aspinquid, a Native American medicine man who died at age 94 in 1682; according to the plaque, 6723 wild animals were sacrificed here at the wise man's funeral. See *To Do* for details about mountain biking and horseback riding. Inquire about the pleasant trail to the summit.

Vaughan Woods, South Berwick. A 250-acre preserve on the banks of the Salmon Falls River; picnic facilities and nature trails. The first cows in Maine are said to have been landed here at Cow Cove in 1634. See directions under *Scenic Drives*.

York Beach

WALKS

Shore Path, York Harbor. For more than a mile you can pick your way along the town's most pleasant piece of shorefront. Begin at the George Marshall Store (see *To See*) and walk east along the river and through the shady Steedman Woods. Go across the Wiggly Bridge (a mini–suspension bridge), then continue across Route 103, past the Sayward House, along the harbor, down the beach, and along the top of the rocks.

Cliff Walk, from York Harbor Beach west along the dramatic rocks and open ocean, below the most elaborate of York Harbor's "cottages." The path is eroded in sections, recommended only if you're in good shape and well shod.

Brave Boat Harbor Trail. The Kittery Land Trust maintains a 43-acre conservation area with a 2-mile trail. Note the pullout on Route 103.

LODGING

In Kittery, Eliot, and South Berwick

Gundalow Inn (439-4040), 6 Water Street, Kittery 03904. Open year-round. An 1890s brick village house just off the Kittery green, across from the Piscataqua River, this makes a good hub for exploring both Portsmouth and Maine's South Coast. The six guest rooms have each been carefully, imaginatively furnished and all rooms have private baths (some with claw-foot tubs). $80–105 double, including a full breakfast. No smoking.

Whaleback Inn (439-9570), Box 162, Kittery Point 03905. Open Memorial Day through October. Part of the Frisbee compound (see *Scenic*

Drives), this coveside house offers three upstairs bedrooms, each with a theme. One room is filled with images and mementos, even a few things that once belonged to Queen Victoria. A room overlooking the harbor is dedicated to the fact and fiction of the Native American, and the smallest room is decorated with antique toys. All have double beds, and the Native American room ($65) has its own bath and TV. The other two ($55) share a bath, and all share a cheery kitchen/breakfast room as their sole common space. Your collector/hosts are Frank Frisbee and Ron Ames, both well versed in local history; rates include breakfast. Small pets and children over 12 are welcome.

☞ **High Meadows Bed & Breakfast** (439-0590), Route 101, Eliot 03903. Technically in Eliot, this pleasant retreat is really just a few miles off Route 1. Open April through October. A 1736 house with five nicely furnished rooms, all with private bath. Our favorite is the Wedgwood Room with its canopy bed and highboy. There's a comfortable common room with a woodstove and a formal living room with a fireplace; there is also a wicker-furnished porch overlooking the landscaped grounds. Walking trails lead through the surrounding 30 acres. No children under 14. All rooms are $80, $70 off-season, full breakfast and afternoon snack included.

☞ **The Moses Paul Inn** (437-1861; 1-800-552-6058), 270 Goodwin Road (Route 101), Eliot 03903. Open year-round. Just 5.5 miles from Kittery's outlets, this red 1780 house has five guest rooms: two downstairs with private baths, three upstairs that share. Moses, a friendly combination greyhound and black Lab, meets you at the door and follows you through the open kitchen and dining area overlooking a mowed meadow; the common room is low beamed and attractive with a fireplace. Your hosts are Joanne Weiss, an interpreter for the deaf, and her husband, Larry James, a merchant seaman. Interestingly, this is one of only two Maine B&Bs we know of that preserve the old tradition of a wife taking in guests while her husband is away at sea, and both houses have ghosts (ask about Henri). $75 private, $65 shared bath; $5 less off-season.

The Academy Street Inn (384-5633), 15 Academy Street, South Berwick 03908. A 1903 mansion just off the main drag in an attractive village, handy to the Piscataqua River, the Sarah Orne Jewett Birthplace, and Hamilton House (see *Scenic Drives*). Paul and Lee Fopeano, the new innkeepers, offer five spacious guest rooms (shared baths); a full breakfast is served at the dining room table. There's plenty of space for relaxing—a large porch as well as parlor. $55–75.

In York Village and York Harbor

INNS

Dockside Guest Quarters (363-2868), PO Box 205, Harris Island Road, York 03909. Open daily May through October, weekends the rest of the year. Two generations of the Lusty family imbue this fine little hideaway with a warmth that few inns this size possess. Situated on a peninsula in York Harbor, Dockside is a 7-acre compound with six buildings: the gracious, 19th-century Maine House, four newer, multiunit cottages, and the Dockside Restaurant (see *Dining Out*). In all there are 21 guest rooms—including six apartment/suites with kitchenettes—all with private decks and water views. Breakfast is served buffet-style in the Maine House. It's a nominally priced, "Continental Plus" (fruit compote, baked goods, etc.), muffins-and-juice breakfast, laid out on the dining room table—a morning gathering place for guests who check the blackboard weather forecast and plan their day. Guests can use a canoe or Boston whaler or take advantage of regularly scheduled harbor and river cruises. Special lodging and cruise packages are offered June through October. Two-night minimum stay during July and August. May through early June and the last half of October: $59—103 for double rooms, $78–153 for cottage units. Ask about off-season packages.

Stage Neck Inn (363-3850; 1-800-222-3238), York Harbor 03911. Open year-round. An attractive 1970s complex of 58 rooms built on the site of the 19th-century Marshall House. Located on its own peninsula, the inn offers water views (by request), a formal dining room, a less formal Sand Pipers Grill (see *Dining Out*), tennis courts, an outdoor pool, a small indoor pool, and a Jacuzzi. The lobby, sitting room, and main dining room are formal; a frequent conference site. $135–150 per room in-season; no meals included.

York Harbor Inn (363-5119; 1-800-343-3869), PO Box 573, York Street, York Harbor 03911. Open year-round. The inn is on Route 1A across from the harbor. The beamed lobby is said to have been built in 1637 on the Isles of Shoals. An exclusive men's club in the 19th century, the inn is now a popular dining spot. Its Cellar Lounge, with an elaborately carved bar, is a local gathering place. The 33 rooms are divided between the inn itself (request one with a working fireplace or ocean view) and the neighboring Yorkshire Building, where three have Jacuzzis and sitting areas. All rooms have private baths, phones, and air-conditioning. $89–195 double, continental breakfast included; ask about special packages.

BED & BREAKFASTS

☞ **Inn at Harmon Park** (363-2031), PO Box 495, York Harbor 03911. Open year-round. A shingled Victorian, this B&B has been Sue Antal's home for more than 20 years. It's attractive and airy, with a comfortable living room; in the middle of the village of York Harbor, within walking distance of the beach and Shore Path. The four guest rooms and one suite (with working fireplace) are all nicely furnished; private baths. The room diaries are filled with thanks to Sue for her unusual hospitality and sound suggestions for enjoying the immediate area. $69–99 includes a full, healthy breakfast on the sun porch. Less off-season.

Edwards' Harborside Inn (363-3037; 1-800-273-2686), PO Box 866, York Harbor 03911. Open year-round. Nicely sited near York Harbor Beach, this solidly built summer mansion is owned by Jay Edwards, a third-generation innkeeper. Breakfast is served in one of the most pleasant rooms in the area: a sun porch with an unbeatable view of the harbor. You can enjoy the vista all day from a lawn chair. Many of the 10 guest rooms also have water views; a suite with a Jacuzzi overlooking the water is $160–230. Other rooms from $90 (shared bath) to $160; $50–80 off-season.

Canterbury House Bed & Breakfast (363-3505), Route 1A, York Harbor 03911. Open year-round. James Pappas is a detail person and his home in the center of York Harbor (within walking distance of beach and paths) is artfully, comfortably furnished. Guests breakfast (dinner also available on request: $29.95) at formally set tables, and there are four carefully furnished rooms, three with private bath. $69–95 double includes continental breakfast and afternoon tea; a suite is $100–110. No children under 12.

Tanglewood Hall (363-7577), 611 York Street, PO Box 12, York Harbor 03911. Open June through mid-October. This shingled 1880s summer mansion was a summer home of bandleader Tommy Dorsey and his brother Jimmy. Set in gardens and woods, it was professionally decorated in 1994 as a show house to benefit the local historical society. The York Harbor Suite ($120) has a fireplace and conservatory but we liked best the Winslow Homer Room (Homer is said to have been a guest; $90); all three rooms have private baths; the octagonal game/music room and many-windowed dining room are also special.

RiverMere (363-5470), 45 Varrell Lane, York Harbor 03911. A spacious 19th-century shingled house just off the harbor with formal gardens and water views from its third-floor suite and another upstairs guest room; $75–125 includes breakfast.

In York Beach 03910

☞ **The Katahdin Inn** (363-1824; in winter: 617-938-0335), 11 Ocean Avenue Extension. Open mid-May through October. "Bed and beach" is the way innkeeper Rae LeBlanc describes her 1890s guest house overlooking Short Sands Beach and the ocean. Eight of the 11 guest rooms have water views. Number 9 on the third floor is small and white with a window and a skylight that seem to suspend it above the water. All rooms have a small fridge. More water views from the living room and two porches (one enclosed), which are equipped with games for poor weather. From $60 (shared bath) to $85 for a large room, private bath; less off-season. No breakfast but tea and coffee.

The Willows B&B (363-9900), 3 Long Beach Avenue. A spacious, turn-of-the-century house on Route 1A within walking distance of Short Sands Beach; four rooms with private baths, four with shared; request a water view. $69–79.

View Point (363-2661), 229 Nubble Road, PO Box 1980. Office open daily in summer, selected days off-season. A nicely designed, oceanfront, condominium-style complex overlooking the Nubble Lighthouse. All suites have a living room, kitchen, porch or patio, gas fireplace, phone, cable TV, CD stereo, VCR, washer/dryer. $200 for one bedroom to $320 for three-bedroom unit in-season; half that in winter. Weekly rates available.

The Anchorage Inn (363-5112), Route 1A, Long Beach Avenue. A total of 178 motel-style rooms, most with water views across from Long Sands Beach. For families, this is a good choice; facilities include indoor and outdoor pools, rooms that sleep four, TV, small fridge. $107–180 per room in high season, $180–230 for spa suites; off-season packages.

In Cape Neddick

Cape Neddick House (363-2500), Box 70, 1300 Route 1, Cape Neddick 03902. Open year-round. Although it is right on Route 1, this Victorian house (in the Goodwin family for more than 100 years) offers an away-from-it-all feel and genuine hospitality. There are five guest rooms with private baths, two with working fireplaces, all furnished with antiques. Breakfast is an event—maybe strawberry scones and ham with apple biscuits—served on the back deck (overlooking garden and woods), in the dining room, or in the homey kitchen. A six-course dinner—from stuffed mushrooms to raspberry cheesecake, all cooked on the 80-year-old Glenwood woodstove—can be reserved in advance. Good value: $65–85 double, $90–95 for a suite, depending on season.

The Riverbed (363-3630), 154 Route 1A, PO Box 730, York Beach 03910. Open Memorial Day through Columbus Day. This 1761 house over-looks the tidal Cape Neddick Harbor. Cassandra and Steve Ewing offer three rooms, two with shared baths and two with decks overlooking the water. A canoe and outdoor hot tub add to the appeal of this place, and a path leads to Cape Neddick Beach and the lobster pound. $69–89 includes breakfast.

Wooden Goose Inn (363-5673), Route 1, Cape Neddick 03902. Open in January and most months but closed in July. The antithesis of its Route 1 surroundings, this is a snug, fussily exquisite retreat. Hosts Tony Sienicki and Jerry Rippetoe have created six air-conditioned guest rooms—and six amazing bathrooms, meticulously decorated with fine fabrics, art, and antiques. Guests are pampered with elaborate teas and breakfasts. $125 all year. No children.

WHERE TO EAT

DINING OUT

Cape Neddick Inn and Gallery (363-2899), Route 1, Cape Neddick. Open year-round for dinner and Sunday brunch; closed Monday and Tuesday from Columbus Day to mid-June. A beautifully designed dining space features artwork. The menu changes, but roast duckling remains a year-round staple along with fish and pasta du jour. Lamb loin with Dijon mustard and Swiss-chard sauce baked in phyllo and broiled haddock with sesame-oyster hollandaise are examples. The desserts are spectacular. Reservations suggested. Entrées are $9–28.

The York Harbor Inn (363-5119), Route 1A, York Harbor. Open year-round for lunch and dinner, also Sunday brunch. Four pleasant dining rooms, most with views of water. The menu is large. The seafood chowder is studded with shrimp, scallops, and crabmeat as well as haddock ($3.95 a cup); milk-fed veal, fresh seafood, and pastas are the specialties. The dinner entrées range from garden lasagna ($14.95) to Yorkshire Lobster Supreme (lobster stuffed with scallop and shrimp filling: $23.95). Sunday brunch is big. For dinner, plan to spend $60 per couple, excluding wine, tax, and tip. The **Cellar Pub** menu runs to burgers, soups, sandwiches, and salads.

Harbor Porches (363-3850), Stage Neck Road, York Harbor. Open year-round for breakfast, lunch, and dinner. The new gilded-era look (harkening back to the glory days of the Marshall House, a grand hotel that occupied this site for many decades) is much more appropriate and pleasant than the former crystal-chandelier decor, and the menu has lightened up too, ranging now from fresh Maine shrimp ravioli ($16.95) to roast rack of lamb provençale ($22.95), also including lighter fare like mussels provençale ($6.50) and warm seafood salad ($12.95).

☞✐ **Cap'n Simeon's Galley** (439-3655), Route 103, Pepperrell Cove. Open year-round for lunch and dinner; closed Tuesdays mid-October to Memorial Day. A special place with one of the best water views of any Maine restaurant. You enter through the original Frisbee Store (the building is said to date back to 1680; the store opened in 1828) to a spacious dining area with picture windows overlooking the cove and beyond to Portsmouth Harbor. Seafood is the specialty, but you can get anything from a grilled cheese sandwich ($2.50) to a New York choice sirloin steak ($12.50), from a quiche and salad ($5.75) to a fisherman's fried seafood platter ($11.95); lobster is priced daily. (Also see *Eating Out*.)

Dockside Restaurant (363-2722), off Route 103, York Harbor. Open for lunch and dinner late May through Columbus Day except Monday. Docking facilities, glass-walled and porch dining overlooking York Harbor. Specializes in seafood from $6.95 for fish-and-chips at lunch to $17.95 for bouillabaisse (including half a lobster) at dinner; roast stuffed duckling is another house specialty. Dinners include "The Salad Deck" as well as breads and veggies. Children get a Dockside Vacation coloring book to use while waiting.

☞✐ **Fazio's** (363-7019), 38 Woodbridge Road, York Village. This popular trattoria is decorated with original murals and photos of Annette Fazio's mother. The menu is traditional—fettuccine carbonara (pancetta, cheese, cream, cracked pepper, and egg) for $8.95, chicken Francese (white wine and lemon sauce served with cheese pasta, $11.95). The pasta is made daily. Patrons would not complain at twice the price. Children's menu.

Mimmo's (363-3807), Long Sands, York Beach. Open for breakfast and dinner June through September and for dinner only the rest of the year, closed on Christmas and Thanksgiving. Named for its colorful chef Mimmo Basileo, this trattoria is a hot spot in summer (reservations necessary). Tables are close packed, the water view is limited to the front dining room, and the menu ranges from eggplant parmigiana ($14.95) through a variety of pastas to seafood "coastazurro" (mussels, shrimp, haddock and calamari sautéed with garlic, $17.95). BYOB.

LOBSTER

The Lobster Barn (363-4721), Route 1, York. Open year-round for lunch and dinner. A pubby, informal, popular dining room with wooden booths and a full menu. Specialties such as scallop and shrimp pie earn this place top marks from locals. In summer, lobster dinners (in the rough) are served under a tent out back. Most of the seafood casseroles are $11.95; lobster is priced daily.

Chauncey Creek Lobster Pound (439-1030), Chauncey Creek Road, Kittery Point. Open during summer only. Lobster in rolls and in the rough; steamed clams and mussels are the specialty. There is also a raw bar. An average dinner with steamers costs $12, but don't expect any extras. The locals bring their own salad, bread, and wine. The setting is great, but service can be slow.

Cape Neddick Lobster Pound (363-5471), Route 1A (Shore Road), Cape Neddick. Open April through December for dinner only. Situated at the mouth of a tidal river, this modern, shingled building has the look of having always been there. Besides lobster and clams, there are temptations such as bouillabaisse or baked sole with Maine shrimp, crab, cheddar, and lemon stuffing, or smoked trout with herb mayonnaise. Moderate to expensive. Live music, dancing after 9 PM.

Warren's Lobster House (439-1630), 1 Water Street, Kittery. Open year-round; lunch, dinner, and Sunday brunch; docking facilities. A low-ceilinged, knotty-pine dining room overlooking the Piscataqua River and Portsmouth, New Hampshire, beyond. An old dining landmark with 1940s decor. The salad bar features over 50 selections ($6.95 as a meal in itself), and the specialty is seafood, fried and broiled. Dinner entrées average $13.

Fox's Lobster House (363-2643), Nubble Point, York Beach. Open daily in-season 11:45–9. A large, tourist-geared place with a water view and a menu ranging from hot dogs ($3.50) to deep-fried lobster tails ($18.95).

EATING OUT

The Goldenrod (363-2621), York Beach. Open Memorial Day through Columbus Day for breakfast, lunch, and dinner. In business since 1896, one of the best family restaurants in New England; same menu all day from 8 AM to 10:30 PM, served up at time-polished, wooden tables in the big dining room with a fieldstone fireplace as well as at the old-style soda fountain. Famous saltwater taffy kisses cooked and pulled in the windows.

A wide selection of homemade ice creams and yogurts, good sandwiches (cream cheese and olive or nuts is still $1.95), daily specials.

Cap'n Simeon's Galley (see *Dining Out*) is also the best bet in Kittery for a fried scallop roll or burger at lunch.

Flo's Hot Dogs, Route 1. Open only 11–3 and not a minute later. The steamers are just $1.50 but that doesn't explain the long lines, and it's not Flo that draws the crowds because Flo sold it to Gail. This is just a great place. It's even fun to stand in line here. Request the special sauce.

Bob's Clam Hut (439-4233), Route 1, Kittery. Open year-round. The best fried clams on the strip. Here since 1956 and now, finally, with indoor seating.

The Line House (439-3401), Route 1 on the Kittery/York line. Open year-round for breakfast (with an amazing variety of egg dishes), lunch, and dinner; family run and geared, a favorite with the local police force. Choose lazy lobster pie or a seafood platter, but this is also one of the few places around featuring smothered liver and onions and baked ziti.

Road Kill Cafe (351-2928), Route 1A, Long Sands Beach. A Maine original (see "Moosehead Lake Area") that's now a chain but still fun, with a hilarious menu and great views across the road to the water.

SNACKS

Brown's Ice Cream (363-4077), Nubble Road, a quarter mile beyond the lighthouse, York Beach. Seasonal. All ice cream is made on the premises. Exotic flavors, generous portions.

Pie in the Sky Bakery (363-2656), Route 1, Cape Neddick, York Beach. Open Monday through Saturday except January; hours vary off-season. The purple house at the corner of River Road is filled with delicious smells and irresistible muffins, pies, tortes, and breads, all baked here by John and Nancy Stern.

ENTERTAINMENT

Hackmatack Playhouse (698-1807), in Berwick, presents summer-stock performances most evenings; Thursday matinees.

Seacoast Repertory Theatre (603-433-4472), 125 Bow Street, Portsmouth. Professional theater productions.

(Also see "Ogunquit and Wells.")

York Beach Cinema (363-2074), 6 Beach Street, York. First-run movies.

SELECTIVE SHOPPING

ART GALLERIES

York Art Association Gallery (363-4049; 363-2918), Route 1A, York Harbor. Annual July art show, films, and workshops.

CRAFTS SHOPS

York Village Crafts (363-4830), 211 York Street, York Village. Open daily 9–5. Housed in the vintage 1834 church in the center of York Village, more than 100 displays of crafts, art, books, and antiques.

YORK OUTLET MALLS

Note: For the Kittery shopping strip, take I-95, exit 3.

At this writing, the 120 discount stores within a 1.3-mile strip of Route 1 in Kittery represent a mix of clothing, household furnishings, gifts, and basics. All purport to offer savings of at least 20 percent on retail prices, many up to 70 percent. Open daily, year-round; hours vary; call 439-7545. The **Kittery Trading Post** (439-2700) is the original anchor store of this strip. A local institution since 1926, the sprawling store is always jammed with shoppers in search of sportswear, shoes, children's clothing, firearms, outdoors books, and fishing or camping gear. The summer-end sales are legendary, and many items are routinely discounted. The strip is divided into a series of malls, among them the **Maine Outlet Mall**, with more than 20 shops, including Banister Shoe, The Children's Outlet, and Dress Barn; **Tidewater Outlet Mall**, a small but quality shopping center, worth the stop for Lenox China and Boston Traders. In the **Kittery Outlet Center** you'll find Royal Doulton, Van Heusen, and Le Sportsac. Eddie Bauer, Benetton, Brooks Brothers, Corning Revere, Polo/Ralph Lauren, Dexter Shoe, and Bass Shoe are also here.

WINERY

The Parsons Family Winery (363-3332), Brixham Road, York. Open Monday through Saturday 10–5; Sunday 12–5. Up Route 91, 4.8 miles off Route 1, turn onto Brixham Road and look for the big white farmhouse that's now an apple winery. Tours and tastings are offered.

SPECIAL EVENTS

Note: Be sure to pick up the area's unusually lively "Summer Social Calendar" at the York Chamber of Commerce (see *Guidance*).

June: **Strawberry Festival,** South Berwick.

July: **Independence Day celebrations,** York—parades, cannon salutes, militia encampment, crafts and food fair, picnic, and dinner. Kittery—Seaside Festival at Fort Foster's Park. **Band concerts,** Wednesday evenings at Short Sands Pavilion, York Beach. **Old York Designers' Show House** sponsored by the Old York Historical Society. **York Days Celebration** (last days of month, see August)—raffle, puppet shows, skits.

August: **York Days Celebration** (beginning of the month)—flower show, church supper, concerts, square dances, parade, and sand castle contest. **Seacoast Crafts Fair** (late in the month).

September: **House Tours. Eliot Festival Days** (late September).

October: **Harvest Fest,** York Village (third weekend)—an ox roast, ox-cart races, hay- and horse rides, militia encampment, music, and live entertainment.

December: **Christmas Open House Tours. Kittery Christmas Parade and Tree Lighting** and **York Festival of Lights Parade.**

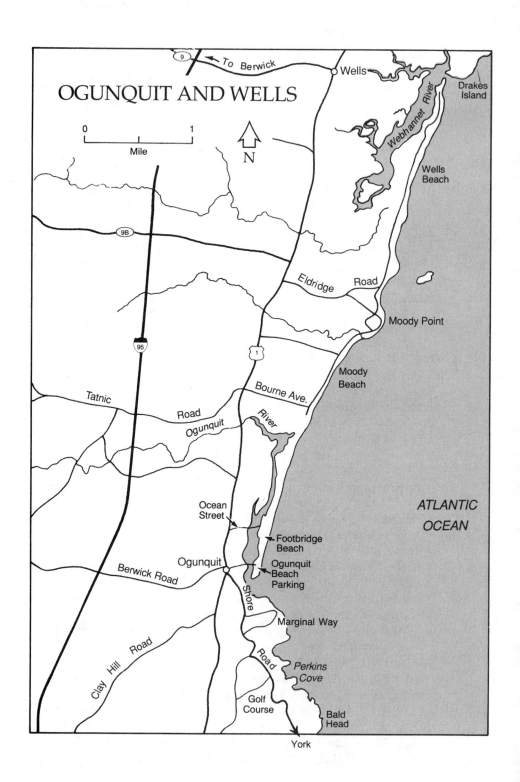

OGUNQUIT AND WELLS

0 — 1
Mile

N

To Berwick
9

Wells

Webhannet River

Drakes Island

Wells Beach

9B

Eldridge Road

Moody Point

95

1

Moody Beach

Tatnic

Bourne Ave.

Road

River

Ogunquit

Ocean Street

ATLANTIC OCEAN

Footbridge Beach

Berwick Road

Ogunquit

Ogunquit Beach Parking

Shore

Marginal Way

Clay Hill Road

Road

Perkins Cove

Golf Course

Bald Head

York

Ogunquit and Wells

Ogunquit and Wells share many miles of uninterrupted sand and the line between the two towns also blurs along Route 1, a stretch of restaurants, family attractions, and family-geared lodging places. The two beach resorts are, however, very different.

Named for the English cathedral town, Wells was incorporated in 1653 and remains a year-round community with summer cottages, condo complexes, and campgrounds strung along the beach and Route 1—parallel strips separated by a mile-wide swatch of salt marsh. Wells is a resort for families, the place to find a reasonably priced weekly rental.

Ogunquit was part of Wells until 1980 but seceded in spirit long before that, establishing itself as summer resort in the 1880s and a magnet for artists in the 1890s. It remains a compact, walk-around resort village clustered between its magnificent beach and picturesque Perkins Cove; these two venues are connected by the mile-long Marginal Way, an exceptional shore path. The village offers two vintage movie houses and the Ogunquit Playhouse, one of New England's most famous summer theaters. Most of Ogunquit's big old wooden hotels were razed during the 1960s and replaced by luxury motels. With the 1980s came condos, B&Bs, more restaurants, and boutiques. Luckily, it also brought trolleys-on-wheels to ease the traffic crunch at Perkins Cove and the beach.

Natural beauty remains surprisingly accessible in both Ogunquit and Wells. Given the vast expanse of sand, you can always find an uncrowded spot, and Wells harbors more than 4000 acres of conservation land, much of it webbed with trails (see *Nature Preserves*).

On weekends a tidal wave of day-tripping Bostonians spreads over the beach and eddies through Perkins Cove, but it recedes on Sunday evenings. Both Ogunquit and Wells are relatively peaceful midweek in summer and especially delightful in September and October.

GUIDANCE
Chamber of Commerce (646-2939; 1-800-639-2442), Route 1, just south of Ogunquit Village. Open weekdays 9–5 year-round and manned by the town as an information center (646-5533) May through Columbus Day, daily (until 8 PM Friday and Saturday). Stocked with pamphlets year-round; public rest rooms.

Wells Chamber of Commerce (646-2451; 1-800-639-2442), 136 Post Road (Route 1, northbound side) in Moody. Open daily Memorial Day through Labor Day, weekdays the rest of the year.

GETTING THERE

By car: Coming north on I-95, take exit 1 (York) and drive up Route 1 to the village of Ogunquit. Coming south on I-95, take exit 2 (Wells).

By bus: **C & J Trailways** (1-800-258-7111) connects Ogunquit and Wells with Portsmouth, New Hampshire; Boston; and Logan airport.

By train: **AMTRAK** service was promised for '96, then '97, now '98, but don't hold your breath. Stay tuned.

GETTING AROUND

Seasonal **open-sided trolleys** make frequent stops throughout the village of Ogunquit, Perkins Cove, at the beach, and along Route 1. They connect with the trolleys that circulate up and down Route 1 and through the beach and lodging areas in Wells. Fare is nominal. Trolley maps are available from the chambers of commerce.

PARKING

Park and walk or take the trolley. In summer this is no place to drive. There are at least seven public lots; rates are $4–6 per day. There is also free parking (2-hour limit) on Route 1 across from the Leavitt Theatre just north of Ogunquit Square or adjacent to Cumberland Farms. Parking at the main entrance to Ogunquit Beach itself is pricey. (For more on beach parking, see *Beaches.*) In Wells, parking at the five public lots is $6 per day; monthly permits are available from the town office.

MEDICAL EMERGENCY

Ambulance/Rescue Squad (646-5111), town of Ogunquit.

York Hospital (363-4321), 24-hour emergency, 15 Hospital Drive, York Village.

Wells Ambulance (646-9911). In Wells, you may be nearer to **Southern Maine Medical Center** (283-3663), 1 Mountain Road, Biddeford.

TO SEE

Perkins Cove. This is probably Maine's most painted fishing cove, with some 40 restaurants and shops now housed in weathered fish shacks. It is the departure point for the area's excursion and fishing boats, based beside the famous draw-footbridge. Parking is nearly impossible in summer, but public lots are nearby, and the trolley stops here regularly. The cove can also be reached on foot via the Marginal Way (see *Walks*).

Ogunquit Museum of American Art (646-4909), Shore Road, Ogunquit. Open July to late September, 10:30–5 daily, Sunday 2–5; $3 adults, $2 seniors, free to members and children under 12. Built superbly of local stone and wood with enough glass to let in the beauty of the cove it faces, the museum displays selected paintings from its permanent collection, which includes the strong, bright oils of Henry Strater and other

NANCY C. HORTON

Beach on Marginal Way in Ogunquit

one-time locals such as Reginald Marsh. Special exhibitions feature nationally recognized artists.

- **Wells Auto Museum** (646-9064), Wells. Open daily mid-June to mid-September, 10–5. More than 70 cars dating from 1900 to 1963, plus nickelodeons, toys, and bicycles.

TO DO

BOAT EXCURSIONS
From Perkins Cove
Finestkind (646-5227). Scenic cruises to Nubble Light, cocktail cruises, and "lobstering trips" (watch lobster traps hauled, hear about lobstering). *Ugly Anne* (646-7202). Half- and full-day, deep-sea-fishing trips with Captain Ken Young Sr. *The Silverlining* (361-3800), a 42-foot, wooden Hinckley sloop, sails out of Perkins Cove on regularly scheduled, 2-hour cruises. Minimum six people, $28; also available for half- and full-day charters. *The Bunny Clark* (646-2214). Half- and full-day, deep-sea-fishing trips with Captain Tim Tower. *Deborah Ann* (361-9501), Perkins Cove, offers whale-watching cruises.

FISHING FROM SHORE
Tackle and bait can be rented at Wells Harbor. The obvious fishing spots are the municipal dock and harbor jetties. There is surf casting near the mouth of the Mousam River.

MINI-GOLF
- **Wells Beach Mini-Golf,** next to Big Daddy's Ice Cream, Route 1, Wells. Open daily in-season 10–10.

✐ **Wonder Mountain,** Route 1, Wells. A mini-golf mountain, complete with waterfalls; adjoins **Outdoor World.**

✐ **Sea-Vu Mini Golf** is another Route 1 option in Wells.

SWIMMING

See *Beaches.*

TENNIS

Three public courts in Ogunquit. Inquire at **Dunaway Center** (646-9361).

Wells Recreation Area, Route 9A, Wells. Four courts.

THEATER

Ogunquit Playhouse (646-5511), Route 1 (just south of Ogunquit Village). Open late June through August. Billing itself as "America's Foremost Summer Theater," this grand old summer-stock theater (now air-conditioned) opened for its first season in 1933 and continues to feature top stars in productions staged every evening during the season except Sunday. Matinees are Wednesday and Thursday. Usually we describe summer stock under *Entertainment* near the end of a chapter, but in this case a visit to the Playhouse is one of the major things to do.

GREEN SPACE

BEACHES

Three-mile-long **Ogunquit Beach** offers surf, soft sand, and space for kite flying, as well as a sheltered strip along the mouth of the Ogunquit River for toddlers. It can be approached three ways: (1) The most popular way is from the foot of Beach Street. There are boardwalk snacks, changing facilities, and toilets, and it is here that the beach forms a tongue between the ocean and the Ogunquit River (parking in the lot here is $2 per hour). (2) The Footbridge Beach access (take Ocean Street off Route 1 north of the village) offers rest rooms and is less crowded. (3) Eldridge Street, Wells. Be sure to park in the lot provided. Walk west onto Ogunquit Beach, not to Moody Beach, now private above the high-water mark.

Wells Beach. Limited free parking right in the middle of the village of Wells Beach, also parking at east end by the jetty station. Wooden casino and boardwalk, clam shacks, clean public toilets, a cluster of motels, concrete benches—a gathering point for older people who sit while enjoying the view of the wide, smooth beach.

Drakes Island. Take Drakes Island Road off Route 1. There are three small parking areas on this spit of land lined with private cottages.

NATURE PRESERVES

Wells National Estuarine Research Reserve at Laudholm Farm (646-1555), Laudholm Road (off Route 1, just south of junction with Route 9), managed by the Laudholm Trust. The reserve consists of 1600 acres of estuarine habitat for the area's wildlife. "Estuarine," by the way, describes an area formed where ocean tides meet freshwater currents (an estuary). The reserve is divided into two parts, each with its own access point. Grounds include meadows and two barrier beaches at the mouth of the Little River. Laudholm Farm is a former estate, owned by the Lord family from 1881 until 1986 (George C. Lord was president of the Boston & Maine Railroad). It is now a visitors center with a slide show, exhibits, rest rooms, and parking ($5 in July and August). Seven miles of trails meander through fields, woods, and wetlands (bring a bathing suit if you want to swim at the beach). The Laudholm Trust grounds are open year-round (gates open daily 8–5), and guided trail walks are offered daily in summer, weekends in spring and fall. This is a birder's mecca.

Rachel Carson National Wildlife Refuge (operated by the US Fish and Wildlife Service), off Route 9, subtly marked. Open sunrise to sunset. The nature trail is 1 mile long—a loop through a white pine forest and along the Little River through a salt-marsh area. Maps and guides are available from the resident manager's office (646-9226) near the entrance to the refuge along Route 9.

WALKS

Marginal Way. In 1923 Josiah Chase gave Ogunquit this windy path along the ocean. A farmer from the town of York just south of here, Chase had driven his cattle around rocky Israel's Head each summer to pasture on the marsh grass in Wells, just to the north. Over the years, he bought land here and there until, eventually, he owned the whole promontory. He then sold off sea-view lots at a tidy profit and donated the actual ocean frontage to the town, thus preserving his own right-of-way. There is very limited parking at the mini-lighthouse on Israel's Head. **Wells Harbor.** Here is a pleasant walk along a granite jetty and a good fishing spot. There is also a playground and gazebo where concerts are held. **Old Trolley Trail.** An interesting nature walk and cross-country ski trail; begins on Pine Hill Road North, Ogunquit. **Mount Agamenticus** is a defunct ski area and the highest hill on the Atlantic between Florida and Bar Harbor. Take the Big A access road off Agamenticus Road, Ogunquit. See "Kittery and the Yorks" for details and information about horseback riding and mountain bike rentals there.

LODGING

RESORT

The Cliff House (361-1000), PO Box 2274, Ogunquit 03907. Open late March to mid-December. The tower-topped, mansard-roofed Cliffscape Building, opened in 1990, is now the centerpiece of this 162-room, 70-acre resort. The new building's multitiered lobby and dining rooms make the most of the oceanside roost atop Bald Head Cliff, and the atmosphere is a rare blend of new amenities (including an indoor lap pool) and family antiques. It's all the work of Kathryn Weare, a great-granddaughter worthy of Elsie Jane Weare, the indomitable lady who opened The Cliff House in 1872.

The family-run resort continued to maintain its status through the Roaring Twenties and shaky '30s, but World War II about did it in. The resort was literally drafted—as a radar station, keeping a 24-hour vigil for Nazi submarines. When the Weares were finally permitted back on their property, they found it in shambles. Discouraged, Charles Weare placed an ad in a 1946 edition of the *Wall Street Journal:* "For sale. 144 rooms. 90 acres, over 2500 feet ocean frontage for just $50,000."

There were no takers. Charles turned the property over to his son Maurice, who went with the times, shaving off the top two floors and transforming it into a "resort motel"—which is what it was until 1990. High-season summer rates range from $155 for a motel-like unit with a limited view to $205 for a one-bedroom suite; off-season rates run $95–125. These prices do not include meals, but a variety of packages bring the rack rate way down. Facilities include outdoor and indoor pools, a sauna and Jacuzzi, an exercise room, a game room, tennis courts, and a summertime trolley into the village and to the beach.

RESORT MOTOR INNS

Our usual format places inns before motels, but in the 1960s, some of Ogunquit's leading resorts replaced their old hotel buildings with luxury "motor inns."

Sparhawk (646-5562), Shore Road, Box 936, Ogunquit 03907. Open early April to late October. The 50 prime units in this complex, each with a balcony, overlook the entrance to the Ogunquit River and the length of Ogunquit Beach. The 20 units in neighboring Ireland House (with balconies canted toward the beach) are combination living room/bedroom suites, and the Barbara Dean, a spacious old village house, has seven suites and three apartments. The Sparhawk Apartment, a three-room house with fireplace and private deck overlooking the ocean, is rented by the week. Guests register and gather in Sparhawk Hall; a continental breakfast is served here, and there are books and comfortable spaces to read and to study local menus. Recreation options include a pool, shuffleboard, croquet, and tennis. One-week minimum stay, June 30 to mid-August; $140–160 in high summer, $70–90 in spring and fall.

Aspinquid (646-7072), Box 2408, Beach Street, Ogunquit 03907. Open mid-March through mid-October. A picture of the old Aspinquid hangs above the check-in counter of this condo-style complex just across the bridge from Ogunquit Beach. Built in 1971 by the owners of the old hotel, the two-story clusters still look modern. They are nicely designed and range in size from motel units to two-room apartments; all have two double beds, phones, and TVs; most have kitchenettes. Facilities include a pool, a lighted tennis court, a sauna, a spa, and a fish pond with waterfall ideal for peaceful reading and relaxation. $60–125 for a motel room, $75–135 for an efficiency unit, $115–205 for an apartment.

INNS AND BED & BREAKFASTS

All listings are for Ogunquit 03907 unless otherwise indicated.

Beachmere (646-2021; 1-800-336-3983), Box 2340. Open late March to mid-December. Sited on the Marginal Way with water views, this fine old mansion has a motel annex; there are also rooms in Mayfair and Bullfrog cottages a half-mile away on Israel's Head Road. Three of the rooms in the old mansion have working fireplaces, and many have decks; all have kitchenettes and cable TV. The large, inviting grounds overlook Ogunquit Beach, and smaller beaches are a few minutes' walk. Rates range from $75 per day for a third-floor efficiency accommodating two to $175 for a suite with fireplace in high season; $60–135 in shoulder season, $50–95 off-season.

The Trellis House (646-7909; 1-800-681-7907), 2 Beachmere Place, PO Box 2229. Open year-round. This is a find. Pat and Jerry Houlihan's shingled, turn-of-the-century summer cottage offers appealing common areas, including a wraparound screened porch (where breakfast is served in nice weather) and comfortable seating around the hearth. Upstairs are three guest rooms, all with full private baths, one with a water view. The most romantic room is a cottage in the garden; there is also a two-bedroom, housekeeping apartment ($850 per week in-season) as well as two more guest rooms in the carriage house. $100–110 in-season, $75 off-season, includes a breakfast (served anytime between 8:30 and 10) that might include a fruit compote and zucchini pie, or maybe apple-cinnamon French toast and sausage. The inn is handy both to the village and to Perkins Cove via the Marginal Way.

☞ **Ye Olde Perkins Place** (361-1119), 749 Shore Road (south of Perkins Cove), Cape Neddick 03902. Open late June through Labor Day. Overlooking the ocean, this 1717 homestead has six rooms, three in a more modern annex. The location is great, away from the village but within walking distance of a pebble beach. $60–70 per room; coffee, juice, and muffins included. No credit cards.

The Pine Hill Inn (361-1004), PO Box 2336. Open mid-May to mid-October. A Victorian summer house set in a rock garden, high above a quiet residential road but within walking distance of Perkins Cove. Walls throughout the house are all tongue-and-groove paneling, the four tastefully furnished guest rooms have private baths, and the large living room and screened-in porch offer plenty of inviting common space. Diana and Charles Schmidt are helpful hosts. Children over age 12, please; younger allowed in the neighboring two-bedroom cottage. $75–95 per room includes breakfast. Three-night minimum for the cottage, $300 ($650 for a week).

Marginal Way House and Motel (646-8801; 363-6566 in winter), Box 697, 8 Wharf Lane. Open late April through October. Ed and Brenda Blake have owned this delightful complex for more than 25 years. Just a short walk from the beach and really in the middle of the village, it is hidden down a back, waterside lane. There are old-fashioned guest rooms with private baths in the inn itself, and six standard motel rooms in a small, shingled, waterside building, as well as seven efficiency apartments (one or two bedrooms). The landscaped grounds have an ocean view. From $40 per room off-season; $79–118 during high season in the inn; apartments are $68–158, rented only by the week in high season.

The Hayes Guest House (646-2277), 127 Shore Road. Open June through October. Elinor Hayes has been renting rooms in her country home at the entrance to Perkins Cove since 1950. The house is furnished with antiques, and Mrs. Hayes's collections of 500 dolls (many of which she made) and 1000 salt dishes and spoons are displayed. There is a small outdoor pool. Guest rooms have air conditioners and private baths ($85 per night); a small "semi-efficiency" is $85 per day, $550 per week; a two-bedroom apartment with a sun porch is $135 per day, $800 per week.

Rose Cottage (646-6552), PO Box 2092, 7 Bourne Lane. This charming house was once part of the Dunelawn estate (since made into condos) by the Ogunquit River, where it hosted famous Playhouse performers such as Rita Hayworth, Mickey Rooney, and Bette Davis. In 1986 the classic, shingle-style house was moved to the other side of the village, within walking distance of the Marginal Way and Perkins Cove. It offers four rooms, ranging from $37.50 (for a single with shared bath) to $70 for a large double with a waterbed, sun room, deck, and private entrance as well as bath. Rates include breakfast. Innkeepers Larry and Marcia Smith also own Ogunquit's Camera Shop.

Morning Dove (646-3891), PO Box 1940, 30 Bourne Lane. Open late June through Labor Day, weekends in spring and fall. On a quiet side street off Shore Road, within walking distance of everything, is this carefully restored 1860s farmhouse. We like the feel of the living room with its white marble fireplace, and of the seven nicely decorated guest rooms; the innkeepers are Jane and Fred Garland. $60–110 (depending on season) per room includes breakfast.

Rockmere Lodge (646-2985) 40 Stearns Road. Open year-round. One of the 1890s summer mansions along the most private stretch of the Marginal Way. Andy Antoniuk and Bob Brown offer eight rooms, each different; our favorite is the Anna-Marie, a corner room on the second floor with an ocean view from the queen-sized wrought-iron bed (there's also a twin) and from the window seat. $98–135 in-season; from $60 off-season.

☞ **The Grand Hotel** (646-1231), 102 Shore Drive. Open April through November. An attractive three-floor, 28-suite hotel that's good value. Outfall from the '80s real estate boom, this was built as a condominium complex, but it makes a great small hotel. All suites are two rooms, with wet bar, fridge, color cable TV, and private sun deck or balcony; fireplaces on the top floor. There's an elevator, an interior atrium, and an indoor pool. $130–180 in high season, $50–125 in winter.

Beach Farm Inn (646-7970), Eldredge Road, Wells 04090. Open mid-June through October. A 19th-century farmhouse, nicely restored. Eight rooms, furnished with antiques, some with private baths. We like the large third-floor room. Set back from the main road, a peaceful setting with a country feel and a pool, handy to the beach and on the trolley line. $50–70 per couple, including breakfast; less off-season and for long stays.

COTTAGES

We have noted just a few of the dozens of cottage, condominium, and motel complexes that line Route 1. The helpful Wells Chamber of Commerce (see *Guidance*) keeps track of vacancies in these and in many private cottages.

Dunes (646-2612), Box 917, Route 1, Ogunquit 03907. Open mid-May to mid-October. Set way back from the highway on 12 acres of landscaped grounds and fronting on the Ogunquit River, the complex offers direct access to Ogunquit Beach by rowboat at high tide and on foot at low tide. Owned by the Perkins family for more than 60 years, this is really a historic property, the best of the coast's surviving "motor courts," as well as a great family find: The 36 units include 19 old-style Maine classics—cottages with white-and-green trim—scattered over spacious, well-kept grounds. Most have fireplaces. Refrigerators and color TVs in all rooms. One- and two-bedroom cottages are $72–90 off-season, $96–133 in-season (June 21 through Labor Day). Two-week minimum stay in July and August. Cottage suites (part of a larger building typically with one or two attached units, with living room/bedroom with fireplace and a kitchen) are $65–100. Motel rooms are $58–78 double off-season, $76–126 in-season.

Cottage in the Lane Motor Lodge (646-7903), Drakes Island Road, Wells 04090. There are 11 housekeeping cottages all facing landscaped grounds under the pines (an artistic play structure and a pool form the center-piece); salt marsh beyond. It's a ¾-mile walk or bike ride to the beach. The quiet setting borders the Rachel Carson Wildlife Refuge and Laudholm Farm (see *Nature Preserves*). $440–465 per week for a three-room cottage accommodating four, and $520–600 for a four-room cottage good for five people; from $42 per night off-season.

MOTELS

Riverside Motel (646-2741), PO Box 2244, Shore Road, Ogunquit 03907. Open late April through late October. Just across the foot-drawbridge and overlooking Perkins Cove is this trim, friendly place with 41 units; also four rooms in the 1874 house. The property has been in Harold Staples's family for more than 100 years. All rooms have color TVs and full baths, and all overlook the cove; continental breakfast is included and served in the lobby around the fireplace or on the sun deck. $50–125, depending on season and location of room. Three-day minimum July 28 through August 17.

Seagull Motor Inn (646-5164), Route 1, Wells 04090. Open April to mid-October. Facilities include 24 motel units, 24 one- and two-bedroom cottages with screened porches, a pool, a playground, and lawn games on 23 acres. Having spent four summer vacations here as a child (40 years ago), Chris Tree is happy to report that the place is still essentially the same family value, with plenty of common space, a water view, and a loyal following. Rentals are nightly or by the week, $360–720 for housekeeping cottages.

WHERE TO EAT

DINING OUT

Arrow's (361-1100), Berwick Road, Ogunquit. Dinner 6–9, late April through October. Considered one of the best—and most expensive—restaurants in Maine, with an emphasis on fresh local ingredients. A 1765 farmhouse is the setting for nouvelle-inspired dishes. Appetizers might include leek and asparagus soup, or a sautéed peekytoe crabmeat pillow with a rice wrapper; entrées could be braised rabbit with herb puff pastry, *haricots verts*, and chive–crème fraîche pearl onions. The chef-owners are Mark Gaier and Clark Frasier. Entrées $25.95–28.95

Hurricane Restaurant (646-6348), Perkins Cove. Year-round, 11:30–10:30 daily. "Our view will blow you away—our menu will bring you back" is the boast of the most popular place to dine in Perkins Cove. Dining rooms maximize the ocean view. The same menu all day ranges from "Soups and Salads" and "Small Plates" like deviled Maine lobster cakes with salsa ($7.25) to dinner entrées like baked salmon and Brie baklava, roast rack of lamb with a mango and port wine demiglaze. Entrées are $14.95–22.95. Desserts like mile-high cheesecake or warm fruit and berry cheesecake are $5.95.

98 Provence (646-989), Shore Road, Ogunquit. Open April through December 1 for dinner (5:30–9:30) except Tuesday. Provençale cuisine that's outstanding. You might begin with *soupe de pecheur* studded with mussels, shrimp, clams, and scallops ($6.95) and dine on hazelnut-crusted chicken breast with sautéed wild mushrooms and leeks ($14.95), or goat cheese ravioli with mussels meunière ($12.95).

Gypsy Sweethearts (646-7021), 18 Shore Road, Ogunquit Village. Open May to October. Dinner nightly in-season and breakfast weekends; closed Monday off-season. Fine dining in a charming old house. A place that all Ogunquit regulars hit at least once in their stay. Chef-owner Judy Clayton's specialties include light seafood dishes like a salad of grilled sea scallops with citrus and mango; entrées from $12.95 for linguine to $22.95 for herbed rack of lamb; many dishes around $15; award-winning wine list.

Barnacle Billy's, Etc. (646-5575), Perkins Cove. Open April through October for lunch and dinner. What began as a no-frills lobster place (the one that's still next door) has expanded to fill a luxurious dining space created for a more upscale restaurant. Lobster and seafood dishes remain the specialty and it's difficult to beat the view combined with comfort, which frequently includes the glow from two great stone fireplaces. Full bar; entrées from $10.45 for fried or grilled chicken to $18.95 for surf and turf.

Cliff House (361-1000), Bald Hill Cliff, Shore Road, Ogunquit. Open for breakfast and dinner most of the year, for lunch in July and August. The dining room is in the Cliffscape Building, with dramatic ocean views. Unique creations like chicken Hyannis, a boneless breast sautéed and served in creamy cranberry chutney sauce with cashews ($13.95), await you; and where else can you try lobster tails lightly breaded in hazelnuts and sautéed in lemon-wine butter ($20.95)?

Dianne's Fine Food & Spirits (646-9703), 111 Shore Road, Ogunquit. Open for dinner early May through Columbus Day, also weekends in spring and fall. Chef-owner Scott Walker, ably assisted by wife Dianne, has created a very pleasant setting for dining from a menu that includes chicken béarnaise ($14.95), lobster Newburg in puff pastry ($16.95), and steak *au poivre* ($17.95).

Clay Hill Farm (361-2272), Agamenticus Road (north of Ogunquit Village). Open year-round for dinner but closed Monday and Tuesday in winter. A gracious old farmhouse with valet parking and an elegant Victorian setting; geared to functions but with a reliable menu that might include veal piccata with prosciutto or grilled eggplant and rice-stuffed grape leaves. Entrées $12.95–22.95.

Poor Richard's Tavern (646-4722), Shore Road and Pine Hill, Ogunquit. This local dining landmark is back where it began 30 years ago, in a charming old house near Perkins Cove. Chef-owner Richard Perkins prides himself on his lobster stew and Infamous Lobster Pie and offers a large menu ranging from meat loaf to charbroiled fillet of salmon. Entrées: $10.95–17.95.

Blue Water Inn (646-5559), Beach Street, Ogunquit. The water view is hard to beat, and the specialty is fish—mako shark as well as mackerel and haddock. Entrées $10.95–17.95.

Roberto's Italian Cuisine (646-8130), 82 Shore Road, Ogunquit. Ogunquit's chef-owned trattoria. Roberto specializes in no-nonsense southern Italian dishes like veal parmigiana, chicken Marsala, and seafood lasagna. Entrées $7.95–15.95.

Grey Gull Inn (646-7501), 475 Webhannet Drive, Moody Point (Wells). Open year-round for dinner. Across the road from the ocean, a dependable dining room with minimal atmosphere. Entrées include maple walnut chicken (lightly breaded and topped with maple syrup and walnuts, $13.95) and Yankee pot roast ($14.50).

EATING OUT

☞ **Lobster Shack** (646-2941), end of Perkins Cove. Open May through Columbus Day weekend. A genuine old-style, serious lobster-eating place since the 1940s (when it was known as Maxwell and Perkins); oilcloth-covered tables, good chowder, apple pie à la mode, wine, beer.

Barnacle Billy's (646-5575), Perkins Cove. Open May through mid-October, 11–10 daily. Order lobster at the counter and wait for your number; beer and wine. Dining on outdoor deck and inside, water views.

Oarweed Cove Restaurant (646-4022), at the entrance to the Marginal Way in Perkins Cove. Open daily mid-May through mid-October for lunch and dinner. Water view; same menu all day; chowder, seafood (none fried).

Litchfield's (646-5711), Route 1, Wells. Open daily, year-round, for lunch and dinner. Reliable food and good value. Lobster served baked and stuffed as well as straight; Aztec chicken, prime rib, seafood dishes.

Lord's Harborside Restaurant (646-2651), Wells Harbor. Open April to November for lunch and dinner, closed Tuesday in spring and fall. A big, ungarnished dining room with a harbor view and a reputation for fresh fish and seafood. Lobster (fried, boiled, and baked).

Fisherman's Catch (646-8780), Wells Harbor. Open Mother's Day through Columbus Day, 9–8 daily. Water views, the feel and taste of a good place; good chowder, lobster stew, and clam cakes.

Billy's Chowder House (646-7588), Mile Road, Wells. Open daily year-round, closed for lunch on Thursday in winter. A knotty-pine and shamrock atmosphere with views of salt marsh and water. The seafood is fresh, and spirits are served.

Jake's Seafood (646-6771), Route 1, Bourne Avenue, Moody. Open for all three meals year-round. Specializes in good American cooking, fresh seafood, homemade ice cream.

Congdon's Donuts Family Restaurant, Route 1, Wells. Open 6:30–2 year-round, seasonal at Wells Beach. Fresh muffins, breads, pastries, and doughnuts; also ice cream made on premises.

Maine Diner (656-4441), Route 1, Wells. Open year-round 7 AM–9 PM, near the junction of Routes 1 and 9. A classic diner with a large menu for all three meals, plus beer, wine, takeout; breakfast all day, great corned beef hash, and outstanding clam chowder. The homemade chicken pot pie takes a few minutes longer, but it's worth the wait.

Ogunquit Lobster Pound (646-2516), Route 1 (north of Ogunquit Village). Open Mother's Day through Columbus Day weekend for dinner. After more than 40 years of ownership by the Hancock family, this is still notoriously expensive, and service is frequently slow, but patrons return year after year. Dine either in the rustic log building or outside on swinging, wood-canopied tables. Beer and wine are available along with cheeseburgers and steak, but lobsters and clams are what the place is about. Don't pass up the deep-dish blueberry pie.

SNACKS

S.W. Swan (646-1178), 117 Shore Road, Ogunquit, is a delightful coffee- and teahouse open from 7:30 AM in summer, from 8:30 off-season, until dark; also a gourmet gift shop. **Bread & Roses Bakery** (646-4227), 28A Main Street (up an alley), Ogunquit. A pleasant source of muffins, coffee, and delectable pastries. **Scoop Deck** (646-5150), Eldridge Road just off Route 1, Wells. Memorial Day through Columbus Day. Mocha almond fudge and dinosaur crunch (blue vanilla) are among the more than 40 flavors; the ice cream is from Thibodeau Farms in Saco. Also yogurt, cookies, brownies, and hot dogs.

ENTERTAINMENT

THEATER
Hackmatack Playhouse (698-1807), Route 9, Berwick. Stages live performances throughout the year. **Leavitt Fine Arts Theatre** (646-3123), Route 1, Ogunquit Village. Open early spring through fall. An old-time theater with new screen and sound; first-run films. **Ogunquit Square Theatre** (646-5151), Shore Road, Ogunquit Village. Another old-time theater with all the latest movies. **Jonathan's** (646-4777), 2 Bourne Lane, Ogunquit. A restaurant with nightly entertainment in summer, from Maine humor to concerts to murder-mystery theater. Summer **Saturday-night concerts** at Hope Hobbs Gazebo, Wells Harbor Park. (See also Ogunquit Playhouse under *To Do—Theater.*)

SELECTIVE SHOPPING

ANTIQUARIAN BOOKS
Boston book lovers drive to Wells to browse in this cluster of exceptional bookstores along Route 1. They include **Douglas N. Harding Map & Print Gallery** (646-8785), huge and excellent: 4500 square feet of old and rare books, maps, and prints, plus some 100,000 general titles. **The Book Barn** (646-4926) specializes in old paperbacks, comic books, baseball cards, and collectors' supplies. **East Coast Books** (646-3584), Depot Street at Route 109, has a large general collection, autographs, prints, drawings, paintings, and historical paperbacks.

ANTIQUES SHOPS
Route 1 from York through Wells and the Kennebunks is studded with antiques shops, among them: **MacDougall-Gionet** (646-3531), open 9– 5 Tuesday through Sunday; a particularly rich trove of country furniture in a barn; 60 dealers are represented. **R. Jorgensen Antiques** (646-9444) has nine rooms filled with antique furniture, including fine formal pieces from a number of countries.

ART GALLERIES
In addition to the Museum of Art of Ogunquit (under *To See*), there is the **Ogunquit Art Association** (646-8400), Shore Road and Bourne Lane, Ogunquit. Open Memorial Day through September, Monday through Saturday 11–5 and Sunday 1–5. The gallery showcases work by mem-

bers; also stages frequent workshops, lectures, films, and concerts. Ogunquit's galleries (all seasonal) also include: **June Weare Fine Arts** (646-8200), Shore Road; open mid-May to mid-October, 10–4. Original prints, paintings, and sculpture. In Perkins Cove look for the **George Carpenter Gallery** (646-5106). A longtime area resident, Carpenter paints outdoors in the tradition and style of new England's '20s marine and landscape artists. **Hearthstone at Stonecrop Gallery** (361-1678), Shore Road at Juniper Lane, three doors south of the Ogunquit Museum; landscape paintings and handsome stoneware by a husband and wife, displayed in their unusual gallery/home. **Shore Road Gallery** (646-5046), 112 Shore Road; open Memorial Day through Columbus Day weekend, daily. Fine arts, jewelry, and fine crafts by nationally known artists. **Bartok Studio/Gallery** (646-7815), 104 Shore Road. Watercolors by John Bartok.

SPECIAL SHOPS

Books Ink. (646-8393), Perkins Cove. A collection of toys, games, cards, wine, books, and other things owner Barbara Lee Chertok finds interesting or educational. Sit on the terrace and look over the cove.

Ogunquit Camera (646-2261), at the corner of Shore Road and Wharf Lane in Ogunquit Village. Open year-round, and features 1-hour film developing. A great little shop that's been here since 1952. It's also a trove of toys, towels, windsocks, beach supplies, and sunglasses.

Harbor Candy Shop, 26 Main Street, Ogunquit. Seasonal. Chocolates and specialty candies are made on the spot; there's also a selection of imported candies.

SPECIAL EVENTS

April: Big **Patriot's Day celebration** at Ogunquit Beach.

June: **Ogunquit Chamber Music Festival** (first week); **Laudholm Farm Day** (midmonth); **Wells Week** (end of the month)—a week-long celebration centering on Harbor Park Day: boat launchings, a chicken barbecue, a sand-sculpture contest, and a crafts fair.

July: **Independence Day fireworks** at Ogunquit Beach. **Sand Castle–Building Contest,** midmonth.

August: **Sidewalk Art Show. Great Inner Tube Race. Kite Day.**

September: **Open Homes Day** sponsored by the Wells Historical Society. **Nature Crafts Festival** at Laudholm Farm (second weekend). **Capriccio,** a celebration of the performing arts.

December: **Christmas parade** in Wells; **Christmas by the Sea** in Ogunquit.

The Kennebunks

Kennebunk is a busy commercial center straddling the strip of Route 1 between the Mousam and Kennebunk Rivers. A 10-minute ride down Summer Street (Route 35) brings you to Kennebunkport. Then there are Kennebunk Beach, Cape Porpoise, Goose Rocks Beach, Cape Arundel, and Kennebunk Lower Village. Luckily, free, detailed maps are readily available.

The Kennebunks have been around under one name or another since the 1620s. They began as a fishing stage near Cape Porpoise, which was repeatedly destroyed by Native American raids. In 1719 the present "port" was incorporated as Arundel, a name that stuck through its peak shipbuilding and seafaring years until 1821, when the name was changed to Kennebunkport. Later, when the novel *Arundel* by Kenneth Roberts (born in Kennebunk) had run through 32 printings, residents attempted to reclaim the old name. They succeeded in doing so in 1957, at least for North Kennebunkport.

In the 1870s, this entire spectacular 5-mile stretch of coast—from Lord's Point at the western end of Kennebunk Beach all the way to Cape Porpoise on the east—was acquired by a Massachusetts group, the Boston and Kennebunkport Sea Shore Company. No fewer than 30 grand hotels and dozens of summer mansions (including Walker Point) evolved to accommodate the wave of visitors that train service brought. The Kennebunks, however, shared the 1940s to 1960s decline suffered by all Maine coastal resorts, losing all but a scattering of old hotels. Then the tourist tide again turned and over the past few decades surviving hotels have been condoed, inns have been rehabbed, and dozens of B&Bs and inns have opened.

You can bed down a few steps from Dock Square's lively shops and restaurants, in the quiet village of Cape Porpoise, or out at Goose Rocks, where the only sound is the lapping of waves on endless sand. Many B&Bs, on the other hand, are housed in the former sea captains' homes grouped along a few stately streets near the river, within walking distance of both Dock Square and the open ocean.

This is the least seasonal resort on the South Coast. Most inns and shops remain open through Christmas Prelude in early December (see *Special Events*), and many never close.

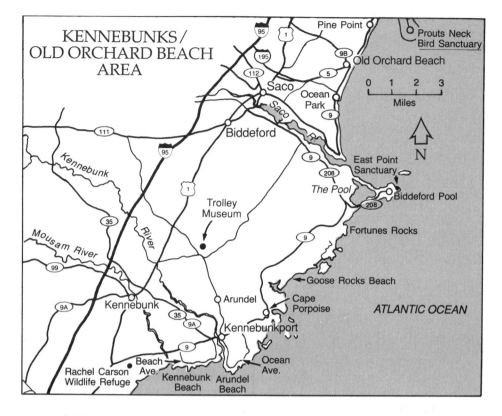

GUIDANCE

Kennebunk/Kennebunkport Chamber of Commerce (967-0857; 1-800-982-4421), PO Box 740, Kennebunk 04043. Open daily year-round in Lower Village. Request a copy of the excellent free guide.
Kennebunkport Information and Hospitality Center (967-8600), open May through mid-December, rest rooms and information in Dock Square.

GETTING THERE

By air: You can fly your own plane into **Sanford Airport;** otherwise Portland International Jetport (see "Portland Area") is served by **JJ's Express** (878-3062), **Lilley's Limo** (773-5765), and **Bob's Airport Luxury Tour** (773-5135).
By land: Drive up I-95 to exit 3, or take **C&J Trailways** (1-800-258-7111) from Boston or Logan Airport.

GETTING AROUND

Intown Trolley Co. (967-3686) offers narrated sight-seeing tours with $6 tickets good for the day, so you can also use them to shuttle between Dock Square and Kennebunk Beach.
Select Tours (985-7946). Barbara Cook's guided 2-hour tours of the

area draw rave reviews. $12 per person.

Bicycles work well here, an ideal way to handle the mile between Dock Square and the ocean or Kennebunk Beach.

PARKING

A municipal parking lot is hidden just off Dock Square behind Alison's restaurant. There are also two free nearby lots: one at St. Martha's Catholic Church on North Street, the other at the Consolidated School, Route 9.

MEDICAL EMERGENCY

Southern Maine Medical Center (283-7000), Medical Center Drive (off Route 111), Biddeford. **Kennebunk Walk-in Clinic** (985-6027), Route 1 North, Kennebunk.

TO SEE

MUSEUMS

The Brick Store Museum (985-4802), 117 Main Street, Kennebunk. Open year-round, Tuesday through Saturday 10–4:30. Admission. A block of early-19th-century commercial buildings, including William Lord's **Brick Store** (1825), a space used for changing exhibits of fine and decorative arts and marine collections. ($3 admission per adult). Architectural walking tours are offered of Kennebunk's National Register District in summer and you can tour the nearby Federal-era **Taylor-Barry House** ($2 admission).

Seashore Trolley Museum (967-2800), Log Cabin Road, located 3.2 miles up North Street from Kennebunkport or 2.8 miles north on Route 1 from Kennebunk, then right at the yellow blinker. Open daily late May to mid-October, varying hours (call to check on special events, which include a Halloween ghost trolley and New Year's Eve celebration). Admission is $7 for adults, $5 seniors, $4 children, and family rates. This nonprofit museum has preserved the history of the trolley era, displaying more than 200 vehicles from the world over. The impressive collection began in 1939, when the last open-sided Biddeford/Old Orchard Beach trolley was retired to an open field straddling the old Atlantic Shore Line railbed. The museum now owns 300 acres as well as cars shipped here from London, Budapest, Rome, and Nagasaki, among other cities. A 4-mile, round-trip excursion on a trolley takes visitors out through woods and fields, along a route once traveled by summer guests en route to Old Orchard Beach.

Kennebunkport Historical Society (967-2751). Based in the Town House School on North Street. Open year-round Wednesday through Friday 1–4. Displays local memorabilia; also maritime exhibits housed next door in the former office of the Clark Shipyard. The society also maintains the **Nott House,** open mid-June through Columbus Day,

CHRISTINA TREE

The Seashore Trolley Museum

Wednesday through Saturday 1–4. A Greek Revival mansion with a Doric colonnade, original wallpapers, carpets, and furnishings. $3 per adult. Inquire about **walking tours.**

HISTORIC SIGHTS

Wedding Cake House, Summer Street (Route 35), Kennebunk. Ann Burnett's studio, featuring artwork on furniture and clothing, is open to the public; the house itself is private. This 1826 house is laced up and down with white wooden latticework. The tale is that a local sea captain had to rush off to sea before a proper wedding cake could be baked, but he more than made up for it later.

South Congregational Church, Temple Street, Kennebunkport. Just off Dock Square, built in 1824 with a Christopher Wren–style cupola and belfry; Doric columns added in 1912.

Louis T. Graves Memorial Library (967-2778), Main Street, Kennebunkport. Built in 1813 as a bank, which went bust, it later served as a customs house. It was subsequently donated to the library association by artist Abbott Graves, whose pictures alone make it worth a visit. You can still see the bank vault and the sign from the customs collector's office. Upstairs, the book saleroom is full of bargains.

First Parish Unitarian Church, Main Street, Kennebunk. Built in 1772–1773 with an Asher Benjamin–style steeple added in 1803–1804, along with a Paul Revere bell. In 1838 the interior was divided into two levels, with the church proper elevated to the second floor.

Kennebunkport Maritime Museum & Shop (967-3218). Open May 15 through October 15, 10–4. $2 admission; children 12 and under free. This "museum" occupies the former boathouse in which author Booth

Tarkington wrote. Exhibits include the last remnants of the schooner *Regina* and a collection of early-19th-century scrimshaw and other nautical memorabilia. There is a museum shop.

SCENIC DRIVE

Ocean Avenue follows the Kennebunk River a mile to Cape Arundel and the open ocean, then winds past many magnificent summer homes, including Walker's Point, former president Bush's summer estate (it fills a private, 11-acre peninsula). Built by his grandfather in 1903, its position was uncannily ideal for use as a president's summer home, moated by water on three sides, yet clearly visible from the pull-out places along the avenue. Continue along the ocean (you don't have to worry about driving too slowly, because everyone else is, too). Follow the road to Cape Porpoise, site of the area's original 1600s settlement. The cove is still a base for lobster and commercial fishing boats and the village is a good place to lunch or dine. Continue along Route 9 to Clock Farm Corner (you'll know it when you see it) and turn right on Dyke Road to Goose Rocks Beach; park and walk. Return to Route 9 and cross it, continuing via Goose Rocks Road to the Seashore Trolley Museum (see *Museums*) and then Log Cabin Road to Kennebunkport.

TO DO

BALLOONING

Balloons over New England (499-7575; 1-800-788-5562) offers champagne flights year-round.

BICYCLING

The lay of this land lends itself to exploration by bike, a far more satisfying way to go in summer than by car since you can stop and park wherever the view and urge hit you. Rental bikes are available from **Cape-Able Bike Shop** (967-4382), Townhouse Corners (off Log Cabin Road), Kennebunkport.

BLUEBERRYING

The Nature Conservancy (729-5181) maintains 1500 acres of blueberry plains in West Kennebunk; take Route 99 toward Sanford.

BOATBUILDING SCHOOL

The Landing School of Boat Building and Design (985-7976), River Road, Kennebunk, offers a September-to-June program in building sailing craft. Visitors welcome if you call ahead.

BOAT EXCURSIONS

A variety of boats offer fishing trips, day sails, and scenic tours; check with the chamber of commerce (see *Guidance*). This is also Maine's prime departure point for whale-watching on Jeffrey's Ledge, about 20 miles offshore. If you have any tendency toward seasickness, be sure to choose a calm day. Chances are you'll see more than a dozen whales. Frequently sighted species include finbacks, minkes, rights, and humpbacks. *The Nautilus* (967-0707), a 65-foot boat carrying up to 100 passengers, offers narrated trips daily from May to October. *Indian Whale Watch* (967-5912), a 75-foot boat holding 72 passengers, is slower and takes longer to reach the whales than some but features narration by a mammalogist (July through October). *First Chance* (967-5507) also offers whale-watching and sunset cruises.

DAY CAMP

Kennebunk Beach Improvement Association (967-2180; September through May: 967-4075) offers weekly sessions for 3–18-year-olds featuring swimming, sailing, rowing, fishing, golf, tennis, arts and crafts, photography, and sand-castle building.

KAYAKING

Kayak Adventures (967-5243), Kennebunkport. Guided ocean and river trips in open-cockpit-design kayaks.

GOLF

Cape Arundel Golf Club (967-3494), Kennebunkport, 18 holes. These are the local links former president Bush frequents. Open to the public except from 11 to 2:30. **Webhannet Golf Club** (967-2061), Kennebunk Beach, 18 holes. Open to the public except from 11:30 to 1. **Dutch Elm Golf Course** (282-9850), Arundel, 18 holes; cart and club rental, lessons, pro shop, snack bar, putting greens.

HAYRIDES

Bush Brook Stables (284-7721), 463 West Street, Biddeford.

CROSS-COUNTRY SKIING

Harris Farm (499-2678), Buzzell Road, Dayton. A 500-acre dairy farm with more than 20 miles of trails. Equipment rentals available. Located 1.5 miles from the Route 5 and Route 35 intersection.

GREEN SPACE

BEACHES

The Kennebunks avoid an overabundance of weekend day-trippers by requiring a permit to park at their major beaches. Day and seasonal passes must be secured from the chamber of commerce or local lodging places. You can also park in one of the town lots and walk, bike, or take a trolley to the beach.

Kennebunk and **Gooch's Beaches** in Kennebunk are both long, wide strips of firm sand backed by Beach Avenue, divided by Oak's Neck. Beyond Gooch's Beach, take Great Hill Road along the water to **Strawberry Island,** a great place to walk and examine tidal pools. Please don't picnic. Keep going and you come to **Mother's Beach,** small and very sandy.

Parsons Beach, south of Kennebunk Beach on Route 9, requires no permit, but in-season you will probably be able to stop only long enough to drop someone off; off-season you have a chance at one of the half-dozen parking spaces. You can always park along the road on the other side of Route 9 and walk down the grand avenue of sugar maples to the sand. It's a splendid place for an early-morning or evening walk.

Goose Rocks Beach, a few miles north of Kennebunkport Village on Route 9, is a magnificent, wide, smooth stretch of sand backed by the road. You can also walk down Ocean Avenue to tiny **Arundel Beach** near the Colony Hotel at the mouth of the Kennebunk River. It offers nice rocks for climbing.

NATURE PRESERVES

Biddeford Pool East Sanctuary, Route 9 (north of Kennebunkport), is a place to observe shorebirds. **Rachel Carson National Wildlife Refuge** encompasses 1600 acres with a mile-long nature trail and is an excellent spot for birding (see *Nature Preserves* in "Ogunquit and Wells"). **Vaughns Island Preserve** offers nature trails on a wooded island separated from the mainland by two tidal creeks. Cellar holes of historic houses are accessible by foot 3 hours before and 3 hours after high tide. (Also see Laudholm Farm described under *Nature Preserves* in "Ogunquit and Wells.")

WALKS

Henry Parsons Park, Ocean Avenue, is a path along the rocks leading to Spouting Rock and Blowing Cave, both sights to see at midtide. A great way to view the beautiful homes along Ocean Avenue.

St. Anthony Monastery and Shrine (967-2011), Kennebunkport. Some 20 acres of peaceful, riverside fields and forests on Beach Road, now maintained by Lithuanian Franciscans as a shrine and retreat. Visitors are welcome; gift shop. Ask about summer lodging in the Guest House.

LODGING

All listings are for Kennebunkport 04046 unless otherwise indicated.

RESORT HOTEL

The Colony Hotel (967-3331 or 1-800-552-2363), Ocean Avenue and King's Highway. Open May through October. With 134 rooms (all private baths) in four buildings, this is one of the last of New England's coastal resorts that are still maintained in the grand style. It's set on a rise, overlooking the point at which the Kennebunk River meets the Atlantic. It's been owned by the Boughton family since 1948; many guests have been coming for generations. Amenities include a saltwater pool, a beach, a putting green, a social program, nightly entertainment, and dancing. A 2-night minimum is required for weekend reservations for July and August. $195–295 double per day includes two meals; $40 per extra person (children under 4, $30) plus $12 for service. Worth it. Handicapped-accessible rooms.

INNS AND BED & BREAKFASTS

Kennebunkport Inn (967-2621; 800-248-2621), Dock Square. Open year-round; dining room closed November to April. Originally an 1890s mansion, but an inn since 1926. Although just a skip from Dock Square, it's set back from the hubbub. The feel here is of a small, personable European hotel, the kind with one innkeeper (Rick Griffin) behind the check-in desk and the other (Martha Griffin) supervising the well-respected kitchen. There are 34 rooms, one with a fireplace. The inn has three sections—the main house; a 1980s Federal-style addition; and a 1930s river house, with smaller rooms and stenciled walls. Each room is individually decorated with antiques, and all have TVs and private baths; many have water views. In summer, a small pool on the terrace is available to guests. The cocktail lounge is dark and friendly with a huge old bar and green-hooded lights, evening piano music. Special packages include meals and a lobster cruise. High-season rates $85–219 per room, off-season $69–199.

Captain Lord Mansion (967-3141), PO Box 800. Open year-round at the corner of Pleasant and Green Streets. This splendid mansion is one of the most romantic inns around. The three-story, Federal-era home is topped with a widow's walk from which guests can contemplate the town and sea beyond. Other architectural features include a three-story, suspended elliptical staircase, and pine doors that have been painted trompe l'oeil–style to simulate inlaid mahogany. There are 16 meticulously decorated rooms, 14 with gas fireplaces, some with high four-posters and canopy beds—and all with antiques and private baths. The gathering room is also very elegant, but the full breakfast is an informal affair, served in the large country kitchen. Now in their 20th season, hosts Bev Davis and Rick Litchfield emphasize warmth and go out of their way to make each guest feel special. Phebe's Fantasy, a separate building, has four more rooms with fireplaces. $144–249 per room in high season, breakfast and tea included; $99–199 off-season.

Old Fort Inn (967-5353; 1-800-828-FORT), PO Box M. Open mid-April to mid-December. An unusual combination of things, but it works. The reception area is in an antiques store in the former barn. This is also where you'll find a spacious sitting room in which guests enjoy a morning buffet breakfast and are otherwise drawn to relax. Grounds and buildings represent the remnants of an 1880s resort, nicely converted to serve 1990s families, with a pool, tennis court, horseshoes, and shuffleboard. The sturdy stone and brick carriage house now offers 16 guest rooms with private baths, antiques, color TV, phones, air-conditioning, and wet bars. Two suites available. A path leads down to the ocean. Unsuitable for children under 12. Two-night minimum during high season. $130–260 in high season, $96–190 off-season, breakfast included.

Bufflehead Cove (967-3879), Box 499, off Route 35. Open year-round except March. This is a hidden gem, sequestered on 6 acres at the end of a dirt road, overlooking an 8-foot tidal cove, but less than a mile from the village of Kennebunkport. It's a Dutch Colonial–style home in which Harriet and Jim Gott raised their children. Harriet is a native of nearby Cape Porpoise, and Jim is a commercial fisherman. There are six pretty guest rooms, some with hand-painted or stenciled wall designs. The Hideaway features a fireplace that opens into the bedroom on one side and into the sitting area on the other. The living room has a hearth and deep window seats; you'll also find an inviting veranda, and woods and orchard to explore. $95–200 includes a full breakfast and afternoon wine and cheese.

Inn on South Street (967-5151; 1-800-963-5151), South Street, PO Box 478A. A Greek Revival home on a quiet street preserves a sense of the era in which it was built. Innkeeper Jack Downs is a professor with a keen interest in the China trade, and the living room decor includes the kind of Chinese furniture and furnishings a Kennebunkport sea captain might well have brought back. There are three guest rooms and a suite. Our favorite, named for "Mrs. Perkins," has a fireplace, a pine four-poster bed with a canopy, Oriental rugs, and a portrait of its namesake tucked in the closet. The first-floor suite has its own sitting room, a four-poster bed and wood-burning stove, a bath with Jacuzzi, a kitchen, and a porch overlooking the herb garden. Eva Downs's amazing breakfasts are delivered to this kitchen, and served upstairs in the dining room to other guests; afternoon tea is also served, and is included in rates that run $90–145 for a double room, $155–185 for the suite.

The Inn at Harbor Head (967-5564), 41 Pier Road, Cape Porpoise. Open year-round. Joan and Dave Sutter offer three rooms and two suites (both with fireplaces) in their rambling, shingled home overlooking Cape Porpoise harbor. The Summer Suite has a view of the picturesque harbor from the bath as well as from the bed. Most rooms have water views and hand-painted seascapes on the walls; all are decorated with florals and antiques. Guests share the dock, terrace, and sitting rooms, with an inviting fireplace in the library. Fresh-baked goods top off large breakfasts; afternoon tea or wine and cheese are served. Beach passes and towels provided for nearby Goose Rocks Beach. No smoking, no TV. $150–250 per room in-season, $95–175 in winter.

White Barn Inn (967-2321), PO Box 560C, Beach Street. Open year-round. The barn is now an elegant dining room (see *Dining Out*) attached to the old inn. Built in 1865 as a farmhouse, later enlarged as the Forest Hills Hotel, this complex midway between Dock Square and Kennebunk Beach now includes 17 rooms and seven suites and represents the height of South Coast luxury and formality. Choose an antiques-furnished room in the original farmhouse, a suite in the carriage house (four-poster king beds, fireplaces, and marble baths with whirlpool tubs), or, most luxurious of all, the cottage with its specially crafted furnishings, a double-sided fireplace, Jacuzzi, and steam shower. $100–400 per couple, including breakfast, afternoon tea, and use of touring bikes. Cheaper off-season. Amenities include a new, landscaped swimming pool.

The Captain Fairfield Inn (967-4454; 1-800-322-1928), corner of Pleasant and Green Streets. Bonnie and Dennis Tallagnon put a Vermont inn on the hospitality map and then sold it, but they say they missed innkeeping too much not to give it another try. They found this Federal-era captain's home and lovingly restored it to its present grandeur. There are nine bedrooms, all decorated with antiques and wicker, four-poster and canopy beds. Each has a private bath, one handicapped accessible, three with fireplaces. Those in the front part of the house are more elegant, while those in the rear wing are air-conditioned. Dennis is an accomplished chef and offers a choice for breakfast, maybe crêpes, blueberry pancakes, or eggs Benedict. $89–175; $25 per extra person.

The Captain Jefferds Inn (967-2311), Pearl Street, Box 691. This strikingly handsome, Federal-era mansion changed hands as this edition went to press but all signs are that it will continue to be a standout.

✐ **Maine Stay Inn and Cottages** (967-2117; 1-800-950-2117), Box 500A, Maine Street. Open year-round. The 1860 house is big, white, and distinctive, with a large cupola. It offers four guest rooms, each with private bath, one with a fireplace and deck and two suites, one with a fireplace. What set this place apart from the other gracious B&Bs in Kennebunkport are the 11 cottages of varying sizes sequestered in nicely landscaped grounds, 5 with fireplaces, all but 1 with efficiency kitchens. This is one of the few attractive places for families to stay within walking distance of Dock Square. A full breakfast is served and might include blueberry blintzes or apricot scones (cottage guests have the option of breakfast delivered in a basket). All guests can enjoy a full afternoon tea in the attractive living room or on the wraparound porch. Carol and Lindsay Copeland are warm hosts, eager to help you make the most of your stay. $125–200 per night; winter, $85–170.

Kylemere House "Crosstrees" (967-2780), 6 South Street. Open April through early December. A graceful, Federal-era house with just four spacious guest rooms, one with a working fireplace. All have period furniture and antiques, private baths, and sitting areas. Guest-room shelves are well stocked with books and there are spacious grounds. Your hosts are Ruth and Helen Toohey. A full breakfast is served in the formal dining room overlooking the gardens. $95–135 in-season, $80–125 in the shoulder months.

The 1802 House (967-5632; 1-800-932-5632), PO Box 646-A, 15 Locke Street. Open year-round. Recently remodeled by innkeepers Ron and Carol Perry, this country retreat offers five guest rooms furnished with antiques, also a three-room suite with fireplace, fridge, and double shower, and a Roman garden room with a double whirlpool tub overlooking a private deck. Most rooms have queen-sized four-posters and fireplaces, and many have whirlpool tubs. The house is away from town on the edge of the Cape Arundel Golf Club, with an out-in-the-country

Near Ocean Avenue in Kennebunkport

feel, shaded by large pines. A ship's bell calls guests to a very full break-fast. Common rooms are airy and comfortable; cozy corners for winter. $89–169 for a room with fireplace and whirlpool; $229–249 for suites.

The Green Heron (967-3315), PO Box 2578, 126 Ocean Avenue. Open daily mid-May to late October and mid-December through January 1, Wednesday through Sunday during the rest of the year, closed in January. Within walking distance of both village and shore, this old house has 10 guest rooms that are attractive, clean, and bright, individually decorated and filled with the spirit of a friendlier, simpler day. There is also a coveside cottage. The famous breakfast is included in the guest rates; it's also available to the public. Ownership has remained in the Reid family for many decades. The front porch is an inviting evening gathering place, and the paved path overlooking the creek leads to steps to a tiny gravel beach. $85–103 in-season, $67–87 off-season; $15 for an extra person, $10 ages 12 and under. Shannon Cottage is $125 in-season, $102 off-. This is one place where both children and pets are welcome.

Chetwynd House Inn (967-2235), PO Box 130TN, Chestnut Street. Open year-round. This was Kennebunkport's first B&B, a gracious 1840s home near Dock Square. Susan Chetwynd offers four antiques-furnished guest rooms with private baths and TVs and a top-floor two-room suite with skylights and a river view. Generous breakfasts—maybe ham and cheese omelets and a quarter of a melon with peaches, blueberries, and bananas—are served family-style at the dining room table; afternoon refreshments are offered in the sitting room/library. $75–160.

Cove House Bed & Breakfast (967-3704), RR 3, Box 1615. Kathy Jones has lived in Kennebunkport most of her life and offers a warm welcome to guests. The 18th-century Colonial house is down by Chick's Cove on the

Kennebunk River, within walking distance of a beach and easy bicycling distance of Dock Square. The three pleasant guest rooms have private baths; there's a book-lined living room with a woodstove. $70–80, $15 per extra person, includes breakfast. A nearby cottage is $395–575 per week.

On the Beach

Tides Inn By-the-Sea (967-3757), RR 2, Box 737, Goose Rocks Beach. Open May to October. Away from Kennebunkport Village but right across from the area's best beach: wide, firm enough for running, long and silvery. This is one of the area's best-kept secrets—a small, very Victorian inn built by Maine's foremost shingle-style architect, John Calvin Stevens, in 1899. Guests have included Teddy Roosevelt and Sir Arthur Conan Doyle. Owned since 1972 by Marie Henriksen and now run jointly with her daughter Kristin Blomberg, it is one of the area's most popular places to eat (see *Dining Out*), but guests also have plenty of comfortable sitting space around the fireplace downstairs. Rooms in the main building are furnished with antiques, and we recommend going for the high-end rooms with both private bath and view. We were lulled to sleep by the sound of the waves in Room 24, a third-floor aerie with an ocean view from the bed. $89–185. This is one place that manages to be both romantic and a family find. Next door, **Tides Too** offers one- and two-bedroom apartments ($1800–2300 per week in-season; from $125 per night, off-).

The Ocean View (967-2750), 72 Beach Avenue, Kennebunk Beach 04043. Open April through mid-December. Bob and Carole Arena's painted lady is right on Kennebunk Beach. The main house has four guest rooms and one suite, a comfortable TV room, and a living room with fireplace. A separate building houses four pretty suites with sitting areas, color TVs, and private terraces. Breakfasts are consciously healthy as well as full. "Breakfast in bed" is served to guests in suites. High-season rates run $150–195; low: $85–140.

Seaside Inn & Cottages (967-4461), PO Box 631, Gooch's Beach. Rooms in the 1756 inn are rented just from July through Labor Day, cottages are rented May through October, the motor inn is year-round. An attractive complex formed by a 1720s homestead, a 1756 inn, a modern 22-room motor inn, and 10 housekeeping cottages—all on a private beach next to one of Maine's best public strands. This property has been in the Severance family for 13 generations. The old homestead is rented as a cottage, and there are still four antiques-furnished guest rooms in the old inn. A buffet breakfast is included in the rates. Cottages are per month in July and August, per week the rest of the season. One-week minimum in oceanfront rooms and 2-day minimum in terrace-side rooms in high season. $148–168 per night for motel rooms, $100–140 for rooms in the 1756 inn; less off-season.

MOTELS

Yachtsman Motel and Marina (967-2511; 1-800-9-YACHTS), PO Box 2609, Ocean Avenue. Open early May through late October. This is a beautifully positioned property, right on the Kennebunk River, a short walk from Dock Square. Units are tastefully decorated with private riverside patios. Slip space for boats available at the marina. $79–169.

🖉 **Idlease Guest Resort** (985-4460; 1-800-99-BEACH), PO Box 3086, Route 9. A terrific family find. A traditional motel and cottage complex, recently renovated. Some cathedral ceilings with skylights were added, giving the cottages a more spacious appearance. Within walking distance of Parsons Beach (one of the most beautiful, least commercial beaches on the South Coast). Facilities include outdoor pool, outdoor hot tub, yard games, horseshoes, basketball, and grills. $55–125; also reasonably priced housekeeping cottages accommodating up to eight, and a two-bedroom, two-bath cottage with living room available (sleeps 6–10). One small single room is $39.

OTHER LODGING

Schooners Inn (967-5333), PO Box 709, Ocean Avenue. Open seasonally. Every room has a water view, some with balconies and skylights, each named after a schooner and furnished with Thomas Moser furniture. Amenities include an elevator, cable TV, phones; the master suite has a raised sitting area, whirlpool bath, and private deck. $125–250 high season, less off-season.

🖉 **Cabot Cove Cottages** (967-5424), PO Box 1082, South Main Street. Open mid-May to mid-October. Fifteen old-style, knotty-pine-walled, freshly furnished cottages on 2 acres bordering a tidal cove. One- and two-bedroom units, all with new kitchen facilities. Within walking distance of Dock Square and a sandy beach. $90–145 per day, $590–920 per week in high season, less off-season.

🖉 **Clover Hill Farm** (490-1105), RR 1, Box 24A, Alfred 04002. Alfred is a 20-minute drive from the coast, and it's a beautiful old village, with the kind of good places to eat you would expect in the York County seat (see *Eating Out*). Clover Hill Farm is a classic white farmhouse 5 miles from the village, with 100 acres of rolling hills and woodland. The three clean, simply furnished guest rooms share baths and cost $65 for a double ($55 single, $10–15 for a third person), with a breakfast that may include freshly laid eggs and pasta garnished with just-picked chives and strawberries. Margit Lassen and her farmers hay the fields and raise sheep, goats, and a couple of pigs. Children can feed and pet lambs and pygmy goats and help gather eggs.

WHERE TO EAT

DINING OUT

White Barn Inn (967-2321), Kennebunk Beach. Open for dinner year-round (closed Mondays in winter); also for Sunday brunch. One of New England's most luxurious barns, still attached to the 19th-century inn for which it was built but with its face now glassed; a warm, candlelight atmosphere. The five-course menu changes frequently but you might begin with a lobster spring roll or boneless quail breast on a potato tart with beans, leeks, mushrooms, and roasted garlic vinaigrette, and dine on roasted rack of lamb and medallions of venison on a flaky pastry of sweet potato and Granny Smith apple puree with celery and red port sauce. Palate cleansers are served throughout the meal to prepare you for the next course. The service is formal and attentive. $56 prix fixe plus cocktails and wine.

Kennebunkport Inn (967-2621), Dock Square, Kennebunkport. Open April through December. Breakfast and dinner daily May through October. Elegant fare in two lacy dining rooms. This is a widely respected favorite, with entrées ranging from the vegetarian dishes or cherrywood-smoked game hen with smoked Kennebunk venison kielbasa ($17.50) to the inn's signature bouillabaisse (lobster, shrimp, scallops, swordfish, mussels, and clams in a tomato-fennel broth, served with hot pepper sauce on the side; $24.95). Lighter fare is served in **Martha's Vineyard** (Martha Griffin is the owner-chef), a pleasant garden just off Dock Square, a pleasant place for a glass of wine with a grilled bruschetta, mussels, a grilled marinated chicken sandwich, or roasted vegetable Napoleon.

Salt Marsh Tavern (967-4500), Route 9, Lower Village, Kennebunk. Open daily for dinner; closed January to mid-March. Offering gracious dining overlooking a salt marsh, this widely respected restaurant is the work of artist Jack Nahil, former owner of the White Barn Inn. Entrées might include wild rice paella (venison sausage, lobster, shrimp, mussels, and scallops; $23.95), or broiled haddock with a pecan crumb topping, mango lobster salsa, and garlic mashed potatoes ($17.95). Save room for a profiterole.

Tides Inn By-the-Sea (967-3757), Goose Rocks Beach, 6 miles northeast of Dock Square. Open for breakfast and dinner daily 6:30–9:30. The preferred tables are on the sun porch with ocean views. The chowder, for starters, is great (oysters and shrimp as well as fish in a light, buttery broth) and the menu is large; specialties include Muscovy duck, sautéed veal medallions, and a hearty lobster and oyster dinner stew. Come early enough to walk the neighboring beach before or after. Entrées run $15.75–22.95.

Cape Arundel Inn (967-2125), Ocean Avenue, Kennebunkport. Open May to mid-October for breakfast and dinner (closed Sunday evenings). The dining room overlooks the ocean, and the dinner menu is Continental. Signature dishes include roast duck breast with sun-dried cherry sauce and Maine seafood bouillabaisse. The breakfast menu features codfish cakes and omelets. Dinner entrées: $16.50–22.95.

Windows on the Water (967-3313), Chase Hill, Kennebunkport. Open for lunch, dinner, and Sunday brunch. A dining room with views of the port through arched windows, screened terrace or alfresco dining, and live entertainment on Friday and Saturday. Seafood is the specialty. Lobster-stuffed potato is popular at lunch. Light-fare selection for smaller appetites. Reservations are a must for dinner. Dinner entrées $9.95–22.90.

The Colony (967-3331), Ocean Avenue, Kennebunkport. The elegant dining room at this resort is open to the public for all three meals. Dinners include a relish tray and rolls, appetizer, soup, main dish, vegetables, salad, beverage, and dessert for $25. Menu selections change each night and might include citrus shrimp and scallops on herbed fettuccine, and baked, maple-cured ham with cider sauce. Sunday brunch is served 11–2, with a different theme (such as Christmas in July) each week.

Seascapes (967-8500), Pier Road, Cape Porpoise. Open for lunch and dinner daily in-season, varying days April through December. Seascapes combines a great location (on a working fishing pier) with well-known local management (Angela LeBlanc has put her Kennebunk Inn on the South Coast dining map). Specialties include roasted lobster, panache of red-tailed deer, and "Christina's Shrimp." Entrées $13.95–24.95.

Schooners Inn (967-5333), 127 Ocean Avenue. Dinner nightly except Tuesday and Wednesday. The view of the Kennebunk River is unbeatable and the ambience is muted, pleasant. Entrées range from chicken sautéed with basil pesto, plum tomatoes, and lemon-garlic-infused cream with polenta ($16.95) to filet mignon ($22.95).

Mabel's Lobster Claw (967-2562), Ocean Avenue, Kennebunkport. April to mid-October, open for lunch and dinner. A favorite with locals, including George Bush. The specialty is lobster, pure or richly dressed with scallops, shrimp, and fresh mushrooms in a creamy Newburg sauce, topped with Parmesan cheese. The lunch special is a lobster roll with Russian dressing and lettuce in a buttery, grilled hot-dog roll. Entrées $11.95–16.95.

☞ **Bartley's Dockside** (967-5050), Kennebunkport (by the bridge). Open 8 AM–9 PM daily. There is candlelight dining by the fire and a water view. Known for its chowder. Dinner entrées start at $10.95.

EATING OUT

Note: This area offers an unusual number of first-rate alternatives to expensive dining.

☞ **The Wayfarer** (967-8961), One Pier Road, Cape Porpoise. Open at 6:30 for breakfast, lunch, and dinner. Closed Monday off-season. The atmosphere is upscale coffee shop with a counter and booths, and the food is superb: haddock chowder ($4.50 bowl), spicy pan-blackened swordfish steak ($14.50), or the night's roast (maybe turkey or Yankee pot roast). Smaller portions on some meals are available for kids. All meals include salad, starch, and hot rolls. BYOB from the general store across the road.

Alison's (967-4841), 5 Dock Square, Kennebunkport. Open at 6:30 for breakfast; also serves lunch and dinner. A pub and grill "where the nicest people meet the nicest people," the true heart of Dock Square. The owners are Pam and Brian MacCillivray and Marie and Michael Condon, and at least one is always there. Our lunch favorite is the salad in a monster tortilla shell with chili, salsa, and sour cream, topped with Monterey jack. Dinner entrées run $12.95–17.95.

The Green Heron (967-3315), Ocean Avenue, Kennebunkport. The place for breakfast, a long-standing tradition, served on a glassed-in, waterside porch. The menu is vast and varied.

Grissini (967-2211), 27 Western Avenue, Kennebunk. Open year-round, except January, for lunch and dinner. A northern Italian trattoria opened in 1996 by the owner of the White Barn Inn, this is a 120-seat, informal, and trendy restaurant with seasonal outdoor terrace dining and an à la carte menu. You might dine on fresh Maine trout steamed in foil with extra-virgin oil, tomato, lemon, white wine, and herbs ($12.50) with a house salad ($4.50).

Portofino (967-5005), Dock Square, Kennebunkport. David Willey and Melissa Kany have created an attractive dining area in the heart of Dock Square (eat inside or out) with a moderately priced menu ranging from manicotti, fettuccine, and eggplant Parmesan to some interesting fish dishes, like fresh baked haddock with bread crumbs and white wine.

Nunan's Lobster Hut (967-4362), Route 9, Cape Porpoise. Open for dinner May through October. This low, shedlike landmark packs them in and charges, too. This is the place for a classic lobster feed—there are sinks with paper towels to wipe off the melted butter. Lobster, clams, and pies are the fare. No credit cards.

Shipyard-Kennebunkport Brewing Company and Federal Jack's Brew Pub (967-4322), 8 Western Avenue, Kennebunk Lower Village. Open for lunch and dinner, offering a variety of handcrafted ales. Standard pub fare.

Leedy's Restaurant (324-5856), Alfred Square, Alfred. Closed Tuesday, otherwise open for all three meals. This is the kind of place you walk into and know immediately that everything is going to taste good. Straight-shooting, all-American cooking specializing in seafood and prime rib. $3.95–15.95.

Chase Hill Bakery (967-2283), Chase Hill, Kennebunkport. Open year-round. Delectable cookies, brownies, and cakes such as "Lemon Cloud." Everything is made from scratch. Soups and sandwiches. A few tables and fresh-ground Green Mountain Coffee if you like to linger.

SEAFOOD MARKETS

Preble Fish (967-4620) and **Cape Porpoise Lobster Co.** (967-4268), both in Cape Porpoise, are where the locals get their fish and steamed lobster to go. **Port Lobster** (967-2081), Ocean Avenue, Kennebunkport. Live or cooked lobsters packed to travel or ship, and lobster, shrimp, and crab rolls to go (several obvious waterside picnic spots are within walking distance). **The Clam Shack** (967-3321; 967-2560),

Kennebunkport (at the bridge). Clams, lobsters, and fresh fish. Look for their seasonal take-out stand at the bridge.

ENTERTAINMENT

Hackmatack Playhouse (698-1807), Route 9, Beaver Dam, Berwick. Local actors, rave reviews.
River Tree Arts (985-4343) stages local productions and happenings.
(Also see *Entertainment* in "Ogunquit and Wells.")

SELECTIVE SHOPPING

ANTIQUES SHOPS
The Kennebunks are known as an antiques center with a half-dozen shops, representing a number of dealers, most on Route 1.
ART GALLERIES
You'll find more than 60 galleries, most of them seasonal; **Mast Cove Galleries** (967-3453) on Maine Street is touted as the "largest group gallery in the area."
SPECIAL SHOPS
Kennebunk Book Port, 10 Dock Square, Kennebunkport. Open year-round. The oldest commercial building in the port (1775) is one of the most pleasant bookstores in New England. Climb an outside staircase into this inviting mecca, which is dedicated to reading as well as to buying. Helpful, handwritten notes with recommendations from staff make browsing even easier. Books about Maine and the sea are specialties.
Lafayette Center, Storer and Main Streets, Kennebunk. Open daily year-round. A former shoe factory has been recycled and is now a complex of upscale shops.
Brick Store Exchange, 4 Dane Street, Kennebunk. Open year-round 10–4; closed Sunday, also Monday in winter. A sweet-smelling, volunteer-run outlet for locally crafted gifts.
Port Canvas (967-2717), Dock Square, Kennebunkport. Open year-round. Canvas totes, suitcases, and hats all made in Kennebunkport.
The Good Earth, Dock Square, Kennebunkport. Open daily May through October, varying hours; closed January to March. Stoneware in unusual designs—mugs, vases, and bowls. Great browsing in the loft showroom.

SPECIAL EVENTS

February: **Winter Carnival Weekend** (first weekend); sleigh rides on Saturday all month.
March: **Kennebunkport tours and food show.**

June: **Bed & Breakfast Inn and Garden Tour.**

July: Old-fashioned **picnic, fireworks, and band concert.**

August: **Riverfest** (first Saturday). **Kennebearport Teddy Bear Show** (second Saturday).

September: **Old-Time Fiddlers Contest** (second Saturday).

December: **Christmas Prelude** (first and second weekends). Dock Square is decked out for Yuletide, and there are church suppers, concerts, and carols.

Old Orchard Beach Area

When Thomas Rogers was granted 12 acres of land in 1657 and planted a fruit orchard, he undoubtedly had no idea his holding would one day become a resort area so popular that its year-round population would multiply by 10 in the summer.

In 1837, E.C. Staples first recognized the region's potential as a summer playground. From taking in boarders on his farm for $1.50 a week, he moved to building the first Old Orchard House. His instincts proved right, for rail travel brought a wave of tourists to the beach from both the rest of the United States and Canada.

The Grand Trunk Railroad did away with the long carriage ride from Montreal, and Canadians discovered that the Maine shore was a great place to vacation. The area is still a popular destination for French Canadian visitors, and you are likely to hear French spoken almost anywhere you go.

When the first pier at Old Orchard Beach was built in 1898, it stood 20 feet above and 1800 feet out over the water and was constructed entirely of steel. The pavilions housed animals, a casino, and a restaurant. In the decades that followed, the original pier was rebuilt many times after being damaged by fire and storms, until a wider and shorter pier of wood was built in 1980. The pier continues to be a focal point in the community and a hub of activity.

An amusement area first appeared in 1902 and grew after World War I. The 1920s brought big-name bands such as Guy Lombardo and Duke Ellington to the Pier Casino, and thousands danced under a revolving crystal ball.

Fire, hard economic times, the decline of the railroad and steamboat industries—all took their toll on Old Orchard Beach over the years. Though the 7 miles of sandy beach and the amusement park near the pier endured, the 1980s saw the area deteriorate and succumb to a younger, wilder crowd.

In the early 1990s, the citizens decided to reclaim their town. A major revitalization plan widened sidewalks, added benches and streetlights, and passed and enforced ordinances. The result is a cleaner, more appealing, yet still lively and fun vacation spot.

Historically diverse, the area is also well known for the camp meetings held beginning in the late 1800s, first by Methodists, then by the Salvation Army. These meetings continue in the Ocean Park community today.

Biddeford and Saco are often called the twin cities, and no two Maine towns are more different or more closely linked. Saco is a classic Yankee town with white-clapboard mansions lining its main street, and Biddeford is a classic mill town with a strong French Canadian heritage and mammoth, 19th-century brick textile mills that have stood idle since the 1950s. A few years back, the largest mills were renamed Saco Island and slated for redevelopment as a combination hotel, office, shop, and condo complex, a project that has yet to be fully developed. Still, Biddeford is worth visiting, especially for *La Kermesse,* the colorful Franco-American festival in late June. Saco's Route 1 strip of family-oriented amusement parks is a big draw for those with children.

Parts of Scarborough's 49 square miles belong more in Casco Bay descriptions, but Pine Point and its surrounding area is the easternmost tip of Old Orchard Beach, and is often a less crowded, quieter spot to visit. A large saltwater marsh in Scarborough is also good for quiet relaxation and exploring.

GUIDANCE

Old Orchard Beach Chamber of Commerce (934-2500), PO Box 600 (First Street), Old Orchard Beach 04064, maintains a seasonal walk-in information center and offers help with reservations.

Biddeford-Saco Chamber of Commerce (282-1567), 170 Main Street, Biddeford 04005.

GETTING THERE

By air: **Portland International Jetport** is 13 miles north, and rental cars are available at the airport. You can also fly your own plane into **Sanford Airport.**

By car: Exits 5 and 6 off the Maine Turnpike (I-95) take you easily to the center of Old Orchard Beach. You can also find the town from Route 1 (turn by the large flea market).

GETTING AROUND

From many accommodations in Old Orchard Beach, you are close enough to walk to the pier, the town's center of activity. The **Biddeford-Saco-OOB Transit** also takes you right to the center of town. Call 282-5408 for schedules. **Mainely Tours** (774-0808) offers excursions to Portland, and will pick up and drop off at all area motels and campgrounds.

PARKING

An abundance of privately operated lots can be found in the center of Old Orchard Beach. Most charge $2–4 for any length of time—10 minutes or all day. There are meters on the street if you don't mind circling a few times to catch an available one, but at 15 minutes for a quarter, you're better off in lots if you plan to stay long.

MEDICAL EMERGENCY
Southern Maine Medical Center (283-7000), Biddeford.

VILLAGES

Ocean Park is a historic community founded by Free Will Baptists and well known for its outstanding religious, educational, and cultural programs. There is a neighborhood association that sponsors lectures, concerts, and other events throughout the summer. There is a recreation hall, shuffleboard, and tennis courts within the community, as well as an old-fashioned ice cream parlor and a smattering of gift shops.

Pine Point. This quiet and less crowded end of the beach offers a selection of gift shops, restaurants, lobster pounds, and places to stay.

TO SEE AND DO

MUSEUMS
York Institute Museum (282-3031), 371 Main Street, Saco. Open Tuesday through Friday 1–4, May through October; also Saturday (same hours) in July and August. November through April it's open Tuesday and Wednesday 1–4, and year-round it's open Thursday 1–8. Admission is $2 per adult, $1 under 16 and over 60 (free under 6). Original paintings, furniture, decorative arts, and tools; also natural history specimens. Trace the history of southern Maine; inquire about frequent lectures, tours, and special exhibits. The institute's **Dyer Library** next door has an outstanding Maine history collection.

HISTORIC SITES
Harmon Historical Museum, 4 Portland Avenue, is open from 1–4 Tuesday through Saturday, June through September, and by appointment. Home of the Old Orchard Beach Historical Society, the building is full of exhibits from Old Orchard Beach's past. Each year, in addition to the regular school, fire, and aviation exhibits, there is a special exhibit on display. Pick up the timeline of the area's history and the walking map of historic sites.

FOR FAMILIES
The Route 1 strip in Saco and nearby Orchard Beach makes up Maine's biggest concentration of kid-geared "attractions." Be prepared to pay.

Maine Aquarium (284-4511), Route 1, Saco. Open daily, year-round. Marine life exhibits include seals, penguins, sharks, tidepool animals. Also nature trails, and picnic grounds. Handicapped accessible. $6.50 adults, $4.50 children 5–12, $2.50 ages 2–4. Interesting but small, and the price is a bit high. There is also a small branch at the end of the pier in the center of Old Orchard Beach.

Funtown/Splashtown USA (284-5139), Route 1, Saco. Open daily (depending on the weather) mid-June through Labor Day, weekends in

ELIZABETH ROUNDY

Attractions at Old Orchard Beach

spring and fall. Water activities and a large amusement park: bumper cars, New England's largest log flume, canoe ride down "Adventure River," hydrofighter, kiddie rides, antique cars.

Aquaboggan Water Park (282-3112), Route 1, Saco. Open June through Labor Day. Water slides, swimming pool, bumper boats, mini-golf, arcade, shuffleboard, toddler area, wave pool.

Pirate's Cove Adventure Golf (934-5086), 70 First Street, Old Orchard Beach. Thirty-six up-and-down miniature golf holes, waterfalls, ponds.

Palace Playland (934-2001), Old Orchard Street, Old Orchard Beach. Open late June through Labor Day. For more than 60 years, fun-seekers have been wheeled, lifted, shaken, spun, and bumped in Palace Playland rides; there's also a 1906 carousel with hand-painted wooden horses and sleighs, a Ferris wheel, and a 60-foot-high water slide. Charge is by the ride or $16.50 for an afternoon pass. $11 kiddie pass good on all two-ticket rides.

Village Park, Old Orchard Beach. On the other side of the pier, across the road from Palace Playland. Arcade, games, kiddie rides. $6 for an all-day pass.

GOLF

Old Orchard Beach Country Club (934-4513), 49 Ross Road, Old Orchard Beach. Nine-hole course. **Biddeford-Saco Country Club** (282-5883), Old Orchard Road, Saco. Eighteen-hole course.

HORSEBACK RIDING

Horseback Riding Plus (883-6400), 338 Broadturn Street, Scarborough. Guided trail rides and beach rides for adults; kiddie and pony rides.

RACING

Scarborough Downs (883-4331), off I-95, exit 6 in Scarborough. The largest harness-racing facility in New England. Live harness racing, as well as thoroughbred and harness racing via simulcast. Downs Club Restaurant (883-3022) is open for dinner and Sunday brunch.

Beech Ridge Motor Speedway (883-5227), Holmes Road, Scarborough. Summer stock-car racing every Saturday night.

TENNIS

The Ocean Park Association (934-9325) maintains public tennis courts, open in July and August.

CROSS-COUNTRY SKIING

Beech Ridge Farm Cross Country Ski Center (839-4098), 193 Beech Ridge Road, Scarborough. One hundred fifty acres of fields and woods with 15 km of groomed tracks. Warming hut, rentals, lessons.

GREEN SPACE

BEACHES

Obviously, **Old Orchard Beach** is the big draw in this area, with 7 miles of sand and plenty of space for sunbathing, swimming, volleyball, and other recreation.

Ferry Beach State Park is marked from Route 9 between Old Orchard Beach and Camp Ellis, in Saco. The 100-acre preserve includes 70 yards of sand, a boardwalk through the dunes, nature trails, a picnic area with grills, lifeguards, changing rooms. $1 per person, free under age 12.

Bay View Beach, at the end of Bay View Road near Ferry Beach, is 200 yards of mostly sandy beach; lifeguards, free parking.

Camp Ellis Beach, Route 9, Saco. Some 2000 feet of beach backed by cottages; also a long fishing pier. Commercial parking lots.

Pine Point, Route 9, the easternmost stretch of Old Orchard Beach, is a small, uncrowded spot, with a restaurant and lobster pound.

NATURE PRESERVES

Scarborough Marsh Nature Center (883-5100, seasonal), Pine Point Road. Open daily mid-June through Labor Day, 9:30–5:30. The largest salt marsh (3000 acres) in Maine. This Maine Audubon Nature Center offers canoe rentals, exhibits, a nature store, guided walking tours, and canoe tours throughout the summer.

LODGING

INNS AND BED & BREAKFASTS

The Carriage House (934-2141), 24 Portland Avenue, Old Orchard Beach 04064. Just off the main drag, this Victorian home with carriage house offers a welcome alternative to the abundance of motels and condominiums lining the beach. There are eight pretty rooms furnished in period antiques in the main house, all with shared bath. One down-stairs room has a beautiful antique brass bed. The carriage-house suite is large and private, with a kitchen and TV. Also available is a five-room apartment with a deck.

The Atlantic Birches Inn (934-5295), 20 Portland Avenue, Old Orchard Beach 04064. Just around the corner from the center of activity is this lovely Victorian, shingle-style home, built in the area's heyday. The guest rooms are named after grand hotels from the era when the inn was built. Decorated in pretty pastel colors, the rooms are bright and cheer-ful with a mix of old and new furnishings. There is space for relaxing in the living room and on the large front porch shaded by white birches. Three newly renovated rooms with private baths are in the recently purchased "cottage" next door. The in-ground pool is perfect on a hot day. $39–75 (for suite) off-season, $59–120 in high season, includes a breakfast of muffins or coffee cake, fruit salad, cereal, coffee, and juice.

☞ **Crown 'n' Anchor Inn** (282-3829; 1-800-561-8865), PO Box 228, Saco 04072-0228. This is a rare find: a Greek Revival, pillared mansion built in 1827 by a local lawyer, sold in 1841 to Stephen Goodale, in whose family it remained until 1925. Obviously, these were all well-to-do folk, and Stephen's son George became a Harvard professor of botany, involved with the planning and execution of the university's botanical museum (he was the man who commissioned those famous glass flowers). Hosts John Barclay and Martha Forester (along with Martha's late husband) ran an inn in Newcastle before acquiring this property. They had looked at it earlier but had been deterred by its dilapidated state—which only increased in ensuing years as it continued to stand empty. We won't attempt to tell the story of why they are here and how the inn came to look the way it does. Suffice it to say, the common space includes a double living room, the front room returned to its traditional look as a "receiving parlor," and all six rooms are painstakingly restored, each with an elegant bathroom. The Normandy Suite with its two working fire-places and Jacuzzi bath is a steal at $90 per night double occupancy. Throughout the inn is a large, intriguing collection of British royal family memorabilia. The inn is just up the street from the York Institute and a 10-minute drive from Saco's relatively uncrowded sands (see *Beaches*). A candlelight breakfast is served on fine china in the small but formal dining room. $60–95 in high season, $50–90 off-season.

☞✐**Country Farm** (282-0208), 139 Louden Road, Saco 04072. Open year-round. Nothing fancy, just a 150-acre working farm (cattle, goats, several kittens, and a horse) that's been in the same family for several genera-tions with two clean, comfortable guest rooms (shared bath) and plenty of space to wander—down to the shore of the Saco River. Arlene and Norman Gonneville seem to enjoy their guests, children included. $45 for a double includes a big breakfast; $10 per additional guest.

✐ **Maine-lly Llamas Farm** (929-3057), Route 35, Hollis. May to November.

A small working farm in a historic area. John and Gale Yohe offer comfortable guest rooms and a chance to learn about the farm or take a nature trek with their gentle llamas. Other animals include turkeys and Angora rabbits. Organically grown vegetable and flower gardens. Rooms are in the carriage house, with a separate staircase, part of an apartment that can be rented with kitchen for $110, including breakfast for up to five guests; otherwise $55 single, $65 double with breakfast. Guided llama treks are $20 per hour for two llamas, $10 for each additional llama.

OTHER LODGING

Old Orchard Beach offers an overwhelming number of motel, cottage, and condominium complexes both along the beach and on main roads. The chamber of commerce publishes a helpful "Old Orchard Beach Vacation Planner" that lists many of your choices (see *Guidance*). A word of caution—some of these establishments have been around for years, with no renovations and poor upkeep. It's a good idea, if possible, to check out a room before making reservations. Generally, condominiums on the beach are better kept, and many have reasonable rates.

Aquarius Motel (934-2626), 5 Brown Street, Old Orchard Beach 04064. A small, family-owned and -operated motel that's exceptionally clean, and right on the beach. Wes and Barb Carter are friendly and eager to help travelers plan their stay. Rates are $82–138 (for a two-room unit with three double beds and kitchenette) in-season. Many special rates in early spring and late fall. Three-night minimum on holiday weekends.

Billowhouse (934-2333), One Temple Avenue, Ocean Park 04063-7543. This 1880 Victorian guesthouse is Mary and Bill Kerrigan's retirement project. Completely renovated, yet retaining some of the old-fashioned charm, like original sinks in guest rooms. There are three ground-level efficiency apartments, and six more kitchenette units in the adjoining motel. The five B&B rooms include a large fourth-floor room with a play loft for children. All accommodations have private baths. Rooms in the guest house share a deck overlooking the ocean; the beach is just steps away. $65–120 for B&B rooms, $99–120 for kitchenette units. Also available on a $650 weekly basis is a three-bedroom cottage nearby.

CAMPGROUNDS

Camping is a budget-minded family's best bet in this area. There are at least a dozen campgrounds here, many geared to families and offering games, recreational activities, and trolley service to the beach in-season. Following are a couple of recommendations; check with the chamber (see *Guidance*) for a full listing.

Bayley's Camping Resort (883-6043), 27 Ross Road, West Scarborough 04074. Just down the road from Pine Point, you hardly have to leave the grounds to have a terrific vacation. Paddleboats, swimming pool, Jacuzzi, horseback riding, fishing, game room, special programs for children and adults—the list goes on and on. $27.50–36.50 depending on hook-ups; lower in spring and fall.

Powder Horn (934-4733; 1-800-934-7038), PO Box 366, Old Orchard Beach 04064. A 450-site campground with plenty of recreation options— playgrounds, shuffleboard, horseshoes, volleyball, rec hall and game room, miniature golf, trolley service to the beach in-season. $22–30 per night.

WHERE TO EAT

DINING OUT

Cornforth House (284-2006), 893 Route 1, Saco. Open for Sunday break- fast and dinner daily year-round. A large, brick house transformed into a fantastic restaurant. A series of small dining rooms creates an intimate but casual atmosphere. Meals are prepared with an emphasis on fresh, local ingredients. Appetizers might include champagne lobster, sautéed and served with a saffron-champagne cream sauce over puff pastry. Entrées may include steak Diane and veal captiva (scaloppine of veal sautéed with lobster meat, garnished with béarnaise). Save room for the delicious homemade desserts. $12.95–15.95.

Village Inn (934-7370), 213 Saco Avenue, Old Orchard Beach. Open for lunch and dinner, with a large and varied menu. Lunch specials include fried seafood, pastas, and chicken cordon bleu. At dinner, there is ev- erything from a large, fried seafood combination to eggplant Parmesan to baked chicken stuffed with broccoli, rice, and cheese and topped with a creamy broccoli sauce.

Joseph's by the Sea (934-5044), 55 West Grand Avenue, Old Orchard Beach. A fine dining tradition in the area since 1968. Enjoy creative seafood specialties, beef or pasta dishes in a romantic setting in two dining rooms overlooking the water. $12.95–20.

EATING OUT

Note: Near the pier and on the main drag of Old Orchard Beach is an abun- dance of take-out stands and informal restaurants serving pizza, burgers, hot dogs, fried seafood, fried dough, pier fries, ice cream, and almost anything else you could want.

Danton's Family Restaurant (934-7701), Old Orchard Beach Street. Easy to overlook on the main road amid all the souvenir shops and take-out stands, but don't. Established in 1946, this little place is still going strong. Home-cooked meals for breakfast, lunch, and dinner at very reasonable prices. Daily lunch specials might include baked ziti, fish- and-chips. Try the homemade pies.

Chowderheads (883-8333), Oak Hill Plaza, Route 114, Scarborough. A few minutes away from the center of activity, but just off Route 1. A small place with a loyal following. The seafood chowder is thick and hearty, and a favorite with locals. Specialties include swordfish steak, salmon pie, and fried seafood dinners at very reasonable prices. Por- tions are quite generous.

The Pier at Old Orchard Beach

Hattie's (282-3435), Biddeford Pool. The local gathering spot for breakfast and lunch. *The* place (the only place) to eat in Biddeford Pool, and it's a find. Former president Bush knows it well.

Wormwoods (282-9679), Camp Ellis Beach, Saco. Open year-round, daily for lunch and dinner. A large, friendly, old-fashioned place that you can count on for a good chowder and family-geared dining if you are exploring this quiet corner of the south coast.

LOBSTER POUNDS

Bayley's Lobster Pound (883-4571), Pine Point, Scarborough. A popular place for lobster and seafood.

Lobster Claw (282-0040), Route 5, Ocean Park Road, Saco. Lobsters cooked outside in giant kettles, stews and chowders, cozy dining room, and takeout available. Twin lobster specials, also steamers, fried seafood. Lobster packed to travel.

COFFEEHOUSE

The Hobo Jungle (934-4266), 32 East Grand Avenue, Old Orchard Beach. A haven for anyone who wants a great cup of coffee and a place to relax. Owner Christopher Tryba has created a comfortable atmosphere with couches and chairs, a working fountain, and live plants. There is a large back billiards room, video games, pinball, a token-operated computer hooked up to the Internet, and plenty of books and games. Open 6 AM–12:45 AM. The owner also operates Sunshine Coffee Co., an espresso bar on the pier.

ENTERTAINMENT

The Ballpark (934-1124), Old Orchard Beach. Once a professional baseball stadium, the park now features a mix of entertainment throughout the summer including sporting events, concerts, fairs, festivals, and family shows. Seating capacity of 12,500, and parking for 2000 cars.

THEATER

City Theater (282-0849), Main Street, Biddeford. A 660-seat, 1890s theater, recently restored, now offering a series of live performances.

SPECIAL EVENTS

Summer: **Fireworks** on the beach every Thursday night through Labor Day.

Late June: La Kermesse **Franco-American Festival,** Biddeford. Parade, public suppers, dancing, entertainment, sand-castle competition. **Beachfest.** Major sand-sculpture exhibit and competitions, entertainment, male and female physique contests, Frisbee tournament, more.

July: **Canada/USA Days,** Ocean Park, festival and parade.

August: Ocean Park **Festival of Lights** and Salvation Army camp meetings in Ocean Park. **Beach Olympics.**

September: **Classic car weekend,** Old Orchard Beach.

December: **Tree-lighting ceremony** with collectible ornaments, crafts.

II. CASCO BAY

SUSAN COOPER, PORTLAND'S DOWNTOWN DISTRICT

Opening parade for the annual Old Port Festival

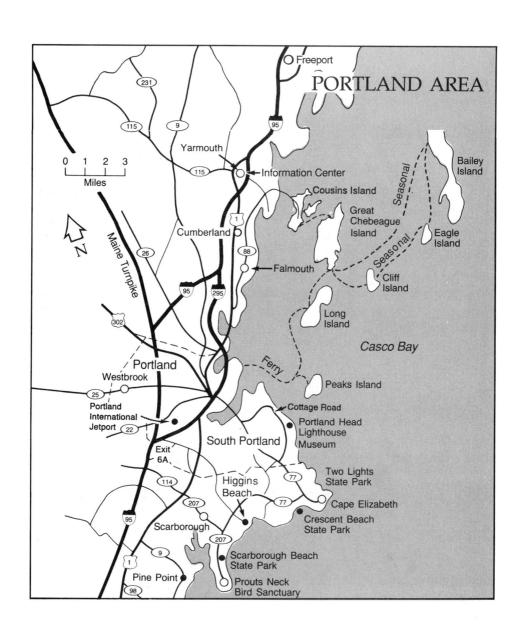

PORTLAND AREA

Freeport

231

115

9

95

Yarmouth

0 1 2 3
Miles

115

Information Center

Cousins Island

Great
Chebeague
Island

Seasonal

Bailey
Island

N

Cumberland

1

26

88

Falmouth

Seasonal

Eagle
Island

Cliff
Island

Maine Turnpike

95

295

Long
Island

Casco Bay

302

Ferry

Portland

Peaks Island

Westbrook

25

Cottage Road

Portland
International
Jetport

22

South Portland

Portland Head
Lighthouse
Museum

Exit
6A

114

Higgins
Beach

77

Two Lights
State Park

207

77

Cape Elizabeth

95

Scarborough

Crescent Beach
State Park

207

9

Scarborough Beach
State Park

1

Pine Point

Prouts Neck
Bird Sanctuary

98

Portland Area

In Portland, seagulls perch on skyscrapers and a smell and sense of the sea prevails. Northern New England's most sophisticated and one of its most important cities since the 1820s, it is blessed with distinguished buildings from every era. Portland provides a showcase for resident painters, musicians, actors, dancers, and craftspeople.

Portland is Maine's largest city, yet it still has a small-town feel. The total population still hovers around 64,000, and downtown is invitingly walkable. Hundreds of shops and galleries and dozens of restaurants are packed into ornate Victorian buildings in one, five-block waterfront neighborhood. Known as the Old Port Exchange, this area was a canker at the city's heart until the 1970s, when it was first slated for urban renewal.

Portland's motto, *Resurgam* ("I shall rise again"), could not be more appropriate. First, the 17th-century settlement was wiped out twice by Native Americans, then once by the British. It was not until after the American Revolution that the community really began to prosper—as witnessed by the Federal-era mansions and commercial buildings like the granite and glass Mariner's Church, built in 1820 to be the largest building in the capital of a brand-new state.

This port is the one that was loved by a small boy named Henry Wadsworth Longfellow, who later wrote:

> *I remember the black wharves and the ships*
> *And the sea-tides tossing free*
> *And the Spanish sailors with bearded lips*
> *And the beauty and mystery of the ships*
> *And the magic of the sea.*

Portland continued to thrive as a lumbering port and railroad terminus through the Civil War and until the Independence Day at that war's end. Then disaster struck again. On July 4, 1866, a firecracker flamed up in a Commercial Street boatyard and quickly destroyed most of downtown Portland. The city rose like the legendary phoenix, rebuilding yet again, this time in sturdy brick. The buildings were replete with the kind of flourishes you would expect of the Gilded Age, years during which these city blocks were the core of northern New England's shipping, rail, and manufacturing businesses.

These very buildings, a century later, were "going for peanuts," in the words of a real estate agent who began buying them up in the late 1960s. The city's prominence as a port had been eclipsed by the opening of the St. Lawrence Seaway in 1959, and its handsome Grand Trunk Station was torn down in 1966. Decent folk did their shopping at the department and chain stores up on Congress Street, itself threatened by the Maine Mall out by the interstate highway.

Down by the harbor, artists and craftspeople were renting shop fronts for $50 per month. They formed the Old Port Association, hoping to entice people to stroll through the no-man's-land that separated the shops on Congress Street from the few famous fish restaurants and the ferry dock on Commercial Street. That first winter they strung lights through upper floors to convey a sense of security, and they shoveled their own streets, a service the city had long ago ceased to provide to that area. At the end of the winter, they celebrated their survival by holding the first Old Port Festival, an exuberant street fair that is still held each June.

Portland's Old Port Exchange continues to thrive, and on its fringes, new semi-high-rise, redbrick buildings blend with the old and link the Old Port with Congress Street.

Condominiums now line a wharf or two, but Portland remains a working port. It's also a departure point for the ferry to Yarmouth (Nova Scotia) and for the fleet of Casco Bay Liners that regularly transport people, mail, and supplies among Casco Bay's Calendar Islands. These range from Peaks Island—accessible in just 20 minutes by commuter ferry, and offering rental bikes, guided sea kayaking, lodging, and dining—to Cliff Island, more than an hour's ride, offering sandy roads and the feel of islands usually found farther Down East. In summer, these ferries bill their longer runs as Casco Bay Cruises and add Music Cruises and a lazy circuit to Bailey Island. Two excursion lines (one from South Freeport) also service Eagle Island, preserved as a memorial to Arctic explorer Admiral Peary. The waterfront is, moreover, the departure point for deep-sea fishing, harbor cruises, and day-sailing.

Art lovers can easily spend a day among Portland's museums and galleries. The Portland Museum of Art quintupled in the 1980s and exhibits American painters like John Singer Sargent, Winslow Homer, George Bellows, and Jamie Wyeth. Next door, the Children's Museum of Maine is sure to please both adults and children with its interactive, educational displays.

Congress Street and the surrounding area have undergone a transformation recently, now emerging as the Downtown Arts District. The old Porteous building is home to the Maine College of Art, and there are small galleries, funky secondhand shops, restaurants, cafés, and theaters nearby. In summer months, there are a variety of concerts and events in Congress Square.

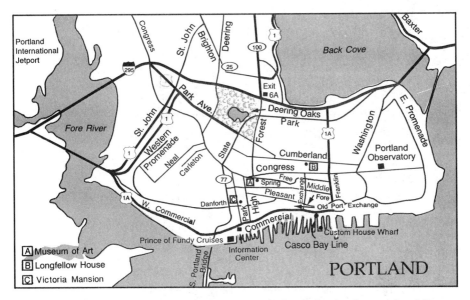

Visitors can find a wide range of food, from Thai and Afghan to seafood and burgers, in the more than 40 restaurants Portland offers. Downtown boasts some appealing bed & breakfasts, as well as a few good hotels. Cape Elizabeth, just south of Portland, offers beaches and birding, and both Falmouth and Yarmouth, just east of the city, are worth exploring.

GUIDANCE

The Convention and Visitors Bureau of Greater Portland (772-5800), 305 Commercial Street, Portland 04101, publishes *Greater Portland Visitors Guide,* listing restaurants, sights, museums, and accommodations. Its walk-in information center at 305 Commercial Street is well stocked with menus and pamphlets, and courtesy phones connect with lodging places and services. There is also a small kiosk in Congress Square, with brochures and maps.

Portland's Downtown District (772-6828), 400 Congress Street, Portland 04101, offers information about performances, festivals, and special events.

The **Maine Publicity Bureau** (846-0833) staffs a major state information center on Route 1 in Yarmouth, just off I-95, exit 17.

For details about guided walking tours of the city, contact **Greater Portland Landmarks** (774-5561), 165 State Street, Portland 04101. Be sure to request the self-guided walking tour leaflets (also available from the visitors bureau) that outline walking tours of Congress Street, the Old Port Exchange, State Street, and the Western Promenade.

GETTING THERE

By air: **Portland International Jetport** (774-7301) is served by Delta Air Lines (1-800-638-7333), Continental Airlines (1-800-525-0280), United (1-800-241-6522), USAir (1-800-428-4322), Northwest Airlink

(1-800-241-2525), Pine State Airlines (1-800-353-6334), and Downeast Express (1-800-983-3247). Car rentals at the airport include National, Avis, Hertz, and Budget.

By bus: **Vermont Transit** (772-6587) stops in Portland daily en route from Boston to points farther up the coast and to inland points north. But the terminal is dingy, inconvenient to the arts district, the Old Port, and ferries, and it closes early, forcing passengers to stand out in the cold and rain. **Concord Trailways** (828-1151) stops in Portland daily en route from Boston to Bangor or coastal points. It offers movies and music on the way.

By ferry: Canadians may cruise to Portland aboard the **Prince of Fundy Cruises Limited** ferry, *Scotia Prince,* out of Yarmouth, Nova Scotia (775-5616; seasonally, 1-800-482-0955 in Maine; 1-800-341-7540 outside Maine). Overnight cruises are offered early May through October. Prices vary, depending on the season, cabin, or special package. Restaurants, shops, live entertainment, and a casino are some of the features passengers enjoy aboard. The luxury cruise vessel accommodates 1500 passengers in 800 cabins, plus 250 cars.

GETTING AROUND

The **Metro** (774-0351) bus transfer system serves Greater Portland. The Metro city buses connect airport and city.

PARKING

Portland meters are limited to 2 hours, hard to come by, and checked often. The city urges visitors to use its many parking garages. The **Fore Street Garage** (439 Fore Street) puts you at one end of the Old Port, and the **Custom House Square Garage** (25 Pearl Street), at the other. The **Casco Bay Garage** (Maine State Pier) and **Free Street Parking** (130 Free Street, just up from the art museum) are also handy. **The Gateway Garage** next to the Radisson Eastland Hotel is close to the arts district.

MEDICAL EMERGENCY

Portland Ambulance Service (dial 911). **Maine Medical Center** (871-0111), 22 Bramhall Street, Portland.

VILLAGES

Cape Elizabeth is a peaceful residential area. The main village of **Pond Cove** is a refuge for many Portland commuters, who live in homes overlooking the Atlantic Ocean. Two Lights State Park and a large, popular beach are also part of this community.

Falmouth is a suburb of Portland. The village, known as **Falmouth Foreside,** has tremendous old houses in the original section of town. A popular marina and restaurant offer terrific views and water access.

Yarmouth has carried the charm of a Colonial village into the 19th century with style. Commercial and tourist-aimed businesses are relegated to

Route 1, leaving the inner village lined with 18th- and 19th-century homes mixed with quaint stores and antiques shops. North Yarmouth Academy's original Greek Revival brick buildings, the 18th-century meetinghouse, and many fine old churches are must-sees for architecture buffs. Several parks are open to the public, including the village green with its historic, round railroad station and Royal River Park, offering recreation in all seasons. In July, Yarmouth really comes alive with the clam festival.

TO SEE

MUSEUMS

Portland Museum of Art (775-6148; for a weekly schedule of events and information, 773-ARTS; 1-800-639-4067), 7 Congress Square, Portland. Tuesday, Wednesday, and Saturday 10–5, Thursday and Friday 10–9, and Sunday noon–5; closed New Year's Day, July 4, Thanksgiving, and Christmas. $6 per adult, $5 per student (with ID) or senior citizen, and $1 per child 6–12. Maine's largest art museum houses an extensive collection of American artists, featuring Maine-based masters such as Winslow Homer, Edward Hopper, and Andrew Wyeth. The adjoining museum buildings include the splendid, Federal-style **McLellan-Sweat** mansion, built for Portland's biggest shipowner in 1800. The museum itself was founded in 1882. In 1991, Joan Whitney Payson's collection was also absorbed into the museum. It includes works by Renoir, Degas, Prendergast, and Picasso, as well as Homer and Wyeth. Changing exhibits also.

Children's Museum of Maine (828-1234), 142 Free Street, Portland. Next door to the Museum of Art, this elaborate museum offers three levels of interactive, hands-on exhibits, designed to help the young and old learn together. Permanent exhibits include Main Street USA (with toddler park, cave, farm, supermarket, bank, and fire department), a space shuttle, a news center, and a computer room with games and learning activities. Enough to keep kids and their parents entertained for an entire afternoon.

The Museum at Portland Head Light (799-2661), 1000 Shore Road in Fort Williams Park. Open June through October, 10–4, and November, December, April, and May, weekends 10–4. $2 per adult, $1 children 6–18. This is the oldest lighthouse in Maine, first illuminated in 1791 per order of George Washington. It is now automated, and the former keeper's house has been transformed into an exceptional lighthouse museum. This is a great spot to come just for the view. Bring a picnic; there are tables with water views as well as the ruins of an old fort in the surrounding **Fort Williams Park,** just 4 miles from downtown Portland: Take State Street (Route 77) south across the bridge to South Portland, then left on Broadway and right on Cottage Street, which turns

Portland Head Light

into Shore Road. On the way back, you might want to check out the
Spring Point Museum (799-6337) on Fort Road, marked from Route
77 in South Portland. Open Memorial Day weekend through October,
Thursday to Sunday 1–4; $2 per adult, $1 children. Sited in a brick repair
shop that was part of Fort Preble and is now part of Southern Maine
Technical College, it mounts changing exhibits on local maritime history
and features an ongoing restoration of the pieces of the *Snow Squall,* an
1850s Portland clipper ship wrecked in the Falkland Islands. The
Spring Point Lighthouse, at the end of a breakwater, is another good
vantage point on the harbor.

Portland Fire Museum, 157 Spring Street. Open mid-June to mid-
September, Monday and Thursday 7–9 PM. Donations requested. Given
Portland's unusual fire-fighting history, this collection of artifacts and pho-
tos is something to see. Housed in a granite Greek Revival firehouse.

Maine Narrow Gauge Railroad Co. & Museum (828-0814), 58 Fore
Street, Portland. Open daily 10–4. Hard to spot if you aren't looking for
it—but you should. From the 1870s to the 1940s, Maine had a unique,
smaller-than-standard railroad system, with rails spaced just 2 feet apart.
The "2-footers" were more economically viable, and five lines carried
visitors to the more remote parts of the state. After the lines went out of
business, a millionaire cranberry grower who loved the 2-footers bought
as much of the equipment and rail cars as he could. His collection
evolved into Edaville, a major tourist attraction until its closing in 1991
due to lease disputes. Phineas Sprague Jr. and a group of railroad
enthusiasts brought the cars and equipment back to Portland and set up
this great little museum. Displays include the world's only 2-foot parlor

car, the "Rangeley," locomotives, a railbus, a model-T inspection car, and a caboose. There is also a short video on 2-footer history, and well-informed, enthusiastic guides show you around. Track has been laid and a short train ride is available daily May through October and other times by special arrangement.

Baxter Gallery of Portland School of Art (775-5152), 619 Congress Street. Art lovers shouldn't miss the photo and primary gallery in this beautiful old building, just south up Congress Street from the Portland Museum of Art.

HISTORIC SITES

Wadsworth-Longfellow House, 485 Congress Street. Maintained by the Maine Historical Society (879-0427), which also offers the Maine History Gallery and an extensive research library next door. Open June through October, Tuesday through Sunday 10–4 (closed July 4 and Labor Day; gallery and library open in winter, Wednesday through Saturday 12–4). $3 per adult, $1 per child under 18. Allow 45 minutes for a guided tour. Built by the poet's grandfather, this was the home of an important Portland family. Peleg Wadsworth was a Revolutionary War hero, and the entire clan of Wadsworths and Longfellows was prominent in the city. The house, in which Henry spent his childhood, is a good example of how such families lived in the 19th century. The garden behind the house has been adapted from gardens of the era, and most furnishings are original. At Christmastime, the Wadsworth-Longfellow House has a popular open house, with decorations and festivities of the season.

Portland Observatory (772-5561), 138 Congress Street. Built in 1807, this octagonal, shingled landmark is the last surviving 19th-century signal tower on the Atlantic. The 102 steps to the top are currently closed to visitors due to the deteriorated state, but Greater Portland Landmarks is working with the city on restoration plans to save the historic building.

Victoria Mansion, the Morse-Libby House (772-4841), 109 Danforth Street (at the corner of Park Street). Open May through October, Tuesday through Saturday 10–4, Sunday 1–5 (closed July 4 and Labor Day). $4 per adult, $2 per child 6–18. About as Victorian as can be, this brownstone Italianate home was built in 1859 for a Maine native who had made his fortune in the New Orleans hotel business. The interior is extremely ornate: frescoed walls and ceilings, a flying staircase with 377 hand-carved balusters of Santo Domingo mahogany, giant gold-leaf mirrors, marble mantels, ornate chandeliers, stained glass, and much more. The Victoria Mansion reopens during the Christmas season for special programs.

First Parish Church (773-5747), 425 Congress Street. Open year-round, by appointment. A vintage 1826 meetinghouse in which the pews are tipped forward—so that dozing parishioners would fall onto the floor. This is the site of the drafting of the Maine Constitution, and now houses artifacts from the 17th century.

Neal Dow Memorial (773-7773), 714 Congress Street. Open year-round, Monday through Friday 11–4. A handsome Greek Revival house built in 1829 by the man responsible for an 1851 law that made Maine the first state to prohibit the manufacture and sale of alcoholic beverages. Currently the headquarters of the Maine Women's Christian Temperance Union, the mansion is a memorial to Neal Dow.

Tate House (774-9781), 1270 Westbrook Street (follow Congress Street west across the Fore River to Westbrook). Open July and August, Tuesday through Saturday 10–3, Sunday 1–4. $4 per adult, $1 per child under 12. George Tate, mast agent for the Royal Navy, built this Georgian house in 1755 to reflect his important position. Both inside and outside are unusual, distinguished by fine windows, a gambrel roof, wood paneling, and elegant furniture. An 18th-century herb garden is part of the historic landscape.

TO DO

BICYCLING

Hundreds of acres of undeveloped land offer some great bicycling. Call **Portland Trails** (775-2411) for designated trails. **Forest City Mountain Bike Tours** (780-8155) offers 2- to 6-hour guided rides of the city and off-road areas. Rentals available, reservations required. **Peaks Island Mercantile** (766-5631) rents bikes for island exploring.

BOAT EXCURSIONS

Casco Bay Lines (774-7871), Casco Bay Ferry Terminal, 56 Commercial Street at Franklin. Founded in 1845, this business was said to be the oldest continuously operating ferry company in the country when it went bankrupt in 1980. The present, quasi-municipal Casco Bay Island Transit District looks and functions much the way the old line did. Its brightly painted ferries are still lifelines to six islands, carrying groceries and lumber as well as mail.

No one seems sure how many islands there are in Casco Bay. Printed descriptions range from 136 to 222. Seventeenth-century explorer John Smith dubbed them the Calendar Islands, saying there was one for every day of the year.

Of the six islands accessible via Casco Bay Lines, five invite exploration. There's a state-owned beach on **Long Island** (also a general store and restaurant), and a classic summer hotel (at the other end of the island from where the ferry docks) on **Great Chebeague.** On **Peaks Island,** a 20-minute ferry ride from Portland, you can spend the night, learn to paddle a sea kayak (see *Sea Kayaking*), dine with a great view of Portland (see Will's under *Dining Out*), or rent a bike at Peaks Island Mercantile (see *Bicycling*) and tour the promontories of the undeveloped Back Shore. Peaks is about 1 mile square (5 miles around).

You can also lunch or dine and sleep on neighboring **Great**

Diamond Island (see The Diamond's Edge restaurant under *Dining Out* and Diamond Cove under *Inns and Bed & Breakfasts*). On **Cliff Island,** a full 1½-hour ferry ride from the rest of the city (though technically part of Portland), you can walk the dirt road to sandy beaches. Each island retains its own rarefied world of 19th-century summer cottages and fishermen's homes, of wildflowers and quiet inlets.

Casco Bay excursions include the year-round, daily mail-boat run (2¾ hours), putting into all the islands in the morning and again in the afternoon, and a variety of seasonal, special excursions including a 5½-hour Bailey Island Cruise (see "Brunswick and The Harpswells"). Also year-round, frequent, daily car-ferry service to Peaks Island.

Eagle Tours, Inc. (774-6498), Long Wharf, Portland. Runs late June through October. The *Kristy K* takes you out to Eagle Island, the former home of Admiral Peary, now maintained by the state as a historic site and nature preserve (see the "Brunswick" and "Freeport" chapters); the 49-passenger *Fish Hawk* is used for a harbor and island cruise and for seal-watching. Group charters available.

Bay View Cruises (761-0496), Fisherman's Wharf, Portland. Daily June through October, weekends from April. Narrated harbor cruises aboard the *Bay View Lady;* harbor lunch cruise (bring your own sandwich) 12:10–12:50, just $3. Otherwise $8 per adult, $7 per child for a 1½-hour cruise; Sunday brunch cruise June through August.

The ultimate cruise out of Portland is the overnight run (early May to late October) to Yarmouth, Nova Scotia (see *Getting There*).

BREWERY TOURS

Microbreweries have popped up all over Portland, many with restaurants alongside them. Most give tours, either on a regular basis or by appointment. For information, contact individual breweries: **Allagash Brewing** (878-5385), 100 Industrial Way; **Casco Bay Brewing** (797-2020), 57 Industrial Way; **D.L. Geary Brewing** (878-2337), 38 Evergreen Drive; **Gritty McDuff's Brew Pub** (772-2739), 396 Fore Street; **Shipyard Brewing** (761-0807), 86 Newbury Street; and **Stone Coast Brewing** (799-4280), 14 York Street.

CANOEING

See Scarborough Marsh Nature Center under *Green Space*.

DEEP-SEA FISHING AND SAILING

Several deep-sea-fishing boats and sailing yachts are based in Portland every summer. Check with the Convention and Visitors Bureau (772-5800) for current listings. Also see *Sea Kayaking* for details about self-propelled cruising through Casco Bay.

FOR FAMILIES

Smiling Hill Farm (775-4814), 781 County Road, Westbrook. Farm with a petting zoo and popular ice cream stand.

Southworth Planetarium (780-4249), University of Southern Maine, Falmouth Street, Portland. Astronomy and laser light shows throughout the year. Special shows for young children in the summer and holidays.

GOLF

There are several popular 9- and 18-hole courses in the area, including **Riverside North** (18 holes) and **Riverside South** (9 holes) in Portland; **Valhalla** (18 holes) in Cumberland; and **Twin Falls** (9 holes) in Westbrook.

HOT-AIR BALLOONING

Hot Fun (799-0193), Box 2825, South Portland. Hot-air balloons carry up to six passengers.

Balloon Rides (761-8373; 1-800-952-2076), 17 Freeman Street, Portland. $150 per person.

ICE SKATING

There are several outdoor rinks in the area, including the pond at Deering Oaks Park. For indoor skating, the **Portland Ice Arena** (774-8553) has public skating times, pro shop.

ROCK CLIMBING

Maine Rock Gym (780-6370). Hours vary by season. Year-round indoor climbing facility, as well as a 40-foot outdoor climbing wall. Clinics for beginners as well as more experienced climbers.

SEA KAYAKING

Maine Island Kayak Co. (766-2373; 1-800-796-2373), 70 Luther Street, Peaks Island. Late May through October. One of the state's leading kayaking outfitters, offering 1- to 10-day (camping) tours as far Down East as Machias; also weekend overnights on Jewell Island—on the outer fringe of Casco Bay—and 7-day expeditions through the islands of the bay. Introductory paddling sessions available. Casco Bay is a great place to learn to sea kayak, given its easy access both to a wide variety of islands and to open ocean.

GREEN SPACE

BEACHES

Crescent Beach State Park (8 miles from Portland on Route 77) is a mile of sand complete with changing facilities, playground, picnic tables, and snack bar. $2.50 adults, $.50 ages 5–11.

Kettle Cove, just down the road from Crescent (follow the road behind the ice cream shop), is small, with a grassy lawn and rocky beach. There is no admission fee, but limited parking.

Higgins Beach, farther down Route 77 in Scarborough, is an extensive strand within walking distance of lodging—but there is no parking on the street. Private lots charge $4.

Scarborough Beach State Park (Route 207, 3 miles south of Route 1 on Prouts Neck) is a superb beach, but only a 65-foot stretch is technically public. Thanks to limited parking, however, the crowd is rarely excessive. $2.50 per person.

PARKS

Deering Oaks, a 51-acre city park designed by Frederick Law Olmstead, has a pond, ducks and swans, paddleboats, fountains, a playground, and a fine grove of oak trees. A farmer's market is held here every Saturday morning throughout the summer and into November. Ice skating on the pond in winter.

Two Lights State Park is open April 15 through November. No swimming, but 40 acres of shore for picnicking and fishing. $2.50 per person. (Also see Fort Williams Park and Spring Point Lighthouse in *To See*.)

NATURE PRESERVES

Gilsland Farm Sanctuary (781-2330), 118 Route 1, Falmouth Foreside (3 miles east of Portland). The headquarters of the **Maine Audubon Society** is located here. The sanctuary is open sunrise to sunset, year-round. The nature-oriented shop is open Monday through Saturday 9–5, Sunday 2–5. Sixty acres of trails, rolling fields, river frontage, and salt marsh. There is also a solar-heated education center with exhibits; special programs and field trips are year-round.

Prouts Neck Cliff Path and Wildlife Sanctuary. Winslow Homer painted many of his seascapes in the small studio attached to the summer home, which was—and still is—part of the exclusive community on Prouts Neck, beyond the Black Point Inn. It's not far from the inn to Winslow Homer Road, where the Cliff Walk (unmarked) begins. It's a beautiful stroll along the rocks, around Eastern Point, and back almost to the inn. You can also walk through the sanctuary between Winslow Homer Road (just east of St. James Episcopal Church) and Library Lane, donated by Winslow's brother Charles. The studio itself is open July and August 10–4, marked only by a STUDIO sign on the shedlike room attached to a private house.

Scarborough Marsh Nature Center (883-5100, seasonal), Pine Point Road (10 miles south of Portland). Open daily mid-June through Labor Day, 9:30–5:30. The largest salt marsh (3000 acres) in Maine. This Maine Audubon Nature Center offers canoe rentals, exhibits, a nature store, guided walking tours, and canoe tours throughout the summer.

Fore River Sanctuary (781-2330), near exit 8, off Brighton Avenue. A 76-acre preserve owned by the Maine Audubon Society. Hidden behind a suburban neighborhood where explorers may not think to look, the 2½ miles of hiking trails offer access to Portland's only waterfall, Jewell Falls. A set of railroad tracks (be careful—they are active) marks the beginning of a trail that leads you through woods and marshland.

WALKS

Eastern Cemetery, Congress Street and Washington Avenue (near the Portland Observatory on Munjoy Hill). More than 4000 souls are interred in these 9 acres, and the headstones, dating back to the mid-17th century, are embellished with angels' and death's heads. Despite its derelict state, this is an utterly fascinating place.

Fort Allen Park dates from 1814 and is on a blustery point on Casco Bay, a sure bet for a fresh breeze on the hottest day, as is the adjacent 68-acre **Eastern Promenade,** part of the turn-of-the-century park system designed by the famous, Boston-based landscape architects the Olmsteads. (The Olmsteads also designed Boston's Emerald Necklace and New York's Central Park.) The **Western Promenade,** first laid out in 1836, is another part of this grand plan. Sited on the edge of a 175-foot-high plateau, it commands a long view to the west (theoretically you can see Mount Washington on a clear day) and serves as the front porch for Portland's poshest and most architecturally interesting residential neighborhood. You might want to pick up a copy of the Portland landmarks leaflet, "Guide to the Western Promenade" ($1), from the visitors bureau (see *Guidance*).

Mackworth Island, off Route 1 north of Portland; follow signs to Governer Baxter School for the Deaf. A walking path circles the island, with views across the bay. Small beach for strolling.

LODGING

HOTELS

There are over 2000 hotel and motel rooms in and around Portland. Right downtown, within walking distance of the Portland Museum of Art and the Old Port, you can choose from the following hotels, all in Portland 04101.

Radisson Eastland Hotel Portland (775-5411; 1-800-333-3333), 157 High Street. A 12-story landmark built in 1927. In the mid-1980s it fell to bankruptcy, and the bank owned the property for 10 years. In 1992 the building was purchased, and major renovations were made to bring back the character of the place. The marble floors in the lobby and 204 guest rooms, many with harbor views, now reflect the elegance of that long-ago era. Geared to business travelers but a distinct cut above most small city hotels, with attractive rooms and many amenities, unusually friendly service (including elevator operators), original art in the hallways, Portland's only rooftop lounge, two restaurants, and complimentary van service to the airport. $99–139 for a double, depending on season; includes breakfast. Ask about special packages, like the romantic pajama party.

Portland Regency (774-4200; 1-800-727-3436), 20 Milk Street. The 95-room hotel, housed in a century-old armory in the middle of the Old Port Exchange, offers rooms decorated with reproduction antiques and equipped with amenities such as TV, two phones, and an honor bar. There is a formal dining room, attractive lounge, and a full health spa. Complimentary coffee with your wake-up call. $115–140 in high season, otherwise $95–130; no meals included.

Holiday Inn by the Bay (775-2311; 1-800-HOLIDAY), 88 Spring Street. With 246 rooms, this is Maine's largest hotel. Rooms on the bay side have

Interior of Pomegranate Inn

a fabulous harbor view. Each year, 75 rooms are completely refurbished, which keeps all of them looking fresh and new. The hotel has 30,000 square feet of meeting space, making it popular for conventions and business meetings. Indoor pool, small fitness center, cable TV and video-game hook-ups, free parking, laundry facility, nice restaurant and lounge.

Hotel Everett (773-7882), 51A Oak Street. Describing itself as an "informal, European-style hotel with a homelike atmosphere," this is an inexpensive option tucked onto a side street. Bright blue walls lend a cheerful air to the place, which is not in any way fancy, but is clean and friendly. $42–65.

Portland Hall (874-3281), 645 Congress Street, is a summer (June through August) AYH hostel with comfortable dormitory lodging right across from the Portland Museum of Art. Under $20 per person.

Note: Portland does have the major chains, but they are mainly located by I-95 at exit 8 in Westbrook or in South Portland by the mall.

INNS AND BED & BREAKFASTS

Pomegranate Inn (772-1006; 1-800-356-0408), 49 Neal Street, Portland 04102. This is an extraordinary place to stay. Isabel Smiles, an interior designer and former antiques dealer, has turned an 1880s Western Promenade house into a work of art. Nothing stiff, just one surprise for the eye after another. Eight amazing rooms furnished in a mix of antiques and *objets,* most with hand-painted walls in bold, original designs. Downstairs, the walls of the wide entryway are a hand-mottled tangerine, and the mantel and four columns in the living room are marbleized. Guest rooms have phones, discreet TVs, and private baths; five have gas fireplaces. The living room is well stocked with art books.

Breakfast is exquisite. Frankly, we're glad we stayed here before its fame spread, because what has since been described as the Pomegranate's "high style" came as a complete surprise. Still, repeat visits have been as good as the first. $125–165 per room in-season, $95–125 off-season, includes breakfast.

The Inn on Carleton Street (775-1910; 1-800-639-1779), Portland 04102. An attractive town house in the Western Promenade area offers seven rooms furnished with marble-topped sinks and Victorian-era antiques. We like the feel of this place. Proprietor Sue Cox makes guests feel welcome, and they tend to form a congenial group around the breakfast table. No smoking. From $55 for a single with shared bath off-season to $115 for a double with private bath in summer.

On Casco Bay Islands

(See the island descriptions under *Boat Excursions.*)

The Chebeague Inn By-the-Sea (846-5155), Chebeague Island 04017. Open Memorial Day through September. A three-story, flat-roofed summer hotel set high on a knoll. We like the large, open-beamed living room with its massive stone fireplace, brightly upholstered chairs, and rainy-day board games. The 21 guest rooms (15 with private bath) have a nice, sea-washed feel and are decorated simply but with taste. All three meals are served in July and August. On sunny days you can play golf (the nine-hole public course is just below the hotel), swim at Hamilton Beach, or explore the island by bike, and on rainy days you can take the 15-minute ferry to Cousins Island, not far from Freeport's shops. Casco Bay Line service to Portland leaves from the other end of the island (shuttle service is available from the hotel). $75–125 (plus tax and gratuity) for a double in high season includes a full breakfast; less in May and June. *Warning:* Be sure to get detailed directions to the Cousins Island ferry and inquire about parking options.

Diamond Cove (772-2992; 766-5804 for reservations), PO Box 3572, Portland 04104 (on Great Diamond Island, served by regular Casco Bay Line service from Portland). Nineteenth-century Fort McKinley on Great Diamond Island has been turned into an exclusive resort area offering townhouse rentals and sales. Amenities include a health club, beaches, a restaurant, tennis courts, a heated pool, and a walking path and woodland area for hiking, biking, and cross-country skiing. In-season there's a 2-night minimum at $160–200 per couple per night; all units have fully equipped kitchens; weekly rates run $1000–1890; 15 percent discount off-season.

Keller's (766-2441), Box 8, Peaks Island 04108. Open year-round. Just up from the ferry landing, a former general store and restaurant now offers five guest rooms, all with water views and full baths. Also a restaurant (766-2149) with a view serving all three meals. Innkeeper Carolyn Parker provides guests with a map of the island, marked with points of interest. Beach on the property. $75 single, $90 double, includes a full breakfast with Belgian waffles, pastries, fresh fruit, and beverages. No credit cards (personal checks accepted).

Beyond Portland

Black Point Inn Resort (883-4126), Prouts Neck 04074. Open early May to late October. Easily one of the most elegant inns in the state; a vintage 1878 summer hotel that is so much a part of its exclusive community that guests are permitted to use the Prouts Neck Country Club's 18-hole golf course and 14 tennis courts. Guests may also rent boats or moor their own at the local yacht club. Public rooms are extensive and elegant with views of the south coast on one side and of the open ocean on the other. Facilities include two sandy beaches, indoor and outdoor pools, two Jacuzzis, a sauna, and a manned elevator. There are 80 rooms, poolside buffets, afternoon tea with a pianist, evening cocktails, and dancing. No children under age 8 mid-July to mid-August. A London taxi serves as a shuttle to the airport and into Portland. $280–370 for double MAP per night plus 15 percent gratuity. A $15 noon buffet is offered. (See Prouts Neck under *Green Space*.)

Higgins Beach Inn (883-6684), 34 Ocean Avenue, Scarborough 04074 (7 miles south of Portland). Open Memorial Day through Columbus Day. An 1890s, three-story, wooden summer hotel near sandy Higgins Beach. The pleasant dining room, open July and August, features home cooking prepared with Gram's secret "receipts." There is also a cocktail lounge, a homey TV room, and a sun porch. Upstairs, the 24 guest rooms are basic but clean and airy, 14 with private bath. Continental breakfast is available after Labor Day. Owners Jack and Carlene Harrison have been improving this old place steadily over the past 27 years and take pride (as they should) in the fact that their rates haven't risen in 5 years. $60–75 for a double per day or $364–455 per week in-season; an even better bargain at $588–679 for a double MAP. Cheaper in shoulder months.

COTTAGES

South of Portland, cottages in the Higgins Beach and Pine Point areas can be found through the Chamber of Commerce of the Greater Portland Region (772-2811), 145 Middle Street, Portland 04101. Seasonal rentals are also listed in the *Maine Sunday Telegram*. For listings on summer cottages in the Casco Bay Islands, contact Casco Bay Development Association, Peaks Island 04108.

Also check the "Maine Guide to Camp & Cottage Rentals," available from the Maine Publicity Bureau (623-0363).

WHERE TO EAT

The claim is that Portland has more restaurants per capita than any other city in America. Take a look at the following partial list, and you will begin to believe it. The quality of the dining is as exceptional as the quantity. People from all over Maine look forward to a reason for dining in Portland. Enjoy!

DINING OUT

In and around the Old Port Exchange

Cafe Uffa (775-3380), 190 State Street (in Longfellow Square near the Portland Museum of Art). Open Wednesday through Saturday 5:30–10, Sunday 9–2. Hugely popular for Sunday brunch (get there early); highly rated for its creative and reasonably priced entrées like wood-grilled salmon, and desserts like chocolate raspberry truffle. Bistro atmosphere, good wine list. Entrées average $9.

Walter's Cafe (871-9258), 15 Exchange Street. Open for lunch and dinner daily. A very popular storefront space that's been deftly transformed into a bistro. Lunch includes unusual soups and salads, with hot entrées ranging from burgers to pasta dishes like sausage and capiccola with olive oil and seasonings on spinach penne. At dinner there are nightly specials; usually also grilled lamb and fish dishes. $10–15.

Cafe Always (774-9399), 47 Middle Street. Dinner Tuesday through Sunday. Recently sold to Maureen Fiterry, a former employee, this intimate, softly redecorated (in yellow and pink) café remains an Old Port standout. Though not right in the middle of all the activity, it's worth finding. The menu changes daily and might include appetizers like salmon cakes with a creasabi aoili; among the entrées may be veal sweetbreads with pancetta and balsamic sauce. Save room for delectable desserts like papaya pineapple sorbet with raspberry sauce. $17–24.

Street & Company (775-0887), 33 Wharf Street. Open for dinner nightly at 5:30. Year-round. A small, informal, incredibly popular seafood place. It is always a good idea to make reservations. The 22 seats they leave open for walk-ins go quickly. Seafood grilled, broiled, pan-blackened, and steamed, much of it served right in the pan it's been cooked in. Specialties include lobster diavolo, mussels provençale, and sole française. Homemade desserts. Entrées $11.95–17.95.

The Pepperclub (772-0531), 78 Middle Street. Open for dinner nightly. Vegetarian heaven: soups, rice and bean dishes; for others, some fish, chicken, organic beef. Zany decor, imported beers. Entrées under $10, no credit cards.

Hugo's Portland Bistro (774-8538), 88 Middle Street. Dinner Tuesday through Saturday. Eclectic, mismatched antiques decor. The varied menu changes monthly; specialties include Maine crabcakes and lobster in lemon cream over fettuccine. Check out the imported beer list. $10.95–16.95.

The Seamen's Club (772-7311), 375 Fore Street. Open 11–11 daily. Try to get a table upstairs in the library by the Gothic window so you can watch shoppers hustling along the brick sidewalks below. Very pleasant service and atmosphere. Best at lunch, but also offering candlelight dining. Often has bands in the bar on weekends. Entrées: $3.95–11.95.

Baker's Table (775-0303; 773-3333), 434 Fore Street (also an entrance on Wharf Street). Open daily, 10–10; Sunday brunch. The lunchtime specials are chowders, sandwiches, and bistro fare. Dinner is full-service dining with candlelight. Diverse European and New England fare (lobster bouillabaise is a specialty); fresh-baked desserts. Dinner entrées: $10.95–18.95.

DiMillo's Floating Restaurant (772-2216), Long Wharf. Open for lunch and dinner. Maine's only floating restaurant, this converted car ferry serves seafood, steaks, and Italian cuisine to customers who come as much for the old nautical atmosphere and the views of the waterfront as they do for the food. Entrées run $8.95–24.95 (shore dinner with chowder, salad, lobster, steamed clams, vegetable, potato, ice cream, and beverage).

Boone's Restaurant (774-5725), 6 Custom House Wharf. Open for lunch and dinner year-round. Still going strong in the same location on the wharf that it has occupied since 1898. Specialties include Mediterranean pasta dishes, lobster, and other fresh seafood. Seasonal patio dining overlooking the water. A real slice of the waterfront's long history. Lunch $4.95–7.95, dinner $10.95–17.95.

Beyond the Old Port

Katahdin (774-1740), 106 High Street. Dinner Monday through Saturday 5–10 PM. No reservations and it is often very busy, so you might want to call for the wait time before you go. Inventive New England entrées include wild mushroom ravioli, and specials might include grilled monkfish coated in Moroccan spices with ginger sauce.

The Roma Cafe (773-9873), 769 Congress Street. Open for lunch and dinner on weekdays, dinner only on weekends. Elegant dining rooms in the Rines Mansion, a great place for a romantic dinner or a special group gathering. Begin with appetizers like chicken-stuffed artichokes, salads. Entrées include a delicious seafood linguine, roast pork tenderloin, and filet mignon. Special requests (like leaving off the shrimp to create a good vegetarian pasta dish) are cheerfully accommodated when possible. $11.95–17.95.

The Diamond's Edge (766-5850), Great Diamond Island. Open in summer for lunch and dinner. Reservations a must. A short ride on the Casco Bay Line brings you to this fairly formal restaurant in a century-old warehouse overlooking Diamond Cove. Fresh Maine seafood is the specialty. Dinner entrées $14.95–21.95.

West Side (773-8223), 58 Pine Street. Serving breakfast, lunch, and dinner; brunch Sunday. A delightful café near the Western Promenade with an informal, friendly atmosphere featuring paintings by local artists. New menus biweekly, with fresh game, Maine seafood, organic produce. Outdoor patio in summer. $10.95–18.95.

☞ **Will's** (766-3322), Island Avenue, Peaks Island. Since there is limited seating inside, the time to lunch or dine at Will's is on a summer day when you

The Seamen's Club in Portland

can sit on the deck and enjoy the view of Portland's waterfront across the harbor. Burgers are always a possibility, but there are also some great seafood specials. Wine by the glass. Under $10 for an entire dinner.

Madd Apple Café (774-9698), 23 Forest Street. Open for lunch Tuesday through Friday, dinner Tuesday through Sunday, and brunch on Saturday and Sunday; adjacent to the Portland Performing Arts Center. Reservations recommended. The dinner menu changes every 2 weeks, with an emphasis on seasonal and local ingredients. Specialties are Maine game and seafood, and the menu might include frogs' legs *meunière* or Carolina pulled-pork barbecue. $13.95–19.95

Back Bay Grill (772-8833), 65 Portland Street. Open for dinner Monday through Saturday. Brightly painted murals add a lively feel to the place. The menu changes monthly, and might include appetizers like confit of duck on a grilled Portobello mushroom, their popular Caesar salad, and entrées like roast lamb and grilled salmon. Their crème brûlée is always a hit. Extensive wine list, single-malt scotches, and small-batch bourbons. $15.95–22.95.

South of Portland

Black Point Inn (883-4126), Prouts Neck. Dinner by reservation in a formal dining room with water views. The menu changes nightly; varies from basics like Yankee pot roast and boiled lobster to Cajun-style sautéed shrimp on angelhair pasta; extravagant desserts. $30 prix fixe plus tax and gratuity.

North of Portland

The Cannery Restaurant at Lower Falls Landing (846-1226), Yarmouth. Open daily for lunch and dinner, Sunday brunch. Built in 1913 as a herring factory; then served as a sardine-packing plant from the 1920s right up until 1980. The building, now part of a complex that includes a marina and some interesting shops, makes an attractive restaurant space with a waterside terrace. $7.95–15.95.

EATING OUT

In the Old Port

Note: Most of the restaurants described under *Dining Out* also serve a reasonably priced lunch.

Norm's Bar-B-Q (774-6711), 43 Middle Street. Open Tuesday through Thursday noon–10, Friday and Saturday noon–11, Sunday 3–9. For a memorable pork sandwich or spareribs, or maybe the rib sampler with onion rings, this is the place. Entrées average $9; beer and wine served.

The Porthole (774-3448), 32 Customs Wharf. Open early for breakfast, also serves lunch and dinner. Great chowder; breakfast dishes at unbeatable prices. Cheerful service at both counter and tables. Great all-you-can-eat fish fry ($3.95 at lunch, $5.95 at dinner). If you stick your head in and don't like what you see, this isn't for you; what you see is what you get. This is the last holdout on the funky former Casco Bay wharf.

Dock Fore (772-8619), 336 Fore Street. Open for lunch and dinner. A sunny, casual pub (most seating is at the bar or side bar) serving hearty fare and homelike specialties. Large portions at good prices.

Village Café (772-5320), 112 Newbury Street. Open for lunch and dinner daily. This is an old family favorite that predates the Old Port renaissance (it's just east of the Old Port). The third generation of the Reali family is now welcoming patrons to the same comfortable place. A large, often crowded space with specialties like fried Maine clams, lobster, veal parmigiana, and steaks.

Anthony's Italian Kitchen (774-8668), 151 Middle Street. This great little place is always crowded at lunchtime. It smells like a real Italian kitchen, and the aromas are not misleading. Terrific pizza and pasta specialties, homemade meatballs, service that makes you feel like an old friend.

Gritty McDuff's (772-2739), 396 Fore Street. A brew pub specializing in its own ales, stouts, and bitters, with such pub fare as fish-and-chips and shepherd's pie. Predictable wood-and-rugby decor.

Carbur's (772-7794), 123 Middle Street. Serves lunch and dinner daily. Be prepared to choose the first menu item on which your eye falls or to study the 20-page menu carefully to select the one thing that appeals to you the very most. This is a fun place, where all the sandwiches (their specialty) are big enough for a meal and come with outrageous names.

Beyond the Old Port

☞ **The Afghan Restaurant** (773-3431), 419 Congress Street. Open for lunch and dinner daily except Sunday. Authentic Afghan food at reasonable prices. This storefront restaurant is hung with scenes of Afghanistan painted by the owner. Try the combination plate. Bring your own wine. Entrée and dessert are less than $10.

Beyond Portland

The Lobster Shack (799-1677), Cape Elizabeth (off Route 77 at the tip of the cape, near Two Lights State Park). Open for lunch and dinner April to mid-October. A local landmark since the 1920s, set below the lighthouse and next to the foghorn. Dine inside or out. This is the place to pick a lobster out of the tank and watch it being boiled—then eat it "in the rough." Herb and Martha Porch are also known for their chowder and lobster stew, fried Maine shrimp, scallops and clams, lobster, and crabmeat rolls.

Spurwink Country Kitchen (799-1177), 150 Spurwink Road (near Scarborough Beach), Scarborough. Open mid-April to mid-October, 11:30–9. Part of this place's beauty is that it's here at all, right where you wouldn't expect to find a place to eat. Then you discover it's a special place, looking much the same and serving much the same food as when Hope Sargent opened it in 1955. Specials vary with the day and include soup, potato, vegetable or rolls, tea or coffee. Great homemade pies.

COFFEE BARS

An abundance of cozy cafés serving coffee and espresso drinks have sprung up in Portland. Our favorites are: **Java Joe's** (761-5637), 13 Exchange Street. A good place to go for late-night coffee and conversation. **Coffee By Design** (772-5533), 620 Congress Street. A friendly, cheerful spot with plenty of tables (sidewalk tables in summer), local artwork shows, and all the usual coffee and espresso choices. **The Daily Fix** (828-8610), 182 Middle Street. Small and cozy, with a bright, interesting mural and a couple of large comfortable chairs by the woodstove. Occasional live entertainment.

And for those who prefer tea:

Sweet Annie's Tea Shop (773-3353), 642 Congress Street, has a large selection of teas, baked goods, accessories, and gifts.

ENTERTAINMENT

Cumberland County Civic Center (775-3481 ext. 2 for 24-hour hotline), 1 Civic Center Square, Portland. A modern arena with close to 9000 seats, the site of year-round concerts, special presentations, ice-skating spectaculars, winter hockey games, and other events. Pick up a free monthly calendar of events.

MUSIC

Portland Symphony Orchestra (773-8191), City Hall Auditorium, 389 Congress Street, Portland. The winter series runs October through April, Tuesdays at 7:45 PM. In summertime, the symphony delights audiences throughout the state at outdoor pops concerts in some of the most beautiful settings, such as overlooking Casco Bay or by Camden Harbor.

LARK Society for Chamber Music/Portland String Quartet (761-1522). This distinguished chamber group grows in stature every year; performances are in a variety of Portland locations as well as around the state.

Portland Concert Association (772-8630). Sponsors orchestra, jazz, opera, musical theater in various locations; throughout Maine in summer.

PROFESSIONAL SPORTS

The **Portland Pirates** (828-4665) play their home games at the Cumberland County Civic Center. The **Portland Sea Dogs,** a double-A baseball team, play in Hadlock Stadium on Park Avenue (next to the Expo).

THEATER

Portland Performing Arts Center, 25A Forest Avenue (just off Congress Street), Portland. The city's old Odd Fellows Hall now houses an elegant, intimate, 290-seat theater that serves as home base for the **Portland Stage Company** (774-0465 for tickets), which performs September through April, and for the **Ram Island Dance Company** (773-2562), which stages weekend performances year-round.

Portland Players (799-7337), Thaxter Theater, 420 Cottage Road, South Portland, stages productions September through June.

Portland Lyric Theater (799-1421), Cedric Thomas Playhouse, 176 Sawyer Street, South Portland. This community theater presents four musicals each winter.

Oak Street Theatre (775-5103), 92 Oak Street. Newly renovated with 90 seats, its performances range from comedy to jazz and classic drama.

SELECTIVE SHOPPING

The Old Port Exchange has become the center for shopping and is filled with handicrafts, imported clothing, art, home furnishings, jewelry, books, and much, much more. Most Old Port shops are owner operated and have been restored individually. We have returned home from Portland laden with purchases ranging from an egg separator to a dining room table. Even when you are not shopping, it is always pleasant to stroll along the Old Port's brick sidewalks, pausing at a bench beneath a gas lamp to watch the shoppers. At Christmastime, with all of the decorations and fairy lights, it resembles an old English village.

The Old Port hosts a half-dozen noteworthy galleries. Other favorite stores include the **Whip & Spoon,** a fascinating Commercial Street emporium that sells every imaginable piece of cookware plus gourmet foods and wines, and **Maine Potters Market,** a 14-member crafts cooperative in the Mariner's Church, Fore Street. **Nancy Margolis Gallery** (367 Fore Street) reserves half its space for special museum-quality shows, the remainder for selling unusual crafts pieces. **Abacus/ Handcrafters Gallery** (44 Exchange Street) offers two floors full of crafted items, from jewelry to furniture. **The Stein Glass Gallery** (20 Milk Street) displays stunning pieces by 40 artists. **Joseph's** (410 Fore Street) features well-tailored clothing for both men and women.

There are stores dedicated to selling records, posters, ballet outfits, tobacco, woodstoves, canvas bags, cheese, woodenware, paper products, art materials, stencil equipment, games, potting supplies, herbs, children's toys and clothing, and more.

Beyond Portland proper is the **Maine Mall** (exit 7 off I-95), whose immediate complex of more than 100 stores is supplemented by large shopping centers and chain stores that ring it for several miles.

BOOKSTORES

In the past couple of years, Portland has become a mecca for book lovers. **Books Etc.** (38 Exchange Street) is a very inviting store. **Bookland's** in-town store at One Monument Way stocks a full range of titles and has a great children's section and bargain table. **Harbour Books** (846-6306), at Lower Falls Landing, Yarmouth, is part of the same rehabbed sardine-cannery complex that includes the Cannery Restaurant. This is a very special independent bookstore, the kind book lovers will feel completely comfortable in and probably walk out of with something they never intended to buy. Soft music, views of the harbor, and bargain tables. Open daily 9–6, Friday until 8, Sunday 12–5. Visible from I-95; take exit 17. **Borders Books and Music** by the mall has a huge selection and you can grab a book and read in its café for hours if you want.

SPECIAL EVENTS

April: **Aucociso,** a 10-day celebration of Casco Bay, centered on the Maine Boatbuilder's show.

First Sunday in June: **Old Port Festival**—special sales and performances in the streets that make up the Old Port.

Mid-July: **Yarmouth Clam Festival** in downtown Yarmouth.

August: **Cumberland Crafts Fair,** Cumberland Fairgrounds. **Sidewalk Art Festival,** Congress Street.

November and December: **Victorian Holiday Portland** with tree lighting, arrival of Father Christmas, costumed carolers, special events through Christmas.

December 31: **Portland New Year's Celebration**—modeled after the First Night begun in Boston, with performances throughout the city from afternoon through midnight.

Freeport

Although many think of Freeport as synonymous with shopping, there is much more to this town. Hidden behind the discounts and bargain stores is a history dating back more than 200 years. The area was granted a charter separating itself from North Yarmouth in 1789. With the War of 1812, shipbuilding became an important industry, with one famous ship inspiring Whittier's poem "The Dead Ship of Harpswell." The town is particularly proud of the fact that in 1820 the papers separating Maine from Massachusetts were signed in the historical Jameson Tavern (see *Dining Out*).

These days, shopping is high on visitors' lists. Each year as many as 15,000 cars per day squeeze up and down the mile of Main Street (Route 1) that is lined on both sides with upscale, off-price shops. L.L. Bean, ranked not only as Maine's number one emporium but also as its number one man-made attraction, has been a shopping landmark for over 75 years. The establishment of more than 100 neighboring outlet stores, however, didn't begin until the early 1980s.

Although the shops are the major draw for most travelers, the village has retained the appearance of older days—even McDonald's has been confined to a gracious old Colonial house, with no golden arches in sight. Some come to the area simply to stroll wooded paths in Wolfe's Neck Woods State Park and the Maine Audubon's Mast Landing Sanctuary. The Desert of Maine is also an interesting sight. The quiet countryside and waterside retreats away from crowds are enjoyed by many.

GUIDANCE

The Freeport Merchants Association (865-1212; 1-800-865-1994), PO Box 452, Freeport 04032, has a new visitors center in a replica of a historic hose tower on Mill Street. Brochures and information, rest rooms, and an ATM can be found here, and the association's office is upstairs. They also gladly respond to telephone and mail requests for information. Among their materials is an excellent, free, visitor's walking map, with a list of all the stores, restaurants, accommodations, and other services. Be sure to get one in advance or pick one up as soon as you arrive in town—almost all the merchants have them.

The Maine Publicity Bureau's welcome center in Kittery stocks some Freeport brochures, and there is a state information center on Route 1 just south of Freeport, in Yarmouth, at exit 17 off I-95.

GETTING THERE

Bus service to Freeport from Boston and Portland is available via **Greyhound. Mid Coast Limo** runs to and from the Portland International Jetport (1-800-834-5500 within Maine; 1-800-937-2424 outside Maine). A number of **bus tour companies** also offer shopping trips to Freeport from Boston and beyond. Most people drive, which means there's often a shortage of parking spaces, especially in peak season. The best solution to this problem is to stay at an inn or B&B within walking distance and leave your car there.

MEDICAL EMERGENCY

Mid Coast Hospital (729-0181), 58 Baribeau Drive, Brunswick.

VILLAGES

South Freeport has been a fishing center from the start. Between 1825 and 1830, up to 12,000 barrels of mackerel were packed and shipped from here each year. Later, the area specialty became crabmeat packing. A very different feel from the chaotic shopping frenzy of downtown Freeport, the harbor is still bustling with activity and offers some great seafood. From here you can take a cruise to explore Eagle Island in summer.

Porter's Landing. Once the center of commercial activity, this is now a quiet residential neighborhood, amid rolling hills, woods, and streams. The village is part of the Harraseeket Historic District on the National Register of Historic Places.

TO SEE AND DO

Desert of Maine (865-6962), Desert Road, Freeport. Open daily, mid-May to mid-October, 9 AM to dusk. Narrated coach tours ($4.75 adults, $2.75 children, $4.25 senior citizens) and self-guided walks through 40 acres of sand that was once the Tuttle Farm. Heavily farmed, then extensively logged to feed the railroad, the topsoil eventually gave way to the glacial sand deposit beneath it, which spread . . . and spread until entire trees sank below the surface. It is an unusual sand, rich in mineral deposits that make it unsuitable for commercial use but interesting to rock hounds. Children love it, especially the gem hunt (stones have been scattered in a section of the desert for children to find). There's a sand art demonstration and a 1783 barn museum, plus gift and souvenir shops; 2.5 miles from downtown Freeport. Overnight camping available.

Freeport Balloon Company (865-1712; 1-800-808-1712), 41 Tuttle Road, Pownal. Year-round hot-air-balloon flights, weather permitting, just after sunrise and a few hours before sunset.

BOAT EXCURSIONS

Anjin-San (772-7168), near town landing, South Freeport. A 34-foot sportfishing boat custom-built for Captain Greg Walts. Day trips for mackerel, bluefish, and shark. Also sight-seeing and diving trips, and charters.

Atlantic Seal (865-6112), Town Wharf, South Freeport. Memorial Day through mid-October. Daily narrated trips aboard this 40-footer out into Casco Bay include 3-hour cruises to Eagle Island, the former summer home of Admiral Robert E. Peary, the first man to reach the North Pole. Seal- and osprey-sighting trips and fall foliage cruises mid-September and October. Lobstering demonstrations are usually included, except Sunday, when lobstering is prohibited by Maine law.

Freeport Sailing Adventures (865-9225), PO Box 303, Freeport. Half- and full-day charters with crew. Longer charters available. You can learn to sail and help, or let them do the sailing while you relax.

CANOEING

The **Harraseeket River** in Freeport is particularly nice for canoeing. Start at Mast Landing, the northeastern end of the waterway; there are also launching sites at Winslow Memorial Park on Staples Point Road and at South Freeport Harbor. Phone the **Maine Audubon Society** in Falmouth (781-2330) for details about periodic, scheduled guided trips through the area. Nearby lake canoeing can be found at **Run Around Pond** in North Pownal (the parking lot is off Lawrence Road, 1 mile north of the intersection with Fickett Road).

GOLF

Freeport Country Club (865-4922), Old Country Road, Freeport. Nine holes.

CROSS-COUNTRY SKIING

The areas listed under *Green Space* are good cross-country skiing spots; rent or purchase equipment from L.L. Bean, which also offers classes in cross-country skiing (see *Special Learning Program*).

SPECIAL LEARNING PROGRAM

L.L. Bean Outdoor Discovery Program (865-3111), Route 1, Freeport. An interesting series of lectures and lessons that cover everything from cross-country ski lessons (on weekends beginning in January) and golf to survival in the Maine woods, making soap, tanning hides, paddling sea kayaks, building fly-rods, cooking small game, and fishing for Atlantic salmon. Call 1-800-341-4341, ext. 6666, for a free program guide.

GREEN SPACE

Winslow Memorial Park (865-4198), Staples Point Road, South Freeport. Open Memorial Day through September. A 90-acre municipal park with a sandy beach and large, grassy picnicking area; also boating and camping. Facilities include rest rooms with showers. Admission fee.

Wolfe's Neck Woods State Park (865-4465), Wolfe's Neck Road (take Bow Street, across from L.L. Bean), Freeport. Open Memorial Day weekend through Labor Day weekend. Day-use fee. A 244-acre park with shoreline hiking along Casco Bay, the Harraseeket River, and salt marshes. Guided nature walks are available; picnic tables and grills are scattered about.

Mast Landing Sanctuary, Upper Mast Landing Road (take Bow Street south), Freeport. Maintained by the Maine Audubon Society, this 100-acre sanctuary offers trails through apple orchards, woods, and meadows and along a millstream. Several paths radiate from a 1-mile loop trail.

Bradbury Mountain State Park (688-4712), Route 9, Hallowell Road, Pownal (just 6 miles from Freeport: From I-95, take exit 20 and follow signs). Open May 15 through October 15. $2.50 per adult, $.50 children ages 5–11, under age 5 free. The summit, accessible by an easy hike (even for young children), yields a splendid view of Casco Bay and New Hampshire's White Mountains. Facilities in the 297-acre park include a small playground, a softball field, hiking trails, toilets, and a small overnight camping area.

Pettengill Farm (phone the Freeport Historical Society at 865-3170), Freeport. Open for periodic guided tours. A saltwater farm with 140 acres of open fields and woodland that overlook the Harraseeket Estuary, with a totally unmodernized, vintage 1810 saltbox house.

LODGING

All entries are for Freeport 04032 unless otherwise indicated.

INN

Harraseeket Inn (865-9377; 1-800-342-6423), 162 Main Street. Just two blocks north of L.L. Bean, this luxury hotel is the largest in the area, with 54 rooms and 4 suites. It has maintained the elegant atmosphere of the 1850 Greek Revival house next door, where this operation first began as a five-room B&B. Nancy and Paul Gray are native Mainers, but their family also owns the Inn at Mystic, Connecticut, and they definitely know how to make the most of their location. Twenty-three of the rooms are decorated with antiques and reproductions and feature canopy beds and Jacuzzis or steam baths; 20 have fireplaces. The inn has its formal dining rooms and the casual Broad Arrow Tavern downstairs (see *Dining Out*). Other public spaces include a drawing room, library, and ballroom. Rates in-season are $145–225; full breakfast and afternoon tea are included. Two-night minimum stay required on some holiday weekends. Package plans available.

BED & BREAKFASTS

The **Freeport Area Bed & Breakfast Association** lists about a dozen members, all of which must meet certain standards established by the association. You can get a copy of its brochure by writing to PO Box 267, Freeport 04032. The majority of Freeport's B&Bs have opened in the past decade, since the shopping craze began. Many are in the handsome, old, white-clapboard Capes and Federal-style houses that stand side by side flanking Main Street just north of the shopping district.

The Isaac Randall House (865-9295), 5 Independence Drive. Open year-round. Historically, this property has been a dairy farm, dance hall, and tourist court. The handsome farmhouse became the first bed & breakfast in Freeport in 1984. Eight air-conditioned rooms with antiques, Oriental rugs, and lovely old quilts. Two have working fireplaces. The Loft, furnished all in wicker (including the king bed), is nice. The newest room is a restored train caboose, a perfect place for families with children (who are welcome here). A full breakfast is served in the beam-ceilinged country kitchen; a playground out back can keep children entertained. Pets are also welcome. On a small street off Route 1, but within walking distance of the downtown shopping area. Doubles are $65–125 (for the caboose), breakfast and snacks included.

One-Eighty-One Main Street (865-1226; 1-800-235-9750), 181 Main Street. Open year-round. This 1840s gray Cape with white trim and black shutters has been featured in *Country Home,* and it's easy to see why. The seven guest rooms, all with private baths, are attractive and cozy. Furnishings include American primitive antiques from hosts David Cates's and Ed Hassett's collections, Oriental rugs, and quilts made by David's mother. There are two parlors with books and games, gardens, a swimming pool, and a resident dog, May Elizabeth, who has appeared in an L.L. Bean catalog. Full breakfast, served at individual tables in the dining room, is included in the $85–100 room rate.

White Cedar Inn (865-9099; 1-800-853-1269), 178 Main Street. Open year-round. This restored, white-clapboard Victorian house was once the home of Arctic explorer Donald B. MacMillan, who went to the North Pole with Admiral Peary. There are six bedrooms with private baths and simple but pretty furnishings. Three have a single bed in addition to a double or queen. The cozy room up under the eaves offers more privacy with its own staircase. When we stopped by, construction of a new room, which will have a private entrance, spiral staircase, two queen beds, and a sitting area, was in progress. Full breakfast, included, is served at small tables in the sun room, adjacent to the country kitchen. Innkeepers Carla and Phil Kerber live in the remodeled ell and barn that extend from the back of the inn. Doubles $80–110 (for new room).

Kendall Tavern Bed & Breakfast (865-1338; 1-800-341-9572), 213 Main Street. Open year-round. Slightly farther up Main Street than the others, but still just a half mile from the shopping district. This early-1800s, yellow-clapboard farmhouse with attached barn offers an indoor spa in addition to seven rooms with private baths, queen or twin beds. Upstairs rooms have two doubles or a queen and a twin. The two downstairs parlors have glowing wide-board floors and fireplaces. One has a Steinway upright piano that is kept tuned and ready to be played; the other offers cable TV. No smoking. Doubles in-season are $100–110 (for a room with a sitting area). Full all-you-can-eat breakfast included.

The James Place Inn ((865-4486), 11 Holbrook Street. Darcy and Bill James opened their five-room B&B in July 1996. Decorated in peaceful pastel colors, all rooms have private baths (one with a Jacuzzi tub), air-conditioning, and cable TV. The upstairs rooms have kitchenettes. A buffet breakfast is served in the glassed-in breakfast/social room. $80–100 double in-season.

Jacaranda House (865-9858), 8 Holbrook Street. Three rooms when we stopped by, with plans to expand to five. Rooms are private and simply furnished with stenciling and touches of bold color scattered throughout. Breakfast is included in the $75 double rate, and the hostess will work around your dining preferences (vegetarian, vegan, etc.)

Porter's Landing B&B (865-4488), 70 South Street. Open April through December. Peter and Barbara Guffin offer three guest rooms in the 1800s post-and-beam carriage house adjacent to their elegant home in the Historic District. Quiet country setting about a mile from L.L. Bean. A fieldstone wall runs along the front of the house, and a brick sidewalk with granite inlay leads to a new roofed porch entrance. The rooms, built to preserve historic architectural details, have private baths and are furnished with antiques and handmade quilts. The large common room has a Count Rumford fireplace; the sunny, airy loft, with sky windows and books lining the walls, is a perfect place to curl up and read. Doubles are $95 in high season, including a full breakfast that might feature Belgian waffles or the special Porter's Landing omelet.

Atlantic Seal B&B (865-6112), Main Street, Box 146, South Freeport 04078. Open year-round. Just 5 minutes from downtown Freeport but eons from the bustle, this 1850 Cape in the village of South Freeport boasts views of the harbor from each of its three guest rooms. Owned and operated by the owners of the *Atlantic Seal* tour boat, it is furnished with antiques and nautical collections. There is a resident dog. Summer rates, including "hearty sailor's breakfast," are $85–135 (for a room with both a queen and a double bed, cable TV, refrigerator, and Jacuzzi). Guests also receive a discount on *Atlantic Seal* morning cruises. Van service from the Portland airport can be prearranged.

The Bagley House Bed & Breakfast (865-6566; 1-800-765-1772), 1290 Royalsborough Road, Durham 04222. Ten minutes from downtown Freeport in a serene country setting. Built as a public house in 1772, this is the oldest home in town. The town's first worship services were held here, and it was the site of the first schoolhouse. Susan Backhouse and Suzanne O'Connor left the Boston area after many years in nursing, to fulfill a lifelong dream of operating a country B&B when they purchased the property in 1993. They have created a welcoming atmosphere, furnishing with antiques and custom-made pieces, as well as hand-sewn quilts. Details like robes in the room, fresh flowers, and cold drinks and cookies available at any time make guests feel right at home. The cozy nook has slanted ceilings, two double beds, and wall-to-wall carpeting. Other rooms have queen beds or a double bed. $100 double in-season, including full breakfast.

MOTELS

On Route 1, south of Freeport near the Yarmouth town line, there are a number of modern motels. Among these is the **Freeport Inn** (865-

3106; 1-800-99-VALUE). Set on 25 acres of lawns and nature trails, all rooms have wall-to-wall carpeting, cable TV, air-conditioning, and in-room phones. Doubles are $100–110 in-season. There's a swimming pool and a pond where you can ice skate in winter. Canoes are available for paddling on the Cousins River. The inn's café and bakery serves breakfast and lunch and they operate the Muddy Rudder (see *Eating Out*) just down the road.

CAMPGROUNDS

Sandy Cedar Haven Campground (865-6254), Baker Road, Freeport. Fifty-eight mostly wooded sites, each with fireplace and picnic table. Water and electricity hook-ups, four with sewer as well. Twelve tent sites. Store with wood, ice, and groceries. Mini-golf, playground, and swimming pond. Two miles from Route 1 and downtown Freeport.

Desert of Maine Campgrounds (865-6962), 95 Desert Road, Freeport. Fifty wooded and open sites adjacent to this natural glacial sand deposit (see *To See and Do*). Hook-ups, hot showers, laundry, convenience store, propane, fire rings and picnic tables, horseshoe pits, nature trails. Campsites are $16–20 per night.

WHERE TO EAT

DINING OUT

Fiddlehead Farm and **Country Café** (865-0466), Independence Drive and Lower Main Street, Freeport. Open year-round. This exceptional restaurant in a restored 1800s Greek Revival farmhouse continues to please diners with attentive but unpretentious service and an imaginative menu. Highlights include scaloppine prepared several ways, plus lamb chops, unusual pasta combinations, and lovely fresh seafood with simple but special sauces. Most entrées are under $20. A fireplace adds warmth to the decor—wide-pine floors, flowered wallpaper, simply swagged curtains. The Country Café offers casual, moderately priced, home-style meals. There's also a bakery on the premises.

Harraseeket Inn (865-9377; 1-800-342-6423), 162 Main Street, Freeport. Open year-round. Continental cuisine and elegant service in three formal dining rooms. The chef uses fresh ingredients from local gardeners and farmers in-season and creates mouth-watering entrées like grilled mushroom risotto, Maine lobster clambake (a complete dinner with dessert), two-texture duckling, and three dishes for two (one is châteaubriand, $50 for two) prepared at the table. Desserts are sure to please here, too. In addition to dinner, the Harraseeket is known for its outstanding Sunday brunch, which often features such delicacies as caviar, oysters on the half shell, and even venison. The inn also serves lunch, high tea, and a breakfast buffet. $14.95–22.95. The dress code at dinner is a collared shirt, and reservations are suggested.

Jameson Tavern (865-4195), 115 Main Street, Freeport. All three meals are served in several inviting dining rooms in the 1779 tavern where the papers separating Maine from Massachusetts were signed in 1820. Specialties include fresh seafood, like bacon-wrapped scallops with maple cream, and chicken Aberdine. Children's menu and outside patio. $10.95–20.95.

EATING OUT

The Broad Arrow Tavern (865-9377), Harraseeket Inn, 162 Main Street, Freeport. Downstairs in this elegant inn, the atmosphere is relaxed and pubby. The menu is appropriate to the setting.

Crickets Restaurant (865-4005), Lower Main Street, Freeport. Open daily for breakfast, lunch, and dinner, plus Sunday jazz brunch. The almost overwhelming lunch/dinner menu offers something for just about everyone, from generous specialty sandwiches ($6–8) to fajitas, from pasta dishes to heavier steak and seafood entrées (most entrées between $9 and $15). We're particularly intrigued with the crumb-coated, deep-fried lobster tails.

Tap Room (865-4195), Jameson Tavern, 115 Main Street, Freeport. This informal tavern to the rear of the building serves inexpensive snacks and sandwiches until late in the evening.

Blue Onion (865-9396), Lower Main Street, Freeport. Open for lunch and dinner daily except Monday. A charming dining room in an old blue roadside house located south of Freeport's downtown traffic squeeze. Soups, salads, quiche for lunch; baked and broiled fish, lobster pie, and other fish, veal, and chicken dishes for supper. No liquor.

Caffe Latte Bistro and Annabelle's Ice Cream Parlour (865-2257), 11 Independence Drive. A coffeehouse with excellent sandwiches. Try the Heartfelt Artichoke on sourdough bread. Salads, soups, pizza, and rollwiches also. Espresso bar and ice cream.

Gritty McDuff's (865-4321), 183 Lower Main Street. The only brew pub in Freeport offers outdoor dining, lobster, seafood, pizza, and pub food. Great ales.

Muddy Rudder (846-3082), Route 1, Freeport. Operated by the nearby Freeport Inn, this popular restaurant overlooks the water and serves a wide selection of seafood dishes plus steaks, sandwiches, and salads; you can also have a full clambake on the deck. The atmosphere is relaxed, with piano music in the evening.

Harraseeket Lunch & Lobster Co. (865-4888), South Freeport (turn off Route 1 at the giant wooden Indian outside Levinsky's, then turn right at a stop sign a few miles down). Open May through October. In the middle of the Harraseeket boatyard; you order lobsters and clams on one side, fried food on the other, and eat at picnic tables (of which there are never enough at peak hours) overlooking a boat-filled harbor. Lobsters are fresh from the pound's boats. Homemade desserts. There is also a small, inside dining room. Worth seeking out.

- **The Corsican** (865-9421), 9 Mechanic Street, Freeport. Lunch and dinner. Seafood, chicken, vegetarian entrées. Nonsmoking restaurant.
- **The Lobster Cooker** (865-4349), 39 Main Street, Freeport. Steamed lobster, fresh-picked lobster and crabmeat rolls, sandwiches, chowders; dining on the outdoor patio. Beer and wine.

SELECTIVE SHOPPING

☞ FREEPORT FACTORY OUTLETS

As noted in the introduction to this chapter, Freeport's 125-plus factory outlets constitute what has probably become Maine's mightiest tourist magnet. *Boston Globe* writer Nathan Cobb described it well: "A shoppers' theme park spread out at the foot of L.L. Bean, the high church of country chic." Cobb quoted a local landlord: "The great American pastime now is shopping, not hiking."

Although hiking and hunting put L.L. Bean on the tourist map in the first place, tourists in Freeport are intently studying the map of shops these days. L.L. Bean has kept pace by selling fashionable, sporty clothing and an incredible range of sporting equipment, books, gourmet products and gifts, as well as its golden boot.

L.L. Bean contends that it attracts at least 2½ million customers annually—roughly twice the population of Maine. In the early 1980s, neighboring property owners began to claim a portion of this traffic. Instead of relegating the outlets to malls (see "Kittery and the Yorks"), they have deftly draped them in brick and clapboard, actually improving on the town's old looks (although longtime shopkeepers who were forced to move because of skyrocketing real estate prices might well disagree). Ample parking lots are sequestered behind the Main Street facade (it's still sometimes tough to find a space). In summer there is a festive atmosphere, with hot-dog and ice cream vendors on key corners. But it is the quality of the shops that ensures a year-round crowd. Just about any well-known clothing, accessory, and home furnishing line has a factory store here. The following is a selected list of some of the outlets here. Many stores claim 20–70 percent off suggested retail prices, and even L.L. Bean has a separate outlet store.

L.L. Bean (1-800-221-4221 for orders; 1-800-341-4341 for customer service), 95 Main Street. Open 24 hours a day, 365 days a year. More than a store—for millions it is the gateway to Maine. Most shoppers arrive having already studied the mail-order catalog (which accounts for 85–91 percent of sales) and are buying purposefully. The store has been expanded several times in recent years to the point where it's hard to find the old boot factory—built by Leon Leonwood Bean—that is at its heart. With its outdoor waterfall, indoor trout pond, and thousands of square feet of retail space, the building now resembles a fancy shopping mall more than it does a single store. It was back in 1912 that Mr. Bean developed his boot, a unique combination of rubber bottom and

The old L.L. Bean Store in the 1930s

leather top. He originally sold it by mail order but gradually began catering to the hunters and fishermen who tended to pass through his town in the middle of the night. L.L. Bean himself died in 1967, but grandson Leon Gorman continues to sell nearly a quarter of a million pairs of the family boots each year. Gorman's leadership, together with an excellent marketing staff, has seen Bean grow substantially in the last few decades. Current stock ranges from canoes to weatherproof cameras to climbing gear. There is a wide variety of clothing as well as every conceivable gadget designed to keep you warm. It is the anchor store for all the outlets in town.

L.L. Bean Factory Store (1-800-341-4341), Depot Street (in the middle of the parking lot across Main Street from the retail store). Seconds, samples, and irregular merchandise are offered here. You never know what you'll find, but it's always worth a look. Unlike the main store, the outlet is not open 24 hours a day.

Dooney & Bourke (865-1366), 52 Main Street (in back). Stylish pocketbooks, shoulder bags, belts, wallets, and portfolios in water-repellent, coarse-grained leather.

Cuddledown of Maine Factory Store (865-1713), Route 1 South. Comforters, pillows, gift items, all filled with goose down. The store bills itself as having the "only European down-filling room in the country that we know of."

Maine Wreath & Flower Factory Outlet (865-3019), 13 Bow Street. Quality Maine dried flowers and wreaths at discount prices.

Buttons and Things Factory Outlet (865-4480), 24 Main Street. A warren of rooms chock-full of buttons, beads, bead books, and other findings.

Casey's Wood Products (865-3244), 15½ School Street. Bins full of wood turnings, craft materials, and toys. Free catalog.

Dansk Factory Outlet (865-6125), 92 Main Street (across from Bean's). Scandinavian-design tableware, cookware, and gifts.

Mikasa Factory Store (865-9441), 31 Main Street. Dinnerware, bone china, crystal, linens, and gifts. Three floors offering a large inventory.

SPECIAL SHOPS

Harrington House Museum Store (865-0477), 45 Main Street, Freeport. This charming house, right in the middle of all the outlet shops, is owned by the Freeport Historical Society. Faced with escalating property taxes, the preservationists came up with a unique way to hold onto their house and keep up with the times. Every room is furnished with 1830- to 1900-era reproductions, all of which are for sale. Pieces, all documented, range from handsome furniture and weavings to artwork, crafts, Shaker baskets, kitchen utensils, and toys. The historical society mounts changing exhibits in the newly renovated barn.

Edgecomb Potters/Hand in Hand Gallery (865-1705), 8 School Street, Freeport. Fine contemporary crafts. Displays colorful porcelain, jewelry, blown glass, and iron.

Brown Goldsmiths (865-4126), 1 Mechanic Street, Freeport. Open Monday through Saturday. Original designs in rings, earrings, and bracelets.

DeLorme's Map Store (865-4171), Route 1 (south of downtown Freeport). The publishing company's own maps, atlases, and pamphlets; also guidebooks and maps of the United States and the world.

Bridgham & Cook, Ltd. (865-1040), 8A Bow Street (behind Polo–Ralph Lauren). Packaged British and Irish foods, toiletries, teas, gifts—a must for the Anglophile.

Just Ship It (865-0421), 15 Bow Street, Freeport. If you've bought something you just can't fit into your suitcase, into the car, or onto the airplane, they'll ship it home for you. And if you forget to buy something while you're in Freeport, give them a call and they'll *buy* it and ship it for you!

20th Maine (865-4340), 49 West Street. Devoted to the Civil War—books, art, music, collectibles.

SPECIAL EVENTS

December: **Sparkle Weekend Celebration** brings caroling, horse-drawn wagons, Santa, and a talking Christmas tree. **All-night Christmas shopping.** Not just L.L. Bean, but all the shops stay open throughout the night the weekend before Christmas to accommodate late shoppers. Adding to the atmosphere are costumed carolers and hot refreshments.

III. MID COAST AND THE ISLANDS

Helping out on a windjammer off Rockland

GREIG CRANNA

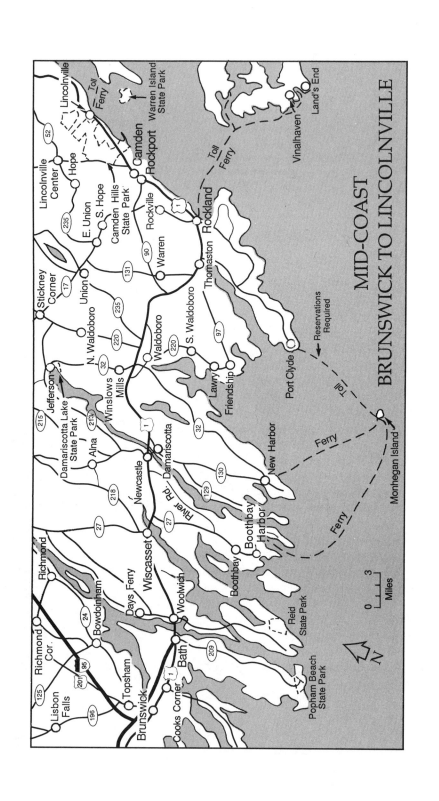

MID-COAST
BRUNSWICK TO LINCOLNVILLE

Mid Coast Area

Beyond Casco Bay the shape of Maine's coast changes—it shreds. In contrast to the even arc of shoreline stretching from Kittery to Cape Elizabeth, the coast between Brunswick and Rockland is composed of a series of more than a dozen ragged peninsulas extending like so many fingers south from Route 1, creating a myriad of big and small harbors, coves, and bays. Scientists tell us that these peninsulas and the offshore islands are mountains drowned by the melting of the same glaciers that sculpted the many shallow lakes and tidal rivers in this area.

The 70 miles of Route 1 between Brunswick and Lincolnville are generally equated with Maine's Mid Coast, but its depth is actually far greater and more difficult to define. It extends south of Route 1 to the tips of every peninsula, from Potts Point in South Harpswell and Land's End on Bailey Island to Popham Beach on the Phippsburg Peninsula and on through the Boothbays to Pemaquid Point, Friendship, Port Clyde, and Spruce Head. Along with Rockland, Camden, and the islands of Monhegan, Vinalhaven, North Haven, and Islesboro, these communities have all catered to summer visitors since steamboats began off-loading them in the mid-19th century. Each peninsula differs in character from the next, but all offer their share of places to stay and eat in settings you rarely find along Route 1.

North of Route 1, this midcoastal area also extends slightly inland. Above Bath, for instance, five rivers meld to form Merrymeeting Bay, and north of Newcastle the tidal Damariscotta River widens into 13-mile-long Damariscotta Lake. This gently rolling, river- and lake-laced backcountry harbors a number of picturesque villages and reasonably priced lodging places.

We would hope that no one who reads this book simply sticks to Route 1.

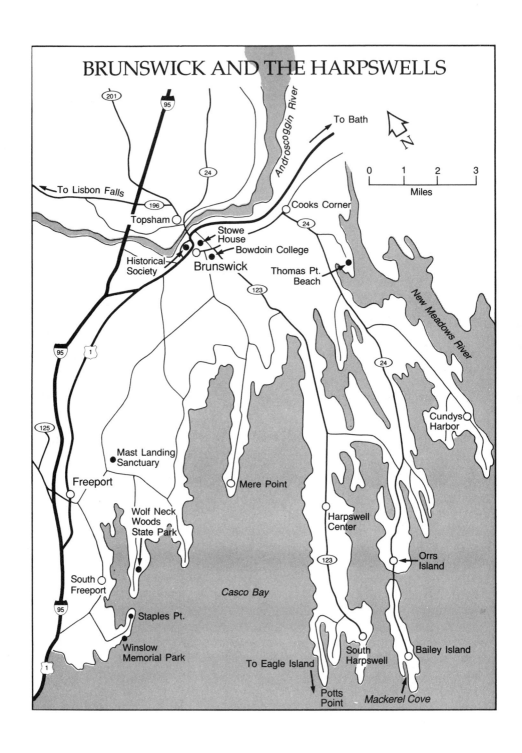

BRUNSWICK AND THE HARPSWELLS

Brunswick and the Harpswells

Brunswick, Maine's oldest college town, is the natural centerpiece for this area. Bowdoin College was founded in 1794, and its campus is still among New England's finest. Brunswick offers summer music and theater, along with some interesting shops, restaurants, and galleries.

Brunswick's Maine Street is a full 12 rods wide—just as it was when the town was laid out in 1717 as an early commercial site near the confluence of the Androscoggin and Kennebec Rivers, which generated power for 19th-century mills. Be sure to turn off Route 1 and drive down Maine Street with its shops and wide grass mall. Given its bandstand and frequent festivities, the town green is often bustling with activity.

Three narrow land fingers and several bridge-linked islands stretch seaward from Brunswick, defining the eastern rim of Casco Bay. Collectively they form the town of Harpswell, better known as "the Harpswells" because it includes so many coves, points, and islands (notably Orrs and Bailey). Widely known for its seafood restaurants, Bailey Island is on the tourist path; but otherwise these peninsulas are surprisingly sleepy, salted with crafts, galleries, and some great places to stay. They are Maine's most convenient peninsulas, yet they seem much farther Down East.

GUIDANCE

Chamber of Commerce of the Bath-Brunswick Region (725-8797), 59 Pleasant Street, Brunswick 04011. Open weekdays year-round, 8:30–5; also open July through Labor Day on Fridays until 8 PM, and Saturdays 3–7 PM. Staff members keep tabs on vacancies and send out lodging and dining information. The walk-in information center displays area menus and stocks a wide range of brochures. From Route 1 North follow Brunswick business district signs (these will take you down Pleasant Street).

GETTING THERE

Bus service to downtown Brunswick from Boston and Portland is via **Vermont Transit/Greyhound** and **Concord Trailways.**

MEDICAL EMERGENCY

Dial **911.**

Parkview Memorial Hospital (729-1641), 329 Main Street, Brunswick. **Mid Coast Hospital** (729-0181), 58 Baribeau Street, Brunswick; and 1356 Washington Street, Bath (443-5524).

TO SEE

Bowdoin College (725-3000), Brunswick. Tours of the 110-acre campus with more than 50 buildings begin at the admissions office. Phone for current hours. Because Maine was part of Massachusetts when the college was founded in 1794, the school is named after a Massachusetts governor. Nathaniel Hawthorne and Henry Wadsworth Longfellow were classmates here in 1825; other notable graduates include Franklin Pierce and Robert Edwin Peary. Founded as a men's college, the school now also welcomes women among its 1350 students. Bowdoin ranks among the nation's top colleges both in cost and in status. It isn't necessary to take a tour to see the sights.

MUSEUMS

Bowdoin College Museum of Art (725-3275), Walker Art Building. Open year-round, Tuesday through Saturday 10–5, Sunday 2–5; closed Monday and holidays. One of New England's outstanding art collections housed in a building designed by McKim, Mead, and White. Colonial- and Federal-era portraits by Gilbert Charles Stuart, Robert Feke, and John Singleton Copley; also paintings by Winslow Homer, Rockwell Kent, John Sloan, and Mary Cassatt; special exhibits.

Peary-MacMillan Arctic Museum (725-3416), Hubbard Hall, Bowdoin College. Open same hours as the Museum of Art. A well-displayed collection of clothing, trophies, and other mementos from expeditions to the North Pole by two Bowdoin alumni. Robert Edwin Peary (class of 1877) was the first man to reach the North Pole, and Donald Baxter MacMillan (class of 1898), who was Peary's chief assistant, went on to dedicate his life to exploring Arctic waters and terrain.

Pejepscot Historical Society Museums (729-6606). Founded in 1888 and named for a local river, this is one of Maine's oldest historical societies. It maintains three downtown Brunswick museums, among which the **Joshua L. Chamberlain Museum** (226 Maine Street; open June through September, Tuesday through Saturday 10–4; $3 per adult, $1 per child) is by far the most popular. Thanks to the recent Civil War series by filmmaker Ken Burns, the entire country now seems to know about Joshua Chamberlain (1818–1914), the college professor who became the hero of Little Round Top in the Battle of Gettysburg and went on to serve four terms as governor of Maine and to become president of Bowdoin College. His formerly forgotten, decaying home—a fanciful mansion with two top floors dating from the 1820s and a Victorian first floor from 1871—has been partially restored over the past few years. Visitation has soared from 300 per season in 1993 to 5000 in 1996. Exhibits include his bullet-dented boots and his governor's chair and desk, and a museum store sells Civil War books and souvenirs. The **Pejepscot Museum,** 159 Park Row (open weekdays year-round, 9–4:30, summer Saturdays 1–4; free), serves as the society's archives and also displays changing exhibits on the history of Brunswick, Topsham, and Harpswell. The **Skolfield-Whittier House,** 161 Park Row, is the 17-room, mid-19th-century, Italianate double house adjacent to the Pejepscot Museum. For over 50 years the mansion was sealed, preserving its original furnishings and decor. Tours in summer, Tuesday through Friday 10–3, Saturday 1–4, are $3 adults, $1 children ages 6–12.

Brunswick Naval Air Station (921-2000). From Route 1, take the Cooks Corner exit just east of Brunswick, then follow Route 24 south to the entrance. Home of the navy's North Atlantic antisubmarine and general patrol squadrons, the base is now open for self-guided, drive-through tours. Pick up a map and directions at the kiosk just inside the gate.

Fishway Viewing Room (725-5521), Brunswick-Topsham Hydro Station, Maine Street, Brunswick. May through June is the best time to view migrating fish; a fish ladder leads to a holding tank beside the viewing room.

SCENIC DRIVE

A tour of the Harpswells, including Orrs and Bailey Islands. Allow a day for this rewarding peninsula prowl. From Brunswick, follow Route 123 south past Bowdoin College 8 miles to the picturesque village of Harpswell Center. The white-clapboard Elijah Kellogg Church faces the matching Harpswell Town Meeting House built in 1757. The church is named for a former minister who was a prominent 19th-century children's book author. Continue south through West Harpswell to Pott's Point, where multicolored, 19th-century summer cottages cluster on the rocks like a flock of exotic birds that have wandered in among the gulls. Stop by the first crafts studio you see here and pick up a map/guide to other members of the Harpswell Craft Guild.

Retrace your way back up Route 123, and 2 miles north of the church turn right onto Mountain Road, leading to busier Route 24 on Great (also known as Sebascodegan) Island. Drive south along Orrs Island across the only remaining cribstone bridge in the world. (Its granite blocks are laid in honeycomb fashion without cement to allow tidal flows.) This bridge brings you to Bailey Island, with its restaurants, lodging places, picturesque Mackerel Cove, and rocky Land's End (there's a small beach, gift shop, and parking lot). Return up Route 24.

TO DO

BOAT EXCURSIONS

Casco Bay Boat Charters (833-2978) and **Sea Escape Charters** (833-5531) both offer fishing trips, scenic cruises, and excursions from Bailey Island to **Eagle Island,** which is also a popular destination for the Bailey-based sloop *Hanoah* (821-6586). A classic one-man's island, just 17 acres, Eagle Island is the site of Admiral Robert E. Peary's shingled summer home where, on September 6, 1909, his wife received the news that her husband had become the first man to reach the North Pole. Peary positioned his house to face northeast on a rocky bluff that resembles the prow of a ship. He designed the three-sided living room hearth, which was made from island stones and Arctic quartz crystals, and stuffed many of the birds that occupy the mantel. The upstairs bedrooms appear as though someone has just stepped out for a walk, and the dining room is strewn with photos of men and dogs battling ice and snow. There is a small beach and a nature path that circles the island and takes you past the pine trees filled with seagulls on the ocean side.

Casco Bay Lines (774-7871) offers a daily seasonal excursion from Cook's Lobster House on Bailey Island. It takes 1½ hours—circles around Eagle Island and through this northern end of Casco Bay.

GOLF

Brunswick Golf Club (725-8224), River Road, Brunswick. Incorporated in 1888, an 18-hole course known for its beauty and challenging nature. Snack bar, lounge, and cart rentals.

SEA KAYAKING

H2Outfitters (833-5257), PO Box 72, Orrs Island 04066. Two-hour clinics include use of equipment; guided day trips and overnight excursions are also offered.

Bethel Point Oar and Paddle (725-6494), Cundys Harbor. Henry Bird rents single kayaks, Alden shells, and canoes by the half and full day, weather permitting.

GREEN SPACE

BEACHES AND SWIMMING HOLES

White's Beach (729-0415), Durham Road, Brunswick. Open Memorial Day through Labor Day. A pond in a former gravel pit (water no deeper than 9 feet). Facilities include a small slide for children. Sandy beach, lifeguards, picnic tables, grills, and snack bar.

Thomas Point Beach (725-6009), Route 24, Cook's Corner. Open Memorial Day through Labor Day, 9–sunset. $2.50 adults, $2 children under 12. This beach is on tidal water overlooking the New Meadows River. There are 64 acres of lawns and groves for picnicking (more than 500 picnic tables plus snack bar, playground, and arcade), and camping. Special events.

Coffin Pond (725-6656), River Road, Brunswick. Phone for current hours and fees. A strip of sandy beach surrounding a circular pool. Facilities include a 55-foot-long water slide, a playground, and changing rooms maintained by the town. Nominal admission.

LODGING

INNS

☞ **Driftwood Inn and Cottages** (833-5461), Bailey Island 04003. Open June through mid-October; dining room (which is open to the public) is open late June through Labor Day. Sited on a rocky point within earshot of a foghorn are three gray-shingled, traditional Maine summer houses that contain a total of 16 doubles and 8 singles (9 with half-baths); there are also six housekeeping cottages. Everyone dines in the pine-walled lodge dining room (so request a room away from the lodge). Almost all views are of the sea. There is a small saltwater swimming pool set in the rocks and plenty of room, both inside and out, to lounge. This is a rustic resort with the kind of atmosphere and value possible only under longtime (over 50 years) ownership by one family. Your hosts are Mr. and Mrs. Charles L. Conrad. $65–70 per couple, $45 single (no minimum stay, no meals). Housekeeping cottages, available by the week, are $400–500. Breakfast is $5; dinner, $12. Weekly MAP rates: $320 per person. No credit cards. Pets are accepted in the cottages.

Captain Daniel Stone Inn (725-9898), 10 Water Street, Brunswick 04011. Twenty-five modern rooms and suites are annexed to a Federal mansion. All have color TV, telephone, VCR, alarm clock/cassette player, and some feature whirlpool baths. Common space includes a handsome living room as well as large function rooms. Breakfast, lunch, dinner, and Sunday brunch are served in the Narcissa Stone Restaurant (see *Dining Out*). Continental breakfast is included in the room rate. $99–175 per room; inquire about packages. Handicapped accessible.

BED & BREAKFASTS

In Brunswick/Topsham

☞ **Brunswick Bed & Breakfast** (729-4914; 1-800-299-4914), 165 Park Row, Brunswick 04011. Open year-round. A beautifully restored, mid-1800s Greek Revival home in the historic district on the town green; within walking distance of shops, museums, and the Bowdoin College campus. The six guest rooms are furnished with antiques and a collection of both new and antique quilts. Four rooms have private baths. Twin parlors with floor-to-ceiling windows overlook the mall. The breakfast (ours included perfect pancakes served with blueberries, strawberries, and melon) is included in the rate: $73–93 single or double occupancy.

Middaugh Bed & Breakfast (725-2562), 36 Elm Street, Topsham 04086. Off Route 1 and I-95 in Topsham's historic district, this Greek Revival house has two very attractive, comfortable second-floor rooms, each with private bath. $60 includes a full breakfast.

In the Harpswells

Harpswell Inn (833-5509; 1-800-843-5509), 141 Lookout Point Road, RR 1, Box 141, South Harpswell 04079. Built as the cookhouse for a boatyard across the way, this three-story white-clapboard has taken in guests under a number of names but has never been quite so gracious as now. Innkeepers Susan and Bill Menz have lived in Hawaii and Texas as well as the South, collecting antiques and furnishings to fill the house—much as though it were owned by a widely traveled sea captain. Guests enter a large living room with plenty of sitting space around a big hearth and windows overlooking Middle Bay. The 13 guest rooms vary widely and come with and without baths and water views, and there are two suites with kitchens. Children must be over 10. No smoking. $58–115 for rooms; suites are $150 in high season. Breakfast is included.

Vicarage by the Sea (833-5480), Route 123, West Harpswell 04079. Open year-round. Built in the 1980s on Curtis Cove, this cozy, Cape-style house is home for Joan Peterson-Moulton, a gracious hostess who offers three rooms, one with a private bath. Some rooms have ocean views, and the rocks that are uncovered at low tide are great for walking and beachcombing. $55–80 includes a full breakfast.

The Lady and the Loon (833-6871), PO Box 98, Bailey Island 04003. Gail Sprague has four antiques- and art-filled rooms with private baths. The house is situated on a bluff overlooking Ragged Island, within walking distance of a private beach. $75–95 includes breakfast. Gail is a gifted painter (the house also includes her shop). She is attuned to the local arts scene and offers landscape painting classes.

Captain's Watch (725-0979), 2476 Cundy's Harbor Road, Harpswell 04011. Built high on a bluff during the Civil War as the Union Hotel, this classic old building with an octagonal cupola has recently been restored by Donna Dillman and Ken Brigham of the Captain Drummond House in Phippsburg. Their 37-foot sloop *Symbion* will be available for short sails and overnight cruises. The five guest rooms include two with fireplaces, one a suite with a deck; all have private baths and water views; two rooms share access to the cupola. $95–110 per room and $140 for the suite includes a full breakfast.

Harborgate Bed and Breakfast (725-5894), RD 2, Box 2260, Brunswick 04011. Open May through October. A modern, redwood home overlooking Quahog Bay, set in woods and flower gardens. The two first-floor guest rooms share a bath and guest living room. You can swim from the dock. $60 per couple includes continental breakfast.

COTTAGES

The Bath-Brunswick Area Chamber of Commerce (see *Guidance*) lists a number of weekly cottage rentals, most on Orrs and Bailey Islands.

MOTELS

Little Island Motel (833-2392), RD 1, Box 15, Orrs Island 04066. Open early May through October. An attractive motel with terrific views. Nine units, each with a small refrigerator and color TV; part of a complex that also includes a gift shop (the Gull's Nest) and a reception area where coffee and a buffet breakfast are served each morning. The complex is set on its own mini-island with a private beach, connected to other land by a narrow neck. $84–114 includes breakfast and use of boats, bicycles, and the outdoor picnic area.

Bailey Island Motel (833-2886), Route 24, Bailey Island 04003. Located just over the cribstone bridge. A pretty, gray-shingled building on the water's edge, offering ocean views and landscaped lawns. The 10 rooms are clean and comfortable, with cable TV. Coffee and muffins are served each morning, included in the $65–85 (depending on season) rates.

Note: If it happens to be a peak travel weekend and you are desperate for a bed, turn north on Route 24 into Topsham, then head up Route 196 toward Lisbon Falls. This truck route is lined with inexpensive motels that never seem to fill.

WHERE TO EAT

DINING OUT
In Brunswick
Note: Brunswick is a college town so you can eat well here fairly reasonably.

Richard's German/American Cuisine (729-9673), 115 Maine Street. Open for lunch and dinner Monday through Saturday. Continental fare like veal Oscar and grilled New York sirloin, but also featuring very satisfying dishes like German farmer soup, *Gemischter salat*, Wiener schnitzel, and *Schlachtplatte*. Nightly specials include *Rindsrouladen* (thinly sliced beef rolled with onions, bacon, mustard, and pickles, braised in a brown sauce). The beer list is impressive. Dinner entrées: $7.95–15.45.

The Great Impasta (729-5858), 42 Maine Street. Open daily for lunch and dinner. A great stop even if you are simply traveling up or down Route 1 (it's at the Route 1 end of Maine Street), but you might want to get there early to get a booth; it's small, popular, and suffused with the aroma of garlic. The specialties are pasta dishes like shells stuffed with spinach and cheeses and topped with marinara and Alfredo sauce ($8.85) and spaghetti with Maine crab and creamy Alfredo sauce ($10.95); cheaper at lunch. Wine and beer served.

Pane Vino II (729-0339), 153 Park Row. An elegant setting in a mansion with outdoor tables in a side garden. Closed Sunday and Monday; open Tuesday through Saturday for breakfast and lunch, dinners Wednesday through Saturday. You might dine on sautéed scallops and roast potatoes on a bed of greens ($13.95) or grilled eggplant with tomato, chick peas, feta, and cilantro salsa served with a mesclun salad ($9.95).

In the Harpswells

J. Hathaway's Restaurant and Tavern (833-5305), Route 123, Harpswell Center. Open from 5 PM for dinner daily except Monday. The Hathaways labor hard to create a casual country atmosphere and delectable dishes that include vegetable lasagna, fish-and-chips, and pork spareribs in the house sauce. They pride themselves on homemade dressings, soups, and desserts. $7.95–13.95.

The Original Log Cabin Restaurant (833-5546), Route 24, Bailey Island. Open mid-March to mid-October, daily for lunch and dinner. A genuine log lodge built as an enormous summer cottage; nice atmosphere with an extensive menu and children's meals. Specialties include chowders and vegetarian dishes. $3–25.

EATING OUT
In Brunswick
Scarlet Begonias (721-0403), 212 Maine Street. Open Monday through Thursday 11–8, Friday 11–9, Saturday noon–9, closed Sunday. In their attractive storefront "bistro," Doug and Colleen Lavallee serve some great sandwiches (we recommend the turkey spinach with mozzarella and basil mayo, grilled on sourdough bread), pastas like Rose Begonia (bacon, chicken, mushrooms, tomato, cream sauce, and fresh herbs over penne), and unusual pizzas.

Joshua's Restaurant & Tavern (725-7981), 121 Maine Street. Open 8 PM–midnight in summer, until 10 in winter. Named for General Joshua Chamberlain (see *Museums*), this is a pubby, pleasant place with seasonal tables on a porch overlooking Maine Street. We can recommend the Chamberlain burger but it's a big menu—plenty of fried and broiled fish, soups, stews, and a wide choice of beers.

Boar's Head New York Style Delicatessen (721-8900), 70 Maine Street. Open 6 AM–8 PM weekdays, weekends from 8, closing 4 PM on Sunday. When you've had one too many lobster or crab rolls this is the place to come for a Reuben, a liverwurst sandwich, maybe even the Lion Tamer (roast beef, ham, turkey, Swiss, tomato, onion, etc.); try a bagel with pastrami for breakfast.

Miss Brunswick Diner (729-5948), 101 Pleasant Street (Route 1, northbound). Open 6 AM–9 PM; Mexican and basic American fare.

Fat Boy's, Route 24, Cooks Corner. This is no '50s reconstruct, just a real drive-in with carhops that's survived because it's so good and reasonably priced (in 1996 a crabmeat roll was $3.50).

In the Harpswells
Holbrook's Lobster Wharf & Snack Bar (725-0708), Cundy's Harbor (4.5 miles off Route 24). Open in-season for lunch and dinner. Lobsters and clams are steamed outdoors. Weekend clambakes; clams, crab rolls, fish-and-chips, homemade salads, and desserts like Barbara's chocolate bread pudding with ice cream. The window boxes are filled with petunias, and you sit at picnic tables overlooking buoys and lobster boats. You can get beer and wine in the shop next door.

The Dolphin Marina (833-6000), South Harpswell (marked from Route 123; also accessible by water). Open year-round, 8–8 daily (but not for breakfast in winter). The nicest kind of small Maine restaurant—family owned and run—with a combo chandlery/coffee shop partitioned from a more formal restaurant by a model of a ketch, overlooking a small but busy harbor. In the morning, fishermen occupy the six stools along the counter; the dining room fills for lunch and dinner (there's often a wait). Chowder, lobster stew, and homemade desserts are specialties, but there is a full dinner menu.

Cook's Lobster House (833-2818), Bailey Island. Open year-round, 11:30 AM–9 PM. A barn of a place, right on the water, adjacent to a working

Maine Festival of the Arts

fishing pier. Save your leftover french fries and muffin crumbs to feed the seagulls on the dock out back. In July and August, try to get there before the Casco Bay Liner arrives with its load of day-trippers from Portland. $2.50–24.

Estes Lobster House (833-6340), Route 123, South Harpswell. Open mid-April through mid-October for lunch and dinner. Another large place on a causeway, with waterside picnic tables across the road. Entrées $2.95–19.95.

Mackerel Cove Restaurant (833-6656), Bailey Island. Open April through mid-October; coffee shop remains open longer. This complex includes a marina, a coffee shop (6 AM–9 PM) that caters to fishermen, and a more formal restaurant (in the pine-paneled, seafood-barn tradition) that serves breakfast, lunch, and dinner. Under new ownership, it specializes in seafood and homemade desserts.

Block & Tackle, Cundy's Harbor Road. Open mid-May to mid-October, 6:30 AM–8 PM. A family-run and -geared restaurant, a real find. Create your own omelet for breakfast; try shrimp stew or a real crabmeat roll for lunch, homemade clam cakes or seafood pie for dinner. The fried lobster platter is top of the menu.

In Lisbon Falls

Graziano's (353-4335), Main Street (Route 196), Lisbon Falls. Open weekdays for lunch and dinner; dinner only on weekends. A much-loved, long-established Italian restaurant, its walls plastered with boxing photos and paintings. You might feast on (large portions of) white pizza with garlic and oil, homemade minestrone, or clams in garlic, olive oil, scallions, and parsley over linguine.

ENTERTAINMENT

Maine State Music Theater (725-8769), Packard Theater, Bowdoin College, Brunswick. Professional musical theater presentations during the summer at 8 PM, except Mondays. Also special children's shows and matinees. **Theater Project of Brunswick** (729-8584), 14 School Street, Brunswick. Serious drama presented year-round. **Bowdoin Summer Music Festival** (725-3322). Performances every Friday evening late June through August. Concerts by music school students, internationally known artists, and music school faculty. Performances are at First Parish Church and Bowdoin College's Kresge Auditorium. **Bowdoin College** (725-3000) performing arts groups from September to May. Concerts and theatrical performances.

SELECTIVE SHOPPING

ARTS AND CRAFTS GALLERIES

Quality galleries at the north end of Brunswick's Maine Street include **O'Farrell Gallery** (729-8228), 58 Maine Street, and **Connections** (725-1399), 56 Maine Street; **Icon Contemporary Art** (725-8157) is around the corner at 19 Mason Street.

Wyler Gallery (729-1321), 150 Maine Street, is a great mix of quality pottery, glassware, jewelry, and fun stuff. Wyler Pottery and Tile Works are also among the studios scattered along Route 123 in Harpswell that welcome visitors; pick up a pamphlet that locates these **Harpswell Craft Guild** members, but call first to make sure they are open.

The Lady and the Loon, Route 24, Bailey Island. Gail Sprague's shop is the kind of place where local residents go for a special gift. Birds and other wildlife are depicted in paintings and on porcelain.

Ma Culley's Old Softies (833-6455), Allen Point Road, just off Route 123 in South Harpswell. Colleen Moser creates truly unusual soft sculptures and says she does not like to sell through stores because she enjoys meeting the people who buy them. She also makes portrait dolls but warns that the recipient must have a sense of humor.

BOOKSTORES

Gulf of Maine Books (729-5083), 134 Maine Street, Brunswick. A laid-back, full-service bookstore with a wide inventory, particularly rich in Maine titles, poetry, and "books that fall through the holes in bigger stores."

Maine Writers & Publishers Alliance (729-6333), 12 Pleasant Street, Brunswick. An inviting bookstore stocking Maine titles and authors, maintained by the state's nonprofit organization dedicated to promoting Maine literature. Frequent workshops, catalog listing, monthly newsletters.

Bookland (725-2313), Cooks Corner Shopping Center, Brunswick. A user-friendly superstore and café in southern Maine's largest bookstore chain.

Old Books (725-4524), 136 Maine Street, Brunswick. Closed Thursday. Upstairs from Gulf of Maine, Old Books features floor-to-ceiling, well-arranged used books and a large stuffed couch, along with friendly nooks for reading.

SPECIAL EVENTS

Throughout the summer: **Farmer's market** (every Tuesday and Friday, May through November) on the downtown Brunswick Mall (the town common). **Beanhole suppers** are staged during summer months by the Harpswell Neck Fire Department.

July: **Annual Lobster Luncheon,** Orrs Island United Methodist Church. **Bailey Island Fishing Tournament** (to register phone Cook's Lobster House at 833-2818). **Great State of Maine Air Show** at the Brunswick Naval Air Station every other year (next in 1997, then in '99).

August: **Topsham Fair** (early), a traditional agricultural fair complete with ox pulls, crafts and food competitions, carnival, and livestock; held at Topsham Fairgrounds, Route 24, Topsham. **Maine Festival of the Arts,** the state's most colorful summer cultural happening, Thomas Point Beach. **A weekend in Harpswell** (late in the month), annual art show, garden club festival in historic homes, and beanhole supper. **Annual Bluegrass Festival,** Thomas Point Beach (off Route 24 near Cooks Corner). **Maine Highland Games,** Thomas Point Beach, a day-long celebration of Scottish heritage, with piping, country dancing, Border collie herding demonstrations, caber tossing, and Highland fling competitions.

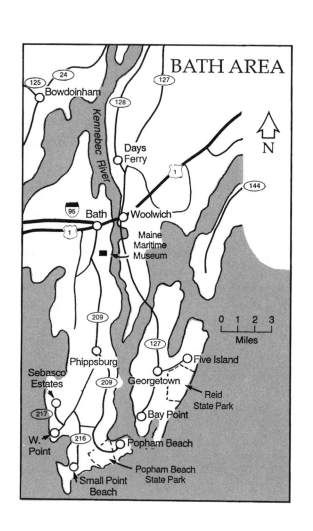

BATH AREA

N

Kennebec River

125
24
Bowdoinham
128
127

Days
Ferry
1
144
95
Bath
Woolwich
1
Maine
Maritime
Museum

209

0 1 2 3
Miles

127
Phippsburg
Five Island
Sebasco
Estates
209
Georgetown
Reid
State Park
217
Bay Point
W.
Point
216
Popham Beach
Small Point
Beach
Popham Beach
State Park

Bath Area

Over the years some 5000 vessels have been built in Bath. Think about it: In contrast to most communities—which retain what they build— here an entire city's worth of imposing structures have sailed away. Perhaps that's why, with a population of fewer than 10,000, Bath is a city rather than a town, and why the granite city hall, with its rounded, pillared facade and cupola (with a Paul Revere bell and a three-masted schooner for a weather vane), seems meant for a far larger city.

American shipbuilding began downriver from Bath in 1607 when the 30-ton pinnace *Virginia* was launched by Popham Colony settlers. It continues with naval vessels that regularly slide off the ways at the Bath Iron Works (BIW).

With almost 9000 workers, BIW employs about the same number of people who worked in Bath's shipyards in the 1850s. At its entrance, a sign proclaims: "Through these gates pass the world's best shipbuilders." This is no idle boast, for many current employees have inherited their skills from a long line of forebears.

Obviously, this is just the place for a museum about ships and shipbuilding, and the Maine Maritime Museum has one of the country's foremost collections of ship models, journals, logs, photographs, and other seafaring memorabilia. It even includes a 19th-century working shipyard. Both BIW and the Maine Maritime Museum are sited on a 4-mile-long reach of the Kennebec River where the banks slope at precisely the right gradient for laying keels. Offshore, a 35- to 150-foot-deep channel ensures safe launching. The open Atlantic is just 18 miles downriver.

In the 1850s Bath was the fourth largest port in the United States in registered tonnage, and throughout the 19th century it consistently ranked among America's eight largest seaports. Its past prosperity is reflected in the blend of Greek Revival, Italianate, and Georgian Revival styles in the brick storefronts along Front Street and in the imposing wooden churches and mansions in similar styles along Washington, High, and Middle Streets.

Today, BIW dominates the city's economy as dramatically as its red-and-white, 400-foot-high construction crane—the biggest on the East Coast—does the city's waterfront. The largest civilian employer in

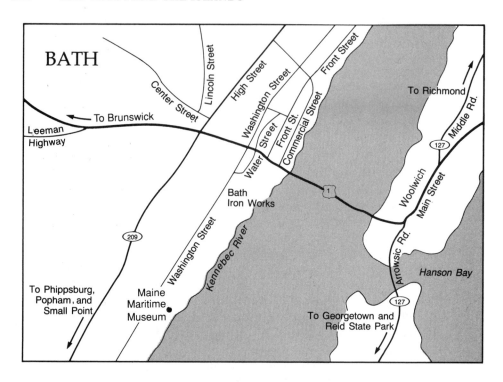

Maine, the company actually produced more destroyers during World War II than did all of Japan, and it continues to keep to its pledge to deliver naval ships ahead of schedule and under budget. Its story is one of many told in the Maine Maritime Museum—for which you should allow the better part of a day. Save another to explore the Phippsburg Peninsula south of Bath. Phippsburg's perimeter is notched with coves filled with fishing boats, and Popham Beach near its southern tip is a grand expanse of sand. Reid State Park on Georgetown Island, just across the Kennebec, is the Mid Coast's only other sandy strand. North of Bath, Merrymeeting Bay draws birders.

GUIDANCE

Chamber of Commerce of the Bath-Brunswick Region (443-9751), 45 Front Street, Bath 04530. Open year-round, weekdays 8:30–5. From mid-June to mid-October, an information center on the northbound side of Route 1, at Witch Spring Hill, is one of the state's busiest. It marks the gateway to Maine's Mid Coast. There are also picnic tables and minimal rest rooms.

For a lodging referral service (including weekends and evenings), phone 725-8797.

GETTING THERE

By car: **Route 1** passes above the city with exits from the elevated road accessing the Carlton Bridge, a bottleneck twice daily when some

9000 employees of BIW come and go to work.

By bus: **Concord Trailways** (1-800-639-3317) stops at the Coastal Plaza on Route 1, and **Mid Coast Limo** (236-2424; 1-800-937-2424) runs to and from the Portland International Jetport.

MEDICAL EMERGENCY

Mid Coast Hospital (443-5524), 1356 Washington Street, Bath. There is also an addiction resource center here.

TO SEE

MUSEUMS

Maine Maritime Museum (443-1316), 243 Washington Street, Bath. Open year-round, 9:30–5 daily; closed Thanksgiving, Christmas, and New Year's Day. Admission is $7 per adult and $4.75 per child ages 6–15 (maximum family admission is $21). Sited just south of BIW on the banks of the Kennebec River, this extensive complex includes the new brick-and-glass **Maritime History Building** and the **Percy & Small Shipyard,** the country's only surviving wooden shipbuilding yard (its turn-of-the-century belts for driving machinery have been restored). The size and solidity of the new building contrast with its setting and the low-slung wooden structures left from the old shipyards. Its exhibits focus, understandably, on the era beginning after the Civil War when 80 percent of this country's full-rigged ships were built in Maine, almost half of these in Bath.

The pride of Bath, you learn, were the Down Easters, a compromise between the clipper ship and old-style freighter that plied the globe during the 1870s through the 1890s, and the big, multimasted schooners designed to ferry coal and local exports like ice, granite, and lime. The museum's permanent collection of artwork, artifacts, and documents is now said to include more than a million pieces, and there is an extensive research library. Permanent exhibits range from displays on Maine's marine industries—fishing and canning as well as shipbuilding and fitting—to the story of BIW.

Did you realize that lobstering in Maine dates back to the 1820s? By the 1880s there were 23 "lobster factories" in Maine, all closed in the 1890s when a limit was imposed on the size of lobsters that could be canned. Visitors are invited to sit on the gunwale of a classic lobster boat and watch a documentary about lobstering narrated by E.B. White.

Woodworkers and wooden-boat buffs will appreciate the lofting models in the mold loft and the details of the cabinetwork in the Joiners Shop, as well as watching the apprentices building wooden boats. Children find hands-on exhibits scattered throughout this sprawling museum—from the World Trade Game in the main gallery to the crow's next in the sandbox boat near the water. Visitors of all ages should take advantage of the narrated boat rides.

Historic District. In the 18th and 19th centuries, Bath's successful ship-building and seafaring families built impressive mansions on and around upper Washington Street. Sagadahoc Preservation, Inc., offers walking tours; ask for a schedule at the chamber of commerce (see *Guidance*). The historical society also produces an excellent folder, "Architectural Tours—Walking and Driving in the Bath Area," available from the chamber of commerce.

✍ **1910 Farmhouse,** Woolwich Historical Society Museum (443-4833), Route 1 and Nequasset Road, Woolwich. Open 10–4 daily, July through Labor Day. $2 per adult, $1 children 6–12. An admirable, small museum run by volunteers, this rambling farmhouse displays an intriguing collection of antique clothing and quilts, plus seafaring memorabilia, all gleaned from local attics.

SCENIC DRIVE

The Phippsburg Peninsula. From the Maine Maritime Museum, drive south on Route 209, down the narrow peninsula making up the town of Phippsburg, pausing at the first causeway you cross. This is **Winnegance Creek,** an ancient shortcut between Casco Bay and the Kennebec River; look closely to your left and you'll see traces of the 10 tidemills that once operated here.

Continue south on Route 209 until you come to the Phippsburg Center Store on your right. Turn left on Parker Head Road opposite, into the tiny hamlet of **Phippsburg Center.** This is one of those magical places, far larger in memory than in fact—perhaps because it was once larger in fact, too. Notice the huge linden tree (planted in 1774) between the stark Congregational church (1802) and its small cemetery. Also look for the telltale stumps of piers on the shore beyond, remnants of a major shipyard. Just off Route 209, note the **Phippsburg Historical Museum** (open in summer Monday through Friday 2–4, and by appointment: 442-7606).

Continue along the peninsula's east shore on the Parker Head Road, past a former millpond where ice was once harvested. At the junction with Route 209, turn left. The road threads a salt marsh and the area at Hoss Ketch Point, from which all traces of the ill-fated **Popham Colony** have long since disappeared. Route 209 winds around **Sabino Head** and ends at the parking lot for **Fort Popham,** a granite Civil War–era fort (with picnic benches) at the mouth of the Kennebec River. A wooded road, for walking only, leads to World War I and II fortifications that constitute **Fort Baldwin Memorial Park;** a six-story tower yields views up the Kennebec and out to sea.

Along the shore at **Popham Beach,** note the pilings, in this case from vanished steamboat wharves. Around the turn of the century, two big hotels served the passengers who transferred here from Boston to Kennebec River steamers, or who simply stayed a spell to enjoy the town's spectacular beach. Now **Popham Beach State Park,** this immense expanse of sand remains a popular destination for fishermen, beach walkers, sunbathers, and even a few hardy swimmers. From Popham Beach return to Route 209 and follow it west to Route 217 and out to **Sebasco Estates,** then back up to Phippsburg Center.

TO DO

BICYCLING
Bath Cycle and Ski (442-7002), Route 1, Woolwich, rents bikes and cross-country skis.

BOAT EXCURSIONS
Maine Maritime Museum Cruises (443-1316). Mid-June to mid-October, the museum (see *To See*) offers periodic daylong special-interest cruises along the Mid Coast, as well as up the Kennebec River and across Merry-meeting Bay.

M/V *Ruth,* based at Sebasco Estates (389-1161), offers a variety of coastal excursions on the New Meadows River and into Casco Bay. **M/V *Yankee*** (389-1788) offers mid-June through Labor Day excursions from Hermit Island Campgrounds at Small Point. **Seguin Navigation Co.** (443-1677), Arrowsic, offers half- and full-day sails. **Lighthouse Lobsterboat Tours** (389-1838; 721-3629) offers fishing and sight-seeing, also lobster dinners aboard a 32-foot "lobster yacht," departing Fort Popham.

CANOE AND KAYAK RENTALS
Taylor Rentals (725-7400), 271 Bath Road, Brunswick, rents canoes to explore Merrymeeting Bay. **Dragonworks, Inc.** (666-8481), in Bowdoinham on Merrymeeting Bay, sells white-water and sea kayaks and offers instruction.

FISHING
Surf fishing is popular at Popham Beach, and there's an annual mid-August Bluefish Tournament in Waterfront Park. Nearly 20 boats offer fishing on the river, and both **Kennebec Charters** (389-1883) and ***Kayla D & Obsession* Sportfishing Charters** (442-8581; 443-3316) offer deep-sea-fishing charters.

GOLF
Bath Country Club (442-8411), Whiskeag Road, Bath. Pro shop, 18 holes. **Sebasco Lodge** (389-1161), Sebasco Estates. Nine-hole course and putting green. Primarily for hotel guests; open to the public by reservation. Late June to early September only.

SWIMMING
If you are traveling with a dog, it is important to know that they are allowed only in picnic areas, not on the beaches.

Charles Pond, Route 27, Georgetown (about 0.5 mile past the turnoff for Reid State Park; 15 miles down the peninsula from the Carlton Bridge). Often considered the best all-around swimming hole in the area, this long and narrow pond has clear water and is surrounded by tall pines.

✐ **Pleasant Pond** (582-2813), Peacock Beach State Park, Richmond. Open Memorial Day through Labor Day. A sand and gravel beach with lifeguards on duty. Water depth drops off gradually to about 10 feet in a 30-by-50-foot swimming area removed from boating and enclosed by colored buoys. Picnic tables and barbecue grills. Admission is $1.50 adults, $.50 ages 5–11; under 5 free.

✐ **Popham Beach State Park** (389-1335), via Route 209 south from Bath to Phippsburg and beyond. A 3-mile-long expanse of sand at the mouth of the Kennebec River. Also a sandbar, tidal pools, and smooth rocks. Never overcrowded, but it can be windy. Day-use fees of $1.50 per adult and $.50 per child ages 5–11 (under 5 free) are charged from mid-April until mid-October.

✐ **Reid State Park** (371-2303), Route 127, Georgetown (14 miles south of Bath and Route 1). Open daily year-round. The bathhouse and snack bar overlook 1½ miles of sand in three distinct beaches that seldom become overcrowded, although the limited parking area does fill by noon on summer weekends. You can choose surf or slightly warmer sheltered backwater, especially good for children. Entrance fees of $2 per adult and $.50 per child ages 5–11 (under 5 free) are charged between mid-April and mid-October.

SPECIAL LEARNING PROGRAM

Shelter Institute (442-7938), 38 Center Street, Bath 04530. A year-round resource center for people who want to build or retrofit their own energy-efficient home. Two- and 3-week daytime courses are offered May to October; Saturday-morning classes are given during the winter. Tuition varies according to course taken.

GREEN SPACE

✐ **Fort Baldwin Memorial Park,** Phippsburg. An undeveloped area with a six-story tower to climb for a beautiful view up the Kennebec and, downriver, out to sea. There are also remnants of fortifications from World Wars I and II. At the bottom of the hill is the site where the Popham Colony struggled to weather the winter of 1607–08, then built the pinnace *Virginia* and sailed away to Virginia.

✐ **Fort Popham Memorial Park** (389-1335 in-season) is located at one tip of Popham Beach. Open Memorial Day through Labor Day. Picnic sites are scattered around the ruins of the 1861 fort, which overlooks the beach.

Josephine Newman Wildlife Sanctuary, Georgetown. Bounded on two sides by salt marsh, 119 acres with 2 miles of walking trails. Look for the sign on Route 127, 9.1 miles south of Route 1.

Bates–Morse Mountain Conservation Area comprises some 600 acres extending from the Sprague to the Morse River and out to Seawall Beach. Allow 2 hours for the walk to and from this unspoiled private beach. There's a great view from the top of Morse Mountain. Pack a picnic and towel, but please, no radios or beach paraphernalia. Seawall Beach is an important nesting area for piping plovers and least terns.

Hamilton Sanctuary, West Bath. Situated on a peninsula in the New Meadows River, offering a 1½-mile trail system and great bird-watching. Take the New Meadows exit off Route 1 in West Bath; turn left on New Meadows Road, which turns into Foster Point Road; follow it 4 miles to the sanctuary sign.

LODGING

RESORTS

Sebasco Lodge (389-1161; 1-800-225-3819), Sebasco Estates 04565. Open late June to early September. A traditional New England summer resort (ownership has changed only once since the 1930s), this 600-plus-acre, self-contained complex includes a saltwater pool and a nine-hole golf course plus putting green. Other amenities include swimming at a private beach, hiking, boating, lobster cookouts, live entertainment, and special evening programs. Choose a cabin, cottage, or lodge room (98 rooms in all). Rates are MAP: $85–155 per person per night, double occupancy. B&B rates available in shoulder seasons; inquire about packages.

Rock Gardens Inn (389-1339), Sebasco Estates 04565. Open mid-June through late September. Next door to Sebasco Estates Lodge, Rock Gardens Inn accommodates just 60 guests, providing a more intimate atmosphere than the larger resort but offering access to all its facilities (see above). The inn perches on the edge of the water, banked, as you'd expect, in a handsome rock garden, and has its own heated swimming pool. Guests gather in the comfortable living room, library, and old-fashioned dining room with round tables and cornflower-blue wooden chairs. There's a welcoming Sunday cocktail party and a weekly lobster cookout. There are three rooms in the inn and 10 cottages, each with living room, fireplace, and sun porch. Most rooms have water views. $148–220 per couple MAP ($93–112 per person); 5-night minimum in July and August. Inquire about weeklong art workshops offered in June, July, and September.

BED & BREAKFASTS

Grey Havens (371-2616), Seguinland Road, PO Box 308, Georgetown 04548. Open mid-April to mid-December. The donor of the land for neighboring Reid State Park also built this turreted, gray-shingled summer hotel, opened in 1904, with a huge parlor window—said to have been Maine's first picture window. The large common room is hung with baskets, furnished comfortably, and warmed with a huge stone fireplace. The long porch, half screened and half open, is well equipped with rocking chairs from which to survey the sweep of islands and bay. The 12 rooms upstairs (private baths) range from small doubles to large, rounded turret rooms; half have water views and all have brass or iron beds and Victorian furniture. While it has been run by members of the same Texas family since 1976, the atmosphere has shifted noticeably as the family members in charge have changed; it's currently casual and friendy. Dinner is no longer served, but guests can cook their own lunch or dinner in the great old hotel kitchen. $100–195 (half that off-season) for a two-room oceanfront suite with balcony; $60–185 for a double. "Hearty continental" breakfast; 2-night minimum on weekends and holidays.

The Inn at Bath (443-4294), 969 Washington Street, Bath 04530. Open year-round. In the historic district, Nick Bayard's rambling, elegantly restored 1810 mansion offers twin parlors with a marble fireplace and six carefully decorated guest rooms with a choice of twin, double, queen, or king beds (all private baths), three rooms with working fireplaces. All guest rooms have air-conditioning, phone, cable TV, VCR, and cassette tape radio alarm. One room is handicapped accessible. Rooms are $65–115; the suite, $115–150. Children welcome and pets accepted selectively. The fee for a third guest is $25.

Fairhaven Inn (443-4391), North Bath Road, Bath 04530. Open year-round. Hidden away on the Kennebec River as it meanders down from Merrymeeting Bay, this 1790s house has eight pleasant guest rooms, six with private bath. The new owners, Dave and Susie Reed, stayed here as guests some 20 times before buying the place. The inn's 16 acres of meadow invite walking in summer and cross-country skiing in winter (the 10-acre golf course nearby makes for even more skiing). Two-night minimum stay on holidays and on weekends in July and August. In-season rates, including a full breakfast, are $70–90.

Captain Drummond House (389-1394), Parker Head Road, PO Box 72, Phippsburg 04562. Open seasonally. Just off Route 209, halfway between Bath and Popham Beach, this historic, circa-1770 home sits on a secluded, 125-foot bluff above the Kennebec River with views of woods, coves, and lighthouses. While innkeepers Donna Dillman and Ken Brigham are now living at their new B&B, the Captain's Watch (see "Brunswick"), this is still a homey but elegant retreat with three guest rooms, one with a private, second-floor balcony and others with private entrances, plus a small suite. $75–100 double; two-room suite $110–130 in-season. Inquire about renting the whole house by the week.

Popham Beach Bed & Breakfast (389-2409), Popham Beach 04562. Open early May until late October. The former Coast Guard Station, built in 1883 right on Popham Beach, has been restored as a posh B&B. Four guest rooms and a tastefully decorated suite with water views, all with private bath; $65–115 in low season and $80–145 in high includes a full breakfast.

Packard House (443-6069), 45 Pearl Street, Bath 04530. Open year-round. A gracious 1790 Georgian home in the heart of the historic district, one block from the Kennebec. Once owned by Benjamin F. Packard, partner in one of the world's most successful shipbuilding companies (the captain's quarters of the clipper *Benjamin F. Packard* are displayed at Mystic Seaport in Connecticut). Three elegant guest rooms with period furnishings. Common space includes a fenced patio. $65 double with private bath, $90 for a suite with private bath and sitting room; includes full breakfast.

Stonehouse Manor (389-1141), HCR 32, Box 369, Route 209, Phippsburg 04563. Open year-round. Set off the road in a large field beside a small lake, this rambling old fieldstone-and-shingle house exudes the style of Maine's grand old cottages. Two of the five large rooms have their own fireplace, and each has a lake or bay view and private bath. Jane and Tim Dennis serve a full breakfast. $75–175 per couple.

The 1774 Inn at Phippsburg Center (389-1774), Parker Head Road, Phippsburg 04562. Open year-round. Once the home of Maine's first congressman, later owned by the area's premier shipbuilder, this house dominates the road through the center of one of the Kennebecs' most picturesque villages. There are four large, Federal-style guest rooms and a beautifully proportioned main stairway you'll want to go up and down again and again. Debbie and Joe Braun plan to add more rooms in the riverside carriage house soon. $75–115.

The Front Porch B&B (443-5790), 324 Washington Street, Bath 04530. Closed January through April. No view but a homey, turn-of-the-century B&B whose atmosphere is a blend of Victorian and country; practically across the street from BIW and the Maine Maritime Museum. In addition to two rooms in the house, there is an efficiency apartment with private bath in the carriage house. Rooms are $55–75; an ambitious breakfast featuring sourdough French toast and homemade blueberry syrup is included. Pets are accepted in the carriage house.

✐ **Small Point Bed & Breakfast** (389-1716), Route 216, Sebasco Estates 04565. A comfortable, informal 1890s farmhouse with three guest rooms and one suite, handy to beaches, boats, and hiking; accepts children and pets by prior arrangement. $55–80, less off-season, full breakfast included.

Riverview (389-1124), HCR-31, Box 29, Phippsburg 04562. Open May through October. Alice Minott's riverside home is one of the oldest Capes (1830) in the area. It's in Phippsburg Center (see *Scenic Drive*). Three guest rooms, one private bath. Two-night minimum weekends and holidays. $30 single, $50 double with continental breakfast.

Coveside–Five Islands Bed and Breakfast (371-2807), Five Islands 04548. Open year-round. Ten miles down Route 127 from Route 1, beyond the turnoff for Reid State Park. Coveside is a 100-year-old farmhouse with a new wing and a large deck, offering three guest rooms (private baths), all with water views. This very special place is currently for sale; it's well worth checking, however.

Glad II (442-1191), 60 Pearl Street, Bath 04530. Open April through October. A 145-year-old home that's an unassuming, old-fashioned bed &

breakfast within an easy walk of downtown shops and restaurants; one twin-bedded room and one double. Common rooms are air-conditioned. $50 double includes breakfast.

Edgewater Farm Bed & Breakfast (389-1322), Route 216, Small Point 04565. A restored, circa-1800 farmhouse set in 4 acres of gardens and fruit trees. New owners Bill and Carol Emerson have added new life to this wonderfully positioned place, just up the road from the entrance to the Bates–Morse Mountain Conservation area (see *Green Space*). There are five guest rooms, a screened sun porch, and a shaded deck. $70 with shared bath, $85 with private.

OTHER LODGING

🖉 **New Meadows Inn** (443-3921), Bath Road, West Bath 04530. Open year-round, with the exception of the cottages (open late May to mid-October). A good family place, with rooms for two, cottages for more, including two log cabins. Dining room with shore dinners, traditional family fare, snacks, salad bar, and buffets. Private docking and marina facilities. Rates: $30–40 for double rooms, $40–60 for cottages.

🖉 **Hermit Island** (443-2101), 42 Front Street, Bath 04530. This 255-acre, almost-island at Small Point offers 275 nicely scattered camping sites, 63 on the water. Only tents and pop-ups are permitted. Owned since 1953 by the Sewall family, Hermit Island also has a central lodge with a recreation room and snack bar where kids can meet. Campers can enjoy the island's private beaches and unspoiled woods and meadows. $22–28 per night; less off-season.

Cottage listings are available from the Chamber of Commerce of the Bath-Brunswick Region (see *Guidance*) and in the Maine Publicity Bureau's "Maine Guide to Camp and Cottage Rentals." (Also see *Cottage Rentals* in "What's Where in Maine.")

WHERE TO EAT

DINING OUT

The Robinhood Free Meetinghouse (371-2188), Robinhood Road, off Route 127, Robinhood. Open daily mid-May through mid-October for dinner (5:30–9) and Sunday brunch. Michael Gagne, the former chef at the nearby Osprey, has turned the vintage 1855 Robinhood Free Meetinghouse into an attractive dining space, decorated with local art, all for sale. The menu is so immense that it's academic to cite selections but the day we visited you could choose from wild mushroom with hazelnut or black bean soup ($4.25 per cup), and appetizers included asparagus in puff pastry ($5.75) and corn-fried oysters with fresh salsa and cream ($8). Among the 37 entrées ($16–20) were veal Oscar with Maine crabmeat, asparagus, and roasted red potatoes and grilled double breast of duck with beurre rouge and five herbs, wild rice, and lingonberry turnovers. The wine list is extensive, as is the choice of wine by the glass ($4–6).

The Osprey (371-2530), at Robinhood Marina, Robinhood (just off Route 127, near Reid State Park). Open spring through fall for lunch and dinner, Sunday brunch; fewer days off-season. Reservations appreciated and a must on summer weekends. Overlooks a boatyard and, yes, there is an osprey nest on the day marker; you can see it from the window. Atmosphere is minimal but the cuisine is elegant. The large menu changes often; it might include such appetizers as local shrimp and crabcakes, roast garlic aioli, and crispy vegetable salsa ($6) and entrées like blackened local tuna steak with roasted potatoes, cucumber salsa, and grilled vegetables ($20). Leave room for raspberries with crème anglaise ($6.50) or dark chocolate mousse with Grand Marnier ($6.50).

☞ **Kristina's** (442-8577), corner of High and Center Streets, Bath. Closed January, otherwise open daily, year-round, Monday through Saturday 8 AM–9 PM, Sunday 9 AM–2 PM. Newly renovated, very attractive dining room, outdoor dining on the tree-shaded deck in summer. What began as a simple room with booths and a bakery case has grown into a sophisticated, two-level restaurant and cocktail lounge. You'll still find the same great quiche, cheesecake, and other incredible breads and pastries (which you can still buy to go at the bakery counter) for which it was first known (inquire about the bread of the day: anadama on Saturday, Swedish orange bread on Tuesday, etc.), plus such entrées as pepper-grilled salmon fillet with Spanish gazpacho sauce or chicken pot pie in cheddar cheese crust. Entrées $8–15.

J.R.Maxwell's (443-4461), 122 Front Street, Bath. Open year-round, in the middle of the shopping district, in a renovated 1840s building that was originally a hotel. Predictable burgers, salads, crêpes, seafood sandwiches, also dinner steaks, chicken, Maine seafood, and Sunday brunch. Children's menu. Exposed old brick walls, hanging plants. Downstairs is the **Boat Builder's Pub,** with live bands on weekends. Dinner for two with wine is around $40.

EATING OUT

✎ **Beale Street Barbeque & Grill** (442-9514), 215 Water Street, Bath. Open 11 AM–9 PM. Brothers Mark and Mike Quigg have built their slow-cooking pits and are delivering the real Tennessee (where Mark lived for six years) goods: pulled pork, ribs, sausage, a big Reuben, also nightly specials (frequently fish) to round out the menu. This place is well worth finding but you almost have to know it's there, in a renovated old BIW building behind Reny's (see *Special Shops*).

✎ **Front Street Deli and Club** (443-9815), 128 Front Street, Bath. Open year-round 8 AM–11 PM. A storefront with inviting booths and standard breakfast and lunch fare, soup of the day, good pies. Downstairs is the Club, mismatched sofas and couches, same food, cocktail lounge

✎ **Spinney's Restaurant and Guest House** (389-1122), at the end of Route 209, Popham Beach. Open weekends in April and daily May to October for lunch and dinner. Our kind of beach restaurant: counter and tables, pleasant atmosphere with basic chowder-and-a-sandwich menu. Pete and Jean Hart specialize in fried fish and seafood but they also serve it steamed and broiled; good lobster and crabmeat rolls. Beer, wine, and cocktails. Inexpensive to moderate.

- **Lobster House** (389-1596), Small Point (follow Route 1 to Route 126). Open summer season only. Mrs. Pye's is a classic lobster place specializing in seafood dinners and homemade pastry; it's down near Small Point, surrounded by salt marsh. Beer and wine are served.
- **The Water's Edge** (389-2756), Sebasco Estates. Open daily 11–9, Mother's Day to mid-September. The Varian family are fishermen who take pride in serving the freshest fish and seafood. Pasta and meat dishes are also on the menu. Right on a commercial fishing wharf, the restaurant is decorated with nets, lobster pots, and photos of old vessels; there's also a take-out window and picnic tables. Reservations are advised for dinner.
- **Georgetown Fisherman's Co-op** (371-2950), 13 miles south of Route 1 on Route 127 at the Five Islands wharf in Georgetown. Open seasonally, specializing in steamed lobsters and clams, lobster rolls; snack bar menu.
- **Sarah's Cafe** (442-0996), Customs House, 1 Front Street, Bath. A branch of the popular Wiscasset restaurant, open for lunch 10–2, specializing in salads, sandwiches, and desserts; some seating on the lawn by the Kennebec.

ENTERTAINMENT

Center for the Arts at the Chocolate Church (442-8455), 804 Washington Street, Bath. Year-round presentations include plays, concerts, and a wide variety of guest artists. Special children's plays and other entertainment are included on the schedule. The handsome church has been completely restored inside. There is also a very nice gallery at the Chocolate Church (so-called because of the chocolate color of this Greek Revival building).

SELECTIVE SHOPPING

ART AND ARTISANS

Georgetown Pottery, Route 127, Georgetown (about a mile south of the Carlton Bridge). Jeff Peters produces an extensive selection of dishes, mugs, and other practical pottery pieces, including hummingbird feeders and soap dishes. **The Five Islands Gallery.** Open seasonally at the wharf at Five Islands at the end of Route 127. This deceptively small gallery is cooperatively run by five genuinely interesting local artists; we especially like the fanciful wood carvings and ceramic pieces by Jack Schnider.

FLEA MARKET

Montsweag Flea Market (443-2809), Route 1, Woolwich (just south of
Montsweag Farm Restaurant). A field filled with tables weighted down
by every sort of collectible and curiosity you could imagine. It is a
beehive of activity every day during the summer and on weekends
in spring and fall. Antiques, rather than flea-market finds, are featured
on Wednesdays.

SPECIAL SHOPS

Bath's Front Street is lined with mid-19th-century, redbrick buildings.
Among the gift shops, don't overlook **Reny's** (86 Front Street), one in a
small chain of Maine department stores that are good for genuine bargains. **Springer's Jewelers** (76 Front Street) is a vintage emporium
with mosaic floors, chandeliers, and ornate glass sales cases.

Woodbutcher Tools (442-7939), 191 Water Street, Bath. The Shelter Institute (see *Special Learning Programs*) maintains this woodworker's
discovery, specializing in hard-to-find woodworking tools.

Dronmore Bay Farm (443-4228), Route 209, Phippsburg. Spread along
the ridge above Cutting Creek, this cheerful spot offers a formal garden
stroll and a wide variety of herbs, wildflowers, fruits, and vegetables.
The shop is a nice mix of antiques, seasonal gifts crafted by local artisans, and Millie Clifford's arrangements of dried flowers.

SPECIAL EVENTS

Three days surrounding the Fourth of July: **Bath Heritage Days,** a grand
celebration with an old-time parade of antique cars, marching bands,
clowns, guided tours of the historic district, craft sales, art shows, musical entertainment in two parks, a triathlon, and Firemen's Follies featuring bed races, bucket relays, and demonstrations of equipment and
fire-fighting techniques. Fireworks over the Kennebec.

Second Saturday in July: **Popham Circle Fair** at the Popham Chapel features the sale of birdfeeders (shaped like the chapel) that residents
make all year; profits keep the chapel going.

July and August: Wednesday-evening concerts by the **Bath Municipal
Band,** Library Park.

December: **"Old Fashioned Christmas,"** all month: competitions, special
events.

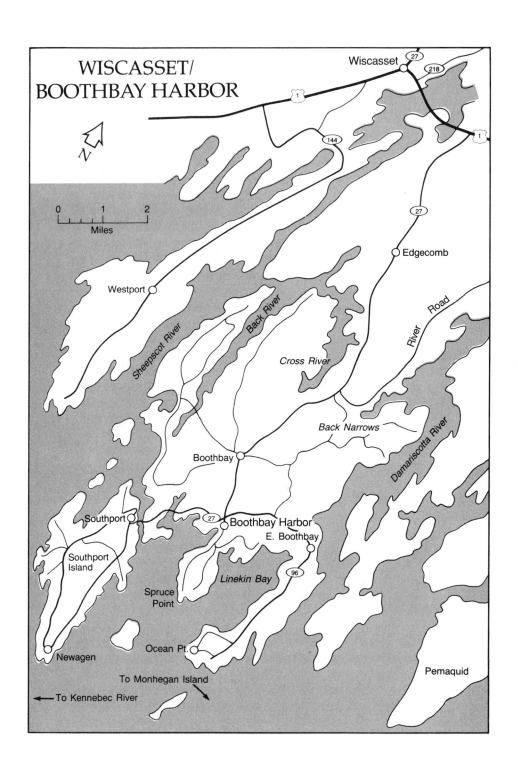

WISCASSET/
BOOTHBAY HARBOR

Wiscasset

N

0   1   2
Miles

Edgecomb

Westport

Sheepscot River

Back River

Cross River

River Road

Back Narrows

Damariscotta River

Boothbay

Southport

Boothbay Harbor

E. Boothbay

Southport
Island

Linekin Bay

Spruce
Point

Newagen

Ocean Pt.

Pemaquid

To Monhegan Island

To Kennebec River

Wiscasset

Wiscasset is Maine's gift to motorists toiling up Route 1. After hours of ho-hum highways, here is finally a bit of what Maine is supposed to look like. Sea captains' mansions and mid-19th-century shops line the road as it slopes toward the Sheepscot River.

Still the shire town of Lincoln County, Wiscasset is only half as populous as it was in its shipping heyday, which—as the abundance of clapboard mansions attests—came after the American Revolution but before the Civil War. Several buildings are open to the public, and many more house shops, galleries, and restaurants. Even in the height of the summer season, this village is a peaceful place to explore. The weathered remains of two early-19th-century schooners, the *Hesper* and the *Luther Little,* are picturesquely positioned just offshore and are purported to be the most photographed shipwrecks in the world.

GUIDANCE

Wiscasset does not have a chamber of commerce, but **Wiscasset Hardware** (882-6622), on Water Street (to your left just before you cross the bridge from Wiscasset to Edgecomb), stocks local brochures. Park at the Water Street entrance and walk up through the appliances; built in 1797 as a chandlery, this hospitable establishment also offers an upper deck on which to get your bearings with a cup of coffee and river view. **Big Al's** on Route 1 just before town also stocks local brochures.

GETTING THERE

Concord Trailways (1-800-639-3317) stops here en route from Portland to Bangor. **Mid Coast Limo** runs to and from the Portland International Jetport (1-800-834-5500 in Maine; 1-800-937-2424 outside Maine). **Downeast Flying Service** (882-6752) offers air charters year-round. **Wiscasset Taxi** (758-1679) serves a 60-mile radius of town, including the airports in Portland, Damariscotta, and Boothbay Harbor.

PARKING

If you can't find a slot along Main Street, you can always find one in the parking lot or elsewhere along Water Street.

MEDICAL EMERGENCY

Bath Memorial Hospital (443-5524), 1356 Washington Street, Bath.

VILLAGES

Sheepscot Village. North on Route 218 from Wiscasset; look for the sign in about 4 miles. An unusually picturesque gathering of 19th-century buildings.

Head Tide Village. Eight miles up Route 218 (follow sign), an early-19th-century village that was the birthplace of poet Edward Arlington Robinson; note the Old Head Tide Church (1838), open Saturday 2–4. Watch for the swimming hole beneath the old milldam.

TO SEE

HISTORIC HOMES

Musical Wonder House (882-7163), 18 High Street. Open daily for guided tours, mid-May to mid-October, 10–5 (fewer tours after Labor Day). An intriguing collection of music boxes, reed organs, pump organs, Victrolas, and other musical machines displayed in a fine 1852 sea captain's mansion. Visitors are taken on tours of the house during which the various machines are played and demonstrated. Tours of just the ground floor are $10 per person (discounts for children and senior citizens); tours of the entire house are by reservation only. They take about 3 hours and are $30 per person, two for $50. The gift shop at the Musical Wonder House is open 10–6 every day that the museum is open (no admission charge). Ask about 8 PM candlelight concerts.

Nickels-Sortwell House, corner of Main and Federal Streets. Open June 1 through September, Wednesday through Sunday 12–5 (last tour begins at 4). $4 adults, $3.50 seniors, $2 children 12 and under. This classic, Federal-era mansion in the middle of town was built by a ship owner and trader. After he lost his fortune, the house became a hotel for many years. In 1895, a Cambridge, Massachusetts, mayor purchased the property; some of the furnishings date from that time. It is now one of five historic house museums in Maine operated by the Society for the Preservation of New England Antiquities. The elliptical staircase is outstanding.

Castle Tucker (882-7364). Open July and August, Tuesday through Saturday 11–4, and in late June and September by appointment; you're also welcome to walk around the grounds when the house is closed. Adults $3, ages 6–12, $.50. An unusual, privately owned mansion overlooking the Sheepscot River. It was built in 1807 by Judge Silas Lee, who overextended his resources to present his wife with this romantic house. After his death it fell into the hands of his neighbors, to whom it had been heavily mortgaged, and passed through several owners until it was acquired in 1858 by Captain Richard Holbrook Tucker. Captain Tucker, whose descendants still own the house, added the elegant portico. Castle Tucker is said to be named after a grand house in Scotland. Highlights include a free-standing elliptical staircase, Victorian furnishings, and original wallpapers.

HISTORIC SITES

Lincoln County Museum (882-6817), Federal Street (Route 218). Open July and August, Tuesday through Sunday 11–4:30 (last tour at 4). $2 per adult, $1 age 12 and under. The museum comprises a chilling 1811 jail (in use until 1913) with damp, thick granite walls (some bearing interesting 19th-century graffiti), window bars, and heavy metal doors; plus the jailer's house (in use until 1953), with displays of tools and changing exhibits. Includes an antiques show in August.

Pownalborough Court House (882-6817), Route 128, off Route 27, Dresden (8 miles north of Wiscasset). Open July and August, Wednesday through Saturday 10–4 and Sunday 12–4. $3 adults, $1 under 13. Worth the drive. The only surviving pre–Revolutionary War courthouse in Maine, it is maintained as a museum by the Lincoln County Historical Association. The three-story building, which includes living quarters for the judge upstairs, gives a sense of this countryside along the Kennebec in 1761 when it was built to serve as an outpost tavern as well as a courtroom. This site is still isolated, standing by a Revolutionary War–era cemetery and a picnic area; there are nature trails along the river. Special events include a mustering of the militia and wreath-laying ceremonies on Memorial Day and a cider pressing in October.

Lincoln County Courthouse. Open during business hours throughout the year. Built in 1824, this handsome redbrick building overlooking the town common is the oldest functioning courthouse in New England.

Fort Edgecomb State Memorial (882-7777), Edgecomb (off Route 1; the turnoff is just across the Sheepscot River's Davey Bridge from Wiscasset, next to the Muddy Rudder restaurant). The fort is open May 30 through Labor Day, daily 9–6. $1; pay in the box. This two-story octagonal blockhouse (built in 1809) overlooks a narrow passage of the Sheepscot River. For the same reasons that it was an ideal site for a fort, it is today an ideal picnic site. Tables are provided on the grassy grounds.

Wiscasset, Waterville, & Farmington Railway Museum, Sheepscot Station, Alna 04535 (about 5 miles north of Wiscasset). Interest in Maine's 2-foot narrow-gauge railroad has rallied in recent years, and this is one of the latest efforts to revive history. The line stopped operations in 1933. The museum includes an engine house/shop, a replica of the original Sheepscot station, an original flatcar, and the oldest 2-footer locomotive in the United States. The goal is to rebuild and run trains on a portion of the original line. Open Saturday 9–5.

OTHER

Sunken Garden, in the center of town. You go down a few steps to this little garden surrounded by a stone wall. Many varieties of flowers and trees, and a couple of benches and chairs.

Morris Farm (882-4080), Route 27, Wiscasset. A community working farm, open to the public during daylight hours for walking, hiking, and picnicking with rolling pastures, forest trails, a pond, waterfall, and streams. Also an education center, offering a day camp for children, farm tours, various workshops throughout the year, and special events. Farmer's market Saturday mornings from May through August.

World's Smallest Church, Route 218. There is barely room for two worshipers in this tiny chapel, maintained as a memorial to a former Boston Baptist minister.

TO DO

✐ **Downeast Flying Service** (882-6752), Wiscasset, offers year-round sightseeing and fall foliage flights ($15 per person for a half hour); must have three passengers.

☞✐ **Maine Coast Railroad** (882-8000; 1-800-795-5404), at the Wiscasset Town Landing (Water Street, next to Le Garage restaurant). Memorial Day through Columbus Day. Excursions through the coastal countryside to Newcastle and back aboard a bright red, restored 1920s train; $10 per adult, $5 per child ages 5–12, $25 per family of two adults and up to four children. Ask about special events and rail/sail packages.

LODGING

INNS

Squire Tarbox Inn (882-7693), RD 2, Box 620 (Route 144), Wiscasset 04578 (turn off Route 1 onto Route 144 just south of Wiscasset). Open mid-May to late October. The inn is on Westport Island, 8.5 miles down a winding country road from Route 1. The handsome, Federal-style farmhouse (begun in 1763, completed in 1825) offers 11 inviting guest rooms and an atmosphere that's a mix of elegance (in the common rooms and dining room) and working goat farm. Guests are invited out to the barn to visit the goats and see how innkeepers Bill and Karen Mitman make their cheeses (Tellicherry pepper, herb and garlic, and jalapeño as well as plain). They can also take advantage of the swing hanging from the barn rafters. Other animals on the farm include a horse, two donkeys, laying hens, and a cat. A path leads through the woods to a saltwater inlet where a screened area is equipped with binoculars and a birding book, and where a rowboat awaits your pleasure. Four large, formally furnished guest rooms are in the original house, while seven more country-style rooms are in the 1820s converted barn. All have private baths and either king or queen beds. Goat cheese is served in the gracious parlor at the cocktail hour, and the player piano in the music room adds a lively touch. A five-course, candlelit dinner (see *Dining Out*) is served at 7 by the big, open fireplace in the attached ell, whose ceiling beams were once ship's timbers. Doubles $139–220, depending on the season, including breakfast and dinner; $85–166 for bed & breakfast; add 12 percent gratuity.

The Bailey Inn (882-4214), Main Street, Wiscasset 04578. A longtime landmark inn (formerly the Ledges), now named for a doctor who lived and practiced here in the early 1900s. The inn was renovated in recent years, and the seven rooms are pleasant, with private baths. Inquire about what's been done to eliminate road noise. $85 including breakfast; $75 off-season.

BED & BREAKFASTS

☞ **Marston House** (882-6010; 1-800-852-4157), Main Street, PO Box 517, Wiscasset 04578. Open May through November. The front of the house is a shop featuring American antiques. In the carriage house behind this building—well away from the Route 1 traffic noise—are two exceptional rooms, each with private entrance, working fireplace, and private bath. They adjoin each other and can become a two-bedroom suite perfect for families. Breakfast is served in the beautiful gardens or in your room, and features fresh fruit, yogurt, home-baked muffins, and fresh orange juice. $75 for a double, $65 single. No smoking.

Snow Squall (882-6892; 1-800-775-7245), corner of Bradford Road and Route 1, Wiscasset 04578. Open year-round (November through April by reservation only, with a 2-night minimum stay). Mary Lou and Bob Madsen offer elegant accommodations in this 1850s house, named for a clipper ship that was wrecked in the Falkland Islands (a piece of the ship is on display at the inn). The seven rooms, each named after a clipper ship built in Maine, offer private baths, king or queen beds. Three are large two-bedroom suites (two in the carriage house are ideal for families). Two guest rooms have fireplaces, as does the library. Doubles are $85–140; carriage house suites accommodating two to four people are $125–195. Full breakfast included.

The Stacked Arms (882-5436), Birch Point Road, Wiscasset 04578. Open year-round except January. Dee Maguire offers two guest rooms with shared bath and one suite with a private bath. Rooms are cozy, and have orthopedic beds and small refrigerators. $65–75 double; $45 single.

OTHER LODGING

Edgecomb Inn (882-6343; 1-800-437-5503), Box 51, North Edgecomb 04556 (off Route 1, across the bridge from Wiscasset). Open all year. Commands a fine view of Wiscasset; 25 rooms (including efficiency suites) and 15 cottages. Next door, the Muddy Rudder serves lunch and dinner daily (see *Eating Out*). Doubles $79–110 in-season.

WHERE TO EAT

DINING OUT

Squire Tarbox Inn (882-7693), Route 144, Westport Island (also see *Inns*). Open mid-May through late October, by reservation only. A candlelit,

A popular eatery in Wiscasset

five-course dinner is served in an 18th-century former barn with a large fireplace reflecting off ceiling beams that were once ship's timbers. Dinner is preceded by a cocktail hour (6 PM) featuring a complimentary selection of savory goat cheeses (made here by innkeepers Karen and Bill Mitman) served variously in the living room, in the less formal game room, by the player piano, or out on the deck. Dinner begins at 7. The menu changes frequently but might include chicken chèvre patisserie, a boneless breast stuffed with herbed goat cheese, encased in pastry, and baked; roast lamb tenderloin; or a seafood medley of lobster, shrimp, scallops, and whitefish in a cream reduction sauce. The light-as-air whey rolls are made with goat's milk. After dessert, which might be a chocolate concoction or homemade vanilla ice cream with a fresh fruit sauce, guests are invited to visit the barn to pat the friendly Nubian goats as they line up for milking. The prix fixe is $31 per person.

☞ **Le Garage** (882-5409), Water Street, Wiscasset. Open year-round, except January, for lunch, dinner, and Sunday brunch. A 1920s-era garage, now an exceptional restaurant with a glassed-in porch overlooking the Sheepscot River (when you make reservations, request a table on the porch). At dinner, many large, wrought-iron candelabra provide the illumination. The menu features plenty of seafood choices, steaks, and vegetarian meals. Entrées are $7.50–17.95. "Light suppers" are also available for $6.95 or $7.95, giving you the option of smaller portions of many menu selections. The lunch menu features omelets and crêpes, soups and salads, as well as sandwiches. Lunch is $5.95–9.95.

The Bailey Inn (882-4214), Main Street, Wiscasset (see *Inns*). Serves breakfast, lunch, and dinner daily, year-round. Light fare is offered in the pub in the attached carriage house. Dinner is served in the more formal dining rooms (linens and candles); a recent menu ranged from broiled or poached salmon with hollandaise sauce and shrimp scampi over egg-and-spinach fettuccine to Moroccan chicken served over a bed of rice with vegetables. $8.95–16.95.

EATING OUT

Red's Eats, Water Street, just before the bridge, Wiscasset. Open April through September until 2 AM on Friday and Saturday, until 11 weeknights, and until 9 on Sunday. Al Gagnon has operated this classic hot dog stand since 1977. Tables on the sidewalk and behind, overlooking the river. A Route 1 landmark for the past 60 years, good for a quick crab roll or pita pocket as well as a hot dog. Special children's meals.

Sarah's Pizza and Cafe (882-7504), Main Street, Wiscasset. Open daily 11– 9. This popular restaurant fills two storefronts. Offerings, prepared from scratch, include exceptionally good pizza (try the Greek pizza with extra garlic), sandwiches in pita pockets or baked in dough, plus delicious homemade breads, soups, desserts, vegetarian dishes, Mexican fare, and lobster 10 different ways. Wine and a wide choice of beers, including Maine microbrews, are also served.

Muddy Rudder (882-7748), Route 1, North Edgecomb (across the bridge from Wiscasset). Open year-round 11–11 daily, Sunday jazz brunch. Extensive menu includes sandwiches, seafood, steaks, and more served in a riverside room with an outdoor deck. Children's menu.

The Sea Basket (882-6581), Route 1 south of Wiscasset. A cheerful diner with lobster stew the *New York Times* has declared to be the best in Maine.

SELECTIVE SHOPPING

ANTIQUES SHOPS

More than a dozen antiques shops (most carry a leaflet map/guide) can be found in town and just south on Route 1; many specialize in nautical pieces and country primitives.

ART GALLERIES

Maine Art Gallery (633-5055), Warren Street (in the old 1807 academy), Wiscasset. Exhibits by Maine artists; special programs are offered year-round.

Wiscasset Bay Gallery (882-7682), Water Street; changing exhibits, specializing in 19th- as well as 20th-century Maine and New England marine and landscape paintings.

ARTISANS

Sheepscot River Pottery (pastel, floral designs), Route 1 just north of Wiscasset in Edgecomb. **Sirus Graphics,** Wiscasset; mostly made-in-Maine crafts, original-design T-shirts. **Feed the Birds,** Port Wiscasset Building, Water Street; birdhouses, feeders, accessories.

Boothbay Harbor Region

The water surrounding the village of Boothbay Harbor brings with it more than just a view. You must cross it—via a footbridge—to get from one side of town to the other, and you can explore it on a wide choice of excursion boats and in sea kayaks. It is obvious from the very lay of this old fishing village that its people have always gotten around on foot or in boats. Cars—which have room neither to park nor to pass each other—are an obvious intrusion. The peninsula's other coastal villages, Southport and East Boothbay, also do not lend themselves to exploration by car. Roads are walled by pines, permitting only occasional glimpses of water.

Boats are what all three of the Boothbays have traditionally been about. Boats are built, repaired, and sold here, and sailing and fishing vessels fill the harbors. Excursions range from an hour-long sail around the outer harbor to a 90-minute crossing (each way) to Monhegan Island. Fishermen can pursue giant tuna, stripers, and blues, and nature lovers can cruise out to see seals, whales, and puffins.

Good public beaches are, unfortunately, something that the Boothbays lack entirely; but the resorts and many of the more expensive motels have pools and private beaches, and there are warm-water lakes and ponds. In the middle of summer, Boothbay Harbor resembles a perpetual carnival: Crowds mill along the wharf eating ice cream cones, fudge, and taffy, shopping for souvenirs, and queuing for excursion boats. You get the feeling it's been like this every summer since the 1870s. Still, you can find plenty of timeless peace and beauty in the Boothbays. Most lodging places and summer cottages hug the ocean.

GUIDANCE

Boothbay Harbor Region Chamber of Commerce (633-2353), PO Box 356, Boothbay Harbor 04538 (open year-round), publishes an annual guide to the area and maintains a Route 27 office (across from the mini-mall) stocked with brochures. **The Boothbay Information Center** (633-4743), farther up Route 27 (open 9–9 daily, Memorial through Columbus Day), is an unusually friendly walk-in center that does its best to help people without reservations find places to stay. It keeps an illustrated scrapbook of options, also a cottage rental list. *Note:* You can call either of the above numbers to find out who has current vacancies.

GETTING THERE

Mid Coast Limo runs to and from the Portland International Jetport (1-800-834-5500 within Maine; 1-800-937-2424 outside Maine). **Wiscasset Taxi** (758-1679) also serves the Boothbays. Boothbay Harbor is 12 miles south on Route 27 from Route 1, 14 miles from Wiscasset, the nearest **Concord Trailways** bus stop (see "Wiscasset").

GETTING AROUND

A free **trolley-on-wheels** runs daily in-season from the parking lot at the Meadow Shopping Center on Route 27. It circulates between the Rocktide Motor Inn on the east side of the harbor and the shops on the west. Runs daily July and August, every 30 minutes, 7–11 AM (check current schedule).

PARKING

In-town parking is limited, and if you can't squeeze into a metered space, the going fee is a flat $5. The large parking lot at the Meadow Shopping Center on Route 27, the trolley terminus, is free.

MEDICAL EMERGENCY

St. Andrew's Hospital (633-2121), Hospital Point, Mill Cove, Route 27 South, Boothbay Harbor. A well-respected shoreside hospital, St. Andrew's serves the community by land and by water (the hospital has a pier).

TO SEE

Boothbay Region Art Foundation (633-2703), 7 Townsend Avenue, Boothbay Harbor. Open daily, 11–5 weekdays and Saturday, 12–5 on Sunday. Three juried shows are held each season in the 1807 Old Brick House. Works are selected from submissions by artists of the Boothbay region and Monhegan Island.

Boothbay Region Historical Society Museum (633-3666), 70 Oak Street, Boothbay Harbor. Open July and August, Wednesday, Friday, and Saturday 10–4; off-season, Saturday 10–2 and by appointment (633-3462).

Hendricks Hill Museum, Route 27, Southport Island. Open July and August, Tuesday, Thursday, Saturday 11–3. An old boardinghouse displays pictures of Southport's old boardinghouses and hotels as well as other village memorabilia, wooden boats, and farm implements.

Boothbay Railway Village (633-4727), Route 27 (1 mile north of Boothbay Harbor). Open daily 9:30–5, mid-June through Labor Day; daily 9:30–4:30 until Columbus Day weekend. Now operated as a museum, the 2-foot, narrow-gauge railway wends its way through a re-created, miniature, turn-of-the-century village made up of several restored buildings including vintage railroad stations, the Boothbay Town Hall (1847), and the Spruce Point chapel (1923). Displays include a general store and a doll museum. More than 50 antique autos (1907–1949) are also on display. Admission is $6 per adult and $3 per child. Many special events, including a large weekend antique auto meet (more than 250 cars) in the latter part of July.

Marine Resources Aquarium (633-9542), McKown Point Road, West Boothbay Harbor. A small aquarium, but well worth the trip. Displays include one touch tank with a shark and skates and another large touch tank with many various species. Daily presentations in July and August at 11, 1, and 3. Open 10–5 daily from Memorial Day weekend through Columbus Day weekend. $2.50 adults; $2 ages 5–18 and over 60; 4 and under free.

TO DO

BICYCLING

Harborside Bike Rental (633-4303; 1-800-734-7171) on Boothbay House Hill rents every kind of bike; **Tidal Transit Co.** (633-7140) rents mountain bikes.

BOAT EXCURSIONS

Balmy Days Cruises (633-2284; 1-800-298-2284), Pier 8, Boothbay Harbor. *Balmy Days II* offers supper cruises and sails every morning early June to late September and weekends in shoulder seasons to Monhegan (see "The Islands"); the crossing is 90 minutes each way, and you have close to 4 hours on the island. A half-hour boat ride around the island is sometimes offered ($2). Bring a picnic and hit the trail. *Novelty* offers 1-hour harbor tours all day, and *Bay Lady* is a 31-foot Friendship sloop that offers five 90-minute sails in the outer harbor, including a sunset sail. *Maranbo II* operates as a harbor ferry during July and August to Southport, Ocean Point, and Spruce Point. Call for schedule. All are available for private charter.

✐ **Boothbay Steamship Company** (633-2500), Pier 6, Fisherman's Wharf. Operates late May to late October. Trips aboard *The Islander* and *Islander III* include seal-watches, lighthouse sight-seeing, sunset and music cruises. Kids under 6 are free. Check the cruise board for specials.

Boothbay Whale and Bird Watch, (633-4574), Tugboat Inn Marina, has whale-watches and sunset nature cruises daily, guided by naturalists; full bar, galley, and rest rooms.

✐ **Cap'n Fish Boat Cruises** (633-3244, 633-2626; 1-800-636-3244), Pier 1 (red ticket booth). Operates mid-May to mid-October, 7 days a week. A variety of cruises including whale-watches, puffin nature cruises, Pemaquid Point lighthouse, seal-watches, and sunset sails. Friday is senior citizens' day on 2-hour trips. Coffee, snacks, soft drinks, beer, wine, and cocktails are available on board (don't bring your own). Children under 12 are half price. Reservations recommended. Check for special cruises, too.

BOAT RENTALS

Holladay Marine (633-4767), Route 27, West Boothbay Harbor. Half- and full-day charters, with or without a captain, aboard a variety of Tartan sloops. Weekly charters also.

Midcoast Boat Rentals (882-6445), Pier 8, Boothbay Harbor, rents powerboats.

DEEP-SEA FISHING

Sportfishing boats include *Yellowbird* and *Buccaneer,* both operated by Captain Fish, and *Breakaway* (633-6990), with Captain Pete Ripley. The catch is mackerel, tuna, shark, bluefish, and stripers.

GOLF

Boothbay Region Country Club (633-6085), Country Club Road (off Route 27), Boothbay. Open spring through late autumn. Nine holes, restaurant and lounge, carts, clubs for rent.

HORSEBACK RIDING

✐ **Ledgewood Riding Stables** (882-6346), Route 27 and Old County Road, Edgecomb. Horses and trails for all levels of expertise. Hourly rates.

SAILING

Several traditional sailing yachts offer to take passengers out for an hour or two, a half day, or a day. These include ***Appledore V*** (633-6598), a 60-foot windjammer that has sailed around the world; and ***Heart's Desire*** (633-6808), a restored, 45-foot schooner built in 1925, taking up to six people sailing from Smuggler's Cove Inn in East Boothbay. The Friendship sloop ***Eastward*** (633-4780) is skippered by Roger Duncan, lecturer on local history and author of the New England sailor's bible, *A Cruising Guide to the New England Coast,* plus several other sailing reference works. (Also see *Bay Lady* under Balmy Days Cruises in *Boat Excursions.*) ***Tribute*** (882-1020), a racing yacht, sails from Ocean Point.

SEA KAYAKING

Tidal Transit Co. (633-7140) offers guided tours.

TENNIS

✐ **Boothbay Region YMCA** (633-2855), Route 27 (on your left as you come down the stretch that leads to town). An exceptional facility open to nonmembers (use-fee charged) in July and August, with special swimming and other programs for children. Worth checking out if you will be in the area for a week or more. A wide variety of programs for all ages: tennis, racquetball, gymnastics, aerobics, soccer, swimming, and more.

Public tennis courts are located across the road from the YMCA, next to the Boothbay Region High School, Route 27, on the way into Boothbay Harbor.

GREEN SPACE

BEACHES

✐ The beaches are all private, but visitors are permitted in a number of spots. Here are four: (1) Follow Route 27 toward Southport, across the Townsend Gut Bridge to a circle (white church on your left, monument in the center, general store on your right); turn right and follow Beach Road to the beach, which offers roadside parking and calm, shallow water. (2) Right across from the Boothbay Harbor Yacht Club (Route 27 south), just beyond the post office and at the far end of the parking lot, is a property owned by the yacht club, which puts out a float by July. There are ropes to swing from on the far side of the inlet, a grassy area in which to sun, and a small sandy area beside the water; but the water is too deep for small children. (3) **Barrett Park,** Lobster Cove (turn at the Catholic church, east side of the harbor), is a place to picnic and get wet. (4) **Grimes Cove** has a little beach with rocks to climb at the very tip of Ocean Point, East Boothbay. (Also see Knickerkane Island Park under *Preserves.*)

PRESERVES

Boothbay Region Land Trust (633-4818) preserves 740 coastal acres, including six properties open to and easily accessible by the public: **Porter Preserve** (19 wooded acres including a beach) on Barter's Island; **Ovens Mouth Preserve** (146 acres with hiking trails by swift tidal water, quiet coves, and salt marshes); **Linekin Preserve** (a 94.6-acre parcel with 2⅓ miles of hiking trails) on Route 96 south of East Boothbay; **Marshall E. Saunders Memorial Park** (22.5 acres) and **Kitzi Colby Wildlife Preserve** (12 acres), both on the Damariscotta River; and **Singing Meadows** (a 16-acre former saltwater farm in Edgecomb).

Knickerkane Island Park, Barter's Island Road, Boothbay. Paths lead from the parking lot onto a small island with picnic tables, swimming.

LODGING

The chamber of commerce lists over 100 lodging places, from resorts to bed & breakfasts to campgrounds and cottages. Families should explore the possibilities of the area's many rental cottages. Because the chamber of commerce is open year-round, it's possible to contact the people there in time to reserve well in advance. See *Guidance* for the numbers you can call to check current vacancies in the area.

RESORTS

Newagen Seaside Inn (633-5242; 1-800-654-5242), Route 27, Southport Island, Cape Newagen 04552. Open mid-May through September. A landmark with a present style dating from the '40s when it was destroyed by fire. Peter and Heidi Larsen rejuvenated this authentic, informal inn at the seaward tip of Southport Island when they purchased the property in 1987. Just 6 miles "out to sea" from Boothbay Harbor, it feels worlds away. Secluded among the pines, the inn's lawn sweeps down to a mile of bold coastline. Sunset Rock is a peaceful place to sit overlooking the water in the evening. There are 26 rooms in the main inn, all with private baths. The four new first-floor rooms all have private decks, and two are completely handicapped accessible. Heated freshwater pool, large saltwater pool, two tennis courts, many lawn games, and rowboats. Meals are served in the new screened dining area. Buffet breakfast is included in rates; lunch and dinner are also available. Doubles $88–175, depending on room and season. Children are just $10–15 extra. Cottages begin at $750 per week; use of all facilities is included.

Ocean Point Inn (633-4200; 1-800-552-5554), PO Box 409, East Boothbay 04544. Open Memorial Day through Columbus Day. Set on 12 acres at the tip of Ocean Point Peninsula, but only 10 minutes from Boothbay Harbor. A cluster of traditional white clapboard buildings adorned with flower boxes filled with red geraniums houses 60 rooms, most with ocean views and porches. David and Beth Dudley have owned the historic inn since 1985, and David worked here for many years before they bought it, creating a real sense of continuity and traditions here. All rooms and cottages have private baths, cable TV, mini-refrigerators, phones; some have fireplaces. Guests can relax in Adirondack chairs by the large heated outdoor pool overlooking a picturesque seawall. The inn offers an oceanfront dining room (see *Dining Out*). $86–135 in-season, cottages from $85.

INNS

☞ **Albonegon Inn** (633-2521), Capitol Island 04538 (follow Route 27 to Route 238 in Southport; look for sign). Memorial Day to mid-October. "Determinedly old-fashioned" and proud of it, this inn is a true haven from the 20th century. It is an integral part of the 1880s gingerbread-style summer colony that fills Capitol Island, linked to the real world by a tiny bridge. Innkeeper Kim Peckham grew up summering on Capitol Island, and her great-grandfather stayed at the Albonegon in the 1890s (his signature is in the guest register); preserving its spirit as well as its structure is a labor of love. The summer's profits are visibly reinvested, most recently in storm windows, new linens, and a new living room rug. The 11 rooms in the main inn are simple but inviting. From the bed in room 35 you can lie on your side and watch a lobsterman setting his traps. Because this place was built as, rather than converted into, an inn, you find that the shared bath system works exceptionally well: Each room is fitted with a sink, and there are half- and full baths for every few rooms. Best of all are the porches, hung over the water and lined with classic green rockers. Guests are welcome to grill their own steaks or burgers right here if they would rather not budge from this incredible view at sunset. Fresh-baked muffins, coffeecake, and breads are served each morning in the informal dining room that shares this view. There are three rooms in separate buildings next to the inn (also on the water's edge) with private bathrooms. Two can be joined to form a cottage with two bedrooms, a kitchen, and a living room. The third, called Barnacle, is small and adorable. $70–120 for a double.

Lawnmeer Inn (633-2544; 1-800-633-7645), Box 505, West Boothbay Harbor 04575 (on Route 27 on Southport Island, 2 miles from downtown Boothbay Harbor). Open mid-May to mid-October. The location is difficult to beat, with broad lawns sloping to the water's edge. Most of the 13 comfortably decorated rooms in the main inn, and the 18 rooms (with decks) in the motel wing, have water views; there's also a small cottage. The Lawnmeer was built as a summer hotel in the 1890s. It has a small, personal feel with lots of attractive common space including the fireplace room with plenty of books, a small lounge, and a porch with a hammock. There is also a popular restaurant (see *Dining Out*). Small pets are accepted, depending on the room. $60–150 single or double occupancy, depending on season. Two-night minimum weekends in July and August.

BED & BREAKFASTS

Five Gables Inn (633-4551; 1-800-451-5048), Murray Hill Road (off Route 96), PO Box 335, East Boothbay 04544. Open mid-May through mid-November. Built around 1865, this rambling building has been renovated into an unpretentious but luxurious B&B. Mike and De Kennedy purchased the inn in 1995, and are preserving the historic feel while offering guests modern conveniences, such as private baths. Fifteen thoughtfully furnished rooms have ocean views; most have queen-sized beds (many with handmade quilts), and five have working fireplaces. There are rocking chairs on the wraparound veranda and a welcoming fireplace in the common room; an extensive buffet breakfast, prepared by Mike, a Culinary Institute of America graduate, is included in $90–155 double. Afternoon tea is also offered. Children over 8 welcome.

Welch House (633-3431), 36 McKown Street, Boothbay Harbor 04538. Open May through late October. A spectacular view of the harbor and islands beyond can be enjoyed from most of the 16 individually decorated rooms (some canopy beds), all with private baths. We prefer the 10 rooms in the 1850 sea captain's house to those in the adjacent Sail Loft (more modern decor). Exceptional views from a third-floor observation deck, main deck, and glass-enclosed breakfast room where an electric kettle can always be used to make tea and coffee. Breakfast buffet includes homemade muffins and granola, as well as hot entrées, maybe banana blueberry pancakes or French toast. $55–125. Two-night minimum stay weekends from July 4 through Labor Day. No smoking in the house.

Hodgdon Island Inn (633-7474), Barter's Island Road, Boothbay (mailing address: Box 492, Boothbay 04571). Open most of the year. On a quiet road overlooking a cove, this B&B offers six attractive rooms with water views in a restored sea captain's house. All have private baths and ceiling fans, and two of the rooms share a porch. Sydney and Joseph Klenk are helpful hosts and justly pride themselves on their heated, chlorine-free swimming pool set in a landscaped garden. Common space includes a room with TV, VCR, books, and games; a large front porch with white wicker furniture; and benches on the waterfront. Full breakfast includes fresh fruit, muffins, cereal, and a hot entrée. $65–95. Two-night minimum stay in July and August and on holiday weekends.

Kenniston Hill Inn B&B (633-2159; 1-800-992-2915), Route 27, Boothbay 04537. Open year-round. A stately, 200-year-old pillared Colonial (one of Boothbay's oldest homes) set back from the road as it curves around to the Boothbay town green. Ten comfortable guest rooms, all with private baths; five have working fireplaces. There are also fireplaces in the dining room and the common area. Relax amid 4 acres of fields and perennial gardens, walk to the Boothbay Country Club for golf, or drive the couple of miles down to the harbor. The full country breakfast may include peaches-and-cream French toast, ham and Swiss in puff pastry, or three-cheese pie with tomato and sweet basil. $69–110 single or double, breakfast included. Inquire about dinner by reservation off-season.

Jonathan's (633-3588), 15 Eastern Avenue, Boothbay Harbor 04538. Open most of the year. Named for that famous seagull, this 100-year-old Cape offers three bedrooms, all with private baths, and a double or twin beds (can be made into a king). In a quiet neighborhood, but just a few minutes' walk from downtown Boothbay Harbor. Grounds include a deck and beautiful gardens, and there is a fireplace in the parlor for colder weather. $65–85, including a full breakfast and afternoon refreshments and sherry. Inquire about special winter weekend packages.

Atlantic Ark Inn (633-5690), 64 Atlantic Avenue, Boothbay Harbor 04538. Open late May through late October. Furnished with antiques and Oriental rugs, this pleasant B&B is removed (but accessible by footbridge) from the bustle of the harbor. Six rooms in the inn, plus a cottage; all have private baths and most have queen-sized beds (some mahogany four-posters). Some rooms have harbor views and private balconies. One of the third-floor rooms has a cathedral ceiling, an oak floor, a Jacuzzi with a view, and French doors opening onto a balcony. This room can be combined with the other third-floor room to form a suite with a private entrance. Full breakfast might include zucchini crescent pie or Scottish popovers. Beverages (spring water, for example) are served in the afternoon. $70–149; $199 for cottage. Two-night stays encouraged on major holiday weekends.

☞✐**Emma's Guest House and Cottages** (633-5287), 110 Atlantic Avenue, Boothbay Harbor 04538. Open May through October. An old-fashioned guest house with five rooms (all with private bath), plus efficiency cottages on Spruce Point and in East Boothbay. A very homey atmosphere, like visiting an old friend. Each room accommodates three or four people. Water views. Pets are accepted in cottages. Rooms are $35–55, including continental breakfast.

COTTAGES

Note: Contact the chambers of commerce (see *Guidance*) for lists of rental cottages; quality is traditionally high and prices are affordable in the Boothbays. In addition the **Boothbay Cottage Connection** (663-6545) represents 80 properties.

☞⌀**Hillside Acres Motor Court** (633-3411), Route 27 (Adams Pond Road), PO Box 300, Boothbay 04537. Open mid-May through mid-October. Seven cabins, including four efficiency units, plus an apartment and two B&B rooms, all on a quiet hillside not far from Boothbay Harbor. Electric heat, showers, color TVs. Swimming pool. Complimentary muffins, coffee cake, and coffee are served mid-June through Labor Day. $40–68; weekly rates, too.

MOTELS

Boothbay Harbor has a number of inviting motels, but we defer to the Mobil and AAA guides.

ISLAND

Fisherman's Island (212-288-0804; Cherokee Station, Box 20692, New York, NY 10021-0073). A mansion built in 1930 on a 68-acre island just off Ocean Point, beyond the Ram Island light. There are now six nicely appointed guest rooms (five doubles and a children's dorm), all with sumptuous baths and, of course, water views. The 55-foot-long beamed Great Room, which has two fireplaces and a cathedral ceiling, is stocked with antique games and plenty of books for foggy days. A powerboat and skipper come with the house, as do memorable meals prepared by Judy Kinson. Her husband, Jim, keeps a herd of sheep on the island. Swimming options include a pool as well as a shingle beach. $12,000 per week includes all meals and shuttle service to and from East Boothbay. It works as a reunion spot for families or friends (ideally five couples with a total of no more than five children). .

WHERE TO EAT

DINING OUT

The Black Orchid (633-6659), 5 By Way, Boothbay Harbor. Seasonal, open daily for dinner except Tuesday. A family-owned trattoria serving classic Italian dishes with a twist, like fettuccine Alfredo with fresh lobster meat and mushrooms, rolled stuffed scaloppine, and baked haddock with tomatoes and lemon pesto. In the less formal **Bocce Club Cafe** upstairs, there are seafood and raw oyster bars. No more than six people per table. No smoking. Entrées $10.95–24.95.

Lawnmeer Inn (633-2544; 1-800-633-7645), Route 27, Southport Island (just across the bridge). Open for breakfast and dinner daily, mid-May through mid-October (open for dinner in June, closed Monday in the fall). Reservations appreciated. This very pleasant dining room sports large windows overlooking the water. The menu changes frequently but might include appetizers like sautéed Maine crabcakes on a spinach bed and entrées like a shrimp tart (gulf shrimp sautéed with caramelized onion and tomato served in puff pastry with fresh rosemary). Some people come just for dessert. $14.95–20.95.

Spruce Point Inn (633-4152), east side of outer harbor at Spruce Point. Open mid-June to mid-September; reservations advised. A gracious, old-fashioned inn with a sophisticated menu to match its decor. Entrées might include marinated breast of chicken with tropical salsa, north Atlantic salmon grilled or pan roasted in a dill sauce, or cioppino. $14.75–24.50.

Newagen Seaside Inn (633-5242), Cape Newagen, Southport Island. Open for breakfast, lunch, and dinner seasonally, closed for dinner on Tuesday. A pleasant, old-fashioned dining room with ocean and sunset views, and splendid grounds to walk off the entrées. Chef Alan Milchik delights diners with entrées like lobster thermidor, tournedos Rossini, and Cajun popcorn. Desserts are wonderful. $23.95 includes a cup of chowder, salad, entrée, and dessert, or you can order à la carte. Breakfast is a delightful buffet.

Brown Brothers Wharf (633-5440), Atlantic Avenue, Boothbay Harbor. Dining room opens in mid-June. One of Maine's better-known seafood restaurants, the largest in the area. Family owned and operated since 1945. Seafood and steaks; a variety of lobster dishes. Breakfast buffet and dinner.

The Harbour High Restaurant (633-3444), Boothbay Harbor (across the street from the post office). Open year-round for lunch and dinner. Entrées include sautéed sole fillet, roast duck teriyaki, and eggplant parmigiana. They also sell smoked Atlantic salmon on the premises. $11.95–18.95; children's portions (and prices) available.

Ocean Point Inn Restaurant (633-4200), East Boothbay. Open mid-June through Columbus Day weekend. This historic inn has been serving dinner for over 100 years. Three informal dining rooms, all with ocean and sunset views. You might dine on lobster brioche, wildberry chicken, or the house specialties, crabcakes, fresh Maine salmon (prepared four ways), and Black Angus steaks. Menu for wee appetites. $4.95–19.95.

EATING OUT

Carriage House (633-6025), Ocean Point Road, East Boothbay. Open year-round, daily 11–10. This friendly eatery offers entrées ranging from a fried fisherman's platter and a wide choice of charbroiled beef cuts to a good selection of pastas and sandwiches. There are luncheon specials and a daily all-you-can-eat haddock fry.

Ebb Tide (633-5692), Commercial Street, Boothbay Harbor. Open year-round. Great breakfasts are served all day plus lobster rolls, club sandwiches, and fisherman's platters. Homemade desserts like peach shortcake are wonderful. An old-fashioned place with knotty-pine walls, booths; look for the red-striped awning.

No Anchovies (633-2130), just off Townsend Avenue, Boothbay Harbor, at the entrance to the public parking lot. A pleasant, informal Italian restaurant with especially good pizza and imaginative toppings.

Fisherman's Wharf (633-5090; 1-800-628-6872), Boothbay Harbor. This is a large place that can accommodate groups and bus tours. It overlooks the water, and has an outside deck. Nicely prepared seafood, boiled lobster, and other standard fare. Three meals are served daily. Reservations recommended for parties of six or more.

1820 House at Smuggler's Cove (632-2800; 1-800-633-3008), East Boothbay. A glass-walled dining room with a very pleasant atmosphere specializing in broiled fish, chicken, and steak. Unique wine selections. Children's menu.

Andrew's Harborside Restaurant (633-4074), Boothbay Harbor (downtown, next to the municipal parking lot and footbridge). Open daily, May through October, for breakfast, lunch, and dinner. The chef-owner specializes in creative seafood and traditional New England dishes. Wonderful cinnamon rolls. Round Top Ice Cream is dispensed from a window at the parking lot level.

✎ **Chowder House Restaurant,** (633-5761), Granary Way, Boothbay Harbor (beside the municipal parking lot and footbridge). Serves lunch and dinner daily mid-June through Labor Day. A restored old building that also houses several small shops. Seating is around an open kitchen and on a waterside deck. There is also a new outdoor boat bar. Chowders, lobster stew, salads, homemade breads, seafood, and full dinners. Homemade pies. Lunch menu offered all day for those with smaller appetites.

MacNab's (633-7222; 1-800-884-7222), Back River Road (first driveway on your left), Boothbay. Open Tuesday through Sunday 11–6. Billed as "the area's only Scottish tea room," serving cock-a-leekie soup, scone sandwiches, and Highland pie as well as tea and scones; afternoon tea ($10.95) and high tea ($21.95) by reservation.

☞ **Everybody's** (633-6113), Route 27. Open year-round for breakfast, lunch, and dinner. A casual, inexpensive place that's very popular with locals. All sorts of salad entrées plus light suppers and dinners. Sandwiches at lunchtime.

J.H. Hawk Ltd. (633-5589), Boothbay Harbor (right on the dock in the middle of town, upstairs). An inviting restaurant liberally decorated with nautical artifacts, offering a large menu ranging from basic burgers to pastas and steaks, pan-blackened fish, and meat in Louisiana Cajun–style. Ask about live entertainment.

✎ **Brud's Hotdogs,** in the middle of the village and on the east side of the harbor. Keep an eye out for Brud's orange motorized cart—he has been selling juicy dogs around town for more than 50 summers.

Crump's (633-7655), 20A McKown Street, Boothbay Harbor. A tiny English dining room serving ploughman's lunches, cappuccino and espresso, and, in the afternoon, authentic Devonshire cream teas with scones and finger sandwiches. There's also a small gift shop on the premises, with many items from Great Britain. Everything on the menu can be packed to go, perfect for a picnic.

Dunton's Doghouse, Signal Point Marina, Boothbay Harbor. Open May through September, 11–8. Good, reasonably priced take-out food, including a decent $4.25 crabmeat roll.

Bravo's (633-7323), 2 Boothbay House Hill. A Mexican restaurant in the former dinner-theater building. A large, cheerful place, with traditional

Mexican entrées as well as more adventurous offerings like lobster tacos and seafood chimichangas. Large portions. Lounge with entertainment and dancing.

LOBSTER POUNDS

Robinson's Wharf (633-3830), Route 27, Southport Island (just across Townsend Gut from West Boothbay Harbor). Open mid-June through Labor Day; lunch and dinner daily. Children's menu. Sit on the dock at picnic tables and watch the boats unload their catch. Pick out your lobster before it's cooked, or buy some live lobsters to prepare at home. Seafood rolls, fried shrimp, clams, scallops, fish chowder, lobster stew, sandwiches, and homemade desserts. Takeout available.

Boothbay Region Lobstermen's Co-op (633-4900), Atlantic Avenue (east side of the harbor). Open mid-May to mid-October, 11:30–8. Boiled lobsters and steamed clams to be eaten at picnic tables on an outside deck on the water or indoors. Corn on the cob, fried seafood dinners, desserts.

Lobsterman's Wharf (633-3443), Route 96, East Boothbay (adjacent to a boatyard). Open mid-May through Columbus Day. Popular with locals. Boiled lobsters to eat at the outside tables over the water or inside. The menu also includes a wide variety of more complex entrées, like fried calamari and barbecued baby-back ribs.

Clambake at Cabbage Island (633-7200). The *Argo* departs Pier 6 at Fisherman's Wharf daily in summer, twice on Saturday and Sunday, carrying passengers to Cabbage Island for a clambake (including steamed lobsters). An old lodge, built in 1900, seats up to 100 people by a huge fireplace.

The Lobster Dock (633-7120), at the east end of the footbridge. Open seasonally noon–8:30. When downtown Boothbay restaurants are packed, you can walk across the footbridge to this relatively peaceful little place, offering both inside and outside lunches and dinners, fried fish, and the usual sandwiches plus lobster and shore dinners, steamed clams and mussels.

SNACKS

Downeast Ice Cream Factory (633-2816), Boothbay Harbor (on the byway). Homemade ice cream and make-your-own sundae buffet; all sorts of toppings, including real hot fudge.

Suzanne's Pastries (633-2200), 15 McKown Street, Boothbay Harbor. Delicious fresh-baked goods and plenty of gourmet coffee choices. Indoor and outdoor seating.

ENTERTAINMENT

Carousel Music Theatre (633-5297), Route 27, near Boothbay Harbor. Performances mid-May to late October. Doors open at 6:30 PM; show begins at 7. Closed Sunday. Light meals (sandwich baskets and such) and cocktails are served by the cast before they hop onto the stage to sing

Broadway tunes cabaret-style and then to present a fully costumed and staged revue of a Broadway play.

Thursday-evening concerts by the Hallowell Band on the library lawn, Boothbay Harbor. July 4 through Labor Day, 8 PM.

Lincoln Arts Festival (633-4676). Concerts throughout the summer in varied locations.

SELECTIVE SHOPPING

ART GALLERIES

The Butke Studio and Gallery (633-3442), Sawyer's Island, Boothbay. Housed in an old barn featuring regional paintings and crafted gifts and clothing.

Footbridge Studio (633-0741), right in the middle of the footbridge, located in the old bridge tender's house. Open Memorial Day through October. Exclusive designs include a collection of miniature buildings by a local artist, pine needle baskets, and prints of Ethel Fowler artwork.

A pamphlet lists several galleries in East Boothbay. Ask for one at the chamber of commerce (see *Guidance*).

ARTISANS

Andersen Studio (633-4397), Route 96 at Andersen Road, East Boothbay. Acclaimed stoneware animal sculptures of museum quality.

Nathaniel S. Wilson (633-5071), East Boothbay. A sailmaker who also fashions distinctive tote bags from canvas. Call for directions.

Hasenfus Glass Shop, Commercial Street, Boothbay Harbor. It's called glassblowing, but it's really the heating and bending of glass tubes into all sorts of imaginative ornaments, from fully rigged sailing ships to tiny animals.

A Silver Lining, 21 Townsend Avenue, Boothbay Harbor. Working metalsmiths. Original sculpture and jewelry in brass, sterling, and gold.

Edgecomb Potter's Gallery, Route 27, Edgecomb. Lovely pottery lamps, bowls, cookware, and jewelry.

Abacus Gallery, 8 McKown Street, Boothbay Harbor. An appealing shop showcasing the very best of contemporary crafts. Many pieces show the artists' wonderful sense of humor. Even if you are not buying, be sure to go browsing here.

Gold Smith Gallery, 63 Commercial Street, Boothbay Harbor. In a white-clapboard house across the street from Abacus. Unusual selection of jewelry in both gold and silver.

SPECIAL SHOPS

Palabra, 85 Commercial Street, Boothbay Harbor, across from Hasenfus Glass. A warren of more than a dozen rooms offering everything from kitschy souvenirs to valuable antiques. Upstairs (open by request) is a Poland Spring Museum with an impressive collection of the Moses bottles this natural spring water used to come in, plus other memorabilia from the heyday of the resort at Poland Spring.

Sherman's Book & Stationery Store, 7 Commercial Street, Boothbay Harbor. A two-story emporium filled with souvenirs, kitchenware, and games, as well as a full stock of books, specializing in nautical titles.

Sweet Woodruff Farm (633-6977), Route 27, Boothbay. Open May through December. One of the oldest homes in Boothbay, this rambling 1767 Cape houses an antiques and herb shop that features herbs that are grown and dried on the premises. Wreaths, potpourris, herb vinegars, and more. Special open houses are held in May and at the end of November.

SPECIAL EVENTS

April: **Fishermen's Festival**—contests for fishermen and lobstermen, cabaret ball, crowning of the Shrimp Princess, tall tale contest, boat parade, and blessing of the fleet.

Late June/early July: **Windjammer Days**—parade of windjammers into the harbor, fireworks, band concert, street dance, church suppers, parade of floats, bands, and beauty queens up Main Street. The big event of the summer.

July: **Friendship Sloop Days**—parade and race of traditional fishing sloops built nearby in Friendship. **Antique Auto Days,** Boothbay Railway Village, Route 27.

October: **Fall Foliage Festival**—boat cruises to view foliage, as well as food booths, craft sales, live entertainment, antique auto museum, steam train rides.

Early December: **Harbor Lights Festival**—parade, crafts, holiday shopping.

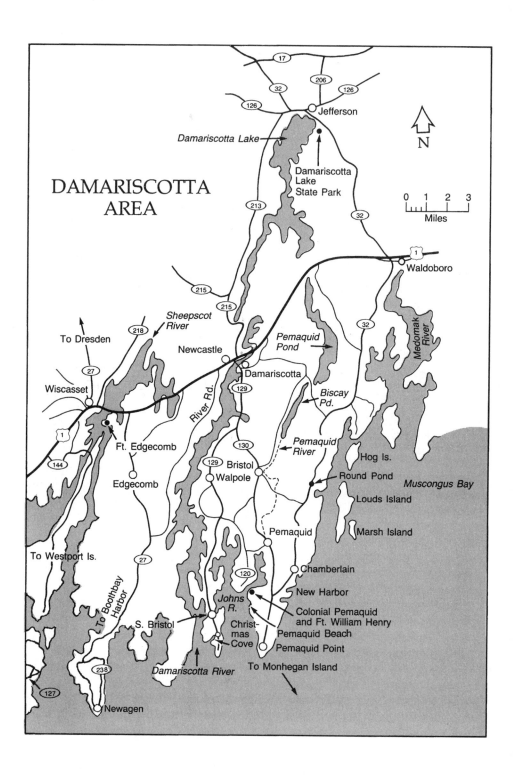

DAMARISCOTTA AREA

To Dresden

Wiscasset

To Westport Is.

To Boothbay Harbor

Newagen

Damariscotta Lake

Damariscotta Lake State Park

Jefferson

Waldoboro

Sheepscot River

Newcastle

Pemaquid Pond

Damariscotta

Biscay Pd.

Ft. Edgecomb

Edgecomb

River Rd.

Pemaquid River

Hog Is.

Bristol

Walpole

Round Pond

Louds Island

Muscongus Bay

Pemaquid

Marsh Island

Chamberlain

New Harbor

Johns R.

Colonial Pemaquid and Ft. William Henry

S. Bristol

Christmas Cove

Pemaquid Beach

Pemaquid Point

Damariscotta River

To Monhegan Island

N

0 1 2 3
Miles

Damariscotta/Newcastle and Pemaquid Area

The Damariscotta region encompasses the Pemaquid peninsula communities of Bristol, Pemaquid, New Harbor, and Round Pond. It also includes the inland villages around Lake Damariscotta as well as the exceptional twin villages of Damariscotta and Newcastle and their German-accented neighbor, Waldoboro. Nowhere else in Maine do you miss quite as much by simply sticking to Route 1.

Damariscotta's musical name means "Meeting place of the alewives," and in spring there are indeed spawning alewives to be seen by the waterfall at Damariscotta Mills, not far from a spot where Native Americans once heaped oyster shells from their summer feasts. Native Americans also had a name for the peninsula jutting 10 miles seaward from this spot: Pemaquid, meaning "long finger."

Pemaquid loomed large on 16th- and 17th-century maps because its protected inner harbor was the nearest mainland haven for Monhegan, a busy fishing area for European fishermen. It was from these fishermen that the Pemaquid Native American Samoset learned the English with which he welcomed the Pilgrims at Plymouth in 1621. It was also from these fishermen that Plimoth Plantation, the following winter, secured supplies enough to see it through to spring. Pemaquid, however, lacked a Governor William Bradford in its history. Although it is occasionally referred to as this country's first permanent settlement, its historical role remains murky.

The site of Maine's "Lost City" is a delightful mini-peninsula bordered by the Pemaquid River and Johns Bay (named for Captain John Smith, who explored here in 1614). At one tip stands a round stone fort (a replica built in the early 1900s). In recent years, more than 40,000 artifacts have been unearthed in the adjacent meadow, many of them now on display at the state-run museum that is part of the Colonial Pemaquid Restoration. An old cemetery full of crooked slate headstones completes the scene.

Since the late 19th century, when steamboats began to put into New Harbor and other ports in the area, this region has supported an abundance of summer inns and cottages. It is especially appealing to families with young children since it offers warm-water-lake beaches as well as saltwater strands and smooth coastal rocks for climbing. No one should fail to clamber around the especially fascinating rocks at Pemaquid Point, one of Maine's most photogenic lighthouses.

GUIDANCE

Damariscotta Information Bureau maintains two offices (both open mid-June through September 10–6, closed Sunday): one on Route 1 in Newcastle just south of the Damariscotta exit (563-3176), and another on Business Route 1, in town, on Church Street (563-3175) at the top of the hill near Chapman-Hall House. Mailed inquiries should be directed to the **Damariscotta Region Chamber of Commerce** (563-8340), PO Box 13, Damariscotta 04543.

GETTING THERE

Concord Trailways (1-800-639-8080) stops in Damariscotta and Waldoboro en route from Portland to Bangor.

Mid Coast Limo runs to and from the Portland International Jetport (1-800-834-5500 within Maine; 1-800-937-2424 outside the state). Most inns on the peninsula will pick up guests in Damariscotta, but basically this is the kind of place where you will want to have a car—or a boat—to get around. **Wiscasset Taxi** (758-1679) also serves the Damariscotta area.

MEDICAL EMERGENCY

Miles Memorial Hospital (563-1234), Bristol Road, Damariscotta.

VILLAGES

Damariscotta/Newcastle. The twin villages of Newcastle and Damariscotta (connected by a bridge) form the commercial center of the region. The main street is flanked by fine examples of 19th-century brick storefronts, many of them now restored. Shops and restaurants are tucked down alleyways. Note the towns' two exceptional churches and check the program of concerts and festivals at the Round Top Center for the Arts on Upper Main Street (see *Entertainment*). Damariscotta Mills, a short drive up Route 215 from Newcastle, has some elegant houses and a great picnic spot on Lake Damariscotta.

Waldoboro. An inscription in the cemetery of the Old German Church (see *To See*) relates the deceptive way in which landholder General Samuel Waldo lured the town's first German settlers here. The church and much of the town overlook the tidal Medomak (pronounced with the emphasis on "Med") River. Bypassed by Route 1, this village includes some architecturally interesting buildings, one of the country's oldest continuously operating five-and-dimes, and a theater presenting films, concerts, and live performances.

Round Pond. The name was obviously inspired by the village's almost circular harbor, said to have been a pirate base (Captain Kidd's treasure may be buried here in the Devil's Oven). It was once a major shipbuilding spot, and still is a working fishing and lobstering harbor (also see *Eating Out*).

New Harbor. About as picturesque a working harbor as any in Maine. Take South Side Road to Back Cove and walk out on the wooden pedestrian bridge for a great harbor view. Note the Samoset Memorial, honoring the Native American who sold land here, creating the first deed executed in New England.

South Bristol. Be prepared to stop and find a parking space as you near this tiny village, a cluster of charming houses and shops around a busy drawbridge.

TO SEE

HISTORIC SITES

✐ **Colonial Pemaquid State Historic Site** (677-2423), Pemaquid (off Route 130). Maintained by the state Bureau of Parks and Recreation and open daily Memorial Day through Labor Day, 9:30–5. In the early 19th century, local farmers filled in the cellar holes of the 17th-century settlement that once stood here. Archaeologists have uncovered the foundations of early-17th-century homes, a customs house, a tavern, and the jail. Inside the museum you view dioramas of the original 1620s settlement and artifacts such as a 16th-century German wine jug and slightly less aged tools and pottery, Spanish oil jars, and wampum—all found in the cellar holes just outside. Nearby is the old burial ground, dating from 1695.

✐ **Fort William Henry,** off Route 130, next to the archaeological museum. Open daily Memorial Day through Labor Day, 9:30–5. Nominal admission. This is a replica (built in 1907) of the third in the series of three English forts and one fortified warehouse built on this one site to fend off pirates and the French. In 1630 a stockade was built, but it was sacked and burned by pirate Dixie Bull. In 1677 Governor Andros built a wooden redoubt manned by 50 men, but this was captured by Baron Castine and his Native American allies in 1689 (see "Castine"). The original of this particular fort, built in 1698, was to be "the most expensive and strongest fortification that has ever been built on American soil," but it was destroyed by the French a year later. Fort Frederick, built in 1729, was never attacked, but during the American Revolution locals tore it down lest it fall into the hands of the British. Inside the fort are exhibits on the early explorations of Maine. The striking 1790 captain's house adjacent to the fort is not open to the public; it serves as the lab for the ongoing research. Picnic tables on the grounds command water views.

✐ **Pemaquid Point Lighthouse** (677-2494/2726), Route 130 (at the end), Pemaquid Point. The point is owned by the town, which charges a $1 entrance fee during the summer (senior citizens $.50, under 12 free). The lighthouse, built in 1824 and automated in 1934, is a beauty, looking even more impressive from the rocks below than from up in the parking lot. These rocks offer a wonderfully varied example of geological up-heaval, with tilted strata and igneous intrusions. The tidal pools can occupy children and adults alike for an entire day—but take care not to get too close to the water since the waves can be dangerous, catching people off balance and pulling them into the water. The rocks stretch for half a mile to Kresge Point. The **Fishermen's Museum,** housed in the former lighthouse keeper's home, is open Memorial Day through Columbus Day, Monday through Saturday 10–5 and Sunday 11–5. It contains fine photographs, ship models, and other artifacts related to the Maine fishing industry, as well as a description of the coast's lighthouses. Voluntary donations are requested of visitors to the lighthouse and museum. The complex also includes the **Pemaquid Art Gallery,** picnic tables, and public toilets. Next door to the lighthouse is The Sea Gull Shop (see *Eating Out*).

Thompson's Ice House (644-8551 in summer; 729-1956 in winter), Route 129 in South Bristol, 12 miles south of Damariscotta. Open July and August, Wednesday, Friday, and Saturday 1–4. One of the few surviving commercial icehouses in New England, this 150-year-old family busi-ness uses traditional tools for cutting ice from an adjacent pond. In sum-mer, a slide and video presentation shows how the ice is harvested (in February); tools are also on display.

Old Rock Schoolhouse, Bristol (follow signs from Route 130 to Route 132). Open during summer months, Tuesday and Friday 2–4. Dank and haunting, this 1827 rural stone schoolhouse stands at a long-overgrown crossroads in the woods.

Shell Heaps. These ancient heaps of oyster shells, left by generations of Native Americans at their summer encampments in what are now Newcastle and Damariscotta, have become incorporated into the tall hillsides along the riverbank. A close look at the soil, however, reveals the presence of the shells. The heaps—or middens, as they are called—are on private land but accessible via the 3-mile Salt Bay Preserve Heri-tage Trail, which begins next to the Newcastle post office. For details, call the Damariscotta River Association (563-1393).

Chapman-Hall House, corner of Main and Church Streets, Damariscotta (in the village, diagonally across from the First National Bank of Damariscotta). Open mid-June to mid-September daily, except Mon-day, 1–5. Built in 1754, this is the oldest homestead in the region. The house has been restored with its original kitchen. There is also an herb garden with 18th-century rosebushes.

Waldoborough Historical Society Museum, Route 220, just south of Route 1. Open late June to early September and weekends in October, 1–4:30. A complex of three buildings—a restored school, town pound, and hall—housing local memorabilia.

Harrington Meeting House, 1772

HISTORIC CHURCHES

This particular part of the Maine coast possesses an unusual number of fine old meetinghouses and churches, all of which are open to the public.

St. Patrick's Catholic Church, Academy Road, Newcastle (Route 215 north of Damariscotta Mills). Open year-round, daily, to sunset. This is the oldest surviving Catholic church (1808) in New England. It is an unusual building: brick construction, very narrow, and graced with a Paul Revere bell. The pews and stained glass date from 1896; and there is an old graveyard out back with forests all around.

St. Andrew's Episcopal Church (563-3533), Glidden Street, Newcastle. A charming, half-timbered building on the bank of the Damariscotta River. Set among gardens and trees, it was the first commission in this country for Henry Vaughan, the English architect who went on to design the National Cathedral in Washington, D.C.

Old Walpole Meeting House (563-5660), Route 129, South Bristol. Open during July and August, Sunday for 3 PM services, and by appointment. A 1772 meetinghouse with box pews and a pulpit with a sounding board.

Harrington Meeting House, Route 130, Pemaquid. Open during July and August, Monday, Wednesday, Friday, and Saturday 2–5. Donations accepted. The 1772 building has been restored and serves as a museum of Old Bristol. A nondenominational service is held here once a year, usually on the third Sunday in August.

Old German Church (832-5100), Route 32, Waldoboro. Open daily during July and August, 1–4. Built in 1772 with square-benched pews and a wine-glass pulpit; note the inscription in the cemetery: "This town was settled in 1748 by Germans who immigrated to this place with the promise and expectation of finding a prosperous city, instead of which they found nothing but wilderness." Bostonian Samuel Waldo—owner of a large tract of land in this area—obviously had not been straight with the 40 German families he brought to settle it. This was the first Lutheran church in Maine; it's maintained by the German Protestant Society.

SCENIC DRIVES

From Newcastle, Route 215 winds along **Damariscotta Lake** to Damariscotta Mills; continue along the lake and through farm country on Route 213 (note the scenic pullout across from the Bunker Hill Church, with a view down the lake) to Jefferson for a swim at **Damariscotta Lake State Park.**

Pemaquid Peninsula. Follow Route 129 south from Damariscotta, across the **South Bristol Bridge** to **Christmas Cove.** Backtrack and cross the peninsula via **Harrington Meeting House Road** to **Colonial Pemaquid** and **Pemaquid Beach** (this corner of the world is particularly beautiful at sunset). Turn south on Route 130 to **Pemaquid Point** and return via Route 32 and **Round Pond;** take Biscay Road back to Damariscotta or continue on Route 32 into Waldoboro.

TO DO

BOAT EXCURSIONS

Hardy Boat Cruises (Stacie Davidson and Captain Al Crocetti: 677-2026; 1-800-278-3346), Shaw's Wharf, New Harbor. May through October the sleek, 60-foot, Maine-built *Hardy III* offers daily service to **Monhegan** (for a detailed description, see "The Islands"). Pick a calm day. It doesn't matter if it's foggy but the passage is more than an hour and no fun if it's rough. An evening cruise circles **Egg Rock,** one of only five Maine islands on which puffins breed; the tours are narrated by an Audubon naturalist (inquire about other special puffin-watching and birding trips). There are also sunset cruises to Pemaquid Point. Parking is free but roughly a quarter mile back up the road. The crew do everything they can to make the trip interesting, like the seal-watching detour on the way back from Monhegan.

BOAT RENTALS

Damariscotta Lake Farm (549-7953) in Jefferson rents boats and motors for use on 13-mile-long Damariscotta Lake. **Lake Pemaquid Camping** (563-5202), Egypt Road, Damariscotta, rents canoes. **Pemaquid River Canoe Rental** (563-5721), Route 130, Bristol (5 miles south of Damariscotta), has canoe sales and rentals.

FISHING

Damariscotta Lake is a source of bass, landlocked salmon, and trout.

GOLF

Wawenock Country Club (563-3938), Route 129 (7 miles south of Damariscotta). Open May to November. Nine holes.

HORSEBACK RIDING
Hill-n-Dale Riding Stables (273-2511) in Warren offers trail rides.
SWIMMING
On the peninsula there is public swimming at **Biscay Pond,** off Route 32, and at **Bristol Dam** on Route 130, 5 miles south of Damariscotta (also see *Green Space*).
SPECIAL LEARNING PROGRAM
National Audubon Ecology Camp, Hog Island (0.25 mile offshore at the head of Muscongus Bay). June through September. Six 1-week programs (the first two focus on birds) for adults and two 10-day camp sessions for 10–14-year-olds focusing on the island's wildlife; also boat trips to see the puffins that were reintroduced to nearby Eastern Egg Rock by the Audubon-related Puffin Project. There are 5 miles of spruce trails, wildflower and herb gardens, and mudflats surrounding rustic bungalows and a dining room in a restored 19th-century farmhouse. For more information and dates, call 203-869-2017 or write to the National Audubon Society Ecology Camps and Workshops, 613 Riverville Road, Greenwich, CT 06831.

GREEN SPACE

BEACHES
Pemaquid Beach Park (677-2754), Route 130, Pemaquid. A town-owned area open Memorial Day through Labor Day, 9–5. Admission is $1 per adult, under 12 free. Bathhouse, rest rooms, refreshment stand, and picnic tables. Pleasant, but it can be windy, in which case try the more pebbly but more sheltered (and free) beach down the road.
Damariscotta Lake State Park, Route 32, Jefferson. A fine, sandy beach with changing facilities, picnic tables, and grills at the northern end of the lake.
NATURE PRESERVES
Rachel Carson Memorial Salt Pond, at the side of Route 32, just north of Round Pond. There's a beautiful view of the open ocean from here, and at low tide the tidal pools are filled with tiny sea creatures. Here Rachel Carson researched her book *The Edge of the Sea.*
Dodge Point Preserve on the River Road south of Newcastle offers a loop trail through pond and marsh to Sand Beach on the river. Roughly a mile south of Newcastle on the River Road, look for FL (Fire Lane) 30 on the river side of the road.
Witch Island, South Bristol. An 18-acre wooded island lies 0.25 mile offshore at the east end of the Gut, the narrow channel that serves as South Bristol's harbor. A perimeter trail around the island threads through oaks and pines, allowing views of Johns Bay. Two sheltered beaches offer swimming, picnicking, and access to a small skiff, kayak, or canoe.

Salt Bay Preserve Heritage Trail and Heritage Center Farm (563-1391). See Shell Heaps under *To See* for a description of the trail; the 98-acre saltwater farm is on Belvedere Road (turn at the yellow blinking light on Route 1 in Damariscotta). Trails have been developed and you can pick up map/guides to local conservation areas. The Damariscotta River Association also maintains Hodgdons Island in the river.

PICNICKING

There are two nice picnic areas on Route 130 in Bristol, one at **Lighthouse Park** and another at **Pemaquid Beach Park.** There are also picnic tables at Damariscotta Lake State Park (see *Swimming* in *To Do*) and by the bridge in Damariscotta Mills.

LODGING

INNS

The Newcastle Inn (563-5685; 1-800-832-8669), River Road, Newcastle 04553. Open year-round. Howard and Rebecca Levitan bought this landmark inn in the fall of '95 and have done some major renovating. There's a woodstove on the sun porch and French doors opening on a deck with water views, and a suite with a gas fireplace and two-person Jacuzzi in the carriage house. The three- or five-course meal (see *Dining Out*) remains the centerpiece of a stay here. The 15 rooms are tasteful and comfortable, all with private baths. Rates are $65–175 double B&B or $135–245 double MAP plus a 15 percent service charge and include a three-course breakfast. Incidentally, the logo and decorating theme of the inn has changed from rabbits to lupines. Inquire about special wine-tasting and holiday weekends. No smoking.

Gosnold Arms (677-3727), Route 32, New Harbor 04554. Open mid-May through mid-October (restaurant opens Memorial Day weekend). Just across the road from the water (and the *Hardy* boat offering day trips to Monhegan and puffin cruises around Egg Rock), this friendly, family-owned and -run inn has been welcoming summer guests since 1925. Nothing fancy, it's a rambling, white-clapboard farmhouse with a long, welcoming porch, an attached barn, and scattered cottages. Eleven guest rooms with unstained pine walls, pleasant furnishings, and firm beds (all with private bath) have been fitted into the barn, above a gathering room with a huge fireplace. There are 14 cottages, some with kitchenettes, fireplaces, and/or water views. Guests breakfast and sup on the enclosed porch overlooking the water; the dining room is also open to the public and has a reputation for fresh, local, simply prepared food (see *Dining Out*). The inn is named for Bartholomew Gosnold, who is said to have sailed into the harbor in 1602. All rates include breakfast. $75–94 double B&B in the inn, $98–124 for cottages; less off-season.

Bradley Inn (677-2105; 1-800-253-1125), 361 Pemaquid Point, New Harbor 04554. Open April through January 2. Chuck and Merry Robinson have restored this turn-of-the-century inn. The 12 guest rooms are nicely furnished (private baths), and the grounds have been handsomely landscaped. Request one of the third-floor rooms with a view of Johns Bay. The entry area also serves two dining rooms (see *Dining Out*), but there is a living room with a fireplace, wing chairs, and a library of nautical books for guests. Bicycles are free, and the inn is nicely positioned for a pleasant walk or bike ride to the lighthouse in one direction and to Kresge Point in the other. From $85 off-season to $175 in-season; also inquire about the Garden Cottage and the carriage house and about special birding weekends.

Coveside Inn (644-8282), Christmas Cove, South Bristol 04568. Motel units are open late May to mid-October; the restaurant and inn rooms, from early June to mid-September. Five old-fashioned guest rooms are in the holly-berry red Victorian inn (all have private baths but some are across the hall), which also has a big living room that is shared with guests in the 10 shorefront motel units (private decks, pine paneling, and cathedral ceilings with skylights). The complex also includes a restaurant, serving all three meals, and a yacht brokerage. $65–95 includes continental breakfast.

The Hotel Pemaquid (677-2312), Pemaquid 04554. Open mid-May to mid-October. A century-old classic summer hotel just 150 feet from Pemaquid Point but without water views. Everything is as neat and tidy, also as fireproof and renovated, as can be. The decor is high Victorian, the living room has a big stone fireplace, and the long porch is lined with wicker chairs. Rooms in the inn itself come with and without private baths, but all rooms in the annex, the bungalows, and the motel units have private baths; there are also handicapped-access rooms and several reserved for smokers. The hotel does not have a restaurant, but coffee is set out at 6:30 AM and The Sea Gull Shop (see *Eating Out*), overlooking the ocean, is a very short walk. From $49 off-season with shared bath to $125 for a suite in August; housekeeping cottage $475–575 per week. Ask about art workshops.

BED & BREAKFASTS

The Flying Cloud (563-2484), River Road, Newcastle 04553. Open most of the year. A magnificent 1840s sea captain's home, expanding on a 1790s Cape. The elegance of the furniture matches that of the floor-to-ceiling windows and fine detailing, but hosts Alan and Jeanne Davis have also taken care to provide comfortable, informal spaces like a den with a TV and sound system and a screened back porch. The five guest rooms (all private baths) are each named and decorated for a port-of-call of the clipper ship *Flying Cloud*, which Alan has researched in depth (our bedtime reading was a fascinating letter written by a passenger on the ship's record-setting voyage around Cape Horn), and the second-floor library will please American-history buffs. San Francisco, New York, and Melbourne all have great water views. Breakfast, served in the formal dining room, may include sourdough blueberry pancakes and always features farm-fresh eggs. $65–90, less off-season.

☞ **The Inn at Middlefield** (529-5009), PO Box 249, Bristol 04539, on Upper Round Pond Road. Checking out lodging places all day can be a drag but the reward is finding a new place as good as this. A classic circa-1800 Federal mansion on a hilltop, set in gardens, orchards, and lawns, it has been painstakingly, tastefully restored to offer five inviting guest rooms, more than ample formal and informal common space, and true hospitality from innkeepers Fred and Lillian Harrigan (former owners of a historic working farm in New Hampshire's Monadnock region). Three guest rooms have fireplaces and another pleasant bedroom has French doors opening onto the garden. $85–110 includes a full country breakfast served on a radiant-heated porch, overlooking the flower garden. The inn is minutes from the good places to eat in Round Pond.

☞✐**Brannon-Bunker Inn** (563-5941), HCR 64, Box 045, Route 129, Damariscotta 04543. Open March to December. A rambling building that includes an 1820s Cape and a barn turned Prohibition-era dance hall turned inn. The upstairs sitting area walls are hung with memorabilia from World War I, and there are plenty of antiques and collectibles around (the adjoining antiques shop is open May through October). This is an unusually relaxed B&B. Your hosts are Mike, Beth, and Jamie Hovance, as well as their parents, Jeanne and Joe; children are welcome. Five rooms have private baths ($65), and two share ($55); there's also a three-bedroom suite with a kitchen, living room, and bath ($115). A path leads to the river . Breakfast features muffins and fruit, and the kitchen is available for guests' use at other times of the day.

✐ **Mill Pond Inn** (563-8014), Route 215, Damariscotta Mills (mailing address: 50 Main Street, Nobleboro 04555). Open year-round. A quiet spot with a back deck overlooking a millpond. Damariscotta Lake is just a few steps away. Wildlife includes a resident bald eagle. There are two 2-person hammocks under the willow trees and a beach at the freshwater swimming hole. The 1780 gray-clapboard house with a red door offers six double rooms (all private baths), one of which has an adjoining smaller room with twin beds. Breakfast might be pancakes with fresh blueberries or omelets with crabmeat and vegetables from the inn's garden. It is served in the dining room, which has a fireplace and a picture window overlooking the lake. In winter, pack a picnic lunch and skate across the lake to a miniature island. In summer, ask for a ride in the 16-foot, restored, antique motorboat on Damariscotta Lake. You can also paddle out in a canoe or explore the rolling countryside on one of the inn's mountain bikes. Owner Bobby Whear, a registered Maine guide, also will arrange fishing trips; the catch is landlocked salmon, brown trout, and smallmouth bass. $75.

The Briar Rose B&B (529-5478), Route 32, Round Pond 04564. Open all year. In the center of the picturesque village of Round Pond, Anita and

Fred Palsgrove offer four large, airy, pleasing, antiques-furnished rooms (three with private bath), and views of the harbor. From $55 double off-season with shared bath to $75 in-season includes a full breakfast served at individual tables in the dining room.

Broad Bay Inn & Gallery (832-6668; 1-800-736-6769), 1014 Main Street, Waldoboro 04572. Closed January. Within walking distance of village restaurants, shops, and performances at the Waldo Theatre, this is a pleasant, 1830s home with Victorian furnishings and canopy beds. The five guest rooms share three baths. Afternoon tea and sherry are served on the sun deck in summer and by the fire in winter. The art gallery in the barn exhibits works by well-known Maine artists, and also sells limited-edition prints, crafts, and gifts. Host Libby Hopkins offers art workshops. Rates include a full breakfast; on Saturday evenings, candle-light dinners may be arranged in advance (for guests and the public). Two-night minimum stay required in July and August. Ask about Thanksgiving, Christmas, and New Year's Eve packages. $50–75 double.

Apple Tree B&B (677-3491), New Harbor 04554. Open year-round. A genuine old Cape a short walk from Pemaquid Beach and Fort William Henry. An attractive first-floor room has a private bath, and the two upstairs bedrooms, one with a working fireplace, share a bath. Pat Landry's kitchen usually smells of the good things served in the dining room or on the patio for breakfast. The comfortable living room has a fireplace and is well stocked with books and magazines. $55–70 double.

Glidden House (563-1859), RR 1, Box 740, Glidden Street, Newcastle 04553. Open most of the year. This Victorian house on a quiet street lined with elegant old homes is a convenient walk to the shops of both Newcastle and Damariscotta. The four guest rooms have private baths. There is also a three-room apartment. Exceptional breakfasts, included in the lodging, are served in the dining room or in the garden. $55 double with shared bath; $60 with private bath; $75 for the apartment.

The Roaring Lion (832-4038), PO Box 756, 995 Main Street, Waldoboro 04572. Open year-round. A 1905 home with tin ceilings, fireplaces, and a big screened porch. The kitchen can cater to special, vegetarian, and macrobiotic diets. One room with private bath; three with shared bath. $55–65 double, $10 less for single occupancy. No smoking.

The Barn Bed & Breakfast (832-5781), RD 3, 2987 Friendship Road, South Waldoboro 04572. On Route 220 between Waldoboro and Friendship, this is a 1793 barn that's been transformed into a charming B&B with three guest rooms (two doubles, one single), set in fields with long views from rockers on the back porch. Helen Power is an interesting as well as hospitable hostess. $60 double, $40 single includes a full breakfast in the brick-floored kitchen.

Le Va Tout B&B, Gallery, and Gardens (832-4969), 218 Kalers Corner Road, Waldoboro. Elizabeth Sweet took on this long-established B&B in 1996 and infused it with an air of hospitality. There are five guest rooms, one with private bath, and a hot tub in the garden (at this writing a sauna is also planned). $60–70 includes a full breakfast. The gallery exhibits contemporary art (no lobster boats).

Inland

✐☞**The Jefferson House** (549-5768), Route 126, Jefferson 04348. Jim and Barbara O'Hallaran's comfortable 1835 farmhouse feels like home the moment you walk in. The large, bright kitchen with its big old cookstove is the center of the house, or you can breakfast on the deck overlooking the village and millpond. Guests can use the canoe on the river. Rooms are homey and comfortable; shared baths. $50 double, $40 single.

Snow Drift Farm Bed & Breakfast (845-2476), 117 Fitch Road, Washington 04574. Open year-round. A restored, mid-1800s farmhouse set in the country with a garden, deck, fields, nature trails, a trout stream, and pond (skating in winter). There's even a professional massage therapist available. From $35 with shared bath to $85 for a two-room suite with private bath.

COTTAGES

☞✐Many rental properties are listed with the Damariscotta area chamber (*see Guidance*); for cottages and apartments down on the peninsula, also request a copy of the current "Map & Guide" published by the Pemaquid Area Association (Chamberlain 04541).

WHERE TO EAT

DINING OUT

The Newcastle Inn (563-5685), River Road, Newcastle. Open nightly June through October; Friday and Saturday off-season. Under new management but still specializing in candlelit dining. The menu changes nightly but might include appetizers like local mussels steamed in a broth of cream, garlic, saffron, and ouzo and entrées like grilled boneless duck breast, served with a raspberry Cassis glaze. A five-course dinner is $35; a three-course is $27.50 (plus tax, gratuity, and wines).

✐ **Anchor Inn** (529-5584), Round Pond. Open daily for lunch and dinner, Memorial Day through Columbus Day. A real find, a tiered dining room overlooking the harbor in this small fishing village. Try the native crabcakes for either lunch or dinner. Dinner options include Italian seafood stew (loaded with fish, shrimp, scallops, and mussels), charbroiled steaks, and linguine with black olives, feta, and roasted vegetables in a sherried tomato sauce. Dinner entrées $11.67–15.87.

Gosnold Arms (677-3727), Route 32, New Harbor. Open Memorial Day weekend through mid-October, 5:30–8. An old-fashioned summer hostelry (see *Inns*) with a public dining room that seats 80. The kitchen specializes in the freshest local seafood in straightforward preparations, such as broiled salmon steak with dill, seafood casserole, and sea scallops broiled or deep fried. Dinner is served on the enclosed porch with a view of the harbor. From $8.95 for a fried boneless chicken breast to whatever the salmon or lobster is priced at. The blackboard specials always include roast lamb on Sundays. Full liquor and beer list.

Bradley Inn (677-2105), Pemaquid Point Road, New Harbor. "Ships" is the more formal of the two dining rooms in this fine old inn. There's live jazz or folk music on Friday and Saturday nights, piano music other nights. The à la carte menu might include pan-poached salmon and haddock with mussels ($17) or a seafood sampler steamed in tomato broth ($23), topped off with a chocolate hazelnut terrine ($8).

Coveside Waterfront Restaurant (644-8282), Christmas Cove, South Bristol. Open June through mid-September; three meals daily. This is a waterside landmark. Dinner specialties include pan-fried crabcakes served with remoulade, grilled marinated shrimp, and steamed seafood in parchment. There are also burgers and seafood salad plates. Dinner runs $30–70 for two.

EATING OUT
On or just off Route 1

⬭ **Moody's Diner** (832-7468), Route 1, Waldoboro. Open 24 hours (except closed midnight–5 AM on Friday and Saturday). A clean and warm, classic old diner run by several generations of the Moody family along with other employees who have been there so long they have become part of the family. Recently renovated, it still retains all the old atmosphere and specialties like cream pies and family-style food; corned beef hash, meat loaf, stews, at digestible prices.

Backstreet Landing (563-5666), Elm Street Plaza, Damariscotta. Open daily, year-round. Just behind Main Street, overlooking the upper Damariscotta River, this very pleasant, low-key restaurant and gathering place has good, dependable food. Three meals are served each day, plus Sunday brunch. Seafood entrées, homemade soups and chowders, quiches, lunch specials, and light late-evening snacks. This is a popular place with locals.

King Edier's Pub (563-6008), 2 Elm Street, Damariscotta. Open year-round 11–11. A family-run newcomer with a warm atmosphere and a sandwich, soup, and burger menu; specials and an assortment of beers.

⬭ **Salt Bay Cafe** (563-1666), Main Street, Damariscotta. Open year-round for lunch and dinner. A pleasant, chef-owned and locally liked restaurant with booths and a fireplace. Serves simple favorites such as fried clams, good salads, sandwiches, and soups; also pastas, steaks, and local seafood.

Schooner Landing, Main Street, Damariscotta. Open year-round for lunch and dinner. A middle-of-town, waterside restaurant with a lounge, deck, and Italian chef specializing in broiled and baked fish.

⬭ **S. Fernald's Country Store** (563-8484), 29 Main Street, Damariscotta. A self-conscious but fun old-fashioned store featuring penny candy up front and a deli in back with some seating in between. Basically, however, this is a great source of picnic sandwiches, like smoked turkey with provolone, tomato, onion, pickle, black olives, and house dressing. A "half" ($2.99) was plenty for us. Soups, salads, and Round Top ice cream.

Pine Cone Bakery and Cafe (832-6337), 13 Friendship Street, Waldoboro. The booths have stained-glass insets, and the brick walls are hung with Eric Hopkins prints. Peasant breads, salads, soups and sandwiches for takeout or for eating in. A back deck overlooks the Medomak River.

The Sea Gull Shop (677-2374), next to the Pemaquid Lighthouse at Pemaquid Point. Open daily in-season, 8–8. The unbeatable ocean view is what this place is all about. Standard menu. BYOB.

Captain's Catch Seafood (677-2396), Pemaquid Beach Road, New Harbor. Open throughout the summer season, 11–8 daily. Indoor and outdoor picnic-style dining. Lobsters, clams (steamed or fried), seafood baskets, and dinners; fish fry every Friday; homemade desserts. Take a truly succulent crab roll or fish sandwich down to the beach for a sunset picnic.

Dana's Chart House (677-3315), at the Pemaquid Restoration. Open Memorial Day through October, lunch through dinner. There's a takeout section adjacent to the pier (you can come by boat) and a large dining room. From $1.50 for a hot dog to $10.95 for lobster pie.

LOBSTER POUNDS

Note: Muscongus Bay is a particularly prime lobster source and genuine lobster pounds are plentiful around the harbors of the Pemaquid peninsula.

✑ **Shaw's** (677-2200), New Harbor (next to the New Harbor Co-op). Open late May to mid-October, daily for lunch and supper. You can't get nearer to a working harbor than this very popular dockside spot. In addition to lobster and steamed clams, the menu includes a variety of basic foods like meat loaf, fish cakes, stews, shrimp, roast turkey, scallops, and sandwiches. Liquor is also served. Choose to sit at a picnic table either out on the dock over the water or in the inside dining room.

New Harbor Co-op (677-2791), New Harbor. Open daily 12–8. Serves boiled lobsters and clams, inside and outside dining. BYOB.

At the picture-perfect harbor in **Round Pond** two competing companies share the town wharf, resulting in satisfying prices. **Muscongus Bay Lobster Company** (529-5528), open daily from 10 AM, has an outdoor sink, and **Round Pond Lobster** (529-5725), open daily 10–7, has a slightly better view. Both offer no-frills (no plumbing) facilities.

Pemaquid Fisherman's Co-op (677-2801), Pemaquid Harbor. Open Saturday and Sunday 11–6. Lobster, steamed clams and mussels, and shrimp to be enjoyed at outdoor tables over the harbor.

✑ **The Antique Cafe** (644-8500), Route 129 at "the Gut" in South Bristol. Open summer months, 11–9 weekends until mid-September. Another classic spot from which to savor a lobstering atmosphere. This complex includes a general store and fish market, and the dining deck is upstairs overlooking the water; a place for lobster stewed as well as steamed, also clams, shrimp, and fried seafood. Beer is on the menu.

SNACKS

✐ **Round Top Ice Cream** (563-5307), Business Route 1, Damariscotta. Open Memorial Day through Columbus Day. You'll find delicious Round Top ice cream offered at restaurants throughout the region, but this is the original Round Top, on the grounds of the farm where it all began in 1924 (an expanded creamery is now just over the hill). The ice cream comes in 36 flavors, including raspberry, Almond Joy, and fresh blueberry. This is the granddaddy of all ice cream stands in the area, and we don't think the interior has changed since 1924. Also on the grounds is the Round Top Center for the Arts, offering concerts, classes, exhibitions, and festivals (see *Entertainment*).

ENTERTAINMENT

Round Top Center for the Arts (563-1507), Upper Main Street, Damariscotta. On the grounds of the old Round Top Farm, this energetic, nonprofit organization offers an ambitious schedule of concerts, exhibitions, classes, and festivals. Check locally for evening outdoor concerts in summer—it could be anything from the Portland Symphony Orchestra to rousing ethnic music by Mama Tongue. Bring a blanket and a picnic and enjoy both the music and the lovely setting.

Waldo Theatre (832-6060), Main Street, Waldoboro. March through December, a schedule of films, concerts, and live performances. Inquire about outlets for advance sales of concert tickets in Damariscotta, Rockland, and Thomaston.

SELECTIVE SHOPPING

ANTIQUES

Antiques shops abound in this area. Pick up a copy of the local antiques pamphlet. Don't miss **Elmer's Barn** (549-7671), up Route 32 in Coopers Mills. Three floors of chairs, clocks, brass beds, woodstoves, player pianos, whatever.

ARTISANS

David Margonelli (633-3326), River Road, Edgecomb. Exquisite, completely handmade furniture with a classic influence. David and Susan make it all themselves.

✐ **Ax Wood Products** (563-5884), Route 129, Walpole. Open year-round. Owner Barnaby Porter is an internationally recognized wood sculptor best known for his whimsical miniature houses and "wild contraptions" built inside tree stumps.

Damariscotta Pottery (563-8121), off Main Street, Damariscotta. Reminiscent of Mallorcan ware, it is decorated in primitive floral and animal designs. You can watch it being made and painted right in the shop.

In Round Pond look for: **Laberge Stained Glass Design** (art glass); **Village Weavers** (table linens, rugs, window hangings, and clothing); **The Scottish Lion Blacksmith** (handwrought ironwork).

SPECIAL SHOPS

☞ **Reny's** (563-3177), Main Street, Damariscotta. First opened in Camden in 1949, Reny's has since become a small-town, Maine institution from Biddeford to Fort Kent. Operated by Robert H. Reny and his two sons, Robert D. and John E., the stores sell quality items—ranging from TVs to sheets and towels and whatever "the boys" happen to have found to stock this week. "We don't know what to call ourselves," Robert H. tells us, "but we have a lot of fun doing it." We enjoy shopping at Reny's too; it's not just the unexpected quality and prices, it's a certain something that's still distinctly Maine. The headquarters for the 15-store chain are in Damariscotta's former grade school; on Main Street look for **Reny's** and **Reny's Underground.**

✐ **Maine Coast Book Shop** (563-3207), Main Street, Damariscotta. One of Maine's best bookstores, with knowledgeable staff members who delight in making suggestions and helping customers shop for others.

✐ **Granite Hall Store** (529-5864), Route 32, Round Pond. Open Tuesday through Sunday 10–5. A general store filled with Scottish-, Irish-, and Maine-made woolens, Eskimo sculptures, a few antiques and baskets, toys, books, a good selection of greeting cards, penny candy, hot roasted peanuts, homemade fudge, and, at an outdoor window, ice cream.

Carriage House (529-5555), Route 32 south of the village of Round Pond. Jean Gillespie continues to run this exceptional antiquarian bookstore, which she established with her husband, Roy, in 1961. Some 15,000 titles line shelves in a barnlike annex to the house. We recently found here a 19th-century Maine guidebook that we had been hunting high and low for, reasonably priced.

Old Post Office Shop (New Harbor center). Open May to December; good selection of gifts, local crafts.

The Roserie at Bayfields (832-6330; 1-800-933-4508), Route 32, just 1.7 miles south of the light on Route 1 in Waldoboro. Open daily April 19 until late July, then Tuesday through Saturday through the growing season. Rose lovers across the country are aware of this unusual nursery, specializing in hundreds of varieties of "practical roses for hard places."

SPECIAL EVENTS

Second weekend in July: **Damariscotta River Oyster Festival,** Damariscotta—a celebration of the oyster aquaculture conducted in the river. Oysters fixed every way (especially au naturel), music, crafts, and a canoe race through the rapids of the Damariscotta River.

Early August: **Olde Bristol Days,** Old Fort Grounds, Pemaquid Beach. **Parade**—fish fry, chicken barbecue, bands, bagpipers, concerts, pancake breakfast, road race, boat race, firemen's muster, crafts, and the annual **Bristol Footlighters Show** (which has been going on for more than 40 years).

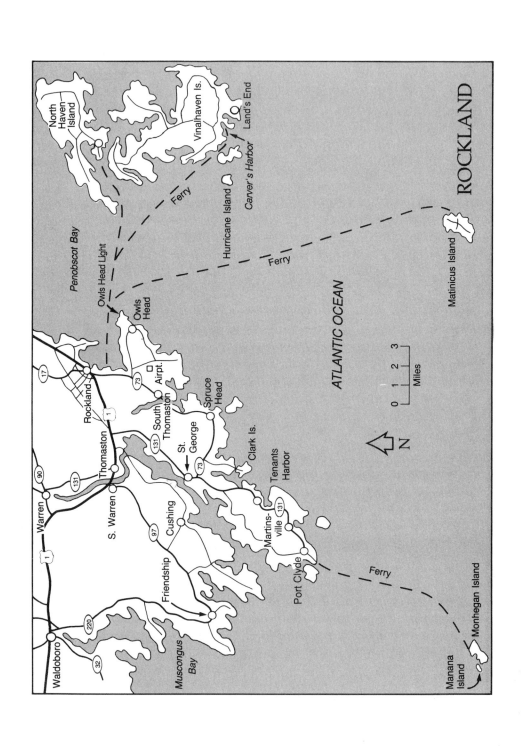

Rockland/Thomaston Area

Rockland's brick downtown is the commercial center for a wide scattering of towns and islands. Long "Lobster Capital of the World," this small city is now recognized as home port for the majority of Maine's windjammers and is increasingly known as home of the Farnsworth Museum, with its exceptional collection of Maine-based paintings, including works by three generations of Wyeths. Still a workaday place, it has attracted a year-round population of artists and musicians. It is also departure point for ferries to the islands of Vinalhaven, North Haven, and Matinicus (see "The Islands").

A century ago summer people heading for Bar Harbor as well as the islands took the train as far as Rockland, switching here to steamboats. Today a similar summer crowd fly into Knox County Airport on Owls Head, just south of town, here transferring to rental cars, air taxis, or windjammers, to the motor yacht *Pauline*, or to charter boats as well as ferries. Wide, deep, and protected by a 4436-foot-long granite breakwater, Rockland's harbor is now clean and amply equipped to accommodate pleasure as well as lobster and fishing boats.

Southwest of Rockland, two peninsulas separate Muscongus Bay from Penobscot Bay. One is the fat arm of land on which the villages of Friendship and Cushing doze. The other is the skinnier St. George Peninsula with Port Clyde at its tip, the departure point for the year-round mail boat to Monhegan Island (again, see "The Islands").

The peninsulas are divided by the 10-mile-long St. George River, at the head of which sits Thomaston, a beautiful old town that has produced more than its share of wooden ships. Although its handsome Main Street mansions stand today in white-clapboard testimony to the shipbuilders' success a century ago, Thomaston is best known as the site of the state prison—and its popular prison shop.

GUIDANCE

Rockland-Thomaston Chamber of Commerce (596-0376), Public Landing, Rockland (write PO Box 508, Rockland 04841). Open weekdays, 9–5 in summer and 8–4 in winter. The chamber's large, comfortable information center in Harbor Park serves the entire Rockland area, which includes Thomaston, the peninsula villages, and the islands. It has cottage listings for North Haven, Vinalhaven, and the area from Owls Head to Cushing.

GETTING THERE

By air: **Knox County Airport** (594-4131), at Owls Head, just south of Rockland, daily service via **Colgan Air** (596-7604; 1-800-272-5488) to Boston, Bar Harbor, Augusta, and New York. Inquire about charter services to the islands. **Mid Coast Limo** (1-800-937-2424) runs to and from the Portland International Jetport. **Schooner Bay Taxi** (1-800-539-5001) is the local reliable.

By bus: **Concord Trailways** (1-800-639-5150) offers service to Rockland with a stop at the ferry terminal.

GETTING AROUND

Rockland's role as transportation hub of Penobscot Bay was underscored in 1996 with the opening of a spacious new **Maine State Ferry Service Terminal** (596-2022), along with the bus stop (see above).

MEDICAL EMERGENCY

Penobscot Bay Medical Center (596-8000), Route 1, Glen Cove, Rockland.

VILLAGES AND ISLANDS

Friendship. Best known as the birthplace of the classic Friendship sloop, first built by local lobstermen to haul their traps (originals and reproductions of this sturdy vessel hold races here every summer). Friendship remains a quiet fishing village with a museum in a former schoolhouse on Martin's Point (it's open July through Labor Day).

Tenants Harbor has a good little library and, beyond, rock cliffs, tidal pools, old cemeteries, and the kind of countryside described by Sarah Orne Jewett in *Country of the Pointed Firs.* Jewett lived just a few bends down Route 131 in Martinville while she wrote the book.

Union is a short ride from the coast but surrounded by gentle hills and farm country (the Union Fair and Blueberry Festival is a big event; see *Special Events*). This place is also a good spot to swim, eat, and explore the unusually interesting Matthews Museum of Maine Heritage at the fairgrounds (open July 1 through Labor Day, daily except Monday, 12–5).

Islands. An overnight or longer stay on an island is far preferable to a day trip. From Rockland you can take a Maine State (car) Ferry to **Vinalhaven** and **North Haven.** Together these form the Fox Islands, with just a narrow passage between them. Yet the islands are very different. On Vinalhaven, summer homes are hidden away along the shore, and what visitors see is the fabulously funky old fishing village of Carver's Harbor. On North Haven, most of the clapboard homes (mainly owned by wealthy summer people) are set in open fields. **Matinicus,** also accessible from Rockland, is the most remote Maine island and quietly beautiful. Tiny **Monhegan,** accessible from Port Clyde, offers the most dramatic cliff scenery and the most hospitable welcome to visitors. For details, see the descriptions of each island in the next chapter.

TO SEE

Farnsworth Art Museum (596-6457), 352 Main Street, Rockland. Open year-round, daily June through mid-October 9–5, Sunday 12–5), otherwise closed on Monday. Admission to the museum and the homestead (see next entry) is $5 adults, $4 senior citizens, $3 students 8–18, under 8 free. This exceptional art museum was established by Lucy Farnsworth, an eccentric spinster who lived frugally in just three rooms of her family mansion. When she died in 1935 at age 96, neighbors were amazed to find that she had left $1.3 million to preserve her house and build the handsome museum next door.

"People come to a museum like this to see what makes Maine unique," observes Chris Crosman, the Farnsworth director credited with catapulting the museum from a way stop to a destination for art lovers.

Since the recent doubling of the museum's exhibit space, the depth and quality of the Farnsworth's 7000-piece collection has become apparent. A permanent exhibit, "Maine in America," traces the evolution of Maine landscape paintings. The museum features Hudson River School artists like Thomas Cole, and 19th-century marine artist Fitz Hugh Lane; American impressionists Frank Benson, Willard Metcalf, Childe Hassam, and Maurice Prendergast; early-20th-century greats like George Bellows, Rockwell Kent, and Charles Woodbury; and such "modernists" as John Marin and Marsden Hartley. It is also well known for its collection of works by three generations of Wyeths: Look for *Eight Bells at Port Clyde* by N.C., *Her Room* by Andrew, and *Portrait of Orca Bates* by Jamie (who worked on nearby peninsulas and islands). Rockland-raised painter and sculptor Louise Nevelson is also well represented. Note the changing exhibit gallery and Main Street museum store. The original Georgian Revival library houses an extensive collection of reference materials and serves as the site for regularly scheduled lectures and concerts. A Main Street sculpture garden and the conversion of a nearby church into The Farnsworth Center for the Wyeth Family in Maine are both in the offing.

Farnsworth Homestead (596-6457), Elm Street, Rockland. Open June through mid-October only, Monday through Saturday 10–5 and Sunday 1–5. Joint admission to the homestead and museum is $5 adults, $4 senior citizens, $3 students 8–18, under 8 free. The Farnsworth Homestead was built in 1850 by Miss Lucy's father, a tycoon who was very successful in the lime industry and also owned a fleet of ships. Brimming with lavish, colorful Victorian furnishings (all original), it remains—according to a stipulation in Miss Lucy's will—just as it was when she died at the age of 96. Curious details of the decor include draperies so

WILLIAM A. FARNSWORTH LIBRARY AND ART MUSEUM

N.C. Wyeth, Portrait of a Young Artist

long that they drag on the floor, to indicate that the family could afford to buy more fabric than was required. Nevertheless, the walls are hung with inexpensive copies of oil paintings known as chromolithographs, a fireplace mantel is glass painted to resemble marble, and doors are not made of fine wood grains but, rather, have been painted to imitate them. How strange that a woman whose home shows so little appreciation for the fine arts should leave all her money for the establishment of an art museum.

The Olson House (596-6457), Hathron Point Road, Cushing. Open June through mid-October, daily 11–4. $3 adults, $1 children 8–18. Administered by the Farnsworth Art Museum, this house served as a backdrop for many works by Andrew Wyeth, including *Christina's World.*

Montpelier (354-8062), Thomaston. Open Memorial Day to mid-October, Tuesday through Saturday 10–4, Sunday 1–4. $4 adults, $3 seniors, $2 children 5–11. A 1926 re-creation of the grand mansion (financed by *Saturday Evening Post* publisher and Camden summer resident Cyrus Curtis) built on this spot in 1794 by General Henry Knox, the portly (5-foot 6-inch, 300-pound) Boston bookseller who became a Revolutionary War hero, then our first secretary of war. He married a granddaughter of Samuel Waldo, the Boston developer who owned all of this area (and for whom the county is named). Inquire about concerts, lectures, and special events.

✐ **Owls Head Transportation Museum** (594-4418), adjacent to the Knox County Airport off Route 73, Owls Head (just south of Rockland). Open year-round. April through October, daily 10–5; November through March, 10–4 weekdays and 10–3 weekends. Regular admission is $5 adults, $3 under 12, under 5 free, $4.50 for senior citizens; more for the frequent special weekends staged spring through fall. One of the country's outstanding collections of antique planes and automobiles, and unique because everything works. On weekends there are special demonstrations of such magnificent machines as a 1901 Oldsmobile and a 1918 "Jenny" airplane; and sometimes rides are offered in a spiffy Model T. In the exhibition hall, you can take a 100-year journey through the evolution of transportation, from horse-drawn carriages to World War I fighter planes; from a 16-cylinder Cadillac to a Rolls Royce; from the Red Baron's Fokker Triplane to a Ford Trimotor. There are also wagons, motorcycles, and bikes. All vehicles have been donated or lent to the museum.

✐ **Shore Village Museum** (594-0311), 104 Limerock Street, Rockland. Open June 1 to October 15, 10–4 daily; by appointment the rest of the year. Free but donations welcome. A large and fascinating collection of historic artifacts of the US Coast Guard, including one of the most extensive collections of lighthouse materials (working foghorns, flashing lights, search-and-rescue gear, buoys, bells, and boats), plus Civil War memorabilia and changing exhibits.

Antique Boats, Maine Waterfront Museum (354-0444; 1-800-923-0444), 4 Knox Street Landing, Thomaston. Open Memorial Day through September. This is a great idea—a collection of antique smallcraft that you can actually get into the water in. But in the summer of 1996 we found little here, certainly nothing worth the admission price of $4 per adult.

LIGHTHOUSES

✐ Maine has more lighthouses (63) than any other state, and Penobscot Bay boasts the largest number of lighthouses of all. Three in the Rockland area are accessible by land. One is the **Rockland Light,** perched at the end of the almost mile-long granite breakwater (turn off Route 1 onto Waldo Avenue just north of Rockland, then follow Samoset Road to the end); the breakwater is a good spot for a picnic. The second lighthouse is the **Owls Head Light,** built in 1825 atop sheer cliffs, but with safe trails down one side to the rocks below—good for scrambling and picnicking. From Rockland or the Owls Head Transportation Museum, take Route 73 to North Shore Drive Road. After about 2 miles you come to a small post office at an intersection. Go down Main Street for 0.25 mile and make a left onto Lighthouse Drive (the road turns to dirt). Just north of the village of Port Clyde (turn off Route 131 onto Marshall Point Road) is the **Marshall Point Lighthouse Museum** (372-6450), open June through September daily, except Monday, 1–5; weekends in May. Built in 1885, deactivated in 1971, this is a small light on a scenic point;

part of the former lighthouse keeper's home is now a museum, but even if it isn't open, this is a great spot to sit, walk, and picnic.

Lighthouse buffs should also be sure to visit the **Shore Village Museum.**

TO DO

BOAT EXCURSIONS

M/V *Monhegan* (596-5660), a former-ferry-turned-excursion boat, offers lunch and dinner cruises and harbor tours from Rockland. ***Windhorse*** (1-800-777-1554), a 33-foot Friendship sloop, offers 2- to 3-hour sails. ***Gladiator*** (354-8036), Town Landing, Friendship. Built in 1902 and sailed by the same owner-captain since 1967, a large, stable, comfortable sloop accommodating six passengers for half and full days; also charters.

Also see the Maine State Ferry Service described above (under *Getting Around*). Ferry passage to North Haven and Vinalhaven is cheap and takes you the distance.

BOAT RENTALS

Midcoast Boat Rentals (594-7714), 5 Commercial Street, Rockland, rents powerboats.

Sail Penobscot Bay (596-7550; 1-800-421-2492) rents day-sailers and bare-boat charters, and runs an ASA sailing school.

COASTAL CRUISES

Motor Yacht *Pauline* (236-3529; 1-800-999-7352) at Windjammer Wharf, Box 1050, Rockland, is a graceful, 83-foot motor vessel, a former sardine carrier, that's been elegantly converted to accommodate 12 guests in six double staterooms, two with double lower berths and four with extra-long twin berths. The large, handsomely decorated deck saloon includes a wood-burning fireplace. High tea and gourmet meals are served. Able to cruise at up to 9 knots, the *Pauline* offers a wider range of travel than do the windjammers. One day she may motor to Monhegan to attend an arts festival; the next, you could be off to Roque Island way Down East. $450 for 3-day cruises, $700–875 for 6-day trips, $1,000 for a week's charter.

Kathryn B (1-800-500-6077), a 105-foot, three-masted, steel-hulled schooner. A luxury version of the traditional windjammer, launched in 1996, accommodating just 12 passengers. Sailing only July through September. Staterooms have private or shared (just two on a head) baths, Victorian detailing and furnishings, and working portholes; the saloon (with fireplace) and dining area (where five-course gourmet meals are served) are topside. Three-day cruises $495–575; 6-day, $1000–1295.

WINDJAMMERS

In 3 days aboard a windjammer you can explore islands and remote mainland harbors that would take hundreds of miles of driving and several ferries to reach. Three- and 6-day cruises range from $335 to $750 (slightly less early and late in the season). For questions to ask when deciding which vessel to take, see *Windjammers* at the front of the book in "What's Where." But you really cannot lose. All the vessels are inspected and certified each year by the Coast Guard.

American Eagle (594-8007; 1-800-648-4544), North End Shipyard, Rockland. One of the last classic Gloucester fishing schooners to be launched (in 1930), this 92-foot vessel continued to fish (minus its original stern and masts, plus a pilothouse) off Gloucester until 1983, when Captain John Foss brought her to Rockland's North End Shipyard and spent the next two years restoring and refitting her. The *Eagle* was built with an engine (so she still has one) as well as sails, and she offers some comfortable belowdeck spaces, well stocked with the captain's favorite books about Maine. The *Eagle* frequently sails farther Down East than most of the other windjammers. She offers 3- and 6-day cruises, accommodating 28 guests in 14 double cabins.

Isaac H. Evans (594-8007; 1-800-648-4544), North End Shipyard, Rockland, is 65 feet long with 11 double cabins for 22 passengers. The vessel is just over 100 years old, having been built in New Jersey in 1886 as an oyster-fishing schooner. It was completely rebuilt in recent years. Captain Ed Glaser is a veteran seaman who plays the guitar and concertina. Ask about special family cruises (children 8 and up).

Heritage (1-800-648-4544; 1-800-542-5030 outside Maine), North End Shipyard, Rockland. Captain Doug Lee likes to describe his graceful, 95-foot, 33-passenger vessel as "the next generation of coasting schooner rather than a replica." He notes that schooners were modified over the years to suit whatever cargo they carried. Here headroom in the cabins and the top of companionways was heightened to accommodate upright cargo, and the main cabin is an unusually airy, bright space in which to gather. Captain Lee is a marine historian who, with his wife and co-captain, Linda, designed and built the *Heritage* in Rockland's North End Shipyard. Their two daughters, Clara and Rachel, have always summered aboard ship and now sail as crew. Both captains are unusually warm hosts.

J&E Riggin (594-2923; 1-800-869-0604) was built in 1927 for the oyster-dredging trade. A speedy 89-footer, she was extensively rebuilt in the 1970s before joining the windjammer trade. Captain Dave Allen is a second-generation windjammer captain, and his family has been sailing vessels out of nearby Brooklin (where the *Riggin* frequently drops anchor) since the War of 1812—so he comes by his Maine humor rightfully. His wife, Sue, is also a Maine native and an excellent cook. The couple rebuilt the vessel themselves. They take 26 passengers in 10 double, 2 triple cabins; no children under 16.

Stephen Taber (236-3520; 1-800-999-7352), Windjammer Wharf (at the State Ferry Landing), Box 1050, Rockland, was launched in 1871 and is the oldest documented US sailing vessel in continuous use. She is 68 feet long and accommodates 22 passengers. She has a hand-held, hot-water shower on deck. Ken and Ellen Barnes, both licensed captains, bought, restored, and continue to sail the *Taber* after careers as (among other things) drama professors. Their enthusiastic following proves that they approach each cruise as a new production, throwing their (considerable) all into each sail. This tends to be a most musical cruise.

Victory Chimes (594-0755; 1-800-745-5651), PO Box 1401, Rockland. "There was nothing special about this boat in 1900 when she was built," Captain Kip Files is fond of telling his passengers at their first breakfast aboard. "But now she's the only three-masted American-built schooner left. And she's the largest commercial sailing vessel in the United States." The *Chimes* is 170 feet long, accommodating 44 passengers in a variety of cabins (4 singles, 2 quads, 1 triple, 12 doubles). In 1991 the vessel returned to the Maine windjammer fleet in which she had served for more than 30 years, before an interlude on the Great Lakes.

Nathaniel Bowditch (273-4062; 1-800-288-4098) comes by her speed honestly: She was built in East Boothbay as a racing yacht in 1922. Eighty-two feet long, she took special honors in the 1923 Bermuda Race and served in the Coast Guard during World War II. She was rebuilt in the early 1970s. A Maine guide from Rangeley, Captain Gib Philbrick came to the coast to sail aboard a windjammer in 1966 and has been at it ever since. He and his wife, Terry, met aboard the *Bowditch* (she was a passenger). They remain a great team. Twenty-four passengers in 11 double-bunked cabins, two single "pullmans"; in-cabin sinks. Children age 10 and up; 3-, 4-, and 6-day cruises.

Wendameen (236-3472), a classic 67-foot schooner, has been beautifully restored by owner-captain Neal Parker, who takes passengers on overnight cruises from Rockland.

Summertime (359-2067; 1-800-562-8290 outside Maine), 115 South Street, Rockland, is a 53-foot pinky schooner offering 3- and 6-day cruises for up to six passengers throughout the summer. In the spring and autumn, she offers day sails out of Stonington, Castine, and Bucks Harbor.

Note: Most of these vessels are members of the Maine Windjammer Association (1-800-807-WIND) or the North End Shipyard (1-800-648-4544).

SPECIAL LEARNING PROGRAMS

Hurricane Island Outward Bound School (594-5548), Box 429, Rockland 04841. Courses lasting 5 to 26 days are offered on Hurricane Island in Penobscot Bay, May to October. There are courses tailored to every age and to both sexes; they focus on sailing, rock climbing, and outdoor problem solving. An international program begun in Wales, Outward Bound challenges participants to do things they never thought they could and then push themselves just a little further.

Merle Donovan's Maine Coast Art Workshops (372-8200), PO Box 236, Port Clyde 04855-0326. Mid-June through September. A well-established program of weeklong landscape workshops (both oil and watercolor) taught by a series of prominent artists from throughout the country. Lodging is in the Ocean House and its Seaside annex in the village of Port Clyde, on a working harbor at the tip of the St. George Peninsula. The ample, attractive studio space is in a converted barn.

GREEN SPACE

BEACHES
Johnson Memorial Park, Chickawaukee Lake, Route 17 (toward Augusta); **Birch Point Park,** Owls Head; and **Ayer Park,** Union.

PICNICKING
Route 1 picnic area overlooking Glen Cove, between the towns of Rockland and Camden; **Johnson Memorial Park,** Chickawaukee Lake, Route 17; **Sandy Beach Park,** Atlantic Street, Rockland.

LODGING

INNS
East Wind Inn (372-6366; 1-800-241-VIEW), PO Box 149, Tenants Harbor 04860. Open April through November; for special functions the remainder of the year. Under longtime ownership of Tim Watts, this is a very tidy and rather formal waterside inn. The parlor is large, with a piano that guests are welcome to play, but the best seats in the house are on the wraparound porch, overlooking picturesque Tenants Harbor. Rooms vary from old-fashioned singles with shared baths ($38–54) to luxurious suites and apartments and are divided among the main inn, waterside Meeting House, and Ginny Wheeler House (with a two-story apartment, a studio apartment, and a two-bedroom housekeeping suite). Rates for double rooms are $55–108 with continental breakfast; suites $99–135; and apartments $260. The dining room, open to the public, serves breakfast and dinner in-season (see *Dining Out*).

Craignair Inn (594-7644; 1-800-320-9997), Clark Island, Spruce Head 04859. Open mid-May to October. Sited on a granite ledge by the shore, this unusual building was originally erected for workers at a nearby granite quarry. The 22 guest rooms are divided between the main house (all shared baths) and units in back (private baths); bedrooms are small but pleasing, furnished with antiques. The water-view dining room, open to the public for dinner, showcases innkeeper Terry Smith's extensive collection of plates and other souvenirs from her travels in the Far East. Walk down the miles of paths meandering from the inn and on Clark Island. There's also good bird-watching and swimming in the old quarry hole. $74–102 (less off-season) includes a full breakfast. Two-night minimum stay on holiday weekends. Weekly rates are available. Dinner is served.

☞ **Ocean House** (372-6691; 1-800-269-6691), PO Box 66, Port Clyde 04855.
Open May through mid-October. The logical place to spend the night
before boarding the morning ferry to Monhegan, a friendly old village
inn run by former islander Bud Murdock. Seven of the nine upstairs
guest rooms in this building have private baths (two share) and several
have water views (also available from the upstairs porch). There are
seven more rooms in neighboring **Seaside.** Note that the inns serve as
a base for **Merle Donovan's Maine Coast Art Workshops** (see *To
Do—Special Learning Programs*). A reasonably priced, family-style
dinner is by reservation (BYOB) and the breakfast is served to both
guests and the public, 7–noon. Rooms are $56–70 double, $47 single.
(In the "Rockport, Camden, and Lincolnville" chapter, also see the Samoset
Resort, which overlooks Rockland Harbor.)

BED & BREAKFASTS

The Captain Lindsey House (596-7950; 1-800-523-2145), 5 Lindsey
Street, Rockland 04841. Built in 1837 as one of Rockland's first inns,
this sturdy brick building just off Main Street was eventually converted
into offices and labs by the Camden-Rockland Water Company. By the
1990s it took real imagination to envision, let alone restore it to, its
original use. Ken and Ellen Barnes, who have also restored the windjammer *Stephen Taber* and turned a former sardine carrier into the
luxury motor vessel *Pauline,* have created a gem of a small hotel with
richly paneled public rooms and nine spacious guest rooms (one handicapped accessible), furnished with flair and theatrical themes (in its
first life the Lindsey House was patronized by thespians). All rooms
have air-conditioning, phones, TVs in cabinets, and baths equipped with
hair dryers. Rates are $95–160, including continental breakfast; lunch
and dinner are served next door at The Water Works (see *Eating Out*).
Ask about discounts for windjammer passengers and value packages in
conjunction with the *Taber* and *Pauline.*

☞ **Old Granite Inn** (594-9036; 1-800-386-9036) Main Street, Rockland 04841.
An 1840s granite mansion attached to a 1790 house, set in a flower and
sculpture garden, right across from the Maine State Ferry Terminal (also
the Concord Trailways stop). The obvious place to stay before boarding
a ferry to Vinalhaven, North Haven, or Matinicus (see "The Islands"),
this is an unusually welcoming and interesting B&B. Innkeepers John
(an artist) and Stephanie (a chef) Clapp have deftly restored the rich
woodwork, creating 10 inviting guest rooms (8 with private bath) with
cottage furniture and other antiques. Though front rooms have views,
you might want to be in back, away from traffic. The living room and
dining room are both delightful, and the Clapps are helpful about
exploring the area. Rooms $49–119 per night; some rooms are wheel-
chair accessible.

☞ **Weskeag Inn** (596-6676; 800-596-5576), Route 73, PO Box 213, South
Thomaston 04858. Open year-round (weekends-only in winter). Conve-

The East Wind Inn

nient to Owls Head Transportation Museum and the Knox County Airport (where they'll gladly pick you up). A hospitable 1830s home overlooking the Weskeag estuary with its reversing falls. From the dining room and deck, you can watch lobstermen hauling their traps. The nine attractive rooms range from singles with shared bath to doubles with private baths; some rooms have two double beds. Request a water view. Rates are $65–85 including full breakfast.

LimeRock Inn (594-2257; 1-800-LIME-ROCK), 96 Limerock Street, Rockland 04841. An 1890s Queen Anne–style mansion on a quiet residential street within walking distance of the Farnsworth Museum, restaurants, and the harbor, the inn has been thoroughly restored, its eight guest rooms (all with private baths) furnished with splendid reproduction antiques (the innkeepers own a furniture store in Intervale, New Hampshire). Rates range from $85 for a small room decorated in floral prints to $180 for a large room with a mahogany four-poster and whirlpool bath or for a turret room with a "wedding canopy" bed. Rates include a full breakfast and afternoon tea.

The Outsiders' Inn (832-5197), corner of Routes 97 and 220, Box 521A, Friendship 04547. Open year-round, except for a few weeks in midwinter. Comfortable atmosphere in an 1830 house. Guests can take advantage of Bill Michaud's kayaking expertise; eight kayaks are available for rent and guided expeditions in nearby Muscongus Bay. Pleasant doubles with private bath are $65; $50 with shared. A small cottage in the garden is $350 per week. Facilities include a sauna. Inquire about sailing seminars and packages on the Friendship sloop *Gladiator.*

Friendship by the Sea (832-4386), PO Box 24, Friendship 04547. A vintage 1805 Cape, set in a meadow, surrounded by woods. Open June through September. Three attractive rooms with shared bath; common rooms include a pleasant living room and dining room with fireplace and deck. Walk to a working harbor or quiet cove. $55 per couple.

Harbor Hill (832-6646), Town Landing Road, PO Box 35, Friendship 04547. Open July and August, also autumn weekends by arrangement. Liga and Len Jahnke's 1800s farmhouse is set on a hillside sloping to the sea, with views of the islands in Muscongus Bay. The three suites all have water views and private baths; $85–90 includes a Scandinavian-style breakfast. A two-bedroom cottage is $500 per week.

The Pointed Fir (372-6213), Box 625, Tenants Harbor 04860. Open June 15 through October 15. Janet Shea's comfortable old house is across Route 131 from a cove but with unobstructed water views from both upstairs guest rooms and handy to a shore path as well as the Monhegan ferry. This is the place for Sarah Orne Jewett fans. $70 per room includes tax as well as breakfast.

Lakeshore Inn (594-4209), 184 Lakeview Drive, Rockland 04841. A much modified 1767 home above Route 17, overlooking Lake Chickawaukee (good swimming), 2 miles north of Rockland. Paula Nicols and Joseph McCluskey offer four air-conditioned guest rooms (private baths) at $85–90, breakfast included. Ask about spa weekends.

COTTAGES AND EFFICIENCIES

A list of cottages, primarily in the Owls Head and Spruce Head areas, is available from the Rockland-Thomaston Chamber of Commerce (see *Guidance*).

WHERE TO EAT

DINING OUT

Jessica's, a European Bistro (596-0770), 2 South Main Street (Route 73), Rockland. Open year-round, nightly for dinner in summer, closed Tuesday in shoulder seasons, also Monday in winter. Reservations are recommended. In a restored Victorian home, chef-owner Hans Bucher serves nicely prepared Swiss and generally Continental cuisine including a wide variety of meat entrées and pastas as well as seafoods. The menu changes quarterly but always includes veal Zürich, $15.50; entrées $11.50–18.50; extensive wine list and full bar.

Cafe Miranda (594-2034), 15 Oak Street, Rockland. Open Tuesday through Sunday 5:30–9:30. Be sure to reserve because chef Kerry Altiero's small, bright dining room—in an array of southwestern colors and flavors—is usually filled with savvy locals. The open kitchen features a brick oven and seafood grill, and the menu, fresh pastas and herbs. Our pink-pottery platter of curried mussels and shrimp (both in the shell) served on polenta with sweet peppers and onions, mopped up with flatbread (olive oil provided), was a bargain at $12.50. Wine and beer, espresso and cappuccino are served. The handwritten menu of 45 items changes daily. Entrées $9.50–15.

East Wind Inn (372-6366), Tenants Harbor. Open for dinner and Sunday brunch. Reservations suggested. A dining room overlooking the working harbor with a porch on which cocktails are served in summer. The menu features local seafood and produce. Dinners might include baked Maine salmon ($15.95) or grilled eggplant torta ($13.95).

(Also see Marcel's at the Samoset Resort, under *Dining Out,* in the "Rockport" chapter.)

EATING OUT

In Rockland

The Water Works (596-7950), Lindsey Street, Rockland. Serving lunch and dinner daily, late light fare. The Barnes family have converted a former eight-bay garage for the Camden-Rockland Water Company into an attractive meeting spot with two distinct atmospheres: a dining area with a striking fountain sculpture (by Captain Ken Barnes) at one end and a pub with congenial, shared tables at the other. Former windjammer chef Susan Barnes is the hand behind the large and satisfying menu. Staples include shepherd's pie, Bermudian fish stew, and pub sausages (Irish bangers wrapped in puff pastry and baked, served with homemade mustard and salad); the blackboard dinner menu changes nightly. The brew list is extensive. Children's menu.

Conte's (596-5579), Harbor Park, Rockland. Open for lunch and dinner, occupying the less rickety end of the former Black Pearl, serving seafood with an Italian accent: haddock with garlic, cherry peppers, and pizziola and salami and scallop marinara on linguine and pasta Napoli.

The Brown Bag (596-6372), 606 Main Street (north of downtown). Open Monday through Saturday 6:30 AM–4 PM, Sunday 7–2. This expanded storefront restaurant offers an extensive breakfast and sandwich menu. Make your selection at the counter and carry it to your table when it's ready.

Second Read Bookstore (594-4123) 328 Main Street. Open 8–5:30, much later on music nights, 12–4 on Sunday. Patrick Reilley and Susanne Ward's recently expanded café seems to serve as a living room for the city's sizable creative community as well as the obvious place for museumgoers to pause for cappuccino and croissants. Try the curried chicken salad or a grilled panini with roasted eggplant, red peppers, and mozzarella. There's frequently folksinging or jazz on Friday and Saturday nights.

The Landings Restaurant & Pub (596-6563), 1 Commercial Street. Right on the harbor with outside as well as inside seating, serves 11–9:30 from a menu that ranges from a hot dog to steak, lobster, and a full-scale clambake. Fried clams, fish-and-chips, and a good selection of sandwiches.

Kate's Seafood (594-2626), Route 1, south of Rockland. A standby for fried, boiled, and steamed seafood, chowder, lobster rolls, etc.

Dave's Restaurant (594-5424), Route 1, between Thomaston and Rockland. Seafood dinners and the area's only smorgasbord, with old-fashioned classics such as macaroni and cheese and beans and franks. Breakfast and lunch buffets, plus a large salad bar. Breakfast is served all day.

Wasses Wagon (found either at 2 North Main Street or the corner of Park and Union Streets); a local institution for hot dogs.

In Thomaston

Harbor View Tavern (354-8173). Open year-round for lunch and dinner. Tucked right down on the harbor on Snow's Pier. Photographs and memorabilia ornament the walls, and contented-looking goldfish swim about in the water tank of a huge, old coffeemaker. Try the broiled scallops, the peel-your-own Maine shrimp, or mussels and cream.

Thomaston Cafe and Bakery (354-8589), Main Street. Open 7–2, also for dinner Friday and Saturday and for Sunday brunch. Homemade soups, great sandwiches, specials like fish cakes with homefries, salads.

Elsewhere

The Harpoon (372-6304), corner of Drift Inn and Marshall Point Road, Port Clyde. Open May through mid-October. In July and August, open for lunch and dinner every day. Spring and fall, dinner only, Wednesday through Sunday. This engaging little seafood restaurant in the seaside village of Port Clyde (just off Route 131, around the corner from the harbor) serves the local catch. Try the Cajun seafood, lazy lobster, fried combo plate, or prime rib.

Dip Net Coffee Shop, Port Clyde. Seasonal. Counter and table seating, but the preferred spot is the deck overlooking this picturesque harbor. Chowder, quiche, lobster stew, and tantalizing desserts.

✐ **Hannibal's Café on The Common** (785-3663), Union. Open year-round from 10 AM Tuesday through Friday; from 7 AM Saturday; Sunday brunch 8–2. Good lunch and dinner; specializing in "classical, ethnic, and vegetarian cuisine," now in an 1839 farmhouse with views of Seven Trees Pond.

LOBSTER POUNDS

Cod End (372-6782), on the Wharf, Tenants Harbor. Open mid-June to mid-September daily 7 AM–9:30 PM; spring and fall 8–6. Hidden down a lane, a particularly appealing longtime family-owned combination fish shop and informal wharfside eatery (tables inside and out) right on Tenants Harbor with a separate cook house: breakfast muffins and eggs, lunch chowders and lobster rolls, dinner lobsters and clams. We recommend the strawberry-rhubarb pie with ice cream. BYOB.

Miller's Lobster Company (594-7406), Wheeler's Bay, Route 73, Spruce Head. Open 10–7, Memorial Day through Labor Day. On a working harbor, old-fashioned, family-owned and -operated, with a loyal following. Tables are on the wharf; lobsters and clams are cooked in seawater.

Waterman's Beach Lobsters (594-2489), off Route 73, South Thomaston. Open daily 11–7 in the summertime. Oceanfront feasting on the deck: lobster and clam dinners, seafood rolls, homemade pies.

ENTERTAINMENT

The Farnsworth Museum (596-6457) stages a year-round series of Sunday concerts, free with museum admission; reservations advised.

Second Read Bookstore (594-4123), 328 Main Street, Rockland, has live music, usually jazz or folksinging, on many Friday and Saturday evenings; also poetry readings.

SELECTIVE SHOPPING

Rockland's Main Street is a relatively well-preserved example of 19th-century commercial architecture, with department, hardware, and furniture stores. Note especially: **The Store,** featuring a wide selection of cooking supplies; **Coffin's,** a family clothing store; **The Reading Corner,** a full-service bookstore with an interesting interior. The **Farnsworth Museum Store** occupies a space that was a florist shop until 1994 (corner of Main and Elm Streets).

ANTIQUES

More than a dozen antiques stores, scattered between Rockland and Thomaston, publish their own guides, which are available locally.

ART GALLERIES

A total of eight galleries have opened around the Farnsworth in Rockland at this writing. These include the **Caldbeck Gallery** (12 Elm Street across from the museum); **Gallery One** (365 Main Street); Thomas O'Donovan's prestigious **Harbor Square Gallery,** which moved down from Camden (where it had been the premier gallery) in 1996 to occupy a former bank building (374 Main Street); and **Between the Mews** on Elm Street. **Gallery-by-the Sea** in the village of Port Clyde is also well worth noting.

BOOKSTORES

The Reading Corner (596-6651), Main Street, Rockland. A full-service bookstore filling two unusual storefronts.

Thomaston Books & Prints (354-0001), 105 Main Street, Thomaston. Open daily. An attractive full-service bookstore.

Lobster Lane Book Shop (594-7520), Spruce Head. Marked from the Off-Island Store. Open June to September, Thursday through Sunday and weekends through October, 12:30–5. Vivian York's stock of 50,000 titles is well known in bookish circles. Specialties include fiction and Maine.

(Also see Second Read Bookstore under *Eating Out* and *Entertainment.*)

SPECIAL STORES

Prison Shop at the Maine State Prison in Thomaston, Main Street (Route 1), at the southern end of town. A variety of wooden furniture—coffee tables, stools, lamps, and trays—and small souvenirs, all carved by inmates. Prices are reasonable and profits go to the craftsmen.

Nobel Clay (372-6468; 1-800-851-4857), Route 131, Tenants Harbor. Open year-round, 10–6. Trish Inman and Steve Barnes produce functional white-and-blue-glazed pottery with whimsical designs.

SPECIAL EVENTS

June: **Warren Day**—a pancake breakfast, parade, art and quilt shows, chicken barbecue, and auction.

July: **Fourth of July** celebrations in most towns, with parades. Thomaston's festivities include a big parade, foot races, live entertainment, a craft fair, barbecue, and fireworks. **Schooner Days** (Friday, Saturday, and Sunday closest to July 4)—see the wonderful windjammers vie for first place in a spectacular race that recalls bygone days. The best vantage point is the Rockland breakwater next to the Samoset Resort. **North Atlantic Blues Festival,** Rockland Public Landing. **Friendship Sloop Days,** Rockland. **Full Circle Summer Fair,** at the Union Fairgrounds sponsored by WERU-FM—the emphasis is on everything natural and on crafts.

Maine Lobster Festival

August: **Maine Lobster Festival** (first weekend in the month plus the preceding Wednesday and Thursday)—this is probably the world's biggest lobster feed, prepared in the world's largest lobster boiler. Patrons queue up on the public landing to heap their plates with lobsters, clams, corn, and all the fixings. King Neptune and the Maine Sea Goddess reign over the event, which includes a parade down Main Street, concerts, an art exhibit, contests such as clam shucking and sardine packing, and a race across a string of lobster crates floating in the harbor. Annual **Transportation Spectacular and Aerobatic Show** at the Owls Head Transportation Museum. **Union Fair and Blueberry Festival** (third week)—a real agricultural fair with tractor- and ox-pulling contests, livestock and food shows, a midway, the crowning of the Blueberry Queen, and, on one day during the week, free mini blueberry pies for all comers.

October: **Farnsworth Festival of Scarecrows:** Rockland community scarecrow contest, dance, related events.

November/December: **Christmas celebrations** beginning Thanksgiving; parade, Santa's Village, sleigh rides.

The Islands

Monhegan, Vinalhaven, North Haven, Matinicus

MONHEGAN

Eleven miles at sea and barely a mile square, Monhegan is a microcosm of Maine landscapes, everything from 150-foot sheer headlands to Cathedral Woods, from inland meadows filled with deer to the smooth, low rocks along Lobster Cove. "Beached like a whale" is the way one mariner in 1590 described the island's shape: headlands sloping down to coves, a low and quiet tail.

Monhegan is known for the quality (also quantity) of its artists and the grit of its fishermen—who lobster only from January through June. The island's first recorded artist arrived in 1858, and by the 1890s a mansard-roofed hotel and several boardinghouses were filled with summer guests, many of them artists. In 1903 Robert Henri, a founder of New York's Ashcan school and a well-known art teacher, discovered Monhegan and soon introduced it to his students, among them George Bellows and Rockwell Kent. Monhegan remains a genuine art colony. Jamie Wyeth owns a house built by Rockwell Kent. Some 20 artists open their studios to visitors (hours are posted on "The Barn") during summer weeks. Cathedral Woods is studded with "fairy houses" (a local art form).

The island continues to draw artists in good part because its beauty not only survives but also remains accessible to all. Prospect Hill, the only attempted development, foundered around 1900. It was Theodore Edison, son of the inventor, who amassed property enough to erase its traces and keep the island's cottages (which still number just 130) bunched along the sheltered Eastern Harbor, the rest preserved as common space and laced with 17 miles of footpaths.

In 1954 Edison helped to organize Monhegan Associates, a nonprofit corporation dedicated to preserving the "natural, wild beauty" of the island. Ironically, this is one of the country's few communities to shun electricity until relatively recently. A number of homes and one inn still use kerosene lamps. Vehicles are limited to a few trucks to haul lobstering gear and visitors' luggage to and from the dock. Deer saunter through the village.

Monhegan has three inns, several bed & breakfasts, and a number of rental cottages; it is also a summer day's destination for day-trippers from Boothbay Harbor and New Harbor as well as Port Clyde—obviously a heavy tide of tourists for such a small, fragile island. Luckily the fog and frequently rough passage, not to mention limited public plumbing, discourage casual visitors. The island's year-round population of substantially less than 100 swells to a little more than 400 (not counting day-trippers) in summer; visitors come to walk, to paint, and to reflect. An unusual number come alone.

GETTING THERE

For details about the *Balmy Days II,* see "Boothbay Harbor," and for the *Hardy III,* see "Damariscotta Area." The Monhegan-Thomaston Boat Line operates both the sleek new *Elizabeth Ann* and the beloved old *Laura B* from Port Clyde (reservations are necessary: Monhegan Boat Line, PO Box 238, Port Clyde 04855; or call 372-8848); parking is $4 per day; the ticket is $24 round-trip per adult, $12 per child, $2 per pet. Service is three times daily in-season, less frequent in spring and fall, and only Monday, Wednesday, and Friday in winter. Come properly shod for the precipitous paths, and bring sweaters and windbreakers. Wading or swimming from any of the tempting coves on the back side of the island tends to be lethal. Flashlights, heavy rubber boots, and rain gear are also good ideas. There is no bank on the island. Camping is prohibited. Do not bring bicycles or dogs (which must be leashed at all times). No smoking outside the village, and please don't pick the flowers.

GETTING AROUND

Several trucks meet each boat as it arrives and provide baggage service for a fee. Otherwise visitors have no access to motorized transport; you need none because distances are all short and there are no paved roads.

TO SEE

The Lighthouse, built in 1824 and automated in 1959, offers a good view from its perch on the crest of a hill. The former keeper's cottage is now the **Monhegan Museum** (open daily July 4 through mid-September, 11:30–3:30), a spellbinding display of island art, artifacts, flora, fauna, some geology, lobstering, and an artistic history of the island, including documents dating back to the 16th century. One upstairs room is dedicated each summer to a show devoted to one of the island's deceased artists. A separate art museum is planned.

Manana Island (across the harbor from Monhegan) is the site of a famous runic stone with inscriptions purported to be Norse or Phoenician. At Middle Beach on Monhegan, you may be able to find someone willing to take you over in a skiff.

The Laura B

TO DO

HIKING

Pick up a trail map before setting out. Day-trippers should take the **Burnt Head Trail** and loop back by the village via **Lobster Cove** rather than trying a longer circuit; allow at least 5 hours (bring a picnic) to go around the island. Our favorite hike is **Burnt Head** to **White Head** along high bluffs, with a pause to explore the unusual rocks in **Gull Cove,** and back through **Cathedral Woods.** On another day head for **Blackhead** and **Pulpit Rock,** then back along the shore to **Green Point** and **Pebble Beach** to watch the action on **Seal Ledges.**

LODGING

INNS

Monhegan House (594-7983; 1-800-599-7983) Box 345, Monhegan 04852. Open Memorial Day through Columbus Day. An 1870s summer inn with 32 rooms, family owned and operated for five generations. No closets, shared baths, but clean, comfortable, and bright; rooms are furnished with antique oak pieces and many have water views. The downstairs lobby is often warmed by a glowing fireplace, and has ample seating for foggy mornings; on sunny days guests tend to opt for the rockers along the porch, a vantage point from which you can watch the comings and goings of just about everyone on the island. The café is a popular spot for all three meals with locals as well as guests of the inn. Singles are $45; doubles $75; $95 for three people.

Island Inn (596-0371; 1-800-722-1269), Monhegan Island 04852. Open late May to mid-October. This waterfront landmark with 32 rooms and four suites changed hands in 1996. Initially some of its old character seemed to have been lost, but we understand that it is in transition. In the two small living rooms (part of the original circa-1850 house that is the nucleus of the 1900 inn), note the hand-painted murals. The large, old-fashioned dining room serves three meals a day to the public as well as to overnight guests. $98–155 double, $88 single including breakfast.

☞ **The Trailing Yew** (596-0440), Monhegan Island 04852. Open mid-May through mid-October. In 1996 Josephine Day died, having operated the Yew since 1926. For the time being, however, we are assured that this quirky institution will remain unchanged: 40 very basic rooms divided among the main house, adjacent buildings, and cottages on the grounds and up the road. Expect shared baths, a combination of electricity (in the bathrooms) and kerosene lamps, and simple food (usually there's some form of cod). Before meals, guests gather around the flagpole outside the main building to pitch horseshoes and compare notes; family-style dining at shared tables features lots of conversation. Birders tend to have their own table. The dining room is open to the public. $54 per person per day, including breakfast and dinner and all taxes and tips; ages 5–10, $15–32.

BED & BREAKFASTS

Shining Sails Guesthouse (596-0041; 1-800-606-9497), Box 346, Monhegan Island 04852. Open year-round. Bill Baker and Amy Melenbacker have renovated an old Monhegan home on the edge of the village. There are three rooms here, two with views of the meadow and of the ocean; also four efficiencies, three with ocean views. All rooms are tastefully decorated, as is the common room, which has a water view and Franklin stove. An ample continental breakfast is served May through Columbus Day. Rooms are $65–85, $432–566 per week; apartments are $85–100 per night, $532–665 weekly.

Hitchcock House (594-8137), Horn's Hill, Monhegan Island 04852. Open year-round. Hidden away on top of Horn's Hill with a pleasant garden and deck. Barbara Hitchcock offers several rooms and efficiencies with views of the meadows. The studio, a separate cabin, has a kitchen and bedroom. Rooms are $48 per night, $320 per week; efficiencies are $72 per night, $440 per week.

COTTAGES AND EFFICIENCIES

Note: Cooking facilities come in handy here: You can buy lobster and good fresh and smoked fish (bring meat and staples) and a limited line of vegetables. **Shining Sails Real Estate** (596-0041) manages two dozen or so rental cottages, available by the weekend as well as by the week.

Monhegan

WHERE TO EAT

Monhegan House Cafe at the Monhegan House is the most attractive and inviting place to eat on the island: homemade breads and omelets for breakfast; luncheon sandwiches like cheese, lettuce, tomato, and avocado on homemade bread, fresh ground peanut butter, or "the ultimate burger"; dinner entrées include vegetarian choices as well as seafood and steak ($8.95–16.95). BYOB.

The Island Inn (mid-June to mid-September). Open to the public for all three meals. Dinner is a set $18 per person ($20 on Sunday, buffet night). You might begin with homemade turkey soup and dine on seafood pot pie in puff pastry (perhaps strawberry pie for dessert). $4 service charge for BYOB wine.

The Trailing Yew (mid-May to mid-October). Open to the public by reservation. Under $15 for fruit cup, entrée, salad, and dessert, whatever is being served that night. Ask when you reserve. The big attraction here is the conversation around communal tables. BYOB.

The Periwinkle serves breakfast, lunch, and dinner. A two-floor restaurant with water views, varied menu, beer and wine. Outside seating at lunch.

North End Pizza, open seasonally 11–7 for lunch and dinner, is good for daily specials as well as a wide variety of pizzas. Run by a young fisherman and his wife.

At the **Fish "R" Us Fish Market,** you'll find smoked products and picnic fixings as well as lobsters.

SELECTIVE SHOPPING

ART GALLERIES
The **Lupine Gallery** (594-8131). Bill Boynton and Jackie Bogel offer original works by 60 artists who paint regularly on the island.

Open Studios: Many of the resident artists welcome visitors to their studios; pick up a schedule, check "The Barn," or look for shingles hung outside listing the hours they're open. To see works by James Fitzgerald, contact his longtime patron, Anne Hubert. In addition, some of the island's most prestigious artists do not post hours, but still welcome visitors by appointment. Several of these, notably Don Stone and Guy Corriero, give occasional workshops.

SPECIAL SHOP
Carina. The spiritual successor of the old Island Spa, with booths, books, quality crafted items, wines, and fresh-baked goods and vegetables.

VINALHAVEN

Vinalhaven is a large (8-mile-long) island 13 miles off Rockland with a year-round fishing fleet of over 200 boats. Summer visitors may outnumber residents five to one, but it still feels like the locals are in charge here. Vinalhaven gets relatively few day-trippers, accommodations are limited, and summer people seem to disappear once off the ferry; most are from families who have been coming here for generations. Unless you are renting a cottage, do not bring a car. Lodging places cluster in **Carver's Harbor,** the 1880s village at which the ferry docks. Bicycles are all you need to reach the quarries (great swimming holes) and nature preserves where you can walk, pick berries, bird-watch, and generally unwind.

In 1880, when granite was being cut on Vinalhaven to build Boston's Museum of Fine Arts and New York's Brooklyn Bridge, 3380 people were living here on the island, a number now reduced to about 1000— a mix of descendants of 18th-century settlers and the stonecutters who came here from Sweden, Norway, Finland, and Scotland. In recent years the island has also attracted a number of artists, including Robert Indiana, who works year-round in the middle of the village.

Vinalhaven makes sense as a day-trip destination only if it's a nice day and if you take the early boat. Pick up the first map you find and don't be discouraged by the walk into Carver's Harbor, along the island's ugliest quarter mile. Don't miss the museum, and rent a bike to get out to Lane's Island. This is a great place to be on the Fourth of July.

GETTING THERE
In the past couple of years, the nightmare quality of taking a car to

Vinalhaven has eased thanks to the addition of a second ferry, but it can still be enough of a hassle in July or August to cancel out the relaxing effect of the island itself. **The Maine State Ferry Service** (in Rockland: 596-2202; in Carver's Harbor: 863-4421) has its own system: Each ferry takes no more than 17 vehicles (usually fewer since there is always a truck or two), and only a handful of these spaces can be reserved (reservations are $5 but must be made at least 30 days in advance). Cars are taken in order of their position in line. For the morning boats you must be in line the night before. During the summer season, getting off the island can entail lining up a day in advance and then moving your car for every ferry (five times a day). It's $24 for car and driver; $8 per adult and $6 per child; $4 per bicycle. Call 867-4621 to find out about shuttle service between Vinalhaven and North Haven.

Penobscot Air Service (596-6211) will fly you in from Portland or Boston as well as Rockland.

TO SEE AND DO

Vinalhaven Historical Society Museum (863-4410; 863-4318), top of High Street; open mid-June though early September, daily 11–3. In the absence of a visitors center, this exceptional museum serves the purpose. It's housed in the former town hall, built in 1830 in Rockland as a Universalist church, brought over in 1875. Displays include photos and mementos from the island's granite and fishing industries. Check out the nearby **Carver Cemetery.**

BICYCLING

Vinalhaven has more than 30 miles of paved roads, but most places you will want to find are a short ride out of Carver's Harbor. **Tidewater Inn** (see *Lodging*) rents bikes.

GREEN SPACE

Lane's Island Preserve lies off the road on the southern side of Carver's Harbor (cross the Indian Creek Bridge and look for the sign on your left). It includes 45 acres of fields, marsh, moor, and beach. **Grimes Park,** just west of the ferry terminal, is a 2-acre point of rocky land with two small beaches. Note the rough granite watering trough once used by horses and oxen. **Armrust Hill** is on the way to Lane's Island, hidden behind the medical center. The first place in which granite was commercially quarried, it remained one of the most active sites on the island for many decades. Notice the many small pits ("motions") as well as four major quarries. The main path winds up the hill for a splendid view. **Booth Quarry.** Continue east on Main Street 1.5 miles past the Union Church to the Booth Brothers Granite quarry (also known as the swamp quarry). This is a town park and popular swimming hole.

Note: This list is just a sampling of possibilities.

LODGING

Fox Island Inn (863-2122), PO Box 451, Carver Street, Vinalhaven 04863. Open Memorial Day through September. A restored, century-old town house near the library, just a 10-minute walk from the ferry landing, through the village and up the hill. Gail Reinertsen, a competitive long-distance runner, is a warm and helpful host, knowledgeable about the island and happy to dispense directions to her favorite beauty spots. Several bikes are available to guests. Rooms are nicely decorated, and the living room is well stocked with books. Breakfast is buffet-style, and guests are welcome to use the kitchen to prepare picnics, light meals, and snacks. There are six rooms, shared (immaculate) baths, and one suite (private bath). Doubles are $50–60; there's also a three-room suite; rates include breakfast. To reserve off-season, call Gail at 904-425-5095.

Tidewater Inn (863-4618), Carver's Harbor, Vinalhaven 04863. Open year-round. Phil and Elaine Crossman's outstanding little motel is located on the water in the heart of the village. There are 11 units and one apartment; some have waterside decks, others kitchens, some both. In July and August $80 double, $92 for waterfront units with kitchens; $65–80 single. The Tidewater also rents bicycles.

Libby House (863-4696; winter: 516-369-9172), Water Street, Vinalhaven 04863. Open July and August. Built in 1869, this handsome, rambling home is furnished with Victorian pieces, including heavily carved beds. The comfortable common rooms are often filled with music; innkeeper Philip Roberts is a music teacher. It's a short walk from here to Lane's Island Preserve. Breakfast is included. $60–100.

COTTAGES

Vinalhaven Realty (863-4474) offers a list and Frank and Ada Thompson (863-2241) specialize in summer rentals.

WHERE TO EAT

The Haven (863-4969), Main Street. Open year-round. In summer for dinner Tuesday through Saturday; off-season, just Wednesday, Friday, and Saturday (call). Two dining rooms—an open-beamed room overlooking the water and a smaller streetside café—flank a kitchen. Dinner in the waterside room is elegant and by reservation for sittings at 6 and 8:15; lighter meals are served in the pub-style street side. Liquor served. No smoking.

Sand Dollar (863-9937), Main Street. Open for breakfast, lunch, and dinner. A good dinner bet: lots of good food, local ambience, BYOB (Boongies is across the street).

Candlepin Lodge (863-2730), Roberts Cemetery Road. Open from 5 daily except Monday, dinner 6–9, Sunday noon–10. A rustic cedar lodge a half mile from the ferry dock with a juke box, candlepin bowling, a soda fountain, a grill, and an appealing restaurant.

The Harbor Gawker (863-9365), Main Street, middle of the village. Open daily, early and late, good for chowder, seafood rolls, and baskets of just about anything.

The Islander (863-2028) Main Street. Open for lunch Monday through Friday, dinner Tuesday through Saturday. Serves good, moderately priced food.

SELECTIVE SHOPPING

The Fog Gallery, featuring the work of such well-known Fox Islands artists as Robert Indiana and Eric Hopkins.

NORTH HAVEN

A low-key, private sort of resort with pebble beaches, very walkable country roads beside rolling, wildflower-filled meadows, vistas of Penobscot Bay, and a pleasant town park on the north side of the island. The **North Island Museum,** operated by the local historical society, will help you understand the island's history.

GETTING THERE

See *Getting There* for Vinalhaven. Same story except you line up in Rockland in the lanes marked NH rather than VH. To reach the Maine State Ferry Service office in North Haven, call 867-4441. For shuttle service from North Haven to Vinalhaven, call 867-4621. Again, you don't need a car; the only place to stay has bicycles.

LODGING

Pulpit Harbor Inn (867-2219), North Haven Island 04853. Open year-round. A 19th-century farmhouse with four guest rooms, two with private baths. While it lacks water views, it is surrounded by pastures, fruit trees, organic gardens, and evergreens. Innkeepers Michelle and Bill Bullock are from mid-Maine; they keep cows and make cheese. $75–95 includes a very full breakfast.

MATINICUS

Home to about 70 hardy souls in winter, most of whom make their living lobstering, Matinicus's population grows to about 200 in summer. A very quiet, unspoiled island, 23 miles at sea on the outer edge of Penobscot Bay. Walking trails thread the meadows and shore and there are two sand beaches, one at each end of the island. **Matinicus Rock** is a protected nesting site for puffins, a lure for birders in June and July.

GETTING THERE

The 40-foot ***Mary and Donna*** (366-3700) takes 2 hours to ply between Matinicus and Rockland, June through September, once a day Friday through Sunday plus one trip midweek (usually Wednesday); $35 round-trip; also day trips to Matinicus Rock to see the puffins on weekends ($10 extra if you aren't taking the boat to or from Rockland that day). **The Maine State Ferry** serves the island about once a month (596-2202) in winter, three times a month in summer. The flying time via **Penobscot Air Service Ltd.** (596-6211) from Owls Head is 12 minutes but flights are often canceled due to weather.

LODGING

Tuckanuck Lodge (366-3830), Box 217, Shag Hollow Road, Matinicus 04851. Open May through October. Pets and well-behaved children welcome. Nantucket islander Bill Hoadley offers five rooms (two shared baths), some with a view of Old Cove and the ocean. $45–80 double, $30–55 single, including breakfast; half rate for children. Lunch and supper are available at the Pirates Galley when it's open; if it's not, guests have kitchen privileges (bring your own fixings); supper at the lodge costs $10–12 (BYOB).

For **cottage rentals:** Call the Matinicus Chamber of Commerce (366-3868), Box 212, Matinicus 04851.

Belfast, Searsport, and Stockton Springs

Belfast has a history of unusual commercial diversification, including a highly successful sarsaparilla company, a rum distillery, and a city-owned railroad, not to mention poultry and shoe enterprises. Belfast can also boast 11 shipyards and over 360 vessels raised in its shipbuilding past. Many sea captains made their homes here, and the streets are lined with a number of their fine old houses, many of which have become bed & breakfasts in recent years. The Victorian brick downtown is now a genuinely interesting place to shop.

East of Belfast, Route 1 follows the shore of Penobscot Bay as it narrows and seems more like a mighty river. With its sheltered harbors, this area was once prime shipbuilding country.

In 1845 Searsport alone managed to launch eight brigs and six schooners. In Searsport's Penobscot Marine Museum you learn that more than 3000 different vessels have been built in and around Penobscot Bay since 1770. Searsport also once boasted more sea captains than any other town its size, explaining the dozens of 19th-century mansions, many now B&Bs, still lining the Searsport stretch of Route 1.

Just north of Searsport lies Stockton Springs, a small town with neither large shopping area nor business district. What it does have is some good restaurants, inns, and Sandy Point, offering great views and a nice little beach.

Pleasant lodging places are scattered along the bay between Belfast and Bucksport, making this a logical hub from which to explore the entire region, from Camden to Bar Harbor.

GUIDANCE

Belfast Area Chamber of Commerce (338-5900) maintains a year-round office and seasonal information booth on the waterfront. Information can be obtained year-round by writing PO Box 58, Belfast 04915.
Searsport & Stockton Springs Chamber of Commerce (548-2213), PO Box 139, Searsport 04974, maintains a seasonal information booth (548-6510) on Route 1 and publishes a guide to the area. It also provides information about antiques shops.

GETTING THERE
By air: **Ace Aviation** (338-2970) in Belfast offers charter service to all points.

By car: The most direct route to this region from points south and west is via I-95, exiting in Augusta and taking Route 3 to Belfast.

MEDICAL EMERGENCY
Waldo County General Hospital (338-2500; 1-800-649-2536), Northport Avenue, Belfast.

VILLAGES

Liberty is home to Lake St. George State Park, and the Liberty Tool Company on Main Street draws large crowds with its bizarre mix of antiques and items found in an old-fashioned hardware store. The octagonal post office houses the historical society and is itself a museum with all of its original equipment. It is open on weekends in the summer.

Northport. A deceptively sleepy-looking little town has a yacht club, a golf club, pretty gingerbread cottages lining the bay, a popular Saturday-night dance club, and a well-known Mexican restaurant.

TO SEE

MUSEUMS
Penobscot Marine Museum (548-2529), Route 1, Searsport. Open Memorial Day to mid-October, Monday through Saturday 10–5, Sunday 12–5. Adults $5, seniors $3.50, children 7–15, $1.50. (The library is open weekdays, year-round.) Housed in a cluster of public and private buildings that formed the town's original core. Displays in the 1845 town hall trace the evolution of sailing vessels from 17th-century mast ships to the Down Easters of the 1870s and 1880s—graceful, square-rigged vessels that were both fast and sturdy cargo carriers. In other buildings there are fine marine paintings, scrimshaw, a variety of lacquerware, Chinese imports, and more. You learn that Searsport didn't just build ships; townspeople owned the ships they built and sailed off in them to the far reaches of the compass, taking their families along. In 1889 Searsport boasted 77 deep-sea captains, 33 of whom manned full-rigged Cape Horners. There are pictures of Searsport families meeting in distant ports, and, of course, there is the exotica they brought home—much of which is still being sold in local antiques shops. The **Fowler-True-Ross house** tells the story of two prominent captains' families. Not everyone led the life of a sea captain, however, and the museum's exhibit "Working the Bay: The Ports and People of Penobscot Bay" focuses on the working-class people who made their living here in the granite, lime, ice, fishing, and lobstering industries. The museum sponsors lecture, film, and concert series and operates a gift store.

✏ **Perry's Tropical Nut House** (338-1630), Route 1, east of Belfast. Open spring through fall until 9:30 PM in high season. A nutty store in every way, this landmark began in the 1920s when the South produced more pecans than it could sell, a situation that inspired a Belfast man who had investments in southern groves to sell pecans to the new tourist traffic coming up Route 1 in Maine. Irving Perry was soon doing so well that he moved his shop to the old cigar factory that it still occupies, along with the original shop building tacked on. He traveled throughout South America and other parts of the world collecting nuts (the display includes every nut species known to man) as well as alligators, monkeys, ostriches, peacocks, gorillas, and other dusty stuffed animals now on display. It's all a bit fusty now, and Perry himself is long gone, but everyone still has to stop and pose next to the various exotica and outsized carved elephants.

Searsport Historical Society (548-6663), Route 1, Searsport. Open July through September, Wednesday through Sunday 1–5. A collection of local artifacts, photos, maps, clothing, and town records.

Belfast Museum (338-2078; 338-1875), 6 Market Street, Belfast. Open Thursday and Sunday in summer, 1–4, and by appointment year-round. Local area artifacts, paintings, scrapbooks, and other displays.

TO DO

AIRPLANE RIDE

Ace Aviation Inc. (338-2970) offers scenic flights from Belfast Municipal Airport; two-person minimum.

BOAT EXCURSION

Balmy Days (338-4652) offers coastal cruises and trips to Castine, also day sails aboard the wooden yacht *Jessamyn Rose.* Check with the Belfast Chamber of Commerce (see *Guidance*) for information about other cruises of the bay.

GOLF

Country View Golf Course (722-3161) in Brooks is the most scenic in the area: nine holes, par 36, cart rental, club rentals, lessons, clubhouse.

KAYAKING

Harvey Schiller (282-6204) offers guided tours from Belfast City Pier using double kayaks; beginners and families welcome.

SWIMMING

Lake St. George State Park (589-4255), Route 3, Liberty. Open May 15 through October 15. A great way station for travelers going to or from Down East. A deep, clear lake with a small beach, lifeguard, bathhouse, parking facilities, 31 campsites, and a boat launch. **Swan Lake State Park,** Route 141, Swanville (north of town; follow signs). This beach has picnicking facilities on Swan Lake. **Belfast City Park,** Route 1, Belfast (south of town). Swimming pool, tennis courts, picnicking facilities, and a gravel beach. **Sandy Point Beach,** off Route 1 north of

Stockton Springs (it's posted HERSEY RETREAT; turn toward the water directly across from the Rocky Ridge Motel). **Mosman Beach Park,** Searsport. There's a town dock, boat ramp, swimming, fishing.

TRAIN EXCURSION

✐ **Belfast & Moosehead Lake Railroad Co.** (338-2330; 1-800-392-5500), May through October, operates 2½-hour excursions from the Belfast waterfront along the Passagassawakeag River to the inland village of Brooks and back. Inquire about rides on Maine's only coal-fired, standard-gauge steam locomotive from Unity station (see *Train Ride* in "Augusta and Mid Maine") and about Rail & Sail combos.

GREEN SPACE

(Also see *Swimming.*)

Moose Point State Park, Route 1, south of Searsport. Open May 30 to October 15. A good spot for picnicking; cookout facilities are in an evergreen grove and an open field overlooking Penobscot Bay.

Fort Pownall and **Fort Point State Park,** Stockton Springs (marked from Route 1; accessible via a 3.5-mile access road). This is the site of a 1759 fort built to defend the British claim to Maine (the Kennebec River was the actual boundary between the English and French territories). It was burned twice to prevent its being taken; only earthworks remain. The adjacent park, on the tip of a peninsula jutting into Penobscot Bay, is a fine fishing and picnic spot. A pier accommodates visitors who arrive by boat. The lighthouse is another great spot. Views from the point are back down to the Camden Hills.

LODGING

INNS AND BED & BREAKFASTS
In Belfast 04915

The Inn on Primrose Hill (338-6982), 212 High Street. One of Maine's more elegant mansions, this Federal beauty was built in 1812 by a local merchant-shipbuilder. Greek Revival touches, added later, include Ionic pillars; in the 1920s the wife of an admiral added a beautifully paneled garden room with a vaulted ceiling and long windows overlooking rose gardens. Linus and Pat Heinz have lovingly restored the house and furnished it appropriately. The Rose Room, with a queen bed, bay view, and private bath, is $85; the Blue Room, same view but shared bath, is $75; two more rooms with garden views are $65. Rates include a full breakfast and afternoon tea featuring Irish oatmeal scones.

The Jeweled Turret Inn (338-2304; 1-800-696-2304), 40 Pearl Street. Open year-round. A handsome gabled and turreted house built ornately inside and out in the 1890s. The fireplace in the den is said to be made of stones from every state in the Union at that time, from the collection of the original owner. Each of the seven guest rooms is decorated in shades reminiscent of the gem it is named for and furnished with antiques and plenty of knickknacks. Private baths. Carl and Cathy Heffentrager serve a full breakfast and tea and take time to visit with guests. $70–95 double, $5 less for singles.

In Searsport 04974

Homeport Inn (548-2259; 1-800-742-5814), Route 1. Open year-round. An 1861 captain's mansion complete with widow's walk that overlooks the bay. Dr. and Mrs. George Johnson were the first Searsport B&B hosts, and they now offer 10 elegantly decorated guest rooms, along with a two-bedroom cottage on the water. Rooms in the front of the house are old-fashioned with shared baths, but those in the back have private baths and bay views. The landscaped grounds include flower gardens and slope to the water. A full breakfast is included in the rates, which range from $35 (single with shared bath) to $85 (double with private bath); lower rates November through April. The cottage is $500 per week.

Captain Green Pendleton B & B (548-6523), Route 1. Open year-round. Another fine old captain's home with 80 acres set well back from Route 1. The three bedrooms, one downstairs (with private bath) and two upstairs, are comfortably furnished with a welcoming feel. All have working fireplaces, and there's a Franklin fireplace in the guest parlor. A path circles the meadow, a cross-country ski trail goes through the woods, and there's a large, spring-fed trout pond. The Greiners are warm and helpful hosts. $65 per night downstairs, $55 upstairs, includes tax as well as a full breakfast; less off-season.

Thurston House B&B Inn (548-2213; 800-240-2213), 8 Elm Street. Open year-round. Carl and Beverly Eppig offer four guest rooms in an attractive 1830s house on a side street in the village, originally built as a parsonage. Two rooms are upstairs and have private baths. The two on the first floor of the carriage house share a bath and have a private entrance (good for a family of five). "Forget-about-lunch" breakfasts and state tax are included in $50–65 high season, $45–55 in the off months; $45 single.

Watchtide (548-6575; 1-800-698-6575), Route 1. Almost too good to be true and we are afraid it may not last. This is a bright house with a 60-foot-long, 19-windowed, wicker- and flower-filled sun porch overlooking fields stretching to the bay. Nancy-Linn Elliott is a warm host who also operates Angels to Antiques—a gift store specializing in angels—in the adjacent barn. The four guest rooms are furnished with antiques; request one of the two in back. $70–85 the first night, less thereafter and off-season.

The Captain Butman Homestead (548-2506), Route 1. A classic 1830s farmhouse on 5½ acres. It's open summers only because hosts Lee and Wilson Flight teach school in Massachusetts. This was home for two generations of Searsport deep-water captains, and there's a right-of-way down to Penobscot Bay. The three guest rooms share 1½ baths. A full breakfast is included in $45 double. If you have high school–aged children, you might want to ask about the Downeast Outdoor Education School, an exciting 2- to 4-week program (Wilson takes a group to Alaska in 1997).

In Stockton Springs 04981

The Hichborn Inn (567-4183; 1-800-346-1522), Church Street, PO Box 115. Open year-round except Christmas. This stately Victorian Italian-ate mansion complete with widow's walk is up a side street in an old shipbuilding village that's now bypassed by Route 1. Built by a prolific shipbuilder (N.G. Hichborn launched 42 vessels) and prominent politician, it remained in the family, preserved by his daughters (there's a tale!), until 1939. For Nancy and Bruce Suppes, restoring this house has meant deep involvement in its story—and its friendly ghosts. Bruce, an engineer on supertankers, has done much of the exceptional restoration work himself. There's a comfortable "gent's parlor," where evening fires burn; also a music room and an elegant library. Elaborate breakfasts are served either in the dining room or on the sun porch. There are four rooms, two with private baths; niceties include books and magazines by all the beds, and hot coffee with your wake-up call. Your hosts will pick you up at the dock in Searsport or Belfast, and provide transport to dinner or for supplies. $60–85 per night, $51–72 off-season.

WHERE TO EAT

DINING OUT

Nickerson Tavern (548-2220), Route 1, Searsport. Open Tuesday through Sunday 5:30–9. Patrons drive from Bar Harbor and Bangor to this handsome 1860s sea captain's house. Under new ownership, the tavern's elegance and quality have been upheld. Entrées include veal sautéed with wild mushrooms, scallions, and sage in a Marsala cream sauce; chicken with a light coating of crushed hazelnuts in raspberry sauce; and shrimp sautéed with Cajun spices, garlic, and ale, finished with sweet butter. Reservations are a must. Entrées are $12.50–18.50.

90 Main (338-1106), Belfast. Open daily for dinner 5–10, Sunday brunch 9–3, and dinner 4:30–9. A reasonably priced dining-out alternative, a storefront with atmosphere and a menu featuring the likes of blueberry chicken (grilled breast in a sauce laced with Bartlett's blueberry wine and Dijon mustard; $11.95), vegetarian dishes, and a variety of fresh pastas as well as a lamb of the day and local salmon (market price).

EATING OUT

Darby's Restaurant and Pub (338-2339), 105 High Street, Belfast. Open for lunch and dinner. A friendly storefront café with salads, burgers, and upscale lunch sandwiches. A reasonably priced dinner find: Entrées might include pan-fried crabcakes ($11.95) or homemade pot pie.

Soups and sandwiches are served all day, along with wine and beer.

90 Main Street (338-1106), 90 Main Street, Belfast. Downstairs, below the restaurant, a deli/bakery (open 7 AM–6 PM) is the source of a half-dozen fabulous breads that change with the day (come on Thursday for the Savory Spinach). Soups, and sandwiches made with the bread. The upstairs lunch menu is broad: nachos, burgers, and vegetarian specials like refried black turtle beans, sauce, and cheese wrapped in a tortilla and topped with sour cream.

Young's Lobster Pound (338-1160), Mitchell Avenue (posted from Route 1 just across the bridge from Belfast), East Belfast. Open in-season 7–6:30. A pound with as many as 30,000 lobsters. Order and enjoy the view of Belfast across the Passagassawakeag River while you wait.

Seafarer's Tavern (548-2465), Route 1, Searsport. Open for lunch and dinner except Sunday. The real heart of Searsport, a great little restaurant good for soups, sandwiches, burritos, pizza, and reasonably priced dinner entrées like smoky barbecue ribs or chicken pot pie. Full bar.

The Griffin House Cafe & More (567-3057), Stockton Springs. Open Wednesday through Sunday 7–2 and Wednesday night 5–7:30 for pasta by reservation. This attractive storefront is good for breakfast omelets and lunch sandwiches like curried tuna salad and thinly shaved ham, with Swiss on a fresh roll with just the right touch of Raye's mustard.

ENTERTAINMENT

The Belfast Maskers (338-9668). A year-round community theater that's making waves with performances in its Waterfront Theater. Check local listings.

SELECTIVE SHOPPING

ANTIQUES SHOPS

Searsport claims to be the "Antiques Capital of Maine." After counting 29 shops on Route 1, we may be inclined to agree. A directory is available at the chamber of commerce (see *Guidance*).

The **Searsport Antique Mall,** open daily year-round, is a cooperative of 74 dealers. Everything from 18th-century furniture to 1960s collectibles is spread over two floors. Next door, **Hickson's Flea Market** has both indoor shops (most have specialties) rented for the season and outdoor tables where anyone can set up. **The Pumpkin Patch,** we're told by an experienced dealer, is one of the best shops in the state. They've been in business close to 20 years and have 26 dealers represented. Mary Harriman ran a truck stop until 1989. When it closed, she opened the **Hobby Horse,** which has since grown to house 20 shops, 30 tables, and a lunch wagon. **The Searsport Flea Market,** held weekends in-season, is also big. Antiques at **Hillman's** (Route 1 across from the Nickerson Tavern): good linens, china, glassware.

ART GALLERIES

Artfellows (338-5776), 16 Main Street, Belfast. Open Monday through Saturday 9–5. A cooperative gallery that represents the work of 40 artists working in a variety of media. Changing exhibits; annual **Invitational Painters Show.**

MH Jacobs Art Gallery (338-3324), 44 Main Street, Belfast. Original paintings.

BOOKSTORES

Victorian House/Book Barn (567-3351), Stockton Springs. Open April through December, 8–8; otherwise by chance or appointment. A large collection of old, out-of-print, and rare books. **Fertile Mind Bookshop** (338-2498), 13 Main Street, Belfast. An outstanding browsing and buying place featuring Maine and regional books and guides, maps, records, and cards. **Canterbury Tales** (338-1171), 52 Main Street, Belfast. A full-service bookstore. **Mr. Paperback** (338-2735), Belmont Avenue, Belfast. A full-service bookstore.

SPECIAL SHOPS

Coyote Moon (338-5659), 54 Main Street, Belfast. A nifty, reasonably priced women's clothing and gift store. **Waldo County Co-op,** Route 1, Searsport Harbor. Open June to October, daily 9–5. A showcase for the local extension service. Dolls, needlework, wooden crafts, quilts, pillows, jams, and ceramics—and lots of them. **Silkweeds** (548-6501), Route 1, Searsport. Specializes in "country gifts": tinware, cotton afghans, rugs, wreaths. **Monroe Saltworks** (338-3460), Route 1, Belfast. This distinctive pottery has a wide following around the country. There are seconds and unusual pieces both here and in the Ellsworth outlets. **Ducktrap River Fish Farms, Inc.** (338-6280), 57 Little River Drive, Belfast. This company produces more than 25 varieties of smoked seafood, sold nationwide. Visitors may view (through windows) the processes involved, and purchase the products in the store. It's best to call first. **Birdworks of Maine** (567-3030), School Street, Stockton Springs. Open weekdays 9–5. Decorative pottery bird feeders, nesting roosts, suet keepers, and much more, all made on the premises.

SPECIAL EVENTS

July: **Belfast Bay Festival**—midmonth week of events; giant chicken barbecue, midway, races, and parade.

December: **Searsport Victorian Christmas**—second weekend in December; open houses at museum, homes, and B&Bs.

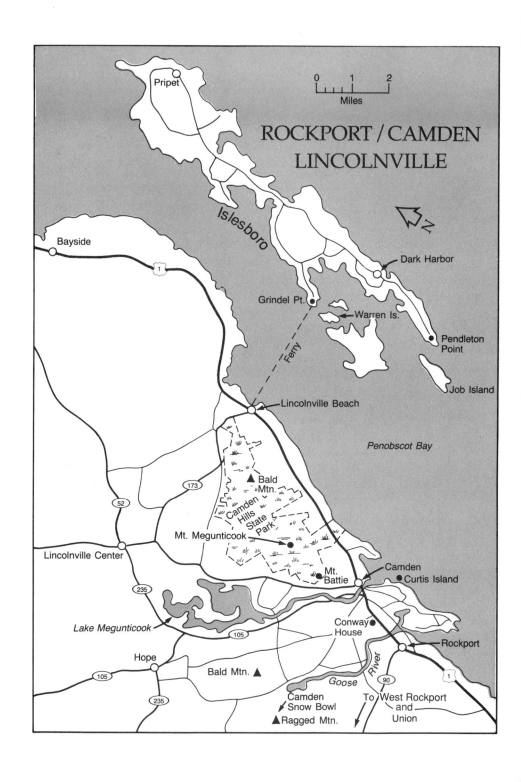

Pripet

0 1 2
Miles

ROCKPORT / CAMDEN
LINCOLNVILLE

N

Islesboro

Bayside

Dark Harbor

1

Grindel Pt.

Warren Is.

Ferry

Pendleton
Point

Job Island

Lincolnville Beach

Penobscot Bay

Bald
Mtn.

173

Camden
Hills
State
Park

52

Mt. Megunticook

Lincolnville Center

Mt.
Battie

Camden
Curtis Island

235

Conway
House

Rockport

Lake Megunticook

105

River

Hope

90

1

105

Bald Mtn.

Goose

235

Camden
Snow Bowl

To West Rockport
and
Union

Ragged Mtn.

Rockport, Camden, and Lincolnville

All I could see from where I stood
Was three long mountains and a wood;
I turned and looked another way,
And saw three islands in a bay.

—Edna St. Vincent Millay

These opening lines from "Renascence" suggest the view from the top of Mount Battie. Millay's hometown—Camden—lies below the mountain on a narrow, curving shelf between the hills and bay.

Smack on Route 1, Camden is the most popular way station between Kennebunkport or Boothbay Harbor and Bar Harbor. Seemingly half its 19th-century captains' homes are now B&Bs. Shops and restaurants line a photogenic harbor filled with private sailing and motor yachts. It's also a poor man's yacht haven.

Here, in 1935, artist Frank Swift refitted a few former fishing and cargo schooners to carry passengers around the islands in Penobscot Bay. He called the boats windjammers. A half-dozen members of Maine's current windjammer fleet are still based here (the rest are in neighboring ports) and several schooners offer day sails. You can also get out on the water in an excursion boat or a sea kayak.

From the water you can see two aspects of Camden that you can't see from land. The first is the size and extent of the Camden Hills. The second is the size and number of the palatial old waterside "cottages" along Beauchamp Point, the rocky promontory separating Camden from Rockport. Here, as in Bar Harbor, summer residents were wise and powerful enough to preserve the local mountains, seeding the creation of the present 6500-acre Camden Hills State Park, one of Maine's more spectacular places to hike.

Camden's first resort era coincided with those colorful decades during which steam and sail overlapped. As a stop on the Boston–Bangor steamboat line, Camden acquired a couple of big (now vanished) hotels. In 1900, when Bean's boatyard launched the world's first six-masted schooner, onlookers crowded the neighboring ornate steamboat wharf to watch.

In contrast to Boothbay and Bar Harbor, Camden has always been a year-round town that's never been overdependent on tourism. Camden's early business was, of course, building and sailing ships. By the mid-1800s, a half-dozen mills lined the series of falls on the Megunticook River, just a block or two from the waterfront. The vast wooden Knox Woolen Co.—the "Harrington Mill" portrayed in the movie *Peyton Place*—made the felts used by Maine's paper mills to absorb water from paper stock. It operated until 1988, and the complex is now the New England headquarters for a major credit card company, the most recent among dozens of companies to locate in Camden.

Culturally enriched by its sophisticated populace—workaday residents, retirees, and summer people alike—Camden (along with Rockport) offers a bonanza of music, art, and theatrical productions surprising in quality. There are also programs in filmmaking, computer science, and photography, as well as the long-acclaimed summertime Salzedo Harp Colony.

Ironically, only a small fraction of the thousands of tourists who stream through Camden every summer take the time to discover the extent of its beauty. The tourist tide eddies around the harborside restaurants, shops, and galleries and continues to flow on up Route 1 toward Bar Harbor. Even in August you are likely to find yourself alone atop Mount Battie (accessible by car as well as on foot) or Mount Megunticook (highest point in the Camden Hills), or in the open-sided Vesper Hill Chapel, with its flowers and sea view. Few visitors see, let alone swim in, Megunticook Lake or set foot on the nearby island of Islesboro.

A dozen years ago you could count on your fingers the number of places to stay here, but Camden has since become synonymous with bed & breakfasts, which, at last count, totaled more than 20. Still, the number of rooms in town is less than 200, and on most summer weekends that's not enough. Be sure to reserve as far ahead as possible.

GUIDANCE

Rockport-Camden-Lincolnville Chamber of Commerce (236-4404), PO Box 919, Public Landing, Camden 04843. Open year-round, Monday through Friday 9–5 and Saturday 10–5; also open Sunday 12–4, mid-May through mid-October. You'll find all sorts of helpful brochures here, plus maps of Camden, Rockport, and Lincolnville, along with knowledgeable people to send you in the right direction. The chamber keeps tabs on vacancies during the high season, as well as on what is open off-season and cottages available to rent (a list is ready for requests each year by January). Be sure to secure their booklet, as well as the Camden-Rockport Historical Society's "A Visitor's Tour," which outlines tours of historic districts in Camden and Rockport.

GETTING THERE

By air: **Knox County Airport,** at Owls Head, about 10 miles from Camden (see the "Rockland" chapter), offers daily flights to and from

Boston. **Bangor International Airport** (see the "Bangor Area" chapter) and **Portland International Jetport** (see the "Portland Area" chapter) offer connections to all parts of the country.

By bus: **Concord Trailways** stops on Route 1 south of Camden en route from Bangor to Portland and Boston.

By limo: **Mid Coast Limo** (1-800-834-5500 within Maine; 1-800-937-2424 outside Maine) offers van service to the Portland and Bangor airports.

PARKING
Parking is a problem in July and August. In-town parking has a stringently enforced 2-hour limit (just 15 minutes in a few spots, so be sure to read the signs). There are a few lots outside the center of town (try the Camden Marketplace and a lot on Mechanic Street). There's an advantage here to finding lodging within walking distance of the village.

GETTING AROUND
The Camden Shuttle (596-6605) is a good alternative to hassling with parking. With two free all-day parking lots outside of town, one south of Camden at the new Country Inn and one north of town at Camden Hills State Park, and several convenient stops in between, it makes sense to use this service—especially since the ride is free. The shuttle runs Monday through Friday 7:30–8 and Saturday and Sunday 9–9. Buses leave the lots on the hour and half hour.

MEDICAL EMERGENCY
Penobscot Bay Medical Center (596-8000), Route 1, Rockport.

VILLAGES AND ISLAND

Rockport's harbor is as picturesque as Camden's, and the tiny village is set high above it. Steps lead down to Marine Park, a departure point in 1816 for 300 casks of lime shipped to Washington, D.C., to help construct the capitol building. A granite sculpture of Andre the Seal recalls the legendary performer who drew crowds every summer in the early and mid-1980s. The village (part of Camden until 1891) includes the restored Rockport Opera House, site of the summer Bay Chamber Concerts, the noted Maine Coast Artists Gallery, the Maine Photographic Workshop program, and a salting of restaurants and shops.

Lincolnville is larger than it looks as you drive through. The village's landmarks—the Lobster Pound Restaurant and Maine State Ferry to Islesboro—serve as centerpieces for proliferating shops, restaurants, and B&Bs.

Islesboro. A 10-mile-long, stringbean-shaped island just 3 miles off Lincolnville Beach, Islesboro is a private kind of place. Its two communities are Dark Harbor (described by Sidney Sheldon in his bestseller *Master of the Game* as the "jealously guarded colony of the super-rich") and Pripet, a thriving, year-round neighborhood of boatbuilders and fishermen. The car-carrying **Maine State Ferry** (789-

5611; 596-2202; $4 per passenger, $12 per car, $2 per bicycle) from Lincolnville Beach lands mid-island, at Grindle Point, next to the old lighthouse and keeper's cottage that's now the seasonal **Sailors' Memorial Museum.** You at least need a bike to get any sense of this place. The **Islesboro Town Office** (734-2253) in Dark Harbor is a friendly source of information and can refer you to local real estate agents who handle cottage rentals. The only place to stay is **Dark Harbor House** (see *Inns*), which also offers dinner by reservation to passing yachtsmen. **Oliver's,** open May through October (734-6543) in Dark Harbor, offers fine dining and lighter fare in a second-floor pub. There are summer musical and theatrical performances at the **Free Will Baptist Church.** Check out the **Up Island Church,** a fine old structure with some beautiful wall stencils and fascinating old headstones in the adjacent graveyard. The luncheonette in **The Dark Harbor Shop** is the local gathering place.

TO SEE

MUSEUMS

Old Conway House Complex (236-2257), Conway Road (off Route 1 just south of Camden). Open during July and August, Tuesday through Friday 10–4; admission $2; students $1, children over 6 $.50. Administered by the Camden-Rockport Historical Society, this restored, early-18th-century farmhouse has been furnished to represent several periods. The barn holds collections of carriages, sleighs, and early farm tools, and there is a Victorian privy and a blacksmith shop.

Knox Mill Museum, MBNA offices, Mechanic Street, Camden. Open weekdays 9–5. A sophisticated little museum dramatizes the 125 years of operation of the Knox Woolen Mill. Exhibits include a video, many photographs, and some machinery. The mill was the prime supplier of felts for the endless belts used in paper manufacturing.

SCENIC DRIVE

Drive or, better yet, bicycle (see *To Do—Bicycling*) around **Beauchamp Point.** Begin on Chestnut Street and follow this peaceful road by the lily pond and on by the herd of Belted Galloway cows (black on both ends and white in the middle). Take Calderwood Lane through the woods and by the **Vesper Hill Children's Chapel,** built on the site of a former hotel and banked with flowers, a great spot to get married or simply to sit. Continue along Beauchamp Avenue to Rockport Village to lunch or picnic by the harbor, and return via Union Street to Camden.

OTHER

Kelmscott Farm (763-4088), RR 2, Box 365, Lincolnville. Open Thursday through Sunday 11–4, late May until Labor Day. $5 adults, $3 children 5–18, under 5 free. Closed when we came through, but we have heard good things about this farm working to preserve rare animal breeds, including several varieties of sheep, the shire horse, and Nigerian dwarf goats. Tours, farm shop and museum, wagon rides, special events.

TO DO

BICYCLING

Fred's Bikes (236-6664), 53 Chestnut Street, across from the YMCA, rents a variety of mountain and road bikes, Kiddie Kart trailers, and accessories, and delivers them to inns and B&Bs. Ask about evening group rides.

Mainely Mt. Bike Tours (785-2703), Union, offers 2- and 3-hour guided mountain bike tours.

Maine Sport Outfitters (236-8797; 1-800-722-0826) rents specialized Crossroads and specialized Rockhoppers, as well as bike trailers and car racks for a day or extended periods. Rentals include helmet, lock, and cable.

BOAT EXCURSIONS

(See also *Windjammer Cruises.*)

Yacht charters are offered spring to autumn along the Maine coast. Most charters run for a week, although sometimes it is possible to charter a boat just for a long weekend, with or without crew. For more information, contact **Windward Mark Yacht Charters** (236-4300; 1-800-633-7900 outside Maine). **Bay Island Yacht Charters** (236-2776; 1-800-421-2492) has yachts available for bare-boat skippered or crewed charters out of Rockland as well as other ports the length of Maine's coast. **Blue Seas Adventure Co.** (236-6904) rents a variety of power- and sailboats by the day or longer.

Appledore (236-8353), an 86-foot schooner (the largest of the day-sailing fleet), has sailed around the world and now offers several trips daily, including sunset cruises.

Surprise (236-4687), a traditional, historic, 57-foot schooner, gets rave reviews from those who take its 2-hour sails. Captain Jack and wife, Barbara Moore, spent seven years cruising between Maine and the Caribbean, educating their four children on board in the process.

Olad and *Northwind* (236-2323), 55- and 75-foot schooners, respectively, offering 2-hour sails.

Shantih II (236-8605; 1-800-599-8605) offers full-day, half-day, and sunset sails out of Rockport for a maximum of six passengers.

Betselma (236-2101), a motor launch, provides 1- and 2-hour sight-seeing trips (owner Les Bex was a longtime windjammer captain) around the harbor and nearby coast.

Lively Lady and *Lively Lady Too* (236-6672), traditional lobster boats, take passengers on 2- and 3-hour cruises that can include watching lobster traps being hauled or an island lobster bake and sunset cruise.

Maine State Ferry from Lincolnville Beach to Islesboro (789-5611). At $4 round-trip per passenger and $2 per bicycle, this is the bargain of the local boating scene; see Islesboro under *Villages and Island.*

GOLF

Goose River Golf Club (236-8488), Simonton Road, Camden. Nine holes, but you can play through twice using different starting tees. Cart rentals. Clubhouse. Tee times recommended for weekends and holidays.

Samoset Golf Course (594-2511; 1-800-341-1650), Rockport, has 18 holes on a course that *Golf Digest* selected as the seventh most beautiful in the country. Many of the fairways skirt the water, and the views are lovely. Carts are available.

HIKING

The Camden Hills are far less recognized than Acadia National Park as a hiking haven, but for the average once-or-twice-a-year hiker, they offer ample challenge and some spectacular views. Mount Battie, accessible by a moderate and sometimes steep half-mile trail just off Route 52, is the only peak also accessible by car. The 1-mile Maiden Cliff Trail (park off Route 52, 2.9 miles from Route 1) is favored by locals for its views from the top of 800-foot sheer cliffs overlooking Lake Megunticook; it connects with the 2½-mile Ridge Trail to the summit of Mount Megunticook (1380 feet). A complete trail map is available from most B&Bs and at Camden Hills State Park (see *Green Space*).

SEA KAYAKING

Ducktrap Sea Kayak Tours (236-8608), Lincolnville Beach, offers 2-hour guided tours in Penobscot Bay. Group tours also available.

Indian Island Kayak (236-4088), 16 Mountain Street, Camden. Specializes in small group trips of any length; kayak sailing, too.

Maine Sport Outfitters (236-8797 or 1-800-722-0826), on Route 1 just south of Rockport, is a phenomenon rather than merely an outfitter. Be sure to stop. They offer courses in kayaking and canoeing, guided excursions around Camden Harbor and out into Penobscot Bay, and island-based workshops. They also rent kayaks and canoes. Contact them for their catalog of activities.

Mt. Pleasant Canoe and Kayak (785-4309), West Rockport, offers a 2-hour sunset trip on Megunticook Lake as well as guided coastal tours.

SWIMMING

Saltwater swimming from Camden's **Laite Memorial Park and Beach,** upper Bayview Street; at **Lincolnville Beach,** Route 1 north of Camden; and in Rockport at **Walker Park.** Freshwater swimming at Megunticook Lake (**Barret Cove Memorial Park and Beach;** turn left off Route 52 northwest of Camden), where you will also find picnic grounds and a parking area; **Shirttail Beach** on Route 105; and at the **Willis Hodson Park** on the Megunticook River (Molyneaux Road). At the **Camden YMCA** (236-3375), Chestnut Street, visitors can pay a day-use fee that entitles them to swim in the Olympic-sized pool (check hours for family swimming, lap swimming, etc.), use the weight rooms, and play basketball in the gym.

TENNIS

There are two public tennis courts at the **Camden Snow Bowl** on Hosmer's Pond Road. In addition, **Samoset Resort** (594-2511), Rockport, has outdoor courts, as do the Whitehall Inn and Rockport Recreation Area.

WINDJAMMER CRUISES

Windjammer cruises are offered mid-June to mid-October. A half-dozen schooners and a ketch sail from Camden and Rockport on 3- to 6-day cruises through Penobscot Bay. For brochures and sailing schedules, contact the **Maine Windjammers Association** (374-5400; 1-800-807-WIND). (See also *Windjammer Cruises* under *To Do* in the "Rockland" chapter and under "What's Where.")

Angelique (236-8873; 1-800-282-9989), PO Box 736, Camden, is a 95-foot ketch that was built expressly for the windjammer trade in 1980. Patterned after 19th-century English fishing vessels, she offers a pleasant deck-level salon and belowdecks showers.

Timberwind (236-0801; 1-800-759-9250), PO Box 247, Rockport, was built in Portland in 1931 as a pilot schooner. This pretty, 75-foot vessel was converted to a passenger vessel in 1969. She has an enclosed, hand-held shower on deck. The *Timberwind* is the only windjammer sailing out of Rockport Harbor.

Roseway (236-4449; 1-800-255-4449), Yankee Schooner Cruises, PO Box 696, Camden, was built in 1925 as a fishing schooner and later spent 32 years as a pilot vessel, escorting ships in and out of Boston Harbor. She was the last pilot schooner active in the United States. *Roseway* has been a passenger vessel sailing out of Camden since 1975. There are enclosed, hot, freshwater showers on deck.

Lewis R. French (594-9411; 1-800-469-4635), PO Box 992 CC, Camden, was launched on the Damariscotta River in 1871. Before becoming a passenger vessel, she carried cargo along the coast. She had three major rebuilds, the most recent in 1976 when she was brought into passenger service. Sixty-five feet long, she accommodates 23 passengers. Hot, freshwater shower on board. Native Maine Captain Dan Pease met his wife, Kathy, when she came aboard for a vacation. Now their sons, Joe and Bill, come along every chance they get. No smoking.

Mary Day (1-800-540-2750 in Maine; 1-800-992-2218 in the US and Canada), Box 798, Camden, was the first schooner built specifically for carrying passengers. She's among the swiftest; Captains Barry King and Jen Martin have extensive sailing experience. Features include a fireplace and parlor organ and hot, freshwater showers on the deck.

Grace Bailey, Mercantile, and *Mistress* (236-2938; 1-800-736-7981), Maine Windjammer Cruises, PO Box 617, Camden. For years known as the *Mattie, Grace Bailey* took back her original name following a thorough restoration in 1990. Built in 1882 in New York, she once carried cargo along the Atlantic coast and to the West Indies. She has belowdecks

The schooner Grace Bailey

showers. **Mercantile** was built in Maine in 1916 as a shallow-draft coasting schooner; 78 feet long, she has been in the windjammer trade since its beginning in 1942. Each cabin has its own private head, and there are belowdecks showers nearby. **Mistress,** the smallest of the fleet, carries just six passengers. A topsail schooner built along the lines of the old coasting schooners, she is also available for private charter. All three cabins have private heads, but there is no shower on board.

SKIING

Camden Snow Bowl (236-3438), Hosmer's Pond Road, Camden. With a 950-foot vertical drop, nine runs for beginner through expert, and night skiing, this is a comfortably sized area where everyone seems to know everyone else. Facilities include a base lodge, a rental and repair shop, and a cafeteria.

Camden Hills State Park also marks and maintains some trails for cross-country skiing, and there's a ski hut on Mount Battie.

Tanglewood 4-H Camp (789-5868), off Route 1 near Lincolnville Beach. Ungroomed scenic trails. Map and description of trails available at the chamber (see *Guidance*).

SPECIAL LEARNING PROGRAMS

Camden Yacht Club Sailing Program (236-3014), Bayview Street, provides sailing classes for children and adults, boat owners and non–boat owners, during July and August; among them is an excellent weeklong course just for women. There is also a lecture series open to the public.

Bay Island Sailing School (236-2776; 1-800-421-2492), headquartered in Camden but based at Journey's End Marina in Rockland, an ASA-certified sailing school offering beginner, coastal cruising, and bareboat certification programs ranging from intensive weekend workshops to 5-day hands-on cruises. $395–995.

Maine Photographic Workshops (236-8581), Rockport. A nationally respected, year-round school offers a choice of 200 programs that vary in length from 1 week to 3 months for every level of skill in photography, cinematography, television production, and related fields. Teachers are established, recognized professionals who come from across the country, as do the students. There is also a gallery with changing exhibitions open to the public. The school provides housing for most of its students and helps to arrange accommodations for others.

Maine Sport Outfitters (236-8797), PO Box 956, Rockport. This Route 1 complex is worth a stop whether you are up for adventure sports or not. This place is more than simply a store or kayaking, canoeing, mountain biking center; it has evolved over the years from a fly-fishing and canvas shop into a multitiered store that's a home base for adventure tours. Inquire about a wide variety of local kayaking tours and multiday kayaking workshops geared to all levels of ability, based at its facilities on Gay Island.

Center for Furniture Craftsmanship (594-5611), 25 Mill Street, Rockport. June through October. One- and 2-week, hands-on workshops for novice, intermediate, and advanced woodworkers.

GREEN SPACE

Camden Hills State Park (236-3109; 236-0849), Route 1, Camden. In addition to Mount Battie, this 6500-acre park includes Mount Megunticook, one of the highest points on the Atlantic seaboard, and a shoreside picnic site. You can drive to the top of Mount Battie on the road that starts at the park entrance, just north of town. Admission through the gate is $2 adults; $.50 ages 6–12; 5 and under free. At the entrance, pick up a "Hiking at Camden Hills State Park" map. For highlights of this 25-mile network, see *Hiking*. In winter many of the trails are suitable for cross-country skiing, given snow. There are 112 campsites here.

Warren Island State Park, also administered by Camden Hills State Park, is just a stone's throw off the island of Islesboro. There are picnic tables, trails, and tent sites here. Accessibility is the problem: You can arrange to have a private boat carry you over from the mainland, rent your own boat in Camden, or paddle out in a sea kayak (see *Sea Kayaking*). Because of this, the island is seldom used and always peaceful.

Marine Park, Rockport. A nicely landscaped waterside area with sheltered picnic tables. Restored lime kilns and a train caboose are reminders of the era when the town's chief industry was processing and exporting lime.

Merryspring (236-4885), Camden. A 66-acre preserve with walking trails, an herb garden, a lily garden, a rose garden, raised beds, a demonstration garden, and an arboretum. The preserve is bisected by the Goose

River and is accessible by way of Conway Road from Route 1 in Camden. Weekly talks in summer. The organization is dedicated to planting and preserving flowers, shrubs, and trees in this natural setting and to interpreting them through workshops and special events. Donations are encouraged.

Fernald's Neck Nature Conservancy Preserve. Near the junction of Route 52 and the Youngtown Road, 315 acres cover most of a heavily wooded peninsula that juts into Lake Megunticook. A brochure of walking trails is available at the registration box near the entrance. One trail leads to 60-foot cliffs. Trails can be boggy: Wear boots or old shoes.

Camden Amphitheatre, Atlantic Avenue, Camden. A magical setting for summertime plays and concerts and a good place to sit, think, and read anytime. Tucked behind the library and across the street from the harbor park—a gentle, manicured slope down to the water.

Curtis Island, in the outer harbor. A small island with a lighthouse that marks the entrance to Camden. It is a public picnic spot and a popular sea-kayaking destination.

LODGING

All listings are Camden 04843 unless otherwise indicated. Rates are for high summer; most have off-season rates as well. *Note:* If you choose one of the many B&Bs in historic houses on Elm, Main, or High Streets (all are Route 1), you might want to ask what pains have been taken to muffle passing traffic.

Camden Accommodations (1-800-236-1920), a reservations service representing most places to stay in the Camden area. It also coordinates rentals for some six dozen cottages and condos.

RESORT

Samoset Resort (594-2511; 1-800-341-1650), 220 Warrenton Street, Rockport 04856. Open year-round, a full-service resort set on 230 oceanside acres, with 132 rooms and 18 suites, some handicapped accessible, many with ocean views, all with balconies or patios, private baths, color TVs, and climate-controlled air-conditioning and heat. Seventy-two time-share units with full kitchens and washer/dryers are also available for nightly rentals. The two-bedroom Flume Cottage, perched on a rocky outcropping above the water, is available by the week in-season and nightly off-season. A scenic, peaceful spot with many amenities, including an outstanding 18-hole golf course, indoor golf center, four outdoor tennis courts, a Nautilus-equipped fitness club, racquetball courts, and indoor and outdoor pools. Spring 1997 will bring a new clubhouse for the golf course, with a full lounge, locker room, and showers. A children's program is offered during the summer months and other school holiday periods. This is a popular meeting and convention site, especially with the addition of a 7000-square-foot exhibit hall. The dining room, Marcel's (see *Dining*

Out), is generally rated among the best on the Mid Coast. The adjacent Breakwater Lounge has a large fireplace and floor-to-ceiling windows overlooking the water. $132–290 in summer; $95–160 in winter. Timeshare units are $270–320 (one bedroom), $315–375 (two bedroom) in summer, less by the week and off-season. Ask about packages.

INNS

The Belmont (236-8053; 1-800-238-8053), 6 Belmont Avenue. Open mid-May through October. An 1890s Edwardian house with a wraparound veranda. The four guest rooms and two suites are each attentively furnished with careful details, such as bedspreads that match the chairs, curtains, and wallpaper. All have private baths. Our favorite is the third-floor room with the canopy bed. In the living room, accented by Oriental rugs on shining wood floors, guests are invited to relax in comfortable wing chairs and chat about the day's adventures or enjoy a cocktail from the bar. Chef Gerald Clare (one of the owners) offers imaginative "New American" fare (see *Dining Out*) in an inviting dining room that's recognized as one of the best on the Maine coast. A full country breakfast—egg dishes or perhaps blueberry pancakes—is included in lodging, and breakfast in bed is available. $95–145 in summer, $75–105 in winter, single or double occupancy. Two-night minimum stay, but single-night stays are accepted on weekdays if guests are also staying for dinner (MAP).

Dark Harbor House (734-6669), Box 185, Main Road, Dark Harbor, Islesboro 04848. Open mid-May to mid-October. The only place to stay on Islesboro and one of the most pleasant inns along the Maine coast. Built on a hilltop at the turn of the century as a summer cottage for the president of the First National Bank of Philadelphia, this imposing, yellow-clapboard inn offers elegance from a past era. Inside you'll find a summery living room with glass French doors opening onto a porch and a cozier library with a fireplace just right for crisp autumn afternoons. Fine antiques are found throughout the Dark Harbor House and its 10 bedrooms. All have private baths, and some feature balconies. There's also a two-room suite with a wet bar and a fold-out sofa bed in its living room, as well as a two-room master suite complete with an enclosed sun-porch sitting room, fireplace, and canopied queen-sized mahogany bed. An à la carte dining and full wine service is offered to guests and to the public with reservations. Entrées might be *paupiettes* of sole with native crabmeat, chicken roulades with leek, Gruyère, and prosciutto, or locally caught steamed lobster. Dessert might be lemon mousse, raspberry-blueberry crisp, or chocolate caramel walnut torte. Picnic baskets can be prepared for day trips. Doubles are $105–245 including a full, four-course breakfast; 2-night minimum on holiday weekends. Dinner entrées run $16.95–21.95.

Whitehall Inn (236-3391), 52 High Street (Route 1). Open Memorial Day through Columbus Day weekend. There's an air of easy elegance and comfort to this rambling inn on Route 1, east of the village. The Dewing family has owned and operated the inn for 25 years. The large, low-beamed lobby and adjoining parlors are fitted with Oriental rugs and sofas, games, and puzzles. The Millay Room, with its vintage 1904 Steinway, looks much the way it did on the summer evening in 1909 when a local girl, Edna St. Vincent Millay, read a poem, "Renascence," to assembled guests, one of whom was so impressed that she undertook to educate the young woman at Vassar. The inn offers 40 guest rooms in the main inn, 5 more in both the Maine House and the Wicker House across Route 1. These rooms are simpler than most to be found in neighboring B&Bs, but each has its appeal. Most have private baths. All have the kind of heavy, old phones your children have never seen. There is a tennis court and shuffleboard, and it's just a short walk to the Salzedo Harp Colony (summer concerts) and a "sneaker" beach (wear shoes because of the rocks) on Camden's outer harbor. Families are welcome but asked to dine early. Doubles are $135–170 MAP July through mid-October; a single room with shared bath is $65 B&B during this period; doubles are $105–135 B&B. Cheaper Memorial Day through June. Add 15 percent service for MAP, 10 percent for B&B.

☞ **The Blue Harbor House** (236-3196; 1-800-248-3196), 67 Elm Street (Route 1). Open year-round. The feel here is that of a friendly B&B but they serve dinner to guests as well as breakfast on the spacious sun porch. We haven't sampled dinner but other guests have raved about it in the logbook. The dinners are multicourse ($30 per person) and might include entrées like beef Wellington or stuffed rack of lamb, or the ever popular Down East lobster dinner. Breakfast is just as delectable, and might be a lobster quiche, Dutch babies (custard-type pancakes with fresh fruit, Maine maple syrup, almonds, and powdered sugar), or blueberry pancakes with blueberry butter. The eight guest rooms vary, but all are pleasantly decorated with country antiques, stenciling, and handmade quilts; all have private baths and telephones, some have air-conditioning, and/or TV/VCR. There are also two carriage house suites (children and pets welcome) with whirlpool tubs. Bicycles are available to guests. Hosts Jody Schmoll and Dennis Hayden are warm and eager to help. Doubles $85–135; 2-day Thanksgiving and winter packages with dinner, $225.

Youngtown Inn (763-4290; 1-800-291-8438), Route 52 and Youngtown Road, Lincolnville 04849. This 1810 farmhouse is 4 miles from Camden Harbor at the end of Megunticook Lake, near Lincolnville Center. The decor is country, with nice touches like stenciling in one room that matches the bedspread. All six rooms have private baths. Rooms 5 and 6 convert to a suite for four. The dining room (see *Dining Out*) and pub downstairs have a genuinely hospitable atmosphere, complete with pumpkin-pine floors, beamed ceilings, and fireplaces. $85–99 single or double occupancy in summer, $70–85 in winter includes a full country

The Maine Stay Inn

breakfast: maybe fresh fruit, muffins, or croissants, French toast stuffed with apple slices, or an egg dish. Ask about packages.

BED & BREAKFASTS

The Maine Stay (236-9636), 22 High Street (Route 1). Open year-round. This is one of the oldest homes in Camden's High Street Historic District. A Greek Revival house with an attached barn, it offers eight guest rooms, two of which are suites. Six have private baths, and all are carefully furnished in antiques. The lower-level guest room in the attached carriage house is especially appealing, with well-stocked, built-in bookshelves, a woodstove, and glass doors opening onto a private patio with lawn and woods beyond (the 2-acre property includes an extensive, well-tended wildflower garden and benches). A new suite in 1996 features a queen brass bed with private bath and a sitting room with a gas fireplace overlooking historic High Street. We also find the third-floor rooms (shared bath) particularly appealing. The two parlors (with fireplaces), the TV den, and dining room are all salted with interesting furnishings and curiosities collected during innkeeper (former captain) Peter Smith's wide-ranging naval career. Peter, his wife, Donny, and her twin sister, Diana Robson, are unusually helpful hosts, offering a personalized area map to each guest, as well as computer printouts of things to do, day trips, etc. A hot breakfast is served at the formal dining room table; afternoon tea is also included in the $75–135 ($55–95 off-season) double-room rate. Needlepointers should inquire about the March Stitch-Inn weekend.

Norumbega (236-4646), 61 High Street (Route 1). Open year-round. With one of the most imposing facades of any B&B anywhere, this turreted stone "castle" has long been a landmark just north of Camden. Inside, the ornate staircase with fireplace and love seat on the landing, formal parlor with fireplace, and dining room capture all the opulence of the Victorian era. Its 12 guest rooms, some with fireplaces and all with king-sized beds and private baths, are located both upstairs and downstairs, the latter with private terrace entrances. We are intrigued by the Library suite, two rooms with a loft balcony full of books, which was the original castle library. There is a billiard room open to guests until 9 PM. Doubles $195–325 in high season, including full breakfast and afternoon wine and cheese; penthouse $450. Two-night minimum on weekends. Inquire about special Murder Mystery weekends

Windward House (236-9656), 6 High Street (Route 1). Open year-round. Tim and Sandy Laplante are the new owners of this handsome, Greek Revival, clapboard home surrounded by a lawn and gardens. The eight welcoming guest rooms each have private baths and are carefully furnished with antiques and small touches. The airy Garden Room is delightful, with its Vermont Castings gas stove, skylights, and gardening decor. The Carriage Room has private parking and a private entrance, pine-board floors, a gas stove, a queen canopy bed, and a claw-foot tub. The common rooms are comfortable and inviting, and the game room is stocked with a wide variety of board and card games. A delicious gourmet breakfast, served in the sunny dining room, is included, and coffee and tea are available anytime. Doubles $75–160.

The Blackberry Inn (236-6060; 1-800-833-6674), 82 Elm Street. Open year-round. The decor in this 1860 Italianate Victorian includes marble mantels, Oriental rugs, and Bar Harbor wicker. The courtyard is a perfect place to relax. All 10 rooms have private baths; some rooms are air-conditioned and others feature king-sized beds, whirlpool baths, TV, wood-burning fireplaces, and ceiling fans. Children are welcome, and the newly renovated carriage house is a good place for families. The garden rooms are private and cozy, with fireplaces and whirlpool baths. $65–145 depending on room and season. A full "gourmet" breakfast in the dining room or alfresco in the courtyard is included, plus an "afternoon hospitality hour."

The Inn at Sunrise Point (236-7716; 1-800-435-6278), PO Box 1344, Lincolnville 04849. Open May through October. Set on a 4-acre waterfront estate just over the town line in Lincolnville, this small, luxurious B&B is owned by Jerry Levitin, author of the *Country Inns and Back Roads* guidebooks. Levitin himself tends to be on the road in summer, but an affable innkeeper is on hand to welcome guests either to one of the three rooms with water views in the main house (all with fireplaces) or to one of the four deluxe oceanside cottages, all skillfully furnished and fitted with fireplaces and Jacuzzis. All accommodations have queen- or king-sized beds, phones, and color TVs with VCRs; plush robes are also provided in each bath. Common rooms include a glass conservatory that lets the sun shine in, plus a snug, wood-paneled library with fireplace that's just right for cooler days. Rooms are $150–200; cottages are $250–350; full breakfast and afternoon appetizers included.

☞ **The Spouter Inn** (789-5171), Route 1, PO Box 176, Lincolnville 04849. Open year-round. Just across the road from Lincolnville Beach and the ferry to Islesboro, this early-1800s home invites guests to enjoy the view from a rocker on the front porch or to relax by the fire in the attractive library and parlor. There are six rooms, named for naval ranks and increasing in luxury accordingly. The Admiral's quarters on the third floor has ocean and mountain views, a deck, fireplace, and Jacuzzi. All but one room have wood-burning fireplaces. Doubles $65–175 ($5 off for singles), depending on room and season. Full breakfast included. Two-night minimum during high season.

Victorian B&B (236-3785; 1-800-382-9817), Lincolnville Beach 04849. Open year-round. A quiet spot overlooking the water and away from the bustle of Route 1. This spacious 1800s house offers six guest rooms, all with queen beds and private baths; all but one have fireplaces. As the name suggests, both the exterior and interior are very Victorian. The third-floor suite has a bathroom sink set into an antique library table, a claw-foot tub, sitting area, and loft with twin beds. We also like the suite with the turret sitting room. $85–125 includes full breakfast and evening sweets.

A Little Dream (236-8742), 66 High Street. Open year-round. If you like ruffles and furbelows, you will love this Victorian confection: all ribbons and collectibles, with a touch of English country. There are tiny details everywhere, with each room's decor telling a little story. We especially like the first-floor room with a turret sitting area and working fireplace. A full breakfast, served in the dining room, may include a smoked-salmon or an apple-Brie omelet, banana-pecan waffles, or lemon-ricotta soufflé pancakes. Doubles $95–139. Two-night minimum on holiday weekends.

OTHER LODGING

All listings are in Camden 04843 unless otherwise indicated.

✐☞ **High Tide Inn** (236-3724), Route 1. Open May through October. Set far enough back from Route 1 to preclude traffic noise, this friendly complex appeals to singles and couples (who tend to choose one of the five rooms in the inn) and families, who opt for one of the six cottages or 19 motel units (some with connecting, separate sleeping rooms). Most accommodations have views. The complex is set on 7 quiet acres—formerly a private estate—of landscaped grounds and meadow that slope to the water, where there's over 250 feet of private beach. Home-baked continental breakfast, included in lodging in-season, is served on the glass-enclosed porch; the living room also has ample windows with views of the bay. The porch, living room, and bar all have working fireplaces. Rates: $60–175 in-season, less May through late June; 2-night minimum weekends in July and August and over holidays.

☞ **The Owl and Turtle Harbor View Guest Rooms** (236-9014), PO Box 1265, 8 Bayview Street. Open year-round. In the middle of all the harbor hubbub but high above it, with the best harbor view in town. Just three rooms, and repeat business is heavy, so book early for the summer months. Each room has air-conditioning, TV, telephone, and private bath; two face directly over the water. Private parking is provided. Downstairs is one of the state's best bookshops. No smoking; no pets. Rates include continental breakfast brought to the room. $80–90 plus tax; less off-season.

Lord Camden Inn (236-4325; 1-800-336-4325), 24 Main Street. Open year-round. In a restored, 1893 brick Masonic hall, the "inn" occupies several floors above a row of Main Street shops. Restored antique furnishings, including some canopy beds, blend with modern amenities: color cable TV, private baths, in-room telephones, and elevator service. Most rooms have two double beds and balconies overlooking the town and harbor or the river and hills beyond; there are also three luxury suites on the first floor. Rates include a full continental breakfast buffet with fresh muffins, juices, cereals, breads, and coffee. $128–175, depending on the view, in summer. $88–118 off-season. Children 16 and younger stay free.

WHERE TO EAT

DINING OUT

The Belmont (236-8053; 1-800-238-8053), 6 Belmont Avenue, Camden. Open for dinner early May through October, 6–9. Closed Wednesday. There is a lot of creativity in the kitchen here, reflected in rave reviews from the *New York Times* and others. Gerald Clare, the only Maine chef featured on the PBS series *Great Chefs of the East*, oversees the 55-seat dining room of this fine inn (see *Lodging*) with co-owner John Mancarella. Pad Thai, a popular appetizer here, reflects Mr. Clare's skill with Asian ingredients like lemongrass, ginger, and Kaffir lime leaves. The dish combines rice noodles and bean sprouts with chicken, shrimp, or lobster. Entrées might include salmon, crisply seared and served in lime-scented broth; desserts are an art form (around $6). $13–25. Reservations recommended.

Marcel's (594-0774), Rockport (at the Samoset Resort). Open every day year-round for breakfast, lunch, dinner, and Sunday brunch. The fare merits the formality it receives; the wait staff wear tuxedos, and jackets are required for gentlemen at dinner. Specialties include tableside service of rack of lamb or châteaubriand for two, and steak Diane. Extensive selection of beer and wine. The children's menu ($5–5.75) features fish-and-chips and fettucine Alfredo prepared tableside among its choices. There's piano music at dinner and entertainment in the adjacent Breakwater Lounge. $16.95–26.95.

✐☞**O'Neil's** (236-3272), 21 Bayview Street, Camden. Open for dinner daily, year-round. Multilevel seating in a distinctive atmosphere. The menu features entrées prepared on a wood-fired brick oven, grill, and rotisseries. You can even have wood-grilled Maine lobster with crab and shrimp stuffing, but the spit-roasted marinated chicken and grilled salmon with braised fennel, cherry tomato salad, and fried leeks can hit the spot, as will any of the one-person pizzas.

✐ **The Sail Loft** (236-2330), Rockport. Open year-round for lunch and dinner daily and Sunday brunch. A family-owned restaurant since 1962, this is a favorite of residents and visitors alike. The Sail Loft overlooks Rockport Harbor and the activities of the boatyard below (owned by the same family). The lunch menu might include scallop Thai pasta, or crabmeat and lobster quiche. At dinner, fresh seafood selections are the specialty, and one option is a shore dinner of clam chowder, steamed clams or mussels, and a steamed lobster. Small, melt-in-your-mouth blueberry muffins come with every meal. Children's menu ($3.50–8). Dinner entrées run $9.95–38.50 (the shore dinner with a 2-pound lobster).

Youngtown Inn (763-4290; 1-800-298-8438 outside of Maine), corner of Route 52 and Youngtown Road, Lincolnville. Open for dinner 5:30–9, daily in July, August, and September; closed Sunday and Monday the rest of the year. Four miles from Camden, this inn's (see *Inns*) dining rooms are warmed by fireplaces on cool evenings. French chef-owner Manuel Mercier serves up a wide variety of French cuisine, which might include lobster ravioli, rack of lamb, and salmon potato crust. There is also a small, cozy lounge. $12–23 or a four-course prix fixe menu for $30.

☞ **Chez Michel** (789-5600), Lincolnville Beach (across the road from the beach). Lunch and dinner. This pleasant restaurant serves exceptional food with a French flair. Moderately priced entrées include bouillabaisse, steak *au poivre*, and pork chops Saint Vincent. Outside dining in-season. A well-kept secret among Camdenites who have become loyal regulars. Dinner entrées run $8.75–14.95.

Frogwater Cafe (236-8998), 31 Elm Street, Camden. Open for lunch and dinner Tuesday through Sunday. A terrific new addition to the Camden dining scene, highly recommended by local innkeepers. Lunch selections might include a BLT, a club sandwich, lobster roll, or veggie burger. At dinner, you might begin with a delicious appetizer of sautéed mushrooms with garlic toast, then continue with entrée selections like spinach crêpes, vegetable lasagna, or fisherman's stew. $8–12.

EATING OUT

✐ **Cappy's Chowder House** (236-2254), Main Street, Camden. Open year-round (hours vary depending on the season). An extremely popular pub—they claim that "sooner or later, everyone shows up at Cappy's," and it's true. Good food with reasonable price tags: eggs, granola, treats from the on-premises bakery for breakfast; croissant sandwiches, burgers, full meals for lunch; seafood entrées, special pasta dishes, meat dishes for dinner. The seafood stew with Maine kielbasa is a big hit and the chowder has been written up in *Gourmet*. Upstairs in the Crow's Nest (open in the summertime only), you will find a quieter setting, a harbor view, and the same menu. Kids get their own menu with selections served in a souvenir carrying box; a place mat with puzzles, crayons for coloring, and sometimes even balloons are provided. This is also a good bet if you're in a hurry and just want a chowder and beer at the bar. They have recently opened an expanded bakery and coffee-house, and company store.

✐ **Sea Dog Brewing Co.** (236-6863), 43 Mechanic Street, Camden. Housed in the former Knox mill with views of the waterfall; a large, cheerful, family-run brew pub decorated with windjammer and other nautical paraphernalia, featuring a large, moderately priced menu and generous portions. Choices range from burgers and crab rolls, to soups and salads, to shrimp and vegetable kabobs and daily specials featuring fresh fish, beef, or pasta. The specialty brews are lagers and ales with a half-dozen staples and several monthly specials.

✐ **Village Restaurant** (236-3232), Main Street, Camden. Open year-round. Long a favorite with locals, this traditional restaurant serves lots of fried seafood and fish chowder. The dining room overlooks Camden Harbor.

✐ **Gilbert's Public House** (236-4320), Bayview Street, Camden. Tucked underneath the shops along Bayview Street (you enter through a side door just off the road), this is a good place for a beer and a sandwich, snacks or light meals for the kids, or a simple supper before the evening's activities. There's an international flavor to the "pub food" offered: Mediterranean shrimp salad, wurst platter, egg rolls, veggie stir fry, and nachos are among the favorites. There's also a frozen drink machine here, plus frothy and colorful daiquiris, margaritas, and the like. Live music for dancing in the evening.

The Helm (236-4337), Route 1, Rockport (1.5 miles south of Camden). Open for lunch and dinner April to late October; closed Monday. There's a French accent to the menu, with such dishes as coquilles Saint-Jacques and bouillabaisse, plus Maine shore dinners. The menu offers about 50 entrées. One dining room overlooks the Goose River. Children's menu, too. At the take-out window you can order real onion soup, fresh rabbit pâté, among other treats, plus delicious crabmeat rolls and sandwiches on French bread.

Mama and Leenie's (236-6300), Elm Street, Camden. Open year-round for breakfast, lunch, tea, and dinner. A warm, mothering atmosphere with fresh meat pies and a fragrant bakery. Hearty home cooking includes soups, sandwiches, salads, cheesecake, and pineapple upside-down cake. No liquor. This is a small place with only a handful of tables inside, plus a few more on an adjacent, shaded, outdoor patio. Service can be slow when they're busy.

Fitzpatrick's Deli Cafe (236-2041), Sharp's Wharf, Bayview Street, Camden. Open March through early January for breakfast, lunch, and dinner. Fitzi's is easy to miss as you walk from Bayview to the public landing. But it's a find: a wide variety of sandwiches and salads plus quiche of the day and special soup-salad-sandwich plates. You order at the counter, and they call you by name when it's time to pick up your food. Popular with regulars. Outside patio for summertime dining.

Camden Deli (236-8343), 37 Main Street, Camden. Over 35 sandwich choices, combining all of the regular deli meats and cheeses, as well as some less expected choices, like chicken broccoli salad or hummus. The Deli Lama has bologna, salami, turkey, capiccola, ham, and all the veggies. The back room overlooks the harbor.

Rockport Corner Shop (236-8361), Rockport. Open year-round for breakfast and lunch. Regulars greet each other warmly at this spot in the heart of the village, but newcomers are made to feel welcome, too. Help yourself to coffee. An exceptional find with almost no decor but plenty of atmosphere. Fresh coffeecakes are baked each morning; all salads are made with garden-grown vegetables. Breakfast specialties include eggs Benedict and Swedish pancakes; lunch offers pocket sandwiches, lobster and crabmeat rolls, and daily specials. No liquor. Very reasonable prices.

Miss Plum's, Route 1, Rockport. Open year-round. All three meals from April through October; breakfast and lunch only from November to March. Painted deep plum, this is a real, old-fashioned ice cream parlor with all flavors made on the premises. There are homemade cones and edible dishes and nostalgic treats such as egg creams and extra-thick frappes. The menu includes hash 'n' eggs and omelets at breakfast, a variety of sandwiches at lunch, and several choices like meat loaf and gravy or chicken pot pie available at lunch or dinner.

CAFÉ

Cork, Inc. (230-0533), 37 Bayview Street, Camden. A wine and espresso café, with a pleasant, relaxing atmosphere. Couches, comfy chairs. Light lunches include cheese platters, salmon pâté, and a French dip sandwich. Desserts include chocolate fondue. A multitude of wine and beer choices, espresso, and soft drinks.

LOBSTER POUNDS

Lobster Pound Restaurant (789-5550), Route 1, Lincolnville Beach. Open every day for lunch and dinner, the first Sunday in May through Columbus Day. Also serves breakfast from July 4 through Labor Day. This is a mecca for lobster lovers—some people plan their trips around a meal here. Features lobster, steamed or baked, also clams, other fresh seafood, roast turkey, ham, steaks, and chicken. This is a family-style restaurant that seats 260 inside and has picnic tables near a sandy beach and take-out window. Always popular (always crowded).

Captain Andy's (236-2312), Upper Washington Street, Route 105, Camden. Call and order your lobsters with all the fixings, and they'll be delivered right to you at the harbor park or town landing for a delicious picnic.

TAKEOUT

The Market Basket (236-4371), Routes 1 and 90, Rockport. The daily menu includes a selection of two or more unusual soups, generously portioned Greek and garden salads, and many specialty entrées such as curried chicken salad with pasta and grapes. Desserts are available. This is a specialty food store, so you can buy French bread (the best we've had anywhere), cheeses, pâtés, slices of cheesecake, and a good bottle of wine or imported beer to top things off. Then head for Marine Park.

☞ **Scott's Place** (236-8751), Elm Street, Camden. This tiny building in the parking lot of a small shopping center serves hundreds of toasted crabmeat and lobster rolls, marinated chicken sandwiches, burgers, hot dogs, and chips. Prices are among the best around: $1 for a hot dog, under $5 for a lobster roll. This is one of several small take-out buildings around town, but it's the only one open year-round.

☞ **Ayer's Fish Market** (236-3509), Main Street, Camden. A great little fish store with live lobsters, too. But the pièce de résistance is what has to be the best lunch bargain in town: a large serving of steamy fish chowder for just $1.50. What goes into it varies from day to day, and it's sometimes chunkier than at other times; but it's always delicious.

(Also see The Helm under *Eating Out* and Captain Andy's under *Lobster Pounds.*)

ENTERTAINMENT

Bay Chamber Concerts (236-2823), Rockport Opera House, Rockport. Thursday- and Friday-evening concerts are given during July and August (also monthly winter concerts from October through May) in this beautifully restored opera house with its gilded interior. Outstanding chamber music presented for more than 30 years. Summer concerts are preceded by free lectures.

Camden Civic Theatre (John Ferraiolo, 594-5161), Camden Opera House, PO Box 362, Main Street, Camden. A variety of theatrical performances are presented in this restored, second-floor theater with plum seats and cream-and-gold walls. Tickets are reasonably priced.

Camerata Singers (Sandra Jerome, director: 236-8704). This award-winning, 15-member, a cappella singing group presents a summer series in July and a Twelfth Night concert in January. Performances are given in Camden, Belfast, and Waldoboro.

Maine Coast Artists (see *Art Galleries*) sponsors a series of lectures and live performances June through September.

Bayview Street Cinema (236-8722), Bayview Street, Camden. Showings daily. A mixed bag of old favorites, foreign and art films, and some current movies.

SELECTIVE SHOPPING

ANTIQUES

At the chamber of commerce (see *Guidance*), pick up the leaflet guide to antiques shops scattered among Camden, Rockport, and Lincolnville.

ART GALLERIES

Maine Coast Artists Gallery (236-2875), Russell Avenue, Rockport. Major exhibitions May through October; open daily 10–5. Ongoing special exhibits off-season; call for details. Free admission, but contributions encouraged. A late-19th-century livery stable, then a firehouse, then the town hall, and, since 1968, one of Maine's outstanding art centers. Showcasing contemporary Maine art, the gallery sponsors several shows each season, an art auction, a crafts show, gallery talks, and an evening lecture series.

Maine's Massachusetts House Galleries (789-5705), Route 1, Lincolnville (2 miles north of Lincolnville Beach). Open year-round Monday through Saturday 9–5; Sunday in summer and fall, 12–5. A large barn gallery that's been a landmark since 1949, exhibiting works by Maine artists: oils, watercolors, and sculpture.

Pine Tree Shop and Bay View Gallery, Bayview Street, Camden. One of the largest galleries in the Mid Coast area. Original paintings and sculptures by contemporary Maine artists plus several thousand posters and prints. Expert custom framing, too.

A Small Wonder Gallery (236-6005), Commercial Street (across from the Camden Chamber of Commerce). A small gallery with well-chosen, limited-edition graphics, watercolors, art glass.

ARTISANS

Anne Kilham Designs (236-0962), 165 Russell Avenue, Rockport. Anne Kilham's distinctive designs on postcards, note cards, and prints are now distributed throughout the country. She is frequently here in her studio and in the shop that sells her watercolors and oils as well as paper products, place mats, and more.

Windsor Chairmakers (789-5188), Route 1, Lincolnville Beach. Filling two floors of an old farmhouse, the inviting display encompasses not only Windsor chairs but also tables, highboys, and four-poster beds, all offered in a selection of finishes including "distressed" (instant antique). The owner welcomes commissions—he's always ready to make a few sketches as you describe your ideas—and enjoys chatting with visitors and showing them around the workshop.

Brass Foundry (236-3200), Park Street, West Rockport (diagonally across from Mystic Woodworks). Custom metal castings in bronze and aluminum. Also handblown glass vases, bowls, and goblets.

James Lea (236-3632), 9 West Street, Rockport. Showroom is open by appointment Monday through Friday. Jim Lea is a third-generation craftsman fashioning museum-quality furniture reproductions using antique tools as well as more modern devices; all work is done on commission.

BOOKSTORES

ABCDef Books (236-3903), 23 Bay View Street, Camden. Open daily except Sunday from July 4 through Labor Day, otherwise closed Monday April through December; closed completely January through March. A Camden literary landmark: an unusually extensive and organized collection of rare and used books featuring maritime, art, New England, and history titles.

Down East (594-9544), Route 1, Rockport. The headquarters for Down East Enterprises (publishers of *Down East, Fly Rod & Reel, Fly Tackle Dealer,* and *Shooting Sportsman* magazines, as well as a line of New England books) is a fine old mansion that includes a book and gift shop.

The Owl and Turtle Bookshop, Bayview Street, Camden. One of Maine's best bookstores. Six rooms full of books, including special ones devoted to arts and crafts, boats, sports, and young adults and children. Special orders and searches for out-of-print books. Great for browsing.

SPECIAL SHOPS

All shops are in Camden and open year-round unless otherwise indicated.

Camden 5 & 10. The Camden Store. "Yes you can buy underwear in downtown Camden!" is the slogan of this huge old five-and-dime on Mechanic Street, just off Main.

Unique 1, Bayview Street. Woolen items made from Maine wool, designed and hand loomed locally. Also some pottery.

Once a Tree, Bayview Street, Camden. Wooden crafts including beautiful clocks, kitchen utensils, desk sets; a large game and toy section.

The Smiling Cow, Main Street. Seasonal. Three generations ago, a mother and five children converted this stable into a classic gift shop, one with unusual warmth and scope. Customers help themselves to coffee on the back porch overlooking a waterfall and the harbor.

Ducktrap Bay Trading Company, Bayview Street. Decoys and wildlife art. Many of these really special pieces have earned awards for their creators. There are also some less expensive carvings, plus jewelry.

Etienne Fine Jewelry, Main Street. Gallery of designer jewelry in 14- and 18-carat gold; contemporary and unusual pieces made on the premises.

L.E. Leonard, 67 Pascal Avenue, Rockport. An old general store with a fine selection of antique and contemporary furnishings from Indonesia and India; pieces range from jewelry to carved beds.

Danica Design Candles (236-3060), Route 90, West Rockport. In a striking building of Scandinavian design, a candle factory and shop.

SPECIAL EVENTS

Late June: **Down East Jazz Festival,** Camden Opera House.

July: **Fourth of July**—a full weekend of special events culminating in fireworks over the harbor. **Great Schooner Race** (see "Rockland/ Thomaston Area").

Late July: **Annual Open House and Garden Day,** sponsored by the Camden Garden Club. Very popular tour of homes and gardens in Camden and Rockport held every year for five decades. Third Saturday and Sunday in July—**Arts and Crafts Show,** Camden Amphitheatre.

Early August: **Maine Coast Artists Annual Art Auction,** Maine's largest exhibit and auction of quality, contemporary Maine art.

Late August: **Union Fair and Blueberry Festival,** Union Fairgrounds (see "Rockland/Thomaston Area").

Labor Day weekend: **Windjammer Weekend,** Camden Harbor—a celebration of the windjammer industry.

Mid-September: **Rockport Folk Festival,** Rockport Opera House.

First weekend in October: **Fall Festival of Arts and Crafts,** Camden Amphitheatre—75 artisans displaying work for sale.

Early December: **Christmas by the Sea**—tree lighting, Santa's arrival, caroling, holiday house tour, refreshments in shops, Christmas Tree Jubilee at the Samoset Resort.

IV. DOWN EAST

East Penobscot Bay Region
Bar Harbor and Acadia Area
Washington County, Campobello, and St. Andrews

Trenton Lobster Pound

KIMBERLY GRANT

Down East

"Down East" is a nautical term that refers to sailing with the prevailing winds. Along the Maine coast these blow dependably from the southwest, ushering sailing vessels ever eastward.

The precise location of "Down East" is another question. State tourism promoters now define it as Hancock and Washington Counties. This Down East divides into three very distinct areas: (1) the series of extraordinarily beautiful peninsulas and islands that define East Penobscot Bay; (2) Mount Desert—the island on which Acadia National Park is the big attraction and Bar Harbor, the big tourist town—and East Hancock County, the coast and peninsulas beyond but still within view of Mount Desert's mountains and aura; and (3) Washington County, with its more than 900 miles of rugged coast stretching east to Quoddy Head, on around Cobscook Bay and along Passamaquoddy, the island-spotted bay that divides Maine from New Brunswick, Canada.

"I live in the other state of Maine: Washington County," bumper stickers proclaim, and it's true. Washington County is far and foggy, but the bleak beauty of this rugged coast becomes more accessible every year as hiking trails, boat excursions, and kayak rentals gradually increase. Lodging and food are more reasonably priced than in more touristed stretches of the coast.

If you have just a couple of extra days, we recommend that, rather than hopping the *Bluenose* ferry at Bar Harbor (which takes 6 hours and lands you in the least interesting part of Nova Scotia), you "do the Quoddy Loop." Continue on down the Maine coast at least another 90 miles to Lubec and cross the bridge to Campobello Island, where Roosevelt International Park offers a glimpse into the life and era of FDR as well as extensive hiking trails. The car ferry rides from Campobello or Eastport to Deer Island and on across Passamaquoddy Bay are both rewarding, bargain-priced cruises, and it's a short ride from the ferry terminal to St. Andrews (the Bar Harbor of New Brunswick) and on back along the bay to Calais (Maine). You can do the Quoddy Loop in 2 days, and we suspect that you will want to return for a longer stay.

East Penobscot Bay Region

Bucksport; Castine; Blue Hill Area; Deer Isle, Stonington, and Isle au Haut

BUCKSPORT

"Gateway" is a much overused touring term but crossing the high, narrow Waldo–Hancock County suspension bridge (vintage 1931) above the confluence of the Penobscot River and Bay, you can't escape the sense of turning a corner in the coast. Beyond is Bucksport, a workaday river and paper mill town with a couple of very good places to eat and a 1916 movie theater/museum showcasing New England films dating back to the turn of the century.

Bucksport began as a major shipping port in 1764. After the British burned it, settlers rebuilt, and it is still a strong shipping force today. Bucksport overlooks New England's biggest fort, a memorial to its smallest war.

GUIDANCE

Bucksport Area Chamber of Commerce (469-6818), Main Street 04416, next to the town offices, is open Monday through Friday 9–1. It publishes a "source book" that includes Orland and Verona Islands. Public rest rooms are at the town dock.

TO SEE AND DO

Fort Knox State Park (469-7719), Route 174 (off Route 1), Prospect (just across the Penobscot from Bucksport). Open daily May 1 to November 1, 9 AM–sunset. $2 per adult. Built in 1844 of granite cut from nearby Mount Waldo, it includes barracks, storehouses, a labyrinth of passageways, and even a granite spiral staircase. There are also picnic facilities. The fort was to be a defense against Canada during the boundary dispute with New Brunswick called the Aroostook War. The dispute was ignored in Washington, and so in 1839 the new, lumber-rich state took matters into its own hands by arming its northern forts. Daniel Webster represented Maine in the 1842 treaty that formally ended the war, but

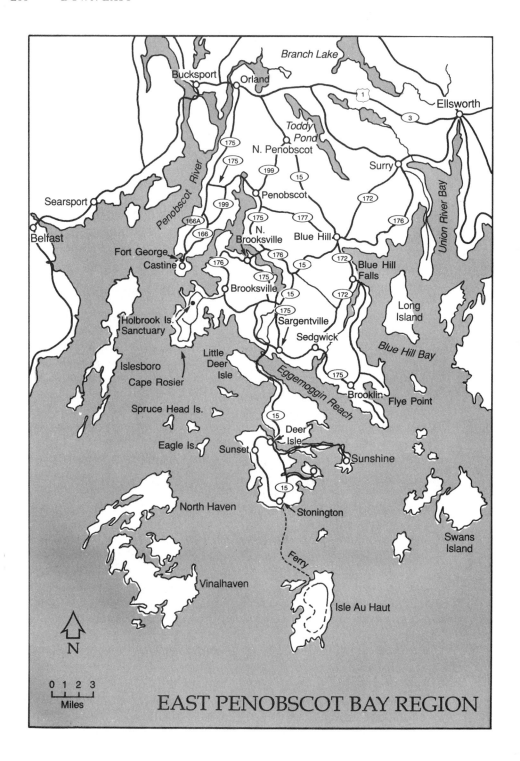

EAST PENOBSCOT BAY REGION

Maine built this fort two years later, just in case. It was never entirely completed and never saw battle.

Bucksport Historical Society Museum (567-3623), Main Street, Bucksport. Open July and August, Wednesday through Friday 1–4, and by appointment. Admission $.50. Housed in the former Maine Central Railroad Station; local memorabilia.

Northeast Historic Film (469-0924), 379 Main Street, Bucksport 04416. Open year-round, Monday through Saturday 9–4. Housed here in the vintage 1916 Alamo Theatre is New England's only "moving image" archives—source of silent, Maine-made films. The museum is devoted to collecting and preserving films depicting New England life, from 1901 to the present. Check out the Saturday matinees ($2). The gift shop features videos and classic posters.

At **Bucksport Cemetery,** near the Verona Bridge (across from the Shop & Save), a granite obelisk marks the grave of Colonel Jonathan Buck, founder of Bucksport. The outline of a leg on the stone has spurred many legends, the most popular being that a woman Judge Buck sentenced to death for witchcraft is carrying through a promise to dance on his grave. Attempts to remove the imprint have failed, and it is still there.

Craig Brook National Fish Hatchery (469-2803), East Orland (turn off Route 1 in Orland, just east of Bucksport). Open daily 8–4:30. Opened in 1871, this is the country's oldest salmon hatchery. Situated on the shore of a lake, it offers a visitors center with aquariums, also a nature trail, picnic tables, and a 19th-century icehouse.

SPECIAL LEARNING PROGRAM

Verna Cox (469-6402; fax: 469-6243) offers multiday rug-braiding and rug-hooking seminars at the River Inn; also inquire about spinning, weaving, crewel, cross-stitching, tatting, and wool-felting workshops.

LODGING

The River Inn Bed & Breakfast (469-3783), 210 Main Street, Bucksport 04416. Open year-round. A sea captain's house with three pleasant guest rooms, $55 with private bath, $50 for a private deck but shared bath. The parlor is equipped with color TV, books, and a player piano. No smoking.

WHERE TO EAT

MacLeods (469-3963), Main Street, Bucksport. Open weekdays 11–9, weekends 5–9. A pubby bar with booths, informal atmosphere, dependable dining. Good lunch specials (try a croissant sandwich). Entrées include scampi and linguine ($12.95), MacLeod's mixed grill ($12.95), and jambalaya ($9.95).

L'Ermitage (469-3361), 219 Main Street, Bucksport. Open for dinner by reservation, Tuesday through Sunday. Enjoy traditional French fare in the dining rooms of a Victorian house. It may be the only place in Maine you will find blueberry trifle. Entrées begin at $12.95.

Sail Inn, Route 1 in Prospect just before the bridge. The name always makes us laugh since there is no way you could sail into this classic diner, perched as it is atop a high bluff. Blackboard specials supplement a menu featuring fried chicken, sandwiches, pizza, seafood chowders, and stews.

Dockside Restaurant (469-7600), Main Street, Bucksport. Open daily for breakfast, lunch, and dinner. Adjacent to the public landing, overlooking the Penobscot and across to Fort Knox. Plain good food, cocktail lounge, a good way stop.

SPECIAL EVENT

Last week in June: **Orland River Days**—an "anything goes" raft contest, live music, crafts in a classic New England town on the Narramissic River.

CASTINE

Sited at the tip of a finger of the Blue Hill peninsula, Castine is one of Maine's most photogenic coastal villages, the kind writers describe as "perfectly preserved." Even the trees that arch high above Main Street's clapboard homes and shops have managed to escape the blight that has felled elms elsewhere.

Situated on a peninsula at the confluence of the Penobscot and Bagaduce Rivers, the town still looms larger on nautical charts than on road maps. Yacht clubs from Portland to New York visit annually.

Castine has always had a sense of its own importance. According to the historical markers that pepper its tranquil streets, Castine has been claimed by four different countries since its early-17th-century founding as Fort Pentagoet. It was an early trading post for the Pilgrims but soon fell into the hands of Baron de Saint Castine, a young French nobleman who married a Penobscot Indian princess and reigned as a combination feudal lord and Indian chief over Maine's eastern coast for many decades.

Since no two accounts agree, we won't attempt to describe the outpost's constantly shifting fortunes—even the Dutch owned it briefly. Nobody denies that in 1779 residents (mostly Tories who fled here from Boston and Portland) welcomed the invading British. The Commonwealth of Massachusetts retaliated by mounting a fleet of 18 armed vessels and 24 transports with 1000 troops and 400 marines aboard. This small navy disgraced itself absurdly when it sailed into town in 1779. The British Fort George was barely in the making, manned by 750 soldiers with the backup of two sloops, but the American privateers refused to attack and hung around in the bay long enough for several British men-of-war to come along and destroy them. The surviving patriots had to walk back to Boston, and many of their officers, Paul Revere included, were court-martialed for their part in the disgrace. The town was occupied by the British again in 1814.

Perhaps it was to spur young men on to avenge this affair that Castine was picked (150 years later) as the home of the Maine Maritime Academy, which occupies the actual site of the British barracks and keeps a training ship anchored at the town dock, incongruously huge beside the graceful, white-clapboard buildings of a very different maritime era.

In the mid-19th century, thanks to shipbuilding, Castine claimed to be the second wealthiest town per capita in the United States. Its genteel qualities were recognized by summer visitors, who later came by steamboat to stay in the eight hotels. Many built their own seasonal mansions.

Only two of the hotels survive. But the town dock is an unusually welcoming one, complete with picnic tables, parking, and rest rooms. It remains the heart of this walking town, where you can amble uphill past shops or down along Perkins Street to the Wilson Museum. Like many of New England's most beautiful villages, Castine's danger seems to lie in the perfect preservation of its beauty, a shell unconnected to the lives that built it. Few visitors complain, however. Castine is exquisite.

GUIDANCE

Castine Merchants Association (326-4884), PO Box 329, Castine 04421. Request the helpful map/guide, available by mail or around town. The obvious place to begin exploring is the Castine Historical Society on the common.

GETTING THERE

By air: See the "Bar Harbor" and "Portland" chapters for air service.
By car: The quickest route is the Maine Turnpike to Augusta and Route 3 to Belfast, then Route 1 to Orland and Route 175; follow signs.

MEDICAL EMERGENCY

Blue Hill Memorial Hospital (374-2836), the largest facility in the area, has a 24-hour emergency room. **Castine Community Health Services** (326-4348) has a doctor on call.

TO SEE

MUSEUMS

Castine Historical Society (326-4118), Abbott School Building, Castine Town Common. July through Labor Day 10–4, from 1 on Sunday; closed Monday. The former high school, converted to a historical society and welcome center for the town's bicentennial in 1996. Center stage is a stunning quilted mural designed by artist Margaret Hodesh and stitched by more than 50 townspeople. An ornate chair, said to be carved from the wood of a sunken English warship, is also displayed, along with vintage photos.

Wilson Museum (326-8545), Perkins Street. Open May 27 through September 30, Tuesday through Sunday 2–5. Housed in a fine waterside building donated by anthropologist J. Howard Wilson, a summer resident who amassed many of the displayed Native American artifacts as well as ancient ones from around the world. There are also changing art exhibits, collections of minerals, old tools, and farm equipment, an 1805 kitchen, and a Victorian parlor. **Hearse House** and a blacksmith shop are open Wednesday and Sunday afternoons in July and August, 2–5. The complex also includes the **John Perkins House,** open only during July and August, Wednesday and Sunday 2–5 ($4 admission); a pre-Revolutionary War home, restored and furnished in period style. Guided tours and crafts and fireside cooking demonstrations.

HISTORIC SITES

Fort George. Open May 30 through Labor Day, daylight hours. The sorry tale of its capture by the British during the American Revolution (see above) and again during the War of 1812, when redcoats occupied the town for 8 months, is told on panels at the fort—an earthworks complex of grassy walls (great to roll down) and a flat interior where you may find Maine Maritime Academy cadets being put through their paces.

State of Maine (326-4311). A new ship is due in '97 but at this writing visiting hours have not been set. Traditionally the vessel used by Maine Maritime Academy cadets is open to visitors weekdays in July and August.

TO DO

BOAT EXCURSION

Balmy Days (338-4652; 596-9041), a 1932 coastal Maine workboat, offers tours of Castine Harbor and around Islesboro, also sunset cruises and trips to Belfast; bicycles and kayaks welcome.

FISHING

We are told that you can catch flounder off the town dock and mackerel at Dyce's Head, below the lighthouse.

GOLF AND TENNIS

Castine Golf Club (326-4311), Battle Avenue. Offers nine holes and four clay courts.

SWIMMING

British Canal, Backshore Road. During the War of 1812, the British dug a canal across the narrow neck of land above town, thus turning Castine into an island. Much of the canal is still visible.

Maine Maritime Academy (326-4311) offers, for a nominal fee, gymnasium facilities to local inn guests. This includes the pool, weight room, and squash and racquetball courts.

GREEN SPACE

Witherle Woods is an extensive wooded area webbed with paths at the western end of town. The ledges below **Dyce's Head Light,** also at the western end of town, are great for clambering. The **Castine Conservation Commission** sponsors nature walks occasionally in July and August. Check local bulletin boards.

LODGING

All lodging listings are for Castine 04421.

☞ **Castine Inn** (326-4365), PO Box 41, Main Street. Open May through October. A rare bird among Maine's current plethora of B&Bs and inns: a genuine, 1890s summer hotel that's been lovingly and deftly restored, right down to the frieze beneath its roof. It offers 20 light and airy, but unfrilly (the furniture is Maine made—solid but not fancy), guest rooms, all with private baths and many with harbor views. Guests enter a wide, welcoming hallway and find a pleasant sitting room and a pub, both with frequently lit fireplaces and interesting, original art. Innkeeper Margaret Hodesh has painted a mural of Castine on all four walls of the dining room (see *Dining Out*)—a delightful room with French doors leading out to a broad veranda overlooking the inn's terraced, formal gardens (a popular place for weddings) and the town sloping to the harbor beyond. Children over 5 welcome. Margaret and cohost Mark Hodesh orient guests to the region, annually updating their own guide to sights and shops. $75–125 ($150 for a two-room suite if occupied by four) includes a full breakfast.

Pentagoet Inn (326-8616; 1-800-845-1701), PO Box 4, Main Street. Open May to October. The main inn is a very Victorian summer hotel with a turret, gables, and a wraparound porch. Rooms in the inn itself are unusually shaped, nicely furnished, and cozy; one room in neighboring **Ten Perkins Street** (a 200-year-old home) has a working fireplace. In all there are 16 guest rooms, each with private bath. There are two sitting rooms and a pink-walled dining room that opens onto the garden. $95–125 per couple B&B includes early-morning coffee, a full breakfast, and evening wine and cheese; children over 12 are welcome.

WHERE TO EAT

DINING OUT

☞ **Castine Inn** (326-4365), Main Street. Open daily for breakfast and dinner. The ambience, quality, and value of this dining room are well known locally, filling it most nights. Crabmeat cakes in mustard sauce are a specialty. Broiled salmon with lemon caper sauce is a real treat, but it's no hardship to settle for the chicken and leek pot pie. The menu changes frequently but always features local seafood and produce. Save room for the chocolate soufflé cake or caramelized apple tart. A mural of Castine wraps around all four walls of the room, punctuated by windows and French doors overlooking the inn's spectacular garden. Entrées are $13–19. Tuesday is buffet night. A short but interesting wine list.

EATING OUT

Bah's Bake House (326-9510), Water Street. Open 7 AM–9 PM daily, until 8 PM on Sunday. A few tables and a great deli counter featuring sandwiches on baguette bread, daily-made soups, salads, and baked goods.

Dennett's Wharf (326-9045), Sea Street (off the town dock). Open daily spring through fall for lunch and dinner. An open-framed, waterside structure said to have been built as a bowling alley after the Civil War. Seafood, smoked fish, and seafood pasta salads, and waterside dining.

The Breeze (326-9034), town dock. Seasonal. When the summer sun shines, this is the best place in town to eat: fried clams, hot dogs, onion rings, and soft ice cream. The public facilities are next door and, with luck, you can dine at the picnic tables on the dock.

ENTERTAINMENT

Cold Comfort Productions (366-3510), PO Box 259. A resident company mounts a series of popular productions from early July through late August. Performances are either in Emerson Hall on Court Street, at the Maine Maritime Academy, or, occasionally, outside.

SELECTIVE SHOPPING

Leila Day Antiques (326-8786), Main Street. An outstanding selection of early American furniture, also paintings, quilts, and Maine-made Shard Pottery. The shop is in the historic Parson Mason House and the approach is through a formal garden.

Chris Murray, waterfowl carver (326-9033), Main Street. Accomplished decoy artist Chris Murray maintains a shop behind his house. He sells the highly detailed birds for which he is known (and the books and tools necessary for making them) and conducts classes in carving.

McGrath-Dunham Gallery (326-9938), Main Street. Open daily May through October. Thirty other artists.

Compass Rose (326-9366; 1-800-698-9366), Main Street. Frances Kimball's fully stocked bookstore features children's titles, summer reading, regional books, and Penguin classics.

Water Witch (326-4884), Main Street. Jean de Raat sells original designs made from Dutch Java batiks, English paisley prints, and Maine-made woolens.

SPECIAL EVENTS

Third weekend in June: **Summer Festival**—craft show, ethnic food, children's activities.

July: **Sea Kayaking Symposium** sponsored by L.L. Bean.

June–October, Tuesday: Windjammers usually in port.

BLUE HILL AREA

In Maine, Blue Hill refers to a specific hill, a village, a town, a peninsula—and also to an unusual gathering of artists, musicians, and craftspeople.

The high, rounded hill overlooks Blue Hill Bay. The white wooden village is graced with no fewer than 75 buildings on the National Historic Register: old mansions, an 1840s academy, a fine town hall, a busy music hall, two gourmet restaurants, some lively cafés, a half-dozen galleries, and two potteries.

Blue Hill is a shade off the beaten path, one peninsula west of Mount Desert and nowhere near a beach; but it always has had its own following—especially among craftspeople, artists, musicians, and writers. Most tourists whiz on by up Route 1 to Mount Desert, and relatively few stray as far as the village of Blue Hill—let alone as far as Deer Isle, attached to the southern tip of the Blue Hill peninsula by Maine's most amazing bridge. Deer Isle itself wanders off in all directions, and a number of its villages, although technically linked to the mainland by causeways, retain the atmosphere of islands.

Pause at the turnout on Caterpillar Hill, the height-of-land on Route 15/175 just north of the Deer Isle bridge, for an overview of this intermingling of land and water that stretches across East Penobscot Bay to the Camden Hills. Follow narrow roads through the countless land fingers around Blue Hill and on Deer Isle, searching out studios of local craftspeople and artists. What you remember afterward is the beauty of clouds over fields of wildflowers, quiet coves, the loveliness of things woven, painted, and blown, and conversations with the people who made them.

GUIDANCE

A map/guide is available from PO Box 520, Blue Hill 04614, or by calling the Liros Gallery at 374-5370 (see *Selective Shopping*).

GETTING THERE

Follow directions to Castine (see *Getting There* in "Castine"), but turn off Route 1 onto Route 15 south instead of Route 175 (it's between Orland and East Orland).

MEDICAL EMERGENCY

Blue Hill Memorial Hospital (374-2836), the largest facility in the area, has a 24-hour emergency room.

TO SEE

Parson Fisher House (374-2001), 0.5 mile south of Blue Hill Village on Route 15/176. Open July through mid-September, Monday through Saturday 2–5. A house built in 1814 by Blue Hill's first pastor, a Harvard graduate who augmented his meager salary with a varied line of crafts and by teaching (he founded Blue Hill Academy), farming, and writing. His furniture, paintings, books, journals, and woodcuts are exhibited. $2 admission.

Holt House, Water Street, Blue Hill. Open during July and August, Tuesday and Friday 1–4. The Blue Hill Historical Society collection is housed in this restored, Federal, 1815 mansion near the harbor, noted for its stenciled walls. The annual quilt show is held here.

Blue Hill Library (374-5515), Main Street. Open daily except Sunday. A handsome WPA project building with periodicals and ample reading space; changing art shows in summer.

Bagaduce Lending Library (374-5454), Blue Hill. Open Tuesday and Wednesday 10–3. This is another Blue Hill phenomenon: some 500,000 volumes of sheet music, some more than a century old, most of it special for one reason or another, all available for borrowing. The collection includes 1400 pieces either about Maine, by Maine composers, or published in Maine. Stop by just to see the fascinating picture over the entrance depicting Blue Hill at the center of concentric, creative circles.

The Good Life Center (326-8211), Harborside, Cape Rosier. Open Memorial Day through Labor Day, Wednesday through Sunday 1–5 and in the fall by appointment. The stone home built in 1953 by Helen and Scott Nearing, coauthors of *Living the Good Life* and seven other books based on their simple, purposeful lifestyle, is now maintined by the Trust for Public Land, open for tours and occasional workshops; off-season call 617-367-6200.

✐ **MERI Resource Center** (359-8078), Brooklin. Open May through August, weekdays 9–5, Saturday 10–4. Frequent walking trips and cruises as well as weeklong programs for youngsters to tune them in to shore and sea life. The center has a small aquarium and a "sea library."

(Also see *Art Galleries* under *Selective Shopping*.)

TO DO

SAILING

Buck's Harbor Marine (326-8839), South Brooksville, is the place from which day-sail charters leave. Captain Gil Perkins (326-4167) offers half- and full-day cruises on his 30-foot sailboat *2nd Fiddle* and power cruiser *Queen Mary*. *Summertime* (359-2067; 1-800-562-8290 outside the state), a 53-foot pinky schooner, offers day sails and longer cruises from several ports around Penobscot Bay.

WOODEN BOAT SCHOOL IN BROOKLIN

Boat building at the Wooden Boat School in Brooklin

SEA KAYAKING

The Phoenix Center (374-2113), Route 175, Blue Hill Falls. With a salt
pond on its acreage, the center is well positioned to teach and guide
half-day and full-day sea kayaking on both sides of the Blue Hill peninsula. Wilderness canoe camping, backpacking, and rock-climbing trips
are also offered. Inquire about the Fantasy Island Escape (a guide
paddles with you to a private island, prepares your dinner, and disap-
pears to return in the morning to make breakfast).

SPECIAL LEARNING PROGRAM

Wooden Boat School (359-4651), off Naskeag Point Road, south of the
village of Brooklin. A spinoff from *Wooden Boat* magazine more than

14 years ago, this seafaring institute of national fame offers more than 75 summer courses between June and October, ranging from building your own sailboat, canoe, or kayak to navigation and drawing and painting. Facilities are a former estate on Eggemoggin Reach, and visitors are encouraged to come to the library and to shop in the Big House. The former brick barn now houses three separate boatbuilding spaces, and you can wander down to the Boathouse, now a classroom and evening gathering spot. For a course catalog write: Wooden Boat School, PO Box 78, Brooklin 04616. Accommodations available.

GREEN SPACE

Blue Hill. Our friends at the Blue Hill Bookstore tell us that this was not the setting for the children's classic *Blueberries for Sal,* by Robert McClosky—a longtime summer resident of the area. But we choose to disbelieve them. It looks just like the hill in the book and has its share of in-season blueberries. The big attraction, however, is the view of the Mount Desert mountains. To find the mile-long trail to the top, drive north from Blue Hill Village on Route 172 and take a left across from the Blue Hill Fairgrounds; after 0.8 mile, a sign on your right marks the start of the path.

CONSERVATION AREA

Holbrook Island Sanctuary is a state wildlife sanctuary of more than 1230 acres, including 2.3 miles of shore. It's accessible by car from Route 176 in West Brooksville. No camping is permitted, but there is a lovely picnic area adjacent to a pebble beach. A network of old roads, paths, and animal trails leads along the shore and through marshes and forest. It's the creation as well as the gift of Anita Harris, who died not many years ago at age 92, the sole resident of Holbrook Island. Her will stipulated that her mansion and all the other buildings on the island (accessible only by private boat) be demolished. She was also responsible for destroying all homes within the sanctuary.

LODGING

RUSTIC RESORTS

Oakland House (359-8521; 1-800-359-RELAX), Brooksville 04617. Open May to late October. The picturesque old mansard-roofed hotel opened by Jim Littlefield's forebears in 1889 now houses only the dining rooms and serves as a centerpiece for this unusually extensive property, with a half mile of frontage on Eggemoggin Reach, and lake as well as saltwater beaches. Sixteen cottages (each different, most with living rooms and fireplaces) are scattered through the woods and along the shore, each accommodating four to six people. Some accept pets and smokers. There are no TVs and firewood is free. Families feel particularly welcome.

Facilities include a dock, rowboats, badminton, croquet, a rec hall full of games, and a choice of hiking trails. Breakfast and dinner are served in the old-fashioned dining rooms, one reserved for families, the other adults-only. After a century of "plain Maine cooking," the menu is now on a par with the best old Acadia hotels (see *Dining Out*). Thursday is lobster picnic night. Cottages rent by the week: $280–795 per adult in-season (children's rates slide) and $355–725 per week (housekeeping) in shoulder seasons. (Also see Shore Oaks Seaside Inn under *Bed & Breakfasts*.)

☞ ✐ **Hiram Blake Camp** (326-4951), Cape Rosier, Harborside 04642. Open mid-May to mid-October. Well off the beaten track, with more than 75 seasons in the same family, this is the kind of place you come to stay put. All cottages are situated within 200 feet of the shore, with views of Penobscot Bay. There are six one-bedroom cottages, five cottages with two bedrooms, and three with three bedrooms; each has a living room with a wood-burning stove; some have a fireplace as well. Each has a kitchen, a shower, and a porch. Guests with housekeeping cottages cook for themselves in the four shoulder months, but in July and August everyone eats in the dining room, which doubles as a library because thousands of books are ingeniously filed away by category in the ceiling. There are rowboats at the dock, a playground, and a recreation room with table tennis and board games; also ample hiking trails. The camp is run by the children, grandchildren, and great-grandchildren of Captain Hiram Blake, who founded it in 1916. $600 per week for a two-bedroom cottage sleeping a family of four, plus $150 per week per adult for meals, $100 for children age 12 and under. Rates drop during "housekeeping months" to $300–500 per week.

INNS AND BED & BREAKFASTS
In Blue Hill 04614

John Peters Inn (374-2116), Peters Point. Open May through October. An imposing mansion, a fantasy place with columns and airy, superbly furnished rooms (nine with fireplaces), is set on 25 shorefront acres, a mile from the center of town. Guest rooms offer great views, private baths; some have outside decks and four have kitchens. There's a glassed-in breakfast room, a pool, and lawns sloping down to the water. A canoe, rowboat, and small sailboat are available to guests. $95–150 includes an ambitious breakfast. Children over age 12.

☞ ✐ **Blue Hill Farm** (374-5126), Box 437. Open year-round. An attractive old farmhouse on 48 acres laced with walking/cross-country-ski trails. The former barn has been reworked as an open-beamed combination breakfast room and living room with plenty of light and space to read quietly alone or mingle with other guests. Innkeepers Jim and Marcia Schatz are usually around, manning the desk or the adjoining kitchen. Upstairs are seven small guest rooms, each with a private bath. The attached farmhouse offers seven more guest rooms with shared baths (including one appealing single) and more comfortable common rooms, one with a woodstove. $78–85 double includes a very full breakfast.

View from Eggemoggin Reach B&B

Blue Hill Inn (374-2844), near the junction of Main Street and Route 177. Open year-round. A classic 1830s inn on a quiet, elm-lined street in the village. The 11 guest rooms, some with sitting rooms and/or working fireplaces, are all carefully furnished with antiques and have private baths. Common rooms are ample and tasteful. In good weather guests gather for cocktails in the garden. A number of Kneisel Hall concerts (see *Entertainment*) are performed here during summer. A full breakfast, five-course candlelight dinner, and hors d'oeuvres are included in $150–190 double, plus 15 percent service charge; B&B rates also available. Inquire about kayaking and sailing packages.

Elsewhere on the Blue Hill peninsula

☞ **Buck's Harbor Inn** (326-8660), Box 268, South Brooksville 04617. Open year-round. Technically in the town of South Brooksville but really smack in the middle of the delightful yachting center of Buck's Harbor. Built in 1901 as an annex to a larger, long-vanished hotel, Peter and Ann Ebeling's mansard-roofed inn offers six bedrooms, 2½ baths, and pleasant common rooms. The dining room is open to the public November to April 1 on Saturday nights, and in summer the neighboring Landing Restaurant (see *Dining Out*) offers fine food and views. We like the feel of this place, from the sea-bright rooms to the glass-faced breakfast room; a full breakfast (Swedish pancake trees if you're lucky) features fresh fruit. Pets are accepted off-season. From $50 single, $65 double; $75 for the suite with an attached room, ideal for a family with one child.

Eggemoggin Reach Bed & Breakfast (359-5073), RR1, Box 33A, Herrick Road, Brooksville 04673. Susie and Mike Canon built this many-windowed waterside house as a retirement retreat but have transformed it into an unusually luxurious B&B with two suites and the spacious former master bedroom in the main house, all with water views and private baths (one suite, The Wheelhouse, also has its own living room and cathedral ceilings). A cottage in the pines offers two attractive "studio" units, each with stove, cathedral ceiling, sitting area, and private, screened-in porch on Deadmans Cove. Another one-bedroom cottage features a large living room and water view and more such cottages are in the making. The common gathering space is tastefully decorated, the venue for (full) breakfast if it's not sunny enough to serve on the porch. A dock with rowboat and canoe await. $134–159 per couple.

Shore Oaks Seaside Inn (359-8521; 1-800-359-RELAX), part of the Oakland House property (see *Rustic Resorts*) and one of the best-kept secrets of the region. Built at the turn of the century as a private "cottage," it eventually became absorbed into the resort complex—where it dozed until Sally, a trained designer, married Jim (Littlefield) and focused her considerable energy on this 10-bedroom stone and shingle building, renovating it totally but preserving the old simple feel of summer life centered on the water (the porch and lawn command sweeping views of the entrance to Eggemoggin Reach) and the big stone hearth. We also appreciated the bedtime reading light and the deep old tub. Guests have full use of all Oakland House facilities and eat breakfast and dinner in the hotel dining room, but this is a place apart. Coffee and tea are available from early morning in the dining room, and the living room and library are delightful. $56–86 per person MAP in-season; B&B rates available, less in shoulder seasons.

The Brooklin Inn (359-2777), Route 175, Brooklin 04616. A casual, friendly old inn on the edge of the village. Lorraine Duffy charges $70 and serves breakfast and dinner. Well-behaved pets permitted.

WHERE TO EAT

DINING OUT

Firepond (374-2135), Main Street, Blue Hill. Open May through December, lunch and dinner daily. This village restaurant is exceedingly popular, and even with its recent expansion, dinner reservations are a good idea. Request a table on the porch, within earshot of an old millstream (and don't forget a sweater). The specialties are delicately flavored veal and lamb, maybe with morels or sun-dried tomatoes, and seafood dishes like scallops with leeks; also roast duckling or tournedos of beef with the chef's sauce of the day. Dinner entrées run $16.95–21.95. You can also dine from the "Light Fare" menu on salads, soups, and entrées ranging from grilled chicken Caesar salad to baked lobster and artichoke hearts.

Jonathan's (374-5226), Main Street, Blue Hill. Open daily year-round for lunch and dinner. Two pleasant dining rooms. The menu is large and features seafood, local produce, and dishes prepared in imaginative ways, like assorted fish and shellfish simmered with a saffron-scented Arborio rice, greens, tomatoes, orange zest, fresh herbs, and imported cheeses. The wine list is extensive. Dinner entrées come with soup, vegetable, and French bread. With his sister, chef-owner Jonathan Chase has authored *Saltwater Seasonings,* a glossy, coastal-Maine cookbook. $16.95–18.95.

The Landing Restaurant (326-9445), Buck's Harbor, South Brooksville. Open May to October, Tuesday through Sunday from 5 PM. Kurt and Verena Stoll, from Zurich (Switzerland), bought this water-view dining room in 1996 and the reports are excellent. The menu ranges from fettuccine with artichoke hearts, roasted tomatoes, and spinach ($12.50) to roasted rack of Australian range lamb with caramelized onion and sun-dried tomato ($21). A prix fixe menu including soup, appetizer, and dessert is $17.50. The wine list is respectable.

Surry Inn (667-5091), Route 172, Contention Cove, Surry. Open nightly for dinner. This pleasant dining room overlooking a cove is well known locally for reasonably priced, fine dining. The menu changes often but always includes interesting soups—maybe Hungarian mushroom or lentil vegetable—and a wide selection that might include veal tarragon, medallions of pork sautéed with herbs and red wine vinegar, spicy garlic frogs' legs, and scallops with pesto and cream. Entrées $14–17.

The Blue Hill Inn (374-2844), Union Street, Blue Hill. Dinner to non-guests is by reservation only, but the candlelit dining room is large enough and the fare ambitious enough to encourage dinner patrons. The $30 prix fixe menu changes nightly. You might begin with a salad of lobster, potatoes, and peas, then dine on salmon with Pernod or beef fillet with blue-cheese sauce, and finish with parfait glacé. Open year-round but serving weekends-only in deep winter.

The Lookout (359-2188), Flye Point (2 miles off Route 175), North Brooklin. Seasonal. Open for dinner from 5:30; Sunday brunch. This classic old summer hotel has a spectacular view of Herrick Bay on one side and the Acadia Range on Mount Desert beyond Blue Hill Bay on the other. It has been in the same family for 200 years and an inn since 1891 (when the farmhouse was enlarged). The menu might include grilled salmon with cucumber dill sauce or grilled quail with maple syrup. Entrées $14–19. Reserve if you want a table with a view (on the porch).

Oakland House Hotel (359-8521), off Herrick Road, Brooksville. Open mid-June through September. The old-fashioned dining room is set with white tablecloths and wildflowers for a five-course dinner that might begin with a delicate soup or an appetizer pork and champagne pâté, then a mesclun salad and a choice among baked, herbed haddock, roast loin of spring lamb, and saffron linguine with olives and white wine. Dessert specialties include baked Maine apple charlotte and Maine blueberry buckle with freshly whipped sweet cream. Complete dinners are $25–33. At this writing wine is not permitted in the dining room, but stay tuned. The menu changes daily and you can check what's for dinner when you call to reserve.

EATING OUT

The Left Bank Bakery and Cafe (374-2201), Route 172, Blue Hill. Open daily 7 AM–10 PM. A sensational success as a place both to eat and to hear nationally known musicians (see *Entertainment*). Under new ownership but there are still exceptional baked goods, soups, freshly picked salads, spinach pie, fruit pies, and reasonably priced dinners like mushroom bean Stroganoff and apricot chicken. In summer, frequent nightly programs pack the place.

Jean-Paul's Bistro (374-5852), Main Street, Blue Hill Village. Open just July through mid-September, 11–4 for lunch and then for tea until 5:30. The view of Blue Hill Bay is unbeatable and is summer light, with a French accent as thick and authentic as Jean-Paul's. "Les Sandwiches" include *croque monsieur* and a walnut tarragon chicken salad with watercress on whole-grain bread, and the "Specialties" include a French farmer's plate (cold cuts, cheese, a baguette, and celery salad) and a sausage tart. We came for tea on a sunny afternoon and sampled the exquisite chocolate truffle terrine with delicate wild strawberries, and the taste will forever be mixed in memory with the view. The preferred seats are outside under umbrellas or, better yet, in one of the Adirondack chairs that can be grouped together around tables on the lawn overlooking the water. Wine and beer served.

Sarah's Shoppe (374-5181), Main Street, Blue Hill. Open 7 AM–9 PM daily. A snug little restaurant that features blueberry pancakes for breakfast, homemade soup du jour and quiche for lunch, and broiled garlic shrimp and steamed crabmeat for dinner.

The Red Bag Deli (374-8800), Water Street, Blue Hill. Open weekdays for breakfast and lunch (9–5 daily, Sunday 10–3). Salads and sandwiches, good source of takeout if you want to picnic.

Pie in the Sky Pizza (374-5570), Mill Street, Blue Hill. Open daily for lunch and dinner: pizzas, calzones, and subs. This is such a popular spot, you may want to plan on coming early to be sure to get a booth or a table on the porch by the brook. The soups are especially good, and we recommend the pesto pizza with a Greek salad.

Captain Isaac Merrill Inn & Cafe, middle of Blue Hill, next to the general store, a new café in an old house. Daytime chowders, baguette sandwiches, soda fountain, moderately priced evening meals like roast Maine turkey and local haddock broiled in herb lemon butter, also Portuguese seafood stew.

Bagaduce Lunch, Route 176, North Brooksville (at the Reversing Falls). A great spot with picnic tables by the river.

Benjamin's Pantry, Sedgwick, next to the post office. Open 6:30–1:30. Breakfast specials include biscuits, blueberry pancakes or muffins, cinnamon rolls, and pie. Homemade soup, sandwiches, and specials such as meat loaf or sweet-and-sour pork for lunch; omelets and root-beer floats all day.

Morning Moon Cafe (359-2373), Brooklin. A tiny oasis in the middle of Brooklin Village. Fresh-dough pizza, full menu: traditional American fare like a really good BLT, fine fish-and-chips. Open daily 7 AM–2 PM, except Monday, also for dinner Thursday through Sunday 5–8.

ENTERTAINMENT

MUSIC

Kneisel Hall Chamber Music Festival (374-2811), PO Box 648, Blue Hill. Faculty and students at this prominent old summer school for string and ensemble music present a series of Sunday-afternoon and Friday-evening concerts, early July through mid-August.

The Left Bank Bakery and Cafe (374-2201), Route 172, northern fringe of the village of Blue Hill. A 55-seat café that's become a stop on the national folk music, jazz, and poetry circuit.

WERU (469-6600), a nonprofit community radio station based on Route 1 in East Orland (89.9 FM), is known for folk music, jazz, and reggae.

Bagaduce Chorale (326-8532), Blue Hill. A community chorus staging several concerts yearly ranging from Bach to show tunes.

Surry Opera Company (667-2629), Morgan Bay Road, Surry. Zen master Walter Nowick founded this company in 1984 and mounts fairly spectacular productions most (but not all) summers, often incorporating performers from Russia and other countries. Performances are held throughout the area, but home base is Walter Nowick's Concert Barn.

SELECTIVE SHOPPING

ART GALLERIES

In Blue Hill: **Leighton Gallery** (374-5001), Parker Point Road. Open June to mid-October. Exhibits in the three-floor gallery change every few weeks, but there are some striking staples: Judith Leighton's own oils, the wonderful variety of sculpted shapes in the garden out back, and the unforgettable wooden animal carvings by local sculptor Eliot Sweet. **Liros Gallery** (374-5370), Main Street, specializes in fine paintings, old prints, maps, and Russian icons. **Jud Hartman Gallery and Sculpture Studio** (374-9917), Main Street, exhibits Hartman's own realistic bronze sculptures of northeastern Native Americans. **S.L. Kinnery Studio and Gallery** (374-5894), the Levy House, Main Street (Tuesday through Sunday 11–6 in summer, otherwise by appointment) displays contemporary American, Native American, shamanistic images; also paintings, photographs, carvings, jewelry.

Quinn Gallery (667-8490), Route 172, Surry. A truly eclectic and quality collection of paintings, photography, jewelry, pottery, blown glass.

ARTISANS

Rowantrees Pottery (374-5535), Union Street, Blue Hill. Open year-round, daily in summer (8:30–5, Sunday from noon) and weekdays in winter (7–3:30). Find your way back behind the friendly white house into the large studio. It was a conversation with Mahatma Gandhi in India that got Adelaide Pearson going on the idea of pottery in Blue Hill by using glazes gathered from the town's abandoned copper mines, quarries, and bogs. Fifty years later, Sheila Varnum continues to make the deeply colored glazes from local granite and feldspar. She invites visitors to watch tableware being hand thrown and to browse through the upstairs showroom filled with plates, cups, vases, and jam pots. Note the prints and original work by a longtime Blue Hill summer resident, artist Frank Hamabe.

Rackliffe Pottery (374-2297), Route 172, Blue Hill. Open Monday through Saturday 9–5, also Sunday afternoon. Phyllis and Phil Rackliffe worked at Rowantrees for 22 years before establishing their own business. They also use local glazes, and their emphasis is on individual small pieces rather than on sets. Visitors are welcome to watch.

Handworks Gallery (374-5613), Main Street, Blue Hill. Open Memorial Day to late December, Monday through Saturday 10–5. An upstairs, middle-of-town space filled with unusual handwoven clothing, jewelry, furniture, rugs, and blown glass.

North Country Textiles, Route 175, South Penobscot (326-4131), and Main Street, Blue Hill (374-2715). Open May through December in Blue Hill, summer months on Route 175. A partnership of three designer/weavers: Sheila Denny-Brown, Carole Ann Larson, and Ron King. The shop displays jackets and tops, mohair throws, guest towels, and coasters, all in bright colors and irresistible textures.

Scott Goldberg Pottery, Route 176, Brooksville. Open daily May to October. Scott Goldberg and Jeff Oestreich display their own stoneware pottery as well as work by others.

Peninsula Weavers (374-2760), next to the Blue Hill Yarn Shop. Four weavers share an upstairs studio using Swedish looms and techniques. Woven rugs, scarves, weaving supplies, Swedish linens and clogs.

Gail Disney (326-4649), Route 176 between South Brooksville and Brooksville Corners. Visitors are welcome year-round. Handwoven cotton and wool rag rugs, custom made.

ANTIQUES

Roughly a dozen antiques shops are scattered through the peninsula, described in a pamphlet guide available at all. Anyone with a serious interest in early American and European painted country furniture should stop by **Anne Wells Antiques** (374-1093) just north of Blue Hill Village on Route 172. Open Monday through Saturday 10:30–5 and by appointment.

BOOKSTORES

Blue Hill Books (374-5632), 2 Pleasant Street (two doors up from the post office). A long-established, full-service, family-run bookstore. **North Light Books** (374-5422), Main Street, Blue Hill. A full-service, family-run bookstore. **Wayward Books** (359-2397), Route 15, Sargentville; mid-May through December, 10–5, Saturday 12–5. A good used bookstore.

SPECIAL SHOPS

Blue Hill Tea & Tobacco Shop (374-2161), Main Street. Open Monday through Saturday 10–5:30. An appealing shop dedicated to the perfect cup of tea or coffee, a well-chosen wine, and the right blend of tobacco.

Blue Hill Yarn Shop (374-5631), Route 172 north of Blue Hill Village. Open Monday through Saturday 10–4. A mecca for knitters in search of a variety of wools and needles. Lessons and original hand knits are sold.

H.O.M.E. Co-op (469-7961), Route 1, Orland. Open daily in-season 9–5. A remarkable complex that includes a Crafts Village (visitors may watch pottery making, weaving, leatherwork, woodworking); a museum of old handicrafts and farm implements; a large crafts shop featuring handmade coverlets, toys, and clothing; a market stand with fresh vegetables, herbs, and other garden produce; and a chapel with services open to the public on Wednesday afternoons. There is a story behind this non-profit enterprise, which has filled an amazing variety of local needs. Be sure to stop.

SPECIAL EVENTS

Last weekend in July: **Blue Hill Days**—arts and crafts fair, parade, farmer's market, antique car rally, shore dinner, boat races.

August: **St. Francis Annual Summer Fair.**

Labor Day weekend: **Blue Hill Fair,** at the fairgrounds. Harness racing, a midway, livestock competitions; one of the most colorful old-style fairs in New England.

December: a weekend of Christmas celebrations.

DEER ISLE, STONINGTON, AND ISLE AU HAUT

The narrow, soaring suspension bridge across Eggemoggin Reach connects the Blue Hill peninsula with a series of wandering land fingers linked by causeways and bridges. These are known collectively as Deer Isle and include the towns of Deer Isle and Stonington, the villages of Sunset and Sunshine, and the campus of the nationally respected Haystack Mountain School of Crafts. Many prominent artisans have come here to teach or study—and stayed. Galleries in the village of Deer Isle display outstanding work by dozens of artists and craftspeople who live, or at least summer, in town. Stonington remains a working fishing harbor, but it too now has its share of galleries. Most buildings, which are scattered on smooth rocks around the harbor, date from the 1880 to World War I boom years during which Deer Isle's pink granite was shipped off to face buildings from Rockefeller Center to Boston's Museum of Fine Arts.

To a degree life still eddies around Bartlett's Supermarket, Billings Diesel and Marine, and the Commercial Pier, home base for one of Maine's largest fishing/lobstering fleets. But the tourist tide is obviously rising. In 1996 a Grasshopper Shop (a Maine boutique chain) opened and the funky old Captain's Quarters was gentrified. On Main Street, you can now buy locally crafted jewelry, pottery, and clothing, pay $6000 for a painting, and lunch on goat cheese and smoked salmon.

Creeping resortification? Only in July and August—when visitors stream over the Eggemoggin Reach bridge to visit crafts studios salted throughout Deer Isle and explore the kind of coves and lupine-fringed inlets usually equated with "the real Maine." Isle au Haut, a mountainous island 8 miles off Stonington, is accessible by mail boat. It's a glorious place to walk trails maintained by the National Park Service.

GUIDANCE

Deer Isle–Stonington Chamber of Commerce (348-6124) maintains a spacious new (seasonal) information booth on Route 15 at Little Deer Isle, just this side of the bridge. Hours are theoretically 10–4, but since this booth is a volunteer effort, it may or may not be open.

The *Annual Bay Community Register,* listing some useful touring information, is available from **Penobscot Bay Press** (367-2200), Box 36, Stonington 04681. The press also publishes *Island Advantages* and the *Weekly Packet,* printed weekly for 111 years.

GETTING THERE

Follow directions to Castine, but continue on Route 1 to Orland and take Route 15 on down through Blue Hill to Deer Isle.

MEDICAL EMERGENCY

Island Medical Center (367-2311), Airport Road, Stonington. (Also see "Blue Hill Area.")

TO SEE

Haystack Mountain School of Crafts (348-2306), Deer Isle (south of Deer Isle Village, turn left off Route 15 at the Mobil station; follow signs 7 miles). Mid-June through Labor Day, 3-week sessions are offered, attracting some of the country's top artisans in a variety of crafts. Visitors are welcome to join campus tours offered Wednesday at 1 PM, June through August, and to shop at Goods in the Woods, the campus source of art supplies and craft books. Phone to check when visitors are also welcome to view student shows and to attend lectures and concerts. The school itself is a work of art: a series of small, spare buildings clinging to a steep, wooded hillside above Jericho Bay.

Salome Sellers House, Route 15A, Sunset. Open July through Labor Day, Wednesday and Friday 2–5. This is the home of the Deer Isle–Stonington Historical Society, an 1830 house displaying ship models, Native American artifacts, and old photos; interesting and friendly.

TO DO

BOAT EXCURSIONS

Isle-Au-Haut Company (367-5193/2355) departs Stonington at least twice daily except Sunday, year-round. See *Green Space* for a description of the island; note that the island's famous hiking trails cluster around Duck Harbor, a mail boat stop only in summer; a ranger usually meets the morning boat to orient passengers to the seven hiking trails, the picnic area, and drinking-water sources (otherwise a pamphlet guide serves this purpose). Be sure to check the schedule, and in July and August come as early as possible for the first ferry. The boat tends to fill up, and it's first come, first served; if you miss the first boat, you can at least make a later one. The boat takes kayaks and canoes for a fee, but not to Duck Harbor.

Palmer Day IV (367-2207). Seasonal 2 PM sailings. Captain Reginald Greenlaw offers narrated cruises of Penobscot Bay. $10 per adult, $5 per child under age 10. Longer excursions to Vinalhaven and North Haven on Thursday.

The Eagle Island Mailboat (348-2817) leaves Sylvester's Cove at Sunset; daily in-season.

GOLF AND TENNIS

Island Country Club (348-2379), in Deer Isle, welcomes guests mid-June through Labor Day; nine holes.

GREEN SPACE

Ames Pond, east of town on Indian Point Road, is full of pink-and-white water lilies in bloom June to early September.

Holt Mill Pond Preserve. A walk through unspoiled woodland and marsh. The entrance is on Stonington Cross Road (Airport Road)—look for a sign several hundred feet beyond the medical center. Park on the shoulder and walk the dirt road to the beginning of the trail, then follow the yellow signs.

Isle au Haut. Isle au Haut (pronounced *eye-la-ho*) is 6 miles long and 3 miles wide; all of it is private except for the 2800 acres of national park that are wooded and webbed with hiking trails. More than half the island is preserved as part of Acadia National Park (see "Bar Harbor and Acadia"). Camping is forbidden everywhere except in the five Adirondack-style shelters at Duck Harbor (each accommodating six people) that are available by reservation only. For a reservation form, phone 288-3338 or write to Acadia National Park, PO Box 177, Bar Harbor 04609; the cost is $25 to secure a site, and the form must be sent on or as soon after April 1 as possible. Camping is permitted mid-May through mid-October, but in the shoulder season you have to walk 5 miles from the town landing to Duck Harbor. In summer months the mail boat arrives at Duck Harbor at 11 AM, allowing plenty of time to hike the island's dramatic Western Head and Cliff trails before returning on the 5:30 boat. Longer trips, like that to the summit of Mount Champlain near the northern end of the island, are also possible. Trails are pine carpeted and shaded, with water views. For more about day trips to the island, see *Boat Excursions*.

Crockett Cove Woods Preserve (a Maine Nature Conservancy property) comprises 100 acres along the water, with a nature trail. Take Route 15 to Deer Isle, then the Sunset Road; 2.5 miles beyond the post office, bear right onto Whitman Road; a right turn at the end of the road brings you to the entrance, marked by a small sign and registration box. From Stonington, take the Sunset Road through the village of Burnt Cove and turn left on Whitman Road.

Barred Island Preserve is a 2-acre island just off Stinson Point, accessible by a wide sandbar; request permission for access from Goose Cove Lodge (see *Rustic Resort*).

LODGING

RUSTIC RESORT

Goose Cove Lodge (348-2508), Sunset 04683. Open mid-May to mid-October. One-week minimum stay during July and August. Sited on a secluded cove, this many-windowed lodge with its fine library and dining, unusually attractive common space and cabins, and waterside/island trails, is a real standout. Joanne and Dom Paris have retained the rustic feel but brightened both the lodge and cabins with well-chosen art, quilts, hooked rugs, and attractive fabrics. Just 15 minutes from Stonington, Goose Cove is at the end of its own 1½-mile road, set in a 70-acre preserve with trails along the shore and low-tide passage to Barred Island, a Nature Conservancy property well known to birders. Guests congregate for evening cocktails and hors d'oeuvres and frequently team up for dinner, although there is no pressure to do so. Children are given a special menu and dine early. Dinners are exceptional (see *Dining Out*) and breakfast might include potato latkes with sweet pepper relish and crème fraîche or baked egg in a dilled crêpe nest with smoked salmon and chèvre. You might want to pack a flashlight if you book one of the more secluded cabins (we recommend Bunchberry); the evening walk through the firs can be inky black despite the stars. Widely scattered, most cottages have water views. Four attached to the lodge also have water views (one doesn't) and rooms in the lodge include a suite. Late June through August, a week's reservation is requested but shorter stays are frequently available due to cancellations. $73–116 per person MAP or $94–140 per couple B&B; sliding rates for children; a three-person minimum is required in high season for some cottages; a 2-day minimum is required.

INNS

In Stonington 04681

☞ **Pres du Port** (367-5007), Box 319, West Main and Highland Avenue. Open June through October—a find. An unusually cheery, comfortable B&B with three imaginatively furnished guest rooms with double beds and screened and glassed-in porches with harbor views. Charlotte Casgrain is a warm, locally knowledgeable hostess who enjoys speaking French. $40–70 double with a buffet breakfast, less for a single.

The Inn on the Harbor (367-2420; 1-800-942-2420), PO Box 69. Open mid-April through December. New Yorker Christina Shipps acquired this 15-unit waterside complex in '95 and has reduced the number of rooms to 13, upgrading all and enlarging some, naming each for one of the Maine windjammers that regularly moor within their view. Most rooms face the harbor and a couple have working fireplaces. In fine weather the large, harborside deck is a great spot to relax all day. Rates are $80–95.

Burnt Cove Bed & Breakfast (367-2392), RFD 1, Box 2905, Whitman Road. Open early May through October. A modern, year-round home designed to maximize its view of Burnt Cove, both from the large, open central room and from the inviting deck. This is the comfortable, genuinely hospitable home of local fisherman Bob Williams and Diane Berlew, a good breakfast chef. The large downstairs bedroom with a cathedral ceiling, full bath, and private entrance is $80 and the two upstairs bedrooms (shared bath) are $45 single, $55 double.

Island House (367-5900), Weedfield Road, RD 1, Box 3227. Open June through September. An ultramodern redwood home with water views, furnished in pastels and southwestern decor, managed by Rebecca Cennamo, who delights in "pampering guests." The five rooms (three with private bath) range from the large, balconied Merchants Room to the tiny top-floor Lookout Room, an enclosed cupola above the trees. Rates $100 up to $200 for the neighboring two-bedroom guest house; a full breakfast and tea included. Amenities include a hot tub, laundry facilities, and a lily pond.

Ocean View House (367-5114), Main Street, Box 261. Open July and August only. A white-clapboard, Victorian inn set on a knoll near the dock, built to board quarry workers employed on Crotch Island. Midwesterners Christine and Jack Custer have created bright, cheerful rooms; the three guest rooms share baths, but all have bay views. $60 per room; breakfast of homemade pastries.

On Deer Isle 04627

The Inn at Ferry Landing (348-7760), Old Ferry Road, RR 1, Box 163. Overlooking Eggemoggin Reach is this 1840s seaside farmhouse with magnificent water views, spacious rooms, patchwork quilts, and a great common room with huge bay windows and a grand piano that innkeeper-musician Gerald Wheeler invites guests to use. The six guest rooms include a huge master suite with a woodstove, skylights, and sunken tub. The Annex, a two-story, two-bedroom fully equipped housekeeping cottage, is perfect for families with small children. $70–95 for double rooms, $125 for the suite, and $900 per week ($150 per night) for the annex. Rates include a full breakfast; minimum of 2 days in high season.

Pilgrim's Inn (348-6615). Open mid-May through mid-October. Squire Ignatius Haskell built this house in 1793 for his wife, who came from Newburyport, Massachusetts, and demanded an elegant home. The story goes that he built the house in Newburyport and had it shipped up to Deer Isle, where it stands in the middle of the village overlooking Northwest Harbor and his millpond. Of the 13 guest rooms, 10 have private baths and 3 on the top floor share one. All rooms have water views, and many have fireplaces. Downstairs there are four common rooms, and a dining room is in the old barn, known for its gourmet fare (see *Dining Out*). Eighteenth-century colors predominate, and the inn is furnished throughout with carefully chosen curtains and rugs, antiques, and local art. $85 single MAP plus 15 percent gratuity; the one-bedroom cottage up the street is $125 EP, $145–205 double MAP. Weekly rates are also available.

Holden Homestead (348-6832), PO Box 221, Route 15. Open May to November. A former church parsonage, this is an 1850s house, owned since the 1860s by the Holden family and restored by Cynthia Bancroft Melnikas, a fifth-generation Holden. Three rooms, one with a private entrance and deck. $43–48 single, $53–65 double, $65 for the suite.

On Isle au Haut 04645

The Keeper's House (367-2261), PO Box 26. This turn-of-the-century lighthouse keeper's house sits back in firs behind its small lighthouse on a point surrounded on three sides by water. Most guests arrive on the mail boat from Stonington just in time for a dip and a glass of sparkling cider before dinner (guests who want something stronger should be advised to bring it). Dinner is by candlelight, and guests tend to sit together, four to a table, and after dinner wander down to the smooth rocks to gaze at the pinpoints of light from other lighthouses and communities in Penobscot Bay. There are four guest rooms in the main house, a self-contained room in the tiny Oil House, and another in the "woodshed." It's a hike to the island's most scenic trails in Duck Harbor on the southeastern end of the island. $250 per couple, $175 single, and $50 per child includes all meals and use of bikes; add $18 per person round-trip for the ferry plus $3–5 per night for parking.

MOTEL

Bridge Inn (348-6115), Little Deer Isle 04650. Open May through mid-October. A nicely sited motel just beyond the Deer Isle suspension bridge, overlooking Eggemoggin Reach. The 20 rooms are clean, and the restaurant serves breakfast, lunch, and dinner. Rooms: $50–60.

COTTAGE RENTALS

Reasonably priced rentals are available on both Deer Isle and Isle au Haut. Check with **Island Vacation Rentals** (367-5095) and **Sargent's Rentals** (367-5156), both in Stonington.

WHERE TO EAT

DINING OUT

Pilgrim's Inn (348-6615), Main Street, Deer Isle Village. Open mid-May to late October. Dinner is by reservation only. Guests congregate at 6 for hors d'oeuvres served in the living room or on the deck and the five-course meal begins at 7, including soup, salad, an entrée that varies with the night: maybe halibut with artichokes and cream, poached salmon with beurre blanc, or paella. Lettuce is from the backyard, chickens from Deer Isle, breads and desserts are baked daily. The dining room is a converted goat barn; tables are covered with checked cloths and lighted by candles. Wine is served. Prix fixe: $29.50.

Goose Cove Lodge (348-2508), Route 15A, Sunset. Open May to mid-October. Outside guests are welcome by reservation, gathering for cocktails and hors d'oeuvres at 6. Friday night always features lobster and one Saturday night we dined on potato-and-horseradish-crusted salmon fillet with chive and pink peppercorn beurre blanc, served with fresh asparagus and greens. Dessert was a chocolate almond terrine with a trio of sauces. Wine is served. Dinner for outside guests is $30.

Eaton's Lobster Pool Restaurant (348-2383), Deer Isle. Seasonal. Monday through Saturday 5–9, Sunday noon–9. A barn of a place with a great view. For the best value, be sure to order lobster à la carte and by the pound instead of the higher-priced "lobster dinner." The restaurant is still in the family that settled the spot, and it is the area's premier lobster pound. BYOB. We've received both rave reviews and complaints from readers.

EATING OUT

Penobscot Bay Provisions (367-2920), West Main Street, Stonington. Open year-round, June through August, Tuesday through Saturday 8–5, Sunday 10–2; shorter hours off-season. This is the best picnic source for many miles around. Rich and May Howe have thrown in the corpo-

CHRISTINA TREE

Stonington

rate towel and gone year-round with this amazing store. A blackboard menu lists sandwiches (the hard salami and goat cheese was memorable), and shelves and a cooler are stocked with made-in-Maine cheeses and bottled, canned, and otherwise preserved products. Breads are baked daily.

Fisherman's Friend Restaurant (367-2442), School Street, Stonington (just up the hill from the harbor). Open daily 11–9, BYOB. Simple decor, reasonably priced food, and fabulous pies. Recently we've received complaints as well as rave reviews.

Bayview Restaurant (367-2274), Sea Breeze Avenue, Stonington (near the dock). Open mid-May to mid-October, daily 8 AM–8 PM or later. A pleasant dining space with reasonably priced candlelight dinners featuring local seafood, broiled and baked as well as fried. BYOB.

The Finest Kind (348-7714), marked from Route 15 between Stonington and Deer Isle Village. Open April through November, lunch and dinner; Sunday breakfast from 8 AM. Neat as a pin, a log cabin with counter and booths. Dinner from $6.25 for chopped steak to $12.95 for prime rib. Pizzas, fried seafood, salad bar, calzones, draft and imported beers.

Eaton's Pier (348-6036), Sunshine Road, Deer Isle. Open mid-May through October, Monday through Saturday 11–8. Theoretically no relation to the Lobster Pool Eatons (see *Dining Out*). A small waterside restaurant with a screened porch, picnic tables, reasonably priced lobster plus corn, steamed shrimp. No alcohol permitted.

The Lobster Deck & Restaurant at North Atlantic Seafood, Stonington. Open year-round, daily 5 AM–9 PM, from 6 on Sundays. A new waterside eatery featuring steamed and fried seafood, lobster, scallop and crabmeat stews.

Austin Wood's Ice Cream, Main Street, Stonington. Open May to December, 8 AM–9 PM. The ice cream is from Hancock County Creamery, and the view is of the harbor. Sandwiches are also available on a deck overlooking the water.

The Bridge Inn Restaurant (348-6115), Little Deer Isle. Open for breakfast, lunch, and dinner, specializing in seafood, pasta, and lobster dinners.

SELECTIVE SHOPPING

Pick up a current (free) copy of the *Maine Cultural Guide* published by the **Maine Crafts Association** (348-9943), which maintains its own gallery featuring the work of over 70 members at 6 Dow Road, marked off Route 15 just before Deer Isle Village. The registry represents 300 members but is particularly helpful in tracking down the art galleries and crafts studios, which are most plentiful here. It's available at most local galleries.

ART GALLERIES AND ARTISANS

Deer Isle Artists Association, Route 15, Deer Isle Village. Open mid-June to September. A series of four-person shows; members exhibition every summer.

Turtle Gallery (348-2538), Route 15, north of Deer Isle Village. Open June through September, Monday through Saturday 10–5 and Sunday 2–6. Newly relocated in the Old Centennial House Barn, this choice gallery now fills two levels with paintings, photographs, prints, sculpture, and outstanding craftswork.

Hoy Gallery (367-6339/5628), East Main Street, Stonington (at the foot of Furlow Hill as you enter the village). Open daily July through September, 10–5. A big, white barn set back from the street, filled with Jill Hoy's bold, bright Maine landscapes. (Note the sample on our cover.)

Eastern Bay Gallery (367-5006), Main Street, Stonington. Open mid-May through October, daily in summer and Monday through Saturday in slow season. In this long-established and outstanding gallery, Kate Fairchild sells works by more than 40 artists and craftspeople within a 50-mile radius. The space, filled with fine clothing, jewelry, pottery, and such, is itself worth the trip to Stonington.

The Blue Heron (348-6051), Route 15, Deer Isle (near the center of the village). Open daily June through September. An old barn attached to Mary Nyburg's pottery studio is filled with fine contemporary crafts featuring work by Haystack Mountain School's faculty (see *To See*).

Pearson's Jewelry (348-2535), Old Ferry Road (off Route 15), Deer Isle. Ron Pearson has an international reputation for creative designs in gold and silver jewelry as well as delicately wrought, tabletop sculpture in other metals. From $22 for small silver earrings to $8000 for a gold necklace. The shop also displays work by local blacksmith/sculptor Douglas Wilson.

Kathy Woell (348-6141), 156 Old Ferry Road, Deer Isle. Open Monday through Saturday 10–5. This home/studio is tucked deep in the pines, filled with soft, vivid scarves and hats, vests, jackets, and coats—each one of a kind. "I put colors together. That's the gift I have," says Woell, a former painter who discovered weaving as her medium at Haystack.

William Mor (348-2822), Reach Road, Deer Isle. Open mid-June through October. Hand-thrown pottery in interesting shapes, functional and handsome. Designs are based on Oriental folk pottery; the studio, kiln, and shop are in a garden setting. Oriental rugs are also sold.

Jutta Graf (348-7751) weaves stunning one-of-a-kind rugs usually on view in local galleries, also at her studio by appointment.

Terrell S. Lester Photography (348-2676), East Main Street, Deer Isle Village. Open in-season Monday through Saturday 10–5; otherwise by appointment. Popular, sharply detailed local landscapes.

SPECIAL SHOPS

Gallery of the Purple Fish, Main Street, Stonington. Open when the windjammers are in port and otherwise by chance. Evelyn and Jan Kok maintain this weathered old waterside building (said to be a former fishermen's church) as a gallery, filled with paintings and wonderful clutter. Evelyn also hand-inks bookmarks and cards and strums on her guitar; visitors may find themselves dancing and singing.

Dockside Books and Gifts (367-2652), West Main Street, Stonington. Seasonal. E.L. Webber's waterside bookstore has an exceptional selection of Maine and marine books, also gifts and a great view with a harbor balcony where you can sit and read, or not read.

The Periwinkle, Deer Isle. A tiny shop crammed with books and carefully selected gifts.

SPECIAL EVENTS

July: **Independence Day** parade and fireworks in Deer Isle Village.
August: **Lobster boat races** and **Stonington Fisherman's Festival.**

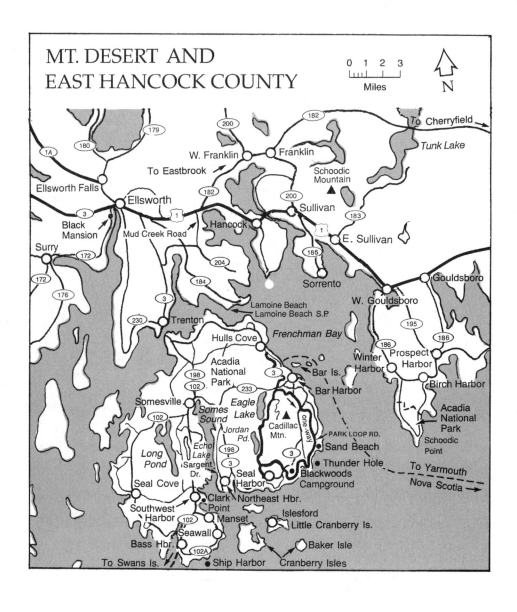

MT. DESERT AND
EAST HANCOCK COUNTY

0 1 2 3
Miles

N

To Cherryfield

182

Tunk Lake

200

179

180

1A

W. Franklin   Franklin

To Eastbrook

Schoodic
Mountain

182

Ellsworth Falls

Ellsworth

200

3

1

Sullivan

183

Black
Mansion

Mud Creek Road

Hancock

E. Sullivan

Surry

172

185

204

Sorrento

172

184

Gouldsboro

176

3

W. Gouldsboro

195

230

Trenton

Lamoine Beach
Lamoine Beach S.P.

186

186

Hulls Cove

Frenchman Bay

Winter
Harbor

Prospect
Harbor

Acadia
National
Park

198

102

3

Bar Is.

Birch Harbor

233

Bar Harbor

Somesville

Eagle
Lake

Acadia
National
Park

102

Somes
Sound

Cadillac
Mtn.

one-way

PARK LOOP RD.

Schoodic
Point

Jordan
Pd.

Sand Beach

Long
Pond

Echo
Lake

198

3

Thunder Hole

To Yarmouth

Seal Cove

Sargent
Dr.

Seal
Harbor

Blackwoods
Campground

Nova Scotia

Southwest
Harbor

Clark
Point

Northeast Hbr.

102

Manset

Islesford

Seawall

Little Cranberry Is.

Bass Hbr.

102A

Baker Isle

To Swans Is.

Ship Harbor

Cranberry Isles

Bar Harbor and Acadia Area

Mount Desert is New England's second largest island, one conveniently linked to the mainland and laced with roads ideally suited for touring by car, bike, or skis. It also includes 120 miles of hiking trails.

The island's beauty cannot be overstated. Seventeen mountains rise abruptly from the sea and from the shores of four large lakes. There are also countless ponds and streams, an unusual variety of flora, and more than 300 species of birds.

Native Americans first populated the area, using it as hunting and fishing grounds. Samuel de Champlain named it L'Isle de Monts Deserts in 1604. Although it was settled in the 18th century, this remained a peaceful, out-of-the-way island even after a bridge was built in 1836 connecting it to the mainland. In the 1840s, however, landscape painters Thomas Cole and Frederic Church began summering here, and their images of the rugged shore were widely circulated. Summer visitors began arriving by steamboat, and they were soon joined by travelers taking express trains from Philadelphia and New York to Hancock Point, bringing guests enough to fill more than a dozen huge hotels that mushroomed in Bar Harbor. By the 1880s, many of these hotel patrons had already built their own mansion-sized "cottages" in and around Bar Harbor. These grandiose summer mansions numbered more than 200 by the time the stock market crashed. Many are now inns.

The legacy of Bar Harbor's wealthy "rusticators" is Acadia National Park. A cadre of influential citizens, which included Harvard University President Charles W. Eliot, began to assemble parcels of land for public use in 1901, thus protecting the forests from the portable sawmill. Boston textile heir George Dorr devoted his fortune and energy to amassing a total of 11,000 acres and convincing the federal government to accept it. In 1916 Acadia became the first national park east of the Mississippi. It is now a 40,000-acre preserve, encompassing almost half the island.

Four-fifths of the park's 3 million annual visitors limit their tour to the introductory film in the visitors center and to the 27-mile Park Loop Road, which includes the summit of Cadillac Mountain, the highest point on the eastern seaboard north of Brazil.

Mount Desert Island is 16 miles wide and 13 miles long, but it

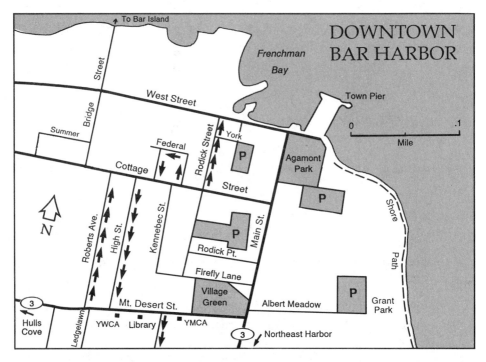

seems far larger because it is almost bisected by Somes Sound, the only natural fjord on the East Coast. Bar Harbor is the big town, and the village holds one of New England's largest clusters of hotels, motels, inns, B&Bs, restaurants, and shops. These are within easy reach of the park visitors center, on the one hand, and the *Bluenose* ferry to Nova Scotia, on the other. The shops and restaurants line Cottage, Mount Desert, West, and Main Streets, which slope to the Town Pier and to the Shore Path, a mile walk between mansions and the bay.

Bar Harbor lost its old hotels and many of its mansions in the devastating fire of 1947, which also destroyed 17,000 acres of woodland. The island's summer social scene has since shifted to Northeast Harbor, where a deceptively sleepy lineup of shops and galleries caters to visiting and resident yachtsmen.

Southwest Harbor lacks the galleries and yachtsmen-geared shops of Northeast Harbor and the crowds of Bar Harbor, but provides easy access to both mountain and shore paths. Bass Harbor, a genuine working fishing village, offers ferry service to Swan's Island.

During July and August, Mount Desert is expensive, crowded, and exquisite. Between Labor Day and Columbus Day it is cheaper, less crowded, and still beautiful. The rest of the year is off-season. If you take advantage of the solitude and bargains available in June or February (when there may be cross-country skiing), be sure you have access to a fireplace.

East of Ellsworth, the shopping center for Maine's eastern coast, Route 1 continues along Frenchman Bay. Superb views of Mount Desert's pink-shouldered mountains can be enjoyed from the shore in Sullivan and from the Hancock and Schoodic Peninsulas. Schoodic Point with its dramatic surf is part of Acadia National Park and this entire peninsula—especially the old resort village of Winter Harbor and the charming fishing village of Corea—are well worth exploring.

GUIDANCE

(Also see *To See—Acadia National Park.*)

Bar Harbor Chamber of Commerce (year-round: 288-5103; 1-800-288-5103), PO Box 158, 93 Cottage Street, Bar Harbor 04609, maintains seasonal information booths. Write for the free vacation guide to sights and lodging.

Mount Desert Island Regional Visitors Center (288-3411) is open daily May to mid-October (9–8 during high season) on Route 3, just after you cross the bridge. It is a walk-in center that offers rest rooms, national park information, and help with lodging reservations on all parts of the island.

Mount Desert Chamber of Commerce (276-5040), Northeast Harbor, maintains a seasonal walk-in cottage at the town dock.

Southwest Harbor Chamber of Commerce (244-9264; 1-800-423-9264), PO Box 1143, Southwest Harbor 04679 maintains a seasonal information booth on Route 102.

Ellsworth Chamber of Commerce (667-5584/2617), 163 High Street, Ellsworth 04605 (in the Ellsworth Shopping Center; look for the Burger King), also maintains a well-stocked, friendly information center.

Schoodic Peninsula Chamber of Commerce (963-7658; 1-800-231-3008), PO Box 381, Winter Harbor 04693; request the helpful pamphlet guide.

GETTING THERE

By air: **Colgan Air** (1-800-272-5488) serves Hancock County/Bar Harbor Airport in Trenton (between Ellsworth and Bar Harbor) from Boston and Rockland. Avis, Hertz, and Budget rental cars are available at the airport. (Also see Bangor International Airport in the Bangor section of "Northern Maine" for connections with most American cities.)

By boat: **Marine Atlantic *Bluenose* ferry** (1-800-432-7344 in Maine; 1-800-341-7981 elsewhere in the continental United States); carries passengers and cars between Bar Harbor and Yarmouth, Nova Scotia. The trip takes 6 hours. Service is daily late June to late September, three times per week in the shoulder seasons, and twice a week in winter. See "Portland Area" for details about the *Scotia Prince* ferry from Yarmouth to Portland.

By private boat: A number of visitors arrive under their own sail; contact the Mount Desert or Bar Harbor Chamber of Commerce (see

Guidance) for details about moorings, or contact the Bar Harbor harbormaster at 288-5571.

By bus: **Vermont Transit** serves Bar Harbor May through October. **Concord Trailways** also serves Bangor from Portland and Boston, and has movies and music en route.

By car: From Boston and New York there are three routes. The longest is Route 1 from Kittery. The shortest is I-95 to Bangor to 395, then to Route 1A to Ellsworth. The third is a compromise: I-95 to Augusta, then Route 3 east to Bar Harbor.

GETTING AROUND

Local ferries: **Beal and Bunker, Inc.** (244-3575), Northeast Harbor, operates daily ferry service to the Cranberry Islands. **Swan's Island Ferry** (244-3254), Bass Harbor, has daily ferry service to Swan's Island; service twice weekly to Frenchboro.

Both **Acadia National Park Tours** (288-3327) and **Oli's Trolley** (288-9899) offer narrated, 2½-hour bus tours through Bar Harbor and along the Park Loop Road, and 1-hour trolley tours, daily in-season.

MEDICAL EMERGENCY

Maine Coast Memorial Hospital (667-4520), Ellsworth. **Mount Desert Island Hospital** (288-5081), Bar Harbor, provides 24-hour emergency care. **Southwest Harbor** (244-5513). **Northeast Harbor** (276-3331).

TO SEE

ACADIA NATIONAL PARK

The park maintains its own visitors center (288-3338) at Hulls Cove, open mid-April through October. From mid-June to August 31, hours are 8–6 daily; during shoulder seasons, hours are 8–4:30. The park headquarters at Eagle Lake on Route 233 (288-3338) is open daily throughout the winter 8–4:30. For more information about the park, write to Superintendent, PO Box 177, Bar Harbor 04609. The glass-and-stone visitors center, set atop 50 steps, shows its 15-minute introductory film every half hour. Books, guides, and postcards may be purchased here. This is also the place to pick up a free map and a copy of the current "Acadia's Beaver Log" (a listing of all naturalist activities), to rent a cassette tape tour, and to sign up for the various programs offered. Special evening programs are scheduled by the national park staff nightly, June through September, at the amphitheaters in Blackwoods and Seawall campgrounds. Children of all ages are eligible to join the park's Junior Ranger Program; inquire at the visitors center.

Within the park are 45 miles of carriage roads donated by John D. Rockefeller. These incredible gravel roads take bikers, hikers, joggers, and cross-country skiers through woods, up mountains, past lakes and streams. The paths also lead over and under 17 spectacular stone bridges. In recent years, volunteers have rallied to refurbish and improve this truly spectacular network.

There is a weekly charge of $5 per car and $3 per hiker or biker along the 27-mile Park Loop Road, the prime tourist route within the park. It is possible, however, to get to mountain trails and some popular spots, such as the drive up Cadillac, without charge.

Sights along the Loop Road include the following: **Sand Beach,** actually made up of ground shells and sand; a great beach to walk down and from which to take a dip, if you don't mind 50-degree water; there are changing rooms and lifeguards. **Thunder Hole.** The water rushes in and out of a small cave, which you can view from behind a railing. The adjacent rocks can keep small children scrambling for hours. **Cadillac Mountain.** From the smooth summit you look out across Frenchman Bay dotted with the Porcupine Islands, which look like giant stepping-stones.

Also in Acadia: **The Ship Harbor,** Route 102A (near Bass Harbor), offers a fine nature trail that winds along the shore and into the woods; it is also a great birding spot.

EAST HANCOCK COUNTY
Schoodic Peninsula. This quiet peninsula includes one of the most spectacular parts of Acadia National Park. The park's one-way loop road begins beyond Winter Harbor. Look sharp (an unmarked left after the Frazier Point Picnic Area) for the side road up to Schoodic Head. Park here and follow the short trail to the summit. The loop road leads to Schoodic Point, where flocks of people feed bread to flocks of seagulls. There are also flat, smooth rocks ideal for clambering, and Little Moose Island with its arctic flora is accessible at low tide. This is one corner of the park that is as popular in stormy as in fair weather because the roiled surf here is magnificent. (Also see Isle au Haut, another part of Acadia National Park, in "Deer Isle, Stonington, and Isle au Haut.")

BEYOND ACADIA
In Bar Harbor
Bar Harbor Oceanarium (288-5005), Route 3 at the entrance to the island. Open 9–5, except Sunday, mid-May to late October. Seal exhibit and everything you ever wanted to know about a lobster; also the Thomas Bay Marsh Walk. $5.95 per adult, $4.25 per child ages 4–12. Tour the lobster hatchery for an additional fee.

College of the Atlantic (288-5015), Route 3, Bar Harbor. The **Ethel H. Blum Gallery**, Gates Community Center, open Monday through Saturday 9–5, is outstanding. The **Natural History Museum** (9–5 daily in summer, weekdays 10–4 Labor through Columbus Day) is housed in the original Acadia National Park headquarters (recently moved to the college campus). It showcases the skeleton of a rare true-beaked whale; detailed dioramas depict plants and animals of coastal Maine. Note the hands-on discovery room, self-guided nature trail, Wednesday-evening lecture series, and museum shop; $2.50 per adult, seniors and teens $1.20, $.50 per child above age 3). Founded in 1969, the College of the Atlantic (COA) is a liberal arts college with a curriculum based on the study of "human ecology." Its 26 waterside acres, an amalgam of four large summer estates, are now a handsome campus for 230 students.

Bar Harbor Historical Society (288-3838), Jesup Memorial Library, 34 Mount Desert Street. Open mid-June to October, Monday through Saturday 1–4, also by appointment. A fascinating collection of early photographs of local hotels, steamers, cottages, the cog railroad, and the big fire of 1947.

The Shore Path. This mile-long path runs from Agamont Park near the Bar Harbor Town Pier and along the bay. It's also accessible from Grant Park, off Albert Meadow at the corner of Main and Mount Desert Streets.

Robert Abbe Museum at Sieur de Monts Spring (288-3519), posted from both Route 3 (south of the Jackson Laboratory) and the Park Loop Road. Open May to October, 9–5 daily during July and August, otherwise 10–4. Don't miss this exceptional collection of New England Native American artifacts: sweet-grass baskets, jewelry, moccasins, a birchbark canoe, dioramas of Native American life during all seasons, an authentic wigwam. Changing exhibits teach about early life on Mount Desert Island, recent archaeological excavations, culture and traditions, and more. $2 per adult, $.50 per child. The museum overlooks the Nature Center and the Wild Gardens of Acadia, a pleasant walk where more than 300 species of native plants are on display with labels.

In Otter Creek

Jackson Laboratory (288-3371), Route 3. June to September, Monday and Wednesday, an audiovisual presentation about one of the world's largest mammalian-genetics research facilities. Cancer, diabetes, and birth defects are among the problems studied.

In Northeast Harbor

Asticou Terraces, including **Thuya Garden** and **Thuya Lodge** (276-5130). Open July to Labor Day, 7–7; the lodge is open daily 10–5. $2 donation. An exquisite, 215-acre municipal park complex begun by landscape artist Joseph Henry Curtis around 1900. Curtis created a system of paths and shelters on Asticou Hill, now open to the public along with his home, Thuya Lodge, which houses an important collection of botanical books and floral paintings. Thuya Garden behind the lodge was designed by landscaper and artist Charles Savage; it's semiformal, with perennial beds and a reflecting pool. The gardens descend in terraces, then through wooded paths to the harbor's edge.

Asticou Azalea Gardens, Route 3 (near the junction of Route 198). Open April through October. Also designed by Charles Savage. A delightful place to stroll down winding paths and over ornamental bridges. Azaleas (usually in bloom the last weeks in June), rhododendrons, laurel, and Japanese-style plantings.

Petite Plaisance (276-3940), South Shore Road. Open mid-June through August by appointment. The former home of French author Marguerite Yourcenar has long been a pilgrimage destination for her fans. English translations of her books are available in local bookstores.

Great Harbor Collection at the Old Firehouse Museum (276-5262), Main Street. Open June through Columbus Day, Monday through Saturday 10–5. A collection of historical artifacts ranging from an early fire engine to a parlor room, a kitchen, photographs, clothing, sleighs, and a player piano; demonstrations.

From Northeast Harbor

Cranberry Isles. Accessible by boat (see *Boat Excursions*) from Northeast Harbor in-season. Note the park ranger–led trips to Baker Island and the guided tours to the Islesford Historical Museum on Little Cranberry Island. The museum is open daily late June through September, varied hours depending on the ferry schedule. It traces the area's history from 1604; there are some juicy smuggling stories told here about the War of 1812.

In Somesville

Mount Desert Historical Society (244-7334), Route 102. Open June through August, weekdays 10–12 and 1–5. Two tidy little buildings, one dating back to 1780, connected by a moon bridge. Collections include mill- and marine-related items, featuring the shipyards for which this village was once widely known.

In Southwest Harbor

Oceanarium, Clark Point Road (244-7330). Open mid-May to mid-October, 9–5 daily except Sunday. A large, old, waterside building filled with exhibits, including 20 tanks displaying sea life, whale songs, a "lobster room," and a touch tank. $5.95 per adult, $4.25 per child.

Wendell Gilley Museum (244-7555), Route 102. Open May through December, 10–4 (10–5 July and August), daily except Monday; Friday through Sunday only in May, November, and December. A collection of more than 200 bird carvings by the late woodcarver and painter Wendell Gilley. $3 per adult, $1 per child under age 12.

(Also see the Ship Harbor trail under *To See—Acadia National Park.*)

From Bass Harbor

Frenchboro Historical Society (334-2929), open seasonally. Old tools, furniture, local memorabilia. A good excuse to explore this very private island 8 miles offshore. Bring a bike. Check with the state ferry service: 334-2929.

Swan's Island Educational Society (526-4350), open seasonally. Six miles offshore, Swan's is a pleasant island that's good biking. The museum, in the Seaside Hall, Atlantic Street, includes a store, school, old tools, and photographs. It's a ¾-mile walk from the ferry (244-3254) to the hall.

Seal Cove Auto Museum (244-9242), Pretty Marsh Road off Route 102, between Bass Harbor and Somesville. Open daily June to September,

10–5. A collection of over 100 antique cars and 30 motorcycles, the life's work of a private collector; $5 per adult, $1.50 per child.

Indian Point Blagden Preserve, a 110-acre Nature Conservancy preserve in the northwestern corner of the island, includes 1000 feet of shorefront and paths that wander through the woods. It offers a view of Blue Hill Bay and is a tried-and-true seal-watching spot. From Route 198 north of Somesville, turn right on Indian Point Road, bear right at the fork, and look for the entrance; sign in and pick up a map at the caretaker's house.

In Ellsworth

Colonel Black Mansion (Woodlawn), West Main Street. Open June to mid-October, Monday through Saturday 10–5 (last tour starts at 4:30). An outstanding Georgian mansion built as a wedding present in 1862 by John Black, who had just married the daughter of the local agent for a Philadelphia land developer, owner of this region. Supposedly, the bricks were brought by sea from Philadelphia, and it took Boston workmen three years to complete it. It is now open to the public, furnished just as it was when the Black family used it (three generations lived there). Besides the fine period furniture and spiral staircase, there is a lovely garden and a carriage house full of old carriages and sleighs. $5 per adult, $2 per child.

Stanwood Homestead Sanctuary and Museum (667-8460), Route 3. Open daily mid-June to mid-October, 10–4; sanctuary open year-round. Don't miss this exceptional place: a 130-acre nature preserve that is a memorial to Cordelia Stanwood (1865–1958), a pioneer ornithologist, nature photographer, and writer. The old homestead (1850) contains family furnishings and a collection of Stanwood's photos. There are gardens, a picnic area, and a gift shop. $2 per adult, $1.50 for seniors, and $.50 per child for the museum; no admission charge for the sanctuary.

FOR FAMILIES

In addition to the whale and lobster oceanariums and auto museum listed above, there are several attractions along Route 3: the Acadia Zoological Park ($4.50 per adult, $3.50 per child), as well as elaborate mini-golf and go-cart options.

SCENIC DRIVES

Mount Desert's Quiet Side: Note that the sights described under *To See* are listed as they appear along a loop tour. From Bar Harbor, follow Route 3 south to Northeast Harbor and on along Somes Sound on Sargent Drive to Somesville, back down along Echo Lake on Route 102 to Bass Harbor and back up through Pretty Marsh to Route 3.

East Hancock County: From Bar Harbor, take Route 3 north to signs for Lamoine Beach and Marlboro, then Mud Creek Road to Route 1 at Hancock (see the map for this region). Turn right (east) at Route 1 to Hancock and note the galleries described under *Selective Shopping*. Also note the turnoff for Hancock Point, the former terminus for the railroad and transfer point to steamers for Bar Harbor, an old summer colony with a tiny octagonal post office. Just beyond Hancock you cross the **Singing Bridge,** a 1926 landmark across the tidal Taunton River, into Sullivan Harbor (note signs for the Barter Family Gallery and for Sullivan Harbor Salmon, both described under *Selective Shopping*). Be sure to stop at the scenic turnout (the site of a former inn) just before **Dunbar's Store** for a spectacular view back across Frenchman Bay. Note the Route 183 turnoff for **Schoodic Mountain** (see *Hiking*); continue on Route 1 to Route 186 south, leading to Winter Harbor, the small village at the entrance to the Schoodic Point loop (described under *Acadia National Park*). Note the eating and shopping places we have described at both ends of the loop. The **Winter Harbor Historical Society** just off Main Street is in the old schoolhouse; it's open 12–2 Saturdays in July and August. Route 186 continues through Birch Harbor and Prospect Harbor. If time permits, turn onto Route 195 and follow it the couple of miles to **Corea,** as picturesque a fishing village as any other in Maine. It's 6 miles on up Route 6 to the village of Gouldsboro just off Route 1. Note signs for the Bartlett Maine Estate Winery (see *Selective Shopping*).

TO DO

AIRPLANE RIDES

Acadia Air (667-5534), Route 3 at Trenton Airport. Flight instruction, aircraft rentals, and a number of well-worth-it sight-seeing and whale-sighting flights. **Island Soaring Glider Rides** (667-SOAR), also at the airport, offers a motorless soaring flight daily.

BICYCLING

The 50-mile network of gravel carriage roads (see *To See—Acadia National Park*) constructed by John D. Rockefeller in 1915 lends itself particularly well to mountain biking.

In Bar Harbor **Acadia Bike & Canoe Company** (288-9605) rents child trailers and every kind of bike; also provides detailed maps. **Bar Harbor Bicycle Shop** (288-3886) also rents a wide variety of bikes and offers handy access to the park. **Northeast Harbor Bike Shop** (276-5480), Main Street, Northeast Harbor, also has rentals. **Southwest Cycle** (244-5856) in Southwest Harbor rents mountain and 10-speed bicycles. Companies offering sunrise rides from the top of Cadillac Mountain seem to vary each season.

Note under *To See—From Bass Harbor* the information about Swan's Island. Rentals on Swan's Island can be reserved by phoning 288-9605.

BIRDING

For special programs led by park naturalists, consult "Acadia's Beaver Log," available at the park visitors center (see *To See—Acadia National Park*).

BOAT EXCURSIONS

We recommend the cruises that operate daily in-season from Northeast Harbor to the Cranberry Islands (**Beal and Bunker Co.:** 244-3575) and the naturalist-guided cruise to Baker Island (**Islesford Ferry Co.:** 276-3717). There are also cruises from Bar Harbor aboard the *Chippewa*, a recently rebuilt 1920s ferry.

BOAT RENTALS

In Bar Harbor, **Harbor Boat Rentals** (288-3757) rents powerboats and sailboats; in Southwest Harbor **Manset Yacht Service** (244-4040) offers sailboat charters, **Island Boat Rentals** (244-4040) rents powerboats, and **Mansell Boat Rentals** rents day-sailers and small powerboats.

CANOEING AND KAYAKING

Most ponds on Mount Desert offer easy access. Long Pond, the largest lake on the island, has three access points. Boats can be launched at Echo Lake from Ike's Point, just off Route 102. Seal Cove Pond is less used, accessible from fire roads north of Seal Cove. Bass Harbor Marsh is another possibility at high tide. Canoe rental sources offer suggestions and directions. Kayaking is a recent but booming sport, easier to master than saltwater canoeing. Outfitters include **Acadia Bike & Canoe Company** (288-9605) and **Coastal Kayaking Tours** (288-9605) in Bar Harbor; **National Park Canoe Rentals** (244-5854) on Long Pond near Somesville; **Life Sports** (667-7819) in Ellsworth; **Atlantic Kayak Tours** (422-3213) just across the Singing Bridge in Sullivan; and **Moose Look Guide Service** (963-7720) in Gouldsboro, which offers guided fishing trips as well as rental canoes and kayaks.

DIVING

Harbor Divers (244-5751) in Bass Harbor offers morning and afternoon dive trips daily in-season. Night dives and all-day charters also available as well as snorkeling packages.

GOLF

Kebo Valley Club (288-3000), Route 233, Bar Harbor. Open daily May through October. Eighteen holes; "oldest golf grounds in America," since 1892. **Bar Harbor Golf Course** (667-7505), Routes 3 and 204, Trenton. Eighteen holes. **Causeway Golf Club** (244-3780), Southwest Harbor. Nine-hole course, club and pull-carts, pro shop.

HIKING

Acadia National Park is a recognized mecca for hikers. Several detailed maps are sold at the visitors center, which is also the source of an information sheet that profiles two dozen trails within the park. These range in difficulty from the Jordan Pond Loop Trail (a 3⅓-mile path around the pond) to the Precipice Trail (1½ miles, very steep, with iron rungs as ladders). There are 17 trails to mountain summits on Mount Desert. Acadia Mountain on the island's west side (2 miles round-trip) commands the best view of Somes Sound and the islands.

Kebo Valley Club, Bar Harbor

Schoodic Mountain, off Route 183 north of Sullivan, provides one of eastern Maine's most spectacular and least known hikes, with 360-degree views, including the peaks on Mount Desert across Frenchman Bay. The Bureau of Parks and Lands (827-5936) has improved the parking area and trail system here. Take your first left after crossing the railroad tracks on Route 183; bear left at the Y and in 0.8 mile bear right to the parking lot. The hike to the top of Schoodic Mountain (1069 feet) should take less than 45 minutes; a marked trail from the summit leads down to sandy Schoodic Beach at the southern end of Donnell Pond (good swimming and a half-dozen primitive campsites); return to the parking lot on the old road that's now a footpath (½ mile). From the same parking lot you can also hike to the bluffs on Black Mountain; from here the trail continues to other peaks, and another trail descends to Schoodic Beach.

HORSE-DRAWN TOURS

Wildwood Stables (276-3622), follow the Park Loop Road from the visitors center; turn left at the sign a half mile beyond Jordan Pond House. Two-hour horse-drawn tours in multiple-seat carriages are offered six times a day.

ROCK CLIMBING

Acadia National Park is the most popular place to climb in Maine; famous climbs include the Precipice, Goat Head, and Otter Cliffs.

Acadia Mountain Guides (288-8186) and **Atlantic Climbing** (288-2521) offer instruction and guiding for beginner through advanced climbers.

SAILING

The *Natalie Todd* (288-4585) sails from the Bar Harbor pier, late June through early October. Maine's only three-masted commercial schooner, it was built in 1941 as a two-masted schooner dragger. Captain Steven Pagels found the vessel in Gloucester in 1986 and rebuilt her as a three-masted, gaff-rigged schooner. The 2-hour cruises through Frenchman Bay are offered several times a day in high season, less frequently in slower weeks. Check current handouts for other day sails.

Mansell Boat Company (244-5625), Route 102A, Manset (near Southwest Harbor), offers sailing lessons; also rents small sailboats. For sailboat charters contact **Classic Charters** (244-7312), Northeast Harbor; **Hinckley Yacht Charters** (244-5008), Bass Harbor; or **Manset Yacht Service** (244-4040).

SWIMMING

Within Acadia there is supervised swimming at Sand Beach, 4 miles south of Bar Harbor, and at Echo Lake, 11 miles west. At Seal Harbor there is a small, free, town beach with parking in a small lot across Route 3.

Lake Wood near Hull's Cove is a pleasant freshwater beach, ideal for children. The trick is finding it: Turn off Route 3 at the Cove Motel and take your second left up a dirt road (there is a small official sign); park and walk the short way to the beach. No facilities or lifeguard, but warm water.

The clearest water and softest sand we have found in the area is at **Molasses Pond** in Franklin.

WHALE-WATCHING

Whale-watching is offered by a number of Bar Harbor–based companies including **Acadian Whale Watcher Co.** (288-9794), **Bar Harbor Whale Watch Co.** (288-2386), and **Sea Bird Watcher Company** (288-2025); **Northeast Whale Watch** (288-9794) departs from Northeast Harbor.

CROSS-COUNTRY SKIING

More than 43 miles of carriage roads at Acadia National Park are maintained as ski-touring trails. Request a "Winter Activities" leaflet from the park headquarters (write to Superintendent, PO Box 177, Bar Harbor 04609).

LODGING

GRAND OLD RESORTS

The Claremont (244-5036; 1-800-244-5036), Claremont Road, Southwest Harbor 04679. Open May to mid-October. Mount Desert's oldest hotel (110 years in 1994), substantially renovated. Sited with spectacular views of Cadillac Mountain across Somes Sound and the waterfront estates in Northeast Harbor. This is a classic, grand but not large resort hotel with rockers on the veranda, spacious common rooms that include a game room lined with books, and a large dining room designed so that every table has a water view. Food is excellent, with an emphasis on fresh fish (see *Dining Out*). In the old resort tradition, jacket and tie are required at dinner, but the atmosphere is relaxed and friendly. Lunch is served at the boathouse, right on the water with splendid views of the mountains and Northeast Harbor. The hotel has 23 old-fashioned double rooms, simply, tastefully furnished and with private baths; there are large suites in Phillips and Clark Houses, also 12 cottages, each with living room and fireplace. Recreation options include tennis on clay courts, croquet, badminton, and water sports; rowboats are available. The Croquet Classic in August is the social high of the season. A room in the hotel is $162–192 double, MAP, in-season; $150–180, EP, in the cottages; $90–130 double, B&B, off-season in the hotel. A gratuity is added: 15 percent in the rooms, 10 percent in the cottages.

Asticou Inn (276-3344; 258-3373), Route 3, Northeast Harbor 04662. Cranberry Lodge is open May to late December, and the main house, mid-June to mid-October. The epitome of elegance, the Asticou Inn offers superb food, simply furnished rooms with water views, luxurious public rooms with Oriental rugs and wing chairs by the hearth, and a vast porch overlooking formal gardens. In all, there are 50 rooms and suites, all with private baths, divided among the main house and annexes, which include Cranberry Lodge across the road. Facilities include a cocktail lounge, tennis courts, and a heated swimming pool. Dinner dances on Thursday evenings in July and August; music many summer nights. $180–255 double, MAP. $69–99 with breakfast in Cranberry Lodge, off-season. Add 15 percent gratuity.

INNS AND BED & BREAKFASTS
In Bar Harbor 04609

The majority of Bar Harbor's 2600 beds, ranging from '20s motor courts to large chain hotels and motels, are strung along Route 3, north of the walkaround town—where 30 or so surviving summer mansions are now B&Bs, commanding top dollar. So be warned: Never come to Bar Harbor in July or August without a reservation. You will find a room, but it may well cost more than $300. We cannot claim to have inspected every room in town, but we offer this partial listing of places that we have actually checked out.

Inn at Canoe Point (288-9511), Box 216. Open year-round. Two miles north of Bar Harbor near the entrance to the Acadia National Park visitors center. Separated from Route 3 by its own small pine forest, overlooking the bay. The five guest rooms have water views and private baths. The master suite, with its fireplace and French doors onto a deck, is ideal for a romantic getaway. The garret suite occupies the whole third floor; the garden room exudes the charm of a traditional Bar Harbor cottage guest room. All rooms have been imaginatively, elegantly furnished. Guests gather in the Ocean Room for breakfast to enjoy the fireplace, grand piano, and 180-degree view. Tom and Nancy Cervelli are the proud new innkeepers. $145–235 in-season; off-season $90–155.

Nannau Seaside B&B (288-5575), Box 710, Lower Main Street. Open May through October. Sited on peaceful Compass Harbor a mile from downtown Bar Harbor and abutting the national park, this vintage 1904, shingled, 20-room "cottage" offers rooms ranging from a third-floor double ($115) to one with a fireplace and a large bay window on the ocean ($145). A two-bedroom suite with ocean views is $165. A large breakfast, maybe eggs Florentine or frittata, is served, and Vikki and Ron Evers invite guests to make themselves at home in the parlor and living room, where there are plenty of books. The couple pride themselves on their organic vegetable garden, young orchard, and perennial flower beds. A path leads down to the water, and there is an easy walk to a point with wonderful views. No smoking.

Mira Monte Inn and Suites (288-4263; 1-800-553-5109), 69 Mount Desert Street. Open May to mid-October. A gracious 1865 mansion with 13 comfortable guest rooms, many with private balconies overlooking the deep, peaceful lawn in back or the formal gardens on the side. A native of Bar Harbor, innkeeper Marian Burns is an avid hiker who likes to steer her guests off the park's beaten path. All rooms have private baths; eight have fireplaces. All are furnished with antiques and equipped with phones, clock radios, and TVs. Two suites in a separate building feature kitchenettes, whirlpool tubs, and private decks. A four-room suite, available by the week, is good for families. Common space includes the inviting library and sitting room with fireplaces as well as the formal Victorian flower garden. Rates include full breakfast and afternoon refreshments. $115–150 per room, $125–180 for suites. Discounts for longer stays and special spring and fall packages.

Ullikana Bed & Breakfast (288-9552), 16 The Field. An 1885 Tudor-style summer cottage with 10 guest rooms, all with private baths, 2 with fireplaces, each decorated with unusual imagination and taste by innkeeper Helene Harton, who obviously has a way with paint and an eye for art as well as a flair for creating exquisite breakfasts like lemon soufflé pancakes and crêpes aux pommes. The "cottage" is handy both to the Shore Path and to downtown shops and restaurants, yet has a secluded feel. $110–190.

The Tides (288-4968), 119 West Street. Open May through October. A vintage 1887 mansion overlooking the "bar" and the harbor, just a short walk from shops and restaurants. At low tide you can walk out to Bar Island. Due to local zoning, the three guest rooms have recently been converted to two-room suites, with sitting rooms, four-poster beds, fireplaces, cable TV, and window seats with water views. The veranda, with its wicker chairs, fireplace, and water views, is the gathering spot for afternoon hors d'oeuvres. $125–260 includes a full breakfast. No smoking, pets, or children.

Manor House Inn (288-3759), 106 West Street. Open May through mid-November. All 14 rooms in this 1887 "cottage" have private baths, and most are furnished with Victorian pieces. Six have working fireplaces. Rare woodwork and nicely preserved details add elegance, as does the full acre of landscaped grounds. We particularly like the guest room and two suites in the Chauffeur's Cottage and the two newly renovated cottages (with gas fireplaces) in the garden. $85–175 per room (less off-season) includes a buffet breakfast.

Canterbury Cottage (288-2112), 12 Roberts Avenue. Open May to mid-October. A small, centrally located B&B whose owners share a lifetime familiarity with the island. The Victorian house is architecturally inter-esting (its original owner was the B&M stationmaster, and its architect specialized in railroad stations), and rooms are comfortably and taste-fully decorated. No children, pets, or smokers. $70–95 double includes breakfast in the country kitchen.

The Maples Inn (288-3443), 16 Roberts Avenue. A pleasant 1903 house is now a six-room B&B (with private baths) on a quiet side street within walking distance of shops and restaurants. Innkeeper Susan Sinclair is known for breakfasts like blueberry-stuffed toast and orange omelet souffle. $90–150 per couple; $60–95 mid-October through mid-June.

Anne's White Columns Inn (288-5357; 1-800-321-6379), 57 Mount Desert Street. Built in the 1930s as a Christian Science church, hence the columns, the interior of the building was designed as a B&B (each of the 10 rooms has a private bath and cable TV). It works and inn-keeper Ann Bahr delights in helping guests explore the park and area. $75–110 in July and August, otherwise $65–95; includes breakfast, wine and cheese.

Bass Cottage in the Field (288-3705), The Field. Open late May to mid-October. This grand old home, just off Main Street but in a quiet byway, has been in Ann Jean Turner's family since 1928. The large, enclosed porch is stacked with magazines and local menus, furnished with wicker. The nine rooms with high ceilings and one suite are simply, tradition-ally furnished; six have private baths. Smoking on porches only. $55–90 double, the $45 single (in-season) is a real find.

In Northeast Harbor 04662

Harbourside Inn (276-3272). Open June through September. An 1880s, shingle-style inn set in 4 wooded acres, with 11 guest rooms and three suites on three floors, all with private baths, some kitchens. There are also working fireplaces in all the first- and second-floor rooms. All are large and bright with interesting antiques and fine rugs. This is a very special place, as only an inn with long-term family management and a returning clientele can be. The flower garden and its yield in every guest room is a special feature. Guests mingle over breakfast muffins served on wicker-furnished sun porches. There is also a comfortable living room, but most guests spend their days in adjacent Acadia National Park (its wooded paths are within walking distance) or on boat excur-sions out of Northeast Harbor, also just down the road. Your hosts, the

NEAL PARENT

Painting on Swans Island

Sweet family, are longtime island residents. $75 (low off-season) to $175 for a suite in August.

In Southwest Harbor 04679

Penury Hall (244-7102), Box 68, Main Street. Open year-round. An attractive village house with three guest rooms sharing two baths, all nicely decorated with interesting art and tempting reading material salted about. This was the first bed & breakfast on the island. Toby and Gretchen Strong take their job as hosts seriously and make guests feel part of the family. Breakfast includes juice, fresh fruit, a choice of eggs Benedict, blueberry pancakes, or a "penurious omelet." A canoe and a 21-foot sloop are available, and you can relax in the sauna after hiking or cross-country skiing. $70–85.

The Inn at Southwest (244-3835), PO Box 593, Main Street. Open May to October. A high Victorian "cottage" in the village with a wraparound porch and harbor views. Pleasant sitting room with fireplace, games, and magazines. All nine rooms have private baths; $60–125 double includes a full breakfast, afternoon refreshments.

Lindenwood Inn (244-5335), Box 1328. Open all year. A turn-of-the-century sea captain's home set among stately linden trees. All nine guest rooms have private baths and many have water views, as do the six housekeeping units in the annex, which have balconies and fireplaces. There are three cottages, one at water's edge. There's an in-ground heated pool and hot tub, also a small in-house restaurant. A full breakfast is served in the paneled dining room (where the fire is lit most mornings). Swing on the porch. $65–195 double; $20 per extra person.

The Island House (244-5180), Box 1006. Open all year. Right across from the harbor, this large 1850s house is part of an early summer hotel (ask to see the scrapbook of historical memoirs). Ann Bradford offers four double rooms with two shared baths, also a cozy efficiency apartment with a loft in the carriage house. $50–65, $10 more for private bath; $95 for carriage house includes breakfast; 2-night minimum in August.

The Heron House (244-0221), 1 Fernald Point Road. Open year-round. After 16 years of vacationing in the area, Sue and Bob Bonkowski re-decorated this comfortable house into a B&B of their own. Three pleasant guest rooms share two baths. Guests are welcome to use the living room and den to relax in. $55–65 depending on season ($15 per extra person), includes full breakfast served family-style.

The Birches (244-5182), Fernald Point Road, PO Box 178. "Great-Grandma bought these 8 acres for $50 and for another $50 she could have had 20 more," Dick Homer quips. The Homer summer home, built in 1916, commands a splendid water view from its tongue-and-groove paneled living room and ample grounds (which include a croquet court). The three simply furnished guest rooms share baths and you feel like a guest in a gracious but informal home. $85 includes a full breakfast.

In Bass Harbor 04653

Pointy Head Inn and Antiques (244-7261), HC 33, Box 2A. Open mid-May to late fall. This rambling old sea captain's home on Route 102A overlooks the ocean. Doris and Warren Townsend offer six guest rooms, some with views of water, mountains, or both, two with private baths, the rest sharing baths. "Mature" children only. An antiques shop with wood carvings by Warren is on the premises. $45–95 per room, $15 per extra person; includes full breakfast.

Bass Harbor Inn (244-5157), PO Box 326. Open May through October. In an 1832 house with harbor views, within walking distance of village restaurants, Barbara and Alan Graff offer eight rooms ranging from doubles with shared baths to a top-floor studio with kitchenette. One room with half-bath has a fireplace. $60–100 in-season, $40–80 off-season, includes breakfast.

In Lamoine 04605

Lamoine House (667-7711), Route 184, Box 180. Open all year. Just a few miles off Route 3, Lamoine is a quiet byway with its own beach and water views. This B&B is a simple, friendly old farmhouse across the road from the water. Two guest rooms, one upstairs and one down, share the family bath and living room. Molly Gilley is a serious gardener and baker, and the reasonable rates—$20–26 single and $26–34 double—include a full country breakfast.

In East Hancock County

Crocker House Country Inn (422-6806), Hancock Point 04640. Open daily mid-April through Columbus Day, weekends (Thursday through

Sunday) late October to New Year's Eve. Just 30 minutes north of Bar Harbor, Hancock Point has a different feel entirely: quiet, with easy access to water, hiking trails, crafts shops, and concerts. The three-story, 1880s inn has 11 guest rooms, 9 in the inn itself and 2 on the second floor of the carriage house. All rooms have private baths (new and nicely done with natural woods) and country antiques, quilts, and stenciling. There is a pleasant, unpretentious air to this inn, and families feel welcome; the common rooms are spacious, and there's more lounging space on the ground floor of the carriage barn near the hot tub. The second smallest post office in the United States sits across the road next to the tennis courts, and the nearby dock is maintained by the Hancock Improvement Association. Breakfast and dinner are served in the dining room, which is open to the public (see *Dining Out*). $75–120 double includes breakfast.

Le Domaine (422-3395/3916; 1-800-554-8498), Route 1, Hancock 04640. Best known for the French fare of its dining room (see *Dining Out*), this European-style inn also has seven rooms, each with private bath. Guests arrive in plenty of time for dinner (check-in ends promptly at 5:30), ideally early enough to stroll through the woods to the tranquil trout pond. Each room is named for a herb and each has obviously been designed and furnished with care for closet, writing, and reading space. There are fresh flowers and interesting books. Request a room facing the wide deck (where your breakfast of fresh croissants and fruit can be served), overlooking the flower garden and lawns stretching to the woods. Our only criticism is that there is only one phone. We had to resort to our bag phone to confirm an invitation with our dinner guest. $200 per couple, MAP, plus tax and 15 percent gratuity.

Island View Inn (422-3031), HCR 32, Box 24, Sullivan Harbor 04664. This is a spacious, gracious, turn-of-the-century summer "cottage" set well back from Route 1 with splendid views of Frenchman Bay and the dome-shaped mountains on Mount Desert. The seven guest rooms, five with private baths and three with water views, are nicely decorated, and there is ample and comfortable common space; a full breakfast is included. $65–85 in-season; no charge for children 5 years and younger, otherwise $10 per extra person in room. An 18-foot sailboat is available for guests to rent and a canoe and rowboat are available at no charge.

Sullivan Harbor Farm (422-3735), Route 1, Sullivan Harbor 04664. Built in 1820 by Captain James Urann, who launched his vessels from the shingle beach across the road. The house, overlooking Frenchman Bay, is cheerfully, tastefully decorated and includes a library and an enclosed porch on which breakfast is served. The three guest rooms with double beds have private baths ($65). Cupcake, a particularly delightful year-round cottage, also has water views and can sleep six ($650 per week). Another great cottage, Milo, sleeps four ($525 per week). A canoe is available, and hosts Joel Franztman and Leslie Harlow delight in tuning guests in to local hiking, biking and paddling possibilities. Their award-winning salmon smokehouse is on the premises.

Oceanside Meadows Inn (963-5557), PO Box 90, Prospect Harbor 04669. Sonja Sundaram has inherited the 200-acre estate. She and her husband, Englishman Ben Walter (they met at an environmental research center in Bermuda), have brought the old place to life, spiffing up the seven bedrooms and three apartments (all with private bath). Sonja's breakfasts, according to guests, are not to be believed. There is a sand beach, also a network of trails through the adjoining woods, meadow, and salt marsh. $75–95 per room, $650–750 per week for two-bedroom apartments.

The Black Duck (963-2689), PO Box 39, Corea 04624. Overlooking a picturesque harbor in a quiet fishing village. Barry Canner and Robert Travers offer four guest rooms, comfortably furnished with antiques, contemporary art, and Oriental rugs. Common areas display collections of antique toys and lamps, and the living room has a cozy fireplace. Twelve acres of land and waterfront property invite hiking, photography, artistic pursuits, and quiet relaxation. Two dog, three cats, and Dolly the pot-bellied pig will welcome you, so please leave your pets at home. Two waterfront cottages are also available. $60–125.

COTTAGES

"Maine Guide to Camp & Cottage Rentals," available free from the Maine Publicity Bureau (623-0363), lists some great rental cottages within easy striking distance of Mount Desert.

Emery's Cottages on the Shore (288-3432), Sand Point Road, Bar Harbor 04609. Open May to mid-October. Twenty-two cottages on Frenchman Bay (14 with kitchens), electric heat, showers, cable TVs, and private pebble beach. No pets. $440–680 per week, $68–98 per day; less off-season.

Eden Village Motel and Cottages (288-4670), Box 1930 (10 minutes north of Bar Harbor on Route 3), Bar Harbor 04609. The housekeeping cottages, set on 25 acres, accommodate two to six people and are equipped with fireplaces and screened porches. $375–659 per week; nightly and lower off-season rates. Motel rooms are $54–72. Inquire about the honeymoon cottage.

HOTELS AND MOTELS

Bar Harbor Inn (288-3351; 1-800-248-3351), Newport Drive, Bar Harbor 04609. With 153 units, this landmark hotel get its share of tour groups, but its downtown waterside location is unbeatable and it's a good value at Bar Harbor prices, especially for families. It's also a genuinely gracious hotel, with a 24-hour front desk, bellmen, a restaurant open for all three meals, and room service. The lobby with its formal check-in desk is grand, and the Reading Room (dining room) began as an elite men's social club in 1887. The 51 guest rooms in the main inn were the first new hotel rooms available in town after the 1947 fire. Recent additions include a 64-unit Oceanfront Lodge with private balconies on the bay and the Newport Building: 38 equally comfortable rooms without views. All rooms have phone, cable TV, and access to the pool, Jacuzzi, and 7 acres of manicured lawns on the water. The lodge is open year-round. In winter rates begin at $59; in summer the range is $115–255, continental breakfast included. Children 15 and under are free; ask about 2- to 4-night packages, which bring the rack rates down.

Atlantic Oakes By-the-Sea (288-5801; 1-800-33MAINE), Box 3, Eden Street (Route 3, next to the *Bluenose* ferry terminal), Bar Harbor 04609. Open year-round. This is a modern facility on the site of Sir Harry Oakes's 10-acre estate: The eight different buildings house 152 units, many with balconies, 12 with kitchens. There's also an eight-room bed & breakfast in the original Oakes summer mansion. Facilities include a pebble beach, heated outdoor pool, indoor pool, five tennis courts, and pier and float handy to the *Bluenose* ferry. $125–158 in-season, $59–85 off-season.

Wonder View Inn (288-3358 or 1-800-341-1553), PO Box 25, 50 Eden Street, Bar Harbor 04609. Open mid-May to mid-October. Both pets and children are welcome in the 79-unit motel built on 14 acres, the site of an estate once owned by Mary Roberts Rinehart, author of popular mystery stories. Near both the *Bluenose* ferry and downtown Bar Harbor, the motel overlooks Frenchman Bay, and its extensive grounds are nicely landscaped. Includes a swimming pool and the Rinehart Dining Pavilion, which serves breakfast and dinner. $55–125.

PUBLIC CAMPGROUNDS

The two campgrounds within Acadia National Park are **Blackwoods** (288-3274), open all year and handy to Bar Harbor; and **Seawall** (244-3600) near Southwest Harbor, open late May to late September. Sites at Seawall are meted out on a first-come, first-served basis, but Blackwoods reservations can be made at least 8 weeks in advance from June 15 to September 15 by calling 1-800-365-2267.

Note: Although Blackwoods and Seawall may fill during July and August, waterside sites in nearby **Lamoine State Park** (667-4778), open mid-May to mid-October, are often empty. This attractive, 55-acre park is just minutes from Route 3 on Route 184 in Lamoine. Facilities include picnicking and a boat launch but no hot showers. The park is just up the road from Lamoine Beach (great for walking and skipping stones). There are also more than a dozen commercial campgrounds in this area.

OTHER LODGING

Bar Harbor Youth Hostel (288-5587; 1-800-444-6111), 41 Mount Desert Street (behind St. Savior's Episcopal Church), PO Box 32, Bar Harbor 04609. Open mid-June through August to AYH members. Two dorms with a total of 20 cheery red and white bunks in a clean, cozy building, kitchen facilities. $15 per person for nonmembers; $3.50 for a pancake breakfast; reservations advised.

Appalachian Mountain Club's Echo Lake Camp (244-3747), AMC/ Echo Lake Camp, Mount Desert 04660. Open late June through August. Accommodations are platform tents; family-style meals are served in a central hall. There is a rustic library reading room and an indoor game room. The focus, however, is outdoors: There are boats for use on the lake, daily hikes, and evening activities. Reservations should be made on April 1. Rates for the minimum 1-week stay (Saturday to Saturday) are inexpensive per person but add up for a family. All meals included. For a brochure, write to Echo Lake Camp, AMC, 5 Joy Street, Boston, MA 02108.

Swan's Island Vacations (526-4350; September through May: 474-7370). Year-round, Maili Mailey coordinates rentals for cottages, houses, and apartments on Swan's Island, a picturesque lobstering island accessible from Bass Harbor. Accommodations $280–900 per week. **Jeannie's Place** (526-4116) on Swan's also offers three rooms; $45 in-season. We love Swan's Island, as genuine a getaway as any other island in Maine with only one general store (no alcohol sold) but a good library, museum, and sense of community.

WHERE TO EAT

DINING OUT
In Bar Harbor

George's Restaurant (288-4505), 7 Stephen's Lane (just off Main Street behind the First National Bank). Open mid-June through October. Dinner 5:30–10 PM. Creative, fresh, vaguely Greek cuisine in a summery house with organdy curtains. Extensive choice of appetizers, grazers, and entrées. You might dine on Very Rich Lobster Bisque and the lamb specialty of the night. All entrées are $23 and the prix fixe for a three-course meal is $32.

The Fin Back (288-4193), 78 West Street. No smoking. Lunch and dinner daily, reservations suggested. A small, chef-owned restaurant with great decor, across the street from the harbor. Entrées might include a smoked seafood risotto ($15.95) and grilled veal chop with prosciutto shiitake (21.95). The bouillabaisse ($20.95) and crabcakes are famous.

Galyn's (288-9706), 17 Main Street. Easy to miss among the shops near the bottom of Main Street, this is one of the best bets in town for seafood at either lunch or dinner. Try the Frenchman Bay stew ($12.95). The large menu actually ranges from jambalaya ($8.95) to rack of lamb ($22.95) and there is lighter fare in the Galley Lounge, featuring weekend jazz until 11 PM.

The Porcupine Grill (288-3884), 123 Cottage Street. Open most of the year for dinner, daily from 6 PM. Reservations recommended. Well-chosen antiques, photos of the Porcupine Islands, and fresh flowers complement imaginative dishes like lobster and sun-dried tomato tart and grilled leg of lamb with mint peppercorn sauce. $16.50–18.50, extensive wine list, cocktails a specialty.

Maggie's Classic Scales (288-9007), 6 Summer Street. Dinner 5–10:30. Chef-owned restaurant featuring New England cuisine well prepared, fresh seafood specialties; the lobster crêpes come highly recommended. Entrées $12.95–18.95.

Cafe Bluefish (288-3696), 122 Cottage Street. Dark wood, books, cloth napkins patterned with different designs, and mismatched antique china create a pleasant atmosphere. Chef-owner Bobbie Lynn Hutchins, a fourth-generation Bar Harbor native, specializes in chicken, vegetarian, and seafood entrées like Cajun-crusted swordfish ($18.95) and herbed salmon strudel ($16.95).

The Reading Room (288-3351), Bar Harbor Motor Inn, Newport Drive. Opened in 1887 as an elite men's club, the horseshoe-shaped, formal dining room commands a splendid harbor view; frequent piano music at dinner. Open for all three meals, specializing in daily lobster bakes on the outdoor terrace. Dinner entrées range from grilled breast of chicken ($14.95) to steak and lobster pie (market price). A Sunday champagne-brunch buffet is 11:30–2:30.

124 Cottage Street (288-4383). Pleasant, flowery atmosphere, a large vegetarian salad bar (included in all meals), and genuine early-bird specials (5–6 PM): a three-course dinner for $12.95. Try the mussels Fra Diablo or crabmeat baked with three cheeses and fresh asparagus (both $14.95).

Poor Boy's Gourmet (288-4148), 1 Stanwood Place, Lower Main Street. Open for dinner nightly. Chef-owner Kathleen Field is dedicated to providing a decent dining experience at reasonable prices. Her wide choice of lobster, seafood, veal, beef, chicken, pasta, and vegetarian entrées is priced from $9.95 (for linguine al pesto) to $15.95 for lobster and shrimp Alfredo. An early-bird menu with entrées like apricot chicken and shrimp marinara is $7.95. Wine and beer served.

Testa's at Bayside Landing (288-3327), 53 Main Street. Open 7 AM–midnight, June 15 through September, when the family moves to its Palm Beach restaurant. In Bar Harbor since 1934, serving three daily meals. Italian and seafood specialties. Children's menu. Dinner entrées from $11.95 for linguine to $18.95 for lobster thermidor.

Elsewhere on Mount Desert

Jordan Pond House (276-3316), Seal Harbor, Park Loop Road. Open mid-May to mid-October for lunch 11:30–2:30, for tea on the lawn 2:30–5:30, and for dinner 5:30–9. First opened in the 1870s, this landmark was beautifully rebuilt after a 1979 fire, with dining rooms overlooking the pond and with a view to the mountains. It's best known for popovers and outdoor tea, but most pleasant, least crowded at dinner (jackets suggested). Specialties include crabmeat au gratin ($14), prime rib ($14.50), and crabmeat and Havarti quiche ($8). Children's menu and half portions available. A lobster salad is $16.

Asticou Inn (276-3344), Northeast Harbor. Open mid-May to mid-October for breakfast, lunch, and dinner. The Thursday-night buffet and dance is an island tradition. Grand old hotel atmosphere with a waterside formal dining room (window seats, however, are reserved for longtime guests). Specialties include filet mignon and lobster *au poivre* (in light beurre blanc with angelhair pasta). Entrées $15–23. Reservations required. The lunch buffet is a good value. Off-season a dining room in Cranberry Lodge opens for dinner on weekends.

Bistro at Seal Harbor (276-3299), Seal Harbor. Mid-June to mid-October, dinner daily, except Monday, from 6 PM. Justly popular. Appetizers might include crabcakes with Creole mustard sauce, or a bistro salad with feta, apples, and spiced pecans; entrées, grilled loin lamb chops with garlic-rosemary butter, or seafood gumbo. Owners Donna Fulton and Teresa Clements spend time in New Orleans (and love Cajun cooking) and California and take pride in their domestic wine list. Desserts might include plum crisp or Seal Harbor chocolate torte. Entrées $16–21.

Redfield's (276-5283), Main Street, Northeast Harbor. This is a trendy storefront café, open for espresso and gourmet takeout during the day and for dinner until 9 PM. The rear dining room doubles as a daytime art gallery. Sample menu includes nightly vegetarian offerings and grilled marinated quail. $17.95–18.95.

The Claremont (244-5036), Clark Point Road, Southwest Harbor. Open late June through Labor Day; lunch at the Boathouse, mid-July through August, also the place for a drink before dinner, with a view that's as spectacular as any on the island. In the formal dining room, most tables have some water view and both food and service are traditional (jacket and tie are required). Dinner choices change frequently, perhaps including tournedos of beef in béarnaise sauce, or grilled lamb tenderloin with mint pesto. Entrées $14–19.

The Burning Tree (288-9331), Route 3, Otter Creek. Open 5–10:30; closed Tuesday except in August. Admired for its fresh fish and organically grown produce, imaginatively prepared. Dine inside or on a lattice-enclosed porch on a wide choice of seafood, chicken, and vegetable entrées like Cajun crab and lobster ($19.50), grilled scallop kabobs ($15.95), and Swiss chard, potato, and artichoke pie ($14).

The Preble Grill (244-3034), 14 Clark Point Road, Southwest Harbor. Open 5:30–10. The specialty here as in Terry Preble's popular Fin Back in Bar Harbor is regional cuisine with a Mediterranean touch. It's an à la carte menu with entrées ranging from grilled andouille sausage ($10.75) or eggplant Napoleon ($13.75) to lobster with Seal Cove chèvre and a tarragon cream sauce over grilled polenta (market price). Reservations suggested.

XYZ Restaurant & Gallery (244-5221), Shore Road, Manset. Open for dinner nightly except Tuesday. Mexican food aficionados alert. Billed as "classical food from the Mexican interior," the fare is authentic and good. Try the sampler plate. Entrées are $11–16. Across the road from the water, this is the dining room of the Dockside Motel, decorated in the white, red, and green of the Mexican flag.

Seafood Ketch (244-7463), on Bass Harbor. Open May to November, 7 AM–9:30 PM daily. Lisa, Stuart, and Ed Branch work hard to make this place special. Known for homemade breads and desserts, also for fresh, fresh seafood. Dinner specialties include baked lobster-seafood casserole and baked halibut with lobster sauce; luncheon fare includes burgers, BLTs, and crabmeat rolls. Dinner entrées $11.95–16.95.

Deck House Restaurant (244-5044), end of Swan's Island Ferry Road, Bass Harbor. A very special place featuring, in addition to an excellent menu, nightly cabaret theater by the serving staff, beginning at 8:30 PM. Entertainment cover. Full bar. Reservations are a must.

East of Mount Desert

Le Domaine (422-3395), Route 1, Hancock. Closed Tuesday night, except August. Nicole Purslow, *propriétaire et chef,* prepares very French entrées, generally rated the best cuisine Down East. The atmosphere is that of a European-style country bistro. Nicole's mother, Marianne Purslow-Dumas, established the restaurant in the 1940s. She fled France during World War II and came to live with a relative, Pierre Monteux, who had established a conducting school—which still thrives and holds summer concerts—in Hancock. Every summer resident in and around Bar Harbor knows this story, along with the shortcut to Le Domaine from Mount Desert (turn off Route 3 onto 204 in Lamoine and follow our map). Dinner should begin with drinks in the lounge, with its bright provençale prints, then proceed into one of the two softly lit dining rooms where a fire frequently glows. The meal might begin with escargots or a tomato salad (tomatoes topped with a wonderful blend of herbs and cheeses), and move on to *escalope de veau sauté aux champignons* (veal medallions sautéed with mushrooms) or a daily special like tuna. Dessert choices include crème brûlée and Nicole's "bread pudding." Needless to say the wine list is extensive. Thursday is bistro night, $30 per person prix fixe.

Crocker House Country Inn (422-6806), Hancock Point. Open nightly for dinner, 5:30–9. A pleasant country inn atmosphere and varied menu; the specialty is Crocker House scallops, sautéed with mushrooms, scallions, garlic, and tomatoes with lemon and wine sauce ($17.50). In summer request the sun porch. Sunday brunch is big here, as are desserts. Entrées $16.95–21.95.

Oceanwood Gallery (963-2653), Birch Harbor. Sited just north of the Park Loop Road on the Schoodic Peninsula, with water views. A great place, especially for lunch. Restaurant profits benefit the Pajaro Jai Foundation, dedicated to practical solutions to rain forest destruction. The gallery features top local artists and Native American baskets, carvings. Lunch ranges from a peanut butter sandwich ($3.50) to crab salad

View of Northeast Harbor from Thuya Garden path

($8.50); dinner, from roast chicken ($9.50) to steak (17.50). Try the finnan haddie pie ($13.50).

EATING OUT

Lobster pounds

We put lobster pounds first in this category because they are the best as well as traditional places to eat lobster—as everyone should. The easiest to find are the clutch around the Trenton Bridge on Route 3. The **Trenton Bridge Lobster Pound** (667-2977), open in-season 8:30–8, has been in George Gascon's family a long time, and the view is great; but the preferred spot (it has a spectacular view) is the **Oak Point Lobster Pound** (667-8548), 4 miles down Route 230 from Route 3. Open in-season for lunch and dinner. Picnic tables and weatherproof dining on Western Bay: lobster rolls, stews, and seafood dinners; excellent blueberry pie.

Thurston's Lobster Pound (244-7600), Steamboat Wharf Road, Bernard. Open Memorial Day through September daily 11–8:30. On a working wharf overlooking Bass Harbor. Fresh and tender as lobster can be, plus corn and pie, also seafood stew, sandwiches, wine and beer.

Beal's Lobster Pier (244-7178; 244-3202), Clark Point Road, Southwest Harbor. Dock dining on picnic tables at the oldest lobster pound in the area. Crabmeat rolls, chowder, fresh fish specialties, and lobster (packed and shipped air freight, too).

In Bar Harbor

Fisherman's Landing (288-4632), 47 West Street. Open in-season 11:30–8. Right on the dock. Boiled lobster dinner, steamed clams, hamburgers, hot dogs, and fried foods; liquor license.

Epi Sub & Pizza (288-5853), 8 Cottage Street. Open 7 AM–11 PM. Tops for food and value but zero atmosphere. Cafeteria-style salads, freshly baked calzone, pizza, quiche, pasta, and crabmeat rolls. Clean and friendly; game machines in back.

Bubba's (288-5871), 30 Cottage Street. Open 11:30 AM–1 AM but serving food to 8:30 PM only. Steam-bent oak and mahogany in art deco–style creates a comfortable atmosphere. Soup and sandwiches, full bar.

Island Chowder House (288-4905), 38 Cottage Street. Open 11–11. A toy train circles just below the ceiling and the atmosphere is bright; good service, homemade soups, thick chowder, seafood pasta, and chicken. Bar. Lunch and dinner specials.

Miguel's Mexican Restaurant (288-5117), 51 Rodick Street. Open 5–10 nightly. Best Mexican food Down East: fajitas, blue corn crabcakes with roasted red pepper sauce.

Lompoc Cafe & Brew Pub (288-9392), 34 Rodick Street. Open daily for lunch, dinner, and late-night dining, specializing in house-made beer, espresso, international and vegetarian entrées; live entertainment.

West Street Cafe (288-5242). Open for lunch and dinner. Features home-made soups and pies, fried and broiled seafood, and four different lobster dishes. Children's menu and early-bird specials are available.

Nakorn Thai Restaurant (288-4060), 30 Rodick Street. Open daily for lunch and dinner, closing Saturday and Sunday at 4 PM. Locally liked, reasonably priced.

Elsewhere on Mount Desert

Chart Room (288-9740), Route 3, Hulls Cove. Open for breakfast, lunch, and dinner. A dependable, family-geared, waterside restaurant with seafood specialties. Moderate.

Docksider (276-3965), Sea Street, Northeast Harbor. Open 11–9. Bigger than it looks with a no-frills, knotty pine interior and great chowder, also salads, burgers, sandwiches, clam rolls, seafoods, and shore dinner. Wine and beer; lunch menu available all day.

Cafe Drydock (244-3886), 108 Main Street, Southwest Harbor. Open May to October, 7 AM–10 PM. An informal dining find specializing in seafood and pasta dishes; specialty drinks like Maine Mudslide and Creamsicle. Entrées $9–17.

The Deacon Seat (244-9229), Clark Point Road, Southwest Harbor. Open daily 5 AM–4:30 PM except Sunday. A great place for breakfast and the local gathering spot, near the middle of the village. A choice of 22 sandwiches to take out for picnics.

Little Notch Cafe (244-3357), 340 Main Street, Southwest Harbor. Open 11–8, specializing in freshly made soups and sandwiches like grilled tuna salad with cheddar on wheat ($3.95) and grilled chicken on focaccia with onions and garlic aioli ($4.95).

Ellsworth

The Mex (667-4494), 185 Main Street, Ellsworth. Open daily for lunch and dinner. Front tiled booths, inner dining room with white stucco walls, beaded curtains, heavy wooden chairs and tables. The Mex serves standard Mexican food—we always order too much. (The bean soup is a meal in itself.) Sangria, margaritas, and Mexican beer.

Maidee's (667-6554), Main Street, Ellsworth. A good road-food bet: a former diner with Oriental and standard American fare.

On the way to Schoodic

The Olde Post Office Restaurant (963-5900), Route 186, South Gouldsboro. The former village post office is now a family-run restaurant serving breakfast, lunch, and supper, specializing in ethnic and vegetarian dishes.

Fisherman's Inn (963-5585), Route 186, Winter Harbor. Open April to October, then weekends until Christmas, dinner only; 4:30–9 on weekdays and Saturday; 12–9 on Sunday. New ownership in '96 upped the prices and tone, but this is still a good place.

Chase's Restaurant (963-7171). Open all day in-season. A convenient, no-nonsense eatery at the entrance to the park. Booths, salad bar, fried lobsters and clams, good chowder; will pack a picnic.

SNACKS

Jordan Pond House (276-3316), Park Loop Road. Tea on the lawn at the Jordan Pond House (served 2:30–5:30) has been de rigueur for island visitors since 1895. The tea comes with freshly baked popovers and homemade ice cream. Reservations suggested.

J.H. Butterfield Co. (288-3386), 152 Main Street, Bar Harbor. FANCY FOODS SINCE 1887, the sign says, and John Butterfield preserves the quality and atmosphere of the grocery that once delivered to every one of Bar Harbor's summer mansions. The reasonably priced sandwiches are the best takeout we've found in town, and the chocolate and lemon cakes are legendary. Carry your order to a bench across the way on the town green or around the corner to Grant Park, overlooking the Shore Path and the bay.

Rooster Brother (667-8675), Route 1, Ellsworth. Just south of the bridge. Gourmet groceries, cheese, fresh-roasted coffee blends, takeout.

Gerrish's Store (963-5575), Winter Harbor. Open May through October, an old-fashioned village store with an ice cream parlor, light lunches, and penny candy.

ENTERTAINMENT

MUSIC

Bar Harbor Music Festival (288-5744), The Rodick Building, 59 Cottage Street, Bar Harbor. Mid-July to mid-August. For more than 25 years this annual series has brought top performers to the island. The 8:30 PM concerts are staged at a variety of sites around town.

Mount Desert Festival of Chamber Music (276-5039), Neighborhood House, Main Street, Northeast Harbor. A series of six concerts presented for more than 25 seasons mid-July through mid-August.

Acadia Mountains from across Frenchman Bay

TOM JONES

Arcady Music Festival (288-3151 or 288-2141). Late July through August. A relative newcomer (this is its 14th season) on the Mount Desert music scene. A series of concerts held at the College of the Atlantic (each concert performed in Bangor and Dover-Foxcroft as well).

Pierre Monteux Memorial Concert Hall (546-4495), Hancock, is the setting for a series of summer concerts presented by faculty and students at the respected Pierre Monteux School for Conductors.

(Also see *Entertainment* in "Blue Hill Area.")

FILM

Criterion Theater (288-3441), Cottage Street, Bar Harbor. A vintage 1932, art deco, 891-seat theater, gorgeous but musty (asthmatics, beware); first-run and art films at 8 nightly. Rainy-day matinees.

Reel Pizza Cinema (288-3828), 22 Kennebec Place, Bar Harbor. Gourmet pizza and first-run art films in a funky setting (beanbag chairs and big sofas). Films at 6 and 8:30 nightly, year-round.

The Grand Theater (667-9500), Main Street, Ellsworth. A classic old theater. When not in use for live performances, first-run and art films are shown.

Ellsworth Cinemas (667-3251), Maine Coast Mall, Route 1A, Ellsworth. Two evening shows; matinees on weekends, holidays, and rainy days. First-run films.

THEATER

Acadia Repertory Theatre (244-7260), Route 102, Somesville. Performances during July and August, Tuesday through Sunday at 8:15 PM, Sunday matinees at 2. A resident theater group based in the Somesville Masonic Hall (8 miles from Bar Harbor) performs a half-dozen popular plays in the course of the season.

The Grand Theater (667-9500), Main Street, Ellsworth. Live performances by singers, comedians, and theatrical groups. Check current listings.

Deck House Cabaret Theatre (244-5044), Swan's Island Ferry Road, Bass Harbor. July and August, dinner at 6:30. Waitstaff stage a cabaret show at 8:15 (see *Dining Out*).

SELECTIVE SHOPPING

ART AND FINE CRAFTS GALLERIES

Worth the trip: The **Barter Family Gallery and Shop** (422-3190), North Sullivan. Open mid-May through December, Monday through Saturday 9–5, or by appointment. We put this one first, although it's way off the beaten track, because it's our favorite. You will find Philip Barter's paintings in the best galleries (we first saw them in a Massachusetts museum). Mostly landscapes, they are primitive, bold, and evocative of northern Maine. The artist's furniture creations are also displayed in this extension of the Barter home, and the gallery shop also features Maine woolens, crafts, and Priscilla Barter's original hooked and braided rugs. Marked from Route 1 not far beyond the Sullivan bridge, less than 15 miles from Ellsworth.

Along Main Street in Northeast Harbor. The quality of the artwork showcased in this small yachting haven is amazing. **The Wingspread Gallery** (276-3910) has changing exhibits in the main gallery and a selection by well-established artists like Rockwell Kent (for a mere $40,000). **Redfield Artisans Gallery** (276-3609) offers a mix of high-end and affordable works.

In Bar Harbor

Eclipse Gallery (288-9048), 12 Mount Desert Street, seasonal. A quality gallery specializing in handblown glass, ceramics, and fine furniture, also showing metal sculpture, fine jewelry, and art photography.

Island Artisans, 99 Main Street, Bar Harbor. A cooperative run by area craftspeople.

Lone Moose (288-4229), West Street, Bar Harbor. A long-established collection of "made in Maine" craftswork.

In East Hancock County

Sugar Hill Gallery (422-8207), daily in summer and fall 9:30–5:30; Sunday noon–4:45. On Route 1, Hancock Village, representing local potters, jewelers, woodcarvers, and weavers, also quality artists like Ragna Bruna (her home gallery on Hancock Point: 422-3291).

Hog Bay Pottery (565-2282), 4 miles north of Route 1 on Route 200 in Franklin. Susanne Grosjean's award-winning rugs and the distinctive table and ovenware by Charles Grosjean are well worth the pleasant drive.

Spring Woods Gallery (442-3007), Route 200, off Route 1 in Sullivan. Open daily 10–5 except Sunday. This gallery represents five members of the Breeden family. It features fine arts, jewelry, and sculpture.

Gull Rock Pottery (422-3990), Eastside Road, Hancock;1.5 miles off Route 1. Open year-round. Torj and Kurt Wray wheel-throw blue and white stoneware with hand-brushed designs.

Pine Tree Kiln, Route 1, West Sullivan. Ruth and Denis Vibert have made this shop standing behind an easy-to-miss clapboard home into an insider's landmark. Their own ovenproof stoneware is outstanding, as is the selection of prints. Books and cards are also sold.

Maine Kiln Works, Route 186, West Gouldsboro. Open year-round, Monday through Saturday 10–5. An amazing number of unusual items: Dinnerware, ceramic sinks, soap dishes, and lamps are made on the spot; there are also unusual quilts and work by other local craftspeople.

The Harbor Shop (963-4117), Route 186, Winter Harbor. The custom-made hardwood furniture by owner John Jandik is center stage in this crafts shop.

Lee Art Glass Studio (963-7004), Main Street, Winter Harbor. It's difficult to describe this fused-glass tableware, which incorporates ground enamels and crochet doilies or stencils. It works.

U.S. Bells (963-7184), Route 186 in Prospect Harbor. Open daily 8–5 except Sunday. Richard Fisher creates (designs and casts) superb and distinctive wind-bells.

BOOKSTORES

Sherman's Bookstore and Stationery (288-3161), Main Street, Bar Harbor. A great browsing emporium; really a combination five-and-dime, stationery store, gift shop, and well-stocked bookshop.

Port in a Storm Bookstore (244-4114), Route 302, Somesville. Open year-round, Monday through Saturday 9:30–5:30 and Sunday 1–5. A 19th-century general-store building with water views, two floors of books, disks and cassettes, soft music, reading nooks, coffee. Linda Lewis and Marilyn Mays have created a real oasis for book lovers.

Mr. Paperback, Maine Mall, Route 1A, Ellsworth; and 227 Main Street, Bar Harbor. Fully stocked bookstores with popular titles and magazines.

Main Street Books (667-0089), 165 Main Street, Ellsworth. An appealing bookstore-café.

✏ **Oz Books** (244-9077), Main Street, Southwest Harbor. A first-rate children's bookstore.

SPECIAL SHOPS

✏ **Darthia Farm** (963-7771), West Bay Road (marked from Route 1), Gouldsboro. Open May through October, 8–6. A 133-acre organic farm with resident sheep, Scotch Highland cattle, turkeys, collies, and cows. Visitors are welcome to inspect the farm as well as the farm stand, justly famed for its vinegars, jams, and cheeses (there's even crème fraîche); **Hattie's Shed,** a weaving shop also at the farm, features coats, jackets, scarves, and shawls.

Sullivan Harbor Salmon (422-3735), Route 1, Sullivan Harbor. The salmon is local and visitors are welcome to tour the smokehouse in which the fish are cured in a blend of salt and brown sugar, then cold smoked in the traditional Scottish way, using hickory and applewood.

Bartlett Maine Estate Winery (546-2408), off Route 1, Gouldsboro. Open June to mid-October, Monday through Saturday 10–5; other times by appointment. Maine's first winery, specializing in blueberry, apple, and pear wines, also limited raspberry, strawberry, and honey dessert wines. An attractive complex in the pines, just off Route 1. Guided tours, tasting rooms, and gift packs. Call for tour times.

L.L. Bean Outlet, High Street, Ellsworth. Clothing, sporting equipment, and a wide variety of discounted items from Maine's most famous store.

Big Chicken Barn (667-7308), Route 1 south of Ellsworth. Maine's largest used bookstore fills the vast innards of a former chicken house on Route 1. Annegret and Mike Cukierski have 80,000 books in stock: hardbacks, paperbacks, magazines, and comics; also used furniture and collectibles. Browsers are welcome.

SPECIAL EVENTS

May: Memorial Day weekend, **Celebrate Bar Harbor.**

Throughout the summer: **Band concerts**—Bar Harbor village green (check current listings).

June: **Antique Auto Rally, Lobster Races,** Bar Harbor.

July: **Independence Day**—midnight square dance with breakfast for dancers, followed by sunrise dance on top of Cadillac Mountain, street parade, and seafood festival. **Art Show**—Bar Harbor's Agamont Park (later in the month). **Dulcimer and Harp Festival,** Bar Harbor. **Southwest Harbor Days**—crafts show, parade, sidewalk sales. **Ellsworth Craft Show** (end of month).

August: **Crafts Show** and **Art Show,** Bar Harbor. **Winter Harbor Lobster Festival,** Winter Harbor—includes road race, lobster feed, and lobster boat races.

September: **Marathon road race, bicycle race,** Bar Harbor.

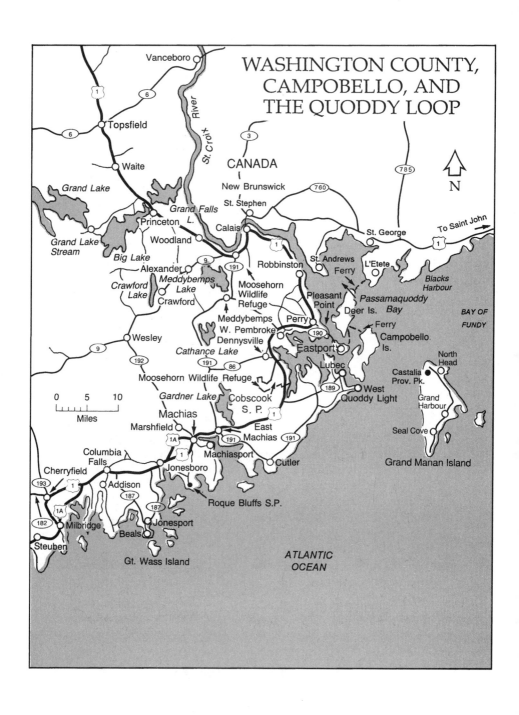

WASHINGTON COUNTY, CAMPOBELLO, AND THE QUODDY LOOP

Vanceboro

Topsfield

Waite

Grand Lake

St. Croix River

CANADA

New Brunswick

St. Stephen

Grand Falls L.

Princeton

Calais

Grand Lake Stream

Big Lake

Woodland

Alexander

Meddybemps

Crawford Lake

Lake

Robbinston

St. Andrews Ferry

L'Etete

Blacks Harbour

Crawford

Moosehorn Wildlife Refuge

Pleasant Point

Passamaquoddy Bay

Deer Is.

BAY OF FUNDY

Wesley

Meddybemps

W. Pembroke

Dennysville

Cathance Lake

Perry

Ferry

Campobello Is.

Eastport

North Head

Moosehorn Wildlife Refuge

Gardner Lake

Lubec

Castalia Prov. Pk.

Cobscook S. P.

West Quoddy Light

Grand Harbour

Machias

Marshfield

East Machias

Seal Cove

Columbia Falls

Machiasport

Cutler

Grand Manan Island

Cherryfield

Jonesboro

Addison

Roque Bluffs S.P.

Milbridge

Jonesport

Steuben

Beals

Gt. Wass Island

ATLANTIC OCEAN

St. George

To Saint John

N

0   5   10

Miles

Washington County, Campobello, and St. Andrews

The Atlantic Coast: Milbridge to Campobello; Eastport and Cobscook Bay; Calais and the St. Croix Valley; St. Andrews, New Brunswick

As Down East as you can get in this country, Washington County is a ruggedly beautiful and lonely land unto itself. Its 921-mile coast harbors some of the most dramatic cliffs and deepest coves—certainly the highest tides—on the eastern seaboard, but relatively few tourists. Lobster boats and trawlers still outnumber pleasure craft.

Created in 1789 by order of the General Court of Massachusetts, Washington County is as large as the states of Delaware and Rhode Island combined. Yet it is home to just 32,000 people, widely scattered among fishing villages, canning towns, logging outposts, Native American reservations, and saltwater farms. Many people (not just some) survive here by raking blueberries in August, making balsam wreaths in winter, and lobstering, clamming, digging sea worms, and diving for sea urchins the remainder of the year.

Less than 10 percent of the visitors who get as far as Bar Harbor come this much farther. The only "groups" you see are scouting for American bald eagles or osprey in the Moosehorn National Wildlife Refuge, for puffins, auks, and arctic terns on Machias Seal Island, or for whales in the Bay of Fundy. You may also see fishermen angling for Atlantic salmon in the tidal rivers or for landlocked salmon and smallmouth bass in the lakes.

Recently word has begun to spread that you don't drop off the end of the world beyond Eastport or Campobello despite the fact that since 1842—when a boundary was drawn across the face of Passamaquoddy Bay—New England maps have included only the Maine shore and Campobello Island (linked to Lubec, Maine, by a bridge), and Canadian maps have detailed only New Brunswick. In summer when the ferries are running, the day trip from either Eastport or Campobello to the resort town of St. Andrews is, in fact, one of the most scenic in the East; you drive one way and take the ferries the other. The drive is up along the St. Croix River to Calais and via Deer Island—which entails two delightful car ferry rides (one of them free) across Passamaquoddy Bay.

For exploring purposes, Washington County is divided into four distinct regions: (1) the 60-mile stretch of Route 1 between Steuben and Lubec (this actually includes some 600 miles of rugged coast), an area for which Machias is the shopping, dining, and information center; (2) Eastport and Cobscook Bay, the area of the highest tides and an end-of-the-world feel; (3) Calais and the St. Croix Valley, including the lake-splotched backwoods and the fishermen's havens at Grand Lake Stream; and (4) St. Andrews, New Brunswick.

Wherever you explore in Washington County—from the old sardine-canning towns of Eastport and Lubec to the coastal fishing villages of Jonesport and Cutler and the even smaller villages on the immense inland lakes—you find a Maine you thought had disappeared decades ago. You are surprised by the beauty of old buildings such as the 18th-century Burnham Tavern in Machias and Ruggles Mansion in Columbia Falls. You learn that the first naval battle of the Revolution was won by Machias men; that some local 18th-century women were buried in rum casks (because they were shipped home that way from the Caribbean); and that pirate Captain Richard Bellamy's loot is believed to be buried around Machias.

And if any proof were needed that this has always been one isolated piece of coast, there is Bailey's Mistake. Captain Bailey, it seems, wrecked his four-masted schooner one foggy night in a fine little bay 7 miles south of Lubec (which is where he should have put in). Considering the beauty of the spot and how far he was from the Boston ship-owner, Bailey and his crew unpacked their cargo of lumber and settled right down on the shore. That was in 1830, and many of their descendants have had the sense to stay put.

Local historians will also tell you why Deer Island, Grand Manan, and Campobello now belong to Canada rather than to the United States. Daniel Webster, the story goes, drank a few too many toasts the night Lord Ashburton sailed him out to check the boundaries. The islands were barely visible to Webster when he conceded them.

GUIDANCE

Washington County (1-800-377-9748); call to request printed information.

The Machias Bay Area Chamber of Commerce (255-4402), PO Box 606, Machias 04654. Request a copy of "Maine's Washington County" as well as the Machias Bay–area directory—a B&B and inn pamphlet. The chamber maintains a seasonal information center in the old railway station on Route 1 in Machias (across from Helen's Restaurant; see *Eating Out*).

Lubec Chamber of Commerce (733-4522), PO Box 123, Lubec 04652, maintains an office on Route 189.

The **Calais Information Center** (454-2211), 7 Union Street, Calais 04619. Open year-round and staffed by the Maine Publicity Bureau, it provides material on the entire county and state.

New Brunswick information of all kinds is available by phoning (within North America) 1-800-561-0123. Request a copy of the "New Brunswick Travel Guide."

(Also see *Guidance* for each region.)

GETTING THERE

By air: See "Bar Harbor and Acadia" chapter, along with "Bangor" chapter in "Northern Maine," for scheduled airline service. Charter service is available to the following airports: **Eastport Municipal** (853-2951); **Machias Valley** (255-8709); **Lubec Municipal** (733-5532); and **Princeton Municipal** (796-2744).

By bus: **Vermont Transit** (1-800-451-3292) and **Concord Trailways** (1-800-639-3317) both serve Bangor year-round; some summers Vermont Transit comes as close as Ellsworth.

By car: There are three equally slow ways to come: (1) I-95 to Augusta, then Route 3 to Belfast (stop at Lake St. George for a swim), then Route 1; (2) I-95 to Bangor, then Route 1A to Ellsworth, then Route 1. (*Note:* For coastal points east of Harrington, you save 9 miles by cutting inland on Route 182 from Hancock to Cherryfield); (3) for eastern Washington County, take I-95 to Bangor, then the Airline Highway (Route 9) for 100 miles straight through the blueberry barrens and woods to Calais. The state maintains camping and picnic sites at intervals along this stretch, and food and lodging can be found in Beddington, Wesley, Alexander, and Baring.

GETTING AROUND

East Coast Ferries (506-747-2159), based on Deer Island, serves both Campobello (45 minutes) and Eastport (30 minutes). Generally these run every hour from around 9 AM to around 7 PM, mid-June to mid-September, but call Stan Lord to check. The Campobello ferry takes 15 cars, and the Eastport ferry (a fishing boat lashed to a barge) takes 12 but gets far fewer passengers. **Deer Island** itself is more than a mere stepping-stone in the bay. Roughly 9 miles long and more than 3 miles wide, it's popular with bicyclists and bird-watchers. It boasts the world's largest lobster pound, the original salmon aquaculture site, a staffed lighthouse, and several B&Bs. The free, 18-car **Deer Island–L'Etete (New Brunswick mainland) Ferry** (506-453-2600) crossing takes 20 minutes, departing April through September every hour, 7–7, but call to confirm.

MEDICAL EMERGENCY

Calais Regional Hospital (454-7531). **Down East Community Hospital** (255-3356), Machias.

THE ATLANTIC COAST: MILBRIDGE TO CAMPOBELLO

GUIDANCE

The **Machias Bay Area Chamber of Commerce** (255-4402); see *Guidance* in the introduction to this chapter. **The Campobello Tourist Bureau** (506-752-7043), at the entrance to the island, is open daily May through Columbus Day.

TO SEE

Entries are listed geographically, traveling east.

Steuben, the first town in Washington County, is known as the site of the 3135-acre **Petit Manan National Wildlife Refuge** (see *Hiking*).

Milbridge, a Route 1 town with a wandering coastline, is the administrative home of one of the oldest wild-blueberry processors (Jasper Wyman and Sons). The town also supports one of the county's surviving sardine canneries, a Christmas wreath factory, a commercial center, and a great little movie theater. **McClellan Park,** overlooking Narraguagus (pronounced *nair-a-gway-gus*) Bay, offers picnic tables, fireplaces, campsites, rest rooms, and drinking water. The **Milbridge Society and Museum** (546-4471), open Tuesday, Saturday, and Sunday 1–4 and by appointment, is a delightful window into this spirited community, with displays on past shipyards, tanneries and Dr. Lawrence Bettridge (1895–1975), the town's Harvard-trained GP who liked to stand on his head. Milbridge Days (late July) have attracted national coverage in recent years; the highlight is a greased cod contest (see *Special Events*).

Cherryfield. A few miles up the Narraguagus River, Cherryfield boasts stately houses and a fine Atlantic salmon pool. The **Cherryfield-Narraguagus Historical Society** (546-7979), Main Street (just off Route 1), is open July and August, Wednesday and Friday 1–4, otherwise by appointment May through October. Picnic tables in **Stewart Park** on Main Street and in **Forest Mill Dam Park** on River Road are on the banks of the river. Cherryfield (why isn't it called *Berryfield*?) bills itself "Blueberry Capital of Maine"; there are two processing plants in town.

Columbia Falls is an unusually picturesque village with one of Maine's most notable houses at its center. **The Ruggles House** (1 mile from Route 1; open June to mid-October, Monday through Saturday 9:30–4:30, Sunday 11–4:30) is a Federal-style mansion built by wealthy lumber dealer Thomas Ruggles in 1818. It is a beauty, with a graceful flying staircase, a fine Palladian window, and superb woodwork. Legend has it that a wood-carver was imprisoned in the house for three years with a penknife. There is an unmistakably tragic feel to the place. Mr. Ruggles died soon after its completion, and his heirs petered out in the 1920s.

Jonesport and **Beals Island.** Jonesport and Beals are both lobstering and fishing villages. Beals is the home of the **Beals Island Regional Shellfish Hatchery** (497-5769), open to the public May through November, daily 9–4. Beals is connected by a bridge to Jonesport and by a shorter bridge to **Great Wass Island,** probably the county's most popular place to walk (see *Hiking*). Jonesport is the kind of village that seems small the first time you drive through but grows in dimensions as you slow down. Look closely and you will find a colorful marina, several restaurants, grocery stores, antiques shops, bed & breakfasts, chandleries, a hardware/clothing store, an art gallery, and more. Together the towns are home for eastern Maine's largest lobstering fleet, but the big buy at the cooperative in Jonesport is crabmeat.

Jonesboro is represented on Route 1 by a general store, a church, and a post office. The beauty of this town, however, is in its shoreline, which wanders in and out of points and coves along the tidal Chandler River and Chandler Bay on the way to **Roque Bluffs State Park** (see *Swimming*), 6 miles south of Route 1. A public boat launch with picnic tables is 5 minutes south of Route 1; take the Roque Bluffs Road but turn right onto Evergreen Point Road.

Machias is the county seat, an interesting old commercial center with the Machias River running through town and over the Bad Little Falls. **The Burnham Tavern** (255-4432), tucked up behind the old-fashioned five-and-dime, is open early June through mid-September, Monday through Friday 9–5; otherwise by appointment. A 1770s, gambrel-roofed tavern, it's filled with period furnishings and tells the story of British man-of-war *Margaretta,* captured on June 12, 1775, by townspeople in the small sloop *Unity.* This was the first naval battle of the American Revolution. Unfortunately, the British retaliated by burning Portland.

Machias was a hotbed of patriotic zeal at the outbreak of the Revolution, an era that can also be savored at **Micmac Farm** in Machiasport. Micmac Farm contains one of Maine's best restaurants (see *Dining Out*), filling two rooms of a low-beamed house built in 1772 by a patriot who fled here from Nova Scotia.

The **University of Maine at Machias** maintains an interesting art gallery featuring paintings by John Marin and sponsors weeklong (live-in) summer workshops for birders. There is summer theater and music, including concerts in the graceful 1836 **Congregational church** (centerpiece of the annual Wild Blueberry Festival). Also note the picnic tables and suspension bridge at the falls and the many headstones worth pondering in neighboring **O'Brien Cemetery.**

Early in the 19th century, Machias was second only to Bangor among Maine lumber ports. In 1912 the town boasted an opera house, two newspapers, three hotels, and a trotting park. (At this writing a railroad museum in the town's 1898 railroad station is planned to open in 1998.) Today Machias retains its share of fine houses and is home to the **Maine Wild Blueberry Company,** which processes 250,000 pounds of berries a day and ships them as far as Japan. Billed as the world's largest processor of wild blueberries, Maine Wild is the brainchild of Dr. Amir Ismail, a courtly and portly Egyptian who is generally recognized as Maine's most colorful and effective blueberry promoter.

Machiasport. This picturesque village includes the **Gates House** (open late May through mid-September, Monday through Friday 12:30–4:30), a Federal-style home with maritime exhibits and period rooms. **Fort O'Brien** is an earthwork mound used as an ammunitions magazine during the American Revolution and the War of 1812. We recommend that you continue on down this road to the fishing village of Bucks Harbor and on to **Jasper Beach,** so named for the wave-tumbled and polished pebbles of jasper and rhyolite that give it a distinctive color. The road ends with great views and a beach to walk in **Starboard.**

Cutler. From East Machias, follow Route 191 south to this small fishing village that's happily shielded from a view of the Cutler navy communications station—said to be the world's most powerful radio station. Its 26 antenna towers (800–980 feet tall) light up red at night and can be seen from much of the county's coast. Cutler is the departure point for Captain Andy Patterson's excursions to see the puffins on Machias Seal Island (see *Boat Excursions*). Beyond Cutler, Route 191 follows the shoreline through moorlike blueberry and cranberry country, with disappointingly few views. Much of this land is now publicly owned and the high bluffs can be accessed via the Bold Coast Trail (see *Hiking*). In South Trescott, bear right onto the unmarked road instead of continuing north on Route 191 and follow the coast through Bailey's Mistake (see chapter introduction) to West Quoddy Light.

West Quoddy Light State Park, South Lubec Road, Lubec. Open mid-April through October, sunrise to sunset. Marking the easternmost tip of the United States, the red-and-white-striped lighthouse dates back to 1858. The park, adjacent to the lighthouse, offers benches from which you are invited to be the first person in the United States to see the sunrise. There is also a fine view of Grand Manan Island, a pleasant picnic area, and a 2-mile hiking trail along the cliffs to Carrying Place Cove. Between the cove and the bay, roughly a mile back down the road from the light, is an unusual coastal, raised-plateau bog with dense sphagnum moss and heath.

Lubec. Most visitors now pass through this "easternmost town" quickly— on their way over the FDR Memorial Bridge to Campobello Island. Take a minute to find the old town landing, where there's a public boat launch and a breakwater and a view of The Sparkplug, as the distinctive little Lubec Channel Light is known. It is just offshore amid very fast-moving currents. Once there were 20 sardine-canning plants in Lubec;

the wonder is that there are still two, one now processing salmon (farmed in pens in the bay).

Roosevelt Campobello International Park (506-752-2922), Welshpool, Campobello Island, New Brunswick, Canada (for a brochure write Box 97, Lubec 04652). Open daily Memorial Day weekend to mid-October, 9–4:45 eastern daylight time (10–5:45 Canadian Atlantic daylight time). Although technically in New Brunswick, this manicured, 2800-acre park with a visitors center and shingled "cottages" is the number one sight to see east of Bar Harbor. You turn down a side street in Lubec, and there is the bridge (built in 1962) and Canadian customs. The house in which Franklin Delano Roosevelt summered as a boy has disappeared, but the airy Roosevelt Cottage, a wedding gift to Franklin and Eleanor, is maintained just as the family left it, charged with the spirit of the dynamic man who contracted polio here on August 25, 1921. During his subsequent stints as governor of New York and then as president of the United States, FDR returned only three times. Neighboring Hubbard Cottage, with its oval picture window, gives another slant on this turn-of-the-century resort. There's a visitors center here with an excellent new historical exhibit that compensates for the vapid 15-minute introductory film. Beyond stretch more than 8 miles of trails to the shore and then inland through woods to lakes and ponds. There are also 15.4 miles of park drives, modified from the network of carriage drives that the wealthy "cottagers" maintained on the island. Beyond the park is **East Quoddy Head Lighthouse,** accessible at low tide, a popular whale-watching station but a real adventure to get to (attempt only if you are physically fit). Note the small car ferry to Deer Island that runs during July and August (see *Getting Around*) and the description of The Owen House under *Inns and Bed & Breakfasts*. Campobello Park was granted to Captain William Owen in the 1760s and remained in the family until 1881, when it was sold to Boston developers, who built large (long-gone) hotels.

TO DO

AIRPLANE RIDES
Sunrise Air-Lubec (733-2124), Lubec. Scenic rides, photos, and fish spotting. **David Rier** (255-8458), scenic rides from the Machias airport.

BIRDING
Summer Workshops for Birders and Ornithologists at the University of Maine at Machias (255-3313). Three 1-week sessions are presently offered, one in early July, focusing on warblers, the others in August, each taught by prominent ornithologists. The workshops include field- and boat trips and dorm lodging.

BOAT EXCURSIONS AND PUFFIN-WATCHING

Machias Seal Island is a prime nesting spot for puffins in June and July, also a place to see razor-billed auks and arctic terns in August and September. Although just 9 miles off Cutler, the island is maintained by Canada as a lighthouse station and wildlife refuge. But **Captain Barna Norton** (497-5933) of Jonesport, who has been offering bird-watching cruises to Machias Seal since the 1940s, refuses to concede the island. Since it was never mentioned in the 1842 Webster-Ashburton Treaty, he insists that it was claimed by his grandfather in 1865. Thus he continues to offer puffin-watching and other birding trips to the island, ably assisted by his son John, emphasizing his views on the island by shading himself with an umbrella displaying an American flag on top.

Captain Andrew Patterson's **Bold Coast Charter Company** (259-4484) is based in Cutler, just 9 miles from Machias Seal Island, to which he also offers frequent bird-watching trips from May to August. Captain Patterson also uses his 40-foot passenger vessel *Barbara Frost* to cruise the coast, to visit the Cross Island Wildlife Refuge at the mouth of Machias Bay, and, on special request, to go to Grand Manan Island.

Idle Tours (546-2136). A 45-foot tour boat offers cruises past the Pond Island and Petit Manan lighthouses from Milbridge. At **Machias Bay Boat Tours** (259-3338), Route 191, East Machias, Captain Martha Jordan offers tours aboard the six-passenger, 34-foot, fiberglass, diesel-powered *Martha Ann*. Destinations include Cross Island and one of several 1700-year-old petroglyph sites in the area.

CANOEING AND SEA KAYAKING

The **Machias River,** fed by the five Machias lakes, drops through the backwoods with technically demanding rapids and takes 3 to 6 days to run. The Narraguagus and East Machias Rivers are also good for trips of 2 to 4 days. For rentals, lessons, advice, and guided tours, see **Sunrise County Canoe Expeditions** (454-7708) in the "Calais and the St. Croix Valley" part of this chapter. **Eastern Outdoor Adventures** (255-4210 or 1-800-396-7664), Machias, offers guided tours to a choice of destinations: the Indian petroglyphs, Bucks Harbor, Roque Bluffs, Cobscook Bay, and Great Wass and Head Harbor Islands. Beginners welcome. At **Machias Bay Sea Kayaking** (259-3338), registered guides Martha and Rick Jordan (see *Boat Excursions*) also offer year-round guided kayaking tours. **Kissing Fish Dive Shack and Kayak Rack** (255-3567), 19 East Main Street (Route 1), Machias, also offers guided tours and kayak rentals.

DIVING

Kissing Fish Dive Shack and Kayak Rack (see above) offers scuba equipment and dive tours.

FISHING

Salmon fishing is the reason many people come to this area (see Cherryfield under *To See*); the Narraguagus and Machias Rivers are popular places to fish mid-May through early June. Six Mile Lake in Marshfield (6 miles north of Machias on Route 192), with picnic facilities, shelters, and a boat ramp, is known for trout. **Eastern Outdoor Adventures** (see *Kayaking*) offers guided fishing expeditions. For information about licenses, guides, and fish, write to the regional headquarters of the **Inland Fisheries and Wildlife Department,** Machias 04654.

GOLF

Great Cove Golf Course (434-2981), Jonesboro Road, Roque Bluffs, offers nine holes, water views, clubhouse, rental clubs, and carts.

Herring Cove Golf Course (506-752-2449), in the Herring Cove Provincial Park (open mid-May to mid-November), has nine holes, a clubhouse restaurant, and rentals.

HIKING

(Also see West Quoddy Light State Park under *To See* and Schoodic Mountain in the "Bar Harbor and Acadia Area" chapter.)

Petit Manan National Wildlife Refuge, Petit Manan Point, Steuben (6 miles off Route 1 on Pigeon Hill Road). A varied area with pine stands, cedar swamps, blueberry barrens, marshes, and great birding; a 5-mile shore path hugs the woods and coastline.

Great Wass Island. A 1540-acre tract at the southern tip of the Jonesport-Addison peninsula. The interior of the island supports one of Maine's largest stands of jack pine and has coastal peat lands maintained by the Maine chapter of The Nature Conservancy. There is a choice of trails; we prefer the 2-mile trek along the shore to Little Cape Point, where children can clamber on the smooth rocks for hours. Bring a picnic.

Western Head, off Route 191, 11 miles south of East Machias. Take your first right after the Baptist church onto Destiny Bay Road and follow it to the end. Parking is minimal but there is a sign. It's an easy 3- to 4-mile loop trail through woods to the shore, with views of the dramatic high rocks. Maintained by the Maine Coast Heritage Trust, Brunswick (729-7366).

The Bold Coast. Look for the trailhead some 4 miles east of Cutler Harbor. Maine's Bureau of Parks and Recreation has constructed a 5½-mile loop trail from Route 191 to the rugged cliffs and along the shore, overlooking Grand Manan Channel. There are also two primitive campsites. This is one we haven't yet hiked ourselves but friends tell us to wear serious hiking boots and to allow the better part of a day. For details, call 827-5936.

Roosevelt Campobello International Park. At the tourist information center, pick up a trail map. We recommend the trail from Southern Head to the Duck Ponds. Seals frequently sun on the ledges off Lower Duck Pond and loons are often seen off Liberty Point. Along this dramatic shoreline at the southern end of the island, also look for whales July through September. At Eagle Hill Bog a boardwalk spans a peat bog with interpretive panels.

PICNICKING

McClellan Park in Milbridge, 5 miles south of town at Baldwin's Head, overlooking the Atlantic and Narraguagus Bay (from Route 1, follow Wyman Road to the park gates). A town park on 10½ acres donated in 1926 by George McClellan, a one-time mayor of New York City and later a professor of economic history at Princeton. There's no charge for walking or picnicking. (Also see *Campgrounds* and *Hiking*.)

SPECIAL LEARNING PROGRAMS (ADULT)

SummerKeys (733-2316; winter 201-451-2338), 6 Bayview Street, Lubec. July through mid-August. New York piano teacher Bruce Potterton offers a series of programs limited to 12 students per week. Beginners to more advanced are welcome. Lodging is at local B&Bs.

Art workshops. At this writing several summer workshops are offered in this area. Check with Susan Dowley (733-4610) in Lubec, Sharp Studio (546-4460) in Milbridge, and the Machias Bay Area chamber.

SWIMMING

Roque Bluffs State Park, Roque Bluffs (6 miles off Route 1). There is a pebble beach on the ocean, frequently too windy to use even in August. A sheltered sand beach on a freshwater pond is the ideal place for children. But the water is COLD. Tables, grills, changing areas with vault toilets, and a children's playground.

Gardner Lake, Chases Mills Road, East Machias, offers freshwater swimming, a picnic area, and a boat launch. **Six Mile Lake,** Route 192, North Machias, is also good for a dip. On Beals Island, the **Backfield Area,** Alley's Bay, offers saltwater swimming.

WHALE-WATCHING

The unusually high tides in the Bay of Fundy seem to foster ideal feeding grounds for right, minke, and humpback whales and for porpoises and dolphins. East Quoddy Head on Campobello and West Quoddy Head in Lubec are favored viewing spots. Two father-and-son teams, the Nortons (see *Puffin-Watching and Boat Excursions*) and the Harrises (see *Boat Excursions* under "Eastport"), offer whale-watching cruises. **Cline Marine** (506-529-4188) also offers 2-hour whale-watching cruises from Head Harbour on Campobello Island.

LODGING

INNS AND BED & BREAKFASTS

Entries are listed geographically, heading east.

☞✐**Ricker House** (546-2780), Cherryfield 04622. Open year-round. A classic Federal house built in 1803 with a double parlor, furnished comfortably with plenty of books and an inviting country kitchen. There are three guest rooms (two with river views), nicely furnished with antiques and old quilts, sharing one bath. A path leads to a picnic table by the river, and the tennis courts across the road are free; there are also lawn games:

horseshoes and croquet. The Conways keep a two-volume photo album, "Adventures from Ricker House," on their coffee table and are delighted to help guests explore the area, especially on foot or by canoe. $50 per couple ($10 per extra person), $45 single, includes a full breakfast.

Moonraker Bed & Breakfast (546-2191), Route 1, Milbridge 04658. Bill and Ingrid Handrahan's very Victorian but informal, middle-of-town house with a big porch and within walking distance of restaurants, movies, and the tidal Narraguagus River. The five guest rooms range from a tiny but inviting single ($40) with a stained-glass window and shared bath to a double with private bath ($60). Inquire about art workshop weeks.

Pleasant Bay Bed & Breakfast (483-4490), PO Box 222, West Side Road, Addison 04606. Open year-round. After raising six children and a number of llamas in New Hampshire, Leon and Joan Yeaton returned to Joan's girlhood turf, cleared this land, and built themselves a large, gracious house with many windows and a deck and porch overlooking the Pleasant River. Opening onto the deck is a large, sunny room with couches, a piano, and a fireplace, and an adjoining open kitchen and dining room, all with water views. A more formal living room is well stocked with puzzles and books for foggy days. This is a 110-acre working llama farm, and guests are invited to meander the wooded trails down to the bay, either accompanied or unaccompanied by llamas. There are three guest rooms, a particularly attractive one with private bath, all with water views. $45–70 per couple ($10 per additional child) includes a splendid breakfast of fresh fruit and, if you're lucky, Joan's popover/pancake. Evening meals are available by prior arrangement.

Tootsie's Bed and Breakfast (497-5414), RFD 1, RRO, Box 252, Jonesport 04649. This was the first bed & breakfast in Washington County, and it is still one of the nicest. Charlotte Beal (Tootsie, as her grandchildren call her) offers two rooms—nothing fancy, but homey and spanking clean—and routinely makes a 6 AM breakfast for guests who need to leave at 6:45 to catch Barna Norton's boat (see *Puffin-Watching*). The shipshape house sits in a cluster of lobstermen's homes on the fringe of this fishing village, handy to Great Wass Island. $25–40 includes a full breakfast. Pets are occasionally accommodated if they are small and well behaved.

Raspberry Shores B&B (497-2463), Route 187, Jonesport 04649. Geri Taylor's Victorian home in the middle of town offers three rooms with shared bath, water views, and full breakfasts. It's right next door to Barna Norton, an obvious place to stay if you are puffin-watching with the captain. $50 per couple.

Riverside Inn & Restaurant (255-4134), Route 1, East Machias 04630. Open year-round. This Victorian house fronts on the road, but the back rooms and deck overlook the East Machias River. Tom and Carol Paul owned an antiques shop in Newport before creating this attractive way station, which is pure 1890s—right down to the antique linens. Note the

BRIAN SWARTZ

Living room in the Roosevelt Cottage on Campobello Island

old train-baggage rack over the claw-foot tub. There are two upstairs rooms in the main house (private baths) and two guest house suites with kitchen facilities, and balconies overlooking the river. $58–85 includes a full breakfast; the specialty is blueberry-stuffed French toast. Carol is well known in the area for the quality of her dinners (see *Dining Out*).

Little River Lodge (259-4437), Box 237, Cutler 04626. Open May through October. Built in 1845 as a logging camp, converted to a hotel in 1870 when the Eastern Steamship ferries stopped here. Less appealing than before it changed hands but still comfortable and the only place to stay in Cutler. $50–65 double includes breakfast.

Downeast Farm House (733-2496), Route 189, Trescott (mailing address: RR 1, Box 3860, Lubec 04652). Open year-round. Just one guest room but a real find. Priscilla and Henry Merrill summered in this vintage 1800 house for many years before retiring here and converting a wing—an attractively furnished living room as well as room and bath—into guest quarters. They also maintain a small antiques shop. Knowledgeable, interesting hosts, they delight in steering guests to nearby West Quoddy Head and Campobello Island. $65 includes a full country breakfast.

Home Port Inn (733-2077; 1-800-457-2077), 45 Main Street, Lubec 04652. Open April through October. Tim and Miyoko Carman offer seven antiques-furnished rooms (two on the ground floor, all with private baths) in a gracious 1880s hilltop home. Each room is individually furnished and one, with twin beds and a water view, is quite grand. While the dining room is popular (see *Dining Out*), guests have their own common space, an inviting living room with TV. $60–75 includes continental breakfast.

Peacock House (733-2403), 27 Summer Street, Lubec 04652. Open May 15 to October 15. An 1860s house on a quiet side street, home to four generations of the Peacock family (owners of the major local cannery). The five guest rooms, like the formal common rooms, are immaculate and furnished with souvenirs from the far-flung places where Chet and Veda Childs previously lived; one room is handicapped accessible. No children under 7. $60–80 with a full breakfast.

Lubecker Gast Haus (733-4385), 31 Main Street, Lubec 04652. Open June through September. Sited on a hilltop with sweeping water views and rear deck overlooking the garden. Robert and Irmgard Swiecicki hail originally from Lubec, Germany, and have furnished their four guest rooms with flair. $65 includes a full breakfast.

☞ **The Owen House** (506-752-2977), Welshpool, Campobello, New Brunswick E0G 3H0, Canada. Open May through September. This amazing inn is reason enough to visit Campobello. Probably the most historic house on the island, it was built in 1829 by Admiral William Fitzwilliam Owen, son of the British captain to whom the island was granted in 1769. Joyce Morrell, an artist who maintains one room as her gallery, has furnished the nine guest rooms (five with private baths) with friendly antiques, handmade quilts, and good art. Guests gather around an immense breakfast table in the formal dining room, also around one of the many fireplaces in the evening. There are 10 acres of land, and you can walk to the Welshpool dock and take the ferry to Deer Island and back to get out on the bay. Birders are particularly welcome. $73–83 Canadian plus 11 percent tax (no GST) includes a full breakfast.

COTTAGES

The choice of rental cottages in Washington County has increased substantially in recent years. The Machias Bay chamber publishes the "Vacation Rental Guide"; a number of additional listings are in the booklet "Maine Guide to Camp & Cottage Rentals," available from the **Maine Publicity Bureau** (see *Information* in "What's Where in Maine"). Summer rentals in this area still begin at around $300 per week.

Micmac Farm Guest Cabins (255-3008), Machiasport 04655. Open May to November. Best known for her restaurant (see *Dining Out*), Barbara Dunn also offers several housekeeping cabins. Each has two double beds and a view of the Machias River through sliding glass doors. A real find at $50–60 daily per unit, $300–375 per week.

MOTELS

Machias Motor Inn (255-4861), Route 1 next to Helen's Resturant, Machias 04654. Bob and Joan Carter maintain a two-story, 35-unit motel; most rooms are standard units, each with two double, extra-long beds, cable TV, and a phone. Rooms feature decks overlooking the Machias River. There are six efficiency units, and Helen's Restaurant, serving all three meals, is part of the complex. A new indoor pool is a welcome addition if you are traveling this foggy coast with kids. $50–65 double, $85 for efficiencies. Pets are accepted.

Blueberry Patch Inn (434-5411), Route 1, Jonesboro 04648. This spick-and-span motel is next door to the White House Restaurant. Each unit has a refrigerator, air-conditioning, phone, TV, and coffee; two efficiencies, a pool, and sun deck surrounded by berries. $32–48 in-season.

Eastland Motel (733-5501), Lubec 04652. A good bet if you are taking the kids to Campobello and want a clean, comfortable room with TV; $50–60.

CAMPGROUNDS

McClellan Park, Milbridge. Open Memorial through Columbus Day. See *Picnicking* under *To Do* for more on this dramatically sited, town-owned park. Free for day use but $3 for tenting, $5 for full campsites; 18 campsites and water are available, but no showers. For details, call the town hall at 546-2422.

Henry Point Campground, Kelly Point Road, Jonesport. Open April through November. Surrounded on three sides by water, this is another great town-owned campground that's usually got space (its crunch weekend is July 4). Neither showers nor water is available, but you can shower and use the coin-operated laundry at the Jonesport Shipyard across the cove. Good water is also available from an outside faucet at the town hall. This is a put-in place for sea kayaks. Turn off Route 187 at the purple house.

Herring Cove Provincial Park (506-752-2396), Campobello Island. Adjoining the Roosevelt Campobello International Park is this campground offering 87 campsites; there's a beach, a golf course, and extensive hiking trails.

(Also see Cobscook Bay State Park in "Eastport and Cobscook Bay.")

WHERE TO EAT

DINING OUT

Micmac Farm Restaurant (255-3008), Machiasport. Open year-round (except for 2 weeks at Christmas), Tuesday through Saturday 6 PM–9 PM, by reservation. Located down a bumpy dirt road off Route 92. You wouldn't think anyone could find it, but it tends to be full most summer evenings. The restaurant is in an exquisite riverside house built in 1776 by Ebenezer Gardner, a patriot-refugee from Nova Scotia. Just 25 diners can be seated in the low-beamed dining room, and meals are served by candlelight. From her minute kitchen, Barbara Dunn produces a choice of five entrées, which might include tenderloin Stroganoff, lobster Graziella, and filet mignon bordelaise. Full dinners run $16–18. BYOB, since the town is dry.

Riverside Inn (255-4134), East Machias. Dinner nightly by reservation. Tables line the sun porch overlooking the East Machias River and fill a lacy, flowery dining room. Innkeeper Carol Paul's reputation as a chef is well deserved. You might dine on Riverside western beef ($16.95), sautéed pork tenderloin marinated in orange wine sauce ($15.95), or seafood pasta ($15.95); dinner prices include appetizers, breads, dessert, and beverage. BYOB.

Seafarer's Wife (497-2365), Main Street, Jonesport. Open Tuesday through Saturday, 5:30–8:30 PM by reservation only; closed January. Two very Victorian rooms, with long-skirted waitresses serving a surprisingly wide choice of entrées ranging from a vegetarian plate ($15.95) and stuffed baked chicken ($14.95) to Fisherman's Bounty, a baked medley of shrimp, lobster, halibut, scallops, and more ($19.95). Faye Carver is the owner-chef and her local reputation is sterling. Dinner prices include hors d'oeuvres, soup, salad, bread, and beverage. BYOB.

The Home Port Inn Restaurant (733-2077), 45 Main Street, Lubec. Open nightly Memorial Day weekend through September. Recognized as the best place to dine in the Campobello/Lubec area, this attractive sunken dining room in the back of an inn is small, so it may be wise to reserve. The menu is large and reasonably priced. Specialties include Down East scampi (a seafood medley of fresh lobster, scallops, and salmon sautéed in a scampi butter with artichoke hearts and black olives) and fresh poached salmon ($12.99).

EATING OUT
Entries are listed geographically, heading east.

Milbridge House (546-2020), Main Street, Milbridge. Open 10:30–8, a great family-owned restaurant that's bigger and more attractive than it looks from the road. Don't pass up the pies. Beer and wine are served.

The Red Barn (546-7721), Main Street (junction of Routes 1 and 1A), Milbridge. Open daily year-round, 6 AM. There is a counter in the back, an abundance of deep booths in the main, pine-paneled dining room, and more seating in the overflow "banquet" room. The menu is large: pastas, burgers, steak, seafood, and fried chicken. Children's menu, great cream pies.

Cherryfield Inn Restaurant (546-3336), Cherryfield. Open year-round 6 AM–9 PM; the $6.95 Friday-night fish-fry is outstanding. Nothing fancy but good road food and in the right place if you are shortcutting on Route 182 (see *Getting There*). We prefer the back to the front room.

The Blue Beary (546-2052), Route 1, Cherryfield. Open 11–9, a friendly dining room; also a picnic area featuring fresh-dough pizza (try the garlic and cheese), homemade soups and pies.

Perry's Seafood, Route 1, Columbia. Open daily 6 AM–9 PM. Easy to pass without noticing, favored by locals for dinner as well as other meals; try the homemade onion rings and the special of the day.

Tall Barney, Main Street, Jonesport. Open 7–7. Don't be put off by the exterior of this local gathering spot, set back behind its parking lot across from the access to the big bridge. Particularly welcoming for breakfast on a foggy morning (papers are stacked on the counter). *Note:* The long table down the middle of the front room is reserved for the local lobstermen, who come drifting in one by one.

The White House (434-2792), Route 1, Jonesboro. Open 5 AM–9 PM. It's not white but the awnings are red-striped. Inside are cheery blue booths, a counter, and friendly service. Memorable breakfasts, outstanding fish chowder (much better than the lobster); specialties include fried seafood platters and delectable pies.

Ocean Farms Fish Market (255-3474), Route 1, Machias. Open year-round, daily 11–6. Primarily a fish market, this obvious winner (opened on the commercial strip south of town in '96) serves chowder and crabmeat rolls, and stocks local delicacies like Becky's mussel salad. At this writing the tables are weather-dependent (outside with umbrellas) but owner Rebecca Hudson promises a small dining space soon.

Helen's Restaurant (255-6506), 32 Main Street, Machias (north of town on the water). Open 6 AM–8 PM. Geared to bus groups en route from Campobello to Bar Harbor, but there's plenty of room for everybody. Generous servings: a wide choice of seafood, meat entrées, salads, fish stews, and sandwiches. "Whipped" pies are a specialty: strawberry, blueberry, and a dozen more. Children's plates.

Blue Bird Ranch (255-3351), Lower Main Street (Route 1). Open year-round for all three meals. A diner atmosphere for breakfast and lunch, but the dining room (with banquet room) features live boiled lobster, seafood, salad bar, homemade pies, and cocktails at dinner. New name and ownership in '96 have put this high on our family dining list.

Joyce's Lobster House, Route 1, Machias (north of town). Open daily April to September for lunch and dinner. The best bet in town for dinner, with a menu that also includes an antipasto salad and eggplant parmigiana, good fish chowder, pleasant atmosphere.

The Waterside Restaurant (733-2500), the Landing, Lubec. Open May through Labor Day, 11 until sunset. Home Port Inn owner Tim Carman has turned a former sardine-packing warehouse into a waterside eatery with picnic tables on the water. We found the prices higher than at other local places but what the heck: good crab rolls, lobster, chowder, specials like ribs; beer served. If all the outdoor tables are taken it's customary to share, and you can always request that another table be moved out (this is still a warehouse with machinery for moving boxes of sea urchins).

43 Water Street (733-0903), Lubec. Open Monday through Friday 11–7. An oasis, along with the neighboring laundry, in Lubec's old main street, one that's otherwise pretty much boarded up. Owner Carolyn Monroe cooks everything to order.

Lupine Lodge (752-2555), Campobello. Open 12–9. Under new ownership, this former log "cottage" features a great hearth and has regained its old charm. The dinner menu ranges from $6.95 to $16.95 and friends recommend the sautéed Fundy haddock. Full license.

Herring Cove Restaurant (752-2467), Campobello. A café at the golf club, good for breakfast, lunch, and informal dinner, specializing in fish-and-chips; vague views of the water.

ENTERTAINMENT

Milbridge Theater (546-2038), Main Street, Milbridge. Open nightly May through November, 7:30 show time; Saturday and Sunday matinees for children's films; all seats $3.75. A very special theater: a refurbished movie house featuring first-run and art films with truly affordable prices. Fresh popcorn, ice cream parlor.

University of Maine, Machias (255-3313, ext. 284), offers both a winter and summer series of plays, performances, and concerts.

Downriver Theater Productions (255-4997) stages plays June through August at Gay's Wreath Building, Marshfield Ridge Road, Machias. Productions are a mix of safe musicals (*The Sound of Music, Cabaret*) and original plays. Tickets are $8 per adult, $7 for seniors and students.

Machias Bay Chamber Concerts (255-3889), Center Street Congregational Church, Machias. A series of six chamber music concerts, July through early August, Tuesday at 8 PM. Top groups such as the Kneisel Hall Chamber Players and the Vermeer Quartet are featured.

SELECTIVE SHOPPING

Entries are listed geographically, heading east.

Sea-Witch (546-7495), Milbridge. Describing itself as "the biggest little gift shop in Washington County," this is a trove of trinkets and treasures: collector dolls, spatterware, stuffed animals, seafood, and berry products.

Columbia Falls Pottery (483-4075; 1-800-235-2512), Main Street, Columbia Falls. Open year-round. Striking, bright, sophisticated creations by April Adams: mugs, platters, kitchenware, lamps, wind chimes, and more, featuring lupine and sunflower designs; catalog.

Crossroads Vegetables (497-2641), posted from Route 187 (off Route 1), Jonesport. Open daily except Saturday, 9–5:30 in-season. Bonnie and Arnold Pearlman built their house, windmill, sauna, and barn, and have reclaimed acres of productive vegetable garden from the surrounding woods. In addition to their outstanding vegetables (salad lovers get their greens picked to order; Bonnie adds the edible parts of flowers like nasturtium), they also sell the hand-hollowed wooden bowls that Arnold carves all winter and the dried-flower wreaths that Bonnie makes.

Whitney Originals (255-3392; 1-800-562-7963), 5 Bridge Street, Machias. While Washington County is studded with Christmas-wreath makers, David Whitney is the first to also make decorative year-round wreaths. Tasteful and fragrant, they range from a "woodland wreath" on a blueberry vine base ($28.95) to an elaborate Floral Fantasy ($56.95). Look for the display on Route 1 just south of the bridge.

Country Duckling (255-8063), 1 Water Street, Machias. Locally made handcrafted gifts.

Downeast 5 & 10 Cents (255-8850), Water Street, Machias. Open Monday through Saturday 9–5 and until 8 on Friday. A superb, old-fashioned Ben Franklin store: two stories of crammed aisles.

Machias Hardware Co. (255-6581; 1-800-543-2250), 26 Main Street. An unexpected source of reasonably priced herbs and spices in 2-ounce and 1-pound packages.

Connie's Clay of Fundy (255-4574), Route 1, East Machias. Open year-round. Connie Harter-Bagley's combination studio/shop is filled with her distinctive glazed earthenware in deep colors with minimal design. Bowls, pie plates, platters, lamps, and a variety of small essentials like garlic jars and ring boxes.

Cottage Garden (733-9792), North Lubec Road, Lubec. Open in-season Wednesday through Sunday 10–5; 4.5 miles from Lubec. Gretchen Mead welcomes visitors to her steadily expanding perennial gardens. A short trail through woods leads to a picnic meadow, and a deck behind the shop (herbs, flower wreaths, toys, Christmas ornaments, bird-houses) overlooks the garden and a small pond.

CHRISTMAS WREATHS

Wreath-making is a major industry in this area. You can order in the fall and take delivery of a freshly made wreath right before Christmas. Prices quoted include delivery. Sources are: **Cape Split Wreaths** (483-2983), Box 447, Route 1, Addison 04606; **Simplicity Wreath** (483-2780), Sunset Point, Harrington 04643; **The Wreath Shoppe** (483-4598), Box 358, Oak Point Road, Harrington 04643 (wreaths decorated with cones, berries, and reindeer moss); and **Maine Coast Balsam** (255-3301), Box 458, Machias 04654 (decorations include cones, red berries, and bow). Also see Whitney Originals, above.

SPECIAL EVENTS

June: Last weekend: the **Down East Rodeo,** Machias fairgrounds.

July: **Independence Day** celebrations in **Jonesport/Beals** (lobster boat races, easily viewed from the bridge); **Cherryfield** (parade and fireworks); and **Steuben** (firemen's lobster picnic and parade); also in **Cutler** and **Machias.**

Last weekend: **Milbridge Days** include a parade, a dance and lobster dinner, and the big feature: the greased codfish relay race.

August: **Wild Blueberry Festival** and **Machias Craft Festival** (third weekend) in downtown Machias, sponsored by Penobscot Valley Crafts and Center Street Congregational Church: concerts, food, major crafts fair, and live entertainment.

EASTPORT AND COBSCOOK BAY

With its flat, haunting light and blank, staring storefronts, Eastport has an end-of-the-world feel and suggests an Edward Hopper painting. The town was occupied by the British for four years during the War of 1812, a tale told in the Barracks Museum. One of the old cannons used to fend off the enemy still stands in front of the Peavey Library. But the town's big claim to fame remains the fact that the sardine-canning process was invented here by Julius Wolfe in 1875, and not long thereafter 18 canneries were operating here.

A "city" of 2500 people (less than half its turn-of-the-century population), Eastport remains a working deep-water port, and large freighters frequently dock at the municipal pier to take on woodland products. The town is also a base for salmon farming but there are many gaps in the old waterfront, now walled in pink granite to form Overlook Park.

This is a good spot from which to get out on Passamaquoddy Bay in an excursion boat, to watch the area's summer gathering of whales, and to view Old Sow, a whirlpool off Deer Island that's billed as the world's second largest. If nothing else, take the small ferry that runs every hour to Deer Island and back.

Eastport is on Moose Island, connected to the mainland by a series of causeways linking other islands. In the center of the Pleasant Point Indian Reservation, situated on one of these islands, the Waponahki Museum tells the story of the Passamaquoddy tribe, past and present.

GUIDANCE

Eastport Chamber of Commerce (853-4644), 78 Water Street, Eastport 04631. Open late May to mid-September, Monday through Friday 11–3. At this writing, plans call for adding a Quoddy Maritime Museum to the storefront visitors center.

TO SEE

Waponahki Museum & Resource Center (853-4001), Route 190, Pleasant Point. Open weekdays 8:30–11 and 12–4. Easy to miss, a small red building near the big (closed) IGA. Curator Joseph Nicholas has created an outstanding museum with photos, tools, baskets, and crafts that tell the story of the Passamaquoddy tribe. A good place to inquire about where to shop for Native American crafts.

Barracks Museum (853-6630) 74 Washington Street, Eastport. Open Memorial Day through Labor Day, Tuesday through Saturday 1–4. Originally part of Fort Sullivan, occupied by the British during the War of 1812, this house has been restored to its 1820s appearance as an officers' quarters and displays old photos and memorabilia about Eastport in its golden era.

Reversing Salt Water Falls. From Route 1 in West Pembroke, take the local road out along Leighton Neck, which brings you to a 140-acre park with hiking trails and picnic sites that view the incoming tidal current as it passes between Mahar's Point and Falls Island. As the salt water flows along at upward of 25 knots, it strikes a series of rocks, resulting in rapids.

TO DO

AIRPLANE RIDES
Quoddy Air (853-0997) offers scenic rides, whale-watching, and charters.
BOAT EXCURSIONS
Whale-watching (853-4303). Captain George Harris and his son Butch offer 3-hour cruises of Passamaquoddy Bay.
Ferry to Deer Island and Campobello. For details about **East Coast Ferries Ltd.** (506-747-2159), based on Deer Island, see *Getting Around* in the chapter introduction.
CANOEING
See "Calais and the St. Croix Valley."

GREEN SPACE

WALKS
Shackford Head (posted from Route 190 south of Eastport) is a new 95-acre park with a mile-long trail from the parking lot to a "viewpoint" overlooking Campobello and Lubec in one direction and Cobscook Bay in the other.
Moosehorn National Wildlife Refuge, Edmunds. Some 6700 acres bounded by Cobscook Bay and the mouth of the Dennys and Whiting Rivers, with several miles of rocky shoreline.
Gleason Point, Perry. Take the right just before The Wigwam on Route 1 (see *Selective Shopping*) and follow signs to the beach and boat landing.

LODGING

INNS AND BED & BREAKFASTS
☞ **Weston House** (853-2907; 1-800-853-2907), 26 Boynton Street, Eastport 04631. Open year-round. An elegant, Federal-style house built in 1810 by a Harvard graduate who became a local politician. There are five large guest rooms, one with a working fireplace, views of the bay and gardens, antiques. You can have the room in which John James Audubon slept on his way to Labrador in 1833. Rates are $53.50–74.90 for a double, including state tax, a sumptuous breakfast in the formal dining room, and sherry. Dinner and a picnic lunch are also available. The common rooms are furnished with Oriental rugs and wing chairs; but if you want to put

QUODDY TIDES

Deer Island Ferry and Landing at Eastport

your feet up, there is a very comfortable back room with books and a TV, and the gardens are also good places for relaxing. Jett and John Peterson decorate the house for holidays and enjoy guests on all occasions.

☞✐**Todd House** (853-2328), Todd's Head, Eastport 04631. Open year-round. A restored 1775 Cape with great water views. Breakfast is served in the common room in front of the huge old fireplace. In 1801, men met here to charter a Masonic Order, and in 1861 the house became a temporary barracks when Todd's Head was fortified. The house has changed little in a century. The four large double rooms vary in decor, view, and access to baths ($45–55). There are also two efficiency suites ($70–80), both with water views. Guests are welcome to use the deck and barbecue. Innkeeper Ruth McInnis welcomes well-behaved children and pets.

The Inn at Eastport (853-4307), 13 Washington Street, Eastport 04631. An early-19th-century house built by the owner of a schooner fleet, now a comfortable, welcoming B&B with four rooms, one with a canopy bed, all with antiques and private baths. Guests can gather in two front parlors (one with a TV) or in the outdoor hot tub. $55–65 includes innkeeper Brenda Booker's very full breakfast, maybe Belgian waffles or scrambled eggs with salmon.

The Milliken House (853-2955), 29 Washington Street, Eastport 04631. The 1840s house built by a wharf owner retains Victorian detailing and some original furniture. Artist/innkeeper Joyce Weber maintains a large studio that guests are welcome to use. The five guest rooms share two baths. $50 single, $60 per couple, $10 per extra guest.

Lincoln House (726-3953), Dennysville 04628. After many years of maintaining this rather remote four-square, vintage 1787 mansion as a full-service inn, Mary Carol and Jerry Haggerty have scaled back to a B&B with six rooms, two front rooms with working fireplaces and private baths and four with shared; $58–85 per couple.

MOTEL

The Motel East (853-4747), 23A Water Street, Eastport 04631. This two-story motel has 14 units, some handicapped accessible, all with water views, some with balconies overlooking Campobello Island. Amenities include direct-dial phones, cable TV, some kitchenettes. $70 per night, $85 for a suite.

COTTAGES

Cinqueterre Farm Vacation Cottages (726-4766), RR1-1264 Ox Cove Road, Pembroke 04666. Gloria Christie, known as one of the area's outstanding chefs, maintains waterside cottages with choice of catered or cook-your-own meals.

CAMPGROUND

Cobscook Bay State Park (726-4412), Route 1, Dennysville. Open mid-May to mid-October. Offers 150 camping sites, most of them for tents and many with water views. There are even showers (unusual in Maine state campgrounds). The 864-acre park also offers a boat-launch area, picnicking benches, and a hiking and cross-country-ski trail. (*Cobscook* means "boiling tides.")

WHERE TO EAT

EATING OUT

The Baywatch Cafe (853-6030), 75 Water Street, Eastport. Open daily 11–9. Homemade chowders are the specialty, along with baked haddock with lobster sauce and baked scallops. As we lunched we watched paper products being loaded onto a giant Norwegian freighter at the municipal pier.

La Sardina Loca (853-2739), 28 Water Street, Eastport. Open daily 4–10 except Tuesday. "The crazy sardine" is so flashy, cheerful, and out-of-character with the rest of Water Street that you figure it's a mirage, or at best somebody's one-season stand. But it's been there for years in the former A&P with its Christmas lights, patio furniture, and posters, and a menu that's technically Mexican, including "la Sardina Loca" with hot chiles and sour cream.

New Waco Diner, Water Street, Eastport. Open year-round, Monday through Saturday 6 AM–9 PM. A friendly haven with booths and a long shiny counter; menu choices are posted on the wall behind. You can get a full roast turkey dinner; there is also beer, pizza, and great squash pie.

Crossroads Restaurant (726-5053), Route 1, "at the Waterfall," Pembroke. Open 11–9 daily. Bigger than it looks from outside, a great road-food stop, serving the best lobster roll in the area; deep-fried seafood pies are specialties; liquor served.

ENTERTAINMENT

Stage East (726-4670), a 100-seat theater in the 1887 Masonic Hall at the corner of Water and Dana Streets, summer-season performances.

SELECTIVE SHOPPING

Raye's Mustard Mill (853-4451; 1-800-853-1903), Route 190 (Washington Street), Eastport. Open daily 9–5 in summer; winter hours vary. In business since 1903, this company is billed as the country's last remaining stone-ground-mustard mill. This is the mustard in which Washington County's sardines were once packed, and it's sensational. Try the samples in **The Pantry.**

The Eastport Gallery (853-4166), 69 Water Street, Eastport. Open daily in summer. A cooperative gallery representing more than 40 local artists. Note the upstairs back balcony over the harbor.

Studio 44, 44 Water Street, Eastport, displays paintings featuring works by Philip Harvey who will do your portrait on the spot.

Earth Forms Pottery, corner of Water and Dana Streets. Daily in-season. Nationally known potter Donald Southerland specializes in large garden and patio pots.

Jim's Smoked Salmon (853-4831), 37 Washington Street, Eastport. Jim Blankman uses an old method to process the town's newest product; also rainbow steelhead trout. Will ship anywhere.

The Wigwam and **The Trading Post,** both on Route 1 in Perry, are outlets for local Passamaquoddy crafts.

Fountain Books, Main Street, Eastport. A funky former pharmacy filled with books, retaining the old soda fountain, adding cappuccino.

SPECIAL EVENTS

July: **Independence Day** is celebrated in **Pembroke** (parade, Canoe races) and for a week in **Eastport,** with parades, an air show, and fireworks. Eastport's is the first flag in the United States to be raised on July 4 itself (at dawn). **Cannery Wharf Boat Race** (last weekend).

Mid-August: **Annual Indian Ceremonial Days,** Pleasant Point Reservation. A celebration of Passamaquoddy culture climaxing with dances in full regalia.

September: **Eastport Salmon Festival,** the weekend after Labor Day—a celebration of Eastport's salmon industry; salmon, trout, and Maine potatoes are grilled dockside, and free tours of fish farms in the bay are offered, along with live entertainment, games, and an art show, antiques auction, fishing derby.

CALAIS AND THE ST. CROIX VALLEY

GUIDANCE

Calais Information Center (454-2211), 7 Union Street, Calais. Open year-round, daily 8–6 July through October 15, otherwise 9–5 (rest rooms). Operated by the Maine Publicity Bureau, a source of brochures for all of Maine as well as the local area. Though it's not set up as a walk-in information center, the **Greater Calais Area Chamber of Commerce** (454-2308) is also helpful.

Grand Lake Stream Chamber of Commerce, PO Box 124, Grand Lake Stream 04637. Request the brochure listing local accommodations and outfitters and get a map showing hiking/mountain biking trails.

GETTING THERE

By car: The direct route to Calais from points west of Washington County is Route 9, the Airline Highway. From the Machias area, take Route 191.

TO SEE

Calais. The largest city in Washington County, Calais (pronounced *cal-us*) is a busy border-crossing point and shopping center for eastern Washington County. Its present population is 4000, roughly 2000 less than it was in the 1870s, the decade in which its fleet of sailing vessels numbered 176.

Moosehorn National Wildlife Refuge (454-3521), PO Box 1077, Calais. Established in 1937, this area is the northeast end of a chain of wildlife and migratory bird refuges extending from Florida to Maine, managed by the US Fish and Wildlife Service. The refuge comprises two units, some 20 miles apart. The larger, 16,000-acre area is in Baring, 5 miles north of Calais on Route 1. Look for eagles, which seem to be nesting each spring at the intersection of Charlotte Road and Route 1.

Grand Lake Stream. A remote but famous resort community on West Grand Lake, with access to the Grand Lake chain. Grand Lake Stream claims to have been the world's biggest tannery town for some decades before 1874. Fishing is the big lure now: landlocked salmon, lake trout, smallmouth bass, also pickerel and white perch. Some of the state's outstanding fishing lodges and camps are clustered here and there are many good and affordable lakeside rental camps, a find for families. Local innkeepers can get you into the historical museum, a trove of Native American artifacts, cannery-era photos, and canoe molding. Inquire about hiking/biking trails and guided kayaking.

St. Croix Island Overlook, Red Beach. Eight miles south of Calais on Route 1, the view is of the island on which Samuel de Champlain and Sieur de Monts established the first white settlement in North America north of Florida. That was in 1604. Using the island as a base, Champlain explored and mapped the coast of New England as far south as Cape Cod.

TO DO

CANOEING
Sunrise Canoe Expeditions (454-7708), Cathance Lake, Grove Post Office 04638. March to October. Offers advice, canoe rentals, and guided trips down the Grand Lake chain of lakes and the St. Croix River along the Maine–New Brunswick border; good for a 3- to 6-day run spring through fall. We did this trip with Sunrise (putting in at Vanceboro) and highly recommend it. In business more than 20 years, Sunrise is headed by photographer and naturalist Martin Brown; expeditions to the Arctic and Rio Grande are offered as well as to the Machias, St. John, and St. Croix Rivers. Canoes for local use are $25 per day.

FISHING
Salmon is the big lure. Ranging from 8 to 20 pounds, Atlantic salmon are taken by fly-anglers in the Dennys and St. Croix Rivers, mid-May through early July. **Grand Lake Stream** is the focal point for dozens of lakes, ponds, and streams known for smallmouth bass and landlocked salmon (May through mid-June). There are also chain pickerel, lake trout, and brook trout. Fishing licenses, available for 3 days to a season, are also necessary for ice fishing. For information on fishing guides, lodges, and rules, write to the **Regional Headquarters of the Inland Fisheries and Wildlife Department,** Machias 04653.

GOLF
St. Croix Golf Club, Calais. A tricky nine-hole course on the banks of the St. Croix River.

SWIMMING
Reynolds Beach on Meddybemps Lake by the town pier in Meddybemps (Route 191) is open daily 9 AM–sunset. Meddybemps is a very small, white, wooden village with a church, general store, and pier; a good spot for a picnic and a swim. **Red Beach** at Calais on the St. Croix River is named for the sand on these strands, which is deep red. There is also swimming in dozens of crystal-clear lakes. Inquire about access at local lodges and general stores.

LODGING

BED & BREAKFAST
Brewer House (454-2385), Route 1, PO Box 94, Robbinston 04671. Open year-round on Route 1, 12 miles south of Calais, this is a striking 1828 mansion with graceful Ionic pillars. The interior, filled with treasures amassed by antiques dealers David and Estelle Holloway, is very Victo-

Indian Days, Pleasant Point Reservation

rian. The living room and five bedrooms, not to mention the baths, are filled with fanciful pieces, and there are views of Passamaquoddy Bay across the road. $55–75 in summer ($45–65 in winter) includes a very full breakfast, not the kind you probably eat at home, elegantly served in the sunny breakfast room. Estelle sells antiques next door at The Landing.

SPORTS LODGES

Weatherby's (796-5558), Grand Lake Stream 04637. Open early May through October 15. A rambling, white, 1870s lodge with flowers along the porch, set in roses and birches by Grand Lake Stream, the small river that connects West Grand Lake with Big Lake. Ken and Charlene Sassi, celebrating their 24th season, make you feel welcome. There is a big sitting room—with piano, TV, and hearth—in the lodge; also a homey, newly redecorated dining room with a tin ceiling and better than down-home cooking (served by the owner-chef). Each of the 15 cottages is unique, but most are log-style with screened porches, bath, and a Franklin stove or fireplace. *Fishing* is what this place is about, and it's a great place for children. $83 per person double occupancy, $105 single MAP (family rates available); motorboats are $40 per day, and a guide, $125; 15 percent gratuity added. Inquire about the canoe/camping option and fly-fishing.

Leen's Lodge (796-5575), Box 40, Grand Lake Stream 04637. November 1 through April 30 write to Newport 04953 or call 368-5699. Heated cabins (one to eight bedrooms), each with a fireplace or Franklin stove and fridge, are scattered along the shore of West Grand Lake. A pine-paneled gathering space equipped with games, books, a TV, and BYOB bar and the dining room overlook the lake. $85–125 per day MAP, family rates, 15 percent gratuity; lunch, boat rentals, and guide service are extra.

Indian Rocks Camps (796-2822; 1-800-498-2821), Grand Lake Stream 04637. Open year-round. Five century-old log cabins and a central lodge compose this friendly compound that caters to families in summer as well as to fishermen, cross-country skiers, snowmobilers, and ice fishermen in winter. Amenities include miniature golf. $62 per person includes all meals; $25 per person (no meals) in the housekeeping cabins. Summer rates in cabins: $375. Inquire about fly-fishing school; guide service. Store on the premises.

Lakeside Inn and Cabins (796-2324), Princeton 04668. Open May through November. A handsome old inn with twin chimneys and seven guest rooms; also five basic housekeeping cabins on Lewy Lake (the outlet to Big Lake, also a source for the St. Croix River). Rooms in the inn are simple and nicely furnished; each has a sink. Although baths are shared, there are plenty. Betty Field is a warm, grandmotherly host. $50 per person includes all meals; $38 double, $23 single B&B in the inn; cabins from $55 per couple per day, no meals.

CAMPGROUND

Georgia Pacific's woodland office in Millinocket (723-5232) dispenses a sportsman's map and information about camping on its extensive woodland holdings ($3).

Also see Cobscook Bay State Park in "Eastport and Cobscook Bay."

WHERE TO EAT

DINING OUT

The Chandler House (454-7922), 20 Chandler Street, Calais. Open 4–11 daily except Monday. Chef-owned, specializing in seafood like blackened whitefish. Entrées $9–18.95.

Bernardini's, 89 Main Street, Calais. Open year-round for lunch and dinner except Sunday. An attractive storefront trattoria, entrées $11–20.

The Townhouse Restaurant (454-8021), 84 Main Street, Calais. Open mid-April to mid-October, daily 11–9 except Sunday. Seafood specialties include haddock with lobster sauce ($12.95).

Redclyffe Dining Room (454-3279), Route 1, Robbinston. Open 5–10 for dinner. The view of the bay is superb, and the food, we're told, is good too.

Heslin's (454-3762), Route 1, Calais (south of the village). Open May through October, 5–9. A popular local dining room specializing in steak and seafood entrées and "French cooking." Moderate.

EATING OUT

Wickachee (454-3400), 282 Main Street, Calais. Open year-round, 6 AM–10 PM. Steak and seafood with a big salad bar are the dinner specialties, but even dinner entrées start at just $4.

Angelholm (454-3066), 63 Main Street, Calais. Open early; good road food, within walking distance of the border.

SELECTIVE SHOPPING

Pine Tree Store, Grand Lake Stream. Open daily, year-round. A general store that also carries many sportsmen's essentials.

The Something Special Shop, Grand Lake Stream. Open Memorial Day through Labor Day. Joan Barton turned her garage into a gift shop more than 20 years ago, and it seems to get better every year. A nice selection of crafts and gifts.

SPECIAL EVENTS

July: **Indian Festival** and **Indian Township,** Princeton. Last weekend: **Grand Lake Stream Folk Art Festival**—bluegrass and folk music, woodsmen's skills demonstrations featuring canoe-building, crafts, dinner cooked by Maine guides.

August: **North Country Festival,** Danforth. **International Festival,** Calais—a week of events (parade, suppers, canoe and raft races).

ST. ANDREWS, NEW BRUNSWICK

As we have already mentioned, St. Andrews is much like Bar Harbor, but a Bar Harbor with the genteel charm and big hotels that it lost in the 1947 fire. The big hotel in St. Andrews is the Algonquin, a 200-room, many-gabled, neo-Tudor resort dating from 1915 and still managed by the Canadian Pacific Railroad. The Algonquin sits enthroned like a queen mother above this tidy town with loyalist street names like Queen, King, and Princess Royal. St. Andrews was founded in 1783 by British Empire loyalists, American colonists who so strongly opposed breaking away from the mother country that they had to leave the new United States after independence was won. Most came from what is now Castine, many of them unpegging their houses and bringing them along in the 1780s. Impressed by this display of loyalty, the British government made the founding of St. Andrews as painless as possible, granting them a superb site. British army engineers dug wells, built a dock, constructed a fort, and laid out the town on its present grid. Each loyalist family was also given a house lot twice the usual size. The result is an unusually gracious, largely 19th-century town, hauntingly reminiscent of Castine. The focal point remains Market Wharf, where the first settlers stepped ashore, now the cluster point for outfitters offering whale-watching, sailing, and kayaking tours, and Water Street, lined with shops specializing in British woolens and china.

GUIDANCE

St. Andrews Chamber of Commerce (506-529-2555), Reed Avenue, St. Andrews, New Brunswick EOG 2XO, Canada; office open year-round, information center, May through October.

Complete lodging listings for both St. Andrews and Grand Manan are detailed in the *New Brunswick Travel Guide,* available toll-free in Canada and the United States (1-800-561-0123), or by writing to Economic Development & Tourism, PO Box 12345, Fredericton, New Brunswick E3B 5C3, Canada.

GETTING THERE

By car: Route 1 via Calais. From the border crossing at Calais, it's just 19 miles to St. Andrews.

By car ferry: See *Getting Around* at the beginning of this chapter.

TIME

Note that New Brunswick's Atlantic time is 1 hour ahead of Maine.

TAXES

The Canadian Goods and Services Tax (GST) is a 7 percent tax imposed on food, lodging, and just about everything else in Canada. Visitors who spend more than $100 on goods and short-term accommodations will get most of it back by mailing in a Revenue Canada application and appending all receipts. New Brunswick also tacks on a food and lodging tax; the latter does not apply to smaller B&Bs.

TO SEE

Ross Memorial Museum (506-529-1824), corner of King and Montague Streets, open daily mid-June through Labor Day 10–4:30, then closed Monday until Thanksgiving. An 1824 mansion displaying the fine decorative art collection of the Reverend and Mrs. Henry Phipps Ross of Ohio.

Sheriff Andrews House Historic Site, 63 King Street. Open June to October, Monday through Saturday 9:30–4:30, Sunday from 1. An 1820 house with fine detailing, nicely interpreted by costumed guides.

Ministers Island Historic Site (506-529-5081), Chamcook, New Brunswick. Open June to mid-October. One of the grandest estates, built around 1890 on an island connected by a "tidal road" (accessible only at low tide) to St. Andrews, **Covenhoven** is a 50-room mansion with 17 bedrooms, a vast drawing room, a bathhouse, and a gigantic and ornate livestock barn. The builder was Sir William Van Horne, the driving force in constructing the Canadian Pacific Railway. Because of the tides and nature of the island, only set, 2-hour guided tours are offered. Phone before coming.

Huntsman Marine Science Centre (506-529-1200), off Route 127, Brandy Cove Road, St. Andrews. Open daily. A nonprofit aquaculture research center sponsoring educational programs and cruises; the aquarium-museum features hundreds of living plants and animals found in the Quoddy region, including resident harbor seals.

Atlantic Salmon Centre (506-529-4581), in Chamcook, 5 miles east of St. Andrews on Route 127. Open spring to fall, 10–5, until 6 in July and August. A staffed interpretation area dramatizes the history of Atlantic salmon and current conservation efforts. A nature trail threads the salmon nursery area and adjoining woods.

Kingsbrae Horticultural Garden (506-529-3335), 220 King Street, St. Andrews. Due to be completed in 1998 but tours of these 10-acre, elaborately re-created formal gardens should be offered in '97. A tearoom and art gallery in a former mansion on the grounds are planned.

TO DO

BIKE TOURS

Outdoor Adventure Company (506-529-4181; 1-800-365-3855), St. Andrews. Historic tours of the town, shore and 3- to 4-day inn-to-inn bike tours.

GOLF

Algonquin golf course (see *Resort*) is New Brunswick's oldest (it dates from 1894) and is considered its best. The 18-hole seaside course was designed by Donald Ross. There is also a nine-hole "Woodland" course. Both are open to the public.

HORSEBACK RIDING

Kerrs Ridge Riding Stables (506-529-4698), St. Andrews, offers trail rides, pony rides, riding lessons.

KAYAK AND CANOE TOURS

In St. Andrews, **Seascape** (506-529-4012) offers guided half- and full-day tours, beginners welcome; the **Outdoor Adventure Company** (1-800-365-3855) offers kayak and canoe tours, also horseback riding, hiking, and biking.

SAILING

S/V *Cory* (506-529-8116), a 72-foot gaff and square-rigged cutter built by her captain in New Zealand, offers 3-hour sails in Passamaquoddy Bay and up the St. Croix River.

SWIMMING

Katy's Cove, Acadia Road, has (relatively) warm water, a sandy beach, and a clubhouse; nominal admission.

WHALE-WATCHING

In St. Andrews along King Street and the adjacent waterfront you can comparison shop: **Cline Maine** (506-526-4188) is the local pioneer in bird- and whale-watching tours; **Fundy Tide Runners** (506-529-4481) features fast, 24-foot, rigid-hulled Zodiac Hurricane boats, and clients wear flashy orange, full-length flotation suits; **Quoddy Link Marine** (506-529-2600) offers Whale Search and Island Cruises aboard a larger (40-passenger), slower vessel.

LODGING

Note: All entries are in St. Andrews, New Brunswick EOG 2XO, Canada. Prices are in Canadian dollars.

RESORT

The Algonquin (506-529-8823; in the United States 1-800-828-7447). Open May to October. The last of the truly grand coastal resorts in northeastern America; a 200-room, Tudor-style hotel with formal common and dining rooms, also banquet space geared to the many groups that keep it in business. Although the golf course is the big draw, amenities include tennis courts, a pool, and spa. The rack rate averages $120 per couple, but special packages, including "mini-vacations" that capitalize on weekends, bring it down to $136 for 2 days, breakfast included, children free. Inquire about golf and "romance" packages.

BED & BREAKFASTS

Check with the Chamber of Commerce for other reasonably priced B&Bs, which seem to change each season.

Pansy Patch (506-529-3834), 59 Carleton Street. Open mid-May to mid-September. Built fancifully in 1912 to resemble a Norman cottage, right across from the Algonquin. Michael O'Connor offers four guest rooms with water views and antiques. We particularly like room 3. Breakfast, which can be served in bed, is included in $95–180 per couple. An art gallery and tea garden are also on the premises and guests have access to an outdoor pool, tennis, and other resort facilities at the Algonquin.

The Hiram Walker Estate (506-529-4210; 1-800-470-4088), 109 Reed Avenue. Built in the grand manner in 1912 as a summer retreat for the Walker (as in Johnny Walker whiskey) family, the châteaulike mansion has a formal drawing room, library, music room, and dining room, and the upstairs suites are opulent by today's standards: working fireplaces, marble baths with Jacuzzis, and such. Rates—from $105 to $385—include a full breakfast by candlelight.

Kingsbrae Arms (506-529-1897), 219 King Street. Still under renovation when we visited in '96, an 1890s hilltop shingled mansion adjoining the Kingsbrae Horticultural Garden with nine ultra-deluxe rooms and suites, priced accordingly.

MOTEL

St. Andrews Motor Inn (506-529-4571), 111 Water Street. A three-story motel with 33 units and a heated swimming pool. All rooms have two queen-sized beds and color TVs, some with kitchenettes, and all have private balconies overlooking Passamaquoddy Bay; $94.95 per couple includes coffee and doughnuts.

CAMPING

Passamaquoddy Park Campground (506-529-3439), Indian Point Road. Maintained by the Kiwanis Club of St. Andrews, this is a beautifully sited campground with full hook-up as well as tent sites.

WHERE TO EAT

All listings are in St. Andrews, unless otherwise noted.

DINING OUT

L'Europe Dining Room and Lounge (506-529-3818), 63 King Street. Open for dinner daily except Monday in-season. Chef-owner Alexander Ludwig's specialties are a pleasing mix of French and German classics ranging from Wiener schnitzel ($15.60) to duck à l'orange ($24) to rack of lamb ($26.90); seafood entrées range from broiled sea bass ($17.50) to lobster with morel mushrooms ($33); prices are Canadian and include homemade pâté and salad as well as breads and vegetable. Candlelight and fine linen but no view.

The Passamaquoddy Dining Room at the Algonquin (506-529-8823), 184 Adolphus Street. The dining room is huge and its most pleasant corner is in The Veranda, with windows overlooking formal gardens. The menu is large, featuring local salmon and lobster. Entrées $17.95–23.50 plus tax. The hugely popular Sunday buffet is $8.95 Canadian.

Rossmount Dining Room (506-529-3351), Route 127, east of St. Andrews. Open for breakfast, lunch, high tea, and dinner. The menu changes frequently, but entrées might include charbroiled New York steak ($18.95) and poached Atlantic salmon ($19.95). This is an 84-acre estate and you might want to walk up its trails to the summit of Chamcook Mountain, the highest point in the Passamaquoddy Bay area.

The Gables (506-529-3440), 143 Water Street. Open 11–10. Reasonably priced, good food, and a tiered, shaded deck with a water view; what more can you ask, especially with wine by the glass and a wide selection of beers? Specialties include fresh fish ranging from fried haddock and chips ($9.50 Canadian) to a seafood platter ($21.95). We recommend the mussels.

EATING OUT

The Pickled Herring (506-529-3766), 211 Water Street. Open year-round for lunch and dinner, an inviting, pubby place with a basics-all-day menu: burgers, fish or clams and chips, salads, chili, and Bay of Fundy pickled herring served with cheese on rye, with a dill pickle. Spirits served.

The Lighthouse Restaurant (506-529-3082), Lower Patrick Street. Open for lunch and dinner May through October. The best weatherproof view of the bay from a restaurant.

SELECTIVE SHOPPING

Cottage Craft Ltd., Town Square, St. Andrews. Dating back to 1915, Cottage Craft showcases yarns, tweeds, and finished jackets, sweaters, and skirts; also distinctive handwoven throws made in homes throughout Charlotte County. Skirt and sweater kits as well as the finished products are the specialties.

V. WESTERN MOUNTAINS AND LAKES REGION

Sebago and Long Lakes Region
Bethel Area
Rangeley Lakes Region
Sugarloaf and the Carrabassett Valley

Lake Country

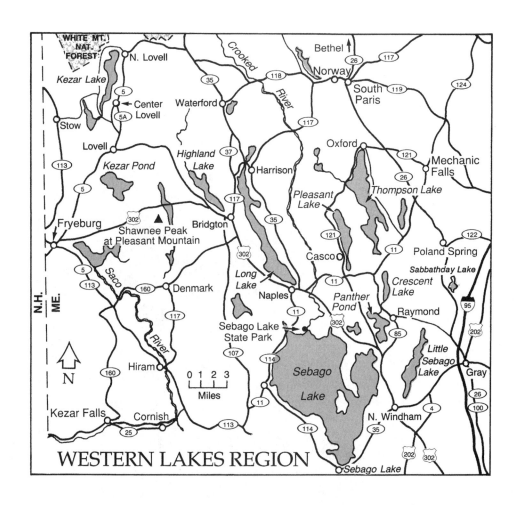

WESTERN LAKES REGION

Western Mountains and Lakes Region

Inland Maine is the most underrated, least explored piece of New England, frequently perceived as an uninterrupted flat carpet of firs.

Larger than Vermont and New Hampshire combined, it is actually composed of several very different regions and distinguished by a series of almost continuous mountain ranges, more extensive than New Hampshire's White Mountains and higher than Vermont's Green Mountains, but lacking a name (why aren't they the Blue Mountains?).

In contrast to the coast, inland Maine was actually more of a resort area a century ago than it is today. By the 1880s trains connected Philadelphia, New York, and Boston with large resort hotels in Rangeley and Greenville, and steamboats ferried "sports" to "sporting camps" in the far corners of lakes. Many of these historic resorts survive but today require far more time to reach, unless you fly in.

Today inland Maine seems even larger than it is because almost a third of it lies beyond the public highway system, a phenomenon for which we can blame Massachusetts and its insistence that Maine sell off the "unorganized townships" (and divide the profits) before it would be permitted to secede in 1820. In the interim, most of this land has been owned and managed by lumber and paper companies, and while debate currently rages about the future of these woodlands (somewhere between a third and almost a half of inland Maine), the reality of the way public roads run—and don't run—continues to physically divide Maine's mountainous interior into several distinct pieces.

The first of these pieces is the Western Mountains and Lakes Region, extending from the rural farmland surrounding the lakes of southwestern Maine, up through the Oxford Hills and into the foothills of the White Mountains and the Mahoosuc Range around Bethel, and into the wilderness (as high and remote as any to be found in the North Woods) around the Rangeley Lakes and the Sugarloaf area—east of which public roads cease, forcing traffic bound for the Moosehead Lake Region to detour south into the farmland of the Lower Kennebec Valley.

The four distinct areas within the Western Mountains and Lakes Region are connected by some of Maine's most scenic roads, a fact not generally appreciated because the area is best known to skiers, accustomed to racing up to Sunday River and Sugarloaf (Maine's most popular ski resorts) by the shortest routes from the interstate.

In summer and fall we suggest following Route 113 through Evans Notch or heading north from Bridgton to Bethel by the series of roads that thread woods and skirt lakes, heading east along Route 2, continuing north to Rangeley via Route 17 through Coos Canyon and over the spectacular height-of-land from which you can see all seven Rangeley lakes and the surrounding mountains. From Rangeley it's just another 19 scenic miles on Route 16 (better known as Moose Alley) to the Sugarloaf area. You can return to Route 2 by continuing along Route 16 to Kingfield, then taking Route 142 through Phillips and Weld. (Also see *Scenic Loop* in "Rangeley Lakes Region.")

Sebago and Long Lakes Region

Fifty lakes can be seen from the summit of Pleasant Mountain, 10 within the town of Bridgton itself.

These lakes are what draw summer visitors. They swim and fish, fish and swim. They cruise out in powerboats or paddle canoes. On rainy days, they browse through the area's abundant antiques and crafts stores. In winter they ski at Shawnee Peak (alias Pleasant Mountain) or cross-country almost anywhere.

Before the Civil War, visitors could actually come by boat all the way to Bridgton from Boston. From Portland, they would ride 20 miles through 28 locks on the Cumberland and Oxford Canal, then across Sebago Lake, up the Songo River, Brandy Pond, and Long Lake to Bridgton. The first hotel atop Pleasant Mountain opened in 1850, and in 1882 the "2-footer" narrow-gauge opened between Hiram and Bridgton, enabling summer visitors to come by train as well.

Today, as in the 1880s, most visitors waste little time getting onto or into water. The Naples Causeway is the base for water sports and departure point for cruises on Long Lake and through the only surviving canal lock. Sebago, Maine's second largest lake, is its most popular waterskiing area.

This southwestern corner of the state offers plenty on land too: golf, tennis, mineral collecting, and such fascinating historic sights as the country's last living Shaker community at Sabbathday Lake.

Fryeburg, just west of the lakes in the Saco River Valley, is the region's oldest community and the site of the state's largest agricultural fair. It is also headquarters for canoeing the Saco River. Sandy-bottomed and clear, the Saco meanders for more than 40 miles through woods and fields, rarely passing a house. Too shallow for powerboats, it is perfect for canoes. There is usually just enough current to nudge along the limpest paddler, and the ubiquitous sandbars serve as gentle bumpers. Tenting is permitted most places along the river, and there are public campgrounds. Outfitters rent canoes and provide shuttle service.

In summer most families come for a week to stay in lakeside cottages—of which there seem to be thousands. The few motels and scattered inns and bed & breakfasts tend to fill on weekends with parents visiting their children at camps—of which there seem to be hundreds.

GUIDANCE

Bridgton–Lakes Region Chamber of Commerce (647-3472), Box 236, Bridgton 04009. The chamber maintains a seasonal walk-in information bureau on Route 302 weekends Memorial Day through October, daily from mid-June through Labor Day; also daily during the early October Fryeburg Fair (see *Special Events*). Request a copy of the chamber's "Bridgton–Lakes Region Map and Guide." Year-round information is also available from the town office (647-8786).

Naples Business Association (693-3285), PO Box 412, Naples 04055, publishes a map/guide to the Sebago/Long Lakes region just south of Bridgton; it also maintains a seasonal information bureau next to the town's historical society museum on Route 302.

Windham Chamber of Commerce (892-8265), PO Box 1015, Windham 04062, maintains a seasonal information booth on Route 302 and publishes a booklet guide.

Oxford Hills Chamber of Commerce (743-2281), PO Box 167, South Paris 04281, publishes a directory to the area and maintains a seasonal information booth on Route 26 in South Paris across from Mario's Pizza.

Fryeburg Information Center (935-3639), Route 302, Fryeburg. The Maine Publicity Bureau staffs this state-owned log cabin on the New Hampshire line. Pamphlets on the state in general, western Maine in particular.

GETTING THERE

By air: The **Portland International Jetport,** served by five minor carriers, is a half-hour to an hour drive from most points in this area. **Rental cars** are available at the airport.

By car: From New York and Boston, take I-95 to the Westbrook exit (exit 8), then Route 302, the high road of the lakes region.

For the Sabbathday Lake/Poland Spring/Oxford area, take I-95 to Gray (exit 11) and Route 26 north.

For Newfield and south of Sebago area, take Route 25 from I-95 at Westbrook (exit 8).

MEDICAL EMERGENCY

Northern Cumberland Memorial Hospital (647-8841), South High Street, Bridgton. **Stephens Memorial Hospital** (743-5933), Norway.

TO SEE

MUSEUMS

Sabbathday Lake Shaker Community and Museum (926-4597), Route 26, New Gloucester (8 miles north of Gray). Open Memorial Day through Columbus Day, except Sunday, 10–4:30. Guided tours (admission charged). Welcoming the "world's people" has been part of summer at Sabbathday Lake since the community's inception in 1794.

GORDON C. PINE

Shaker Village at Sabbathday Lake

Founded by Englishwoman Ann Lee in 1775, Shakers numbered 6000 Americans in 18 communities by the Civil War. Today, with fewer than 10 Shaker Sisters and Brothers, this village is the only one that still functions as a religious community rather than as a museum. These men and women still follow the injunction of founder Mother Ann Lee to "put your hands to work and your heart to God." Guided tours are offered of the 17 white-clapboard buildings; rooms are either furnished or filled with exhibits to illustrate periods or products of Shaker life. The Shaker Store sells Shaker-made goods including oval boxes, knitted and sewn goods, homemade fudge, yarns, souvenirs, antiques, Shaker-style furniture, and Shaker herbs. During warm-weather months, services are held at 10 AM on Sundays in the 18th-century meetinghouse on Route 26. Sit in the World's People's benches and listen as the Shakers speak in response to the psalms and gospel readings. Each observation is affirmed with a Shaker song—of which there are said to be 10,000. This complex includes an extensive research library housing Shaker books, writings, and records open to scholars by appointment. Inquire about special workshops, fairs, and concerts.

Willowbrook at Newfield (793-2784), Newfield (off Route 11). Open May 15 to September 30, daily 10–5. Admission charged. This is a quiet, peaceful place that shouldn't be missed. Although it's off the beaten track, the drive through the quiet countryside is easy and relaxing, and, once you get there, well worth it. Devastated by fire in 1947, the village was almost a ghost town when Donald King began buying buildings in the 1960s. The complex now includes 37 buildings displaying more than

11,000 items: horse-drawn vehicles, tools, toys, a vintage 1894 carousel, and many other artifacts of late-19th-century life. Linger in the ballroom, ring the schoolhouse bell, picnic in the area provided. This is a perfect place to get away from it all. A restaurant and ice cream parlor for light lunches, an old-time country store, and a Christmas gift shop open most of the year are located on the premises.

The Jones Museum of Glass and Ceramics (787-3370), Douglas Hill (off Route 107), Sebago. Open mid-May to mid-November, Monday through Saturday 10–5 and Sunday 1–5. $5 per adult, $3 per student. More than 7000 works in glass and china. Displays include ancient Egyptian glass, Chinese porcelains, Wedgwood teapots, and French paperweights. There are also gallery tours, frequent lecture-luncheon seminars, and identification days (visitors bring their own pieces to be identified).

Orlin Arts Center at Bates College (786-6255), Campus Avenue, Lewiston. Lovers of artist Marsden Hartley may want to seek out this small but excellent collection of bold, bright canvases by Hartley, a Lewiston native (call ahead to find out what's on display).

HISTORIC BUILDINGS AND MUSEUMS

Daniel Marrett House, Route 25, Standish. Tours mid-June to September 1, Tuesday, Thursday, Saturday, and Sunday noon–5. Admission charged. Money from Portland banks was stored in this Georgian mansion for safekeeping during the War of 1812. Built in 1789, it remained in the Marrett family until 1944; architecture and furnishings reflect the changing styles over 150 years, and the formal gardens bloom throughout the summer.

Parson Smith House (892-5315), 89 River Road, South Windham. Open mid-June through Labor Day, Tuesday, Thursday, Saturday, and Sunday 12–5; admission. A Georgian farmhouse with an exceptional stairway and hall; some original furnishings.

Narramissic, Ingalls Road (2 miles south of the junction of Routes 107 and 117), Bridgton. Open June 5 through Labor Day, Tuesday through Sunday 10–4. Nominal admission. A Federal-period home and a Temperance Barn in a rural setting; includes a blacksmith shop, the scene of frequent special events; check with the **Bridgton Historical Society Museum** (647-3699), Gibbs Avenue, which also maintains a 1902 former fire station. The collection (open same hours) includes slides on the old narrow-gauge railroad.

State of Maine Building from the 1893 World's Columbian Exposition in Chicago, Route 26, Poland Spring. Open July and August, daily 9–1; June and September, weekends 9–1. Admission. A very Victorian building that was brought back from the 1893 World's Columbian Exposition in Chicago to serve as a library and art gallery for the now-vanished Poland Spring Resort (the water is now commercially bottled in an efficient, unromantic plant down the road). Houses the Poland Spring Preservation Society with museum displays from the resort era on the second floor and art on the third. While you are there, peek into the All Souls Chapel next door for a look at its nine stained-glass windows and the 1921 Skinner pipe organ.

Hamlin Memorial Library and Museum, (743-2980), Paris Hill, off Route 26. Open year-round, Tuesday through Friday 11:30–5:30, and Saturday 10–2; also Wednesday 7–9. The old stone Oxford County Jail now houses the public library and museum. Worth a stop for the American primitive art; also local minerals and displays about Hannibal Hamlin (who lived next door), vice president during Abraham Lincoln's first term. This stop may not sound very exciting, but the setting is superb: a ridgetop of spectacular, early-19th-century houses with views west to the White Mountains.

Naples Historical Society Museum (693-6790), Village Green, Route 302, Naples. Open July and August, Tuesday through Friday 10–3. The old brick complex includes the old jail, some great memorabilia, and slide presentations on the Cumberland and Oxford Canal, the Sebago/Long Lake steamboats, and vanished hotels like the Chute Homestead.

Hopalong Cassidy in the Fryeburg Public Library (935-2731), 98 Main Street, Fryeburg. Open year-round, varying days; housed in an 1832 stone schoolhouse. It is decorated with many paintings by local artists and also contains a collection of books, guns, and other memorabilia belonging to Clarence Mulford, creator of Hopalong Cassidy. **The Fryeburg Historical Society Museum** next door is also open seasonally and by request at the library.

OTHER

✐ **The Game Farm and Visitors Center** (657-4977), Route 26/100 north, Gray. Open mid-April through Veterans Day 10–4; adults $2.50, children $1.50. This 1300-acre farm, set up to breed ring-necked pheasants, has become a refuge for injured or threatened animals: moose, deer, raccoons, bears, bobcats, porcupines, minks, skunks, fishers, coyotes, and a variety of birds and fish. Exhibits, nature trails, and picnic facilities.

Oxford Plains Speedway/Dragway (539-8865), Route 26, Oxford. Open April to September; races Friday at 7:30 PM, Sunday at 2 PM. The Oxford 250, which draws competitors from throughout the world, is held on Saturdays and Sundays during July.

Songo Locks, Naples (2.5 miles off Route 302). Dating from 1830, the last of the 27 hand-operated locks that once enabled people to come by boat from Portland to Harrison. It still enables you to travel some 40 watery miles. The boat traffic is constant in summer.

TO DO

AIR RIDES

Western Maine Flying Service (693-3129), Naples. Operates daily in-season, scenic flights.

Parasailing (693-3888), Naples Causeway.

Destinations Unlimited (743-9781; 1-800-526-TOUR), Norway. Hot-air-balloon rides.

BICYCLING

Shawnee Peak (647-8444), Route 302, Bridgton, offers lift-accessed riding, a terrain park, and rental mountain bikes, weekends in season.

BOAT EXCURSIONS

Songo River Queen II (693-6861), Naples Causeway. Operates daily July through Labor Day; weekends during June and September. Offers a 2½-hour Songo River ride and a 1-hour Long Lake cruise. The 90-foot-long stern-wheeler was built in 1982; snack bar and rest rooms. The ride is across Brandy Pond and through the only surviving lock from the 1830 canal. It is a pleasant ride to the mouth of Sebago Lake down the Songo River, which is about as winding as a river can be. The distance is just 1.5 miles as the crow flies, but 6 miles as the Songo twists and turns. **Mail Boat Rides** cruises (1½ hours) are also offered daily in-season except Sunday. This pontoon offers varied rides on Songo and Long Lakes (no toilets on board).

BOAT RENTALS

Available region-wide. Inquire at local chambers. (See also *Canoeing.*)

CANOEING

Saco River Canoe and Kayak (935-2369), PO Box 111, Route 5, Fryeburg (across from the access at Swan's Falls). "For canoeing, the Saco is the number one river east of the Mississippi," enthuses Fred Westerberg. "Nowhere else can you canoe so far without having to portage. Nowhere else can you find this kind of wilderness camping experience without the danger of remoteness. Nowhere on the river are you far from help if you need it." Westerberg, a registered Maine guide, runs Saco River Canoe and Kayak with the help of his wife, Prudy, and daughters, Beth and Chris. They also offer shuttle service and canoe rentals, which come with a map and careful instructions geared to the day's river conditions.

Saco Bound (603-447-2177/3801), Route 302, Center Conway, New Hampshire (just over the state line, south of Fryeburg). The largest canoe outfitter around. Offers rentals, guided day trips during the summer (Tuesdays and Thursdays in July and August), white-water canoeing on the Androscoggin River, a campground at Canal Bridge in Fryeburg, and a shuttle service. Its base is a big, glass-faced store stocked with kayaks and canoes, trail food, and lip balm. Staff members are young and enthusiastic.

Canal Bridge Canoes (935-2605), Route 302, Fryeburg Village. Pat and Carl Anderson offer rentals and a shuttle service.

Woodland Acres (935-2529), Route 160, Brownfield. Full-facility camping, canoe rentals, and a shuttle service.

FISHING

Fishing licenses are available at town offices and other local outlets; check marinas for information. Salmon, lake trout, pickerel, and bass abound.

GOLF AND TENNIS

Bridgton Highlands Country Club (647-3491), Bridgton, has an 18-hole course, snack bar, carts, and tennis courts. Nine-hole courses include **Lake Kezar Country Club** (925-2462), Route 5, Lovell; **Naples Country Club** (693-6424), Route 114, Naples; and **Summit Golf Course** (998-4515), Poland Spring.

Tennis at Brandy Pond Camps (693-6333), old Route 114, Naples; also at **Bridgton Highlands Country Club.**

HIKING

Douglas Mountain, Sebago. A Nature Conservancy preserve with great views of Sebago and the White Mountains. The trail to the top is a 20-minute walk, and there's a ¾-mile nature trail at the summit; also a stone tower with an observation platform. Take Route 107 south from the town of Sebago and turn right on Douglas Mountain Road; go to the end of the road to find limited parking.

Pleasant Mountain, Bridgton. Several summits and interconnecting trails, the most popular of which is the Firewarden's Trail to the main summit: a relatively easy, 2½-mile climb from base to peak through rocky woods.

Jockey Cap, Route 302, Fryeburg. Watch for the Jockey Cap Motel beside a general store. The arch between them is the entrance to one of New England's shortest hikes to one of its biggest rewards. A 10-minute climb up the path (steep near the top) accesses a bald, garnet-studded summit with a sweeping view of the White Mountains to the west, lesser peaks and lakes to the east and south, all ingeniously identified on a circular bronze monument designed by Arctic explorer Admiral Peary (see *Bed & Breakfasts*).

HORSEBACK RIDING

Sunny Brook Stables (787-2905), Sebago, offers trail rides pitched to beginners and intermediate riders. $15–18 per hour. **Secret Acres Stables** (693-3441), Lambs Mill Road, Naples (1 mile off Route 302), offers trail rides and lessons.

MINI-GOLF

Steamboat Landing (693-6429), Route 114, Naples. Open weekends Memorial Day to late June, then daily through Labor Day 10–10 (1–10 Sunday). A lovely 19-hole course with a Maine theme in a wooded setting.

Maplewood Miniature Golf and Arcade (655-7586), Route 302 across from State Park Road, Casco. Eighteen holes and a full arcade with video games, pinball, snacks.

ROCKHOUNDING

This area is particularly rich in minerals. Rock hounds should stop at:

✐ **Perham's of West Paris** (674-2341; 1-800-371-GEMS), Route 26, West Paris. Open 9–5 daily. Looking deceptively small in its yellow-clapboard, green-trim building (right side, heading north), this business has been selling gemstones since 1919. Aside from displaying an array of locally mined amethyst, tourmaline, topaz, and many other minerals, as well as selling gem jewelry, Perham's offers maps to five local quarries in which treasure-seekers are welcome to try their luck. Whether you're a rock hound or not, you'll want to stop by this mini-museum, said to attract 90,000 visitors per year.

✐ **Snow Falls Gorge,** off Route 26, West Paris. Whether you are hunting for gems or not, be sure to stop by this beautiful spot (you can ask directions at Perham's). A waterfall cascades into the gorge, and there's a bridge for great viewing; also hiking trails.

SWIMMING

Sebago Lake State Park (693-6613, June 20 through Labor Day; 693-6231 otherwise), off Route 302 (between Naples and South Casco). The day-use area includes beaches, tables, grills, a boat ramp, lifeguards, and bathhouses. There is a separate camping area (see *Campgrounds*) with its own beach; also a summer program of conducted hikes on nature trails and presentations in the amphitheater. Songo Lock is nearby.

The town of Bridgton maintains a tidy little beach on **Long Lake** just off Main Street, another on **Woods Lake** (Route 117), and another on **Highland Lake.** The town of Fryeburg maintains a beach, with float, on the **Saco River,** and **Casco** maintains a small, inviting beach in its picturesque village.

Range Pond State Park (998-4104), Poland, offers swimming and fishing.

Pennesseewasee Lake in Norway is well off the road but public and equipped with lifeguards.

In addition, most camps, cottages, and lodges have their own waterfront beaches and docks, and there are numerous local swimming holes.

CROSS-COUNTRY SKIING

Carter's Farm Market (539-4848), Route 26, Oxford. Extensive acreage used to grow summer vegetables is transformed into a ski center during the winter. Equipment rentals, lessons, 10 km of groomed trails, some lighted trails for night skiing, and food.

DOWNHILL SKIING

Shawnee Peak at Pleasant Mountain (647-8444), Route 302, Bridgton. An isolated, 1900-foot hump, 1 mile west of the center of town. Maine's oldest ski area, it has a vertical drop of 1300 feet, 30 trails, 98 percent snowmaking, and extensive night skiing. Lifts include one triple chair and three double chairs. Other amenities include ski school, rentals, and childcare.

LODGING

RUSTIC RESORTS

The western lakes area offers some unusual old resort complexes, each with cabin accommodations, dining, and relaxing space in a central, distinctively Maine lodge. In contrast to similar complexes found farther north, these are all geared to families or to those who vacation here for reasons other than hunting and fishing.

Migis Lodge (655-4524), PO Box 40, South Casco 04077 (off Route 302). Open early June through Columbus Day weekend. There are seven rooms in the two-story main lodge, and 30 cottages scattered in the pines on 97 acres. All cottages have fireplaces, and guests enjoy use of the private beach, tennis, lawn games, waterskiing, sailboats, canoes, and boat excursions. Children under 4 are not permitted in the dining room during the high season (July through Labor Day), so the resort provides a supervised dining and play time 6:30–8:30; older children are also welcome to join in. $230–360 per couple includes three meals; children's rates;15 percent service charge; handicapped access.

Quisisana (925-3500; off-season: 914-833-0293), Lake Kezar, Center Lovell 04016. Late June through Labor Day. One-week minimum stay in high season. Founded in 1917 as a place for music students and music lovers to relax in the pines by one of Maine's clearest lakes. Each evening climaxes with performances in the lakeside hall: musical theater, opera, and concerts performed by staff recruited from top music schools. There are 16 guest rooms in two lodges; also 38 one- to three-room cottages (some with fireplaces) scattered through the woods and around the soft beach, which curves to a grassy point. Waterskiing, boats, and fishing guides are all available. The white-frame central lodge includes a big, homey sitting room and the kind of dining room you don't mind sitting in three times a day, especially given the quality of the food. $220–284 per couple per day with three meals.

Northern Pines (655-7624), 559 Route 85, Raymond 04071. Open Memorial Day weekend through Labor Day; September and October weekends; Christmas, New Year's week, and 2 weeks in February. A very pleasant holistic health resort housed in an expanded rustic women's camp on the shores of Crescent Lake. A total of 50 rooms are divided between the lodge and cottages. The daily regimen includes aerobics and yoga, meditation and stretch, and frequently there are evening lectures. Meals are vegetarian and delicious. Summer facilities include sailboats, canoes, paddleboats, and a lakeside hot tub; cross-country skiing and ice skating January through March. There are two lodges, one closed in winter. Personal services such as massage, seaweed wraps, and flotation tank are available. Ten percent service added. Handicapped access.

Aimhi Lodge (892-6538), North Windham 04062. Open summer season. More than 70 years in the same family, this classic complex accommodates 75 guests in the lodge, with 25 cabins on Little Sebago Lake. The cabins have one to three rooms, Franklin stoves, and screened porches. Down-home cooking; turkey every summer Sunday since the 1930s, at least. Facilities include game rooms, lawn games, a beach, sailboats, and canoes.

INNS

✐ **Tarry-A-While** (647-2522), Ridge Road, Bridgton 04009. Open June through Columbus Day. This resort has a delightful Swiss ambience. This turreted, vintage 1897 summer hotel has acquired a new lease on life with new owners Marc and Nancy Stretch. Set in 23 lakeside acres, it offers 28 rooms (private and shared baths) divided among the inn, cottages, and a two-bedroom apartment. A beach, social hall, canoes, rowboats, pedal boats, and tennis are all part of the resort and an 18-hole golf course is next door. $100 double includes an expanded continental breakfast. Dinner is served (see *Dining Out*).

The Waterford Inne (583-4037), Box 149, Waterford 04088. This striking, mustard-colored, 1825 farmhouse with its double porch is sequestered up a back road, set on 25 acres of fields and woods. Mother and daughter Rosalie and Barbara Vanderzanden have been welcoming guests since 1978, offering tasteful, spacious rooms (five in the old house and five more carved into the old ell). Common rooms are ample and tastefully furnished; the standout is the Chesapeake Room with a fireplace and the second-story porch. A full breakfast is included in $74–99 per room; dinner, available to the public (see *Dining Out*), is $31.

Oxford House Inn (935-3442), Fryeburg 04037. Open year-round, this spacious 1913 house in the middle of Fryeburg has a view across the Saco River to the White Mountains. The public restaurant is popular for dinner (see *Dining Out*), but there is ample space for inn guests to relax. John and Phyllis Morris offer five upstairs guest rooms, all large and nicely decorated, with private baths. Request one with a view. $75–95, includes a full breakfast.

Kedarburn Inn (583-6182), Route 35, Waterford 04088. London natives Margaret and Derek Gibson bring an English accent to this pleasant 1850s house. The inn offers seven guest rooms, including two with private baths and one 2-room suite with private bath. Margaret has also recently opened a crafts shop on the ground floor, filled with items made by local artists as well as her own crafts, including her specialty quilts. $71–88 double ($50 single), breakfast and an English afternoon tea included. Children and pets are welcome.

Center Lovell Inn (925-1575), Route 5, Center Lovell 04016. Closed November and April. A striking old inn with a cupola and a busy public dining room (see *Dining Out*). Janice and Richard Cox saw their dream come true when they won the inn through an essay contest in May

1993. They run the inn with the help of Janice's mother, Harriet, and her husband, Earle (known to guests as Mom and Pop). There are four guest rooms on the second floor (the two with shared bath can become a suite), nicely furnished with antiques and art. In the 1835 Harmon House there are five smaller rooms, some with private bath. $87–144 MAP (more for suite).

BED & BREAKFASTS

Noble House (647-3733), Box 180, Bridgton 04009. Open year-round, but October 15 to June 15 by reservation only. There is a suitably formal feel to the grand piano, crystal, and Oriental rugs in the parlor of this former senator's manor, set among stately oaks and pines. Back beyond the kitchen, however, is a comfortable den/breakfast room, and the welcome guests receive from Jane and Dick Staret is anything but stiff. The nine guest rooms are divided between the original house (ranging from a single to a family suite under the eaves) and newer doubles and suites in the former ell (three with whirlpool bath); all are furnished with antiques. The private beach (with a hammock, canoe, and dock) on Highland Lake is just across the road; in winter, both downhill and cross-country skiing are nearby. $74–125 double, includes full breakfast and use of a canoe and pedal boats. Singles are $5–10 less; $15 more per child.

Admiral Peary House (935-3365; 1-800-237-8080), 9 Elm Street, Fryeburg 04037. If he returned today we suspect that Robert E. Peary, Maine's famed Arctic explorer, would be pleased with what's happened to the house in which he lived with his mother after graduating from Bowdoin College and before surveying the Panama Canal. The large old home stands on a leafy side street and guests enter from the back, through a large, wicker-filled screened porch overlooking a perennial garden. Next comes a spacious informal living room with barnboard walls and a large hearth, equipped with TV, a billiards table, a stereo, and games. The more formal spaces (a handsome dining room, living room, and library) are off in the front of the house, beyond an open kitchen. The four large guest rooms, each with private bath and air-conditioning, are furnished with oversized beds and antiques. The top-floor North Pole room, with its king brass bed, features mountain views. Amenities include an outdoor spa, bicycles, and well-maintained clay tennis courts; innkeepers Nancy and Ed Greenberg are both tennis pros and offer tennis lessons to guests. $95–118 in season includes a full breakfast; from $70 off-season. Inquire about quilting and artists' water-color weekends. Seven-day off-season packages (can include a weekend) are $385. Nearby Fryeburg Academy maintains a network of cross-country-ski trails.

Sebago Lake Lodge (892-2698), PO Box 110, White's Bridge Road, North Windham 04062. A rambling, old white inn on a narrows between Jordan Bay and the Basin, seemingly surrounded by water. Debra and Chip

Lougee, both Maine natives, have refurbished the rooms to create eight units with their own kitchens (one is a suite with an enclosed porch) and four standard rooms with kitchen privileges. A light buffet breakfast is set out in the gathering room, a pleasant space to read, play games, or watch TV. There are also nine moderately priced cottages. Facilities include an inviting beach, picnic tables, and grills; there is also a fishing boat, rowboat, canoe, and motorboat rentals. Fishing licenses are available. $48 for a room, $98–120 per housekeeping unit; cheaper off-season. Cottages $395–695 per week.

Lake House (583-4182; 1-800-223-4182), Routes 35 and 37, Waterford 04088. Open year-round. A graceful old stagecoach inn with vestiges of the old ballroom under the eaves, offering five spacious guest rooms, including a two-room suite and a one-room cottage, all with private baths. Lake Keoka is across the street. $79–125.

Bear Mountain Inn (583-4404), Routes 35 and 37, South Waterford 04081. Open year-round. One of the area's first farmhouses to take in guests, still with an informal farmhouse feel. Lorraine Blais offers seven guest rooms, four with full baths, and a two-room suite with bath. The 48 acres include frontage on Bear Pond. A 45-minute hiking trail to the top of Bear Mountain begins across the street. Three canoes, a rowboat, and a sailboat are available to guests. $85–125 per room with a full breakfast in the dining room in front of the double-sided fireplace.

The Inn at Long Lake (693-6226), PO Box 806, Naples 04055. Built in 1906 as an annex to the (vanished) Lake House Resort, this four-story, clapboard building has been renovated and is again an inn. Irene and Maynard Hincks offer 16 guest rooms, ranging from small to two-room suites, each with private bath, TV, and air conditioner. The best rooms and views are on the fourth floor. The Great Room on the ground floor has a magnificent fieldstone fireplace. $85–130 per room, $55–90 in winter. Discounts for multiday stays.

Tolman House Inn (583-4445), PO Box 551, Tolman Road, Harrison 04040. Open year-round. A former carriage barn with nine guest rooms (private baths) and a dining and lounging area overlooking gardens. The inn is situated on a hillside sloping to the tip of Long Lake. There is a game room in a former icehouse. Children under 2 stay free, but there are no cribs. $115 double; $90 single includes full breakfast.

✎ **Moose Crossing Farm** (743-7656), 203 Christian Ridge Road, South Paris 04281. This is a nicely renovated, 18th-century farmhouse set high on Christian Ridge with long views west to the White Mountains. Anne and Allen Gass raise black and brown sheep; they offer woodland trails (good for cross-country skiing), two comfortable guest rooms, a hearty breakfast. $55 per room, shared bath.

COTTAGES

The **Bridgton–Lakes Region Chamber of Commerce** (see *Guidance*) publishes a list of more than two dozen rental cottages and many for this area are also listed in the "Maine Guide to Camp & Cottage Rentals," free from the **Maine Publicity Bureau** (see *Information* in "What's Where"). One set of cottages that deserves special mention is **Hewnoaks** (925-6051), Center Lovell 04016. Six unusually attractive, distinctive cottages built as an artists colony and imaginatively furnished (in no way are these your usual summer camps) are scattered on a landscaped hillside above pristine Lake Kezar. Moderately priced.

OTHER LODGING

Wadsworth Blanchard Farm Hostel (625-7509), RR2, Box 5992, Hiram 04041. Open May through October. An attractive Hosteling International (HI) facility that's an 18th-century farmstead, and handy to canoeing on both the Saco and Ossippee Rivers. Sally Whitcher and Edward Bradley offer two dorms with four beds each, one family room with a queen bed; access to the kitchen is included in all rates. $10 per person, $30 per family, half price for children 12 and under.

CAMPGROUNDS

See *Canoeing* for information about camping along the Saco River. In addition to those mentioned, the **Appalachian Mountain Club** maintains a campground at Swan's Falls. The "Maine Camping Guide," available from the **Maine Campground Owners Association** (782-5874), 655 Main Street, Lewiston 04240, lists dozens of private campgrounds in the area.

Sebago Lake State Park (693-6613; 693-6611 before June 20 and after Labor Day), off Route 302 (between Naples and South Casco). Open through mid-October. On the northern shore of the lake are 1300 thickly wooded acres with 250 campsites, many on the water; the camping area has its own beach, hot showers, a program of evening presentations, and nature hikes. For information about reservations, call 1-800-332-1501, or 207-287-3824 from outside the state.

✐ **Point Sebago** (655-3821), RR 1, Box 712, Casco 04015. More than just a campground: 500 campsites, most with trailer hookups, on a 300-acre lakeside site, plus 160 rental trailers ranging from small trailers to large models of near mobile home size. Campers have access to the beach, marina, dance pavilion, children's daycare, teen center, excursion boats, soccer and softball fields, horseshoe pitches, 10 tennis courts, video-game arcade, general store, and combination restaurant/nightclub/gambling casino; full daily program beginning with 8 AM exercises and ending at 1 AM when the club closes.

✐ **Papoose Pond Resort and Campground** (583-4470), RR 1, Box 2480, Route 118, 10 miles west of Norway in North Waterford 04267-9600. Family geared for 40 years, this facility is on 1000 wooded acres with a half mile of sandy beach on mile-long Papoose Pond; facilities include 25 cabins with baths, 18 cabins without baths, 10 housekeeping cottages, 8 bunkhouse trailers, 13 tent sites, 59 tent sites with electricity and water, 28 more with sewage as well, a dining shelter, and a kitchen and

bathhouse. Amenities include a recreation hall, store, café, movie tent, sports area, 50 boats (canoes, rowboats, sailboats, paddleboats, kayaks), fishing equipment, and a vintage 1916 merry-go-round.

WHERE TO EAT

DINING OUT

The Waterford Inne (583-4037), Waterford (ask directions when you call to reserve). Dinner by reservation in the common rooms of a classic country inn. Our dinner began with mini-popovers and a squash-orange soup, followed by greens and chopped walnuts, then perfectly grilled lamb chops with fresh mint, roasted potatoes, and grilled tomato, topped with a glorious pear dessert. Wine can be purchased at Springer's Store down the road. $31 prix fixe.

Peter's (583-6265) at the Kedarburn Inn, Route 35, Waterford. Chefs Peter and Emma Bodwell offer good fare in the dining rooms of an 1858 house. The menu ranges from chicken sautéed in garlic and fresh rosemary served on linguine with a pesto and roasted red pepper sauce ($9.95), to beef tournedos topped with shiitake mushrooms in a rich burgundy sauce ($17.50).

Lake House (583-4182; 1-800-223-4182), Routes 35 and 37, Waterford. Open from 5:30 PM daily. A fine old inn with two intimate dining rooms. In the past the Lake House has been known for its wine list and creative entrées in the $16–21 range.

Center Lovell Inn (925-1575), Center Lovell. Open nightly in summer, Friday through Sunday off-season (reservations requested). You might begin with smoked pheasant ravioli ($8.95) and dine on chef-owner Richard Cox's northern Italian specialties like veal piccata ($18.95) There are two pleasant dining rooms and a wraparound porch in summer.

Tarry-A-While Restaurant (647-2522), Highland Road, Bridgton. The timber-beamed dining room in this old lakeside summer hotel is the setting for serious dining from a menu that might include grilled Tequila Lime Swordfish ($19.95) and Pasta Paellaya (southwestern smoked sausage, chicken, shrimp, and clams, sautéed with fresh vegetables, served over linguine; $18.95), also Vegetarian Wellington (fresh vegetables, herbs, and ricotta rolled and baked in a crispy puff pastry shell, served with plum tomato sauce and aioli; $11.95). A bistro and children's menus are also available.

The Olde House (655-7841), just off Route 302 on Route 85, Raymond. Open for dinner daily year-round. Candlelight dining in a 1790 home. Specialties include Weiner schnitzel (sautéed veal with lemon sauce) and coquilles Saint-Jacques mornay (scallops in light cream sauce with duchess potatoes topped with dilled Havarti). $11.95–19.95.

Venezia Ristorante (647-5333), Bridgton Corners, Routes 302 and 93. Open daily 5–10 in summer, otherwise Wednesday through Saturday. Dependable, moderately priced Italian dishes.

Oxford House Inn (935-3442), 105 Main Street, Fryeburg. Open nightly in summer and fall, winter and spring hours modified. Entrées include veal Oxford and scallops à l'orange (both $21). The setting is the former living room and dining room of a handsome 1913 house.

Maurice Restaurant Francaise (743-2532), 113 Main Street, South Paris. Open daily for lunch and dinner and for Sunday brunch (no lunch on Saturday). A reasonably priced, classic French restaurant with four dining rooms. The specialty is scampi à la provençale. Reservations recommended. $11.25–15.50.

EATING OUT

Bray's Brew Pub (693-6806), Routes 302 and 35, Naples. Open year-round for lunch and dinner daily. A mansard-roofed landmark formerly housing a gourmet restaurant is now an inviting way stop. Mike and Rich Bray brew American ales as they are known in the Pacific Northwest, using North American grains and malted barley, Oregon yeast and Washington hops. Specials might include lobster stew, Maine crabcakes and mussels stewed in beer. The dinner menu runs from grilled salmon ($12.95) to petit filet mignon ($14.95); pub menu served all day.

Mountain View Family Restaurant (935-2909), 107 Main Street, Fryeburg. Open from 6 AM through dinner. The Mutrie family have tacked this pine-paneled dining room onto the back of their Village Variety, with large windows overlooking the White Mountains. For breakfast try the Belgian waffles with blueberries; go with a special like fried haddock at dinner. Burgers and sandwiches are fine, and don't pass up the pies.

Olde Mill Tavern (583-4992), Maine Street, Harrison. Open daily, 11–11. Replacing the Cracked Platter, this slick eatery opened in 1996 and was an instant success with local residents, featuring "family-style dinners" (for two or more) like whole roasted chicken at $7.95 per person and a choice of "big plates" (which run as high as $19.95 for rack of lamb) and "small plates" like mill tavern meat loaf and fajita chicken salad; also "hand-carved sandwiches," flat breads, and Sunday brunch.

Black Horse Tavern (647-5300), Route 302, Bridgton. We must have hit the chef's night off. The signature chicken and smoked sausage gumbo was inedible, but a salad was fine. Large menu and informal atmosphere.

Shaner's Family Dining (743-6367), 193 Main Street, South Paris. Open for breakfast, lunch, and dinner, a large, cheerful, family restaurant with booths; specials like fried chicken, liver and onions, and chicken pie; creamy homemade ice cream in an unusual choice of flavors.

Cole Farms (657-4714), Route 100/202, Gray. Open 5 AM–10:30 PM daily except Monday. Maine cooking from family recipes. Specialties include the fried fish plate and seafood Newburg. Everything from soups and chowders to ice cream and pastries made on the premises. No liquor.

SNACKS

Crestholm Farm Stand and Ice Cream (539-2616), Route 26, Oxford. Farm stand, cheeses, honey, ice cream, and a petting zoo: sheep, goats, pigs, ducks, more.

ENTERTAINMENT

FILM

Magic Lantern, Main Street, Bridgton, presents film classics and first-run cartoons.

Windham Hill Mall, Route 302, has a cinema that shows first-run movies.

MUSIC

Sebago/Long Lakes Region Chamber Music Festival (627-4939), DeerTrees Theater, Harrison. A series of concerts held mid-July through mid-August.

THEATER

DeerTrees Theater (583-6747), Harrison. Once a popular 1930s summer theater, abandoned until the 1980s, when the town of Harrison and volunteers turned it into a nonprofit organization. It is once again becoming a cultural center for the area, with the chamber music festival, comedians, and shows by the resident theater company, the Dear Deer Players.

Celebration Barn Theater (743-8452), South Paris. Summer workshops in acrobatics, mime, and juggling by resident New Vaudeville artists, who stage concerts Friday and Saturday nights in summer.

SELECTIVE SHOPPING

ANTIQUES SHOPS

Route 302 seems to be regaining its '50s and '60s reputation as an antiques alley.

BOOKSTORES

Books 'n' Things (743-7197), Oxford Plaza, Route 26, Oxford. Billing itself as "Western Maine's Complete Bookstore," a fully stocked store with a full children's section. **Downtown Bookshop** (743-7245), 200 Main Street, Norway. Closed Sunday. A source of general titles, stationery, cards, and magazines. **Bridgton Books** (647-2122), 74 Main Street. Extensive stock, books on tape, stationery, music.

CRAFTS SHOPS

Craftworks (647-5436), Upper Village, Bridgton. Open daily. Filling a former church and two neighboring buildings, selective women's clothing, pottery, books, linens, handmade pillows, crafted jewelry, etc.

Cry of the Loon (655-5060), Route 302, South Casco. Ten rooms of gifts, crafts, sculpture garden.

Frances Riecken Pottery (928-2411), Center Lovell. Ceramic cookware, porcelain, and other functional pots, made for the past 40 years in this studio on Kezar Lake.

The Maine Theme (647-2161), 36 Main Street, Bridgton. Open daily. Two floors of New England–crafted work and widely assorted gifts.

SPECIAL SHOPS

Sportshaus (647-5100), 61 Main Street, Bridgton. Open daily. Known for its original Maine T-shirts; also a selection of casual clothes, canvas bags, tennis rackets, downhill and cross-country skis, athletic footwear, swimwear, and golf accessories. Canoe, kayak, sailboat, and sailboard rentals.

United Society of Shakers (926-4597), Route 26, New Gloucester. Open Memorial Day through Columbus Day; sells Shaker herbs, teas, handcrafted items.

SPECIAL EVENTS

July: **Independence Day** is big in both Bridgton and Naples. Bridgton events include a lobster/clambake at the town hall, a road race, a concert, arts and crafts fair, and fireworks. In Naples, the fireworks over the lake are spectacular. Also in early July, the **Oxford 250 NASCAR Race** draws entrants from throughout the world to the Oxford Plains Speedway, and **Harrison** celebrates **Old Home Days. Founders Day** on **Paris Hill** is observed mid-month. In late July, a major **crafts fair** at the town hall is sponsored by the Bridgton Arts and Crafts Society; the 3-day **Lakes Region Antique Show** is held at the high school; and the **Bean Hole Bean Festival** in Oxford draws thousands.

August: **Gray** and **Windham Old Home Days,** both in the beginning of the month, include a parade, contests, and public feeds. In Lovell, the **Annual Arts and Artisans Fair** (midmonth) is held on the library grounds: chicken barbecue, book and crafts sale.

September: **Oxford County Agricultural Fair** in West Paris is usually held during the second week.

October: **Fryeburg Fair,** Maine's largest agricultural fair, is held for a week in early October, climaxing with the Columbus Day weekend. This is an old-fashioned agricultural happening—one of the most colorful in the country.

December: **Christmas open house and festivals** in Harrison, Paris Hill, and Naples.

Bethel Area

Bethel is a natural farming and trading site on the Androscoggin River. Its town common is the junction for routes west to the White Mountains, north to the Mahoosucs, east to the Oxford Hills, and south to the lakes.

When the trains from Portland to Montreal began stopping here in 1851, Bethel also became an obvious summer retreat for city people. But unlike many summer resorts of that era, it was nothing fancy. Families stayed the season in the big, white farmhouses, of which there are still plenty. They feasted on home-grown and home-cooked food, then walked it off on nearby mountain trails.

Hiking remains a big lure for summer and fall visitors. The White Mountain National Forest comes within a few miles of town, and trails radiate from nearby Evans Notch. Just 12 miles northwest of Bethel, Grafton Notch State Park also offers some short hikes to spectacles such as Screw Auger Falls and to a wealth of well-equipped picnic sites. Blueberrying and rockhounding are local pastimes, and the hills are also good pickings for history buffs.

The hills were once far more peopled than they are today—entire villages have vanished. Hastings, for example, now just the name of a national forest campground, was once a thriving community complete with post office, stores, and a wood alcohol mill that shipped its product by rail to Portland, thence to England.

The Bethel Inn, born of the railroad era, is still going strong. Opened in 1913 by millionaire William Bingham II and dedicated to a prominent neurologist (who came to Bethel to recuperate from a breakdown), it originally featured a program of strenuous exercise—one admired by the locals (wealthy clients actually paid the doctor to chop down his trees) as well as by the medical profession. The inn is still known for at least two forms of exercise—golf and cross-country skiing.

Bethel is best known these days as a ski town. Sunday River, 6 miles to the north, claims to "offer the most dependable snow in North America" and, despite its relatively low altitude, has managed to produce reliably good snow conditions on its eight mountains throughout the season. Powered by its snow guns (powered in turn by water from the Androscoggin), the family-geared resort has doubled and redoubled

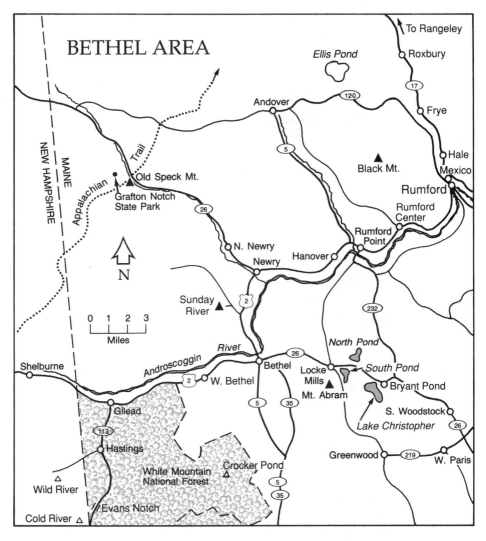

its trails, lifts, and lodging over the last 17 years. Its owner, Les Otten, recently stunned new England by acquiring five of the region's major ski resorts, including Killington in Vermont (by far the East's largest ski resort) and its long-time Maine competitor, Sugarloaf. So it happens that Bethel is now the address of the American Skiing Company, the largest ski resort–operating company in North America. Mount Abram, a few miles south of the village, by contrast remains one of New England's friendliest old-fashioned family ski areas.

Skiers tend to see Bethel as "a quick hit" that you simply get to— and out of—without stopping on the way to the snow-covered trails 75 miles north of Portland. In summer, it's a very different story. As it has been since settlement, Bethel is a natural way station—between the

White Mountains and the coast, and between the lake resorts and children's camps to the south and Rangeley to the north.

For Bethel, however, tourism has remained the icing rather than the cake. Its lumber mills manufacture pine boards, furniture parts, and broom handles. Three dairy farms ship 7000 gallons of milk per week. Bethel is also home to Gould Academy, a coed prep school with a handsome campus. Brooks Brothers is still the name of the hardware store, not a men's clothier, and Preb's pharmacy is still the prime local source of envelopes, diapers, liquor, ice cream, Timex watches, toys, and stationery.

GUIDANCE

Bethel Area Chamber of Commerce (824-2282), PO Box 439, 30 Cross Street, Bethel 04217, publishes an excellent area guide and maintains a reservation service (824-3585; 1-800-442-5826). The chamber occupies a sleek new depot-style building in Bethel Station, off Lower Main Street (Route 26).

Sunday River maintains its own toll-free reservation number (1-800-543-2SKI), good nationwide and in Canada; the service is geared toward winter and condo information, but also serves local inns and B&Bs.

GETTING THERE

By air: The **Portland International Jetport,** served by Continental Express, United, Delta, USAir, and TW Express, is 75 miles from Bethel. All major car rentals are available at the airport. **Bethel Air Service** (824-4321) offers air taxi/charter service; the **Bethel Airport** (824-4321) has a paved 3150-foot runway.

By car: Bethel is a convenient way stop between New Hampshire's White Mountains (via Route 2) and the Maine coast. From Boston, take the Maine Turnpike to Gray, exit 11; Bethel is 55 miles north on Route 26. There are restaurants en route in South Paris (see "Sebago and Long Lakes Region").

MEDICAL EMERGENCY

Bethel Area Health Center (824-2193), or Sheriff's Department (1-800-482-7433).

TO SEE

HISTORIC HOUSES AND MUSEUMS

Moses Mason House (824-2908), 15 Mason Street, Bethel. Open July and August, 1–4 daily except Monday, and by appointment the rest of the year; $2 per adult, $1 per child. This exquisite Federal-style mansion, home of the Bethel Historical Society, is proof of the town's early prosperity. Restored to its original grandeur when it was owned by Dr. Moses Mason, one of Bethel's most prominent citizens in the 1800s, it has Rufus Porter murals in the front hall and fine furnishings, woodwork, and special exhibits.

Woodstock Historical Society Museum (665-2450), Route 26, Bryant Pond. Open Memorial Day through Labor Day, Saturday 1–4 or by appointment. An old barn housing a collection of old furniture, glass, uniforms, books, wooden toys, pictures, and, of course, a crank phone.

COVERED BRIDGE

Artist's Covered Bridge, Newry (across the Sunday River, 5 miles northwest of Bethel). A weathered town bridge built in 1872 and painted by numerous 19th-century landscape artists, notably John Enneking. A great spot to sun and swim. Other swimming holes can be found at intervals along the road above the bridge.

SCENIC DRIVES

Evans Notch. Follow Route 2 west to Gilead and turn south on Route 113, following the Wild and then the Cold River south through one of the most spectacular mountain passes in northern New England. (Also see *Hiking* and *Campgrounds*.)

Grafton Notch State Park. A beautiful drive even if you don't hike (see *Hiking*). Continue on beyond Upton for views of Lake Umbagog; note the loop you can make back from Upton along the old road to Andover (look for the vintage 1867 Lovejoy Covered Bridge across the Ellis River), then south on Route 5 to Route 2.

Patte Brook Multiple-Use Management Demonstration Area, a 4-mile, self-guided tour with stops at 11 areas along Patte Brook near the national forest's Crocker Pond campground in West Bethel. The tour begins on Forest Road No. 7 (Patte Brook Road), 5 miles south of Bethel on Route 5. A glacial bog, former orchards and homesites, and an old dam and pond are among the clearly marked sites.

Rangeley and **Weld Loops.** See the introduction to "Western Mountains and Lakes" for a description of these rewarding drives. You can access either by following Route 2 north from Bethel along the Androscoggin, but back-road buffs may prefer cutting up the narrow rural valleys threaded by Rumford Road or Route 232 from Locke Mills; both join Route 2 at Rumford Point.

TO DO

AIRPLANE RIDES

Bethel Air Service (824-4321). Steve Whitney and Dan Bilodeau offer daily scenic flights of the area with views of the Bethel and Appalachian Mountain areas year-round. They also offer flight instruction, air taxi/charter, and a public lounge.

BICYCLING

Sunday River's Mountain Bike Park (824-3000; 1-800-543-2SKI), Sunday River Ski Area, Newry. Two chairlifts access 60 miles of bike trails. Lift and trail passes are sold at South Ridge Base Lodge. Lodging, lift, and meal packages are available. Rental bikes are available.

Bethel Outdoor Adventures (836-3607) offers scheduled, guided mountain bike tours as well as custom tours. Rental bikes are also available in Bethel from **Mahoosuc Mt. Sports** (824-3786), Main Street, Bethel; **The Great American Bike Renting Company** (824-3092) rents tandems as well as mountain bikes.

CANOEING AND KAYAKING

Popular local routes include the **Ellis River** in Andover (13 easy miles from a covered bridge in East Andover to Rumford Point); the **Androscoggin River** has become far more accessible in recent years with 10 put-in points mapped and shuttle service offered between Shelburne on the New Hampshire line and the Rumford Boat Landing; the **Sunday River** (beginning at the covered bridge) also offers great white water in spring. A chain of water connects **North, South,** and **Round Ponds** and offers a day of rewarding paddling, with swimming holes and picnic stops en route.

Bethel Outdoor Adventures (836-3607; 1-800-533-3607), Route 2 in West Bethel, offers shuttle service, canoe and kayak rentals, guided trips, and kayak clinics; also operates Riverside Campground in Bethel. Guided trips and rentals are available from **Mahoosuc Guide Service** (824-3092) and from **Wild River Adventure Guide Service** (824-2608).

CHAIRLIFT RIDES

Sunday River Ski Resort (824-3000) offers scenic chairlift rides up the mountain (you must walk down, since the chair is not equipped to carry passengers down). Weather permitting, Memorial Day through July 4 weekends and daily through Columbus Day weekend.

DOGSLEDDING

Mahoosuc Mountain Adventures (824-2073), Bear River Road, Newry 04261. Polly Mahoney and Kevin Slater offer combination backcountry skiing and mushing trips. You can be as involved with the dogs as you want: an hour, a day, or a 3-day, 2-night trip.

FISHING

Temporary nonresident licenses are available at the **Bethel, Newry,** and **Woodstock Town Offices;** also at **Dave's Store** in Andover, **Bob's Corner Store** in Locke Mills, and **Bethel Outdoor Adventures** in West Bethel.

GOLF

Bethel Inn and Country Club (824-2175), Bethel. An 18-hole, championship-length course and driving range. Mid-May to October the inn's Guaranteed Performance School of Golf offers 3- and 5-day sessions (classes limited to three students per PGA instructor); golf cart rentals are available.

HIKING

White Mountain National Forest, although primarily in New Hampshire, includes 41,943 acres in Maine. A number of the trails in the Evans Notch area are spectacular. Trail maps for the Baldface Circle Trail,

Basin Trail, Bickford Brook Trail, and Caribou Trail are available from the Evans Notch Ranger District (824-2134), Bridge Street, Bethel— open Monday through Friday 8–4. Pick up detailed maps from the chamber (see *Guidance*).

Grafton Notch State Park, Route 26, between Newry and Upton. From Bethel, take Route 2 east to Route 26 north for 7.8 miles. Turn left at the Getty station (Newry Corner) and go toward New Hampshire for 8.7 miles. **Screw Auger Falls** is 1 mile farther—a spectacular area at the end of the Mahoosuc Range. Other sights include **Mother Walker Falls** and **Moose Cave,** a ¼-mile nature walk. The big hike is up **Old Speck,** the third highest mountain in the state; up Old Speck Trail and back down the Firewarden's Trail is 5½ miles.

Step Falls can be found just before the entrance to Grafton Notch State Park. From Newry Corner, go 7.9 miles. On your right will be a white farmhouse, followed by a field just before a bridge. There is a road leading to the rear left of the field, where you may park. The well-marked trail is just behind the trees at the back. Please respect the private property adjoining the trail and falls. This scenic area on Wight's Brook, maintained by The Nature Conservancy, has been enjoyed by local families for generations.

In Shelburne there are hiking trails on **Mount Crag, Mount Cabot,** and **Ingalls Mountain,** and there are more trails in **Evans Notch.** For details, check the AMC *White Mountain Guide,* and *50 Hikes in Southern and Coastal Maine* by John Gibson, published by Backcountry Publications, Woodstock, VT 05091.

Mount Will Trail. Recently developed by the Bethel Conservation Commission, this is a 3¼-mile loop; many people choose only to climb to the North Ledges (640 vertical feet in ¾ mile), yielding a view of the Androscoggin Valley, which only gets better over the next 1½ miles— climbing over ledges to 1450 feet and then descending the South Cliffs. The trailhead is a chained-off logging road on Route 2 just 1.9 miles beyond the Riverside Rest Area (which is just beyond the turnoff for Sunday River).

HORSEBACK RIDING
Speckled Mountain Ranch (836-2908), Flat Road, West Bethel, offers lessons and riding.

LLAMA TREKKING
Telemark Inn & Llama Farm (836-2703), RFD 2, Box 800, Bethel 04217. Treks offered April through October for guests of the Telemark Inn.

ROCKHOUNDING
This corner of Oxford County is recognized as one of the world's richest sources of some minerals and gems. More than a third of the world's mineral varieties can be found here. Gems include amethyst, aquamarine, tourmaline, and topaz. Mining has gone on around here since tourmaline was discovered at Mount Mica in 1821. Although **Perham's**

of West Paris (see "Sebago and Long Lakes Region" and *Rockhounding* under "What's Where in Maine") is the famous old rockhounding mecca, Jim Mann's **Mt. Mann** (824-3030) on Main Street, Bethel, has recently expanded to include "Maine's most extensive mineral museum." In the cellar are Crystal Caves for Kids (of all ages): a dimly lit "mine" in which rock hounds can fill their cardboard buckets (for a nominal fee) and then identify them back in the museum. Actual mine tours are also planned.

SWIMMING

There are numerous lakes and river swimming holes in the area. It is best to ask the chamber (see *Guidance*) about where access is currently possible. "Never-fail" spots include the following:

Artist's Covered Bridge. Follow Sunday River signs north from Bethel, but continue on Sunday River Road instead of turning onto the ski-area access road. Look for the covered bridge on your left. Space for parking, bushes for changing.

Wild River in Evans Notch, Gilead, offers some obvious access spots off Route 113, as does the **Bear River,** which follows Route 26 through Grafton Notch.

CROSS-COUNTRY SKIING

Sunday River Ski Touring Center (824-2410), Bethel (based at Sunday River Inn, near the ski area). A total of 40 km of double-tracked trails loop through the woods, including a section to Artist's Covered Bridge. Thanks to the high elevation, careful trail prepping, and heavy-duty grooming equipment, snow tends to stick here when it's scarce in much of Maine. The center offers guided night skiing, rentals, instruction, and snacks.

Bethel Inn and Country Club (824-2175), Bethel. Trails meander out over the golf course and through the woods, offering beautiful mountain views, solitude, and challenges suitable for all levels. Skating and classic trails, rental equipment, and lessons available.

Carter's X-Country Center (539-4848), Middle Intervale Road (off Route 26 south of the village), Bethel. Dave Carter, a member of one of Bethel's oldest families and a longtime cross-country pro, maintains some 65 km of wooded trails on 1000 acres, meandering from 600 up to 1800 feet in elevation; an easy loop connects two lodges and runs along the Androscoggin River. Reasonably priced equipment rentals and lessons.

Telemark Inn & Llama Farm (836-2703), West Bethel. These 20 km of high-elevation, wooded trails and unlimited backcountry skiing terrain frequently represent the best cross-country skiing in the area—but Steve Crone issues only 15 passes a day, preserving the wilderness feel of his resort for Telemark Inn guests. Inquire about skijoring behind huskies!

Also see Mahoosuc Mountain Adventures under *Dogsledding* and contact the Bethel Ranger Station for details about cross-country trails in the White Mountain National Forest (see *Hiking*).

DOWNHILL SKIING

Ski Mount Abram (875-5003), Locke Mills. Not so long ago Rick and Micki Hoddinott got together with four other partners and saved this old-style ski area from extinction. The area now includes 35 trails and slopes, which hold some pleasant surprises, including two black diamond trails and a "cruiser" trail. The vertical drop is 1030 feet.

Facilities include 65–70 percent snowmaking; two double chairlifts and three T-bars; an expanded "barn red" lodge with lounge, snack shop, Keenan Co. ski shop, nursery, and ski rentals; and 60 condominiums. PSIA ski school is offered, and there is a variety of special programs, including two-for-one skiing on Tuesdays. Family-friendly rates: On weekends $30 adults, $18 juniors; half-day $14. During midweek $20 adults, $15 juniors. Special student, senior, and group rates. Thursday- and Friday-night skiing.

Sunday River Ski Area (824-3000; resort reservations: 1-800-543-2SKI), Newry 04217. Sunday River has become synonymous with snow. Powered by the incessant output of its snow guns and grooming fleet, it has shown substantial growth annually for the past 16 years. In Bethel's introduction we noted that owner Les Otten now heads the American Ski Company, the largest ski resort–operating company in New England—and North America. It includes Killington, the mammoth Vermont ski resort for which the 23-year-old Otten first came to 12-trail Sunday River. That was in 1972, an era when environmentalists were calling the shots in Vermont, curtailing Killington's growth—so it happened that a big Vermont resort bought a little Maine ski area. Killington's Sherburne Corporation installed a chairlift and some snowmaking equipment, then got the green light to expand again on its own turf. In 1980 it sold Sunday River to Otten. It was from Killington that Otten imbibed an obsession with snowmaking and a sense of how trails can multiply along a range of mountains. What it lacks in altitude (the highest peak is just 3140 feet) the resort makes up for in easy access to water, the essential ingredient in snowmaking.

At Sunday River, 121 trails and glades now lace eight interconnected mountain peaks, including the Jordan Bowl. Challenges include a 3-mile run from a summit and White Heat—"the steepest, longest, widest lift-served expert trail in the East." The trails are served by seven quad chairlifts (three high-speed detachable), five triple chairlifts, and two doubles. The vertical "descent" is 2300 feet. Snowmaking is on 92 percent of the skiing terrain.

Facilities include three base lodges and a Mountaintop Peak Lodge, ski shops, and several restaurants; a total of 5400 beds are in condominium hotels with pools and Jacuzzis, town houses, a new slope-side Summit Hotel, a Snow Cap Inn (really a lodge), and the Snow Cap Ski Dorm (geared to groups).

The ski school offers Guaranteed Learn-to-Ski in One Day and

Bethel Inn

Perfect Turn clinics, Mogul Mites for ages 4–6, Mogul Meisters for ages 7–12, a Junior Racing Program, and a Maine Handicapped Skiing Program. A halfpipe is lit for snowboarders at the White Cap Base Lodge.

Lift tickets are $86 per adult and $54 per junior for 2 days on weekends; less midweek. Many lodging packages available.

ICE SKATING

In winter, a portion of Bethel's common is flooded, and ice skates can be rented from the cross-country center in the Bethel Inn. Skate rentals are also available at the public skating rink at Sunday River's White Cap Base Lodge.

SNOWMOBILING

Local enthusiasts have developed a trail system in the area. Contact the chamber (see *Guidance*) for information on where to get maps. Maine and New Hampshire also maintain 60 miles of trails in the Evans Notch District. **Sun Valley Sports** (824-7553) on Sunday River Road rents snowmobiles.

SLEIGH RIDES

Telemark Inn, Sunday River Inn, and the **Bethel Inn and Country Club** all offer sleigh rides.

LODGING

Also see the Waterford Inne, Lake House, and Kedarburn Inn in "Sebago and Long Lakes Region."

INNS

Bethel Inn and Country Club (824-2175), Bethel 04217. This rambling, yellow structure with mansionlike cottages dominates the town common. There are 57 rooms in the inn and guest houses, all with phones and private baths. The common rooms downstairs are large and formal, but there is nothing starchy about the downstairs Mill Brook Tavern. The formal dining room is one of the loveliest around, with a fireplace and windows overlooking the mountains (see *Dining Out*). There are also 40 one- and two-bedroom town houses, and a recreation center with a pool and hot tub, two saunas, exercise room, game room, and lounge. The pool is outdoors but heated to 91 degrees for winter use. The 18-hole golf course, with 7 holes dating from 1915, 11 more added by Geoffrey Cornish, is a big draw, with golf school sessions offered throughout the season. Facilities also include a tennis court, a boathouse with canoes and sailfish, and a sandy beach on Songo Pond, as well as an extensive cross-country ski network (see *Golf, Cross-Country Skiing,* and *Sleigh Rides*). $95–140 per person double occupancy (no meals); $140–360 per town house (no meals). Many packages are available, especially off-season.

Telemark Inn (836-2703), RFD 2, Box 800, Bethel 04217. It is a challenge to describe this unusual retreat, set among birch trees 2.5 miles off the nearest back road, surrounded by national forest. The feel is that of a north woods sporting camp—with a herd of llamas. Steve Crone offered the first llama treks in New England and he delights in taking guests on 4- to 6-hour treks into the surrounding wilderness. Hiking, canoeing, and mountain biking are also offered, and winter brings exceptional cross-country skiing and the opportunity to try skiing behind huskies. Jo, Steve's ever-cheerful and competent assistant, draws on the inn's substantial herb and vegetable garden to produce memorable meals served family-style at the round cherrywood table, supported by tree trunks. Built in classic "Maine rustic"–style as a millionaire's retreat, the inn has five rooms sharing two baths and accommodates 12 to 17 guests, with plenty of common space including a large semi-enclosed porch and a living room with a magnificent mineral-studded fireplace. $90 per couple, $75 single with breakfast; $75 per day for a llama trek; $399 per adult for 3 days of activities and meals; many packages; children's rates.

Sunday River Inn (824-2410), RFD 2, Bethel 04217. Primarily a winter inn; open only to groups in summer and fall. A large fireplace, a selection of books, and quiet games are in the living room, and an adjacent room can be used for small conferences. A game room, sauna, and wood-heated hot tub just outside the back door are also available to guests. Sleeping arrangements range from dorms to private rooms in the inn or adjacent chalet. The inn maintains its own extensive cross-country trail system and is handy to Sunday River Ski Area. $44–80 per person includes two meals; children's rates.

L'Auberge (824-2774; 1-800-760-2774), Mill Hill Road, Bethel 04217. A former barn (belonging to a long-vanished mansion), has for 20 years been a gracious inn. Recently renovated, the five guest rooms and two suites are furnished with antiques, and all have private baths. The Theater Suite includes a dressing room (where cots can be put) and a staircase and balcony—left over from the days when the building was a theater (this room was the stage). Guests enter a large double living room (a great space for groups to gather) with a baby grand Steinway and elegant hearth. The dining rooms by contrast are small, but well lit; dinner is served to the public (see *Dining Out*). Village shops and restaurants are just around the corner. $65–120 for a double with breakfast.

Sudbury Inn (824-2174; 1-800-395-7837), Lower Main Street, Bethel 04217. A nicely restored village inn built in 1873 to serve train travelers (the depot was just down the street). The 10 guest rooms, seven suites are all different shapes and decors, but all have private baths. The dining room is open to the public and the basement-level Suds Pub (see *Eating Out*) is a year-round evening gathering spot. $50–150 double, includes a full, "made-to-order" breakfast.

(Also see Summit Hotel under *Ski Lodges and Condominiums*—Sunday River.)

BED & BREAKFASTS

Chapman Inn (824-2657), Bethel 04217. A find for both families and singles. A rambling white Federal house on the common in the National Historic District presents a variety of options under one roof: six spacious, carefully furnished rooms (two private, four sharing two baths) and three apartments with full kitchens. In addition to the living room and dining room, common space in the attached barn includes a game room with pool table and two saunas, and a dormitory that sleeps 24. Handy to cross-country trails at the Bethel Inn, also to village shops and restaurants. Hot drinks and baked goods greet guests in late afternoon. $45–95 per room or apartment, $10 less for singles, $25 per person for the dorm; all rates include a full breakfast; midweek and ski-week specials.

Douglass Place (824-2229), Bethel 04217. A handsome, 20-room home that once took in summer boarders. Dana and Barbara Douglass have raised four daughters here and now graciously welcome guests. There are four guest rooms—one with a queen-sized bed and three with twin beds—a game room (with piano, pool table, and Ping Pong table), a Jacuzzi, and a big homey kitchen where breakfast is served. Attractive living and dining rooms, grounds, a gazebo, and a large barn. $50–60 includes continental breakfast with homemade muffins and fresh fruit; special rates for singles and children.

The Ames Place (824-3170), 46 Broad Street, Bethel 04217. Sally and Dick Taylor's pleasant 1850s home on the common has two spacious guest rooms, one with an extra-long double four-poster and a single bed in a corner ell ($80) and the other with an extra-long antique spool bed, a working fireplace, and a sitting area ($90). Neither room is fussy but both have pleasing details like hooked rugs, fresh flowers, and well-chosen country antiques. The barn, accessible through the country kitchen, is filled with antiques—an array of furniture, furnishings, clothing, and jewelry, all gathered from the Bethel area. Common rooms include a comfortable living room and a sunny breakfast room in which a full breakfast is served. The grounds stretch back 6 acres with perennial gardens and an orchard.

The Briar Lea B&B (824-4717), Route 2/26, Bethel 04217. Gary and Carol Brearley have renovated this handsome old farmhouse beautifully and offer six rooms, all with private bath. The living room with its polished floors and deep blue wallpaper is particularly attractive, as is the neighboring breakfast room in which a full breakfast is served buffet-style. From $42 per couple off-season to $89 on winter weekends.

Holidae House (824-3400; 1-800-882-3306), PO Box 851, Bethel 04217. A gracious Main Street house (the first in Bethel to be electrified), built in the 1890s by a local lumber baron. Two guest rooms with private bath, a studio, and a three-bedroom apartment are furnished in comfortable antiques; each has cable TV, phone, and private bath. Common space includes a family room with a woodstove. $45–60 double, includes breakfast. Efficiencies $65 and up off-season to $150 in-season for four in the apartment that sleeps 8 to 10 (each extra person is $25).

✎ **The Norseman** (824-2002), Route 2, Bethel 04217. A fine old farmstead with 10 light, pleasant guest rooms and 22 more units in the old barn. Guests in the house have access to the big, comfortable living room, with its fireplace made from local stones, and the dining room, with a similar hearth where breakfast is served. The motel units are spacious and handicapped accessible; amenities include laundry room and game room. $52–118 includes continental breakfast.

SKI LODGES AND CONDOMINIUMS

✎ **Sunday River** (824-3000; resort reservations: 1-800-543-2SKI), PO Box 450, Bethel 04217. Now offers more than 5000 "slope-side beds." There are nine condominium hotels, ranging from studios to three-bedroom units. Each complex has access to an indoor pool, Jacuzzi, sauna, laundry, recreation room, and game room; **Cascades** and **Sunrise** offer large common rooms with fireplaces, and **Fall Line** has a restaurant. **Merrill Brook Village Condominiums** have fireplaces, and many have whirlpool tubs. **South Ridge** also offers fireplaces in each unit—from $135 for a studio to $520 for a three-bedroom unit; rates are lower off-season. Rooms in the 68-room **Snow Cap Inn,** which has an atrium with fieldstone fireplaces, exercise room, and outdoor Jacuzzi, are $110–150, and a bunk in the Snow Cap Ski Dorm is $25–35. The 147-room **Summit Hotel and Conference Center,** with both standard and kitchen-equipped units and a health club with tennis courts, pool, and conference facilities, offers rooms and studios ($109–249) as well as one-bedroom ($159–400) and two-bedroom ($299–590) efficiency units (less for multi-day stays) in winter, much less in summer.

Pine-Sider Lodge (665-2226), 481 Gore Road, Bryant Pond 04219-6113. Bill and Ernestine Riley designed and built Pine-Sider for families and groups. The lodge is divided into four efficiency units (the Rileys live in one), sleeping four to eight people. $250–325 per week in summer; $75–150 per night in ski season.

☞✑ **The River View** (824-2808), Route 2, 357 Mayville Road, Bethel 04217. Each of the 32 two-bedroom units has a balcony or patio facing the Androscoggin River across a field. Each also has a kitchen, living room, dining area, and bath, sleeps four comfortably, and has cable TV, phone, air-conditioning, and daily maid service. The town's riverside nature path adjoins the property and there is a playground, game room, and tennis court, and—in winter—Jacuzzi and sauna. $50 double in summer ($65 for four people), $69–90 double in winter ($89–140 for four), plus $2 gratuity.

CAMPGROUNDS

In the **Evans Notch area** of the White Mountain National Forest there are five campgrounds: Basin (21 sites), Cold River (12 sites), Crocker Pond (7 sites), Hastings (24 sites), and Wild River (11 sites). All accept reservations during the May 13 to October 11 season. Phone: 1-800-280-2267, Monday through Friday (Pacific time, so from the East Coast, phone between noon and 9 or, on Saturday and Sunday 1 and 6). For information, phone the Evans Notch Ranger Station (824-2134), Bridge Street, Bethel.

Littlefield Beaches (875-3290), RFD 1, Box 4300, Bryant Pond 04219. Open Memorial Day to October. A clean, quiet family campground surrounded by three connecting lakes. Full hook-ups, laundry room, miniature golf, game rooms, swimming. Daily and seasonal rates are available, reduced rates in June and September.

Also see Papoose Pond under "Sebago and Long Lakes."

OTHER LODGING

The Maine House and the Maine FarmHouse (1-800-646-8737), Lake Road, Bryant Pond. An unusual lodging option, two self-service guest houses geared to groups. The Maine House, sited on Lake Christopher, offers eight rooms (sleeping up to 29) sharing 6½ baths and features a large recreation room with a floor-to-ceiling hearth, a living room with Franklin stove, a fully equipped kitchen, cable TV and VCR, a steam room, washer and dryer, and a dock with canoes. The recently restored FarmHouse (75 feet from the Maine House), which can sleep 24, offers similar amenities (but no steam room); it can be rented as one- and two-bedroom suites ($44–78 per couple).

WHERE TO EAT

DINING OUT

Bethel Inn and Country Club (824-2175), Bethel Common. An elegant, formal dining room with a hearth and large windows overlooking the golf course and hills, with a year-round veranda. All three meals are open to the public. The menu offers a choice of a dozen entrées, including charbroiled marinated duck breast, roasted fresh garlic and herbed lamb loin, and maple walnut–scented venison medallions; $14–21 including salad, starches, and vegetable. Leave room for dessert.

☞✐**Mother's** (824-2589), Main Street, Bethel. Open daily for lunch and dinner. A green-and-white gingerbread house with three dining rooms, eclectically furnished with books, old pictures and oddments, and stoves. At dinner, entrées range from $7.50 to $14.95. Pastas are a specialty. At lunch try the Maine crabcake sandwich ($7). Children's menu.

L'Auberge (824-2774; 1-800-760-2774), Mill Hill Road, Bethel. A country inn with three intimate dining rooms and a first-class chef. You might begin with crabmeat puffs ($8) or escargots en croûte ($6.50) and dine on roasted duck with Chambord-soaked cherries, bouillabaisse, or stuffed pork loin. Entrées $13–24.

Sudbury Inn (824-2174), Main Street, Bethel. Breakfast, lunch, and dinner. A pleasant dining room and sun porch in a 19th-century village inn. The dinner menu includes chicken in pastry and baked Maine haddock filled with spinach and shiitake mushrooms. Entrées $12–23.

EATING OUT

The Sunday River Brewing Co. (824-4ALE), junction of Sunday River Road and Route 2. Dining areas surround brewing kettles and tanks. Patrons can choose from a variety of house brews to wash down soups and salads, burgers, and pizza. Often has live entertainment evenings.

Matterhorn Wood-Fired Pizza and Fresh Pasta (824-OVEN), corner of Main and Cross Streets. Swiss owner-chefs and atmosphere, great pasta, seafood, pizza, salads, and desserts.

Cafe di Cocoa (824-JAVA), 125 Main Street, Bethel. Open daily for breakfast, lunch, and takeout. Cathy di Cocoa's cheerful eatery specializes in crunchy and vegetarian dishes. Fresh juices, gourmet coffees.

Suds Pub, downstairs at the Sudbury Inn. Entertainment Thursday through Saturday, otherwise a friendly pub with 5 draft and 25 bottled beers; a reasonably priced pub menu. Open year-round.

Breau's (824-3192), just west of Bethel on Route 2. Will deliver, and the pizza is good. Homemade clam "chowdah," chili, burgers, subs, and salads are on the menu, too. Open from 7 AM for full breakfast.

Iron Horse Bar and Grill (824-0961) at Bethel Station. Open 5–12 daily, vintage rail cars featuring steaks and seafood.

Mexico Chicken Coop Restaurant (364-2710), Route 2 in Mexico. Don't let the outside put you off. This is a great way stop if you are heading north up Route 17 from Bethel to Rangeley. The specialties are Italian, chicken, a huge salad bar, and fresh-baked pastries.

Cisco & Poncho's (824-2902), Snows Falls, Route 26. Closed Monday. Relocated from Bethel, this place still serves outstanding Mexican cuisine, but beware: Hot means *hot*.

ENTERTAINMENT

Casablanca Cinema (824-8248), a four-screen cinema in the new Bethel Station Development (Cross Street), shows first-run films.

SELECTIVE SHOPPING

ARTISANS

Bonnema Potters (824-2821), Lower Main Street, Bethel. Open daily 8:30–5:30. Distinctive stoneware, noteworthy for both design and color: lamps, garden furniture, dinnerware, and the like produced and sold in Bonnema's big barn. Seconds are available.

GEM SHOPS

As noted in *To Do—Rockhounding*, this area is rich in semiprecious gems and minerals. Jim Mann at Mt. Mann (824-3030), Main Street, Bethel, mines, cuts, and sets his own minerals and gems. **Sunday River Gems** (824-3414), Sunday River Road (open Friday through Sunday), and **Mt. Mica Rarities** (875-3060), Route 26 in Locke Mills, are also sources of reasonably priced Maine gemstones.

SPECIAL SHOPS

Maine Line Products (824-2522), Main Street, Bethel. Made-in-Maine products and souvenirs, among which the standout is the Maine Woodsman's Weatherstick. We have one tacked to our back porch, and it's consistently one step ahead of the weatherman—pointing up to predict fair weather and down for foul.

Groan and McGurn's Tourist Trap and Craft Outlet (836-3645), Route 2, West Bethel. Begun as a greenhouse—to which the owners' specially silk-screened T-shirts were added. Now there is so much that an ever-changing catalog is available.

Preb's Marketplace (824-2820), Main Street, Bethel. Open Monday through Saturday 8:30 AM–10 PM. A full-service pharmacy; also the Western Union agent, Agency Liquor Store, and local source of Ben & Jerry's ice cream.

Playhouse Antiques (see The Ames Place under *Bed & Breakfasts*) specializes in antiques from Bethel-area homes.

Mountain Side Country Crafts (824-2518), Sunday River Road, Newry. Made-in-Maine gifts.

Philbrook Place, 162 Main Street, includes an interesting assortment of enterprises including **Books 'n' Things** (a full-service bookstore), the **Hayloft Gallery** (paintings, stained glass), **The Toy Shop,** and **True North Adventure** (sleeping bags, maps, footwear, clothing).

SPECIAL EVENTS

February: **L.L. Bean XC Ski Festival** at Gould Academy.

March: **Sunday River Langlauf Races** at the Sunday River Touring Ski Center (first Saturday)—for all ages and abilities.

April: **Pole, Paddle and Paw Race**—a combination ski and canoe event at the end of ski season, always the first Saturday in April.

July: **Bethel Open Air Art Fair** (first Saturday). **Strawberry Festival,** Locke Mills Union Church (date depends on when strawberries are ready; announced in local papers). **Mollyockett Day** (third Saturday)—road race, parade, bicycle obstacle course, fiddler contest, fireworks. Festivities honor an 18th-century medicine woman who helped the first settlers. **Annual Maine State Triathlon Classic,** Bethel (last Saturday).

August: **World's Fair,** North Waterford; **Andover Old Home Days** (both on the first weekend). **Sudbury Canada Days,** Bethel—children's parade, historical exhibits, old-time crafts demonstrations, bean supper, and variety show (second weekend).

October: **Blue Mountain Crafts Fair** at Sunday River Ski Resort (Columbus Day weekend).

December: A series of Christmas fairs and festivals climax with a **Living Nativity** on the Bethel Common the Sunday before Christmas.

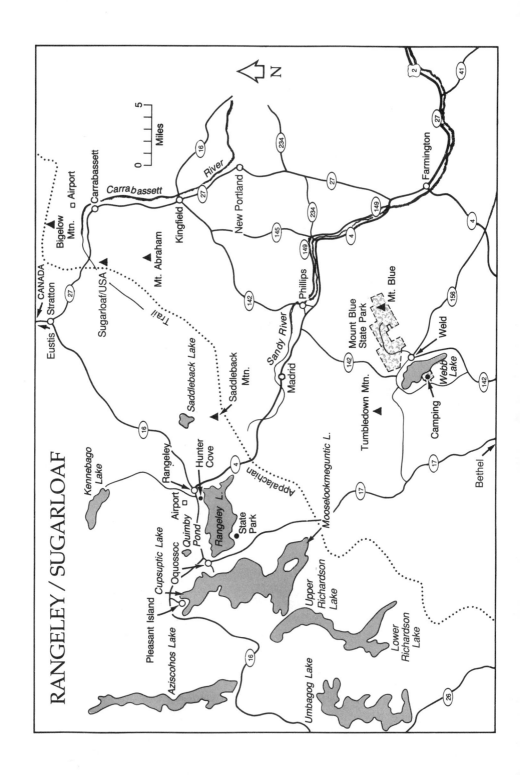

RANGELEY / SUGARLOAF

Rangeley Lakes Region

Seven lakes—Aziscohos, Richardson, Cupsuptic, Mooselookmeguntic, Kennebago, Umbagog, and Rangeley—plus dozens of ponds are scattered among magnificently high, fir-covered mountains, all within a 20-mile radius of the village of Rangeley. The big summer lures are fishing (landlocked salmon and brook trout) and hiking, and in winter there's snowmobiling and both alpine and cross-country skiing.

The Rangeley lakes region offers a sense of splendid isolation, thanks to 450 square miles of commercially forested and conservation trust land, plus the mountains that hump up in every direction, inviting you to climb.

This has been a resort area since steamboat days, as evidenced by the dozens of vintage, rustic log lodges and cottages. Resort hotels are a thing of the past here, but photographs and postcards of days gone by can be found everywhere.

In summer the town's population quadruples, but in winter, loggers outnumber skiers in the IGA. The skiers are here for Saddleback Mountain—a 4116-foot, 40-trail mountain with a high-altitude touring network that may just be New England's best-kept ski secret. On snowy weekends, it generally attracts only about 800 skiers. About the same number of snowmobilers take advantage of one of Maine's most extensive and best-groomed trail networks, found in the Rangeley area.

Doc Grant's Restaurant proclaims that Rangeley is 3107 miles from the North Pole and the same distance from the equator. It feels like a million miles from everywhere, especially if you spend some days in one of the traditional sporting camps scattered widely through surrounding woodland. The Maine classic *We Took to the Woods*, written by Louise Dickinson Rich around 1940 near Lower Richardson Lake, conveys a sense of the splendid isolation still possible.

GUIDANCE

Rangeley Lakes Region Chamber of Commerce (864-5364; 1-800-MT-LAKES), PO Box 317, Rangeley 04970. Open year-round, Monday through Saturday 9–5. The chamber maintains a walk-in information center in the village, publishes a handy "Accommodations and Services" guide and an indispensable map, keeps track of vacancies, and makes reservations.

GETTING THERE

By air: **Mountain Air Service** (864-5307) will pick you up at the **Portland International Jetport** as well as other New England airports; also serves remote ponds and camps.

By car: From points south, take the Maine Turnpike to exit 12 (Auburn), then Route 4. From New Hampshire's White Mountains, take Route 16 east. From the Bethel area, take Route 17 north (see *Scenic Loop*).

MEDICAL EMERGENCY

Rangeley Region Health Center (864-3303; after hours 1-800-398-6031), Dallas Hill Road, Rangeley. **Rangeley Ambulance** (911).

TO SEE

MUSEUM

Wilhelm Reich Museum (864-3443), off Route 4/16, Rangeley. Open July and August, Tuesday through Sunday 1–5, Sundays in September 1–5; admission. The 200-acre property, Orgonon, is worth a visit for the view alone. Wilhelm Reich was a controversial pioneer psychiatrist and scientific thinker concerned with "objectifying the presence of a ubiquitous life force." He is buried on a promontory overlooking a sweep of lake and mountains next to one of his many inventions, a "cloudbuster." There are nature trails, children's activities, and a bookstore. The museum occupies a stone observatory that Reich helped design; it contains biographical exhibits, scientific equipment, paintings, and a library and study that remain as Reich left them.

HISTORICAL MUSEUMS

Rangeley Lakes Region Historical Society (864-3317), Main and Richardson Streets, Rangeley. Open mid-June through mid-September, Monday through Saturday 10–noon. This is a great little museum occupying the only brick building in the middle of town, featuring photographs and local memorabilia from Rangeley's days of grand old hotels, trains, and lake steamers. Note the basement jail cell.

Phillips Historical Society (639-2881). Open August, Friday and Saturday 2–4, and by appointment June through October. The library and historical society are both in an 1820 house in the middle of the village. The collection includes many pictures of the region's bygone railroad (see below) and an attic full of clothes to try on.

Weld Historical Society (585-2586), Weld Village. Open July and August, Wednesday and Saturday 1–3, and by appointment. The 1842 house is filled with period furniture, clothing, and photographs. The original Town House (1845) houses farming, logging, and ice-cutting tools.

SCENIC LOOP

Route 4 to Phillips and Route 142 to Weld. Follow Route 4 from Rangeley 12 miles south to Small's Falls (see *Green Space*) and on to Phillips, once the center of the Sandy River/Rangeley Lakes "2-footer" line, now a quiet residential area. Plan to come the first or third Sunday of the month to ride the rails behind the steam train (see *To Do*). Continue on to Weld, a quiet old lake village with several good hiking options, including Tumbledown Mountain and Mount Blue. You can also swim at Mount Blue State Park. The Kawanhee Inn overlooks Lake Webb.

Weld to Byron. From Weld it's 12 miles to Byron. Drive 2 miles north on Route 142 to the State Beach sign; turn left, go ½ mile, and turn right on the first gravel road. This is Byron Road, well packed. Soon you follow the Swift River (stop and pan for gold) down into Coos Canyon; the picnic area and waterfalls are at the junction with Route 17. It's said that this is the first place in America where gold was found.

Route 17. From the picnic area, drive north on Route 17 for 10 miles to the Height O'Land (the pullout is on the other side of the road), from which the view is a spectacular spread of lakes and mountains; the view from the Rangeley Lake Overlook (northbound side of the road, a couple of miles farther) is the other direction.

TO DO

AIRPLANE RIDES
Mountain Air Service (864-5307) offers 15-minute scenic flights, longer fire patrol flights, and flight instruction.

BOAT EXCURSIONS
Half a dozen places offer tours by appointment; check in the chamber of commerce "Visitor's Guide" pamphlet (see *Guidance*). **Expeditions North** (864-3622), Route 17, Oquossoc, offers regularly scheduled party-boat tours of Rangeley Lake.

BOAT RENTALS
Check with the chamber of commerce (see *Guidance*) about the more than a dozen places in town that rent motorboats, canoes, sailboats, and waverunners, and be sure to rent one, because you're not really in Rangeley unless you're out on a lake one way or another.

CANOEING
Rangeley is the departure point for an 8-mile paddle to Oquossoc. On **Lake Mooselookmeguntic** there is a 12-mile paddle to Upper Dam, then a portage around the dam and another 8 miles to Upper Richardson Lake through the Narrows to South Arm. Check with the chamber of commerce about campsites and canoe rentals (see *Guidance*).

FISHING
Brook trout are plentiful in local streams. In the lakes, the big catch is landlocked salmon, for which the season is early spring through September. A number of fishing camps supply boats, equipment, and guides. The **Rangeley Region Sport Shop** (864-5615), Main Street, Rangeley, specializes in fly-fishing and -tying equipment; also a source of advice on where to fish and with whom (a list of local guides is posted).

GOLF

Mingo Springs Golf Course (864-5021), Proctor Road (off Route 4), Rangeley, offers 18 scenic holes; instruction, carts, and club rentals.

HIKING

The regional map published by the chamber of commerce (see *Guidance*) outlines more than a dozen well-used hiking paths, including a portion of the Appalachian Trail that passes over **Saddleback Mountain.** The longest hike is up **Spotted Mountain** (4½ miles to the top), and the most popular is the mile trail to the summit of **Bald Mountain;** both yield sweeping views of lakes, woods, and more mountains. Other favorites are Bemis Stream Trail up **Elephant Mountain** (6 hours round-trip) and the mile walk in to **Angels Falls**—which is roughly 4 miles off Route 17; be sure to use a current trail guide.

In Weld, the tried-and-true trails are **Bald Mountain** (3 miles round-trip), **Mount Blue** (3¼ miles), and **Tumbledown Mountain** (a particularly varied climb with a high altitude).

MOOSE-WATCHING

Registered Maine guide **Rich Gacki** (864-5136) in Oquossoc offers guided canoe trips departing the Rangeley Inn most days at 5 AM. This is a 3-hour expedition; reservations are required by 6 PM the previous day.

RAILROAD EXCURSION

Sandy River/Rangeley Lakes Railroad (353-8382). Runs May through October on the first and third Sundays of each month, and continuously through Phillips Old Home Days in late August and Fall Foliage Days in early October. $3 per adult, $1.50 per child 6–12. From 1873 until 1935, this narrow-gauge line spawned resort and lumbering communities along its 115-mile length. Begun as seven distinct lines, it was eventually acquired by the Maine Central, which built shops and a large round-house in Phillips. Over the past dozen years, volunteers have produced a replica of the old steam locomotive and the roundhouse, and others have helped lay a mile of track so that you can rattle along in an 1884 car just far enough to get a sense of getting around Franklin County "back when." A depot houses railroad memorabilia.

SWIMMING

Rangeley Lake State Park offers a pleasant swimming area and scattered picnic sites (see *Green Space*). Day-use fee; free under age 12. There is also a town beach with lifeguards and a playground at **Lakeside Park** in the village of Rangeley. Almost all lodging places offer water access.

Mount Blue State Park also has a nice swimming area (see *Green Space*).

SKIING

Saddleback Mountain (864-5671; snow phone: 864-3380), Box 490, Rangeley 04970. This is a very big downhill ski area with a very small, fiercely loyal following. Saddleback itself, 4116 feet high and webbed with 40 trails, forms the centerpiece in a semicircle of mountains rising above a small lake. Twelve thousand acres—comprising most of this natural bowl—are now under Saddleback ownership, and a major four-

Dogs and sled in the Rangeley Lakes region

season resort is planned. Trails and slopes include glade skiing, a 2½-mile beginner trail, and an above-treeline snowfield in spring. The vertical drop is 1830 feet. Most trails are a shade narrower and twistier than today's average, but most intermediate runs such as Haymaker and White Stallion are memorable cruising lanes. Experts will find plenty of challenge on Bronco Buster, Powderkeg, and the Nightmare Glades terrain. Facilities include a cafeteria, lounge, ski school, shop, rentals, nursery, and mountain warming hut. Lift tickets are $32 weekends ($18 juniors), $18 midweek.

Nordic Touring Center at Saddleback (864-5671) claims to be the highest-altitude (2500 feet) cross-country touring center in New England. It offers 40 km of groomed trails, guided tours, rentals, instruction, norpining, and special events. We have seldom skied anything as beautiful as the isolated Rock and Midway Pond Trails—high, sheltered, and tracked by coyotes, bobcats, and snowshoe rabbits as well as by machine.

Mount Blue State Park (585-2347) also offers extensive cross-country skiing trails.

SNOWMOBILING

Rangeley Lake State Park offers 3 miles of marked trails with access to the lake; also a connecting trail with 20 more miles of groomed trails in **Mount Blue State Park.** Rangeley's snowmobile club maintains more than 140 miles of trails.

GREEN SPACE

(Also see *Campgrounds*.)

Rangeley Lake State Park (864-3858) covers 691 acres, including more than a mile of shoreline on the southern rim of Rangeley Lake between

Routes 17 and 4. Open May 15 to early October. There are 40 scattered picnic sites, a pleasant swimming area, a boat launch, and children's play area; $2 per person.

Mount Blue State Park (585-2347), Weld (off Route 156). Open May 30 to October 15. The 6000-acre park includes Mount Blue itself, towering 3187 feet above the valley floor, and a beachside tenting area (136 sites) on Lake Webb. The lake is 3 miles wide and 6 miles long, good for catching black bass, white perch, pickerel, trout, and salmon. Boats may be rented from the ranger, and there is a recreation hall complete with fireplace. The view from the Center Hill area looks like the opening of a Paramount picture. Despite its beauty and the outstanding hiking, this is one of the few state camping facilities that rarely fills up. $1.50 per person admission.

Small's Falls, Route 4 (12 miles south of Rangeley). The Sandy River drops abruptly through a small gorge, which you can climb behind railings. A popular picnic spot. You can follow the trail to the **Chandlers Mill Stream Falls,** equally spectacular.

Hunter Cove Wildlife Sanctuary, off Route 4/16 west of Rangeley Village. Offers color-coded trails, winding in and out of the trees along a cove.

Rangeley Lakes Heritage Trust (864-7311), Oquossoc. Since the trust's founding in 1991, over 10,000 acres have been preserved, including 20 miles of lake and river frontage, 10 islands, and a 2443-foot mountain. Request the map/guide.

LODGING

INNS AND LODGES

Kawanhee Inn (585-2000), Weld 04285. (In winter contact Sturgis Butler and Marti Strunk, 778-3809 evenings; 7 Broadway, Farmington 04938.) Dining room open mid-June through Labor Day; lodging from May to October 15; cottages available from mid-May to mid-October. A traditional Maine lodge set atop a slope overlooking Lake Webb. The 14 guest rooms in the inn have recently been reduced to 6 larger, more comfortable rooms with added insulation and private baths (request a lake view). The 12 one- and two-bedroom cabins are exceptional, each with a screened porch, fireplace, kitchen, and bath. All but Pine Lodge (really a house hidden away in the pines down the road from the inn) have lake views, and the latter compensates with its skylights, privacy, added amenities, and the fact that it is set up to accommodate pets. Meals are served in the large pine dining room and on the screened veranda overlooking the water (see *Dining Out*) and the open-beamed, pine-paneled living room has a massive central fireplace, a pool table, and numerous corners in which to read and talk. There is a private beach and dock; canoes are available, and the local hiking is outstanding. Be sure to get back in time to hear Sturgis play taps. Rooms: $65–95 double; cabins: $500–700 per week; less in shoulder seasons. Room rates include continental breakfast.

*   **Bald Mountain Camps** (864-3671), PO Box 332, Oquossoc 04964. Open mid-May to mid-September. This is the surviving part of a complex that dates from 1897. Nicely old-fashioned, with fireplaces in 15 cabins and a log-style dining room, a safe sand beach, tennis courts, and lawn games. Right on Mooselookmeguntic Lake and exuding the kind of hospitality found only under long-term ownership. Stephen Philbrick is your host. $100 per person, all meals included; less for children and during May and June; some pets accepted.

Rangeley Inn and Motor Lodge (864-3341), Rangeley 04970. Open year-round. A blue-shingled, three-story landmark, partly an annex to a vanished grand hotel that stood across the road, overlooking the lake; the classic old hotel lobby dates from 1907. There are 50 guest rooms, 12 with claw-foot tubs, some with water views; also 15 nicely decorated motel units, some with kitchenettes, whirlpool baths, and woodstoves, overlooking Haley Pond, a bird sanctuary. Popular with bus groups, but also a good spot for couples. Rates that include breakfast and dinner are available. $69–114 double.

Country Club Inn (864-3831), PO Box 680, Rangeley 04970. Open year-round except April and November. Surrounded by an 18-hole golf course and overlooking the lake, this is a golfer's dream. Built by a millionaire sportsman in the late 1920s, this place has the feel of a private club. Massive stone fireplaces face each other across a gracious living room walled in knotty pine and stocked with books and puzzles. You are drawn to the view of lakes and mountains from the deck, from the pub, and from tables in the dining room. Steve and Margie Jamison offer 20 rooms with picture windows and private baths. In winter you can cross-country ski from the door, and in summer there's an outdoor pool. $110 per couple B&B, $154 MAP, less in winter.

BED & BREAKFASTS

*   **Mallory's B&B Inn** (864-2121/5316; 1-800-722-0397), Box 9, Hyatt Road, Rangeley 04970. Open June 15 through Columbus Day. A turn-of-the-century estate on the north shore of Rangeley Lake, with five bright guest rooms, four with water views, sharing three full baths. Our favorite is Anna Maria, with an antique double bed and windows on two sides. The large common room has comfortable couches, a fireplace, a piano, and a decorative "rocking moose." Upstairs, a TV, board games, and plenty of books are on hand for rainy days. The landscaped lawns slope to the lake out front, and there's a floating dock for swimming. A canoe, paddleboats, a hobie cat, and outboard motorboat, as well as mountain bikes, are available, and the heated indoor basketball court can be a blessing on rainy days. Mingo Springs (see *Golf*) is next door. Jane Mallory is a delightful host who serves unusually healthful as well as tasty

breakfasts. Children welcome, pets possible; $56–72 double includes breakfast, $15 per extra child 12 and up, $10 for ages 2–11.

Lake Webb House (585-2479), PO Box 127, Route 142, Weld 04285. Open year-round. A pleasant, welcoming old farmhouse-boardinghouse with a big porch, near the lake and village. Cheryl England makes the quilts that grace the beds in her three guest rooms (which share two baths) and also sells them. There's a pleasant family room with a woodstove. $45–55 double ($35 single!) includes a full breakfast. Cheryl's breakfasts are well enough known locally to draw outside guests (June 15–Labor Day); it's amazing how many people also find their way to her Morning Glory Bake Shop (behind the house), good for breads, oversized cookies, and box lunches.

Piper Brook Bed & Breakfast (864-3469), PO Box 139, Rangeley 04970. Just 3 miles from town, but frankly, we almost gave up a couple of times, following what seems like a logging road up and up to this new house on a wooded flank of Saddleback. But the effort was rewarded by the expansive lake view from the porch and gracious living room (with a fireplace and baby grand piano). Martha Bekeny offers four large guest rooms, $70 for one with a king-sized bed, whirlpool, and view, $65 for another with private bath, $55 for two with shared baths; $10 per extra person; breakfast included.

SPORTING CAMPS

Geared to serious fishermen in May, June, and September, and to families in July and August. These are true destination resorts, but don't expect organized activities.

☞ **Bosebuck Mountain Camps** (243-2945; 486-3238 in winter), Wilsons Mills 03579. Open May through November. Accessible by boat or by a 14-mile private gravel road (phone to check gate times before you decide to drop by), the camps are sited at the remote end of Aziscohos Lake. The lodge houses a dining room overlooking the water and a sitting room filled with books; all heat is from woodstoves, and the nine cabins have electric lights powered by a generator that runs 8 hours a day. Tom Rideout caters to serious fishermen, giving access to the Parmachenee area and to the Big and Little Magalloway Rivers (fly-fishing only). Three full meals are included in the rate: $78 per person per night ($75 for stays of longer than 3 days). If the moosehorn (radio phone) doesn't answer, keep trying. Dogs welcome. Family rates in July and August ($56 per person) when fishing eases off. Fishing package rate available in July.

Grant's Kennebago Camps (864-3608; 282-5264 in winter; 1-800-633-4815), PO Box 786, Rangeley 04970. Open after ice breaks up and through September. A serious fly-angler's haven located 9 miles up a private dirt road on Kennebago Lake. Large, excellent meals are served in the comfortable dining room with terrific lake views. Cabins are rustic, knotty pine with woodstoves and a screened-in front porch overlooking the water. Each has a dock and boat exclusively for your use during your stay. $100 per adult, $30 per child including all meals; less for a 7-day stay.

Lakewood Camps (summer: 243-2959; 392-1581 in winter), Middledam–Richardson Lake, Andover 04216. Open after ice breaks up through September. The specialty is landlocked salmon and trout; fly-fishing in 5 miles of the Rapid River. Twelve truly remote cabins; meals feature fresh-baked breads, cakes, and pies. Access is from Andover. This is very much the same place described in Louise Dickinson Rich's *We Took to the Woods*. $88 per person (2-day minimum), double occupancy includes three full meals; $40 per child under 12, $15 under age 5, pets $15. Tax and gratuity not included.

COTTAGES

Rangeley still has an unusual number of traditional, family-geared "camps."

Sundown Lodge and Cottages (864-3650; 516-485-3059 in winter), Box 40, Oquossoc 04964. Open June to September. Just three delightful one- and two-bedroom cottages right on Mooselookmeguntic Lake, and another 4 miles away. Fireplaces, lawn games, and rental bikes, boats, canoes. $460–600 weekly.

Hunter Cove (864-3383), Mingo Loop Road, Rangeley 04970. Open year-round. Eight cottages on Rangeley Lake set on 6 wooded acres, each accommodating 2–6 people. Recently renovated; a half mile to golf, Saddleback, and the village. Daily $100–150, weekly $600–850.

Mooselookmeguntic House (864-2962), Haines Landing, Oquossoc 04964. The grand old hotel by this name is gone, but the eight log cabins are well maintained and occupy a great site with a beach and marina. Many of the one- and two-bedroom cabins are on the water and have fireplaces or woodstoves. $375–625 per week.

North Camps (864-2247), PO Box 341, Oquossoc 04964 (write to E.B. Gibson). Open spring through hunting season. Fourteen cottages on Rangeley Lake among birches on a spacious lawn. Cottages have fireplaces or woodstoves, screened porches, and access to the beach, tennis, sailboats, fishing boats, and canoes. During July and August, rentals are available by the week only. Nightly rates and rates that include all three meals are available in spring and fall. $325–575 weekly.

Clearwater Sporting Camps (864-5424), Oquossoc 04964. Five cottages, all different, are scattered on private waterfront ledges along Mooselookmeguntic Lake. Michael and Tina Warren also offer boat rentals, a boat launch, swimming, and guide service. Camps $80 per day double; $560 per week.

Note: Some of the area's most famous old cottage clusters have been subdivided but are still available through local rental agents. The former Flybuck, Quimby Pond, Rangeley manor, and Saddleback Lodge properties are all now handled by local rental agents. **Rangeley Lakes Region Chamber of Commerce** (see *Guidance*) also keeps listings of available cottages.

CONDOMINIUMS

Saddleback Ski and Summer Lake Preserve (864-5671), Box 490, Rangeley 04970. There are two condo complexes at the ski resort—most units are exceptionally luxurious, with views over the lake. Some two dozen are usually available for rent. From three to five bedrooms, many with hot tubs, cable TV; all have access to the clubhouse with its game room. $170–325 per night in summer, $180–395 in winter; weekly rentals also available.

CAMPGROUNDS

For information and reservations in both the state parks described below, call 287-3821.

Rangeley Lake State Park (864-3858), between Routes 17 and 4, at the southern rim of Rangeley Lake. Some 50 campsites are well spaced among fir and spruce trees; facilities include a beach and boat launch, picnic sites, and a children's play area. $16 for nonresidents. There are also a number of private campgrounds and wilderness sites accessible only by boat; inquire at the chamber of commerce (see *Guidance*).

Mount Blue State Park (585-2347), Weld. Campsites tend to get filled up after those in better-known parks (see *Green Space*).

WHERE TO EAT

DINING OUT

Also see restaurants described in "Sugarloaf and the Carrabassett Valley." **Porter House** in Eustis and **The White Wolf** in Stratton are popular dining destinations for Rangeley visitors.

Rangeley Inn (864-3341), Main Street, Rangeley. Closed mid-April to late May; otherwise open for breakfast and dinner daily. A large hotel dining room with a high, tin ceiling and a reputation for fine dining. Entrées might include salmon with orange ginger sauce ($16.95) and crabcakes with horseradish cream ($14.95–21.95)

Kawanhee Inn (585-2000), Weld. Open for dining nightly, mid-June to September. One of Maine's most picturesque, traditional-style lodges is the setting for candlelight meals in the open-beamed dining room or screened porch overlooking Lake Webb. Fresh flowers garnish the tables, and meals are thoughtfully prepared. The chef is recognized as one of the best around, making all baked goods from scratch; the menu might include baked chicken breast stuffed with onion, feta, and spinach, served with creamy Parmesan sauce ($12.95), a Caesar salad with grilled shrimp ($9.95), a selection of pastas (from $10.95), and poached salmon with a lobster Boursin sauce ($15.95). Entrées include salad, vegetables, and warm breads.

Country Club Inn (864-3831), Rangeley. Open every evening summer and fall, weekends in winter by reservation only. The inn sits on a rise above Rangeley Lake, and the dining room windows maximize the view. The menu might include veal sautéed with Swiss cheese, tomatoes, and parsley, or baked jumbo shrimp with crab stuffing. Entrées run $10.95–16.50.

EATING OUT

The Oquossoc House Restaurant (864-3881), junction of Route 17 and Route 4, Oquossoc. Open for lunch and dinner. A barn of an old place, a local favorite, good for deep-fried seafood or chicken, prime rib, or a burger; full liquor license.

People's Choice Restaurant (864-5220), Main Street, Rangeley. Open daily 6 AM–9 PM. Lunch choices include fresh-dough pizza, and the dinner specialty is a barbecue platter with pork chops, a half chicken, and a slab of ribs. The lounge features weekend bands and the largest dance floor around (everyone comes).

White Birch Cafe (864-5844), Main Street and Richardson Avenue, Rangeley. Open for breakfast and lunch; Sunday for breakfast only. Knotty-pine walls, the favorite place in town for breakfast: pancakes, bagels, Belgian waffles. Fresh Maine seafood and homemade desserts.

Red Onion (864-5022), Main Street, Rangeley. Open daily for lunch and dinner. A friendly Italian American dining place with a sun room and *Biergarten;* fresh-dough pizzas and daily specials.

Road Kill Cafe (864-3351) Main Street, Rangeley. Open for lunch and dinner. One in the zany northern New England chain that began in Greenville. We recommend the fungus burger.

The Four Seasons Cafe (864-5291), Oquossoc. Don't be put off by the Budweiser sign. Inside there is a bar, along with a woodstove, tables with checked green cloths, and a big menu with Mexican dishes, salads, good soups, sandwiches, and reasonably priced specials.

Fineally's (864-2955), Saddleback Mountain Road, Rangeley. Open Tuesday through Sunday year-round for dinner. Most enjoyable in summer when a screened deck is the best place around from which to dine while watching the sun set over the mountains. Mexican specialties and standard fare like veal Marsala ($10.95) and linguine with meatballs ($6.95).

Doc Grant's Restaurant and Cocktail Lounge, Main Street, Rangeley. Open for breakfast and lunch only now; seafood rolls, chicken in a basket, omelets.

ENTERTAINMENT

Rangeley Friends of the Performing Arts sponsors a July and August series of performances by top entertainers and musicians at local churches, lodges, and the high school. For the current schedule check with the chamber of commerce (see *Guidance*).

Lakeside Youth Theater (864-5000), Main Street, Rangeley. Movies daily in summer; otherwise on weekends.

(Also see People's Choice under *Eating Out*.)

SELECTIVE SHOPPING

Rodney Richard's Woodcarving (864-5072), Main Street, Rangeley. The Mad Whittler, known for his chain-saw sculptures, welcomes visitors.

First Farm (864-5539), Gull Pond Road, Rangeley. Open seasonally, Monday, Tuesday, Friday, Saturday 10–5. Roughly a mile north of town, marked from Route 16. Kit and Linda Casper's farm and farm shop have become a Maine legend.

North Winds Furniture and Cabinetmakers (864-2500), 38 Main Street, Rangeley. Randy Goodwin makes finely crafted furniture, also carries work by other Maine craftspeople.

Yarn Barn Crafts School (864-5917), Bald Mountain Road, Oquossoc. Open Monday through Saturday 10–5. A wide selection of yarns, cross-stitch kits, canvas, floss, weaving supplies, fleece for spinning, books, classes.

(Also see Rangeley Region Sport Shop under *Fishing*.)

SPECIAL EVENTS

January: **Rangeley Snodeo.**

March: **Annual Sled Dog Race. Bronco Buster Ski Challenge** at Saddleback.

July: **Independence Day** parade and fireworks; **Old-Time Fiddlers Contest;** and **Logging Museum Festival Days. Heritage Day Fair** in Weld Village is held on the final Saturday.

August: **Sidewalk Art Festival; Annual Blueberry Festival;** and **Phillips Old Home Days** (third week).

November: **Hunter's Ball.**

December: **Christmas Fair** at the Episcopal church; and **Walk to Bethlehem Pageant,** Main Street, Rangeley. **Giving Tree Celebration.**

Sugarloaf and the Carrabassett Valley

The second highest mountain in the state, Sugarloaf/USA faces another 4000-footer across the Carrabassett Valley—a narrow defile that accommodates a 17-mile-long town.

Carrabassett Valley is a most unusual town. In 1972, when it was created from Crockertown and Jerusalem townships, voters numbered 32. The school and post office are still down in Kingfield, south of the valley; the nearest drugstore, supermarket, and hospital are still in Farmington, 36 miles away. There are just around 300 full-time residents, but there are now more than 5000 "beds." Instead of uptown and downtown, people say "on mountain" and "off mountain."

On mountain, at the top of Sugarloaf's access road, stands one of New England's largest self-contained ski villages: a dozen shops and a more than a dozen restaurants, a seven-story brick hotel, and a church. A chairlift hoists skiers up to the base lodge from lower parking lots and from hundreds of condominiums clustered around the Sugarloaf Inn. More condominiums are scattered farther down the slope, all served by a chairlift. From all places you can also ski down to the Carrabassett Valley Ski Touring Center, Maine's largest cross-country trail network.

More than 800 condominiums are scattered among firs and birches. To fill them in summer, Sugarloaf has built an 18-hole golf course, maintains a serious golf school, fosters a lively special events program, promotes rafting, mountain biking, and hiking, and even seriously attempts to eliminate blackflies.

Spring through fall the focus shifts off mountain to the backwoods hiking and fishing north of the valley. Just beyond the village of Stratton, Route 27 crosses a corner of Flagstaff Lake and continues through Cathedral Pines, an impressive sight and a good place to picnic. The 30,000-acre Bigelow Preserve, which embraces the lake and great swatches of this area, offers swimming, fishing, and camping. Eustis, a small outpost on the lake, caters to sportsmen and serves as a PO box for sporting camps squirreled away in the surrounding woodland.

Kingfield, at the southern entrance to the Carrabassett Valley, was founded in 1816. This stately town has long been a woodworking center

413

and produced the first bobbins for America's first knitting mill; for some time it also supplied most of the country's yo-yo blanks. It is, however, best known as the one-time home of the Stanley twins, inventors of the steamer automobile and the dry-plate coating machine for modern photography. The Stanley Museum includes fascinating photos of rural Maine in the 1890s by Chansonetta, sister of the two inventors. Kingfield continues to produce wood products and also offers some outstanding lodging and dining.

The Carrabassett River doesn't stop at Kingfield. Follow it south as it wanders west off Route 27 at New Portland, then a short way along Route 146, to see the striking, vintage 1841 Wire Bridge. Continue on Route 146 and then west on Route 16 if you are heading for The Forks and the North Woods; to reach the coast, take Route 27 south through Farmington, a gracious old college town with good road food.

GUIDANCE

Sugarloaf Area Chamber of Commerce (235-2100), RR #1, Box 2151, Carrabassett Valley 04947. The chamber is well stocked with brochures on the area as well as statewide information. It also offers an areawide, year-round reservation service (235-2500; 1-800-THE-AREA) for lodging places on and off the mountain. Sugarloaf's toll-free reservations and information number for the eastern seaboard is 1-800-THE-LOAF; you can also call 237-2000.

GETTING THERE

By air: **Portland International Jetport** (779-7301), 2½ hours away, offers connections to all points. **Riverbend Express** (628-2877) offers ground transport year-round. **Rental cars** are available at the Portland International Jetport.

By car: From Boston it theoretically takes 4 hours. Take the Maine Turnpike to exit 12 (Auburn), then Route 4, to Route 2, to Route 27; or take I-95 to Augusta, then Route 27 the rest of the way. (We swear by the latter route, but others swear by the former.)

GETTING AROUND

In ski season, the **Valley Ski Shuttle Bus** runs from the base lodge to the Carrabassett Valley Ski Touring Center and Route 27 lodges.

MEDICAL EMERGENCY

Franklin Memorial Hospital (778-6031), Farmington.

Sugarloaf/USA has its own emergency clinic, and the **Kingfield Area Health Center** (265-4555) has both a full-time nurse and a physician's assistant.

TO SEE

MUSEUMS

Stanley Museum (265-2729), School Street, Kingfield. Open year-round except April and November, Tuesday through Sunday 1–4. Suggested donation: $2 per adult, $1 per child. Housed in a stately wooden school donated by the Stanley family in 1903, this is a varied collection of inventions by the Stanley twins, F.O. and F.E. (it was their invention of the airbrush in the 1870s that made their fortune). Exhibits range from violins to the steam car for which the Stanleys are best known. Three Stanley Steamers (made between 1905 and 1916) are on exhibit; also fascinating photos of rural Maine in the 1890s and elsewhere through the 1920s by Chansonetta Stanley Emmons, sister of the two inventors.

✎ **The Western Maine Children's Museum** (235-2211), RR 1, Box 2153, Carrabassett Valley 04947. Open winter weekends. Hands-on exhibits include math and science tables, a dress-up corner, computers, and a real plane where kids hear the control tower as they take off. Admission.

Nordica Homestead Museum (778-2042), Holley Road, off Route 4 in Farmington. Open June through Labor Day, Tuesday through Sunday 10–noon and 1–5; also September and October by appointment. Admission. This 19th-century farmhouse is the unlikely repository for the costumes, personal mementos, and exotic gifts given the opera star Lillian Norton, who was born here (she later changed her name to Nordica).

Nowetah's American Indian Museum, Route 27, New Portland. Open daily 10–5. Don't dismiss the sign as just another tourist trap. Nowetah Timmerman, a member of the Susquehanna and Cherokee tribes, displays Native American artifacts from the United States, Canada, and South America. A special room holds over 300 Maine baskets and bark containers.

HISTORIC SITES

Kingfield Historical Society (265-2729), Church Street, Kingfield. Open August and September, Sundays 1–4; also by appointment. Local memorabilia of the narrow-gauge railroad, the Stanley family, and Maine's first governor, William King; also 19th-century clothes, dolls, and a general store.

Dead River Historical Society (246-2271), Stratton. Open weekends in summer 11–3. Displays memorabilia from the "lost" towns of Flagstaff and Dead River, flooded in 1950 to create the present 22,000-acre, 24-mile Flagstaff Lake. When the water is low you can still see foundations and cellar holes, including that of a round barn in the Dead River.

BRIDGES

Wire Bridge, on Wire Bridge Road, off Route 146 (not far) off Route 27 in New Portland. Nowhere near anywhere, this amazing-looking suspension bridge across the Carrabassett River has two massive, shingled stanchions. The bridge is one of Maine's 19th-century engineering feats (it was built in 1841). There's a good swimming hole just downstream and a place to picnic across the bridge; take a right through the ball field and go 0.5 mile on the dirt road. Note the parking area and path to the river.

Fly-fishing near Sugarloaf

SUGARLOAF NEWS BUREAU

TO DO

BICYCLING

Mountain bikers are discovering that the winter ski trails on Sugarloaf make for some great rides. Bring your own or rent a bike at the **Sugarloaf Mountain Bike Shop** (237-6998), where maps and information are also available; there's no lift but a shuttle runs Friday through Sunday.

FISHING

Thayer Pond at the Carrabassett Valley Recreation Center, Route 27, is a catch-and-release pond open to the public, with fly-fishing lessons, boat rentals, and fish for a fee. The village of Eustis, north of Stratton, is serious fishing country, with the **Arnold Trail Sport Shop** serving as a source of equipment, information, and canoe rentals. In Eustis, both **Tim Pond** and **King & Bartlett Sporting Camps** are traditional fishing enclaves. **Arnold Trail Service Station** (Irving), **Pines Market,** and **Northland Cash Supply** in Stratton also carry fishing gear. Inquire about fly-fishing schools at Sugarloaf.

GOLF

Sugarloaf Golf Club (237-2000), Sugarloaf/USA. A spectacular, highly rated, 18-hole course designed by Robert Trent Jones II, teaching pro. Weekend and midweek golf schools and packages offered in-season.

HIKING

There are a number of 4000-footers in the vicinity and rewarding trails up **Mount Abraham** and **Bigelow Mountain.** The Appalachian Trail signs are easy to spot on Route 27 just south of Stratton; popular treks include the 2 hours to Cranberry Pond or 4 hours plus (one way) to Cranberry Peak. Pick up detailed hiking maps locally or check the *AMC Mountain Guide* or *50 Hikes in Southern and Coastal Maine* (Backcountry Publications) by John Gibson, which detail several spectacular hikes in the 17-mile Bigelow Range (35,027 acres now lie within the Bigelow Preserve).

SWIMMING

Cathedral Pines, Route 27, Stratton. Just north of town, turn right into the campground and follow signs to the public beach on Flagstaff Lake. Free. (Also see Wire Bridge in *To See.*)

CROSS-COUNTRY SKIING

Carrabassett Valley Ski Touring Center (237-2205). Open in-season 9 AM–dusk. This is Maine's largest touring network, with 95 km of trail loops, including race loops (with snowmaking) for timed runs. Rentals and instruction are available. The center itself includes the Klister Kitchen, which serves soups and sandwiches; space to relax in front of the fire with a view of Sugarloaf; and a rental area.

Titcomb Mountain Ski Touring Center (778-9031), Morrison Hill Road (off Route 2/4), Farmington. A varied network of 25 km of groomed trails and unlimited ungroomed trails; used by the University of Maine at Farmington.

Troll Valley Cross-Country Ski and Fitness Center (778-3656), Red Schoolhouse Road, Farmington. Gently rolling terrain and scenic views; 40 km of groomed trails designed for tourers rather than racers. Ski school, rentals, guided tours, lodge with snack bar, and fitness center.

DOWNHILL SKIING

Sugarloaf/USA (general information: 237-2000; snow report is ext. 6808; on-mountain reservation number is 1-800-THE-LOAF). Sugarloaf Mountain Corporation was formed in 1955 by local skiers, and growth was steady but slow into the 1970s. Then a boom decade produced one of New England's largest self-contained resorts, including a base village complete with a seven-story brick hotel and a forest of condominiums. Sugarloaf has been expanding and improving snowmaking and services ever since. Snowmaking now even covers its snowy cap. In 1996 Sugarloaf was absorbed by the Bethel-based American Skiing Company.

Trails number 118 and glades add up to 43 miles. The vertical drop is a whopping 2820 feet. The 14 lifts include a SuperQuad, a four-passenger gondola, two quad chairs, a triple chair, eight double chairs, and one T-bar. Facilities include a Ski Development Center, a Perfect Kids school, ski shop, rentals, base lodge, cafeteria, nursery (day and night), game room, and a total of 20 bars and restaurants. The nursery is first-rate; there are children's programs for 3-year-olds to teens; also mini-mountain tickets for beginners.

Call for current 1-day lift rates (also multiday, early- and late-season, and packaged rates). Under age 6, lifts are free.

DOGSLED RIDES

T.A.D. Dog Sled Services (246-4461; 237-2000), PO Box 147, Stratton 04982. Tim Diehl offers rides by his team of Samoyeds, "The White Howling Express." The 1½-mile rides leave approximately every half hour throughout the day during ski season from his base on Route 27 just north of the Sugarloaf access road. Drop by just to see his friendly, frisky dogs, all of whom were "unwanted pets" until Diehl adopted and trained them. He owns 19 and usually uses a team of 10 to pull the light, two-person (a child can also be snuggled in under the blanket) toboggan sled. You glide along low to the ground (lower than the feathery tails of the white Samoyeds), through the woods on trails Diehl maintains. In summer, cart rides are offered.

ICE SKATING

Sugarloaf Ski Touring Center (237-2205) maintains a lighted rink and rents skates.

SNOWMOBILING

Snowmobile trails are outlined on many maps available locally; a favorite destination is **Flagstaff Lodge** (maintained as a warming hut) in the Bigelow Preserve. Local rentals available.

LODGING

On Mountain

Sugarloaf/USA Inn and Condominiums (1-800-THE-LOAF; 237-2000), Carrabassett Valley 04947. Some 330 ski-in, ski-out condominiums are in the rental pool. Built gradually over the last 20 years (they include the first condos in Maine), they represent a range of styles and sites; when making a reservation, you might want to ask about convenience to the base complex, the Sugarloaf Sports and Fitness Center (to which all condo guests have access), or the golf club. $119–140 for a studio; $600 for an outsized condo during ski season; less in summer and through special packages. The 42-room **Sugarloaf Inn** offers attractive standard rooms and fourth-floor family spaces with lofts. There's a comfortable living room with fireplace, a solarium restaurant (see *Dining Out*), and a 24-hour, manned front desk, handy to the health club, also to the mountain. $93–185 per night, less in summer.

Sugarloaf Mountain Hotel (1-800-527-9879), RR 1, Box 2299, Carrabassett Valley 04947. So close to the base complex that it dwarfs the base lodge, this is a massive, seven-story, 119-room brick condominium hotel with a gabled roof and central tower. Rooms are large and well furnished, and most have small refrigerators and microwaves. There are also two 2-bedroom suites, each with a living room and kitchen, and two palatial tower penthouses, each with three bedrooms, three baths, and a hot tub. There's a library and a health club with a large hot tub and plunge pool, sauna, and steam room. $90–160 per night, multiday discounts, less in summer; handicapped access.

Off Mountain
INNS AND BED & BREAKFASTS

Even some skiers prefer to stay a full 17 miles south of the mountain in Kingfield, a classic Maine village.

The Herbert (265-2000; 1-800-THE-HERB), PO Box 67, Kingfield 04947. Open year-round. "We're away from 'condomania,'" says Bud Dick, a longtime Sugarloaf skier who has lovingly restored this three-story hotel, billed as a "palace in the wilderness" when it opened in 1918 in the center of Kingfield. In 1982, when Dick purchased it, the hotel was downright derelict, with 230 broken water pipes and no electricity. The "fumed oak" walls of the lobby now gleam, and there's a fire in the hearth beneath the moose head. Soak up the warmth from richly upholstered chairs and enjoy music from the grand piano. The attractive dining room is now frequently filled, and the fare is exceptional (see *Dining Out*). The 28 rooms and four suites are comfortably furnished with antiques, and many bathrooms feature Jacuzzis. $52–99 per couple in summer, more in foliage season, and in winter $98–131 per couple, $75–82 single for standard rooms; packages begin at $119 per couple for 2 nights' lodging, breakfast, and one dinner; midweek ski and stay for $49 per person.

Three Stanley Avenue (265-5541), Kingfield 04947. Designed by a younger brother of the Stanley twins, now an attractive bed & breakfast next to the more ornate One Stanley Avenue, also owned by Dan Davis (see *Dining Out*). There's a nice feel to this place, and each room is different. Number 2 has twin beds and a bath with claw-foot tub; number 1, an ornate sleigh bed with claw-foot tub. We also like number 6 (no bath), and number 4 is good for a family (one double, one twin bed). Although there's no common room, guests are welcome to use the elegant sitting room with floc wallpaper and grandfather clock next door at One Stanley Avenue. In summer, the lawns and woods are good for walking. Breakfast is included. $50–60, less midweek and summer.

Inn on Winter's Hill (1-800-233-9687), RR 1, Box 1272, Winter Hill Road, Kingfield 04947. A Georgian Revival mansion designed by the Stanley brothers for Amos G. Winter (his son, Amos Jr., founded the Sugarloaf Mountain Ski Area). In the house itself, four rooms share a private upstairs sitting area. Another 16 units are in the new section, a replica of the original (burned) barn. Amenities include a pool, hot tub, tennis, lounge, and elegant dining room. $75–125 summer, $68–138 winter.

River Port Inn (265-2552), Route 27, Kingfield 04947. An 1840 roadside house on the edge of town with eight comfortable, nicely decorated guest rooms, a three-room suite, a living room, and a big, friendly dining area in which guests tend to linger over home-baked breakfasts and bottomless cups of coffee. $45–55 per couple, small room for $50.

Tranquillity Bed & Breakfast (246-4280), PO Box 9, Stratton 04982. Open Memorial Day through November. Guy Grant has transformed an old barn into an informal lodge with an attractive living/dining room overlooking Flagstaff Lake. The boat ramp is just across Route 27. Private baths, full breakfast included in $50.

SKI LODGES AND MOTELS

Spillover Motel (246-6571), PO Box 427, Stratton 04982. An attractive, two-story, 20-unit (12 nonsmoking) motel just south of Stratton Village. Spanking clean, with two double beds to a unit, color cable TV, phone. $48–68, $5 for each additional person; includes continental breakfast.

SPORTING CAMPS

Tim Pond Wilderness Camps (243-2947), Eustis 04936. Open after the ice breaks up through November. In business since the 1860s and billed as "the oldest continuously operating sporting camp in America." The lure in spring and September is fly-fishing for native square-tailed trout. There are 10 log cabins, each with a fieldstone fireplace or woodstove; three meals are served in the lodge. Canoes and motorboats are available for use on this clear, remote lake, surrounded by 4450 acres of woodland, also good for hiking. $98 single per night, includes three meals; half price for children under age 12; no charge under age 5. Closed in August.

The Sugarloaf Area Chamber of Commerce (see *Guidance*) keeps a list of second homes, ranging from classic old A-frames to classy condos; the average price is $100 a day in ski season for a fully equipped house sleeping at least six; less in summer.

WHERE TO EAT

DINING OUT

Porter House (246-7932), Route 27, Eustis. Serving dinner "364 days a year." A country farmhouse located 12 miles north of Sugarloaf; also a pilgrimage point for Rangeley Lake visitors. There are four small dining rooms, a fire, and candlelight. Sip a drink while you study the menu, which (of course) includes Porter House steak. Entrées run from $7.95 for Salisbury steak with mushroom sauce or vegetable stir fry to $16.95 for top sirloin with roast duckling; the duckling alone comes in $8.95 and $14.50 servings; children's menu available. All breads, soups, and desserts are homemade. Full bar and wine list. Your chef-hosts are Beth and Jeff Hinman.

One Stanley Avenue (265-5541), Kingfield. Closed May to December; otherwise open after 5 PM except Monday. Reservations are a must. Small, but generally considered one of the best restaurants in western Maine. Guests gather for a drink in the Victorian parlor, then proceed to one of the two intimate dining rooms. Specialties include veal and fiddlehead pie, sweetbreads with applejack and chives, maple cider chicken, and saged rabbit with raspberry sauce. We have seldom savored more tender meat or moister fish, and the herbs and combinations work well. Owner-chef Dan Davis describes his methods as classic, the results as distinctly regional. $15–30 includes fresh bread, salad, vegetables, starch, coffee, and teas, but it's difficult to pass on the wines and desserts.

The Herbert (265-2000), Main Street, Kingfield. Dinner is served after 5 PM, Wednesday to Monday. Sunday brunch 12–2:30. This elegant old hotel dining room is decorated in lacy colors and gleams with cut glass; service is friendly; dress is casual; and the wine list is extensive. A recent summer menu included free-range chicken breast with a cranberry, walnut, and herb stuffing, topped with a tangy cranberry glaze ($13.95); and shrimp Athens (sautéed with tomatoes, garlic, dill, and black olives, topped with feta cheese, $15.95). Thursday is twofer night.

Hug's Italian Cuisine (237-2392), Route 27, Carrabassett Valley. Closed summer and fall; open Tuesday through Sunday, November through April. A small eatery featuring northern Italian delicacies such as tomato, basil, and garlic linguine with basil pesto topped with jumbo shrimp, and veal piccata (both $16.95); from $12.95 for sausage and pasta. Reservations recommended.

The Seasons (237-6834), Sugarloaf Inn, Carrabassett Valley. Breakfast daily, and dinner 6–9. Request a table in the glass-walled section of the dining room. The menu ranges from roasted vegetable cassoulet ($12.95) to filet mignon with a foie gras mousse and a puff pastry hat ($19.95).

EATING OUT

Longfellow Restaurant & Riverside Lounge (265-4394), Kingfield. Open year-round for lunch and dinner (from 5 PM). An attractive, informal dining place in a 19th-century building decorated with photos of 19th-century Kingfield. There's a pubby area around the bar, an open-beamed dining room, and an upstairs dining space with an outdoor deck overlooking the river. Great for lunch (homemade soups, quiche, crêpes, and a wide selection of sandwiches); a find for budget-conscious families at dinner.Children's plates are available. $5.50–12.75.

White Wolf (246-2922), Stratton. Open weekends for breakfast, daily for lunch and dinner. A find featuring homemade soups, reasonably priced entrées with local ingredients (dinner includes full salad bar), and some of the best desserts (try the peanut butter pie) in western Maine. The sure touch belongs to Sandy Isgro, a former chef's assistant at One Stanley Avenue (see *Dining Out*). There's a nice feel to the front dining room with its flowery curtains by the bar (breakfast and lunch) and to the larger space in back where dinner is served. Breakfast from 8 AM, $.99 and up; lunch specials from $2.25; and dinner (the board changes daily according to what is fresh and in-season) runs from $3.95 for a Big Beef Burger to $16.95 for a venison game combo.

The Wirebridge Diner (628-6229), Route 27, New Portland. Open 6 AM–2 PM, closed Mondays. A classic diner with wooden booths and stained glass, originally opened in Haverhill, Massachusetts, moved to Waterville, Maine, in the '40s, here in the '60s: great onion rings and sandwiches (a cheeseburger is $1.99). It's not on the menu, but order "the Bud": a BLT with tuna, cheese, and sweet onion. Ask directions to the Wire Bridge (see *To See*).

✎ **The Woodsman,** Route 27, Kingfield, north end of town. Pine paneled, decorated with logging tools and pictures, a friendly, smoky barn of a place, good for stacks of pancakes, great omelets, endless refills on coffee, homemade soups and subs, local gossip.

Theo's Microbrewery & Pub (237-2211). Home of the Sugarloaf Brewing Company's pale ale. Burgers, steaks, salads, and pastas also served.

In Farmington

F.L. Butler Restaurant & Lounge (778-5223), Front Street. Open for lunch weekdays, dinner Monday through Saturday; Sunday 10–8. Steaks, a variety of fish dishes, and Italian dishes served in a brick-walled tavern. $6.95–16.95. A good way stop en route to Sugarloaf.

The Granary (779-0710), 23 Pleasant Street. Open daily 11–11. Home of the Narrow Gauge Brewing Company, obviously popular with local college students and faculty, featuring a large menu of soups, sandwiches, and moderately priced entrées like chicken stir fry and ribs. The half-dozen house brews are all American-style ales; draft stout is also served.

SELECTIVE SHOPPING

Ritzo & Royal Studio Gallery (265-4586), at the "Brick Castle," Route 27 on the northern fringe of Kingfield. Open Thursday through Sunday, 11–5:30. An exceptional selection of locally crafted jewelry, rugs, pottery, furniture and other woodwork, glass, and Patricia Ritzo's own paintings.

Kingfield Wood Products (265-2151), just off Depot Street, Kingfield. Open weekends 9–4. A trove of small and interesting wooden items made on the spot: wooden apples and other fruit, toys, and novelty items.

Keenan Auction Company (265-2011), Kingfield. Open daily. A great family clothing store featuring brand names at discounts: Woolrich, Oshkosh, Maine Guide, and Nike are all here, plus bargain baskets full of ski mittens, goggles, and the like.

Devaney, Doak & Garret (778-3454), 29 Broadway, Farmington. The outstanding general bookstore in the area.

SPECIAL EVENTS

January: **White White World Winter Carnival**—broom hockey, chili cookoff, bartenders' race, and discounts at Sugarloaf/USA.

March: **Sugarloaf Corporate Challenge Weekend;** and **St. Patrick's Day Leprechaun Loppet**—a 15-km, citizens' cross-country race.

April: **Easter Festival**—costume parade, Easter egg hunt on slopes, and sunrise service on the summit; **Reggae Festival** weekend.

May: **Sugarloaf Marathon.**

August: **Kingfield Days Celebration**—4 days with parade, art exhibits, potluck supper; **Old Home Days,** Stratton-Eustis-Flagstaff; **weekend jazz series.**

September: **Kingfield 10k Foot Race and Sugarloaf Uphill Climb; Franklin County Fair,** Farmington.

October: **Skiers' Homecoming Weekend,** Sugarloaf Mountain.

December: **Yellow-Nosed Vole Day,** Sugarloaf Mountain; and **Chester Greenwood Day,** Farmington, which honors the local inventor of the earmuff with a parade and variety show in Farmington.

VI. THE KENNEBEC VALLEY

Augusta and Mid Maine
The Upper Kennebec Valley and Jackman

Participants in the Great Kennebec River Whatever Week

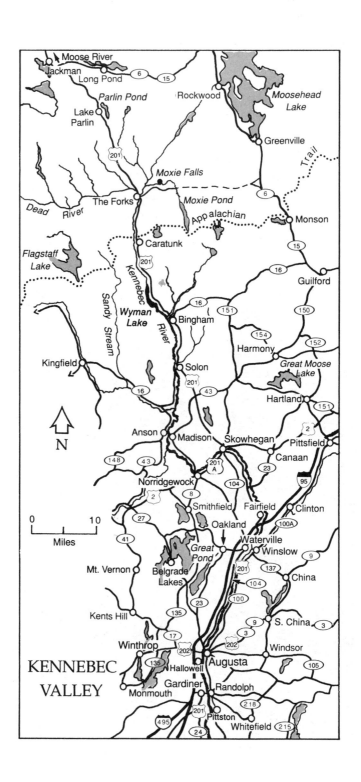

Augusta and Mid Maine

Augusta, the capital of Maine, rises in tiers above the Kennebec River at its head of shipping navigation. This position provided a good hunting and fishing ground for the area's earliest inhabitants, the Norridgewock and Kennebec tribes of the Algonquians. In 1625 the Pilgrims sailed to this spot and traded "seven hundred pounds of good beaver and some other furs" with the Native Americans for a "shallop's load of corn." They procured a grant to the Kennebec, from Gardiner to a waterfall halfway between Augusta and Waterville, with a strip of land 15 miles wide on either side of the bank. At the Native American village of Cushnoc (present-day Augusta), they built a storehouse and, with the proceeds of their beaver trade, were soon able to pay off their London creditors.

With the decline of the fur trade and rising hostilities with the Native Americans, these settlers sold the tract of land to four Boston merchants for just 400 pounds. The merchants had plans—farming, timber, and shipyards. War halted these plans, however, and the settlers fled, but they returned in 1754 when the British built Fort Western. The area was selected as the capital in 1827, and a statehouse, designed by Charles Bulfinch and built of granite from neighboring Hallowell, was completed in 1832. During the mid-19th century, this area boomed: Some 500 boats were built along the river between Winslow and Gardiner, and river traffic between Augusta and Boston thrived. The era is still reflected by the quaint commercial buildings lining the river downstream in Hallowell and Gardiner, both good places to shop and dine.

Today Augusta remains worth a visit, if only to see one of the most interesting state museums in the country; exhibits vividly depict many aspects of landscape, industry, and history

This lower Kennebec Valley is rolling, open farmland, spotted with lakes. Just north of the city the seven lakes in the Belgrade Lakes region form an old resort area, blessed with cottage colonies that need not advertise and plenty of recreation, from mail boat excursions and canoe rides to relaxation plain and simple. East of the city, the China Lakes form another low-profile haven. Good summer theater can be found in Waterville (upriver), Monmouth (another old resort area west of town), and Skowhegan (also known for its art school). In the past few years, attractive old homes and family farms throughout this region have opened their doors to guests—who are discovering not only the beauty of the immediate area but also that "Mid Maine" is the only true hub in this sprawling state, handy to many parts of the coast, the western lakes and mountains, and the North Woods.

GUIDANCE

Kennebec Valley Chamber of Commerce (623-4559), PO Box E, University Drive, Augusta 04332. The office is off I-95 (the exit for Route 27) in the civic center complex. This is a year-round source of information, primarily on the area from Augusta to Gardiner.

Belgrade Lakes Region, Inc., PO Box 72, Belgrade 04917, maintains a seasonal (late June to September) information booth on Route 27 and also publishes a pamphlet guide to the area.

China Area Chamber of Commerce (445-2890), Box 317, South China 04358. Year-round.

Mid-Maine Chamber of Commerce (873-3315), PO Box 142, Waterville 04903. Open year-round.

GETTING THERE

By air: **Colgan Air** (1-800-272-5488) connects Augusta with Boston. **Pine State Air** (1-800-353-6334) offers the only interstate air travel in Maine, with scheduled service from Augusta to Presque Isle.

By bus: **Vermont Transit** serves Augusta and Waterville.

By car: You don't have to take the Maine Turnpike to reach the Augusta area; from points south, I-95 is both quicker and cheaper (I-95 and the turnpike merge just south of Augusta). If you are not in a hurry, the most scenic route to Augusta from points south is to follow the Kennebec River up Route 24 through Bowdoinham and Richmond.

MEDICAL EMERGENCY

Kennebec Valley Medical Center (626-1000), 6 East Chestnut Street, Augusta. **Mid-Maine Medical Center** (873-0621), North Street, Waterville. **Waterville Osteopathic Hospital** (873-0731), Waterville, also offers emergency service. **Redington-Fairview General Hospital** (474-5085), Fairview Avenue, Skowhegan.

VILLAGES

Richmond. If you follow the Kennebec River from Brunswick to Gardiner, you will be rewarded with views of Merrymeeting Bay and then of rolling farmland sloping to the river. Richmond, at first glance, seems to be just another small mill town, but its onion-domed churches recall its Russian population, which numbered as many as 500 in the 1950s and 1960s. Cross the bridge in the middle of the village to find the Pownalborough Court House, which we have described in "Wiscasset."

Hallowell. This village is much the same as it was over 100 years ago. The store names may be different, but the Water Street commercial blocks, with two- and three-story, vintage mid-19th-century buildings, are definitely worth a stroll; known throughout New England for its number of antiques shops. Also note the restaurants described under *Where to Eat.*

Gardiner. Located where the Kennebec and Cobbossee Rivers meet, this old industrial (shoe, textile, and paper) town has been nicely restored. Nineteenth-century Main Street remains a great place in which to stroll and eat; also see *Entertainment.*

TO SEE

State House (287-2301), State Street, Augusta. Open year-round, Monday through Friday 8:30–4:30. Much modified since the original design by Charles Bulfinch; its size has actually doubled. A 180-foot dome replaces the original cupola. There are markers that will lead you on a self-guided tour, but guided tours are available.

Blaine House (287-2301), State Street, Augusta. Open year-round, Monday through Friday 2–4, and by appointment. A 28-room mansion built in the 1830s by a Captain James Hall of Bath, later purchased by James Blaine, a Speaker of the US House of Representatives, a US senator, and twice secretary of state. Blaine was known as the plumed knight when he ran for the presidency in 1884, battling "Rum, Romanism, and Rebellion." His daughter gave the mansion to the state in 1919, and it has since served as home for Maine governors.

Colby College (872-3000), Waterville (2 miles from exit 33 off I-95; marked). Founded in 1813, Colby College enrolls close to 1700 students from almost every state and more than 25 countries. Its campus is set on over 700 acres, with traditional brick and ivy-covered buildings, and there are several attractions worth noting, including **The Colby College Museum of Art,** which houses a permanent collection of American artists, among them Winslow Homer, John Singleton Copley, Andrew Wyeth, and John Marin; **Perkins Arboretum and Johnson Pond,** a 128-acre arboretum and bird sanctuary with nature trails and a picnic area; **The Portland String Quartet,** in residence here, with several concerts throughout the year as well as a summer string quartet institute; and **The Strider Theater,** offering a variety of programs and performances throughout the year.

MUSEUMS

Maine State Museum (287-2301), State Capitol Complex, State Street (Route 201/27), Augusta. Open weekdays 9–5, Saturday 10–4, and Sunday 1–4. Free. Turn into the parking lot just south of the capitol building. This outstanding museum isn't even marked from the street! You have to know that it's in the State Library in order to find it.

Without question, this is the best state museum in New England. Allow at least an hour. The exhibit "12,000 Years in Maine" traces the story of Maine's Native Americans with reproductions of petroglyphs

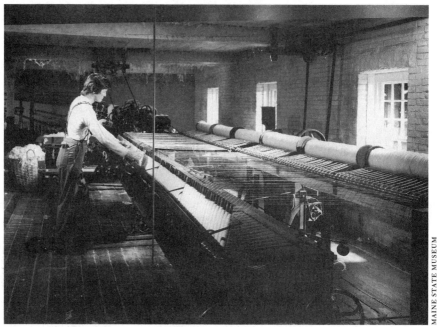

MAINE STATE MUSEUM

Nineteenth-century spinning machines at the Maine State Museum

and genuine ancient artifacts. This fascinating exhibit also dramatizes early European explorations and 19th-century attempts to explore the state's antiquities. Elsewhere, the museum re-creates a variety of Maine's landscapes and traditional industries: fishing, agriculture, granite quarrying, ice harvesting, shipbuilding, and lumbering. "Made in Maine" depicts more than a dozen 19th-century industrial scenes: textile mills and shops producing shoes, guns, fishing rods, and more. What makes these scenes most fascinating is their incredible, lifelike quality and the attention to detail. The 1846 narrow-gauge locomotive "Lion" stands like a mascot in the lobby. The fourth-floor addition houses an exhibit featuring highlights of 25 years at the museum.

Children's Discovery Museum (622-2209), Water Street, Augusta. A small but excellent hands-on museum, with displays that include a life-sized board game that teaches about the Atlantic salmon, a stage where kids can videotape a performance and then watch themselves on TV, post office, diner, and supermarket play areas. When we stopped by, they were in the process of adding an upstairs weather station and a workbench area with tools. Days and hours of operation vary; call for information.

HISTORIC SITES

Fort Western Museum on the Kennebec (626-2385), City Center Plaza, 16 Cony Street, Augusta. Open Memorial Day to July 4, 1–4 daily; July 4 to Labor Day, 10–4 weekdays, 1–4 weekends; Labor Day through Columbus Day, 1–4 weekends only. Groups and school programs year-round. $4.50 adults, $2.50 children. The original 16-room garrison house has been restored to reflect its use as a fort, trading post, and lodge from 1754 to 1810. The blockhouse and stockade are reproductions. Costumed characters answer questions and demonstrate 18th-century domestic activities. Special events on summer Sundays, as well as many annual events.

Redington Museum and Apothecary (872-9439), 64 Silver Street, Waterville. Open mid-May through September, Tuesday through Saturday 2–6, and by appointment. $2 admission; $1 age 18 and under. The local historical collection: furniture, Civil War and Native American relics, a children's room, period rooms, and a 19th-century apothecary.

Monmouth Museum (933-4444), Monmouth (at the intersection of Routes 132 and 135). Open Memorial Day through September, Tuesday through Sunday 1–4; year-round by appointment (933-2287 is the answering machine, or call Annie Smith: 933-2752). $3 per adult, $1 per child. A collection of buildings: 1787 Blossom House, stencil shop (1849), blacksmith shop, freight shed, and carriage house.

Waterville-Winslow Two Cent Bridge, Front Street, Waterville. Until recently the only known remaining toll footbridge in the country. Toll-taker's house on Waterville side. Free.

Fort Halifax, Route 201, Winslow (1 mile south of the Waterville-Winslow bridge at the junction of the Kennebec and Sebasticook Rivers). Just a blockhouse remains, but it is original, built in 1754—the oldest blockhouse in the United States. There is also a park with picnic tables here.

Cumston Hall, Main Street, Monmouth. Open year-round, weekdays during business hours. Vintage 1900, this ornate wooden building would look more at home in India than Mid Maine. Monmouth native Harry H. Cochrane not only designed but also decorated the building with murals, detailing, and stained glass. He also composed the music and conducted the orchestra at the building's dedication. It houses the town offices, library, and the Theater at Monmouth, a repertory company specializing in Shakespeare (see *Entertainment*).

Arnold Historical Society Museum (582-7080), off Route 17, Pittston. Open July and August, Saturday, Sunday, and holidays 10–4, and by appointment. $1.50 per adult, $.50 per child over age 6. An 18th-century house in which Benedict Arnold and Aaron Burr stayed for a couple of nights in the fall of 1775 on their way to attempt to capture Quebec. The army camped on Swan Island in Richmond (see *Green Space*), and about 600 men and supplies continued upriver in *bâteaux*—the flat-bottomed boats that are exhibited here in the barn. The house is furnished to period, and picture panels depict the Arnold expedition.

Norlands Living History Center (897-4366), RD 2, Box 1740, Livermore 04254. Take Norlands Road off Route 108 between Livermore and Livermore Falls. Open July and August, daily 10–4, for general tours of all buildings. $4.50 per adult, $2 per student. Also open by reservation for live-in weekends and weeklong programs, year-round. An incredible 450-acre, living history complex re-creates life in the late 19th century. The working farm with barn and farmer's cottage, church, stone library, and Victorian mansions of the Washburn family are open to visitors. This is the genuine 1870–1890 rural experience; visitors become scholars in the one-room schoolhouse and hear the story of the famous Washburn sons. Those living-in assume the identity of a 19th-century character, carrying out chores (cooking, mending, working the farm) just as they would have if they had been living here then. Chris's husband and oldest son went for a weekend and have never been the same. Try it. Come for a special weekend like Heritage Days in June, the Autumn Celebration in late September, or Christmas in early December. Three-day live-in weekends are also offered in February, April, May, and November.

TO DO

BALLOONING
Sails Aloft (623-1136), Augusta, offers sight-seeing flights in central and midcoast Maine. Starts at $125 per person.

BOAT EXCURSIONS
Great Pond Marina (495-2213; 1-800-696-6329), Belgrade Lakes Village. Operates the mail-boat on Great Pond (the inspiration for the book and movie *On Golden Pond*); the mail boat ride costs $7 per adult, $5 per senior, $4 per child. Also moorings, boat rentals (canoes, sailboards, sailboats, fishing boats), and service.

FISHING
Belgrade Lakes are known as a source of smallmouth bass; **Day's Store** in Belgrade Lakes Village devotes an entire floor to fishing gear. Boat rentals are available (see *Boat Excursions*).

FOR FAMILIES
Inside Out Playground (877-8747), Sterns Cultural Center, 93 Main Street, Waterville. Indoor playground includes a toddler area, wooden pirate ship structure, toy cars and trucks. Open year-round; great for rainy days. Ask about special programs.

GOLF AND TENNIS
Natanis Golf Club (622-3561), Webber Pond, Vassalboro. Twenty-seven-hole course; tennis courts. **Waterville Country Club** (465-7773), Waterville (off I-95). Eighteen holes, clubhouse, carts, and caddies.

SWIMMING
Peacock Beach State Park, Richmond (just off Route 201, 10 miles south of Augusta). A small, beautiful sand beach on Pleasant Pond; lifeguards and picnic facilities. $1 per adult, free under age 12.

Public beaches include **Sunset Camps Beach** on North Pond in Smithfield, and **Willow Beach** (968-2421), China. Although public access is limited at the Belgrade and China lakes, every cottage cluster and most rental "camps" there are on the water.

Lake St. George State Park (589-4255), Route 3, Liberty. A pleasant, clean, clear lake with a sandy beach and changing facilities, a perfect break if you are en route from Augusta and points south to the coast.

TRAIN RIDE

Belfast & Moosehead Lake Railroad (1-800-392-5500), One Depot Square, Unity. Unity station, painted bright red with green and white trim, is hardly what you expect to see as you drive down the quiet roads of this area. There is a gift shop, rest rooms, snack bar, and waiting area with a stuffed black bear, plenty of cushioned seats, and historical photos on the walls. A Swedish steam engine carries passengers on a 1½-hour narrated journey. Pre-ride demonstration as the engine is turned on the old Armstrong turntable. $14 adults, $7 children.

CROSS-COUNTRY SKIING

Natanis Golf Club (622-3561), Webber Pond, Vassalboro, has groomed trails and rental equipment. **Pine Tree State Arboretum** (see *Green Space*) also has lots of space for good skiing.

GREEN SPACE

Pine Tree State Arboretum (621-0031), 153 Hospital Street, Augusta. (At Cony Circle—the big rotary across the bridge from downtown Augusta—turn south along the river; it's a short way down on the left, across from the Augusta Mental Health Institute.) Open daily dawn to dusk. Visitors center open 8–4 weekdays. There are 224 acres, with trails through woods and fields, with more than 600 trees and shrubs (including rhododendrons and lilacs), as well as hostas and a rock garden. Cross-country-ski trails too.

Swan Island. A state-owned wildlife management area. Day use and overnight camping; prior reservations (287-1150) necessary for both, since only 60 visitors are allowed on the island at any one time. $3 day visit, $5 overnight camping. The landing is in Richmond Village, where Department of Inland Fisheries and Wildlife employees transport visitors to the island. Tours are available in an open, slat-sided truck; plenty of area for walking. The southern portion is restricted, but staff will accompany you on a tour (also see *Campgrounds*).

(Also see *Swimming.*)

LODGING

BED & BREAKFASTS

Maple Hill Farm (622-2708; 1-800-622-2708), RFD 1, Box 1145, Hallowell 04347. Little more than 4 miles from the turnpike and downtown Augusta, this pleasant old house with a new addition sits on 62 acres. Scott Cowger bought the property at auction and he and Vincent Hannan now run the comfortable, welcoming place. There are seven rooms, furnished in a pretty country style, some with bedspreads that were made in Hallowell. All have phones and air-conditioning, and one suite has a Jacuzzi tub. Although there were some shared baths when we stopped by, plans were in the works to convert to all private baths. There is also a fully handicapped-accessible room with a private entrance. As you meander up the driveway by the big red barn, watch for chickens (which provide the morning eggs) happily pecking by the side of the road. Other animals on the farm include a goat, two sheep, a llama, two cows (one a dwarf), and a dog. A trail through the woods leads to a spring-fed swimming hole by a quarry, and the carriage house has been transformed into a roomy function space. Full breakfast served in the dining room/art gallery is included in the $60–100 double rates.

Home-Nest Farm (897-4125), Baldwin Hill Road, Box 2350, Kents Hill 04349. Closed March and April. This is a wonderful old family estate, with three historic homes on the extensive property. The main house, built in 1784, offers a panoramic view of the White Mountains. Lilac Cottage (1800) and the Red Schoolhouse (1830) are available for rent as separate units. The property has been in host Arn Sturtevant's family for six generations; his grandchildren are the eighth generation to sleep there. Arn can relate some interesting family tales while showing you Civil War memorabilia. The sheep are a lot of fun to watch. $50 per room, $80–95 for houses with one to three bedrooms; breakfast included.

Independence Farm (622-0284), R1, Box 6857, Vassalboro 04989. This 1820s farmhouse overlooks Webber Pond. Now that their eight children are grown, Pat (a craftsperson with her own store in Hallowell) and Bob Riedman raise llamas on their 55-acre spread, as well as geese, chickens, and a couple of dogs. Two large guest rooms have private baths, and a third is frequently used for children, who are very welcome here. There's a canoe for summer use, and in winter cross-country-ski rentals and trails are available at the nearby 27-hole golf course. $55 double includes a full farm breakfast.

Richmond Sauna and Bed and Breakfast (737-4752), off Route 197, Richmond 04357. Open year-round. A handsome Federal home with five guest rooms, kitchen privileges, sauna, hot tub, and pool. There are actually six saunas, available by the hour. Visitors should be aware that clothing is optional here, and there are those who opt not to wear any. Use of all facilities for guests, who pay $60 per couple, $50 single.

CAMPS AND COTTAGES

Bear Spring Camps (397-2341), Route 3, Box 9900, Oakland 04963. Open mid-May through September. A gem of a family resort with 75 percent repeat business. Serious anglers come in early May for trout and salmon, and in July there's still bass. Each of the 32 cottages has a bathroom, hot and cold water, shower, and heat, as well as an open fireplace. They are right on the water, each with its own dock and motorboat (sailboat rentals are available). There's a tennis court and a variety of lawn games, and the swimming is great (the bottom is sandy). Meals are served in the main house. Weekly rates from $405 per couple in shoulder months to $1440 for eight in high season, including all meals.

Castle Island Camps (495-3312), Belgrade Lakes 04918. Open May through mid-September. In winter, contact Horatio Castle, 1800 Carambola Road, West Palm Beach, FL 33406 (407-641-8339). A dozen comfortable-looking cottages clustered on a small island (connected by bridges) in 12-mile Long Pond. This is the second generation of Castles to maintain the camps, geared to fishing (the pond is stocked; rental boats are available). Meals are served in the small central lodge. There is an open fireplace in the community building, and a rec room with pool tables, Ping-Pong, and darts. Weekly and children's rates are available. $56 per person per night; $374–385 per week, including all three meals.

CAMPGROUNDS

Steve Powell Wildlife Management Area (Swan Island), in Merrymeeting Bay off Richmond. State-owned Swan Island is managed as a wildlife preservation area in Merrymeeting Bay, a vast tidal bay that's well known among birders. Limited camping is available, along with a motorboat shuttle from Richmond, only through the Department of Inland Fisheries and Wildlife: 287-1150.

Lake St. George State Park (589-4255), Route 3, Liberty, offers 38 campsites and a boat launch ($13 for nonresidents).

WHERE TO EAT

DINING OUT

Slate's (622-9575), 167 Water Street, Hallowell. Breakfast, lunch, and dinner Tuesday through Friday, brunch and dinner Saturday, brunch only on Sunday. Coffeehouse atmosphere in three adjoining storefronts with brick walls, tin ceilings, changing art, a great bar, and a patio in back. The brunch menu is huge and hugely popular. The dinner menu changes daily but might include scrod baked with Brie and fresh blueberries, or cashew chicken on rice. Live music Friday and Saturday night, and during Sunday brunch. $8.95–14.95.

Village Inn (495-3553), Route 27, Belgrade Lakes. Open year-round for dinner nightly and lunch on Sunday. Lunch served in July and August. A rambling old place with a lake view and early-bird specials. The specialty is duckling, roasted for up to 12 hours and served with a choice of sauces. Entrées $9.95–16.95.

Bachelders Tavern (268-4965), Route 126 and Hallowell Road, Litchfield. Open daily for lunch and dinner. Dutch chef-owners Clare and Dirk Keijer create memorable meals in an elegant old stage stop, center of the village. A screened summer deck overlooks a pond and garden. Specialties include Mediterranean dishes, Maine seafood, and certified Black Angus beef. Entrées $10.95–21. Reservations recommended.

Johann Sebastian B. (465-3223), 40 Fairfield Street, Oakland. Open Wednesday through Saturday for dinner in summer; Friday and Saturday the rest of the year. A Victorian house in the Belgrade Lakes area. Specialties include chicken cordon bleu and sauerbraten; homemade European pastries and dessert drinks. $11–21.50.

River Cafe (622-2190), 119 Water Street, Hallowell. Open for lunch and dinner daily except Sunday. Mediterranean/American specialties include shish kebab and shish Tawook (marinated chicken tips cooked over an open flame and rolled in Lebanese bread). Reservations required for dinner. $10.95–16.95.

Senator Restaurant (622-5804), 284 Western Avenue, Augusta. Open daily from 6:30 AM through dinner. A big, all-American dining room (buses are welcome). Seafood specialties include seafood medley (shrimp, haddock, crabcake, and scallops) and lobster Newburg in puff pastry; full (generous) salad bar. Entrées $12.95–16.95.

EATING OUT

The A-1 Diner (582-4804), 3 Bridge Street, Gardiner, is a popular spot for any meal. Open Monday through Saturday for all three meals, but just 7 AM–noon on Sunday (open 5 AM weekdays, 6 AM Saturday). A vintage 1946 Worcester diner with plenty of Formica, blue vinyl booths, blue and black tile, a 14-stool, marble-topped counter, and a neon blue and pink clock with the slogan TIME TO EAT. The waitress seems to know everyone in the place at breakfast, and everyone seems to know each other.

You won't find just typical diner fare here, however. The breakfast menu includes banana-almond French toast and a wide variety of omelets, as well as eggs and hash; the meat loaf has a Cajun accent, the split-pea soup, an Italian, and the chili, a Latin. Greek lemon soup is a specialty. Beverages range from herbal tea to imported beers and wines. But you can always get tapioca pudding, and the route to the rest room is still outside and in through the kitchen door.

Burnsie's Homestyle Sandwiches (622-6425), State Street, Augusta, between the Capitol and the rotary. Open 8–4 weekdays only. This is the perfect place if you're visiting the Maine State Museum. Keep your car parked where it is and walk up past the Capitol to this out-of-place house, a source of famous lobster rolls, Reubens, and a variety of sandwiches, many named for local legislators. Although there is no real place to eat in the shop, if it's a nice day the picnic tables in the park just across the river, adjoining Fort Western, offer the best view in town.

Pedro's (582-5058), 161 Water Street, Gardiner. Open for lunch and dinner Tuesday through Saturday. A comfortable, casual place with a Mexican and southwestern menu.

Third Rail Cafe (873-6526), adjacent to the Railroad Square Cinema, Waterville. Lunch and dinner. A good place to go before or after a show. Menu includes such unique choices as roasted vegetable tart and Mediterranean lamb stew.

COFFEE HOUSES

Jorgensen's Cafe (872-8711), Main Street, Waterville. A large, funky café with at least a dozen flavored coffees, as well as tea and espresso choices. The deli serves quiche, soups, salads, and sandwiches with several bread options. Coffee and tea supplies, gourmet foods.

Java Joe's (622-1110), Water Street, Augusta. Cozy place with baked goods, as well as the usual coffee and espresso drinks.

ENTERTAINMENT

Theater at Monmouth (933-2952), PO Box 385, Monmouth. Performances Wednesday through Sunday in July, Tuesday through Sunday in August; matinees and children's shows vary. Housed in Cumston Hall, a striking turn-of-the-century building designed as a combination theater, library, and town hall. A resident company presents classics (last season included Shakespeare's *As You Like It*) and contemporary shows.

Waterville Opera House (873-7000) has a number of shows throughout the year, including music performances and theater productions. It also offers ballet, jazz, tap, acting, and other classes.

Gaslight Theater (626-3698), 1 Winthrop Street, Hallowell, has several productions per season.

Johnson Hall (582-3730), Water Street, Gardiner. The second-floor 450-seat theater, dating from 1864, is presently under restoration, but a 100-seat studio performance space designed for workshops and small performances has already been restored. This is home for the Institute for the Performing Arts (classes in magic, juggling, etc.) offered by Benny and Denise Reehl, the powers behind the semiannual New England Vaudeville Festival. Check local calendars for periodic performances.

Railroad Square Cinema (873-6526), Main Street, Waterville. Heading north on Route 201 (College Avenue), turn left between Burger King and the railroad tracks. Art and foreign films in a casual atmosphere. Rebuilt after a fire, now in a separate building with a café (see *Eating Out*).

SELECTIVE SHOPPING

The mid-19th-century commercial buildings along Water Street in Gardiner have hatched some interesting shops.

The heart of the Belgrade Lakes Village is **Day's Store** (495-2205). Open year-round, recently expanded to serve as general store; state liquor store; fishing license, gear, boot, and gift source; and rainy-day mecca. **Maine Made Shop,** open late May through Labor Day, stocks pottery, books, and Maine souvenirs.

GALLERIES

A dozen galleries in public buildings and private homes, within a short drive of each other, are listed in an art tour brochure promoting this as the Kennebec Valley Art District.

ANTIQUES SHOPS

The picturesque riverside lineup of shops in Hallowell harbors fewer antiques dealers than it did a few years ago, but it is still a worthwhile browsing street. **Dealer's Choice,** 108 Water Street, is a 70-plus dealer mall with a wide range. **Hatties Antiques,** 148 Water Street, specializes in fine antique jewelry, antique lamps, clocks, and art glass.

BOOKSTORES

Children's Book Cellar (872-4543), 5 East Concourse, Waterville.

Leon H. Tebbets Bookstore, 164 Water Street, Hallowell, is a book lover's delight; 36,000 closely packed titles (closed Sunday in winter).

Barnes & Noble Booksellers (621-0038), The Marketplace at Augusta, directly across from the Augusta Civic Center. A new full-service bookstore with music and computer software sections, as well as a café.

FACTORY OUTLETS

Carleton Woolen Mills Factory Outlet (582-6003), Griffin Street, Gardiner. Fabrics, woolens, and notions.

Cascade Fabrics, Oakland. Open Monday through Saturday 8:30–4:30. A genuine mill store.

Dexter Shoe Factory Outlet (873-6739), Kennedy Memorial Drive, Waterville.

SPECIAL EVENTS

July: **The Great Kennebec River Whatever Week**—10 days of activities ending with the Kennebec River Whatever Race, running downriver from Augusta to Gardiner (beginning of the month). **China Connection**—public supper, pageant, road race, pie-eating and greased pig contests in China. **Old Hallowell Days** (third week). **Annual Scottish Games & Gathering of the Scottish Clans,** sponsored by the St. Andrew's Society of Maine, Thomas College, Waterville.

September: **Common Ground Fair,** Windsor—Maine's celebration of rural living, a gathering of organic farmers and Maine craftspeople.

The Upper Kennebec Valley and Jackman

Commercial rafting on the Kennebec began in 1976 when fishing guide Wayne Hockmeyer discovered the rafting potential of up to 8000 cubic feet of water per second (released every morning from late spring through mid-October from the Harris Hydroelectric Station) churning through dramatic, 12-mile-long Kennebec Gorge.

On his first ride through the gorge, Hockmeyer had to contend with logs hurtling all around him, but, as luck would have it, 1976 also marked the year in which environmentalists managed to outlaw log runs on the Kennebec. More than 15 rafting companies now vie for space on the Kennebec, but no more than 800 rafters are allowed on the river at a time. In order to compete, outfitters based in and around The Forks have added their own lodging, and the more elaborate "base camps" now remain open year-round.

Empty as it seemed when rafting began, this stretch of the Upper Kennebec had been a 19th-century resort of sorts. The 100-room, three-story Forks Hotel was built at the confluence of the Kennebec and Dead Rivers in the middle of The Forks in 1860 and was well known for its steady flow of liquor (Maine was legally dry at the time). Nineteenth-century guests were well aware of the area's many miles of wilderness hiking trails and sights (such as spectacular Moxie Falls). A half-dozen remote sportsmen's camps on fishing ponds date from this period.

Route 201, following the Kennebec River north through Skowhegan and Solon to Bingham, The Forks, and Jackman, traverses lonely but beautiful wilderness. Wildlife abounds: More than 100 species of birds have been seen in the region, and this section of the Kennebec is the only US river supporting five types of game fish. The route is known as the Arnold Trail because Benedict Arnold came this way in 1775 to Quebec City, which—it's worth noting—is just 86 miles north of Jackman.

GUIDANCE

Upper Kennebec Valley Chamber of Commerce (672-4100), PO Box 491, Bingham 04920, maintains a seasonal storefront, walk-in information booth with a friendly, helpful staff on Route 201 in the middle of Bingham. Open daily.

Skowhegan Chamber of Commerce (474-3621), PO Box 326, Skowhegan 04976, maintains a seasonal information center in town on Route 201 north. This is actually the gateway to the Upper Kennebec Valley and serves as a source of advice on lodging throughout the valley.

Jackman–Moose River Chamber of Commerce (668-4094) also maintains a seasonal information center on Route 201 in Jackman, but it was not open when we came through in mid-July.

MEDICAL EMERGENCY

Bingham Area Health Center (672-4808); Ambulance Service (672-4410).

TO SEE

Skowhegan History House (474-2415), Norridgewock Avenue, Skowhegan. Open June to mid-September, Tuesday through Friday 1–6. A Greek Revival brick house exhibiting 19th-century furnishings, artifacts, and local maps. Admission by donation.

Margaret Chase Smith Library Center (474-7133), Skowhegan. Open year-round, Monday through Friday 10–4. Set above the Kennebec, an expanded version of Senator Smith's home is a research and conference center housing records, scrapbooks, news releases, tape recordings, and memorabilia from over three decades in public life.

Skowhegan Indian and Norridgewock Monument. Billed as "the world's largest sculptured wooden Indian," this 62-foot-high statue is dedicated to the memory of the Maine Abenakis. It's just off Route 201 near the Kennebec. Abenaki heritage is particularly strong in this area. In the early 18th century, French Jesuit Sebastian Rasle established a mission in nearby Norridgewock, insisting that Native American lands "were given them of God, to them and their children forever." Rasle and his mission were wiped out by the English in 1724. The site of the village is marked by a pleasant riverside picnic area in a pine grove. (Take Route 201A from Norridgewock toward Madison across the bridge and up a steep hill. Turn left 3 miles from the top of the hill on Father Rasle Monument Road; it's 3 more miles to the cemetery and picnic site.) Note that Route 201A rather than 201 follows the Kennebec here. In the middle of Norridgewock, you might also want to stop by Oosoola Park to see the totem pole topped by a frog (this is also a good picnic spot and boat-launch site). Ancient Native American petroglyphs have been found in Emden.

TO DO

FLOATPLANE FLIGHT

Windfall Outdoor Center (668-4814), Moose River, offers a 20-minute ride over the region. Rates are for a minimum of three passengers per flight.

CANOEING

The Moose River Bow Trip is a Maine classic: A series of pristine ponds form a 42-mile meandering route that winds back to the point of origin, eliminating the need for a shuttle. The fishing is fine, remote campsites are scattered along the way, and the put-in place is accessible. One major portage is required. Canoe rentals are available from a variety of local sources (check with chambers of commerce; see *Guidance*), and guided canoe trips can be arranged through some of the larger rafting companies.

FISHING

Fishing is what the sporting camps are all about. The catch is landlocked salmon, trout, and togue. Rental boats and canoes are available (see *Rustic Resorts*).

GOLF

Moose River Golf Course (668-5331), Moose River. Mid-May through mid-October; club rental, putting green, nine holes.

HIKING

Hiking possibilities abound in this area. *Take a Hike* by Susan Varney (available locally) describes 20 hikes in the Upper Kennebec Valley region. The standout is Moxie Falls, an 89-foot waterfall considered the highest in New England, set in a dramatic gorge. It's an easy ⅔-mile walk from the trailhead (it can be very muddy and wet). Turn off Route 201 onto Moxie Road on the south side of the bridge across the Kennebec in The Forks. Park off the road at the trailhead sign on your left.

MOOSE-WATCHING

The best time to see a moose is dawn or dusk. Favorite local moose crossings include Moxie Road from The Forks to Moxie Pond; the Central Maine Power Company road from Moxie Pond to Indian Pond; the 25 miles north from The Forks to Jackman on Route 201; and the 30 miles from Jackman to Rockwood on Route 6/15. Drive these stretches carefully; residents all know someone who has died in a car-moose collision.

MOUNTAIN BIKING

Local terrain varies from old logging roads to tote paths. Rentals are available from **Sky Lodge Resort** (1-800-416-6181) and **Northern Outdoors** (1-800-765-RAFT).

WHITE-WATER RAFTING

See the introduction to this chapter. Selecting an outfitter can be the most difficult exercise of the rafting trip. The safety records for all are excellent, or they wouldn't be in this rigorously monitored business. April through October all offer the basics: a river ride with a hearty steak cookout at its end and a chance to view (and buy) slides of the day's adventures. Standard charges are around $75 weekdays, $95 weekends. If you don't like getting your feet wet (especially early and late in the season when the water is frigid), you might ask about self-bailing rafts, but the big variant among outfitters is the nature of the lodging. It ranges from tent sites to inns and cabins to condo-style units—which they package into rates. To save phoning around for availability, you might call **Raft Maine** (1-800-723-8633; Monday through Friday 9–5, Saturday 9–noon), representing 11 outfitters.

✎ *Note:* Although white-water rafting began as a big singles sport, it is becoming more and more popular with families, who combine it with a visit to Quebec City, just 86 miles north of Jackman.

Northern Outdoors Inc. (663-4466; 1-800-765-RAFT), PO Box 100, The Forks 04985. Wayne and Suzie Hockmeyer were the first rafters on the Kennebec, and Northern Outdoors is still the biggest outfitter. Its "Outdoor Resort Center" at The Forks includes an attractive open-timbered building with high ceilings, a huge hearth, comfortable seating, a cheerful dining room (see *Dining Out*), a bar, a pool, a private lake, platform tennis, a sauna, and a hot tub. Fishing and mountain biking are also available. Accommodations vary from camping to cabins, from lodge double rooms to "logdominiums" (condo-style units with lofts and a kitchen/dining area). In addition to rafting, they offer sportyak and guide-your-own raft adventures, fishing trips, rock climbing, a ropes course, and canoe and kayak clinics. In winter the lodge caters to snowmobilers and cross-country skiers.

New England Outdoor Center (723-5438; 1-800-766-7238), 240 Katahdin Avenue, Millinocket 04462. The second largest outfitter offers some of the fanciest and funkiest lodging in the area; the Sterling Inn in Caratunk, a 19th-century stage stop, dates from 1816 and offers country inn–style guest rooms. The Sterling Guest Houses are on Wyman Lake, and each has two bedrooms, a full bath and kitchen, a living room, and a loft with lots of additional sleeping space. Campsites and cabin tents are other options. The Osprey Outdoor Center has a dining room, shower and changing facilities, outfitter shop, and main lodge.

Wilderness Expeditions (534-2242; 1-800-825-WILD), PO Box 41, Rockwood 04478. Wilderness maintains a base camp in The Forks with a pleasant central lodge, campsites, riverside cabin tents, and recently added cottages. Facilities include swimming pool, hot tub, and volleyball court. Meal packages are available. This is an offshoot of The Birches Resort in Rockwood, a beautifully sited, full-service resort (see "Moosehead Lake"); some packages combine Kennebec and Dead River rafting with stays at The Birches.

Crab Apple White Water (663-4491; 1-800-553-RAFT), The Forks 04985. The Crab Apple Acres is an 1830s edifice with a fanlight over the door and flowery wallpaper in the seven guest rooms. Neighboring motel units serve as the base camp.

Maine Whitewater (672-4814; 1-800-345-MAIN), Gadabout Gaddis Airport, PO Box 633, Bingham 04920. Jim Ernst operates the second oldest rafting company on the river. His Bingham base complex includes a restaurant and lounge, game room, hot tub, a private airport, and a campground. The llamas that share the premises are fun to watch.

Rafting the Kennebec River

Downeast Whitewater (603-447-3002; 1-800-677-7238), PO Box 119, Center Conway, NH 03813, maintains the attractive, seasonal, Dew Drop Inn bed & breakfast on Pleasant Pond in Caratunk, as well as the Kelley Brook Resort with a restaurant, lounge, log cabins, cabin tents, and camping on Route 201. This company offers canoe and kayak trips and rentals from its base in New Hampshire, along with inflatable kayak trips on the Dead River.

Unicorn Rafting Expeditions (725-2255; 1-800-UNICORN), PO Box T, Brunswick 04011, has many packages for families at its Lake Parlin Resort, which offers lakefront cabins sleeping 4 to 10. Facilities include a main lodge with fieldstone fireplace, lounge, pool table, hot tub, and heated swimming pool. Packages combining mountain biking, canoe trips, and/or funyaking are offered. Guided fishing expeditions, too.

Magic Falls Rafting (663-2220; 1-800-207-7238), PO Box 9, The Forks 04985, has a base camp with a bed & breakfast, cabin tents, and campsites on the banks of the Dead River in The Forks. Also offers "funyaks" (an inflatable cross between a canoe and a kayak) and rock climbing.

Mountain Magic Expeditions (663-2233; 1-800-464-2238), PO Box 12, The Forks 04985. The base camp on Route 201 offers campsites and tent rentals, a lounge, board games and movies, and hot showers.

Moxie Outdoor Adventures (663-2231; 1-800-866-6943), SR 63, Box 60, The Forks 04985, operates out of Lake Moxie Camps, one of the oldest and best-known sporting camps around. Mountain biking, fishing, canoes and kayaks, hiking, and family-style meals in addition to rafting.

Professional River Runners of Maine, Inc. (663-2229; 1-800-325-3911), PO Box 92, West Forks 04985, is a smaller company specializing in extended trips from 1–6 days. It operates a campground at a base camp near the Kennebec.

Windfall Rafting (668-4818; 1-800-683-2009), PO Box 505, Moose River 04945. Based at Sky Lodge, accommodations can be motel rooms, cottages, or the lodge itself (for groups of 12 or more). It also offers mountain biking, wilderness canoeing, hiking, and floatplane flights.

SNOWMOBILING

Snowmobiling is big in this region, with miles of trails through woods and fields, over rivers and lakes. Jackman prides itself on the quality of its groomed trail system with many long views. Rentals are available locally. Overnight accommodations at many of the rafting base camps as well as other area lodging establishments.

GREEN SPACE

Moxie Falls (90 feet high) is said to be the highest falls in New England. The view is striking, and well worth the detour from The Forks (see *Hiking*). **Caratunk Falls** is a 36-foot falls located near Solon. **Wyman Dam** (155 feet high) walls the Kennebec River between Moscow and Bingham. It was built in the 1930s by Central Maine Power. It raises the river 123 feet, creating the most popular rafting route in the Northeast. **Wyman Lake** stretches out for many miles behind it, and there is a public boat access from Route 201.

Attean View. Heading north toward Jackman from The Forks, only one rest area is clearly marked. Stop. The view is splendid: Attean Lake and the whole string of other ponds linked by the Moose River, with the western mountains as a backdrop. There are picnic tables.

LODGING

RUSTIC RESORTS

These are classic sporting camps geared to fishermen and hunters.

Harrison's Pierce Pond Sporting Camps (672-3625; this is a radiophone, so let it ring and try again if it doesn't work; Columbus Day to May 15, or when unable to get through, call 603-279-8424), Box 315, Bingham 04920. Open May through Columbus Day. Sited on the Appalachian Trail, 20 miles from Bingham, 15 of it a dirt road. Fran and Tim Harrison have brought new life to this classic, old log camp set on a hillside and overlooking a stream with a waterfall in the distance. Nine-mile-long Pierce Pond is a short walk across the stream and through the woods. Five of the nine log cabins have a half-bath, and there are three full-facility bathhouses on the premises. Rates include three abundant meals per day. Word has gotten out about Fran's cooking, and some people actually drive the bumpy road for Sunday turkey or Friday lobster. $60–66 per person per day or $365–395 per week, includes all meals (based on double occupancy and 2-night minimum); half price for children, special summer rates July 12 through August 11 (3-night minimum), group rates for eight or more people.

Cobb's Pierce Pond Camps (628-2819 in summer; 628-3612 in winter), North New Portland 04961. There are 12 guest cabins, accommodating from two to eight people; each has a screened porch, woodstove, bathroom, and electricity. Home-cooked meals and between-meal snacks are served in the main lodge. This traditional sporting camp dates from 1902, and the Cobb family has been running it for almost four decades; 90 percent of the guests are repeats. It's the kind of place that doesn't advertise. It has a loyal following among serious fishermen; sand beaches nearby. Guiding services available. $67 per person per day includes three meals; children are $25–50 per day.

Attean Lake Resort (668-3792; 668-7726 in winter), Jackman 04945. Sited on an island in Attean Lake, surrounded by mountains. This resort has been in the Holden family since 1900; 20 seasonal cabins, luxurious by sports lodge standards, with full baths, Franklin fireplaces and even a small Oriental carpet, kerosene lamps, and maid service daily. The resort also maintains three cabins along the Moose River trip (see *Canoeing*). Fishing boats and canoes are available. A great place for canoeing, kayaking, sailing, and hiking. The resort is easily accessible from Jackman; you phone from the shore, and a boat fetches you. $150 single, $200 double includes meals.

OTHER LODGING

☞ **Mrs. G's Bed & Breakfast** (672-4034; 1-800-672-4034), Box 389, Meadow Street, Bingham 04920. A tidy house on a side street in the middle of town. Frances Gibson (Mrs. G) delights in orienting guests to the full range of local hiking, biking, rafting, and cross-country skiing possibilities. There are four cheerful guest rooms; also a delightful loft dorm room with nine beds, perfect for groups; shared baths. $30 per person includes a fabulous full breakfast and state tax.

Sky Lodge Resort (668-2171), PO Box 428, Jackman 04945. Open year-round. Splendidly built, known as the largest log cabin in Maine. This lodge on Route 201 has a two-story fieldstone hearth, and plenty of couches and interesting reading in the living room. Five of the comfortable guest rooms in the lodge have fireplaces ($125 suite; $99 for other rooms) and there are five fully equipped, three-bedroom log cabins ($100 for four people) and a motel ($59 double). The lodge will outfit you for mountain biking, canoeing, white-water rafting, snowmobiling, and cross-country skiing; facilities include a seasonal pool and hot tub, a billiards/game room, and a gym with basketball, table tennis, and exercise equipment. Restaurant on the premises open Wednesday through Sunday in the summer months.

(Also see the lodging described for each *White-Water Rafting* outfitter.)

WHERE TO EAT

DINING OUT

The Village Candle Light (474-9724/2978), 1 Madison Avenue, Skowhegan. Open for dinner except Monday. The specialties are seafood, local vegetables, home baking. Entrées $6.95–13.95.

Harrison's Pierce Pond Camps (672-3625; 1-800-478-8951), Bingham. We don't want to understate the taxing trip into Harrison's (see *Rustic Resorts*), but if you happen to be spending a few days in this area and want a very special meal, it's worth the ride for the turkey dinner on Sunday, baked stuffed pork on Monday, steak teriyaki "Juline" on Tuesday, and so on. Lobster is served on Friday night. Breakfast served to Appalachian Trail hikers daily 7:30–8:30 with advance reservations; dinner is served promptly at 5:30, with reservations required at least one day in advance. $9.95 to market price for seafood.

Northern Outdoors (663-4466; 1-800-765-RAFT), Route 201, The Forks. The pine-sided dining room in the lodge is open daily year-round for all three meals. Informal, with great photos of The Forks in its big-time logging and old resort days adorning the walls. The food is very good, offering dinner choices like grilled swordfish and jumbo Florentine ravioli, as well as nightly specials. $5–12.

Loon's Look-Out Restaurant at Tuckaway Shores Cabins (668-3351) on Big Wood Lake, Jackman. Take Spruce Street off Route 201, bear right onto Forest Street, and it's at the end on the right-hand side. Open year-round, Friday through Sunday 5–9; they will open other days and times for groups of 10 or more. Takeout available. A great little Italian place with specialties like mozzarella bread nibblers, lasagna, and *bistecca a la pazzarella* (steak chunks with bell peppers, onions, mushrooms, sauce, and spices). Reservations recommended. $5.95–15.95. Children's menu $3–5.

EATING OUT

Old Mill Pub (474-6627), 41-R Water Street, Skowhegan. Open Monday through Saturday for lunch and dinner; also open Sunday in summer. A picturesque old mill building set back from the main drag with a seasonal deck overlooking the Kennebec. A friendly bar and scattered tables; sandwiches (a good Reuben), quiche, and specials for lunch; spinach lasagna or stir-fry shrimp for dinner.

Bloomfield's Cafe & Bar (474-8844), 40 Water Street, Skowhegan. Open daily 11 AM–1 AM. Stained glass, ferns, tile floors, and an exquisite copper moose head create a pleasant atmosphere in this corner store eatery. Pete's Wicked Ale and Moosehead are available, and the selection of sandwiches is wide; try Bloomie's Bomber.

☞ **Thompson's Restaurant** (672-3245), Main Street, Bingham. Open daily for all three meals year-round. This inviting eatery has been in business since 1939 and still has an old-fashioned look, complete with red awning and deep booths. The menu includes homemade doughnuts, fresh fish, and often favorites like pea soup, baked beans, and custard pie; pizza, wine, and beer also served.

ENTERTAINMENT

Lakewood Theater at Skowhegan, the Cornville Players (474-7176), RFD 1, Box 1780. Mid-June through August. A community group performs in one of Maine's oldest summer theaters. Broadway plays and children's performances. **Park Street Players** at Constitution Hall, Skowhegan State Fair Grounds, Route 201, Skowhegan. A regional theater staging summer plays and musicals. Curtain time is 8 PM.

SPECIAL EVENTS

August: **Skowhegan State Fair,** one of the oldest and biggest fairs in New England—harness racing, a midway, agricultural exhibits, big-name entertainment, tractor and oxen pulls.

September: **Oosoola Fun Day,** Norridgewock, includes the state's oldest frog jumping contest (up to 300 contestants) around a frog-topped totem pole; also canoe races, crafts fair, flower and pet contests, live music, barbecue. **Fly-in,** Gadabout Gaddis Airport, Bingham.

VII. NORTHERN MAINE

Moosehead Lake Area
Bangor Area
Katahdin Region
Aroostook County

Katahdin

TIMOTHY ELLIS JR.

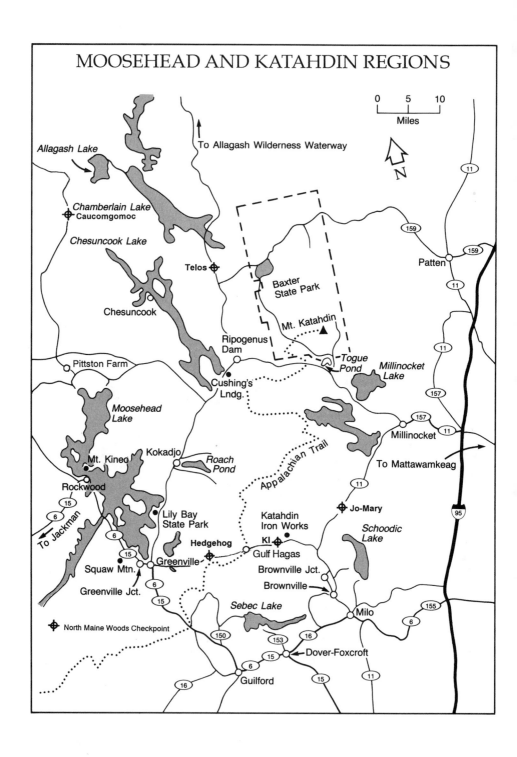

MOOSEHEAD AND KATAHDIN REGIONS

Miles
0   5   10

N

Allagash Lake

To Allagash Wilderness Waterway

Chamberlain Lake
Caucomgomoc

Chesuncook Lake

Telos

Patten

Baxter
State Park

Chesuncook

Mt. Katahdin

Ripogenus
Dam

Togue
Pond

*Millinocket
Lake*

Pittston Farm

Cushing's
Lndg.

*Moosehead
Lake*

Millinocket

Mt. Kineo   Kokadjo

*Roach
Pond*

To Mattawamkeag

Rockwood

Appalachian Trail

11

95

To Jackman

Lily Bay
State Park

Katahdin
Iron Works

Jo-Mary

*Schoodic
Lake*

Squaw Mtn.

Hedgehog

KI

Gulf Hagas

Greenville

Brownville Jct.

Greenville Jct.

Brownville

North Maine Woods Checkpoint

Sebec Lake

Milo

Dover-Foxcroft

Guilford

The North Woods

Like "Down East," Maine's "North Woods" may seem a bit of a mirage, always over the next hill. In fact, 17.6 of Maine's 22 million acres are forested, and much of that woodland lies in what we've described in this book as the "Western Mountains and Lakes Region."

Still, one particular tract of forest tends to be equated—mostly by out-of-staters—with the North Woods. That section is the 6½ million acres bordered to the north and west by Canada, which on highway maps shows no roads. This is the largest stretch of unpeopled woodland in the East, but wilderness it's not.

Private ownership of this sector, technically part of Maine's 10½ million acres known as the Unorganized Townships, dates from the 1820s when Maine was securing independence from Massachusetts. The mother state, her coffers at their usual low, stipulated that an even division of all previously undeeded wilderness be part of the separation agreement. The woods were quickly sold by the legislature for 12½ to 38 cents per acre, bought cooperatively by groups to cut individual losses.

The vast inland tracts, mostly softwood, increased in value in the 1840s when the process of making paper from wood fibers was redis-covered. It seems that the method first used in A.D. 105 had been for-gotten, and New England paper mills were using rags at the time.

By the turn of the century, pulp and paper mills had moved to their softwood source and assumed management responsibility and taxes for most of the unorganized townships. Mergers have since increased the size (decreased the number) of these companies, and ownership of some of the largest (namely Great Northern) is now based in Britain and South Africa. North Maine Woods, Inc., a consortium of more than 20 landowners, now pays the lion's share of the area's land tax and the cost of maintaining thousands of miles of private gravel roads, the ones not shown on the state highway maps but open to visitors who pay a fee and promise to abide by the rules (rule number one: Drive slowly and pull over to permit logging trucks to pass).

The private roads have multiplied since the end of log drives in the 1970s and have changed the look and nature of the North Woods. Many remote sporting camps, for a century accessible only by water, and more recently by air, are now a bumpy ride from the nearest town.

Many of the sporting camps themselves haven't changed since the turn of the century. Some have hardly altered since the 1860s, the era when wealthy "sports" first began arriving in Greenville by train from New York and Boston, to be met by Native American guides. The genuine old camps are Maine's inland windjammers: unique holdovers from another era. Many simply cater to descendants of their original patrons.

For the general public, two North Woods preserves have been set aside to provide a wilderness experience. These are 200,000-acre Baxter State Park and the 92-mile ribbon of lakes, ponds, rivers, and streams designated as the Allagash Wilderness Waterway.

There are three major approaches to this "North Woods." The longest, most scenic route is up the Kennebec River, stopping to raft in The Forks (see "The Upper Kennebec Valley and Jackman"), and along the Moose River to the village of Rockwood at the dramatic narrows of Moosehead Lake, then down along the lake to Greenville, New England's largest seaplane base. (You can, of course, also drive directly to Greenville, exiting from I-95 at Newport.)

From Greenville you can hop a floatplane to a sporting camp or set off up the eastern shore of Moosehead to the woodland outpost of Kokadjo and on to the Golden Road, a 98-mile, private logging road running east from Quebec through uninterrupted forest to Millinocket. As Thoreau did in the 1850s, you can canoe up magnificent Chesuncook Lake, camping or staying in the tiny old outpost of Chesuncook Village. With increased interest in rafting down the West Branch of the Penobscot River through Ripogenus Gorge and the Crib Works, this stretch of the Golden Road has become known as the West Branch Region.

For those who come this distance simply to climb Mount Katahdin and to camp in Baxter State Park, the quickest route is up I-95 to Medway and in through Millinocket; it's 18 miles to the Togue Pond Gatehouse and Baxter State Park.

Northern reaches of Baxter State Park and the lakes beyond are best accessed from the park's northern entrance via Patten. Both Ashland and Portage are also points of entry, and Shin Pond serves as the seaplane base for this northernmost reach of the North Woods.

GUIDANCE

North Maine Woods (435-6213), Box 421, Ashland 04732, is a consortium of more than 20 major landowners that manages the recreational use of 2.8 million acres of commercial forest in northwestern Maine. It publishes map/guides that show logging roads and campsites, as well as a canoers guide to the St. John River, a pamphlet about the organization that tells a bit of history and details the regulations and fees, and a list of outfitters and camps that are licensed and insured to operate on the property.

Maine Sporting Camp Association, PO Box 89, Jay 04239, publishes a booklet guide to its members. See *Sporting Camps* in "What's Where."

Moosehead Lake Area Including Lower Piscataquis

Moosehead Lake is 40 miles long with some 320 miles of mountainous shoreline, most of it owned by lumber companies. Greenville is the sole "organized" town.

Around the turn of the century, you could board a Pullman car in New York City and ride straight through to Greenville, there to board a steamer for Mount Kineo, a palatial summer hotel perched on an island in the lake. Greenville began as a farm town, but it soon discovered its most profitable crops to be winter lumbering and summer tourists—a group that, since train service and grand hotels have vanished, now consists largely of fishermen, canoeists, white-water rafters, and hunters, augmented in winter by skiers, snowmobilers, and ice fishermen.

But you don't have to be a sportsman to enjoy Moosehead Lake. Immense and backed by mountains, it possesses unusual beauty and offers a family a wide choice of rustic, old-fashioned "camps" at reasonable prices. The town remains a lumbermen's depot and jump-off point for excursions into the wooded wilderness to the north. Greenville is New England's largest seaplane base, with three competing flying services ready to ferry visitors to remote camps and campsites.

The community of Rockwood, a half-hour drive north of Greenville on the lake's west shore, is even more of an outpost: a cluster of sporting camps and stores between the lake and the Moose River. The river connects with a chain of rivers and ponds that trail off to the west all the way to Jackman. Rockwood sits at the lake's narrows, across from its most dramatic landmark: the sheer cliff face of Mount Kineo, a place revered by Native Americans. According to local legend, the mountain is the petrified remains of a monster moose sent to Earth by the Great Spirit as a punishment for sins. It was also the Native Americans' source of flint. The Mount Kineo House, which once stood at the foot of this outcropping, accommodated 800 guests. The resort flourished for many years under the ownership of the Maine Central Railroad (which offered service to Rockwood) and had a golf course, a yacht club, and stables.

The big hotel has long since vanished, but a defunct, three-story annex, a row of shingled Victorian "cottages"—one now a small inn serving meals to the public—and the nine-hole golf course survive. The old hotel has recently been purchased, with the intent of complete renovation to recapture some of its previous grandeur. The annex is slated for use as lodging for the many snowmobilers who take advantage of this area each winter. We are eager to watch the progress of this project as it develops. Accessible only by shuttle boat from Rockwood, much of Kineo is now a state-owned nature preserve with exceptional hiking trails.

Most Greenville visitors explore Moosehead's eastern shore at least as far as Lily Bay State Park, and many continue to the outpost village of Kokadjo (population: 5), prime moose-watching country. It's another 40 miles northeast over paper company roads to Chesuncook Lake and to Ripogenus Dam, from which logging roads lead north into the Allagash and east to Baxter State Park and Millinocket.

GUIDANCE

Moosehead Lake Region Chamber of Commerce (695-2702), PO Box 581, Greenville 04441. A four-season resource. The walk-in information center up on Indian Hill (Route 15 south of town) is open daily in summer; 6 days a week from October through May.

Moosehead Vacation and Sportsmen's Association (534-7300), PO Box 366, Rockwood 04478, a source of year-round information about the Rockwood area.

GETTING THERE

By air: **Folsom's Air Service** (see *Getting Around*) offers charter service to Bangor, Augusta, and Portland.

By car: From points south, take the Maine Turnpike to exit 39 (Newport). Proceed up Route 7 to Dexter, then continue north on Route 23 to Sangerville (Guilford), then up Route 15 to Greenville. Note the longer, more scenic route up through The Forks and Jackman suggested in our introduction to this part.

GETTING AROUND

By air: **Folsom's Air Service** (695-2821), Greenville. Billed as "Maine's largest seaplane operator," founded by Dick Folsom in 1946, now headed by his son Max. Until recently, Folsom's radio phone was the only link with the outside world for many camps; his fliers are adept at landing their seaplanes at most North Woods camps. Folsom's will also book you into a camp and transport you and your canoe into the Allagash, or just give you a scenic flight.

Currier's Flying Service (695-2778), Greenville Junction. Offers day trips, scenic flights including Allagash, Mount Katahdin, Mount Kineo, and others, service to camps; will book camps and guides or set up guided backcountry, cross-country ski trips.

Jack's Flying Service (695-3020) caters to Allagash canoe trips and also offers fly-in to housekeeping cottages.

By boat: Service to Mount Kineo from Rockwood is offered regularly in summer (every hour) via the **Kineo Shuttle;** call 534-8812. **The**

Wilderness Boat (534-7305) based at The Birches and **Moosehead Water Taxi** (534-8847) also serve the peninsula.

By car: If you plan to venture out on the network of private roads maintained by the lumber companies, be forewarned that it may be expensive, in terms of both gate fees and damage to your car's suspension. You need a high car, and preferably four-wheel drive.

MEDICAL EMERGENCY

Charles A. Dean Memorial Hospital and ambulance service (695-2223), Greenville. Emergency aid is also available from **Maine State Police Headquarters** (1-800-452-4664).

TO SEE

Moosehead Marine Museum (695-2716 in-season; for year-round information write: PO Box 1151, Greenville 04441). Home for the S/S *Katahdin*, a restored, vintage 1914 steamboat that cruises daily late June through September, weekends after Memorial Day (9–5). One of 50 steamboats on the lake at its height as a resort destination, the *Katahdin* was the last to survive, converted to diesel in 1922 and in the 1930s modified to haul booms of logs, something we can remember her doing in 1975, the year of the nation's last log drive. This graceful, 115-foot, 150-passenger boat was restored through volunteer effort and re-launched in 1985. The museum's displays depict the lake's steamboat history from 1836. The 3-hour cruise is $12 per adult, $10 per senior, $6 per child over 5. Six-hour Thursday trips to Mount Kineo, with time to walk around the island, are $18 per adult, $16 per senior, and $10 per child. Private charters available.

Eveleth-Crafts-Sheridan House (695-2992), Main Street, Greenville. Historical tours offered in July and August, $1 donation requested. Home of the Moosehead Historical Society, a genuinely interesting 19th-century home, with displays on the region's history, including an 1880s kitchen, lumbering exhibit, and changing exhibits on the "sunporch."

SCENIC DRIVES

Along the Western Shore

Follow Route 6/15 north through Greenville Junction. If **Squaw Mountain's** chairlifts are running (see *To Do*), the ride is well worth taking for the views. Continue to **Rockwood** and take the shuttle (see *Getting Around*) to **Mount Kineo;** allow the better part of a day for exploring this dramatic spot (see *Hiking* and *Eating Out*). From Rockwood you can continue north for 20 miles to the Northern/Bowater checkpoint ($8 gate fee for out-of-staters, $4 for Maine resident vehicles). **Pittston Farm,** a short distance beyond, was once the hub of Great Northern operations for this entire western swath of North Woods. It's now a lodge known for lumber camp–style cooking (see *Eating Out*). Note that from Rockwood you can also continue on to Quebec City (via Jackman).

Along the Eastern Shore

Lily Bay State Park (695-2700), 8 miles north of Greenville, offers a sandy beach, a grassy picnicking area, and camping.

Kokadjo, 18 miles north of Greenville, is a 100-acre island of independently owned land on First Roach Pond, in the center of lumber company–owned forest. Most of the buildings here were once part of a lumbering station and are now camps attached to the Kokadjo Trading Post (see *Eating Out*); Northern Pride Lodge (see *Inns*) rents canoes and boats. If you continue north a few miles, you will hit the Bowater/Great Northern Paper checkpoint at **Sias Hill** ($8 per out-of-state vehicle and $4 per Maine license plate). The road surface improves here and is fairly smooth (but you must now pull over to let lumber trucks pass); it improves even more in a dozen miles when you hit the **Golden Road** (see part introduction). Turn right (east).

Cushing's Landing, at the foot of Chesuncook Lake, is worth a stop. The woodsman's memorial here was created from a post in the doorway of a Bangor tavern; it is decorated with tools of the trade and an iron bean pot. This is also the logical boat launch for visiting **Chesuncook Village,** one of the few surviving examples of a 19th-century North Woods lumbermen's village, now on the National Register of Historic Places. In summer, access is by charter aircraft from Greenville or by boat from Chesuncook Dam. In winter, you can come by snowmobile. Writing about the village in 1853, Henry David Thoreau noted, "Here immigration is a tide which may ebb when it has swept away the pines." Today a church, a graveyard (relocated from the shore to a hollow in the woods when Great Northern raised the level of the lake a few years ago), an inn, and a huddle of houses are all that remain of the village. (See Chesuncook Lake House under *Inns* for lodging and boat shuttle.)

Ripogenus Dam, just east of Chesuncook Lake, is the departure point for a number of white-water-rafting expeditions (see *White-Water Rafting/Kayaking*). This is one of the two major centers for white-water rafting in Maine—the other is The Forks (see "The Upper Kennebec Valley and Jackman"). Beginning at the dam, the West Branch of the Penobscot drops more than 70 feet per mile—seething and roiling through Ripogenus Gorge—and continues another 12 miles with stretches of relatively calm water punctuated by steep drops. You can get a view of the gorge by driving across the dam. **Pray's Store** (723-8880) sells most things you might need and rents cottages (open year-round).

The Telos Road leads to the **Allagash Wilderness Waterway,** a 92-mile-long chain of lakes, ponds, rivers, and streams that snake through the heart of the North Woods. The traditional canoe trip through the Allagash takes 10 days, but 2- and 3-day trips can be worked out. Brook trout, togue, and lake whitefish are plentiful. For details see *Canoeing the Allagash* in "What's Where," and *Canoe Rentals and Trips,* below.

TO DO

AIRPLANE RIDES

All the flying services listed under *Getting Around* also offer scenic flights.

BOAT EXCURSIONS

See **S/S *Katahdin*** at the Moosehead Marine Museum under *To See*.

Jolly Rogers Moosehead Cruises (534-8827/8817). Roger Lane's *Socatean* sails from Moose River in Rockwood late May through Columbus Day, offering narrated cruises around the lake; ask about luncheon Mount Kineo and sunset cruises.

CANOE RENTALS AND TRIPS

Allagash Canoe Trips (695-3668), Greenville. A family business since 1953, offering professional guides and top equipment. Weeklong expeditions into the Allagash Wilderness Waterway (also special teen trips); a 4-day trip on the Penobscot River and on Chesuncook Lake.

Allagash Wilderness Outfitters (695-2821), PO Box 620R, HCR 76, Greenville 04441. Supplies gear for a canoe camping trip.

Wilderness Expeditions (534-2242 , 534-7305 or 1-800-825-WILD), PO Box 41, Rockwood 04478. Based at The Birches Resort, this is a good source of rental equipment and advice. Guided trips on the West Branch of the Penobscot or into the Allagash Wilderness Waterway; towing service and ground transportation. Canoe and kayak clinics are offered.

Note: All the flying services will ferry canoes into remote backcountry (see *Getting Around*).

CHAIRLIFT RIDES

Chair Lift Ride at Squaw Mountain (695-1000), Route 6/15 between Greenville and Rockwood; generally weekends in summer and fall, but call ahead. Spectacular view of lake and mountains.

FISHING

Troll for salmon and trout in Moosehead Lake and fly-fish in the many rivers and ponds—rental boats and boat launches are so plentiful that they defy listing.

There are two prime sources of fishing information: the **Inland Fisheries and Wildlife** office (695-3757) in Greenville and the **Maine Guide Fly Shop and Guide Service** (695-2266), Main Street, Greenville. At the Fly Shop, Dan Legere sells 314 different flies and a wide assortment of gear; he also works with local guides to outfit you with a cabin cruiser and guide or to set up a river float trip or a fly-in expedition. For a list of local boat rentals as well as a list of local guides,, check with the **Moosehead Lake Area Chamber of Commerce** (see *Guidance*). Also see listings in *Rustic Resorts,* all of which are on water and cater to fishermen.

Ice fishing begins January 1 and ends March 30. Ice house rentals are available from several area businesses. Inquire at the chamber.

Gulf Hagas

GOLF

Squaw Mountain Village Resort on Moosehead Lake (695-3609). A nine-hole course with lounge and restaurant.

Mount Kineo Golf Course (695-2229), a spectacularly sited, nine-hole course at Kineo, accessible by frequent boat service from Rockwood; carts and club rentals.

HIKING

Moosehead Hiking Tours (695-2441), Greenville. Specializes in guided day hikes for all ages and abilities; 3- to 4-hour hikes. Rates include transportation, snack, gate fees, and a guide.

For those who prefer to guide themselves, easy hikes featuring great views can be found on:

Mount Kineo, an islandlike peninsula that offers steep but rewarding paths to the lookout tower at the top of the 750-foot-high cliff; a shore path also circles the peninsula. It's accessible from Rockwood by shuttle (see *Getting Around*).

Gulf Hagas, billed as the Grand Canyon of Maine, is just 8 miles east of the Wilson checkpoint near the Greenville airport (see the "Katahdin Region" for details).

Borestone Mountain Sanctuary, 10 miles out the Eliotsville Road from Route 6/15 at Monson, offers an information center (June 1 through October 1, 8 AM–dusk) maintained by the National Audubon Society; it's at Sunrise Pond, halfway up the 3-mile trail leading to a summit with a 360-degree view.

The Moosehead Lake Region Chamber of Commerce (695-2702) also furnishes information on climbing **Big Spencer, Elephant Mountain,** and walking into **Little Wilson Falls,** a majestic, 57-foot cascade in a forested setting.

HORSEBACK RIDING AND WAGON RIDES

Northern Maine Riding Adventures (564-3451/2965), PO Box 16, Dover-Foxcroft. Judy Cross, a registered Maine guide and skilled equestrian, offers 1-hour trail rides, centered riding clinics, and day trips from her four-season facility; also overnight treks based at her camp in the back-woods around Katahdin Ironworks. Special-needs riders are welcome.

Rockies Golden Acres (695-3229), Greenville. Trail rides: 1½- to 2-hour rides through the woods to Sawyer Pond; mountain views. Call after 7 PM, or leave a message.

MOOSE-WATCHING

"Moosemainea," sponsored by the Moosehead Lake Chamber of Commerce mid-May through mid-June (see *Moose-Watching* in "What's Where"), makes up the largest, most colorful moose-watching event in New England; but chances are you can spot the lake's mascot any dawn or dusk, especially if you go on a guided moose-watching tour. The chamber has a pamphlet that lists seven options by land, air, and boat.

MOUNTAIN BIKING

North Woods Mountain Bikes (695-3288), Main Street, Greenville. Rents bikes and has trail information available.

The Birches (534-7305; 1-800-825-WILD), Rockwood, offers mountain bike rentals for use on its extensive cross-country-ski network.

SWIMMING

See Lily Bay State Park under *To See.*

WHITE-WATER RAFTING/KAYAKING

Moosehead Lake is equidistant from Maine's two most popular rafting routes—Kennebec Gorge and Ripogenus Gorge. **Wilderness Expeditions** (534-2242; 1-800-825-WILD), PO Box 41, Rockwood 04478, based at The Birches in Rockwood (see *Rustic Resorts*), is a family-run business specializing in half-day white-water-rafting trips on the Kennebec at East Outlet (minimum age is 7); longer expeditions on the Kennebec from a base camp in The Forks and on the Penobscot from another base near Baxter State Park.

CROSS-COUNTRY SKIING

Formal touring centers aside, this region's vast network of snowmobile trails and frozen lakes constitutes splendid opportunities for backcountry skiing. We've skied from the cabins at Chesuncook Lake House and Northern Pride Lodge in Kokadjo (see *Lodging*), all open in winter for cross-country skiers as well as snowmobilers.

Birches Ski Touring Center (534-7305), Rockwood. The resort maintains an extensive network of trails, recently expanded to take advantage of an 11,000-acre forested spread across the neck between Brassua Lake and Moosehead. You can ski to Tomhegan, 10 miles up the lake, or out past the ice-fishing shanties to Kineo. Rentals and instruction; snowshoes, too.

Little Lyford Pond Camps (see *Rustic Resorts*) offers groomed trails. In Chesuncook Village, both **Chesuncook Lake House** and **Katahdin View Lodge** cater to cross-country skiers.

DOWNHILL SKIING

Big Squaw Mountain Resort (695-1000), Box 430, Greenville 04441. A ski resort since 1963, with one of New England's first base-area hotels, owned by Scott Paper (1970–1974) and then sold to the state, under whose ownership it languished for 11 years. It has continued to struggle, but seems to be headed in the right direction under present owners James and Karen Confalone. Billed as a family mountain, it has a vertical drop of 1750 feet and 22 trails at beginner, intermediate, and expert levels. Skiers have terrific views of Moosehead Lake and Mount Katahdin. Lifts include a double chair, a triple chair, a T-bar and a pony lift. Other facilities include a base lodge and cafeteria, ski school, ski shop, and lodging in 54 rooms. There are also plans to have a swimming pool and restaurant open by the 1996–1997 ski season.

SNOWMOBILING

Snowmobiling is huge in this area. The chamber publishes and sells a map of area snowmobile trails, which also offers information on area businesses catering to snowmobilers. **Moosehead Riders Snowmobile Club** proudly proclaims the area the "hub" of snowmobiling and offers a 24-hour trail condition report (695-4561). Its clubhouse is open Saturday and Sunday in winter. The club also sponsors guided tours. Interconnecting Trail System (ITS) routes 85, 86, and 87 run directly through the area, and there are many locally groomed trails as well. The new Moosehead trail goes around the lake, avoiding formerly dangerous ice-out situations. Snowmobile rentals are available from **Kokadjo Trading Post** (695-3993) in Kokadjo, **Greenwood Motel** (695-3321), Greenville Junction, and from **Rockwood Sales & Service** (534-7387), Rockwood.

LODGING

INNS

Greenville Inn (695-2206 or 1-888-695-6000), Norris Street, Box 1194, Greenville 04441. Open all year (B&B November through May). A true lumber baron's mansion set atop a hill just off Main Street, with a sweeping view of Moosehead Lake. Rich cherry, mahogany, and oak paneling, embossed walls, working fireplaces, and an immense, leaded-glass window depicting a single spruce tree—all contribute to the sense of elegance. There are six second-floor rooms (two with fireplaces), also a more rustic suite in the carriage house (ideal for families). Two pine-paneled cottages were moved back to make way for four new cottages, all with views. The dining room, open to the public, is considered the best in northwestern Maine (see *Dining Out*). Your hosts are Elfi, Susie, and Michael Schnetzer. $95–165 in-season (includes European breakfast buffet), less mid-October to late May; $15 for extra person in room.

The Lodge at Moosehead (695-4400), Box 1175, Lily Bay Road, Greenville 04441. Jennifer and Roger Cauchi have transformed a vintage 1916 hunting lodge into a phenomenon. Each of the five guest rooms (four with lake views) has been designed with immense care around a theme. In the "trout" room, for instance, brightly painted leaping trout have been sculpted into the bed's four-posters and matching mirrors; the fabric-covered walls are patterned with hooks and flies. Each room features equally spectacular carved four-poster beds depicting its theme (moose, bear, loon, totem). All rooms have cable TVs, gas fireplaces, and baths with Jacuzzi tubs. The Cauchis plan to convert the carriage house into three more suites, even more luxurious than the present ones, to be ready for occupancy in the spring of 1997. Roger delights in playing concierge, arranging fishing, hiking, rafting, or whatever else guests may desire. Common areas are comfortable and vast, including a downstairs billiards room, where there is always a puzzle in progress. A full breakfast is served in the glass-walled dining room, and dinner is also available to guests. Double-occupancy rates, including breakfast, are $145–195 June 1 through October 31; $145–175 off-season, including dinner as well as breakfast.

Chesuncook Lake House (745-5330; c/o Folsom's: 695-2821), Box 656, Route 76, Greenville 04441. Open year-round. An unpretentious, 1864 farmhouse built on the site of an older log cabin that served as the center for the lumbering camp (see Chesuncook Village under *To See*). There are 12 guest rooms and three housekeeping cabins. Maggie McBurnie, a native Parisian, serves three meals a day in summer; her husband, Bert, born and schooled in Chesuncook, meets guests at Cushing's Landing at the south end of the lake and ferries them in. Otherwise you can fly in from Greenville. Registered Maine guides and boats are available. In winter, cross-country ski tours are offered. $85 per person includes three meals in the inn, which closes in winter; the year-round rate in the cabins is $25 per person per day with a 3-day minimum; $35–38 per person per day in the summer.

Northern Pride Lodge (695-2890), HCR 76, Box 588, Kokadjo 04441. Open year-round. Built as a lumber baron's hunting lodge in this wilderness outpost (year-round population: 5), the lodge offers six guest rooms, each with enough beds for a family or group of friends; shared baths. The living room has a hearth, stained-glass windows, and a sense of opulence; the dining room, on a glassed-in porch overlooking First Roach Pond, is open to guests daily and to the public Thursday through Sunday. There are also 24 campsites, rental canoes, motorboats, and mountain bikes. In winter the lodge caters to snowmobilers and cross-country skiers. $80 per couple May through November; $70 per couple December through April (includes breakfast). $59 per night for single; rates with all three meals are also offered.

BED & BREAKFASTS

Sawyer House (695-2369), PO Box 521, Lakeview Street, Greenville 04441. Open year-round. Handy to the flying services, and an ideal stop if you fly in from Portland en route to a remote sporting camp or inn; good for anyone who likes being in Greenville with a view of the lake. There's a first-floor suite that can accommodate up to four and two second-floor rooms with private bath. $60–70 double in high season, $5 less for singles. Rates include a full breakfast, with hot popovers or homemade breads, bacon or sausage, and a choice of eggs, French toast, or pancakes. Pat Zieten is a warm, helpful host.

Devlin House (695-2229), PO Box 1102, Greenville 04441. A modern home high on the hill west of town with splendid views over meadows to the lake; a ground-level suite with a sitting room, and two rooms with king-sized beds, private baths, air-conditioning, and TV. Ruth Devlin is a long-time local resident who enjoys sharing her knowledge of the area. $75–95.

Pleasant Street Inn (695-3400) PO Box 1261, Greenville 04441. Hostess Sue Bushey has turned this Victorian home into a wonderful resting spot. Rooms range from one decorated all in white, with a queen bed and deep old-fashioned tub, to a smaller, simply decorated one with twin beds. The comfortable second-floor TV room with a large movie library is perfect for rainy days. There is also a turret sitting room that is a peaceful place to read, or you can relax on the large wraparound porch. Rates include a delicious, very filling breakfast.

Kineo House (534-8812), PO Box 397, Rockwood 04478. Open year-round except April, but there is sometimes difficulty getting there in early winter and early spring, when neither boats nor snowmobiles can cross the lake. The only place to stay on Kineo, a nature preserve at the narrows of Moosehead Lake. The six guest rooms (most with private baths) are in one of the cottages once clustered around a mammoth—now all but vanished—grand hotel. The classic, old, nine-hole golf course survives, and hiking trails now lead up the sides of the sheer-faced Mount Kineo for which the old hotel was named. It is also a great place for mountain biking and snowmobiling. In each of the rooms, there is at least a glimpse of a water view. At night this is the quietest place around because of the absence of traffic. Lynn and Marshall Peterson serve lunch to the public, dinner by reservation, and operate the Kineo shuttle (see *Getting Around*). Shuttle and breakfast are included in $70 double, $15 per extra person.

RUSTIC RESORTS

The Birches Resort (534-7305/2241; 1-800-825-WILD), PO Box 41, Rockwood 04478. Open year-round. The Willards have turned this '30s sporting camp into one of the most comfortable family-geared resorts in the North Woods. It's sited in a birch grove overlooking Mount Kineo. Fifteen hand-hewn log cabins are strung along the lake, each with a porch, a Franklin stove or fireplace in a sitting room, and one to three bedrooms.

All of the cabins have kitchens (some don't have ovens), but three meals are available in summer. The main lodge includes a cheerful, open-timbered dining room, an inviting lobby with a trout pool, and a living room with hearth room. Upstairs are four guest rooms with decks overlooking the lake (shared bath); there are also 12 "cabin tents" near the lodge and several yurts scattered through the resort's 11,000 acres. Facilities include an outside hot tub and sauna; windsurfers, sailboats, kayaks, canoes, fishing boats, and mountain bikes are available. Cross-country-skiing rentals and expeditions are also offered. From $76 double with breakfast in the lodge. Housekeeping cottages are $650–950 per week in summer (less off-season) without meals. Cabin tents begin at $22 single per day. A variety of rafting, canoeing, and other packages are also available. The dining room is open to the public (see *Dining Out*).

Little Lyford Pond Camps (Folsom's radio phone: 695-2821), Box 1269, Greenville 04441. Open whenever it is feasible for guests to get in/out. Reservations are required. Sited in a sheltered, alpine-looking valley, these camps were built in the 1870s as a logging company station on a tote road. The seven shake-roofed log cabins (without plumbing or electricity) sleep from two to seven. Each has a private outhouse. Three meals are served in the main lodge; facilities also include a conference center, sauna, and solar shower. Gulf Hagas is a short hike and cross-country-ski trails are maintained. In winter you can ski or fly in, but in summer the pontoon planes don't like to land. The camps are 3.5 miles off the Appalachian Trail, 12 miles via a gated logging road from Greenville. $85 per person includes all meals, plus use of canoes. Children under 12 are half price.

Nugent's Chamberlain Lake Camps (695-2821), HCR 76, Box 632, Greenville 04441. Open year-round. Dates just from the 1930s, but built entirely by Al and Patty Nugent. This is one of the most remote camps, nicely sited and still so old-fashioned that it should be on the National Register of Historic Places. In 1987 the state awarded the lease of these camps to John Richardson and Regina Webster. Within the Allagash Wilderness Waterway, 50 miles north of Millinocket between Baxter State Park and Allagash Mountain, they are best reached via Folsom's Air Service (see *Getting Around*); otherwise it's a 5-mile boat or snowmobile ride up Chamberlain Lake. The eight housekeeping cabins have the traditional front overhang and outhouses; they sleep 2 to 10. Boats are available. AP, MAP, or housekeeping plans available. $22–60 per person. Pets and children welcome.

West Branch Ponds Camps (695-2561), PO Box 1153, Greenville 04441. A 10-mile drive from the main road at Kokadjo. Open after the ice breaks up and through September; inquire about winter season. First opened as a moose-hunting lodge in the 1880s; the newest log cottage was built in 1938. Directly across the pond is the majestic bulk of White-cap Mountain. Wonderfully weathered old cabins (with log beds, heat, electricity, bath; three have Franklin stoves) and a square central lodge with a bell on top. Andy and Carol Stirling are third-generation owners, and Carol is well known for her cooking. Motorboats and canoes are available. The lodge has plenty of books and comfortable corners. $54 per person per day includes three meals and use of a canoe; children are half price.

☞ **Maynards in Maine** (534-7703), Rockwood 04478. Open May through hunting season. "The only thing we change around here is the linen," says Gail Maynard, who helps run the sportsmen's camp founded by her husband's grandfather in 1919. Overlooking the Moose River, a short walk from Moosehead Lake, Maynards includes a dozen tidy, moss green frame buildings with dark Edwardian furniture, much of it from the grand old Mount Kineo Hotel. The lodge is filled with stuffed fish, moose heads, and Maynard family memorabilia, and furnished with stiff-backed leather chairs. A sign cautions DO NOT WEAR HIP BOOTS OR WADERS INTO THE DINING ROOM. Two meals a day are served and one "packed." $50 per person with three meals, $288 per week for cabins.

CAMPS

Tomhegan Wilderness Resort (534-7712), PO Box 308, Rockwood 04478. Open year-round. A 10-mile ride up a dirt road from Rockwood Village; 1.5 miles of frontage on Moosehead Lake. Nine hand-hewn cottages along a wooden boardwalk with kitchens and living rooms, rocking chairs on the porches, full baths, and woodstoves; also efficiency units in the lodge. Very remote and peaceful; deer are frequently seen at close range. Boats and canoes are available; cross-country skiing and snowmobiling in winter. $472 weekly for four people in most camps; $710 per week for six people in the largest camp; efficiency units $65 per day for a double.

✐ **Rockwood Cottages** (534-7725), Box 176, Rockwood 04478. Open year-round. Ron and Bonnie Searles maintain clean, comfortable housekeeping cottages with screened-in porches overlooking the lake and Mount Kineo just across the narrows. They are happy to advise about exploring Kineo and this less developed end of the lake. Boats, motors, and fishing licenses are available, and guests have free docking. There's also a sauna, a barbecue, and an impressive moose head. $65 per couple, $10 per additional person; $395 per couple per week, $60 per additional person. Pets welcome.

Beaver Cove Camps (695-3717; 1-800-577-3717), Greenville 04441. Open year-round. Eight miles north of Greenville on the eastern shore of Moosehead Lake are six fully equipped housekeeping cabins, each with full kitchen and bath. Owner Jim Glavine is a registered Maine guide specializing in fly-fishing. Guided hunting and snowmobile or ski touring also offered. $70 per night or $420 double per week.

☞ **Spencer Pond Camps** (radio service: 695-2821), Star Route 76, Box 580, Greenville 04441. Open May to mid-November. Bob Croce and Jill

Martel are continuing the traditions of this long-established cluster of six housekeeping camps (sleeping 2 to 10) in an unusually beautiful spot, accessible by logging road from Lily Bay Road. The hosts are warm and helpful, with plenty of suggestions for enjoying the wilderness. Guests are welcome to fresh vegetables from the garden. Gas and kerosene lights and hand-pumped water; each cottage is stocked with cooking utensils and dishes, and has a private shower room and outhouse. A base for birding, hiking, and mountain climbing. Canoes and boats available. Reasonable rates: $17–20 per person; 2-night minimum stay for two people.

Medawisla (radio phone year-round: 695-2690), HCR 76, Box 592, Greenville 04441. Open May through November. In this remote corner of the woods, the LeRoys offer six fully equipped cabins with woodstoves, flush toilets, and hot showers. Each can sleep from 2 to 10 people. These camps cater to a quiet clientele, and there is plenty of open space for peaceful relaxation. The "reading room" is a spot outside overlooking a dam that was once the only road in. Popular for fishing in spring, hunting in fall, and as a getaway in summer. Meals available during deer season only. Boats and canoes are available, and they specialize in 1- to 3-day canoe trips with overnight accommodations on the upper West Branch of the Penobscot River. The loons of the sound track from the movie *On Golden Pond* were taped here. $60–90 double, housekeeping; weekly rates.

CAMPGROUNDS

Lily Bay State Park (695-2700), 8 miles north of Greenville. Ninety-three sites, many spaced along the shore; boat launch and beach.

Maine State Bureau of Forestry (695-3721) maintains free (first-come, first-served) "authorized sites" (no fire permit required) and "permit sites" (permit required), scattered on both public and private land along Moosehead Lake and on several of its islands.

Bowater/Great Northern Paper woodlands office in Millinocket (723-5131) is also the source of a map detailing roads and primitive campsites in that company's vast domain. After paying the gate fee ($8 for out-of-state vehicles, $4 for Maine plates), sites are $6 per out-of-state vehicle, $3 for Maine plates.

WHERE TO EAT

DINING OUT

Greenville Inn (695-2206 or 1-888-695-6000), Norris Street, Greenville. Dinner served nightly by reservation from 6 PM. Elfi Schnetzer has turned over the kitchen to her daughter Susie, who continues to delight diners with appetizers like smoked bluefish pâté and basil zucchini soup, and an ever-changing selection of entrées, which might include spicy maple-glazed salmon fillet with basmati rice or sirloin steak with green peppercorn sauce and roasted red potato. Leave room for dessert, maybe

chocolate truffle tart with pecan crust or lemon cheesecake with strawberry sauce. $17–27 (for full rack of lamb).

The Birches (534-2242), Rockwood. Open year-round: daily in summer,
sporadically after that (call for times). This popular resort (see *Rustic
Resorts*) has one of the area's most attractive dining rooms—log-sided
with a massive stone hearth, a war canoe turned upside down in the
open rafters, and hurricane lamps on the highly polished tables. The
menu has undergone a transformation, offering healthier grilled or
baked options. Specialties include prime rib and pork tenderloin with
chutney. $9.95–16.95. Reservations suggested.

Northern Pride Lodge (695-2890), Kokadjo. The dining room in this classic lumber baron's hunting lodge (see *Inns*) is a modified sun porch
overlooking First Roach Pond. Dinner is served to the public Thursday
through Sunday and ranges from spaghetti to filet mignon; $9.95–14.95.
Reservations suggested.

EATING OUT

Pittston Farm (call Folsom's Air Service: 695-2821). Open year-round
except for the last 2 weeks in April. "Authentic" only begins to
describe this classic outpost, a wilderness farm built around 1910 as a
major hub of Great Northern's logging operations. Sited at the
confluence of the North and South Branches of the Penobscot River a
little more than 20 miles north of Rockwood, the white-clapboard
lodge and its outlying barns and fields are now owned by Ken Twitchel
(a veteran lumber camp cook) and his wife, Sonja. Visitors are welcome for all-you-can-eat meals, which include thick, tasty soups and
at least two kinds of meat, several vegetables (some grown outside), a
salad bar, and freshly baked rolls, bread, and pastries. Buffet suppers
($8.95) are served at 5 and 6 PM; reservations are appreciated.
(Folsom's will fly you in and back from Greenville for $50–60 per
person including the meal). Lunch is $8.95 if it's a buffet, or it might
be short order (prices vary by item), and breakfast, $4.95. Upstairs
lodging is available, with a number of quilt-covered beds, shared baths,
$35 per person, meals included. There's also a campground on the
premises. See *Scenic Drives* for toll-road fees.

Kineo House (534-8812), Kineo. Open May through October and December through April. Accessible in summer by shuttle boat from
Rockwood (see *Bed & Breakfasts*). It would be a shame to spend a few
days in the Moosehead area and not explore Kineo, with its dramatic
walks and hiking trails as well as its golf course. Kineo House serves
lunch (burgers and sandwiches), has a pleasant pub, and also offers dinner ($9–15) by reservation.

Kokadjo Trading Post (695-3993), Kokadjo. Open 6 AM–11 PM, earlier
in hunting season. Fred and Marie Candeloro offer a cozy dining
room/pub room with a large fieldstone fireplace and a view of First
Roach Pond.

The Indian Store in Greenville

In Greenville

Flatlander's Pub (695-3373), Pritham Avenue, Greenville. Open except Tuesday, 11 AM "til close." Hamburgers, chicken wings, deep-fried mushrooms, deli sandwiches; beer on tap and house wines; homemade chili, a good pea soup, and pies. Nice atmosphere, the preferred middle-of-town place.

Kelly's Landing (695-4438), Greenville Junction. Open 7 AM–9 PM. A breakfast bar and large salad bar, fried seafood platter, roast chicken, sandwiches. A big, cheerful place with tables on the deck by the lake.

The Road Kill Cafe (695-2230; fax 207-695-3851), Route 15, Greenville Junction. Open daily 11:30–close. The café's subtitle is, "Where the food used to speak for itself." Loud, funky, and fun, the decor runs from hubcaps to license plates, and the menu features moose wings, piglips, chicken that didn't make it across the road, and misteak on the lake. Children's menu.

Cangiano's (695-3314), Route 6/15, Greenville Junction. Open daily 11:30–9. A cozy restaurant with American-Italian gourmet cuisine. Lobster, prime rib, and specialties that include chicken marsala and shrimp cacciatore. Homemade desserts, full bar. Children's menu. The lunch menu is available at dinner for those who prefer a lighter meal.

The Lost Lobster (695-3900), North Main Street, Greenville. A touristy place, with outside deck for dining alongside an old lobster boat. Plenty of lobster choices, fried seafood, sandwiches.

Auntie M's Restaurant (695-2238), Main Street, Greenville. Open for all three meals but best for breakfast; homemade soups and specials. Caters to truckers, rafters, and kids.

SELECTIVE SHOPPING

Indian Hill Trading Post (695-3376), Greenville. Open daily year-round, Friday until 10 PM.

[clip icon] **The Indian Store** (695-3348), corner of Main Street and Pritham Avenue, Greenville. Since 1929 Ida Faye's store has sold baskets, feathers, candies, souvenirs, and knickknacks of every description. Every inch is filled.

The Corner Shop (695-2142), corner of Main and Pritham (across from the Indian Store), Greenville; gifts, books, magazines.

Sunbower Pottery (695-2870), Scammon Road, Greenville, home of the "moose mug"; locally made gifts, artwork.

SPECIAL EVENTS

February: **Winter Festival and Moosehead Riders Moosehead Magic,** Greenville—snowmobile events and poker runs.

Mid-May through mid-June: **Moosemania** month, sponsored by the chamber of commerce, takes place throughout the area. It's big; see "What's Where."

August: **Forest Heritage Days,** Greenville.

September: **The International Seaplane Fly-In Weekend** is held in Greenville.

Bangor Area

It is no coincidence that the year 1820—when big-city merchants began buying timberland along the upper reaches of the Penobscot River—was also the year in which the Massachusetts District of Maine became a state and planted a white pine in the center of its official seal.

By the 1830s the Penobscot River was filled with pine logs, all of which were processed in the sawmills just above Bangor, where they were loaded aboard ships. By 1834–1836 land broker offices were springing up as land speculation reached its peak. Townships and lots were sold sight unseen several times over. In 1835 it was reported that two paupers who had escaped from Bangor's almshouse had each cleared $1800 by speculating in timberland (the land offices worked around the clock) by the time they were caught the next morning.

By the 1850s, Bangor was the world's leading lumber port, handling over $3 million worth of lumber in its peak year. During this boom, a section of the city came to be known as the Devil's Half Acre, where loggers flooded in after a long winter's work (and with a long winter's pay) to frequent the numerous taverns and brothels.

The Bangor of today is substantially different. The only Paul Bunyan around now is the 31-foot-high statue next to the chamber of commerce office. A 1911 fire wiped out the business district, and the end of the logging boom combined with urban renewal left the Devil's Half Acre a distant memory. Still, Bangor is Maine's second largest city, and Bangor International Airport is the departure point for craft (admittedly air instead of sailing) bound for faraway points on the globe. The Bangor area also makes for a good resting spot for those venturing into the northern part of the state, to either the Baxter State Park region or the vast expanse of Aroostook County.

Two neighborhoods actually hint at the city's past grandeur. One is the West Market Square Historic District, a mid-19th-century block of shops. The other is the Broadway area, studded with the Federal-style homes of early prominent citizens and lumber barons' mansions. Across town, West Broadway holds a number of even more ornate homes, including the turreted Victorian home of author Stephen King (look for the bat-and-cobweb fence).

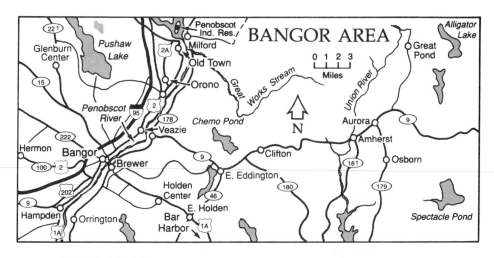

GUIDANCE

Greater Bangor Chamber of Commerce (947-0307), 519 Main Street (just off I-95 exit 45 to 495 East/exit 3B; across from the Holiday Inn), maintains a seasonal visitors information office (947-0307) in Paul Bunyan Park on lower Main Street (Route 1A).

The **Maine Publicity Bureau** maintains two rest area/information centers on I-95 in Hamden between exits 43 and 44: northbound (862-6628) and southbound (862-6638).

GETTING THERE

By air: **Bangor International Airport** (942-0384) is served by Delta Airlines, Northwest Airlink, and USAir Express. **Rental cars** are available at the airport.

By bus: **Greyhound** (942-1700) offers daily service to the downtown terminal. **Concord Trailways** (945-5000; 1-800-639-5150) has express trips, complete with movies and music, daily from Portland and Boston. **Cyr Bus Line** offers daily scheduled service all the way to Caribou, with stops in between.

By car: I-95 from Augusta.

GETTING AROUND

The Bus (947-0536) runs Monday through Saturday to Brewer, Bangor, Hamden, Veazie, Orono, and Old Town.

MEDICAL EMERGENCY

Eastern Maine Medical Center (973-7000), Bangor. **St. Joseph Hospital** (262-1000), Bangor.

VILLAGES

Hampden. Adjacent to Bangor, but offering a more rural setting. The academically excellent Hampden Academy and a well-known truck stop are found here.

Orono. Home of the University of Maine, but still a small town. Downtown there are some nice shops and local dining landmarks, and on campus a multitude of cultural activities are available.

Old Town. Definitely a mill town, also the home of the famous Old Town Canoe factory. There's a great little museum worth visiting.

Indian Island. In 1786 the Penobscot tribe deeded most of Maine to Massachusetts in exchange for 140 small islands in the Penobscot River; they continue to live on Indian Island, which is connected by a bridge to Old Town. The 1970s discovery of an 18th-century agreement that details the land belonging to the tribe (much of it now valuable) brought the island a new school and a large community center, which attracts crowds to play high-stakes bingo (call 1-800-255-1293 for the schedule). A general store in the center sells locally made crafts, as does the Moccasin Shop at Ernest Goslin's house on Bridge Street. A **Penobscot Nation Museum** (827-6545), 6 River Road, is theoretically open weekdays 1–4, but it was not open when we stopped by. The island is accessible from Route 2, marked from I-95, exit 51.

Winterport. An old river town, once home of many sea captains, now a quiet little area with a historic district. Walking tour brochure available from area businesses.

TO SEE AND DO

MUSEUMS

Cole Land Transportation Museum (990-3600), 405 Perry Road (junction I-95 and 395), Bangor. Open May 1 to early November, daily 9–5. $2 per adult, senior citizens $1, age 18 and under free. A collection of 19th- and 20th-century Maine vehicles: snowplows, wagons, trucks, sleds, rail equipment, and more.

Hose 5 Fire Museum (945-3229) 247 State Street, Bangor. Open Wednesday evenings, Saturday afternoons, and by special arrangement. A working fire station until 1993, now a museum with firefighting artifacts from the area. Three fully restored fire engines, wooden water mains, and plenty of historical pictures. Free, but donations gladly accepted.

University of Maine museums, Route 2A, Orono. **Hudson Museum** (581-1901) has tours in July and August at 1:30 on Tuesday, or you can browse on your own. There is an exceptional anthropological collection including a special section on Maine Native Americans and Maine history. **University of Maine Museum of Art** (581-3255), 109 Carnegie Hall (open weekdays 9–5, Saturday 1–4), shows a fraction of its 4500-work collection; changing exhibits.

Old Town Museum (827-7256), North Fourth Street Extension, Old Town. Open early June through the end of August, Wednesday to Sunday 1–5. A former waterworks building houses a great little museum with exhibits on the Penobscot tribe and on local logging; early photos; an original birch-bark canoe; well-informed guides.

Maine Forest and Logging Museum (581-2871), Leonard's Mills, off Route 178 in Bradley (take Route 9 north from Brewer; turn left on 178 and watch for signs). Open during daylight hours. "Living History Days" on two weekends, one in mid-July and another in October, with people in period attire performing various activities. A covered bridge, waterpowered sawmill, millpond, saw pit, stone dam, barn, and trapper's line camp mark the site of a late-19th-century logging community.

HISTORIC HOMES AND SITES

Bangor Historical Society Thomas A. Hill House (942-5766), 159 Union Street (at High Street), Bangor. Open March to mid-December, Tuesday through Friday 12–4 (also Sunday, July through September). Admission is $2 per adult, $.50 per student. Downstairs has been restored to its 19th-century grandeur with Victorian furnishings and an elegant double parlor, while changing exhibits of city memorabilia are housed upstairs in this Greek Revival house. Architecture buffs might also want to check out the neighboring **Isaac Farrar Mansion** (941-2808), 166 Union Street, open weekdays 9–4 ($1 admission). A restored English Regency lumber baron's mansion with marble fireplaces, mahogany paneling, and stained-glass windows.

Mount Hope Cemetery in Bangor is one of the nation's oldest garden cemeteries, designed by noted Maine architect Charles G. Bryant. Hannibal Hamlin's grave is here.

BUS TOURS AND BOAT EXCURSIONS

Best of Bangor Bus Tours, sponsored by the Bangor Historical Society, are offered on Thursday and the first Saturday of the month July through September, departing from the Bangor Visitors Information Office at 519 Main Street (see *Guidance*) at 10:30 AM; $5 per adult, children under 12 free.

Voyageur (948-5500), Bangor's 193-passenger vessel, offers 1½-hour cruises on the Penobscot River in summer. Combined rail and sail excursions are also available, featuring a ride on the Belfast & Moosehead Railroad along with the river cruise.

FISHING

Bangor Salmon Pool. A gathering spot for salmon traveling upstream to spawn; located 2 miles south of Bangor, Route 9 off North Main Street, Brewer.

GOLF

Bangor Municipal Golf Course (945-9226), Webster Avenue; 27 holes. **Penobscot Valley Country Club** (866-2423), Bangor Road, Orono; 18 holes. **Hermon Meadow Golf Club** (848-3741), Hermon; nine holes.

SWIMMING

Jenkins' Beach. Popular beach on Green Lake for families with children. Store and snack bar.

Violette's Public Beach and Boat Landing (843-6876), East Holden (between Ellsworth and Bangor). $2 admission. Popular spot for college students and young adults. Swim float with slide, boat launch, and picnic tables.

DOWNHILL AND CROSS-COUNTRY SKIING

Hermon Mountain (848-5192), Newburg Road, Hermon (3 miles off I-95 on exit 43 Carmel, or off Route 2 from Bangor). Popular local ski area, with 17 runs (the longest is 3500 feet); rentals available; base lodge, night skiing, snowboarding.

Hermon Meadow Ski Touring Center (848-3471). Approximately 6 miles of groomed trails on a golf course.

LODGING

The Phenix Inn (947-0411), 20 Broad Street, Bangor 04401. Renovated and reopened in 1995, this historic inn is located in the heart of downtown Bangor. Some rooms have antique brass fixtures or mahogany beds. All have private bath, air-conditioning, and TVs. Continental breakfast is included in the $64.95 single, $74 double rates.

Highlawn Bed and Breakfast (866-2272; 1-800-297-2272), 193 Main Street, Orono 04773. This majestic white house with front columns has been a bed & breakfast for more than a decade. Six of the 17 rooms in this 1803 house are pretty guest rooms, but only 3 are rented at a time, giving each a private bath. Five minutes from the University of Maine. Full breakfast (maybe pancakes or omelets) is included in $55–65.

The Lucerne Inn (843-5123; 1-800-325-5123), RFD 2, Box 540, Lucerne-in-Maine 04429. A 19th-century mansion on Route 1A, overlooking Phillips Lake in East Holden. Best known as a restaurant (see *Dining Out*), it also has 25 rooms with private baths, working fireplaces, heated towel bars, whirlpool baths, phones, and TVs. $59–99 depending on the season for standard rooms, $89–129 for suites, including a continental breakfast.

Hamstead Farm (848-3749), RFD 3, Box 703, Bangor 04401. Open year-round. Barns and outbuildings trail picturesquely behind a snug 1840s farmhouse. There are three pleasant guest rooms (one with private bath) with cozy, country-style decor. Resident animals include 175 turkeys, 40 cows, two brood sows, 20 feeder pigs, two barn cats, and two dogs. The farm is set on 150 acres, with a deck overlooking the backyard; a path leads into the village of Hermon. $45–50 double, $35–40 single includes a farm breakfast.

Note: Bangor also has many hotels and motels, mainly located by the mall and near the airport.

WHERE TO EAT

DINING OUT

The Lemon Tree (94-LEMON), 167 Center Street, Bangor. A welcome addition to Bangor's dining scene. Open for lunch Monday through Saturday, dinner Tuesday through Sunday, and Sunday brunch. A small place with plenty of atmosphere, as well as delectable menu choices. "Great Beginnings" include fried dill pickles (try them!), and entrées feature plenty of pasta choices, salads, sandwiches, and several house specialties. $4.95-13.95.

Lucerne Inn (843-5123), Route 1A, East Holden (11 miles out of Bangor, heading toward Ellsworth). Open for dinner daily, as well as a popular Sunday brunch. A grand old mansion with a view of Phillips Lake. Specialties include shrimp niçoise and veal Normandy. $11.95-19.95.

Pilot's Grill (942-6325), 1528 Hammond Street (Route 2, 1.5 miles west of exit 45B off I-95), Bangor. Open daily 11:30-9:30 (until 8 on Sunday). A large, long-established place with 1950s decor and a huge, all-American menu. $7-15.

The Greenhouse (945-4040), 193 Broad Street, Bangor. Open for lunch Tuesday through Friday, dinner Tuesday through Saturday. Tropical plants and an exotic menu are not what you'd expect to find in Bangor. We suggest coming for lunch on a warm summer day: There's a large riverside deck. $10-18.

EATING OUT

Captain Nick's (942-6444), 1165 Union Street, Bangor. Open daily for lunch and dinner. A big place with good seafood, steaks.

Bagel Shop (947-1654), 1 Main Street, Bangor. Open Monday to Thursday 6-6, Friday 6-5, Sunday 6-2. A genuine, reasonably priced kosher restaurant, delicatessen, and bakery that features egg dishes, bagels, and chocolate cheesecake.

✐ **Governor's Take Out and Eat In** (947-7704), 643 Broadway in Bangor; and Stillwater Avenue in Stillwater (827-4277). Open from early breakfast to late dinner: big breakfast menu, hamburgers to steaks, specials like German potato soup, fresh strawberry pie, ice cream.

Momma Baldacci's (945-5813) 12 Alden Street, Bangor. A longtime family-owned and -operated restaurant open for lunch and dinner, and serving Italian specialties at reasonable prices.

Dysart's (942-4878), Coldbrook Road, Hermon (I-95, exit 44). Open 24 hours. Billed as "the biggest truck stop in Maine"—one room for the general public and another for drivers. Known for great road food and reasonable prices. Homemade bread and seafood are specialties.

Pat's Pizza (866-2111), Mill Street, Orono. A local landmark, especially popular with high school and university students and families. Now franchised throughout the state, but this is the real thing with booths and a jukebox, back dining room and downstairs tap room, plus Pat and his family still in charge. Pizza, sandwiches, full dinners.

BREW PUB

Bear Brew Pub (866-BREW), 36 Main Street, Orono. An upscale brew pub with a creative menu that includes crabmeat, spinach, and mushroom strudel, as well as sandwiches like lemon pepper chicken breast. Five brews, as well as their own root beer, cream soda, and ginger ale.

COFFEEHOUSE

West Market Cafe (942-3611) 32 Broad Street, Bangor. Coffee specialty drinks include espresso drinks, drip coffee, Melior brewed, Turkish brewed, and a variety of steamed drinks and iced options. Pastries, bagels, soups, and sandwiches as well.

ENTERTAINMENT

Maine Center for the Arts, at the University of Maine in Orono, has become *the* cultural center for the area. As well as hosting a wide variety of events, it is home to the **Bangor Symphony Orchestra** (942-5555), the oldest continuously running community symphony orchestra in the US.

Penobscot Theater Company (942-3333), 183 Main Street, Bangor. For over 20 years this company has been putting on shows. It has a 9-month season and in summer sponsors the Shakespeare on the River festival and the Creative Arts Program for young people.

Maine Masque Theater (581-1963). Classic and contemporary plays presented October through April by theater students at the University of Maine, Orono.

Theatre of the Enchanted Forest (945-0800), 9 Central Street, Bangor. Children's theater.

Bass Park (942-9000), 100 Dutton Street, Bangor. Complex includes **Bangor Auditorium, Civic Center, State Fair,** and **Raceway** (featuring harness racing, Thursday through Sunday, May through July). Band concerts in Paul Bunyan Park Tuesdays in summer.

Blue Ox (941-2337) is the new professional baseball team in town. They play at Mahaney Diamond at the University of Maine. Tickets $4–6.

SELECTIVE SHOPPING

BOOKSTORES

Betts' Bookstore (947-7052), 26 Main Street, Bangor, a full-service bookstore specializing in Maine and Stephen King titles.

Mr. Paperback. Bangor is home base for this eastern Maine chain, with stores here at Main Square (942-6494) and Airport Mall (942-9191). All are fully stocked stores with Maine sections.

BookMarc's (942-3206), 10 Harlow Street, Bangor. A great little full-service bookstore, with a cozy café.

The Booksource, Crossroads Plaza, Bangor. A superstore with special emphasis on multimedia and children's books.

Borders (990-3300), off Hogan Road at Bangor Mall. A new book and music sensation, with a café serving espresso, too.

CANOES

Old Town Canoe Factory Outlet Store (827-5513), 130 North Main Street, Old Town. Varieties sold include fiberglass, wood, Kevlar, Crosslink, and Royalex. Factory tour video shows how canoes are made.

SPECIAL SHOPS

Winterport Boot Shop, Twin City Plaza, Brewer. Largest selection of Redwing workboots in the Northeast. Proper fit for sizes 4–16, all widths.

The Briar Patch (941-0255), on West Market Square, Bangor. A large and exceptional children's book and toy store.

The Grasshopper Shop (945-3132), West Market Square, Bangor. So many items, they now have two stores across the street from each other. Trendy women's clothing, toys, jewelry, gifts, housewares.

The Bangor Mall, Hogan Road (just west of the I-95 exit 49 interchange). Boasts more than 80 stores and has spawned a number of satellite minimalls. Since this is precisely the kind of strip most visitors come to Maine to escape, we won't elaborate; but it certainly has its uses.

SPECIAL EVENTS

July: **Bangor State Fair,** Bass Park—agricultural fair with harness racing. **Shakespeare on the River Festival** (late July to early August)—two shows presented in rotation, food vendors.

August: **WLBZ Downtown Arts Sidewalk Festival.**

September: **Riverfest,** a 2-day celebration with parade, crafts, food, entertainment, and children's games.

Katahdin Region

Mile-high Mount Katahdin is the centerpiece not only for Baxter State Park but also for a surprisingly large area from which it is clearly visible. Like a huge ocean liner in a relatively flat sea of woodland, the massive mountain looms above the open countryside to the east, the direction from which it's most easily accessible.

Though the mountain and park are unquestionably its biggest drawing card, the Katahdin region offers its share of wooded lake country and represents one of the most reasonably priced destinations in Maine for families who want to get away together to hike and fish. Whitewater rafting companies are also based near the Togue Pond gatehouse to Baxter State Park, handy both to the park and to rafting on the Western Branch of the Penobscot.

Like Acadia National Park, Baxter State Park's acreage was amassed privately and given to the public as a gift. In this case, it was one individual—Governor Percival Baxter—who bought all the land himself, after unsuccessfully attempting to convince the state to do so during his political term. At the time (1931), no one seemed able to conceive why Maine, with all its forest, needed officially to preserve a swatch of woods as wilderness.

Decades of subsequent logging and present concerns for the future of this woodland have heightened the value of Governor Baxter's legacy and his mandate—the reason camping and even day-use admission to the park are strictly limited—to preserve at least these 201,018 acres of Maine's North Woods as wilderness.

The restaurants and beds nearest to Baxter State Park are in Millinocket, a lumbering outpost built by the Great Northern Paper Company around the turn of the century. The town is still centered on the big paper mills and the logging industry that feeds it.

GUIDANCE

The **Baxter State Park** information phone is 723-5140, or you can write to park headquarters, 64 Balsam Drive, Millinocket 04462. For details about making reservations, see *Green Space*. The attractive visitors center, which offers picnic tables, rest rooms, and a selection of published as well as free guides to the park, is 1 mile east of Millinocket on Route 11/157.

Millinocket Chamber of Commerce (723-4443), 1029 Central Street, Millinocket 04462. The chamber maintains a seasonal information center on Route 11/157 east of Millinocket; it serves as a year-round source of information about the motels and restaurants that are chamber members.

Northern Katahdin Valley Regional Chamber of Commerce, PO Box 14D, Patten 04765, publishes a brochure focusing on the Patten area and points north and east.

Bowater/Great Northern Paper (723-5131, ext. 1229), One Katahdin Avenue, Millinocket 04462, the largest landowner in this area, maintains thousands of miles of roads and hundreds of campsites. The company's map/guide to its lands is available at checkpoints on its roads and by writing to the office, attention "Public Relations."

GETTING THERE

The most direct route is I-95 to exit 56 at Medway (50 miles northeast of Bangor), and 10 miles into Millinocket. From here, it's about 10 miles to Millinocket Lake, and from there another few miles to the Togue Pond entrance to the park.

GETTING AROUND

Katahdin Air Service Inc. (723-8378), PO Box 171, Millinocket. Available May through November to fly in to remote camps and shuttle in canoes and campers; will also drop hikers at points along the Appalachian Trail. **Scotty's Flying Service** (528-2626) at Shin Pond also serves wilderness camps.

MEDICAL EMERGENCY

Millinocket Regional Hospital (723-5161), 200 Somerset Street, Millinocket.

TO SEE

The Katahdin Iron Works. Open May through mid-October, 6 AM–8 PM. Turn at the small sign on Route 11, 5 miles north of Brownville Junction, and go another 6 miles up the gravel road. This state historic site is really not worth the effort unless you plan to continue on down the gravel road to hike in Gulf Hagas or to camp (see *Hiking* and *Campgrounds*). The spot was a sacred place for Native Americans, who found their yellow ocher paint here. Then from the 1840s until 1890, an ironworks prospered in this remote spot, spawning a village to house its 200 workers and producing 2000 tons of raw iron annually. Guests of the Silver Lake Hotel (1880s–1913) here came on the same narrow-gauge railroad that carried away the iron. All that remains is a big old blast furnace and iron kiln. Tours and books on the ironworks are offered by local author and backwoods guide Bill Sawtell (965-3971).

Patten Lumberman's Museum (528-2650), Shin Pond Road (Route 159), Patten. Open Memorial Day through September, Tuesday through Saturday 9–4 and Sunday 11–4. $2.50 per adult, $1 per child. The museum, which encompasses more than 4000 displays housed in 10 buildings, was founded in 1962 by bacteriologist Lore Rogers and log driver Caleb Scribner. Exhibits range from giant log haulers to "gum books," the lumberman's scrimshaw: intricately carved boxes in which to keep spruce gum, a popular gift for a sweetheart. There are replicas of logging camps from different periods, dioramas, machinery, and photos, all adding up to a fascinating picture of a vanished way of life. This road leads to the Matagamon Gate, the northern, less trafficked corner of Baxter State Park.

A.J. Allee scenic overlook, some 15 miles beyond the Medway exit. The view is of Mount Katahdin rising massively from woods and water.

TO DO

BOAT EXCURSION

Katahdin View Pontoon Boat Rides (723-5211). Seasonal sight-seeing cruises on a 24-foot pontoon boat along Millinocket Lake and into Mud Brook. Approximately 2 hours; the sunset cruise is a little longer and very popular (reservations suggested.) Departs from Big Moose Cabins, Millinocket.

CANOE RENTALS

Penobscot River Outfitters (746-9349 in Maine; 1-800-794-5267 outside the state), Route 157, Medway 04460. Old Town rentals; also specializes in 1- to 7-day canoe trips on the East and West Branches of the Penobscot.

Katahdin Outfitters (723-5700), in Millinocket, offers canoe rentals, trip planning, transport, and shuttle for trips on the Allagash, St. John, and Penobscot.

Canoe rentals are also available in Peaks-Kenny Park (see *Campgrounds.*)

For a more complete list of guide services, contact the **North Maine Woods office** (435-6213) in Ashland.

SCENIC FLIGHT

Katahdin Air Service Inc. (723-8378), offers scenic flights daily, ranging from a 15-minute flight along the base of Mount Katahdin to a day exploring Henderson Pond and Delosconeag Lake.

HIKING

Baxter State Park. Ever since the 1860s—when Henry David Thoreau's account of his 1846 ascent of "Ktaddn" began to circulate—the demanding trails to Maine's highest summit (5267 feet) have been among the most popular in the state. Climbing Katahdin itself is considered a rite of passage in Maine and much of the rest of New England. The result is a steady stream of humanity up and down the Katahdin trails, while other peaks, such as 3488-foot Doubletop, offer excellent, little-trafficked hiking trails and views of Katahdin to boot. Many hikers base themselves at

The Chimney Pond Trail in Baxter State Park

Chimney Pond Campground and tackle Katahdin from there on one of several trails. *50 Hikes in the Maine Mountains* by Cloe Chunn details many of Baxter's trails far better than we can here. We did, however, climb the **Sentinel Mountain Trail,** which we were told was the easiest climb up a mountain peak in the park. It was approximately 6½ miles round-trip, a moderate climb with lots of rocks and roots on the path. The trail can be wet and muddy, but the trees were so thick that even in a light rain, we didn't get soaked. At one point on the trail, you have to cross a brook on a wooden log bridge about 2 or 3 feet above the water. It's sturdy, but not great for people who aren't crazy about heights. The last bit of this trail is steeper, leading to the peak, where there is a loop trail. Assumably, the view is good on a day that is clear rather than foggy. From the same starting point (Kidney Pond Camps) you can choose the **Daicey Pond Trail,** a flat loop around the pond that we hear is a good spot to see moose. Just before Kidney Pond Camps is the **Doubletop Mountain Trail.** We were also told that the **South Turner Mountain** trail from Roaring Brook via Sandy Stream Pond is a good wildlife-watching trail. In all, there are 46 mountain peaks and 175 miles of well-marked trails. Allow 3 to 5 days at a campground like Trout Brook Farm Campground in the northern wilderness area of the park, or base yourself at Russell Pond (a 7- or 9-mile hike in from the road) and hike to the Grand Falls and Lookout Ledges. A free "Day Use Hiking Guide" is available from the park headquarters (see *Green Space*).

Gulf Hagas is most easily accessible (3.1 miles) from the Katahdin Iron Works (see *To See*). Billed as the "Grand Canyon of Maine," this 2½-mile canyon with walls up to 40 feet high was carved by the West Branch of the Pleasant River. The approach is through a 35-acre stand of virgin white pine, some more than 130 feet tall, a landmark in their own right (known as The Hermitage) and preserved by The Nature Conservancy of Maine. The trail then follows the river, along the Appalachian Trail for a ways, but turns off along the rim of the canyon toward dramatic Screw Auger Falls and on through The Jaws to Buttermilk Falls, Stair Falls, and Billings Falls. Allow 6–8 hours for the hike and plan to camp at one of the waterside campsites within the KI–Jo Mary preserve (see *Campgrounds*).

WHITE-WATER RAFTING

Several white-water rafting companies maintain bases near the Togue Pond entrance to Baxter State Park; there are mid-May to mid-September departure points for day trips down the West Branch of the Penobscot River through Ripogenus Dam and the Cribworks. **Northern Outdoors** (1-800-765-RAFT), **New England Outdoor Center** (1-800-766-RAFT), and **Wilderness Expeditions** (1-800-825-WILD) share **The Penobscot Outdoor Center** on Pockwockamus Pond, where facilities include a bar, restaurant, hot tub, sauna, canoes, kayaks, and windsurfers; lodging is at campsites and in cabin tents. **Unicorn Rafting** (1-800-UNICORN), based at Big Moose Inn on Millinocket Lake, also offers a 6-day Penobscot expedition tracing Thoreau's journey in the Maine woods.

CROSS-COUNTRY SKIING AND SNOWSHOEING

Katahdin Country Skis and Sports (723-5839), One Colony Place, Millinocket, offers rental skis; trail maps to close to 60 miles of free groomed and backcountry trails are available here and from the local chamber.

SNOWMOBILING

Snowmobiling is big. There are over 350 miles of groomed trails in the region, and more than 10 snowmobile clubs in the area to consult. A snowmobile map is available at the chamber (see *Guidance*), showing the ITS trails, as well as containing advertisements for many snowmobiling-geared businesses.

GREEN SPACE

BAXTER STATE PARK

This 201,018-acre park surrounds Mount Katahdin, the highest peak in the state (5267 feet). There are only two entry points: **Togue Pond Gate** near Millinocket, by far the most popular, is open 6 AM–9 PM, May 15 through October 15. **Matagamon Gate,** in the northeast corner of the park, is open 6 AM–9 PM. Nonresident vehicles pay an $8 day-use fee at the gate ($25 for the season). Vehicles with Maine plates are admitted free. Day-trippers should be aware that the number of vehicles allowed in the park is restricted, because of limited parking; arrive early to avoid being turned away.

The park is open daily, but note the restricted camping periods and the special-use permits required from December 1 through March. Orchids, ferns, alpine flowers, and dozens of other interesting plants here delight botanists. Geologists are intrigued by Baxter's rhyolite, Katahdin granite, and many fossils. Birds and wildlife, of course, also abound. Rental canoes are available at several locations in the park.

Camping is only permitted May 15 to October 15 and December to April 1. As a rule, campsites are booked solid before the season begins; don't come without a reservation. In all there are 10 widely scattered campgrounds. Daicey Pond and Kidney Pond each offer traditional cabins with beds, gas lanterns, firewood, and table and chairs ($17 per person per night minimum, $30 for a two-bed cabin, $40 for a three-bed cabin, and $50 for a four-bed; children ages 1–6 are free, 7–16 are $10 per person). Six more campgrounds, accessible by road, offer a mix of bunkhouses, lean-tos, and tent sites. There are two more backcountry, hike-in campgrounds, at Chimney Pond and Russell Pond, which are among the most popular. Beyond that there are several backcountry sites, available by reservation for backpackers. Some of these sites have restrictions, so be sure to contact the park before planning your trip. In 1996, tent and lean-to sites were $6 per person, minimum $12 per site. Space in the bunkhouses was $7 per person.

Summer season reservations (only accepted for the period between May 15 and October 15; dates vary a little according to campground opening and closing dates; request information from park headquarters) must be made in person or by mail with the fee enclosed (check or cash), posted no earlier than December 26 of the year before you are coming (Baxter State Park, 46 Balsam Drive, Millinocket 04462). Send a stamped, self-addressed envelope if you want to receive a confirmation. No refunds.

LODGING

Note: For details about a choice of motels handy to I-95, check with the Millinocket Chamber of Commerce (723-4443).

INNS AND BED & BREAKFASTS

Big Moose Inn (723-8391), Millinocket Lake, Millinocket 04462. Open June through October, but will open the lodge in winter for groups. A classic old summer inn has been a family-run business since 1976, offering 11 simple, pleasant guest rooms with double or twin beds, 11 cabins, and a 24-site campground. Plenty of comfortable common areas in the lodge, as well as green rockers on the porch. Beautifully situated on the water, and not far from the Togue Pond entrance to Baxter State Park. Also a base for white-water rafting. The dining room is open to the public (see *Where to Eat*).

The Birches Resort in Rockwood

The Sweet Lillian B&B (723-4894), corner of Katahdin and Pine Streets (88 Pine Street), Millinocket 04462. Donna Cogswell has named this hospitable way station for her deceased mother. Cogswell is warm and helpful, and offers six clean, comfortable guest rooms with shared bath (third floor can be rented as a three-bedroom suite with private bath). Common living room on the first floor. $40–50 includes full breakfast.

Carousel B&B (965-7741), Brownville 04414. Open mid-May through November. We have yet to see this place, but it has been enthusiastically recommended to us. There are three rooms, one with a private bath and a double bed. The other two, one with twins, one with a queen, share a bath. This is the most convenient lodging to Gulf Hagas. $45 for private bath, $40 shared, includes a full breakfast.

REMOTE RUSTIC CAMPS

Katahdin Lake Wilderness Camps, Box 398, Millinocket 04462, at the end of a private, 3½-mile tote trail from Roaring Brook Road in Baxter State Park; it's an hour's walk. Al Cooper will meet you with packhorses, or you can fly in from Millinocket Lake. Ten log cabins (two to seven people per cabin) and a main lodge built on a bluff overlooking the lake; firewood, linens, kerosene lamps, and outhouses go with each cabin, and several also have gas stoves for housekeeping. Sandy beaches. Moderately priced with all meals. Rental boats available.

Bradford Camps (746-7777), Box 729, Ashland 04732. Open following ice-out through November. Sited at the Aroostook River's headwaters, Munsungan Lake. Virtually inaccessible by land (unless you want to weather 47 miles on logging roads), this unusually tidy lodge has well-tended lawns and eight handhewn log cabins on the waterfront, all with full private baths. $100 per person per night includes meals, but boat and motor are extra. Family rates in July and August.

CAMPGROUNDS

KI–Jo Mary Multiple Use Forest (695-8135). Open May through October, a 200,000-plus-acre tract of commercial forest stretching almost from Greenville on the west to the Katahdin Iron Works on the east and north to Millinocket. Seasonal checkpoints are open 6 AM–8 PM (Thursday through Saturday until 10 PM in May, June, and August, 10:30 PM in July). Primitive sites. **The KI–Jo Mary Lake Campground** (723-8117) is located within the forest, but offers modern facilities with flush toilets, hot showers.

Gulf Hagas (see *Hiking*), with 50 miles of the Appalachian Trail, 96 lakes, and 125 miles of brooks, streams, and rivers within its boundaries, along with 150 miles of roads over which lumber trucks have rights-of-way. There are over 60 authorized campsites, some on rivers and lakes. The day-use fee (for those between ages 15 and 70) is $4 for residents, $7 for nonresidents; the camping fee is a flat $4 per person. For reservations (valid only at least a month in advance), write North Maine Woods, Box 382, Ashland 04732.

Peaks-Kenny State Park (564-2003), Route 153, 6 miles from Dover-Foxcroft. Open mid-May through September for camping and for swimming in Sebec Lake.

Mattawamkeag Wilderness Park (746-4881), Mattawamkeag (off Route 2; a half-hour drive from the I-95 Medway exit). Fifty campsites, 11 Adirondack shelters, bathrooms, a small store, a recreation building, picnic facilities, 15 miles of hiking trails, and 60 miles of canoeing on the Mattawamkeag River with patches of white water. An 8-mile gravel road leads into the park.

Scraggly Lake Public Lands Management Unit (contact the Bureau of Public Lands, Presque Isle: 764-2033), a 10,014-acre forested preserve laced with ponds and brooks. It has 12 "authorized" campsites (no fire permit needed). Scraggly Lake is good for salmon and brook trout; a half-mile hiking trail loops up Owls Head.

Katahdin Shadows Campground (746-9349; 1-800-794-KAMP), Route 157, Medway. This is a full-service, family-geared campground with a central lodge with a game room and board games, swimming pool, weekend hayrides, a big playground, athletic fields, free morning coffee, kitchen facilities, tent and hook-up sites, hutniks, and well-designed cabins with kitchen facilities ($39 per couple). Rick LeVasseur also offers canoe and boat rentals, hiking, cross-country skiing, and snowmobiling information. Rabbits everywhere.

(For camping in **Baxter State Park,** see *Green Space.*)

WHERE TO EAT

Big Moose Inn and Restaurant (723-8391), Millinocket Lake, 8 miles west of Millinocket on the Baxter Park road, across from the lake. Open for dinner Wednesday through Saturday, June through early October. A popular place; reservations suggested. A pleasant Maine woods atmosphere with choices like seafood casserole, grilled or blackened swordfish, and pineapple-glazed baked ham. $9.95–15.95. No credit cards.

Angie's Restaurant (943-7432), Milo. Just in case you happen to be cutting over to the Katahdin Iron Works and Gulf Hagas from I-95 (take the Howland exit and the unnumbered woods road through Medford to Milo)—or for whatever other reason you happen to be in Milo—Angie's (across from the cemetery) is open for all three meals. Great road food, homemade sandwich bread, wooden booths, blue frilly curtains, dinner specials ranging from liver and onions to salmon steak.

River's Edge Restaurant (965-2881), Brownville Junction. Open Tuesday through Saturday 4–9. Johanna and James McGuinness have created an attractive dining room featuring seafood and pasta dinners. You can also get liver and onions or prime rib.

Schootic Inn/Penobscot Room (723-4566), Penobscot Avenue, Millinocket. Open for lunch and dinner. George and Bea Simon are third-generation owners. Menu choices include pizza, calzones, seafood, and prime rib. Liquor. Children's menu.

SPECIAL EVENTS

July: **Fourth of July celebration** in Millinocket features a weekend full of activities, and a fireworks display.

October: For 3 weeks before Halloween, the scariest, most elaborate **haunted trolley ride** in Maine, sponsored by Jandreau's Greenhouse, Millinocket.

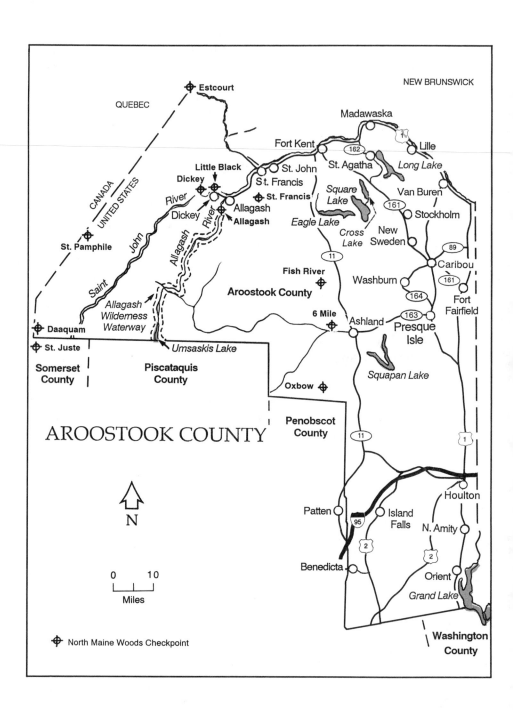

Aroostook County

Almost the size of Massachusetts, Aroostook is Maine's largest and least populated county. It's referred to simply as The County in Maine, and, contrary to its image as one big potato field, it's as varied as it is vast. Four million of Aroostook's 5 million acres are wooded—land that includes many major mountains, most of the Allagash Wilderness Waterway, and more than 1000 lakes.

The Upper St. John Valley at the top of The County, a broad ribbon of river land backed by woodland in the west and by a high, open plateau in the east, has its own distinctly Acadian look, language, and taste. Central Aroostook—the rolling farmland around Fort Fairfield, Presque Isle, and Caribou—is generally equated with the entire county. It, too, has its appeal, especially around Washburn and New Sweden, sites of two of New England's more interesting museums. Houlton, the northern terminus of I-95 and the county seat, is in southern Aroostook, a mix of farmland, lonely woods, and lakes.

"Aroostook" is said to mean "bright," actually the best word we can think of to describe the entire county since the luminosity of its sky—broader than elsewhere in New England—is The County's single most striking characteristic, along with its location. Bounded by Canada on two sides and the North Woods on the third, Aroostook is so far off any tourist route that many New England maps omit it entirely. Maine pundits are fond of noting that Portland is as far from Fort Kent, the northern terminus of Route 1, as it is from New York City.

The conventional loop tour around The County is I-95 to its terminus at Houlton, then Route 1 north to Fort Kent and back down Route 11. We suggest doing it in reverse.

Many visitors actually enter The County in canoes, paddling up the Allagash River, which flows north and empties into the St. John River at Allagash, a minuscule hamlet that's become widely known as Mattagash to readers of novels (*The Funeral Makers, Once Upon a Time on the Banks,* and *The Weight of Winter*) by Allagash native Cathie Pelletier. Local residents will tell you that the names of Pelletier's characters have been changed only as slightly as that of her town and that the interplay between Catholics and Protestants (descendants of Acadian and Scottish settlers, respectively) chronicled in her books remains very real. From the 1940s to the 1960s French was a forbidden language in local schools, and students were punished for speaking it anywhere on school grounds.

Acadians trace their lineage to French settlers who came to farm and fish in Nova Scotia in the early 1600s and who, in 1755, were forcibly deported by an English governor. This "Grand Derangement," dispersing a population of some 10,000 Acadians, brutally divided families (a tale told by Longfellow in "Evangeline"). Many were returned to France, only to make their way back to a warmer New World (Louisiana), and many were resettled in New Brunswick, from which they were once more dislodged after the Revolution when the government gave their land to American loyalists.

In a meadow overlooking the St. John River behind Madawaska's Tante Blanche Museum, a large marble cross and an outsized wooden sculpture of a *voyageur* in his canoe mark the spot on which several hundred of these displaced Acadians landed in 1785. They settled both sides of the St. John River, an area known as Mattawaska ("Land of the porcupine"). Not until 1842 did the St. John become the formal boundary dividing Canada and Maine.

The 1842 Webster-Ashburton Treaty settled the Aroostook War, a footnote in American history recalled in the 1830s wooden blockhouses at Fort Kent and Fort Fairfield. Until relatively recently this bloodless "war" was the area's chief historic claim, but the valley's distinct Acadian heritage is gaining increasing recognition.

In 1976 a "Village Acadien" consisting of a dozen buildings was assembled just west of Van Buren. It's an interesting enough little museum village, but it only begins to tell the story evinced in the very shape of the St. John Valley towns—the houses strung out like arms from cathedral-sized Catholic churches at their centers.

Aroostook County still produces 1½ million tons of potatoes a year, but the family farms—once the staple of The County's landscape and social fabric—are fading, replaced by consolidated spreads that grow other crops, notably broccoli, barley, and sugar beets. The family potato farm is already the stuff of museum exhibits. Our favorites are in the New Sweden Museum, which commemorates not only family farms but also one of the most interesting immigration stories in American history.

The County is as far removed in time as it is in distance from Maine's more commercialized "Vacationland." You shop in craftspeople's and farmers' homes, ask locally for directions to the best places to walk, ski, and fish, feast on fiddleheads and *ployes* (buckwheat crêpes) rather than lobster. Most visitors, moreover, come in winter—to snowmobile or dogsled. Winter driving, we're told, is less daunting here than elsewhere in the Northeast because, thanks to the region's lowest temperatures, the snow is drier (no ice) as well as more plentiful. Summer temperatures also tend to be cooler than elsewhere, and in early July the potato fields are a spread of pink and white blossoms. Fall colors, which usually peak in the last weeks of September at the end of potato harvest, include reddening barley fields as well as maples.

GUIDANCE

As noted in the introduction, The County comprises three distinct regions. For details about northern Aroostook (the Upper St. John Valley), contact the **Greater Fort Kent Chamber of Commerce** (834-5354), PO Box 430, Fort Kent 04743. A walk-in information center at the blockhouse, staffed by the Boy Scouts, is open seasonally. For central Aroostook, contact the **Presque Isle Chamber of Commerce** (764-6561), PO Box 672, Presque Isle 04769; and for southern Aroostook, the **Houlton Chamber of Commerce** (532-4216), 109-B Main Street, Houlton 04730. The county has recently been trying to market itself as a tourist destination, with color brochures inviting people to "discover the other Maine." This campaign is headed by the **Northern Maine Development Commission** (1-800-427-8736), which will send you fact sheets that list lodging, dining, and recreational options for all three regions.

The big walk-in information center in The County is maintained by the **Maine Publicity Bureau,** just off I-95 in Houlton (532-6346).

Note the **North Maine Woods** information office on Route 1 in Ashland described in the introduction to this part.

GETTING THERE

By car: I-95 to Benedicta or Sherman Mills, then Route 11 up through Patten, Ashland, and Eagle Lake to Fort Kent, from which you can explore west to Allagash and east along the Upper St. John Valley to St. Agatha and/or Van Buren. Stop at the New Sweden Museum, for a meal in Caribou, and for a final overnight in the Houlton area.

By plane: Regularly scheduled service is limited to **Pine State Air** (1-800-353-6334), which has daily flights between Portland, Augusta, Presque Isle, and Frenchville (its base). **Scotty's Flying Service** (528-2626), Shin Pond, is a commercial seaplane operation geared to shuttling canoeists, hunters, and anglers in to remote lakes and put-in places along the St. John, Allagash, and Aroostook Rivers.

By bus: **Cyr Bus Lines** (532-6868), Houlton, runs daily between the Greyhound terminal in Bangor and Caribou, with stops in between.

MEDICAL EMERGENCY

Northern Maine Medical Center (834-3155), 143 East Maine Street, Fort Kent.

Houlton Regional Hospital (532-9471), 20 Hartford Street, Houlton.

TO SEE

MUSEUMS

A brochure detailing the county's historical museums and attractions is available from most chambers. Following are those we found of particular interest (in order of suggested routing).

See *To See* in the "Katahdin Region" chapter for details about the **Lumberman's Museum** in Patten.

Camper driving on logging road in northern Maine wilderness

JOSEPH DENNEHY

Fort Kent Historical Society Museum (834-5121), Main and Market Streets. Open weekends mid-May through Labor Day. The former Bangor & Aroostook Railroad depot is filled with local memorabilia and exhibits on the economic and social history of the area, focusing on lumbering and agriculture.

Madouesk Historic Center and Acadian Cross Shrine (728-4518), Route 1, Madawaska. Open early June through Labor Day, weekdays 9:30–4:30, Sunday 1:30–4:30. The complex includes the **Tante Blanche Museum** (local memorabilia) and, if you follow the dirt road behind the museum to the river, the 18th-century **Albert Homestead,** plus the *Voyageur* statue and stone cross described in the introduction to this chapter.

Acadian Village (566-2691 or 866-3972), Route 1, Van Buren. Open mid-June through mid-September, Monday through Saturday 12–5, and by appointment. The 16 buildings include a school and store, a barbershop, a train station, old homesteads with period furnishings, and a reconstructed, 18th-century log church. $3 per adult, $1.50 per child.

Ste. Agathe Historical Society Museum (543-6364/6911), St. Agatha. The oldest house in this unusually pleasant village on Long Lake, the Pelletier-Marquis home dates just from 1854; it's filled with a sense of the town's unusually rich ethnic and social history.

New Sweden Historical Society Museum (896-5639), just east of Route 161, New Sweden. Open June through August, Tuesday through Saturday 12–5, Sunday 2–5, and by appointment. Entering the community's reconstructed Kapitileum (meetinghouse), you are faced with the imposing bust of William Widgery Thomas, the Portland man sent by President Lincoln to Sweden in 1863 to halt the sale of iron to the Confederacy. Thomas quickly learned Swedish, married two countesses (the second after her sister died), and eventually devoted his sizable energies to establishing a colony of Swedish farmers in Maine. In 1870 the House of Representatives authorized the project, granting 100 acres of woodland to each Swedish family. A pink granite memorial in a pine grove behind the museum complex commemorates the arrival and hardships of those who settled here between 1870 and 1875. Despite the severe climate and thin soil (Thomas had been struck by the similarities between Sweden and northern Maine), New Sweden prospered, with 1400 immigrants in 1895 and 689 buildings, including three churches, seven general stores, and two railroad stations. New Sweden's annual festivals draw thousands of local descendants. The museum remains a cultural touchstone for Swedes living throughout the Northeast, and the town continues to attract visitors from Sweden, even an occasional immigrant. The museum complex includes hilltop Thomas Park and a picnic area; also an authentic immigrant cottage and restored blacksmith shop.

The Salmon Brook Historical Society (455-4339), Route 164, Washburn. Open weekends mid-June to Labor Day 1–4, and by appointment. The pleasant 1852 **Benjamin C. Wilder Farmstead** and the **Aroostook Agricultural Museum** (potato-harvesting tools and trivia housed in the neighboring barn) offer a sense of life and potato farming in the late 19th century. Washburn's Taterstate Frozen Foods claims to have invented the frozen french fry.

- **Nylander Museum** (493-4209), 393 Main Street, Caribou. Open Wednesday through Sunday 1–5 Memorial Day through Labor Day, and weekends 1–5 March through May and September through December. A small but intriguing museum displaying permanent collections of fossils, minerals and rocks, shells and other marine life, butterflies and moths, birds, and early-man artifacts, most collected by Swedish-born Olof Nylander; also changing exhibits, and a medicinal herb garden in the back with over 80 specimens.

Caribou Historical Center (498-3095), Route 1, Caribou. Open June through early September, Tuesday through Saturday 9–5, or by appointment. This new log building is filled with local memorabilia from the mid-19th century to the 1930s, including antiques, historical papers, photographs, home furnishings, and tools. Also a replica of an 1860s one-room school with a bell in the cupola.

Aroostook County Historical and Art Museum (532-4216), 109 Main Street, Houlton. Open by appointment. Same building as the Houlton Area Chamber of Commerce and if there is enough staff, someone from the chamber will take you up. A large, well-organized, labeled, and well-maintained collection of local memorabilia.

Webb Museum of Vintage Fashion (862-3797; 463-2404), Route 2, Island Falls. Open Monday through Thursday, late May through September. $3 adults, $2 seniors, children under 12 free. This 14-room Victorian-era house is filled with some 6000 articles of clothing amassed by Frances Stratton—hats, jewelry, combs, and mannequins dressed to represent the specific people to whom their outfits once belonged. It's a spooky, fascinating place, chronicling life in a small town as well as what its inhabitants wore from the 1890s to the 1950s. Each room has its own theme. *Note:* This museum can be accessed either from Route 11 (it's 9 miles east of Patten) or from I-95.

Fort Kent Blockhouse Museum, off Route 1. Open Memorial Day through Labor Day, usually 9–dusk, maintained by the town and the local Boy Scout troop. This symbol of the northern terminus of Route 1 is a convincingly ancient, if much restored, two-story, 1830s blockhouse with documents and mementos from the Aroostook War. Be sure to wander down to the Fish River behind the blockhouse, a pleasant walk to picnic and tenting sites. When we visited, a rainbow seemed to underscore the legend that a pot of gold is buried hereabouts.

CHURCHES

As noted in the introduction to this chapter, tall, elaborate, French Canadian–style Catholic churches form the heart of most Upper St. John Valley villages: **Saint Leonard** in Madawaska, **Saint Louis** in Fort Kent (with distinctive open filigree steeples and a fine carillon), **St. David's** in the village of St. David, and **St. Luce** in Frenchville. When the twin-spired wooden church dominating the village of Lille was condemned, it was purchased by local resident Don Cyr, who is converting it into an Acadian cultural center and a setting for concerts and workshops (895-3339).

OTHER ATTRACTIONS

A.E. Howell Wildlife Conservation Center and Spruce Acres Refuge (532-6880/0676), Lycette Road off Route 1, North Amity (14 miles south of Houlton). Open May through November, 9–sunset; $3 adults, free under age 18. Art Howell, one of the best known and respected of Maine's more than 90 wild animal "rehabilitators," nurtures bald eagles, bears, foxes, otters, and many more creatures that have been wounded and are being readied, if possible, for return to the wild. This is 64 acres of woods with a picnic area and a pond stocked with fish for children; also a camping area for environmental groups. No dogs, please.

New Brunswick Botanical Garden (506-735-3074), Route 2, Saint-Jacques, New Brunswick. Open June through mid-October, daily 9–dusk. More than 50,000 varieties are represented in this spread of flowers, varying with the month.

SCENIC DRIVES

Flat Mountain. The single most memorable landscape that we found in all of Aroostook is easily accessible if you know where to turn. The high plateau is well named Flat Mountain and is just above but invisible from Route 1 east of Fort Kent. Ask locally about the road through the back settlements from Frenchville to St. Agatha, a lake resort with several good restaurants.

Watson Settlement Covered Bridge. Follow Main Street through Houlton's Market Square Historic District (a "Walking Tour Guide" to this area is available from the chamber of commerce) until it turns into Military Street (dating from the Aroostook War). Turn north on Foxcroft Road; in 2 miles note your first view of Mars Hill Mountain (the area's only mountain at 1660 feet). The mountain's ownership was disputed in the Aroostook War; it is now a ski area. At roughly 3½ miles, note the road on your left descending to a small iron bridge across the Meduxnekeag River; the covered bridge, built in 1902, is midway down this hill. The road rejoins Route 1 ten minutes north of Houlton.

TO DO

CANOEING

Canoes-R-Us (834-6793), 2 Church Street, Soldier Pond (off Route 11 on the Fish River south of Fort Kent). Canoe rentals and help planning trips from Eagle Lake to Soldier Pond, from Soldier Pond to Fort Kent, and 1- to 3-day camping trips along the Fish River chain.

Allagash Guide Service (398-3418), Allagash, rents paddles and canoes, also offers transport and car pickup for those canoeing the Allagash Waterway.

Maine Canoe Adventures/Cross Rock Inn (398-3191), Route 162, Allagash. Gorman Chamberlain offers 5- to 7-day trips on the St. John and Allagash, also guided trips into the nearby Debouille area departing from his lodge; also offers three guest rooms ($35 double), tenting area, canoe rentals.

Eagle Valley Adventures (506-992-2827), Clair, New Brunswick, offers river trips on the Madawaska and St. John Rivers.

(Also see *Canoeing the Allagash* under "What's Where.")

Note: The map/guide to the Allagash and St. John (DeLorme Publishing, $4.95) is useful.

FISHING

The catch is so rich and varied that it is recognized throughout the country. Salmon grow to unusual size, and trout are also large and numerous. The 80-mile Fish River chain of rivers and lakes (Eagle, Long, and Square Lakes) is legendary in fishing circles. Fish strike longer in the season than they do farther south, and fall fishing begins earlier. Contact the Maine Department of Inland Fisheries and Wildlife in Ashland (435-3231, or in-state: 1-800-353-6334).

GOLF

The County's topography lends itself to golf, and the sport is so popular that most towns maintain at least a nine-hole course. The most famous course is 18 holes at **Aroostook Valley Country Club,** Fort Fairfield (476-8083), with its tees split between Canada and Maine. The 18-hole **Jo-Wa Golf Course** (463-2128) in Island Falls and the **Presque Isle Country Club** (764-0439) are also considered above par.

HIKING

See the Debouille preserve and Aroostook State Park under *Green Space.*

Fish River Falls. Ask locally for directions to the trail that leads from the former Fort Kent airport down along the river, an unusually beautiful trail through pines. Note the swimming holes below the falls. **The Dyke in Fort Kent** is also worth finding: a half-mile walk along the Fish River. The trail up **Mount Carmel** (views up and down the river valley) begins on Route 1 at the state rest area near the Madawaska/Grand Isle town line.

CROSS-COUNTRY SKIING

The same reliable snow that serves out-of-state snowmobilers allows residents to take advantage of hundreds of miles of trails maintained exclusively for cross-country skiing by local towns and clubs. Any town office or chamber of commerce (see *Guidance*) will steer you to local trails.

SNOWMOBILING

Snowmobiling is the single biggest reason that visitors come to The County (update: 728-7228). For a "Trail Map to Northern Maine" detailing

1600 miles of trails maintained by The County's no fewer than 42 snowmobile clubs—the "highest rated trail riding in New England"—send $2 to any Aroostook County chamber of commerce (see *Guidance*).

GREEN SPACE

Debouille Management Unit, including Debouille Mountain and several ponds, is a 23,461-acre preserve managed jointly by the state and North Maine Woods (charging gate and camping fees), accessible by gated logging roads from St. Francis and Portage. Campsites are clustered around ponds (good for trout) and near hiking trails leading to the distinctive summit of Debouille Mountain. For details, contact the Bureau of Public Lands in Presque Isle (764-2033).

Aroostook State Park (768-8341), marked from Route 1, just 4 miles south of Presque Isle. Open May 15 through October 15. A 600-acre park with swimming and picnicking at Echo Lake; also 30 campsites (June 15 through Labor Day only) at 1213-foot Quaggy Joe Mountain—which offers hiking trails with views from the north peak across a sea of woodland to Mount Katahdin. Note the monument in the small **Maxie Anderson Memorial Park** next door; a tin replica of the *Double Eagle II* commemorates the 1978 liftoff of the first hot-air balloon to successfully cross the Atlantic.

Aroostook Valley Trail and **Bangor and Aroostook Trail** (493-4224). A 71½-mile recreational trail system connecting Caribou, Woodland, New Sweden, Washburn, Perham, Stockholm, and Van Buren. Many bogs, marshes, wetlands, and streams are along these trails, which are owned by the Maine Bureau of Public Parks and Land. Several parking lots and rest areas on the trails. Good for biking, walks, cross-country skiing, and snowmobiling.

(Also see **Allagash Wilderness Waterway** under "Canoeing the Allagash" in "What's Where").

LODGING

Given the unusual warmth and hospitality of Aroostook residents, we look forward to the day when more homes and farms will welcome visitors.

BED & BREAKFASTS

Daigle's Bed & Breakfast (834-8503), 96 East Main Street, Fort Kent 04743. This cheery modern house features a sunny, glass-walled, flower-filled dining room in which guests tend to linger over Doris Daigle's generous breakfast. The five guest rooms range from small with shared bath, to a spacious double with twin beds, to a room decorated in red and black with a refrigerator, TV, and phone. Guests are also welcome to join Elmer and Doris in the evening for drinks and snacks by the living room fireplace. $45–75 double.

Auberge du Lac (728-6047), Birch Point Road, St. David. Open year-round. This small place is very quiet and private. From the road, you can hardly tell it is a B&B, but inside Grace Oulette's attention to detail is obvious. The Oulettes live downstairs, leaving visitors in the three guest rooms (one with private bath) to share a large, comfortable living room with a fireplace and a picture window overlooking Long Lake. Across the street is a stretch of land on the water with Adirondack chairs. $55–65 double includes a full breakfast.

Rum Rapids Inn (455-8096), Route 164, Crouseville 04738. Not far from Presque Isle, one of the oldest houses in The County (vintage 1839) is set in 15 acres on the Aroostook River. Innkeeper Clifton (Bud) Boudman offers candlelight dinners as well as two rooms (private baths) with all the comforts of home, including robes, TV/VCR with movie selections, and an honor snack bar. The common area is filled with interesting things to look at. Bud is happy to help with travel plans in Maine and the Maritimes. Dinners are by reservation only, and they only book one party per night. It's a multicourse event, and there are 17 entrée choices (each party must choose only 2) including Tuscana Primavera (a delicious pasta dish), steamed Maine lobster, and roast beef with Yorkshire pudding. Entrées $23–36. Room rates are $48.50 double including a full "Scottish breakfast."

Old Iron Inn (492-4766), 155 High Street, Caribou. Kate and Kevin Mc-Cartney offer four rooms with shared baths decorated with antiques they have painstakingly chosen themselves. In the common areas, there is an extensive collection of antique irons (hence the name). There is no TV in the place, but there is a reading room and they subscribe to close to 40 magazines. $39–49 includes a full breakfast.

Sweet Water Inn, RR2, Box 241D, Houlton. Actually several miles south of Houlton in a country setting 4 miles off Route 1. No one was home the afternoon we dropped by, but the grounds were wooded, quiet, and peaceful, and the shingled house looked inviting. Run by professional musicians who offer to provide guests with an evening of music. $65–100 double (for room with a hot tub).

SPORTING CAMPS

Allagash Gardners Sporting Camps (398-3168), Box 127, Allagash 04774. Open May through December. Five tidy camps along a ridge overlooking the confluence of the St. John and Allagash Rivers across the road from Roy and Mande Gardner's welcoming old farmhouse. Bed & breakfast and hiking, hunting, camping, and fishing guide service also offered. $30 double, $100 per week.

Moose Point Camps (435-6156), Portage 04768. Open May 10 to early December. Ten log-hewn camps on the east shore of Fish Lake (5 miles long and connecting with other lakes linked by the Fish River). The central lodge features a library, a large stone fireplace, and a dining room overlooking the lake where meals are served (BYOB). The camps are 17 miles from Portage up a paper company road. $300 per person per week or $65 per person per day in spring and summer; ask about children's rates and hunters packages. Boats and canoes available.

Libby Sporting Camps (435-8274), Drawer V, Ashland 04732. Open ice-out through November. One of the original sporting camps, family operated for 100 years. Features hearty meals in the lodge and guides to take you to 40 lakes and ponds from the eight cabins. Also nine outpost cabins on remote ponds and streams. $105 per person per night includes meals. Sited at the headwaters of the Aroostook and Allagash Rivers. Boats and seaplane available.

Chiputneticook Lodge (448-2929), Boundary Road, Orient 04471. Open year-round. Not exactly a sporting camp but, rather, a rustic lodge on East Grand Lake (good for lake trout, salmon, bass), just minutes off Route 1. Also a good base camp for grouse and deer hunters. Guided birding excursions; boat and canoe rentals. Host Peter Roach and his wife rent rooms in the lodge on a B&B or housekeeping basis. There is also a private cottage available overlooking the water. Reasonable rates.

MOTEL

Long Lake Motor Inn (543-5006), Route 162, St. Agatha 04772. Ken and Arlene Lermon pride themselves on the cleanliness and friendliness of this motel (which still looks brand new) overlooking Long Lake. There is a lounge, and continental breakfast is included in $45 for standard room ($39 single), $65 for the suite, which has a Jacuzzi.

WHERE TO EAT

DINING OUT

Sirois' Restaurant (834-6548), 84 West Main Street, Fort Kent. Henry Sirois operates this hospitable, homey restaurant with an extensive menu. Choices range from chicken to seafood, steaks, and Italian specialties. $6.95–18.95. Children's menu $2.95–3.95.

Long Lake Sporting Club (543-7584; 1-800-431-7584), Sinclair. Open daily July and August; the rest of the year closed on Monday. Sit down in the lounge with a drink, order, and then go to your table when it's all ready. Specialties include steaks, seafood, jumbo lobsters (3–4 pounds). Right on Long Lake, with terrific views, dance floor, full-service marina. $8.95–16.95.

Lakeview Restaurant (543-6331), St. Agatha. Open daily for lunch and dinner. Set on a hilltop with a view across the lake and valley. Steak and seafood are the specialties. Live entertainment on summer weekends. Most entrées are around $10.

Daniel's (868-5591), 52 Main Street, Van Buren. A large restaurant and lounge open for lunch and dinner. At lunch, choose from sandwiches and light entrées like chicken stir-fry. The dinner menu includes linguine with white clam sauce, ribeye steak, and filet mignon. Also

The Can Am Crown dogsled race in Fort Kent

serves pressure-fried chicken dinners (party boxes available to go). Dinner entrées $8.75–13.95.

✐ **Joe Hackett's Steak & Seafood Restaurant & Butcher's Market** (496-2501), Route 1 south of Caribou. Open for dinner daily, lunch and dinner on Sunday. One of the best places to eat in central Aroostook, a modern, family-style restaurant specializing in prime beef and fresh fish. Dinner entrées range from Down East midgets (fried or broiled shrimp) to Broncobuster's Splurge (a 22-ounce Porterhouse steak); the "junior executive" menu includes a "buckaroo's wallet with a cow's blanket" (a cheeseburger). $7.50–13.95 (children's menu $2.25–3.75).

EATING OUT

Lil's (435-6471), Route 1, Ashland. Open 6 AM–8 PM. A counter and orange vinyl booths, homemade bread, pizza, outstanding sandwiches and pies, daily specials.

Ma & Pa's Sunrise Cafe (543-6177), Cleveland Road, St. Agatha. Open daily year-round, 5:30 AM–8 PM. Our favorite kind of eatery: a counter, tables, and a view. Features local items as specials, like chicken stew and *ployes* (buckwheat crêpes).

Doris's Cafe, Fort Kent Mills, open for breakfast and lunch; everything prepared from scratch.

Pierrette's Kitchen (834-6888), 57 East Main Street, Fort Kent. Pizza and sandwiches, plus specials like "road kill chili" in a bright, friendly atmosphere. Ice cream, too.

The Dicky Trading Post, Allagash, open 5 AM–7 PM. A combination general store (with stuffed bobcat and lynx), sporting goods shop, and Formica-topped coffee shop.

Stan's Grocery, Route 161 north of Jemtland. Home of Stan's 10-cent cup of coffee, to be savored in a back booth of this indescribable store, the center for the surrounding summer community on Madawaska Lake. The pay phone next to the piano is roto-dial.

Elm Tree Diner (532-3181), Bangor Road, Houlton. Open early and late, an outstanding classic diner with everything made from scratch, daily specials.

SELECTIVE SHOPPING

Fish River Brand Tackle (834-3951), call for directions. Tackle made by Don Baker—one of his big metal flashers secured the $10,000 grand prize in the Lake Champlain Fishing Derby in 1994.

Bouchard Family Farm (834-3237), Route 161, Fort Kent. Stop by the family kitchen and buy a bag of *ploye* mix. *Ployes* are crêpelike pancakes made with buckwheat flour (no eggs, no milk, no sugar, no oil, no cholesterol, no fat—*c'est magnifique*).

Goughan Farms (496-1731), Route 161, Fort Fairfield. Open weekdays 10–5, Sundays 12–5. Pick-your-own strawberries, also a farm stand, animal barn.

SPECIAL EVENTS

February: **Mardi-Gras** in Fort Kent. The 5 days before Ash Wednesday bring a parade, ice sculptures, kids' day, Franco-American music, and exhibitions.

Early March: **The Can Am Sled Dog Race,** Triple Crown 60- and 250-mile races, starting and ending at Fort Kent.

June: **Acadian Festival** in Madawaska, with parade, traditional Acadian supper, and talent revue. The weekend nearest June 21, **"Midsommar,"** is celebrated at Thomas Park in New Sweden with Swedish music, dancing, and food.

July: **Maine Potato Blossom Festival** features 'Roostook River Raft Race, mashed potato wrestling, Potato Blossom Queen pageant, parade, and fireworks.

August: **Northern Maine Fair,** Presque Isle. **Potato Feast Days** in Houlton has arts and crafts, potato barrel–rolling contest, potato games, more.

General Index

Lodging Index

Books from The Countryman Press

EXPLORER'S GUIDES
The alternative to mass-market guides with their homogenized listings, Explorer's Guides focus on independently owned inns, motels, and restaurants, and on family and cultural activities reflecting the character and unique qualities of the area.

Cape Cod: An Explorer's Guide Second Edition
Connecticut: An Explorer's Guide Second Edition
Massachusetts: An Explorer's Guide
New Hampshire: An Explorer's Guide Third Edition
Rhode Island: An Explorer's Guide
Vermont: An Explorer's Guide Seventh Edition
The Hudson Valley and Catskill Mountains:
  An Explorer's Guide Second Edition

A SELECTION OF OUR BOOKS ABOUT MAINE
  AND THE NORTHEAST

Fifty Hikes in Southern and Coastal Maine Second Edition
Fifty Hikes in the Maine Mountains Second Edition
25 Bicycle Tours in Maine
Hiking Trails of Nova Scotia Seventh Edition
The Architecture of the Shakers
Seasoned with Grace: My Generation of Shaker Cooking
The Story of the Shakers
The New England Herb Gardener
Living with Herbs

We offer many more books on hiking, fly fishing, travel, nature, and other subjects. Our books are available at bookstores and outdoor stores everywhere. For more information or a free catalog, please call 1-800-245-4151 or write to us at The Countryman Press, PO Box 748, Woodstock, Vermont 05091. You can find us on the Internet at www.wwnorton.com.